Presented to

Kingwood Branch Library

By

Friends of the
Kingwood Library

**Harris County
Public Library**
your pathway to knowledge

The Greenwood Encyclopedia of African American Civil Rights

The Greenwood Encyclopedia of African American Civil Rights

From Emancipation to the
Twenty-First Century
Volume II
S–Z and Primary Documents

Charles D. Lowery and
John F. Marszalek, Editors
Thomas Adams Upchurch, Associate Editor

Foreword by David J. Garrow

Greenwood Press

Westport, Connecticut • London

Library of Congress Cataloging-in-Publication Data

The Greenwood encyclopedia of African American civil rights : from emancipation to the twenty-first century / Charles D. Lowery and John F. Marszalek, editors ; Thomas Adams Upchurch, associate editor ; foreword by David J. Garrow.—2nd ed.
    p. cm.
    Rev. ed. of: Encyclopedia of African-American civil rights. New York : Greenwood Press, 1992.
    Includes bibliographical references and index.
    ISBN 0–313–32171–X (set : alk. paper)—ISBN 0–313–32766–1 (v. 1 : alk. paper)—ISBN 0–313–32767–X (v. 2 : alk. paper)
    1. African Americans—Civil rights—History—Encyclopedias. 2. Civil rights movements—United States—History—Encyclopedias. 3. United States—Race relations—Encyclopedias. I. Lowery, Charles D., 1937– II. Marszalek, John F., 1939– III. Upchurch, Thomas Adams. IV. Encyclopedia of African-American civil rights.
E185.61.E54   2003
323.1'196073'003—dc21   2003040837

British Library Cataloguing in Publication Data is available.

Library of Congress Catalog Card Number: 2003040837
ISBN: 0–313–32171–X (set code)
           0–313–32766–1 (Vol. I)
           0–313–32767–X (Vol. II)

First published in 2003

Greenwood Press, 88 Post Road West, Westport, CT 06881
An imprint of Greenwood Publishing Group, Inc.
www.greenwood.com

Printed in the United States of America

The paper used in this book complies with the Permanent Paper Standard issued by the National Information Standards Organization (Z39.48–1984).

10 9 8 7 6 5 4 3 2 1

In Memory of Those Who Died
So Others Might Be Free

CONTENTS

FOREWORD TO THE SECOND EDITION

David J. Garrow

The updating and expansion of this wonderfully rich research aid is a most welcome event. Ten years ago, reviewing the original manuscript for this volume, I was deeply impressed with how many leads for more extensive future research a large number of these short essays called to mind.

Disappointingly, however, this past decade has unfortunately not witnessed anywhere near as much of a progression in African American civil rights and freedom struggle historiography as there ideally should have been. A number of landmark volumes have appeared, such as Charles Payne's *I've Got the Light of Freedom* (1995) on Mississippi and Adam Fairclough's *Race and Democracy* (1995) on Louisiana, but the overall breadth and scale of "movement" scholarship still falls far short of what one might optimistically have imagined 15 or 20 years ago. When one looks at the tremendous explosions of scholarly energy that in recent years have marked the fields of labor history, women's history, and gay and lesbian history, black freedom struggle scholarship is still waiting for a similar burst of activity. Younger scholars such as Timothy Minchin (*Hiring the Black Worker*, 1999 and *The Color of Work*, 2001) are showing just how many available avenues there are for creatively original research, but presently there are not as many young scholars proceeding down these paths as there should be. That need is all the more pressing as the ongoing passage of time gets to the point where more and more surviving veterans of 1950s and 1960s activism reach the ages where their future time with us threatens to draw to a close.

Undergraduate or graduate students perusing this volume should keep those thoughts in mind, for an expanded pipeline of younger people who are interested in preserving and telling the movement's story in all of the multifaceted local richness that it merits is crucial if freedom struggle historiography is to grow. The range of contributions to this encyclopedia suggests just how many possible paths there are, many of them in areas that are more "cultural" than the political and economic developments that are oftentimes most intriguing to those of us who are traditional historians. And while many topics from the 1950s and 1960s still merit further attention, scholars have been relatively slow to turn their gaze toward post-1968 developments in black America. As a new and younger generation of black elected officials begins to succeed more experienced representatives who in many instances were firsthand veterans of the movement, the political agenda of black America reflects more and more change, with new issues such as black communities' interest in school vouchers being added to more traditional and painful concerns such as racial profiling and police brutality.

But this emerging generation of prospectively "postracial" African American elected officials is only one of a plethora of subjects that ought to interest students and young scholars. The opportunities for new and important work of African American civil rights are almost limitless, and I hope deeply that this new and expanded edition of this rich encyclopedia will stimulate a significant number of young people to take up that task.

FOREWORD TO THE FIRST EDITION

David J. Garrow

This *Encyclopedia of African American Civil Rights* is a valuable and informative reference volume, but it is also so rich a source of important sketches and instructive bibliographical references that it deserves—and encourages—a fairly thorough reading even by knowledgeable senior scholars.

The range and breadth of entries is oftentimes as impressive as it is informative. Most importantly, any thoughtful perusal of the volume—whether thorough or cursory—will quickly bring home to any reader what a large number of individuals, organizations, and events there are from these last ten decades of Afro-American history which deserve greater and more extensive historical research and study than has yet been the case.

As many scholars now recognize, current and future research in Afro-American history will increasingly treat a wider and wider range of participants and events. To date a disproportionate amount of historical attention has been focused on nationally prominent individuals and on organizations that received significant contemporaneous news coverage, but there is widespread appreciation that increased attention to "grass roots" individuals and organizations is our future direction, just as there also is a growing appreciation of the importance of "local" history and events. Less and less will Afro-American history look at the black experience in America largely through a prism of national news and/or national politics.

No one can peruse this volume without thinking again and again about otherwise obscure and/or often unremembered individuals, protests, and court cases that merit a greater presence in secondary sources and textbook surveys than is presently the case. Probably every contributor hopes that this encyclopedia's publication will further stimulate and encourage such a broadening of secondary historical coverage, and such a hope is quite likely to be fulfilled, While many contributors to this encyclopedia are relatively senior scholars such as John Kirby, Steven Lawson, Jo Ann O. Robinson, Hans Trefousse, and Jerry Ward, many of the most thorough and impressive contributions come from promising junior scholars such as Cheryl Greenberg, Patricia Behlar, Peter Wallenstein, Francille Wilson, Lillie Johnson Edwards, and Glenn T. Eskew.

One very important and as yet largely unmined resource for an expanded and enriched Afro-American history since the late nineteenth century, which a number of significant entries highlight or touch upon, is black newspapers. Although many issues of a number of significant publications most tragically seem to have not been preserved, both national papers such as the *Pittsburgh Courier* and more regionally or locally oriented papers such as the *Birmingham World* can be exceptionally rich and instructive sources for future historical studies. Few scholars enjoy spending hundreds upon hundreds of hours reading microfilm, but there is no escaping the fact that far more use can and will be made of black newspapers as a significant historical source than has yet been the case.

The historical importance of black newspapers is just one notable research path that this rich and valuable volume suggests. Notwithstanding the thoroughness of many of this encyclopedia's more than eight hundred articles, hardly any scholar or student will be able to peruse the useful bibliographies that follow each entry without recognizing a significant number of subjects and individuals who undeniably deserve further or greatly increased research attention. If this volume's publication can stimulate even a modest number of such new research interests, it will have provided a significant scholarly service in addition to the very notable long-term reference value that it will offer to innumerable scholars and students. Such a goal is one which undeniably deserves to be fulfilled.

INTRODUCTION TO THE SECOND EDITION

More than a decade has elapsed since we introduced the first edition of this encyclopedia in 1992. During that time there have been many significant developments in the ongoing struggle for African American civil rights. The unending march of history thus compels us to bring our work up-to-date.

Over the past ten years, notable progress has been made in some areas of American race relations, which offers hope that the worst is behind us and that better days lie ahead. For example, blacks can now be found not merely working at the highest levels of government, business, entertainment, sports, and the professions, but excelling in their positions. At the same time, however, devastating setbacks have occurred in other areas, revealing that much remains to be done to make this country truly a land of liberty and justice for all people. Shocking cases of hate crimes, lynchings, police brutality, racial profiling, and race riots have served to remind us that to be black in America—even at the end of the twentieth century and the beginning of the twenty-first—is still to be different. Provocative debates over reparations for slavery, affirmative action, and reverse discrimination, among other issues, have likewise shown us just how complex the racial issues are that this generation of Americans faces. Appallingly high negative demographic statistics—the black male incarceration rate, the percentage of black teen pregnancies and unmarried mothers, the proportion of black families living in poverty or well below the national average, and the prevalence of drug addiction in black communities—continue to demonstrate that African Americans, as a whole, do not yet share fully in the American Dream.

The generation now coming of age has only scant knowledge of the history of the civil rights struggle. Young Americans find it difficult in 2003 to believe that racial segregation was once considered normal and necessary in some parts of the United States. Indeed, separate public schools, movie theaters, restaurants, bus seats, and water fountains seem incredible to the current generation, while spectacle lynchings, church bombings, assassinations of civil rights leaders, acquittals of white murderers of blacks by all-white juries, and government approbation of such injustices seem utterly inexplicable. Ignorance of past racial tragedies, sadly, retard continued progress in race relations.

It is, therefore, important for all people to understand the history of the struggle for civil rights. It is not a matter of having arcane information or memorizing trivia, but rather of realizing that some courageous and noble human beings endured insults, braved dangers, risked their careers, and even sacrificed their very lives so that those who followed after them could enjoy a greater degree of freedom, equality, and opportunity.

This encyclopedia, in the 10 years of its existence, has served students and teachers, average Americans and professional historians alike, as a convenient source for information on the history of the black civil rights struggle. The book has become a standard reference in a wide variety of public and academic libraries, providing essential information and offering bibliographical references for further information. The editors are pleased that this book, in its first edition, received such an enthusiastic reception, and they are happy to provide this revised second edition.

In this edition we have tried to ensure that the essays and bibliographies present the civil rights story as up-to-date to September 2003 as possible. We contacted, or attempted to contact, all the authors of the original essays and bibliographies, asking each to evaluate his or her original contributions carefully and make revisions as appropriate. We also asked for suggestions for new entries. We then invited new authors to write essays dealing with issues and events of the 1990s. We also asked new authors to add a section of primary documents and to update and expand the chronology. Similarly, we updated the bibliography and index. Whenever possible, we also provided in the individual bibliographies accompanying each entry a World Wide Web (WWW) site for readers who wish to use the Internet for further research.

Despite our exhaustive efforts to do so, it proved impossible to contact about one-third of the original contributors. Some had moved without leaving a forwarding address; some did not respond to several letters and e-mails; a few said they did not wish to revise their essays; and a number had passed away over the past decade. The list of contributors, therefore, contains the present affiliation of most authors, but those authors who could not be located are listed in the past tense at their institution of record when they composed their essays 10 years ago. If an author is deceased, that fact is so noted.

The editors have carefully edited all the original essays, whenever possible with the assistance of the original authors. We also added approximately 60 new essays and deleted approximately 15 entries from the first edition because we did not believe them relevant any longer. Each completed essay in the second edition, therefore, has received a thorough reevaluation. In some cases, the decision was to leave an essay exactly as it appeared in the first edition; in most cases, however, changes were made in the text and the bibliography to bring both up-to-date to September 2003.

The result of this effort is a second edition that reflects the philosophy and direction of the first yet is significantly different in content. The editors hope that this new edition will serve the reading public as well as did the first one. African American civil rights remains a subject of immense importance, and we hope that our effort will play a role in educating the public about it.

In order to expeditiously complete the revision of this encyclopedia, we invited a former student to join us as associate editor. We are pleased to welcome Thomas Adams Upchurch, a promising young historian of American race relations, to our team. He has brought to this project energy, efficiency, and insight. His scholarly contributions in the revisions and in the selection of documents have expedited the project.

Many others also made important contributions to the timely completion of this work. Mississippi State University student assistant Lindley Carruth Shedd's organizational abilities kept the editors, publisher, and authors moving forward together. It was her dedicated efficiency that allowed the editors to concentrate on the historical details, because we knew she had everything else under control.

We also thank Patsy Humphrey and Lonna Reinecke of the Mississippi State University History Department for their word-processing skills; Peggy Bonner of that same department for all that she has done to expedite this book and all the past projects of the editors; Horace Nash, Sara Morris, Mike Butler, Marvin Thomas, and David Canton for assisting with revisions; Buck Foster for his producing the index and Tony Iacono for his expansion of the chronology; Cynthia Harris of Greenwood Press for her constant encouragement and ready answers to any questions we posed to her; and finally, our wives, Susie, Jeanne, and Linda, for their loving support over the years.

AN AID TO USING THE ENCYCLOPEDIA

The entries on individuals, organizations, books, events, concepts, and court cases that constitute this encyclopedia are arranged in alphabetical order. The entries are cross-referenced through the use of boldface; that is, any person, group, occurrence, or court case mentioned in an entry that has its own entry is set in boldface. A detailed index provides a convenient way to locate desired information. Each entry includes a brief bibliographical list to guide the reader to other printed sources that contain valuable data on the subject in question.

Judicial citations conform to standard practice. Supreme Court decisions are officially published in *United States Reports* and are cited by volume and page number. The *Plessy v. Ferguson* opinion, for example, cited as 163 U.S. 537, is found in volume 163 of *United States Reports* at page 537. Recent opinions of the federal appeals courts are in *Federal Reporter, 2d Series*. Thus, the appellate decision in *Collins v. Walker*, cited as 339 F.2d 100, is in volume 339 of *Federal Register, 2d Series* at page 100. Federal district court opinions appear in *Federal Supplement* (F. Supp.), also cited by volume and page number.

INTRODUCTION TO THE FIRST EDITION

The African American's struggle for freedom and equality is one of the truly heroic episodes in American history. From earliest colonial days to the present, that enduring struggle, in all its myriad forms, has been as relentless as it has been inevitable. Regardless of when they lived, black Americans have shared with white Americans—and all people everywhere—the innate, timeless, indomitable desire to be free. It is a cruel irony that a people who could so boldly assert as self-evident truth that "all men are created equal" and are "endowed by their Creator" with such "inalienable rights" as "life, liberty, and the pursuit of happiness," could at the same time so resolutely deny to blacks the exercise of these rights. In failing to remain faithful to their own creed, white Americans underscored the hypocrisy and deception, the contradiction of purpose and spirit, that characterized their relationship to blacks.

From the earliest time tragedy has marked race relations in America. The institution of slavery dominated the country's early years until a bloody Civil War opened the possibility for a new racial relationship. The coming of "Jubilee" contained more promise than reality, however, and slavery was soon replaced by segregation, at first through custom and then more firmly by law. Slave codes became Black Codes and then Jim Crow state constitutions and laws. Freed people saw their emancipation turn into the new prison of segregation. The United States Supreme Court in the landmark *Plessy v. Ferguson* case of 1896 legitimated this "separate but equal" Jim Crowism. The law of the land allowed segregation and enforced "separate" conditions for African American citizens in all aspects of their lives, but the "equal" side of the equation was conveniently ignored.

For most of the twentieth century, the average black American's citizenship was a cruel hoax. Even when the Supreme Court in the momentous 1954 *Brown v. Board of Education* decision eliminated the constitutional justification for segregation, the battle was not won. Several more decades of struggle were required to achieve even minimal integration.

At the same time, though, there existed another dimension of race relations. There were blacks and whites who found slavery and segregation to be intolerable, and they battled it as best they could. The African who committed suicide rather than board a slave ship; the plantation slave who broke tools or nurtured aspects of the African past; the black and white abolitionists who served as national conscience; the free blacks who met in conventions of protest; and the politicians who finally took a stand, led the nation through a war of emancipation, and passed the Thirteenth Amendment—all these and many more individuals fought to eliminate the peculiar institutions.

Once slavery was abolished, those who believed that the battle was over withdrew from the fray. Others, both blacks and whites, saw that the nation had much to do if the former slaves were ever really to be free. Theirs was a long, lonely, and often dangerous battle to try to eliminate pervasive racism and provide full citizenship to America's black population.

The battle seemed unending, and it had many fronts. These included the right to vote and hold public office; the chance for a good job and promotion; the opportunity for an education from kindergarten to professional school; access to decent medical treatment; the opportunity to eat in restaurants or at lunch counters, go to theaters, sleep in motels, use public restrooms and waiting areas, worship in churches; the chance to join the military, appear in films or on the stage, participate on amateur and professional athletic teams, have articles and books published, argue cases in court or serve on juries or testify as a witness; live in a decent home in a pleasant neighborhood; live without fear; and enjoy respect, courtesy, and acceptance. From 1865 through the twentieth century the term "civil rights" came to mean the freedom and opportunity to enjoy, unimpeded, this whole complex of American citizenship rights. The civil rights movement, especially in its intensification in the 1950s and 1960s, was the long struggle to bring African Americans into the promise of the American Dream.

Throughout this period, historical writing reflected the bias that the dominant American white society felt against black people. Assumptions of white superiority and black inferiority were as deeply embedded in the history books as they were in society as a whole. When blacks were mentioned in the texts, if they were, it was in the most depreciative language. Favorable books or articles, when they saw print, were patronizingly or forcefully suppressed.

During the years of the modern civil rights struggle, workers in the movement have labored first and foremost to liberate black people, but they also have tried to liberate America's history. A torrent of literature on all aspects of the black-white experience poured forth when the dam of literary discrimination was breached. This literature has both influenced the civil rights struggle and been influenced by it. In the important body of books on race relations, however, there is a conspicuous void. There is no reference book that presents under a single cover an overview of the century-long struggle for civil rights. Excellent books and articles exist on all aspects of this subject, but there is no one convenient, accurate reference source.

This *Encyclopedia of African American Civil Rights* was prepared to fill this void. It contains over eight hundred short articles on a wide variety of individuals, organizations, events, and court cases focusing on the period since emancipation. Librarians of all types of libraries, from the largest reference to the smallest public, will find it a convenient source for information on this topic. The bibliographical references with each article will also provide ready entry into the vast literature in the field.

In organizing and completing this volume, the editors faced several difficult decisions. The topic is broad and the available pages necessarily limited. The editors decided to include, for the most part, only that which, in their judgment, made a significant positive contribution to the advancement of black civil rights. Every state and community had its share of brave, resourceful individuals, influential organizations, and locally significant events and court cases. Unfortunately, all could not be included here, not because they were not important, but because there simply is not space enough for all of them. In order to include as many subjects as possible and be consistent with the purpose of an encyclopedia, the editors have kept the articles brief.

Another difficult decision concerned whether to include those who opposed the civil rights movement. Individuals such as Eugene "Bull" Connor, Ross Barnett, Orval Faubus, and George C. Wallace, and groups such as the Ku Klux Klan, the White Citizens' Council, and the State Sovereignty Commissions, were legion, outnumbering in the South, certainly, those people and organizations championing racial equality. In a perverse way the opponents of black civil rights, because of the depth of their racism and the brutish violence of their opposition, promoted the cause of freedom. But it would require another book to deal with them, and rather than include some and neglect others, we did not include any.

Similarly, we did not include presidents of the United States or every congressman, Supreme Court justice, black novelist, playwright, newspaperperson, soldier, sports figure, or "first black" whose activities contributed to the movement. We are acutely aware of how much we have omitted, but we also think that we have included a representative cross-section of the most significant people, organizations, events, and court cases of the black civil rights movement.

We were fortunate to be able to work with an outstanding group of conscientious and talented authors. They include some of the foremost scholars in the field as well as individuals just beginning their professional careers. We naturally appreciate the support of the former, but we particularly want to express our gratitude to the latter. Their willingness to undertake a wide variety of assignments enabled us to carry the project forward. All editors have horror stories to tell about working on a book such as this, and we have ours, too. Fortunately, our happy experiences far outnumber the unpleasant ones.

We are deeply indebted to a number of other people who have been instrumental in bringing this project to fruition. Undergraduate student-helper Marzett Jordan undertook a wide variety of clerical and research tasks and accomplished them in his usual quietly efficient manner. Graduate Assistant James Stennett was similarly productive, and Research Assistant Danny Blair Moore provided valuable assistance during the last stages of the project. Jean Whitehead and Karen Groce typed goodly portions of the manuscript. Peggy Y. Bonner and Lonna Reinecke not only typed the manuscript and letters to the authors, but provided invaluable assistance in other ways as well. Their organizational skills and their ability to remember where everything was filed saved us from a host of editorial problems. To say that this book could not have been completed without them is no exaggeration. To Professors David J. Garrow and Willard B. Gatewood, Jr., who read the manuscript and offered many discerning suggestions and criticisms, we are especially indebted. Our friend and colleague Allen Dennis not only authored entries for the *Encyclopedia*, but he also compiled the index for the volume. He has long experience as a professional indexer, and the finished product attests to his skill. We thank him for his help. At Greenwood Press, Executive Editor Cynthia Harris has provided, from the outset, guidance and encouragement, for which we are deeply grateful. Production editor Penny Sippel has skillfully managed the editorial responsibilities of bringing the volume into production. Finally, to our wives, Susie and Jeanne, we are most indebted, not just for the freedom they gave us to complete this project, but for their support, love, and companionship in all things.

CONTRIBUTORS

Cassandra August is Assistant Professor of Family and Consumer Sciences at Baldwin-Wallace College.

Dorothy A. Autrey is Associate Professor of History at Alabama State University.

James L. Baggett was a graduate student in history at the University of Mississippi.

Michael B. Ballard is Professor and Coordinator of Congressional and Political Research Center at Mississippi State University.

Larry T. Balsamo is Professor of History at Western Illinois University.

Charles T. Pete Banner-Haley is Associate Professor of History at Colgate University.

Alwyn Barr is Professor of History at Texas Tech University.

Able A. Bartley is Associate Professor of History, University of Akron.

Jennifer J. Beaumont was a graduate student in history at the University of Maryland, Baltimore.

Patricia A. Behlar is Assistant Professor of Political Science at Pittsburgh State University.

Robert A. Bellinger is Assistant Professor of History at Suffolk University.

Manfred Berg is a faculty member in the John F. Kennedy Institute for North American Studies, Free University of Berlin, Germany.

Amos J. Beyan is Associate Professor of History at Western Michigan University.

Monroe Billington is Emeritus Professor of History at New Mexico State University.

Thomas E. Blantz is Professor of History at the University of Notre Dame.

Robert Bonazzi was Editorial Director of *Latitudes*.

James Borchert is Professor of History at Cleveland State University.

Joseph Boskin is Professor of History at Boston University.

Dorsey Oles Boyle was a graduate student in history at the University of Maryland, Baltimore.

Ray Branch is a doctoral graduate of the Department of History, Mississippi State University.

Jeff Broadwater was Director of the John C. Stennis Oral History Project at Mississippi State University.

Brenda M. Brock was a graduate student in English at the State University of New York at Buffalo.

Lisa Brock is Assistant Professor of Liberal Arts at The School of the Art Institute of Chicago.

Lester S. Brooks is Professor of History at Anne Arundel Community College in Maryland.

Michael Butler is Assistant Professor of History at South Georgia College.

Joe Louis Caldwell is Associate Professor of History at the University of New Orleans.

Robert A. Calvert, now deceased, was Professor of History at Texas A&M University.

David Canton is Assistant Professor of History at Georgia Southern University.

Dominic J. Capeci, Jr., is Distinguished Professor of History at Southwest Missouri State University.

JoAnn D. Carpenter is Professor of History at Florida Community College.

Jessie M. Carter is Lecturer in African American Studies at the State University of New York at Buffalo.

William Cash is Emeritus Professor of History at Delta State University.

Joan E. Cashin is Professor of History at Ohio State University.

Suzanne Ellery Green Chapelle is Professor of History and Geography at Morgan State University.

Lawrence O. Christensen is Distinguished Teaching Professor of History and Political Science at the University of Missouri-Rolla.

James R. Chumney is Associate Professor of History at Memphis State University.

Eric C. Clark is a holder of a doctorate in history and the Secretary of State of Mississippi.

Thomas D. Cockrell is Professor and Chair of the Social Sciences Division at Blue Mountain College.

Willi Coleman is Associate Professor of History at the University of Vermont.

Edwin L. Combs III is a history doctoral student at the University of Alabama, Tuscaloosa.

W. Lance Conn lives in London.

Norlisha Crawford is Assistant Professor of English at Bucknell University.

Stephen Cresswell is Professor of History at West Virginia Wesleyan College.

Jeffrey J. Crow is Adjunct Associate Professor of History at North Carolina State University.

Charles Crowe, now deceased, was Professor of History at the University of Georgia.

Lorenzo Crowell is Associate Professor of History at Mississippi State University.

Donald Cunnigen is Associate Professor of Sociology at the University of Rhode Island.

Robert Cvornyek is Associate Professor of History and Secondary Education at Rhode Island College.

Richard V. Damms is Associate Professor of History at Mississippi State University.

Marsha J. Tyson Darling is Professor of History and Director of the African American and Ethnic Studies Program at Adelphi University.

Jack E. Davis is Associate Professor of History at the University of Alabama at Birmingham.

Thomas J. Davis is Professor at Arizona State University College of Law.

Allen Dennis is Professor of History and Chair at Troy State University.

Vincent P. DeSantis is Emeritus Professor of History at the University of Notre Dame.

Kenneth DeVille was a law student at the University of Texas.

Nancy Diamond was a graduate student in history at the University of Maryland, Baltimore.

Bruce J. Dierenfield is Professor of History at Canisius College.

Bernard Donahoe is Professor of History at Saint Mary's College, Indiana.

Michael S. Downs was Staff Historian, U.S. Air Force Space Command at Peterson Air Force Base, Colorado.

W. Marvin Dulaney is Professor and Chair of History at the University of Charleston.

Aingred G. Dunston is Associate Professor of History at Eastern Kentucky University.

Brenda M. Eagles was Research Librarian and Bibliographer at the Center for the Study of Southern Culture at the University of Mississippi.

Charles W. Eagles is Professor of History at the University of Mississippi.

Lillie Johnson Edwards is Associate Professor of History at Drew University.

David P. Eldridge is Instructor of History at Florence-Darlington Technical College.

Glenn T. Eskew is Associate Professor of History at Georgia State University.

Robert Fikes, Jr., is Librarian at San Diego State University.

Nancy E. Fitch was Assistant Professor of History at Lynchburg College.

Marvin E. Fletcher is Professor of History at Ohio University.

Linda G. Ford was Assistant Professor of History at Keene State College and is now in private business.

Tony A. Freyer is University Research Professor of History and Law at the University of Alabama.

David J. Garrow is Professor of Political Science, Emory University.

Phillip A. Gibbs is Associate Professor of History at Middle Georgia College.

Bruce A. Glasrud is Dean of Arts and Sciences and Professor of History at Sul Ross State University.

Ira Glunts was Head of Technical Services at the American International College Library.

Kenneth W. Goings is Professor and Chair of African American Studies at Ohio State University.

Daniel Gomes was a graduate student in history at the University of Maryland, Baltimore.

Hugh Davis Graham, now deceased, was Holland McTyeire Professor of History at Vanderbilt University.

Barbara L. Green is Assistant Professor of History at Wright State University.

George N. Green is Professor of History at the University of Texas at Arlington.

Cheryl Greenberg is Professor of History at Trinity College.

Bernice F. Guillaume was Associate Professor of History at St. Louis University.

Michele M. Hall was a graduate student in history at the University of Maryland, Baltimore.

David A. Harmon is affiliated with Alabama Public Television.

Alferdteen Harrison is Professor of History and Director of the Margaret Walker Alexander National Research Center for the Study of the Twentieth-Century African American at Jackson State University.

Merrill M. Hawkins, Jr., is Assistant Professor of Religion, Carson-Newman College.

Wanda A. Hendricks is Associate Professor of Women's Studies, University of South Carolina.

Clarence Hooker is Associate Professor of American Thought and Language at Michigan State University.

Leonne M. Hudson is Associate Professor of History, Kent State University.

Gary J. Hunter is Professor of History at Rowan College.

Marshall Hyatt was Director of the Center for Afro-American Studies at Wesleyan University.

Anthony J. Iacono is a historian and assistant dean at Indian River Community College.

Jacquelyn Jackson is Associate Professor of English at Middle Tennessee State University.

Robert L. Jenkins is Associate Professor of History at Mississippi State University.

Lavaree Jones was a Community Organizer for the Child Development Group of Mississippi.

Maxine D. Jones is Professor of History at Florida State University.

Maghan Keita is Associate Professor of History at Villanova University.

Judith N. Kerr, now deceased, was Assistant Professor of History at Towson State University.

Amm Saifuddin Khaled is Professor and Chair of History at the University of Chittagong, Bangladesh.

Wali Rashash Kharif is Professor of History at Tennessee Technological University.

Allen Kifer is Emeritus Associate Professor of History at Skidmore College.

Elizabeth Kight was a graduate student in history at the University of Maryland, Baltimore.

John B. Kirby is Emeritus Professor of History at Denison University.

Stephen P. Labash was a graduate student in history at the University of Maryland, Baltimore.

Jane F. Lancaster is a doctoral graduate of the Department of History at Mississippi State University.

Steven F. Lawson is Professor of History at Rutgers University.

Janice M. Leone is Professor of History at Middle Tennessee State University.

Eric Love is Assistant Professor of History, University of Colorado, Boulder.

Charles D. Lowery is Emeritus Professor of History at Mississippi State University.

Andrew M. Manis is on the Social Sciences faculty at Macon State College, Georgia.

John F. Marszalek is W. L. Giles Distinguished Emeritus Professor of History at Mississippi State University.

James Marten is Professor of History at Marquette University.

Robert F. Martin is Professor of History at the University of Northern Iowa.

Michael S. Mayer is Associate Professor of History at the University of Montana.

Earlean M. McCarrick was Associate Professor of Government and Politics at the University of Maryland.

Phillip McGuire, now deceased, was Dean of Arts and Sciences at Fayetteville State University.

Neil R. McMillen is Emeritus Professor of History at the University of Southern Mississippi.

Tennant S. McWilliams is Dean of the School of Social and Behavioral Sciences at the University of Alabama at Birmingham.

Mark E. Medina was a student at the Yale University Law School.

Stephen Middleton is Assistant Professor of History at North Carolina State University.

Gary B. Mills, now deceased, was Professor of History at the University of Alabama.

Dennis J. Mitchell is Professor of History, Mississippi State University, Meridian.

Gregory Mixon is Assistant Professor of History at the University of North Carolina at Charlotte.

Christopher Mobley is Assistant Professor of Political Science at DePaul University.

Danny Blair Moore is Associate Professor and Chair of History at Chowan College.

Betsy Sakariassen Nash is a school administrator in San Antonio, Texas.

Horace D. Nash teaches history at Alamo Community College District.

William A. Paquette is Professor of History at Tidewater Community College.

Randall L. Patton is Associate Professor of History at Kennesaw State University.

Glenn O. Phillips is Associate Professor and Chair of History at Morgan State University.

Betty L. Plummer was Assistant Professor of History at the University of Tennessee.

James B. Potts is Associate Professor of History at the University of Wisconsin-LaCrosse.

Steve Rea was a graduate student in history at the University of Mississippi.

Linda Reed is Associate Professor of History at the University of Houston.

Richard W. Resh, now deceased, was Associate Professor of History at the University of Missouri at St. Louis.

Charles A. Risher is Professor of History and Political Science at Montreat College.

Edward J. Robinson is a history graduate of Mississippi State University.

Jo Ann O. Robinson is Professor of History and Geography at Morgan State University.

William "Brother" Rogers is Assistant Director of the Stennis

Center for Public Service, Starkville, Mississippi.

William Warren Rogers, Jr., is Associate Professor of History at Gainesville College.

Steve Sadowsky was a graduate student in history at Middle Tennessee State University.

Jeffrey Sainsbury resides in France.

Loren Schweninger is Professor of History at University of North Carolina at Greensboro.

James E. Sefton is Professor of History at California State University, Northridge.

Lindley Carruth Shedd is a student at Mississippi State University.

Carole Shelton was Assistant Professor of History at Middle Tennessee State University.

Malik Simba is Professor and Chair of History at California State University, Fresno.

Frederick G. Slabach was Associate Dean of the Mississippi College School of Law.

James G. Smart is Emeritus Professor of History at Keene State College.

Elizabeth M. Smith is Assistant Professor of History, Kent State University.

Gerald L. Smith is Professor of History at the University of Kentucky.

Thaddeus M. Smith is Professor and Chair of History at Middle Tennessee State University.

Allan H. Spear is Emeritus Associate Professor of History at the University of Minnesota.

James W. Stennett is an executive with a professional baseball team.

Arvarh E. Strickland is Emeritus Professor of History at the University of Missouri.

Quintard Taylor is Scott & Dorothy Bullitt Professor of American History at the University of Washington.

Marvin Thomas is Professor of History at Gordon College.

William J. Thompson was Adjunct Professor of History at Essex Community College, Baltimore.

Hans L. Trefousse is Distinguished Professor Emeritus of History at City University of New York.

Thomas Adams Upchurch is Assistant Professor of History, East Georgia College, Statesboro Branch.

Gloria Waite, now deceased, was Assistant Professor of History at Southeastern Massachusetts University (now University of Massachusetts, Dartmouth).

George E. Walker was Associate Professor of History at George Mason University.

Peter Wallenstein is Associate Professor of History at Virginia Polytechnic Institute and State University.

Jerry Ward is Professor of English at Tougaloo College.

Vibert L. White was Assistant Professor of African American Studies at the University of Cincinnati.

Lawrence H. Williams is Professor of African and Afro-American Studies and History at Luther College, Iowa.

Lee E. Williams, II is Professor of History at the University of Alabama in Huntsville.

LeRoy T. Williams is Associate Professor of History at the University of Arkansas in Little Rock.

Carol Wilson is Associate Professor of History at Washington College.

Francille Rusan Wilson is affiliated with University of Maryland, College Park.

Irvin D. S. Winsboro is History Program Director at Florida Gulf Coast University.

Barbara A. Worthy is Associate Professor of History at Southern University in New Orleans.

Bertram Wyatt-Brown is Milbauer Professor of History at the University of Florida.

Paul Yandle was a graduate student in history at Wake Forest University.

Dean K. Yates was a graduate student in history at the University of Maryland, Baltimore.

Alfred Young is Associate Professor of History at Georgia Southern College.

Robert L. Zangrando is Emeritus Professor of History at the University of Akron.

S

Sam, Alfred Chief (1879, Akyen Abuakwa District, Ghana, West Africa, date and place of death unknown). An African who became a Pan-Africanist in the United States in 1913, Sam arrived in Ofuskee County, Oklahoma, in the summer of 1913. Immediately after his arrival, Sam began urging the blacks there to develop all black towns in the state. (In the 1890s blacks had tried to make the Oklahoma Territory a black state.) The result of Sam's idea was the establishment of 25 predominantly black towns in Oklahoma. Later Sam founded the Akim Trading Company for the purpose of sending blacks to Africa. Despite opposition from other blacks, Sam was able to send 60 blacks to Ghana in 1914. His movement died when the British government stopped colonization.

Selected Bibliography William Bittle and Gilbert Geis, *The Longest Way Home* (1964); Wilson J. Moses, *The Golden Age of Black Nationalism, 1850–1925* (1978).

Amos J. Beyan

Scarborough, William Sanders (16 February 1852, Macon, Ga.–9 September 1926, Wilberforce, Ohio). Educator, political activist, and early champion of political and social equality for blacks, Scarborough was the first African American to achieve scholarly distinction as a student of classical philology. Though born a slave, he learned to read and write as a child. In 1869 he entered **Atlanta University,** where he was introduced to Latin and Greek. He continued his education at Oberlin College, from which he received the B.A. degree in 1875 and an M.A. in classics in 1878. In 1877 he was appointed professor of Latin and Greek at Wilberforce University, where he spent his academic career, teaching, writing, and filling various administrative offices, including that of the university president from 1908–20. In 1881, he published a widely used textbook, *First Lessons in Greek,* which was followed by other scholarly monographs and articles in professional journals. In recognition of his substantial scholarly achievements, he was elected to membership in the American Philological Association in 1882, a rare honor at that time for one of his race.

Scarborough also worked to improve educational, political, and economic opportunities for blacks. Beginning in the late 1880s he published a number of controversial articles in national magazines, including *Forum* and *Arena,* calling for equality of opportunities for blacks. Challenging the **Booker T. Washington** model of industrial education, he argued that classical studies should be open to everyone regardless of race. Blacks were no less able than whites, he asserted, to enjoy the fruits of a liberal education. Scarborough spoke at numerous educational meetings and political rallies concerned with racial problems. Active in the Republican party in Ohio, he played a major role in securing legislation abolishing legal segregation of blacks in the state's schools. He was president of the **Afro-American League** of Ohio, which was established to advance black rights, and which challenged **Jim Crow** railroad cars coming into the state from the South. To a remarkable degree, Scarborough combined the life of the scholar with that of the political activist. He did not think it was enough for educated blacks to be good scholars and professionals; they must also assume a leadership role in municipal and national affairs, acting together to fight racism wherever it existed.

Selected Bibliography Rayford W. Logan and Michael R. Winston, *Dictionary of American Negro Biography* (1982); *New York Times,* 12 September 1926; W. J. Simmons, *Men of Mark* (1887); "Notes," *Journal of Negro History* 11 (October 1926), 689–92; Francis P. Weisenburger, "William Sanders Scarborough: Scholarship, the Negro, Religion, and Politics," *Ohio History* 72 (January 1963), 25–50.

Charles D. Lowery

Schnell v. Davis, 336 U.S. 933 (1949) In 1944 the Supreme Court in **Smith v. Allwright** struck down a Texas law that allowed state political parties the right to determine their membership qualifications. According to the Court, the Democratic party, with the approval of the state, had used this provision to exclude blacks from voting. In response to the Court's decision, many southern states adopted other measures for eliminating black participation. In 1949 Alabama added the **Boswell amendment** to its constitution. This amendment required that prospective voters be able not only to read and write, but also to "understand and explain" any part of the United States Constitution to the satisfaction of a board of registrars. In Alabama, three whites, none of whom was trained in constitutional law, made up the board of registrars in each county. Few blacks, consequently, were allowed to vote. The federal district court that heard the case declared the Boswell amendment an unconstitutional scheme designed to deny blacks their voting rights. Despite the lower court's decision, however, southern states found other ways to dis-enfranchise blacks, including **poll taxes** and lengthy voter application forms.

Selected Bibliography Derrick A. Bell, *Race, Racism and American Law* (1980); Earl and Merle Black, *Politics and Society in the South* (1987); Dewey W. Grantham, *The Life and Death of the Solid South: A Political History* (1988); William C. Havard, ed., *The Changing Politics of the South* (1972); Steven F. Lawson, *Black Ballots: Voting Rights in the South, 1944–1969* (1976).

Phillip A. Gibbs

Schuyler, George S. (25 February 1895, Providence, R.I.–31 August 1977, New York, N.Y.). A maverick African American writer who moved from socialism to conservatism, Schuyler was born in Providence, Rhode Island, and grew up in Syracuse, New York. In 1923 he began contributing to **The Messenger,** a radical journal edited by **A. Philip Randolph.** At the height of the **Harlem Renaissance,** he dismissed the notion of a unique African American character: "Your American Negro is just plain American." Such views were anathema to **Langston Hughes** and the **New Negro movement.** By the 1930s, Schuyler had abandoned socialism, mocked the New Deal, and shared the iconoclastic views of his mentor, H. L. Mencken. As editor of the **Pittsburgh Courier,** a prominent black newspaper, he denounced the intern-ment of Japanese Americans during World War II and Randolph's proposed **March on Washington.** Later he criticized **Martin Luther King, Jr.,** and rejected the teaching of black history as a separate discipline. The nation's mil-itary involvement in Vietnam cheered him, and when he died he was eulo-gized by the conservative *National Review.* Schuyler's longer works include: *Black No More* (1931); *Adventures in Black and White* (1960); and an autobi-ography, *Black and Conservative* (1971). His views exasperated liberals, but he was a superb stylist and relished his role as a scoffer.

Selected Bibliography Nathan Irvin Huggins, *Harlem Renaissance* (1971); Michael Peplow, *George S. Schuyler* (1980); Oscar R. Williams, "The Making of a Black Conservative: George S. Schuyler" (Ph.D. diss., Ohio State University, 1997).

Richard W. Resh

Schwerner, Michael Henry (6 November 1939, New York, N.Y.–21 June 1964, Neshoba Co., Miss.). Michael Schwerner grew up in New York City and in Westchester County. A 1961 graduate of Cornell University, he studied social work at Columbia University and was a social worker in Manhattan. He married Rita Levant in June 1962, and they joined the **Congress of Racial Equality** (CORE) early in 1963. In January 1964 they became CORE field workers in Meridian where they prepared for the **Freedom Summer of 1964** in Mississippi. One of their closest coworkers there was **James Earl Chaney.** In June the Schwerners and Chaney helped train workers for the Summer Project in Ohio where they met **Andrew Goodman.** After they returned to Mississippi, Schwerner, Chaney, and Goodman went to Longdale on June 21 to visit a church that had been burned by the Ku Klux Klan because it was going to be used to house a freedom school. On their way back to Meridian, the three men were arrested. Late that evening they were released from the Neshoba County jail only to be stopped again on a rural road where local whites shot them and buried them in a dam. After an intensive search, FBI agents uncovered the bodies on 4 August. In October 1967, seven whites were convicted in federal court of conspiring to deprive Schwerner, Chaney, and Goodman of their civil rights.

Selected Bibliography Michael R. Belknap, *Federal Law and Southern Order: Racial Violence and Constitutional Conflict in the Post Brown South* (1987); Seth Cagin and Philip Dray, *We Are Not Afraid: The Story of Goodman, Schwerner, and Chaney and the Civil Rights Campaign for Mississippi* (1988); William Bradford Huie, *Three Lives for Mississippi* (1965).

Charles W. Eagles

Scott, Emmett Jay   (13 February 1873, Houston, Tex.–12 December 1957, Washington, D.C.). An African American intellectual, journalist, and administrator, Scott received his early education in Houston. He enrolled at Wiley College, in Marshall, Texas, where he earned his M.A. in 1901. He was employed by the *Houston Post,* and he later became editor of the *Texas Freeman,* a newspaper that addressed the problems of blacks. Scott became **Booker T. Washington**'s special assistant at **Tuskegee Institute,** and he served as secretary of that Institute from 1912 to 1919. Scott was appointed by President Woodrow Wilson as a special assistant to the Secretary of War during World War I. He served as business manager of **Howard University** from 1919 to 1934. Scott's publications on blacks include: *The History of the American Negro in the World War* (1919); *Negro Migration during the War* (1920); *Tuskegee and its People* (1910); Emmett J. Scott and Lyman B. Stowe, *Booker T. Washington, Builder of a Civilization* (1916).

Selected Bibliography Rayford W. Logan and Michael R. Winston, eds., *Dictionary of American Negro Biography* (1982); *New York Times,* 14 December 1957; Jessie Carney Smith, ed., *Notable Black American Men* (1998).

Amos J. Beyan

Scottsboro Trials   On 25 March 1931 nine black youths (aged 12 to 19) were arrested for the alleged rape of two white girls on a freight train in northern Alabama. Two weeks later in Scottsboro the "boys" were tried and convicted, and eight were sentenced to die in the electric chair. Their number and age and the unseemly haste with which they were condemned aroused the concern of several civil rights organizations. In particular, the International Labor Defense (ILD) Committee, a **Communist Party** affiliate, assumed the defense of the "Scottsboro boys'" in mid-1931 and prepared an appeal. The party, meanwhile, conducted an international propaganda campaign, including mass demonstrations, meetings, and petitions on the boys' behalf. In 1932, the Supreme Court in *Powell v. Alabama* overturned the convictions on the ground that the accused had not received proper counsel. In a second trial in 1933, in Decatur, Alabama, even though one of the alleged victims confessed that neither she nor her companion had been assaulted—the all-white jury

The "Scottsboro boys" with the National Guard, March 26, 1931. © Library of Congress.

returned a guilty verdict. On appeal by ILD lawyers, the Supreme Court in **Norris v. Alabama** (1935) set aside the conviction because the arbitrary exclusion of blacks from jury service violated the defendants' **Fourteenth Amendment** rights. The Communist Party subsequently invited to the defense team other civil liberties groups including the **NAACP,** which dominated a newly formed Scottsboro Defense Committee (SDC). The SDC won the acquittal of four defendants in 1937 and laid the groundwork for the pardon of the others. The last "boy" was released on 9 June 1950, 19 years and 2 months after his arrest.

Selected Bibliography Richard Bardolph, ed., *The Civil Rights Record: Black Americans and the Law, 1849–1970* (1970); Dan T. Carter, *Scottsboro: A Tragedy of the American South* (1969); Kwando M. Kinshasa, *The Man from Scottsboro: Clarence Norris and the Infamous 1931 Alabama Rape Trial, In His Own Words* (1997); Hugh T. Murray, "The Scottsboro Rape Cases, 1931–1932," in Bernard Sternsher, ed., *The Negro in Depression and War: Prelude to Revolution, 1930–1945* (1969); Wilson Record, *The Negro and the Community Party* (1951).

James B. Potts

Screws v. United States, 325 U.S. 91 (1945) In the 1940s, the Department of Justice resurrected dormant remnants of Reconstruction legislation protecting civil rights because there were no such contemporary laws. One section of the **Civil Rights Act of 1866,** codified as Title 18, Section 242, provides punishment for "whoever, under color of law, . . . willfully" deprives an individual of national rights. Screws, a Georgia sheriff, was convicted for violating the **Fourteenth Amendment** due process rights of a black prisoner whom he had beaten to death. He challenged the constitutionality of Section 242 insofar as it made due process deprivations a crime, arguing that the meaning of due process was so vague that he could not have known that his actions violated Section 242. Since it is clear, however, that due process condemns vagueness in criminal statutes, Section 242 violated his due process rights. The Supreme Court upheld the constitutionality of Section 242 and its applicability to due process deprivations, thus authorizing federal prosecution of state officials for civil rights violations; it held that due process was understandable because "willfully" means intent to deprive a person of a specific constitutional right. It also held that "color of law" means "pretense" of law, rather than authorized by law. But it reversed Screws' conviction; the trial judge had misconstrued "willfully." Upon retrial, Screws was acquitted.

Selected Bibliography Derrick A. Bell, Jr., *Race, Racism, and American Law* (1980); Robert Carr, *Federal Protection of Civil Rights: Quest for a Sword* (1947); Robert J. Harris, *The Quest for Equality: The Constitution, Congress, and the Supreme Court* (1960); Frederick M. Lawrence, "Civil Rights and Criminal Wrongs: The Measure of Federal Civil Rights Crimes," *Tulane Law Review* 67 (1993), 2113–29.

Earlean M. McCarrick

Seale, Bobby (22 October 1936, Dallas, Tex.–). As cofounder and chairman of the **Black Panther party,** Seale was instrumental in fashioning part of the militant political ideology that characterized the late 1960s civil rights movement. With his compatriot, **Huey P. Newton,** he drafted the Ten Point Program that became the constitution of the party, helped write and edit the *Black Panther* newspaper, and wrote a personal history of the Panthers, *Seize the Time: The Story of the Black Panther Party and Huey P. Newton* (1968). Seale was one of those put on trial in the Chicago Eight Conspiracy case for his protest activities during the 1968 Democratic National Convention. He captured nationwide attention when Judge Julius Hoffman ordered him bound and gagged during the trial. Seale was later charged with murder in a Panther killing in New Haven, Connecticut, but he was acquitted after deliberations ended in a hung jury. During the course of his activist political career, he forced a runoff election against the incumbent mayor of Oakland, California. Seale's contributions to the movement were his ideological stance, powerful rhetoric, and symbolism as a victim of American oppression. In 1999, he was campaign manager for David Hilliard, former Panther Chief of Staff in his unsuccessful run for the Oakland City Council. In 2003 he and other original Black Panthers were battling an anti-Semitic "New Black Panther Party" over the use of the name.

Selected Bibliography Earl Anthony, *Picking Up the Gun: A Report on the Black Panthers* (1970); Curtis J. Austin, "The Role of Violence in the Creation, Sustenance, and Destruction of the Black Panther Party, 1966–1972" (Ph.D. diss., Mississippi State University, 1999); Philip S. Foner, ed., *The Black Panthers Speak* (1970); Gene Marine, *The Black Panthers* (1969); Bobby Seale, *A Lonely Rage* (1978); Bobby Seale, *Seize the Time: The Story of the Black Panther Party and*

Bobby Seale (left) and Huey Newton. © Library of Congress.

Huey P. Newton (1968); Gail Sheehy, *Panthermania: The Clash of Black against Black in One American City* (1971).

Marshall Hyatt

Selma to Montgomery March (1965)   In 1965 following an unsuccessful voter registration drive by the **Student Nonviolent Coordinating Committee** (SNCC) centered on Selma, Alabama, Dr. **Martin Luther King, Jr.,** and the **Southern Christian Leadership Conference** (SCLC) selected Selma to dramatize the need for a federal voter registration law. King and the Reverend **Ralph David Abernathy** led a mass march on 1 February that culminated in the arrest of 770 people. On 16 February Sheriff James G. "Bull" Clark punched a civil rights worker in the face while TV news cameras recorded the scene, and two days later in Marion, state troopers killed **Jimmy Lee Jackson.** Demands arose for a march on the state capital. On Sunday, 7 March, 1965, between five and six hundred marchers led by **Hosea Lorenzo Williams** and

Selma to Montgomery civil rights march, 1965. © Alabama Department of Archives and History, Montgomery, Alabama.

John Lewis marched from Selma. After they crossed the Edmund Pettus Bridge at the edge of Selma, they were stopped by state troopers and a posse including men on horseback. The mounted men rode down the fleeing marchers, and TV cameras captured "Bloody Sunday" for the evening news. Dr. King called for a ministers' march on Tuesday, 9 March, but Federal Judge **Frank M. Johnson** ordered the SCLC not to march. The Justice Department's Community Relations Service arranged a compromise whereby the marchers would cross the bridge and then be stopped. On Tuesday King led the marchers. At the prearranged point when the marchers stopped and prayed, the troopers opened the road. Dr. King ordered the marchers to return to Selma. Many were outraged at the apparent betrayal. White supremacists then attacked three white ministers in Selma and killed the Reverend **James Reeb.** President Lyndon Johnson called Governor George Wallace to the White House for consultation. On 15 March the President, in an address to Congress and a national TV audience, announced that he would submit voter registration legislation. On 17 March Judge Johnson ruled in favor of the march. The President nationalized the Alabama National Guard and sent regular troops, FBI agents, and marshals to secure the route. On Sunday, 21 March, some eight thousand people set out from Selma. Three hundred camped by the road that evening while the rest returned to Selma. On Thursday, 25 March, some twenty-five thousand people assembled before the Alabama State Capitol where King and others spoke. Wallace's executive secretary accepted a petition while the Governor peeked out of his office window. For safety the participants left Montgomery hurriedly. That night while **Viola Fauver Gregg Liuzzo** was returning marchers to Selma, a Ku Klux Klansman shot and killed her. On 6 August President Johnson signed the **Voting Rights Act of 1965.**

Selected Bibliography Thomas R. Brooks, *Walls Came Tumbling Down: A History of the Civil Rights Movement 1940–1970* (1974); David J. Garrow, *Protest at Selma: Martin Luther King, Jr., and the Voting Rights act of 1965* (1978); Stephen B. Oates, "The Week the World Watched Selma," *American Heritage* 33 (1982), 48–63; Juan Williams, *Eyes on the Prize: America's Civil Rights Years, 1954–1965* (1987).

Lorenzo Crowell

Sengstacke, John H. (25 November 1912, Savannah, Ga.–28 May 1997, Chicago, Ill.). John H. Sengstacke, publisher of the *Chicago Defender* and founder of the **Negro Newspaper Publishers' Association** (NNPA), helped save the black press from being shut down for seditious libel during World War II. He joined the staff of the *Defender* in 1934 as assistant to its founder and his uncle, **Robert S. Abbott.** Shortly before the U.S. entrance into World War II, he succeeded his uncle as publisher and editor.

Throughout the war period, the *Defender*, like other African American publications, criticized the treatment of black servicemen and advocated the integration of the armed forces. When the federal government considered indicting black publishers for sedition in order to silence the black press, Sengstacke worked out a compromise with the Justice Department. According to the deal, black newspapers would tone down their criticism and be more cooperative with the war effort if black journalists were given access to government officials. Sengstacke also helped gain accreditation for Harry S. McAlpin, the first black White House correspondent; was involved in the signing of **Jackie Robinson** by the Brooklyn Dodgers; and served on the Committee on Equality Treatment and Opportunity in the Armed Forces, which resulted in the desegregation of the United States military.

Selected Bibliography Wallace Best, "The *Chicago Defender* and the Realignment of Black Chicago," *Chicago History* 24 (No. 3, 1995), 4–21; Caryl A. Cooper, "The *Chicago Defender*: Filling in the Gaps for the Office of Civilian Defense, 1941–1945," *Western Journal of Black Studies* 23 (No. 2, 1999), 111–18; Chester Higgins, "Is the Black Press Dying?" *Crisis* 87 (No. 7, 1980), 240–41; Brent Staples, "John H. Sengstacke: Citizen Sengstacke," *New York Times Magazine* (4 January 1998), 27–28; Patrick S. Washburn, *A Question of Sedition: The Federal Government's Investigation of the Black Press during World War II* (1986).

Danny Blair Moore

Separate-but-Equal This legal doctrine was established as the law of the land by the Supreme Court in its *Plessy v. Ferguson* decision of 1896 and was overturned in its 1954 *Brown v. Board of Education* decision. In the *Plessy* decision, the court declared that a Louisiana law requiring separation by race of passengers on a railroad was a "reasonable" exercise of the state's police power that did not violate the **Fourteenth Amendment.** This doctrine provided the precedent for legal and unequal segregation ranging from rest rooms to schools until it was undermined in a series of cases brought by the **NAACP** between 1938 and 1950 and overturned in 1954.

Selected Bibliography Albert P. Blaustein and Robert L. Zangrando, *Civil Rights and the American Negro: A Documentary History* (1968); James Oliver Horton and Michele Gates Moresi, "Roberts, Plessy, and Brown: The Long Hard Struggle against Segregation," *Magazine of History* 15 (2001), 14–16; Richard Kluger, *Simple Justice: The History of Brown v. Board of Education and Black America's Struggle for Equality* (1976); C. Vann Woodward, *The Strange Career of Jim Crow* (1955).

Lorenzo Crowell

Sharpton, Alfred, Jr. (3 October 1954, Brooklyn, N.Y.–). Al Sharpton, an itinerant minister and political activist in New York, has preached in African American Pentecostal churches since he was four years of age. By the 1960s, he added political activism to his religious activities, gaining the attention of **Adam Clayton Powell, Jr.,** and **Jesse Jackson,** who gave him a position with Operation Breadbasket. After cultivating political connections during the 1970s, including an unsuccessful run for New York State Senate, Sharpton emerged as a leader in that state's African American community. He stepped onto the national scene in 1987 as a leading advocate of justice for Tawana Brawley, whose claims of rape by white police officers attracted much national attention. When Brawley recanted her claims, Sharpton's rise to leadership appeared to have come to a quick end. In 1989, though, Sharpton led protests in response to the murder of African American Yusef Hawkins in Bensonhurst, New York. His leadership in protests regarding police abuse of Abner Louima and **Amadou Diallo** repaired the fiasco of his support for Tawana Brawley. He was a candidate for the 2004 Democratic nomination for president.

Sharpton represents that tradition of African American social and political leadership that is closely wedded to the institutional church. A competitor of sorts with Jesse Jackson for leadership with this group, Sharpton gained an increased voice after Jackson admitted that he had fathered a child with his former mistress.

Selected Bibliography Michael Klein, *The Man Behind the Soundbite: The Real Story of Reverend Al Sharpton* (1991); Hal Marcovitz, *Al Sharpton* (2001); Al Sharpton, *Go and Tell Pharaoh: The Autobiography of Reverend Al Sharpton* (1996).

Merrill M. Hawkins, Jr.

***Shaw v. Hunt,* 116 S. Ct. 1894 (1996)** In *Shaw v. Reno* the U.S. Supreme Court invalidated an oddly shaped majority-black district in North Carolina for classifying voters by race in violation of the **Fourteenth Amendment.** Upon remand, a U.S. District Court nevertheless upheld the districting plan, because it was narrowly tailored to serve the state's compelling interest in complying with the **Voting Rights Act.** Since the Court had already decided in *Miller v. Johnson* that compliance with the Voting Rights Act did not constitute a compelling state interest, if the challenged district was not "reasonably necessary under a constitutional reading" of the Act, the plan was again struck down in *Shaw v. Hunt.* Critics have charged that the Court's *Shaw v. Reno* rulings have transformed the Voting Rights Act from an instrument to prohibit disenfranchisement and vote dilution into a device to diminish minority political power.

Selected Bibliography J. Morgan Kousser, *Colorblind Injustice: Minority Voting Rights and the Undoing of the Second Reconstruction* (1999); Stephan Thernstrom and Abigail Thernstrom, *America in Black and White: One Nation Indivisible* (1997); Carol M. Swain, "The Future of Black Representation," in Stephen Steinberg, ed., *Race and Ethnicity in the United States: Issues and Debates* (2000), 172–78.

Manfred Berg

Shaw v. Reno, **509 U.S. 630 (1993)** In this controversial five-to-four ruling, the U.S. Supreme Court held that the creation of majority-black congressional districts violated the equal protection clause of the **Fourteenth Amendment,** if it separated voters by race without regard for "traditional districting principles" such as geographical boundaries and political subdivisions. The Court invalidated a North Carolina reapportionment plan that contained an oddly shaped majority-black district that stretched for about one hundred and sixty miles along Interstate 85. Even for remedial purposes, racial gerrymandering was impermissible, the majority argued, because it reinforced racial stereotypes and bloc voting and threatened to "balkanize" the American political system. The dissenting justices and numerous other critics have characterized the notion of a color-blind political process as fictitious and accused the majority of ignoring the difference between racial discrimination and empowering minority voters.

Selected Bibliography J. Morgan Kousser, *Colorblind Injustice: Minority Voting Rights and the Undoing of the Second Reconstruction* (1999); Stephan Thernstrom and Abigail Thernstrom, *America in Black and White: One Nation Indivisible* (1997); Carol M. Swain, "The Future of Black Representation," in Stephen Steinberg, ed., *Race and Ethnicity in the United States, Issues and Debates* (2000), 172–78.

Manfred Berg

Shelley v. Kraemer, **334 U.S. 1 (1948)** In the first of the four restrictive covenant cases (*McGhee v. Sipes, Hurd v. Hodge* and *Urciolo v. Hodge*) decided in 1948, the U.S. Supreme Court held racially restrictive property deeds unenforceable. From World War I to 1948, restrictions placed in deeds by developers or neighborhood organizations became a major legal device urban whites used to segregate African Americans (and others by race, national origin, and religion) from white neighborhoods. In St. Louis, where the *Shelley* case originated, covenants restricted more than five square miles. When the Shelleys, an African American family, purchased a home covered by a covenant, the Kraemers, a white family, sought an injunction to block occupancy. The circuit court refused, but Missouri's Supreme Court reversed this decision. The **NAACP** coordinated lawyers George Vaughn (*Shelley*), **Thurgood Marshall** (*McGhee*), and **Charles H. Houston** (*Hurd and Urciolo*); briefs drew heavily on sociological data and theory. Chief Justice Frederick Vinson's unanimous but limited opinion found racially restrictive covenants, voluntarily maintained, permissible, but state action for enforcement violated **Fourteenth Amendment** "rights to acquire, enjoy, own and dispose of property." A major victory, *Shelley* failed to stop private discrimination or violence against black homebuyers, and federal agencies often refused to comply.

Selected Bibliography Tom C. Clark and Philip B. Perlman, *Prejudice and Property: An Historic Brief Against Racial Covenants* (1948); Peter Irons, *The Courage of Their Convictions: Sixteen Americans Who Fought Their Way to the Supreme Court* (1988); Kenneth T. Jackson, *Crabgrass Frontier: The Suburbanization of the United States* (1985); Herman H. Long and Charles S. Johnson, *People vs. Property: Race Restrictive Covenants in Housing* (1947); B. T. McGraw and George B. Nesbitt, "Aftermath of *Shelley v. Kraemer* on Residential Restrictions by Race," *Land Economics* 29 (August 1953), 280–87; Stephen Grant Meyer, *As Long As They Don't Move Next Door: Segregation and Racial Conflict in American Neighborhoods* (2000); Clement E. Vose, *Caucasians Only: The Supreme Court, the NAACP, and the Restrictive Covenant Cases* (1959).

James Borchert

Shepherd v. Florida, **341 U.S. 50 (1951)** In 1949 Samuel Shepherd and Walter Irvin, both black men, were accused of raping a 17-year-old white girl at gun point. They were indicted by an all-white grand jury, convicted, and sentenced to death by an all-white trial jury. The **NAACP** in representing the defendants before the Supreme Court argued that Shepherd and Irvin were denied their constitutional rights to due process because blacks had been systematically excluded from the jury. In addition, despite the sensational nature of the case and the fact that black citizens in the county had been forced to flee for their lives, the defendants were denied a change of venue. The Supreme Court reversed the convictions. Justice Robert Jackson, with Justice Felix Frankfurter concurring, declared that racial discrimination in the selection of a jury was a violation of the Constitution's due process and equal protection. And Jackson declared, "for the court to reverse these convictions upon the sole ground of jury selection is to stress the trivial and ignore the important. . . . I do not see, as a practical matter how any Negro on the jury would have dared to cause a disagreement of acquittal. The only chance these Negroes had of acquittal would have been in the courage and decency of some sturdy and forthright white person of sufficient standing to face and live down the odium among his white neighbors. . . . "

Selected Bibliography Robert J. Harris, *The Quests for Equality: The Constitution, Congress, and the Supreme Court* (1960); Herman Pritchett, *Civil Liberties and the Vinson Court* (1954); Rowland L. Young, "Review of Recent Supreme Court Decisions," *American Bar Association Journal* 37 (1951), 528.

Kenneth W. Goings

Shuttlesworth, Fred L. (18 March 1922, Mt. Meigs, Ala–). The leader of the Birmingham, Alabama, civil rights movement, he survived two bombings, a mob beating, and numerous jailings in his efforts to achieve racial equality. After he earned his A.B. degree at Selma College in 1951 and his B.S. degree from Alabama State College in 1952, Shuttlesworth returned to Birmingham as pastor of Bethel Baptist Church in 1953. He organized the **Alabama Christian Movement for Human Rights** on 5 June 1956 and he served as president until 1969. A colleague of **Martin Luther King, Jr.,** and **Ralph David Abernathy,** Shuttlesworth joined them and others in forming the **Southern Christian Leadership Conference** (SCLC), where he held the position of secretary from 1958 to 1970. King called Shuttlesworth "the most courageous civil rights fighter in the South." On Christmas night of 1956, the charismatic Shuttlesworth survived a bomb blast that destroyed his house. The next day he led a challenge to bus segregation. In 1957 a mob of whites beat him with whips and chains during an attempt to integrate an all-white public school. Shuttlesworth witnessed the **Greensboro, North Carolina, sit-ins** in 1960 and helped the **Congress of Racial Equality** (CORE) with the 1961 **Freedom Rides.** Shuttlesworth asked King and the SCLC in 1962 to assist him in conducting mass demonstrations against segregation in Birmingham. King agreed and the SCLC prepared **Project C.** The **Birmingham Confrontation** began 3 April 1963 and ended with Shuttlesworth reaching a negotiated accord on 10 May 1963. During the interim, he was arrested on 6 and 12 April 1963 and hospitalized on 7 May 1963 after being slammed against a wall by water from firehoses. The demonstrations in Birmingham led to the **Civil Rights Act of 1964.** A veteran of the St. Augustine and **Selma to Montgomery march** campaigns, Shuttlesworth remained active in the movement after his move to Cincinnati, Ohio, in the early 1960s. He served on the boards of the Southern Conference Education Fund and CORE. Shuttlesworth is pastor of the Greater New Light Baptist Church, which he organized in 1966, and is also director of the Shuttlesworth Housing Foundation, which helps the poor buy homes. In 2001, the SCLC named him chairman and Leader of the Direct Action Campaign in Florida in reaction to the disputed 2000 presidential election. His statue stands before the entrance to the Civil Rights Institute in Birmingham.

Selected Bibliography *Cincinnati Enquirer*, 15 January 1989; Glenn T. Eskew, *But For Birmingham: The Local and National Movements in the Civil Rights Struggle* (1997); Lewis W. Jones, "Fred L. Shuttlesworth, Indigenous Leader," in David J. Garrow, ed., *Birmingham, Alabama, 1956–1963* (1989); Jacksonville *Free Press*, 2 May 2001; Andrew M. Manis, *A Fire You Can't Put Out: The Civil Rights Life of Birmingham's Reverend Fred Shuttlesworth* (1999); *Pittsburgh Courier*, 14 February 1959; Marjorie L. White and Andrew Manis, eds., *Birmingham's Revolutionary: The Reverend Fred Shuttlesworth and the Alabama Christian Movement for Human Rights* (2000).

Glenn T. Eskew

"The Silent South"　　The essay, "The Silent South," was written by George Washington Cable for inclusion in the September 1885 issue of *Century* magazine. Intended as a response to the racially conservative writings of Henry Grady of the *Atlanta Constitution*, it served as one of the most thoughtful criticisms of southern racial policy during the postbellum era. In the essay, Cable suggested that there was in the South a silent and conscientious majority of southerners who supported a just and compassionate approach to race relations. Cable's frustration with the South's inability to progress racially and politically resulted in his eventual move to Northampton, Massachusetts, where he continued to analyze conditions in the South.

Selected Bibliography Edward L. Ayers, *The Promise of a New South: Life after Reconstruction* (1992); George W. Cable, "The Silent South," in *The Silent South with an Introductory Essay* (1969); Louis D. Rubin, Jr., *George W. Cable: The Life and Times of a Southern Heretic* (1969); Arlin Turner, ed., *Critical Essays on George W. Cable* (1980); Arlin Turner, *George W. Cable: A Biography* (1966); C. Vann Woodward, *Origins of the New South, 1877–1913* (1951).

JoAnn D. Carpenter

Silver, James Wesley (28 June 1907, Rochester, N.Y.–25 July 1988, Tampa, Fla.). James W. Silver began teaching history at the University of Mississippi in 1936. A popular professor, he quickly became a lightning rod for suspicious Mississippians who saw him as a dangerous radical. He survived a series of relatively minor inquisitions in the 1940s and 1950s, which presaged the firestorm surrounding the publication of his *Mississippi: The Closed Society* (1964). A scathing and meticulous indictment of Mississippi political and racial practices, the book drew copious amounts of praise and scorn. In the wake of this controversy, Silver joined the history faculty at Notre Dame in 1964, and later (in 1969) went to the University of South Florida. He retired in 1979. Silver was less an activist than an advocate of simple human rights. He often downplayed his role in the civil rights movement, calling himself a "paper radical" and a "quiet reformer." In his later writings, Silver faulted some black leaders for separatist thinking, seeing them as little better than the architects of white supremacy he had earlier excoriated.

Selected Bibliography James W. Silver, *Mississippi: The Closed Society* (1964); James W. Silver, *Running Scared: Silver in Mississippi* (1984); Obituary, *The Journal of Southern History* 54 (November 1988), 695–97.

Allen Dennis

***Simkins v. City of Greensboro*, 149 F. Supp. 562 (M.D. N.C., 1957)** This 1957 case grew out of a legal battle that had begun in December 1955, when George Simkins, Jr., a Greensboro, North Carolina, dentist and head of the local **NAACP,** and a number of his colleagues were arrested and put on trial for attempting to play on the segregated Greensboro public golf course. The defendants were convicted, sentenced, and fined, although their sentences were later commuted. Simkins subsequently brought a federal discrimination suit against the City of Greensboro. Until 1949 the Gillespie Park Course had been an 18 hole public golf course restricted to whites and located on land leased by the city from the board of education. In an effort to comply with **Plessy v. Ferguson,** the city also operated a 9 hole golf course for African Americans, known as Nacho Park Golf Course. After a group of black citizens applied for permission to play on the Gillespie course in 1949, the city and the board of education leased the entire course to the Gillespie Park Golf Club, which then operated as a private, nonprofit corporation. Annual membership and green fees were established. In practice, however, white nonmembers were allowed to play on the course by paying only the green fees, while blacks who asked to play were denied such, always being told that they were not members. On 20 March 1957 in this *Simkins* case, the U.S. District Court ruled that the City of Greensboro and the City Board of Education could not avoid giving equal treatment to black citizens by leasing an entire golf course to a nonprofit corporation. In order for the golf course to remain open, it could not discriminate against any citizens of Greensboro on account of race. In reaction to this decision, the city closed both golf courses.

Selected Bibliography Richard Bardolph, ed., *The Civil Rights Record, Black Americans and the Law, 1849–1970* (1970); William H. Chafe, *Civilities and Civil Rights, Greensboro, North Carolina, and the Black Struggle for Freedom* (1980).

Charles A. Risher

Simkins v. Moses H. Cone Memorial Hospital, **323 F.2d 959 (4th Cir., 1963)** This case resulted in a landmark decision in the struggle against segregation. The Fourth Circuit Court of Appeals in November 1963 held that governmentally owned, operated, or subsidized hospitals practicing racial discrimination violated the due process clause of the Fifth Amendment and the equal protection clause of the **Fourteenth Amendment.** Black physicians, dentists, and patients brought the suit in 1962 against two Greensboro, North Carolina, hospitals that practiced exclusionary policies based on race. The plaintiffs argued that since the defendant hospitals received federal funds under the Hill-Burton Hospital Survey and Construction Act, they were subject to constitutional restraints against racial discrimination. The Justice Department intervened in support of the plaintiffs' contention that a provision of Hill-Burton permitting separate but equal facilities in recipient hospitals was unconstitutional. Reversing lower court decisions, a divided Court of Appeals ruled in favor of the plaintiffs. This decision became an important precedent in lawsuits dealing with the discriminatory policies of nongovernmental medical facilities. It and other related cases helped to establish the premise for Title VI of the **Civil Rights Act of 1964,** which prohibited racial discrimination in federally assisted programs and activities.

Selected Bibliography Derrick A. Bell Jr., *Race, Racism, and American Law* 2nd ed. (1980); William H. Chafe, *Civilities and Civil Rights: Greensboro, North Carolina, and the Black Struggle for Freedom* (1980); Loren Miller, *The Petitioners: The Story of the Supreme Court of the United States and the Negro* (1966); Stephen L. Wasby, Anthony A. D'Amato, and Rosemary Metrailer, *Desegregation from Brown to Alexander: An Exploration of Supreme Court Strategies* (1977).

Jack E. Davis

Singleton, Benjamin "Pap" (1809, Nashville, Tenn.–1892, St. Louis, Mo.). Born a slave, Singleton was sold south several times but always managed to return to Nashville. He finally escaped to Canada, but recrossed the border and settled in Detroit, Michigan. There, Singleton harbored other runaways.

After the Civil War, he returned to Nashville where, by the 1870s, he had become involved in the millenarian movement. In 1874 he and several others established the Edgefield Real Estate and Homestead Association. Between 1877 and 1897, the association directed hundreds of landless and persecuted black southerners to Kansas. Thus, by the time Singleton testified before the Senate committee on the exodus, he claimed to be the "father" of the millenarian exodus.

Selected Bibliography Walter L. Fleming, "'Pap' Singleton, the Moses of the Colored Exodus," *American Journal of Sociology* 15 (July 1909), 61–82; Ray Garvin, "Benjamin or 'Pap' Singleton and his Followers," *Journal of Negro History* 33 (January 1948), 7–23; Nell Irvin Painter, *Exoduster: Black Migration to Kansas Following Reconstruction* (1977); U.S. Senate, *Report and Testimony of the Select Committee . . . to Investigate the Causes of the Removal of the Negro from the Southern States to the Northern States*, U.S. 46th Cong., 2nd Sess., Senate Report 693 (1880), 3:379–91.

Judith N. Kerr

Sipuel v. Board of Regents of the University of Oklahoma, 332 U.S. 631 (1948) Ada Lois Sipuel graduated with an excellent academic record from Langston University. In 1946 she applied to the only law school in the state at the University of Oklahoma. The university refused her application, telling her a law school for blacks would be opened as soon as the demand justified the expense. Sipuel sued for immediate admission but lost in state court. On appeal, the Supreme Court held that plans to establish a school did not satisfy the equal protection clause of the **Fourteenth Amendment.** The Court in **Missouri ex rel Gaines v. Canada** required the states to furnish blacks the same opportunities given to white students. The Court affirmed this doctrine in *Sipuel*, requiring the school to offer the opportunity for a legal education to blacks at the same time it was available to whites. The university quickly responded by establishing a law school for blacks in the state capitol. Sipuel argued that the "Negro law school" did not provide her an education equal to whites. The Court refused to consider the question, with only two justices dissenting.

Selected Bibliography Richard Bardolph, *The Civil Rights Record: Black Americans and the Law, 1849–1970* (1970); Derrick A. Bell, Jr., *Race, Racism and American Law* (1980); E. W. Broore, Jr., "Notes and Comments," *Boston University Law Review* 28 (1948), 240–42; Laurence R. Marcus and Benjamin D. Stickney, *Race and Education: The Unending Controversy* (1981); Fred Powledge, *Free at Last: The Civil Rights Movement and the People who Made It* (1991); Geoffrey R. Stone, *Constitutional Law* (1986); Mark V. Tushnet, *The NAACP's Legal Strategy against Segregated Education, 1925–1950* (1987).

Stephen Middleton

Sissle, Noble (10 July 1889, Indianapolis, Ind.–17 December 1975, Tampa, Fla.). African American orchestra leader and lyricist, Sissle was educated in the public schools in Indianapolis and in Cleveland, Ohio, where his family lived from 1909 to 1913. He attended DePauw University, in Greencastle, Indiana (1913) and Butler University, in Indianapolis (1914–15). A protege of black orchestra leader **James Reese Europe,** Sissle toured with Europe from 1917 to 1919, first as a member of his dance orchestra, then, during World War I, as drum major of the 369th Infantry Regiment Band, which Europe led. In the fall of 1917, while stationed with the 15th New York Infantry in Spartanburg, South Carolina, Sissle almost precipitated a race riot when he went into a white hotel to purchase a newspaper and was assaulted by whites. Sissle was best known as pianist-composer Eubie Blake's lyricist partner. They toured the vaudeville circuit from 1919 to 1920. In 1921 they collaborated in the production of the Broadway production *Shuffle Along,* which began their career as writers of musicals. The partnership ended in 1927, after which Sissle formed his own orchestra (1928–31). In 1937, he was one of the founders of the Negro Actor's Guild.

Selected Bibliography Rudi Blesh, *Combo USA* (1971); Robert Kimball and William Bolcom, *Reminiscing with Sissle and Blake* (1973); Obituary, *New York Times,* 18 December 1975.

Judith N. Kerr

The Slater Fund   Established in 1882 with a million dollar endowment by Connecticut industrialist John Fox Slater, the Slater Fund was dedicated to the elevation of black southerners through education. Conservative white businessmen, churchmen, educators, and politicians, including former President Rutherford B. Hayes, were the charter members of the Fund's board of trustees. They agreed that black students would reap the most benefits from training in the manual occupations. For the first 29 years of its life, the Slater Fund gave the lion's share of its aid to black colleges offering industrial training. **Tuskegee** and **Hampton Institutes** received the greatest portion of the appropriations. After 1911 the fund gave a significant amount of aid to county/parish training schools. Its aim was to increase the pool of trained black elementary school teachers in the rural South. Segregation was not an issue of concern for directors of the Slater Fund, most of whom endorsed separate schools. However, by filling the financial void of underfunded black schools and colleges in the South, the Slater Fund, unwittingly perhaps, helped lay the foundation for a middle-class, college-bred black leadership elite that worked with white allies in tearing down the walls of **Jim Crow.**

Selected Bibliography Will W. Alexander, "The Slater and Jeanes Funds, an Educator's Approach to a Difficult Social Problem," Washington, D.C.: Trustees of the John F. Slater Fund, Occasional Papers, No. 286 (1948); Henry Allen Bullock, *A History of Negro Education in the South: From 1619 to the Present* (1967); Leslie H. Fischel, Jr., "The John F. Slater Fund," *Hayes Historical Journal* 8 (No. 1, 1988), 47–51; Lamar Monroe Curry Papers, Manuscript Division, Library of Congress; John E. Fisher, *The John F. Slater Fund: A Nineteenth Century Affirmative Action for Negro Education* (1986); Edward E. Redcay, *County Training Schools and Public Secondary Education for Negroes in the South* (1935).

Joe Louis Caldwell

***Slaughterhouse Cases,* 83 U.S. 36 (1873)**   Challenging a Louisiana statute that gave a 25-year monopoly on the business of slaughtering cattle in New Orleans to one favored company, the rival butchers asserted that section one of the **Fourteenth Amendment** protected their property rights. The law, they said, deprived them of the equal protection of the laws, took their property without due process, and abridged the privileges and immunities of citizenship. Justice Samuel Miller, writing for a five-to-four majority, rejected each of these claims. The equal protection clause prohibited only state laws that discriminated against blacks as a class; the due process clause had only procedural meaning, not substantive; and the privileges and immunities protected against state intrusion were only those, largely undefined, that derived from federal citizenship. While the opinion thus recognized the intent of the equal protection clause, this first Supreme Court interpretation of the Fourteenth Amendment was so narrow that it left very little opportunity for protection of civil rights. The case marks the beginning of a 10-year period that culminated in the *Civil Rights Cases* (1883), during which the Court, through narrow interpretations of the **Thirteenth Amendment** and Fourteenth Amendment, blunted most federal efforts to legislate on civil rights.

Selected Bibliography Charles Fairman, Mr. *Justice Miller and the Supreme Court, 1862–1890* (1939); Charles Fairman, *History of the Supreme Court of the United States, vol. 7: Reconstruction and Reunion, 1864–1888, Part 1* (1986); William Gillette, "Samuel Miller," in Leon Friedman and Fred Israel, eds., *The Justices of the United States Supreme Court, 1789–1969: Their Lives and Major Opinions* (1969); Robert C. Palmer, "The Parameters of Constitutional Reconstruction: Slaughter-House, Cruikshank, and the Fourteenth Amendment," *University of Illinois Law Review* (1984), 739–70; John A. Scott, "Justice Bradley's Evolving Concept of the Fourteenth Amendment from the Slaughterhouse Cases to the Civil Rights Cases," *Rutgers Law Review* 25 (1971), 552–69.

James E. Sefton

Smalls, Robert (5 April 1839, Beaufort, S.C.–22 February 1915, Beaufort, S.C.). Born a slave in Beaufort, South Carolina, Robert Smalls became a Civil War hero after he abducted the *Planter*, a Confederate steamer, and navigated it into Union lines in 1862. He became a major figure in South Carolina Republican politics during Reconstruction, championing black economic, political, and social rights. Smalls attended the 1867 state constitutional convention, represented Beaufort County in the General Assembly, the state senate and in the United States Congress. Even though his congressional career ended in 1888, Smalls continued to wield considerable power and influence in local politics. He was appointed Collector of Customs for the Port of Beaufort in 1888. During World War II a training camp for black naval officers at Great Lakes Naval Station was named after him.

Selected Bibliography Edward A. Miller, Jr., *Gullah Statesman: Robert Smalls from Slavery to Congress, 1839–1915* (1995); Deborah Moore, "The King of Beaufort" (M.A. thesis, Columbia University, 1968); Willie Lee Rose, *Rehearsal for Reconstruction: The Port Royal Experiment* (1964); Dorothy Sterling, *Captain of the* Planter: *The Story of Robert Smalls* (1958); Okon Edet Uya, *From Slavery to Public Service: Robert Smalls 1839–1915* (1971).

Maxine D. Jones

Smiley, Glenn (19 April 1910, Loraine, Tex.–17 September 1993, Los Angeles, Calif.). **Martin Luther King, Jr.,** once wrote: "I rode the first integrated bus in Montgomery with a white minister, and a native Southerner as my seatmate." That seatmate was Glenn Smiley, credited with guiding King in the transition from advocating nonviolent resistance as a tactic to adopting it as a way of life. Smiley conducted nonviolence training workshops during the Montgomery campaign (1955–56) and stumped the nation interpreting the protest. Staff member of the **Fellowship of Reconciliation** from 1952 until 1967 (imprisoned 1944–45 as a conscientious objector), Smiley cultivated nonviolence in Latin America during the years 1967–70. Appointed to the Board of Advisors of the New York State Institute on Nonviolence in 1987 and founder of the Martin Luther King Center for Nonviolence in Los Angeles, Smiley published a nonviolence training manual in 1990.

Selected Bibliography Taylor Branch, *Parting the Waters: America in the King Years, 1954–63* (1989); Vera Brittain, *The Rebel Passion* (1964); Margaret Cavin, "Glenn Smiley Was a Fool: The Use of the Comic as a Strategy of Nonviolence," *Peace and Change* 26 (April 2001), 223–42; David J. Garrow, *Bearing the Cross: Martin Luther King and the Southern Christian Leadership Conference* (1986); Aldon D. Morris, *The Origins of the Civil Rights Movement: Black Communities Organizing for Change* (1984); Juan Williams, *Eyes on the Prize: America's Civil Rights Years, 1954–1965* (1987).

Jo Ann O. Robinson

Smith, Frank Ellis   (21 February 1918, Sidon, Miss.–2 August 1997, Jackson, Miss.). After serving as an artillery officer in World War II, Smith returned to Greenwood, Mississippi, to be the managing editor of the *Morning Star.* He was elected to the Mississippi state senate, worked in John Stennis's 1946 election campaign, and went to Washington, D.C. with Stennis. In 1950 Smith was elected to the U.S. House of Representatives, and in 1962 John F. Kennedy appointed him to the Tennessee Valley Authority (TVA) board. Smith condemned Mississippi's efforts to prevent the integration of the University of Mississippi, and he published his autobiography, *Congressman from Mississippi* (1964), to inspire white southerners to integrate. He served as "confessor" to Mississippians who disagreed with their state's policies and aided exiles who made their views known and had to flee. He counseled state politicians who worked for integration, spoke to groups interested in furthering integration, and used his public role as a TVA director to argue for political and economic justice for blacks. He published his arguments for integration in *Look Away From Dixie* (1965). To provide biracial role models, Smith published a series of short biographies entitled *Mississippians All* (1968). Smith also served on the **Southern Regional Council** and worked with their **Voter Education Project** to register and encourage blacks to vote.

Selected Bibliography Dennis J. Mitchell, *Mississippi Liberal: A Biography of Frank E. Smith* (2001); James W. Silver, *Mississippi: The Closed Society* (1963); Frank Smith, *Congressman From Mississippi* (1964).

Dennis J. Mitchell

Smith, Lamar   (1892–13 August 1955, Brookhaven, Miss). Lamar Smith was not a typical Lincoln County, Mississippi, black man; he owned land and wealth. His active participation in the civil rights movement also set him apart. Although warned to "stay out of white folks' politics," Smith organized black voters throughout the county. He was intensely involved in a county supervisor election during the summer of 1955. His activities figured prominently in the events of Saturday, August 13. While arguing with several whites on the courthouse grounds in Brookhaven, Smith was shot and killed. Although at the time—10 A.M.—many blacks and whites were present, gaining a clear understanding of what had occurred proved difficult. Some witnesses mentioned a blood-spattered white man who sped away in a truck, but Sheriff Robert Case first reported "nobody knows nothing." Before the week had passed, however, three local white men were in custody. A coroner's jury concluded they had committed the crime. Yet, subsequently, due to a lack of evidence, the grand jury failed to return any indictments. District Attorney E. C. Barlow put the murder of the 63-year-old black man in perspective when he attributed the death to "local politics."

Selected Bibliography Sara Bullard, ed., *Free At Last* (1989); *Jackson Clarion-Ledger*, 14, 15, 16, 17, 19 August 1955; James W. Silver, *Mississippi: The Closed Society* (1963).

William Warren Rogers, Jr.

Smith, Lillian (12 December 1887, Jasper, Fla.–28 September 1966, Clayton, Ga.). A southern writer and teacher, she devoted much of her talent and energy to exploring the causes and implications of white racism and being an advocate for black equality and racial understanding. Through the pages of *South Today,* which she coedited, Smith publicized the works of black writers, attacked the racial assumptions of popular novels like *Gone with the Wind,* and probed the historical sources of southern racism and segregation. She directly challenged **Jim Crow** and often criticized fellow white liberals for not confronting the full terror of race separation and violence in the South. In 1944, she published *Strange Fruit,* a novel that looked at the tragic effects of a love affair between a white man and a black woman. Despite being banned in Boston and elsewhere for sexual and racial references, it became a national best seller. *Killers of the Dream,* a collection of essays on the psychological and historical meaning of southern racism, published in 1949, further enhanced Smith's stature as the South's foremost critic of racism. Because of her views, Smith was often harassed by state and local government officials and was attacked by the Ku Klux Klan. During the 1950s and 1960s, she celebrated the civil rights movement, giving special praise to the philosophy and tactics of **Martin Luther King, Jr.,** and to the young black students who initiated sit-in protests in Georgia and elsewhere. A board member of the **Congress of Racial Equality** (CORE), she resigned prior to her death in 1966 in protest against what she felt was CORE's failure to maintain a commitment to integration and **nonviolent resistance**. A courageous advocate of equality, Lillian Smith embodied the best of southern white race liberalism.

Selected Bibliography Louise Blackwell and Frances Clay, *Lillian Smith* (1971); John B. Kirby, *Black Americans in the Roosevelt Era* (1980); Morton Sosna, *In Search of the Silent South*

(1977); Anne C. Loveland, *Lillian Smith, A Southerner Confronting the South: A Biography* (1986).

John B. Kirby

Smith v. Allwright, 321 U.S. 649 (1944)   On 3 April 1944, the U.S. Supreme Court ruled that the **white primaries** of the Texas Democratic party were unconstitutional because, on the basis of race, they denied African Americans the right to participate in the electoral process. **NAACP** General Counsel **Thurgood Marshall** and Dallas lawyer William J. Durham argued the case for the plaintiff, Houston dentist Lonnie E. Smith. Smith was denied a ballot in the 1940 Harris County primary by election Judge S. E. Allwright. To eliminate the Texas white primary, the Supreme Court had to reverse its 1935 **Grovey v. Townsend** decision that had stated that Democratic party primaries were private affairs and not subject to state regulation. In 1941, however, the Supreme Court ruled in the **United States v. Classic** case that party primaries constituted state action because the state delegated to political parties the power to choose candidates to hold elective office. Using this ruling in the *Classic* case, the Supreme Court ruled that African Americans had as much right to participate in party primaries as in general elections and that the denial of their participation violated the Constitution. This landmark case won by the NAACP in Texas removed a major barrier that had prevented African Americans from participating in the electoral process in the South.

Selected Bibliography Darlene Clark Hine, *Black Victory: The Rise and Fall of the White Primary in Texas* (1979); Darlene Clark Hine, "The Elusive Ballot: The Black Struggle Against the Texas Democratic White Primary, 1932–1945," *Southwestern Historical Quarterly* 81 (April 1978), 371–92; Steven F. Lawson, *Black Ballots: Voting Rights in the South, 1944–1969* (1976); *New York Times,* 4 April 1944; Papers of the NAACP, Part 4: The Voting Rights Campaign, 1916–1950.

W. Marvin Dulaney

Smith v. State of Texas, 311 U.S. 128 (1940)   This U.S. Supreme Court case helped define what constituted racial discrimination in the selection of grand juries as proscribed under the "equal protection" clause of the **Fourteenth Amendment.** Edgar Smith, a black resident of Harris County, Texas, was convicted of rape in the State District Court in 1938. His appeal, which reached the Supreme Court in November 1940, contended that his conviction had come under an indictment returned by a grand jury from which blacks had been systematically excluded—as indicated by their almost complete absence on such panels from 1931 to 1938. He had been denied, he argued, the equal protection of law. The court accepted Smith's argument, holding that it is not sufficient that state law merely promise equal protection, as did the Texas grand jury-selection statute; equal protection must actually be provided. The fact that, for example, only one black had served on Harris County grand juries in the four years between 1935 and 1938 indicated the existence of a pattern of discrimination by race in the selection of grand jury members. Regardless of whether that discrimination had been accomplished deliberately or innocently, the fact deprived Smith of the equal protection of the laws. The Court invalidated his conviction.

Selected Bibliography Richard Bardolph, *The Civil Rights Record: Black Americans and the Law, 1849–1970* (1970); Thomas I. Emerson et. al., *Political and Civil Rights in the United States* (1967); *New York Times*, 26 November 1940.

Robert A. Calvert

The Souls of Black Folk   In 1903 **W.E.B. Du Bois,** scholar and intellectual, rose to national prominence as a political propagandist when he published an intensely personal manifesto of 14 essays on the spiritual, cultural, and political significance of being black in America. Using the motif of a "veil" that had created for African Americans a "double-consciousness," Du Bois assessed the past, present, and future of American race relations.

In a national environment of increased racial violence, discrimination, disenfranchisement, and scientific racism, Du Bois offered a prophetic vision of black nationalism for the legal recognition of black human rights and the assertion of an African American cultural identity. In doing so, Du Bois challenged and rejected the leadership and philosophy of **Booker T. Washington,** not only in the one essay entitled "Of Mr. Booker T. Washington and Others," but in the entire book. In place of Washington's accommodationist policy of economic development, Du Bois confronted and challenged what he called the Problem of the Twentieth Century: the color line.

Selected Bibliography David W. Bight, "Up from 'Twoness': Frederick Douglass and the Meaning of W.E.B. Du Bois's Concept of Double Consciousness," *Canadian Review of American Studies* 21 (No.3, 1990), 301–19; Francis L. Broderick, *W.E.B. Du Bois: Negro Leader in a Time of Crisis* (1959); W.E.B. Du Bois, *The Souls of Black Folk* (1903); Manning Marable, *W.E.B. Du Bois: Black Radical Democrat* (1986); Arnold Rampersad, *The Art and Imagination of W.E.B. Du Bois* (1976); Elliott M. Rudwick, *Propagandist of the Negro Protest* (1968); Roumiana Velikova, "W.E.B. Du Bois vs. 'The Sons of the Fathers: & Reading of the *Souls of Black Folk* in the Context of American Nationalism," *African American Review* 34 (No. 3, 2000), 431–42.

Lillie Johnson Edwards

South Carolina Electric and Gas Co. v. Fleming, **351 U.S. 901 (1956)** Sara Mae Fleming boarded a crowded bus in Columbus, South Carolina, in 1954, and went to the back as city law required. No seats were available so she stood in the isle until a white passenger got off. Fleming then took the empty seat in the front of the bus, which was reserved for whites. The driver ordered her to return to the Negro section, but Fleming chose to get off at the next stop. She was closer to the front and would have exited there, but the driver stopped her, insisting that she use the rear door, as blacks were expected to do. When she refused, the driver assaulted her, and she sued for damages. A state court dismissed the complaint on the grounds that the driver had only enforced **Plessy v. Ferguson.** A federal court stating **Brown v. Board of Education** left "no doubt that the separate but equal doctrine [had] . . . been repudiated, reversed the state court decision. On appeal the Supreme Court agreed, but due to a technicality did not reverse in this case. Instead the

Supreme Court dismissed the bus company's appeal. Many people understood the opinion to mean that the court had ended racial segregation in public transit, though the court itself would not say so directly until it decided the Montgomery bus case.

Selected Bibliography Chester J. Antieau, ed., *Federal Civil Rights Acts: Civil Practice* (1980); Catherine A. Barnes, *Journey from Jim Crow: The Desegregation of Southern Transit* (1983); Mark V. Tushnet, *Making Civil Rights Law: Thurgood Marshall and the Supreme Court, 1936–1961* (1994).

Stephen Middleton

South Carolina v. Katzenbach, 383 U.S. 301 (1966)   In a suit filed by the State of South Carolina, the Supreme Court upheld the constitutionality of key provisions of the **Voting Rights Act of 1965,** legislation based upon Section 2 of the **Fifteenth Amendment,** authorizing Congress to enforce the amendment by appropriate legislation. The Court held that the coverage formula, bringing under coverage of the act states and subdivisions of states using "tests or devices" as prerequisites for voting and having less than 50 percent of their otherwise eligible voters registered and voting in the presidential election of 1964, was appropriate legislation. The suspension of literacy tests and other devices in covered jurisdictions, and the authorization of federal examiners to register voters, was also legal. In an even more controversial move, it upheld the requirement that covered states and subdivisions must preclear any changes in laws regarding voting and elections with either the Attorney General or the Federal District Court for the District of Columbia before they could go into effect. In dissent, Justice Hugo L. Black asserted that the preclearance requirement violated principles of federalism. Significantly increasing the minority electorate and the number of minority elected officials, the Voting Rights Act of 1965 and the decision upholding its constitutionality revolutionized southern politics.

Selected Bibliography Alexander Bickel, "The Voting Rights Cases," *Supreme Court Review* (1966), 79–102; Richard Claude, *The Supreme Court and the Electoral Process* (1970); Chandler Davidson and Bennard Grofman, eds., *Quiet Revolution in the South: The Impact of the Voting Rights Act, 1965–1990* (1994); United States Commission on Civil Rights, *The Voting Rights Act: Unfulfilled Goals* (1981).

Patricia A. Behlar

South v. Peters, 339 U.S. 276 (1950)   This Supreme Court case involved a 1917 Georgia statute that established a county unit system, which gave sparsely populated rural counties a vote in primary elections disproportionately larger than the vote of more populous urban counties where much of the black population was located. Plaintiff Bernard South and other black residents of Atlanta argued that because they resided in a large county, their vote had, in effect, only one-tenth the value it would have had in less populated counties. James Peters, chairman of the state Democratic party, defended the statute by arguing, and the Court agreed, that "federal courts consistently refuse to exercise their equity powers in cases posing political issues arising from a state's geographical distribution of electoral strengths among its political subdivisions." Justices William Douglas and Hugo Black dissented. Douglas wrote that "I suppose that if a state reduced the vote of Negroes, Catholics, or Jews so that each got only one-tenth of a vote, we would strike the law down. . . . The discrimination against citizens in the more populous counties of Georgia is plain." Although the county unit vote was upheld in this case, the Court would revisit this issue in *Baker v. Carr* and *Reynolds v. Sims*, ultimately deciding that even though it involved a political issue, federal courts had a duty to ensure the equity of votes.

Selected Bibliography Richard Claude, *The Supreme Court and the Electoral Process* (1970); Richard C. Cortner, *The Apportionment Cases* (1970).

Kenneth W. Goings

Southern Burlington County NAACP, Ethel Lawrence et al. v. Mt. Laurel Township, New Jersey, 67 N.J. 151, 336 A. 2d 713 (1975) In 1950, Mt. Laurel, New Jersey, was a sprawling 22-square-mile township located 15 miles northeast of Philadelphia with a population of only 2,817 people engaged almost exclusively in farming. About four hundred African Americans lived there, most of them descendants of pre–Civil War fugitive slaves. Most were people of modest means who worked largely as laborers on nearby farms. Over the next decade Mt. Laurel experienced rapid suburban development. Small industries and commercial establishments arrived, and the population had quadrupled by 1970. In 1964 the township's council and zoning board adopted a general land use ordinance that prohibited the construction of multiunit apartments, attached townhouses, and mobile home parks. Furthermore, the ordinance mandated minimum house lot sizes of 9,375 to 20,000 square feet with homes having at least 1,100 square feet of living space. Developers were discouraged from selling or leasing to households with more than two children. The zoning code meant that only people of middle and upper income would be able to live in the township. Ethel Lawrence, a fourth generation African American resident of Mt. Laurel, pointed out that most black youth had to leave because they could not afford to purchase or rent housing in their hometown. In conjunction with the local branch of the **NAACP,** she sued Mt. Laurel Township for using restrictive zoning ordinances to exclude from residency certain racial and socioeconomic groups. The Superior and Supreme Courts of New Jersey agreed and found exclusionary zoning so pervasive that they ordered every region and municipality in the state to affirmatively provide housing for low and moderate income families.

Selected Bibliography Gary Hunter, *Up South: The Civil Rights Movement in Southern New Jersey 1940–1973* (1990); Derrick Bell, Jr., ed., *Race, Racism, and American Law* (1980).

Gary J. Hunter

Southern Christian Leadership Conference The Southern Christian Leadership Conference (SCLC) was established in 1957 in order to "coordinate local, nonviolent **direct-action** protest movements" in the South. The key officers were ministers, mostly Baptist. The first executive director was Reverend **Wyatt Tee Walker,** who, by 1963, headed a staff of 50 and supervised 85 affiliated groups. But the key leader, the essence of the SCLC, was **Martin Luther King, Jr.** The organization shared his goal, inspired by Mohandas K. Gandhi, to achieve full equality for blacks through the use of mass nonviolent resistance to win public sympathy and support, and to apply "redemptive love" to heal America's troubled society.

The group's first action, in 1957, was a **prayer pilgrimage to Washington,** led by King, which attracted twenty-five thousand people. It was followed in 1959, by a youth march on Washington, attended by forty thousand. Mass marches were followed by dramatic, televised sit-ins, used to publicize the wrongs of segregation, beginning with the **Greensboro, North Carolina, sit-in** in 1960. The aim of the next series of SCLC campaigns was to fight segregation and to secure voting rights, as in the activities of the **Freedom Riders,** the **Albany, Georgia, sit-in,** the **Birmingham Confrontation** with Commissioner Bull Connor, and the 1964 St. Augustine fight against segregation and the Ku Klux Klan. The SCLC brilliantly mobilized blacks, organizing and leading marches, filling up jails, and displaying to an international television audience the mindless violence of many southern whites. In 1964, influenced by the SCLC-led mass protest movement, Congress finally passed the **Civil Rights Act of 1964.** The SCLC clashed with the **Student Nonviolent Coordinating Committee** (SNCC) in Selma (1965) over tactics and philosophy, with SNCC members feeling the SCLC took too much credit for local movements they had initiated. The SCLC also opposed their burgeoning black supremacy ideas as another form of tyranny. The violence in Selma, including killings, which occurred during the **Selma to Montgomery march,** moved President Lyndon B. Johnson to urge the passage of the **Voting Rights Act of 1965.** The SCLC quickly registered eighty-five thousand new voters within four months.

After the 1964 and 1965 bills were passed, the SCLC turned to the problems of northern cities, such as segregation, job discrimination, and poverty. The Chicago Freedom Movement and Operation Breadbasket in 1967 resulted in violent white resistance. Chicago's Mayor Richard J. Daley eventually promised to enforce city housing laws against discrimination, but clearly northern cities presented a huge challenge. King, by 1967, was speaking out against the Vietnam War, which did not help his popularity. In 1968 the SCLC organized the **Poor People's March on Washington** as a civil disobedience action. While taking time out from this campaign to support sanitation workers in Memphis, Tennessee, King was assassinated in April 1968. The campaign continued, but the movement had lost its articulation. Regrouping under the leadership of the Reverend **Ralph David Abernathy,** SCLC continued the struggle on the local level, fighting against the evils of race discrimination and poverty. Its political influence in the South, as well as its role in changing the national conscience, has been enormous. In 2003, Martin

Luther King III served as president and the organization was battling **racial profiling,** the death penalty, and a host of other social and political issues.

Selected Bibliography Taylor Branch, *Parting the Waters: America in the King Years, 1954–1963* (1988); Taylor Branch, *Pillar of Fire: American in the King Years, 1963–1965* (1998); Adam Fairclough, *To Redeem the Soul of America: The SCLC and Martin Luther King, Jr.* (1987); David J. Garrow, *Bearing the Cross: Martin Luther King, Jr. and the Southern Christian Leadership Conference* (1986); David J. Garrow, ed., *We Shall Overcome: The Civil Rights Movement in the United States in the 1950s and 1960s* (1989); Stephen B. Oates, *Let the Trumpet Sound: The Life of Martin Luther King, Jr.* (1982); Pat Watters, *Down to Now: Reflections on the Civil Rights Movement* (1971); Web site: www.sclcnational.org.

Linda G. Ford

Southern Commission on the Study of Lynching   This commission began in June 1930 in response to the "marked increase" in lynchings. It included some of the most prominent African Americans of the day: **John Hope,** B. F. Hubert, **R. R. Moton,** and **Monroe Nathan Work.** Its work was summarized in two reports, *Lynchings and What They Mean* and *The Mob Murder of S. S. Mincey.* The commission concluded that lynching would be eliminated when all Americans have "opportunities for development and are accorded fundamental human rights."

Selected Bibliography Arthur F. Roper, *The Tragedy of Lynching* (1933); Robert L. Zangrando, *The NAACP Crusade against Lynching, 1909–1950* (1980).

Maghan Keita

Southern Conference for Human Welfare   The Southern Conference for Human Welfare (SCHW) was formed in 1938 to promote civil liberties and to provide the South's answer to the National Emergency Council's *Report on the Economic Conditions of the South,* which labeled the region "the nation's No. 1 economic problem." Chaired in the early years by University of North Carolina President **Frank P. Graham,** the SCHW campaigned against the **poll tax** and in favor of expanding the New Deal to attack southern poverty. The organization held interracial meetings and allied itself with the Congress of Industrial Organizations for a time. Following a "popular front" strategy, the Conference did not exclude Communists from membership. This policy led to exaggerated charges of Communist influence within the organization, and the "red" label was a significant factor in the demise of the organization in 1948.

Selected Bibliography Thomas A. Krueger, *And Promises to Keep: The Southern Conference for Human Welfare, 1938–1948* (1967); Randall L. Patton, "Southern Liberals and the Emergence of a New South, 1938–1950" (Ph.D. diss., University of Georgia, 1990); Morton Sosna, *In Search of the Silent South: Southern Liberals and the Race Issue* (1977); Linda Reed, *Simple Decency and Common Sense: The Southern Conference Movement, 1938–1963* (1991).

Randall L. Patton

Southern Courier   Two student veterans of the 1964 Mississippi Freedom Summer, Ellen Lake and Peter Cummings, founded the *Southern Courier* newspaper in 1965 to provide a more accurate source of information for southerners regarding racial problems in the region and to promote liberal reform in the

South. Lake and Cummings were editors of the Harvard *Crimson* student newspaper, and they initially recruited their staff from like-minded New England college students. With funding from northeastern liberals, the weekly newspaper began publication on 16 July 1965 in Atlanta, Georgia, before moving permanently to Montgomery, Alabama. Under the general editorship of former Chicago *Daily News* reporter Michael Lottman, the *Courier* set out to provide more balanced coverage of black life than any other Alabama newspaper and highlighted local successes in the civil rights struggle. The newspaper educated its readers regarding the mechanics of registering to vote and securing assistance from various federal and state bureaucracies. The *Courier* also trained black Alabamians in journalistic skills, and eventually most staff positions were held by local African Americans. Financially, however, the *Courier* never became self-sustaining. As liberal reformers focused their energies on opposing the Vietnam War, support for the newspaper dried up. On 7 December 1968, the *Courier* ceased publication.

Selected Bibliography Robert Jefferson Norrell, "Reporters and Reformers: The Story of the *Southern Courier*," *South Atlantic Quarterly* 79 (Winter 1980), 93–104; Robert Jefferson Norrell, "Reporters and Reformers: The Story of the *Southern Courier*" (M.A. thesis, University of Virginia, 1978).

Richard V. Damms

Southern Education Board Formed in 1901 with a donation from banker George Foster Peabody, this organization promoted a tax-supported southern school system, with the long term goal of solving complex problems arising from southern poverty, ignorance, and racial tension. By 1914 when the Southern Education Board went out of existence, annual expenditures for education in the South had quadrupled. Although board members considered their efforts successful, historians have criticized the board as a conservative organization that failed to challenge a growing white supremacy movement at the turn of the century. Instead, the board emphasized the education of southern whites to the detriment of southern African Americans, thus contributing to the growth of separate and unequal schools.

Selected Bibliography Charles W. Dabney, *Universal Education in the South* (1936); Raymond B. Fosdick, *Adventure in Giving* (1962); Louis Harlan, *Separate and Unequal* (1958); Louis R. Harlen, "The Southern Education Board and the Race Issue in Public Education," *Journal of Southern Education* 23 (May 1957), 189–202.

Janice M. Leone

Southern Education Reporting Service The Southern Education Reporting Service (SERS) was started in the spring of 1954 by a group of southern editors and educators who wanted "to tell the story, factually and objectively, of what happened in southern education as a result of the Supreme Court's May 17 opinion." It was incorporated in Tennessee, located in Nashville, and funded primarily by the Ford Foundation. Executive directors included Edward D. Ball, Don Shoemaker, C. A. "Pete" McKnight, and Reed Sarrat. The board of directors included Frank Ahlgren, Virginius Dabney, Alexander Heard,

Charles S. Johnson, Thomas R. Waring, Luther H. Foster, John Siegenthaler, **P. B. Young,** and John Popham. For the first decade its staff included only briefly one black. Its most important publications were the monthly *Southern School News,* a periodical "Statistical Summary of School Segregation-Desegregation in the Southern and Border States," and a quarterly *Race Relations Law Reporter.* SERS's library gathered information on race relations throughout the United States by clipping more than fifty newspapers and most news magazines and by collecting books, speeches, reports, and other documents. It made its collections available on microfilm as "Facts on Film." On 1 September 1969, SERS ceased to exist when the Race Relations Information Center began operation in Nashville.

Selected Bibliography Patrick J. Gilpin, "Charles S. Johnson and the Southern Education Reporting Service," *Journal of Negro History* 63 (July 1978), 197–208; *Race Relations Law Reporter; Southern Education Report; Southern School News.*

Charles W. Eagles

Southern Homestead Act (1866)   This law was passed by Congress after the Civil War as an extension of the Homestead Act of 1862, which offered 160 acres of free public land in the Midwest and West to any person who could pay a $10 registration fee and cultivate the land for five years. It was intended to encourage land and home ownership among newly freed slaves in five ex-Confederate states. Applications could be made on homesteads of no more than 80 acres (160 after mid-1868) on the public lands of Alabama, Arkansas, Florida, Louisiana, and Mississippi, which would be reserved exclusively for this purpose. The law failed to convert the freedmen into small independent farmers, however, because many of the 46 million acres of southern federal lands were inferior quality swamp and "overflow" lands or reserved prewar railroad grants. Homesteads were also allowed on timber lands, which encouraged wealthy speculators to misuse the law by hiring men to file claims and then taking over the deeds. Three-quarters of the applicants were white, although a higher percentage of blacks than whites were later able to prove their claims. Many black and white applicants found themselves at the mercy of inefficient, corrupt officials and of endless red tape. Only 25 percent of white applicants and 35 percent of black applicants were able to prove their claims successfully during the 10 years of the law's operation. In June 1876, as support for Radical Reconstruction waned, Congress rescinded the exclusive homestead provision regarding southern public lands and opened them to sale.

Selected Bibliography Michael Les Benedict, *A Compromise of Principle: Congressional Republicans and Reconstruction, 1863–1969* (1974); William R. Brock, *An American Crisis: Congress and Reconstruction, 1865–1867* (1966); Eric Foner, *Reconstruction: America's Unfinished Revolution, 1863–1877* (1988); Michael L. Lanza, *Agrarianism and Reconstruction Politics: The Southern Homestead Act* (1990); James M. McPherson, *Ordeal By Fire: The Civil War and Reconstruction* (1982); Claude F. Oubre, *Forty Acres and a Mule: The Freedmen's Bureau and Black Landownership* (1978); C. Vann Woodward, *Reunion and Reaction: The Compromise of 1877 and the End of Reconstruction* (1951).

Marvin Thomas

Southern Negro Youth Congress   Organized in February 1937 at a convention in Richmond, Virginia, the Congress's mission was to encourage young blacks to join trade unions. The congress joined forces with the **National Negro Congress** in May 1937 to coordinate a wildcat strike by predominantly black tobacco workers in Richmond. After an 18-month campaign, the two organizations had organized seven local unions in the Richmond tobacco processing industry representing several thousand black workers. The union locals were then turned over to the Congress of Industrial Organizations for permanent jurisdiction. The Southern Negro Youth Congress was an important ally of the CIO in its efforts to organize black workers in the late 1930s. The congress did not exclude Communists from membership, and this policy led to the organization's demise after World War II.

Selected Bibliography Philip S. Foner, *Organized Labor and the Black Worker, 1619–1973* (1974); C. Alvin Hughes, "We demand Our Rights: The Southern Negro Youth Congress, 1937–49," *Phylon* 48 (No. 1, 1987), 38–50; Nell I. Painter, ed., *The Narrative of Hosea Hudson: His Life as Negro Communist in the South* (1979); Johnetta G. Richards, "The Southern Negro Youth Congress: A History" (Ph.D. diss., University of Cincinnati, 1987).

Randall L. Patton

Southern Poverty Law Center   Founded in 1971 by **Morris Dees** and Joseph J. Levin, Jr., the Southern Poverty Law Center (SPLC) is a nonprofit, legal

Visitors tour the Civil Rights Memorial outside the Southern Poverty Law Center in Montgomery, Alabama, 1999. © AP/Wide World Photos.

organization dedicated to the advancement of tolerance and civil rights issues. Throughout the 1970s the center participated in a series of legal actions that focused on integration and due process for minority defendants. In notable successes the center assisted death row inmates in North Carolina and helped integrate the Montgomery, Alabama, YMCA and the Alabama State Troopers. The SPLC's efforts shifted in the 1980s as it became embroiled in a lengthy legal battle against the United Klans of America. The conflict began after the SPLC protected Vietnamese immigrants from Klan intimidation in Texas; it culminated in a $7 million civil judgment against the Klan for the lynching of David Donald, a black Alabamian. The large award bankrupted the Klan and encouraged the center to file similar suits against other racist groups. The SPLC collects and monitors racist literature, chronicling the activities of hate groups through publications such as *Klanwatch*, and the quarterly *Intelligence Report*. The center has branched into public education by producing useful materials for school children on diversity and tolerance.

Selected Bibliography Morris Dees, with Steve Fiffer, *A Season for Justice: The Life and Times of Civil Rights Lawyer Morris Dees* (1991); Web site: www.splcenter.org.

Edwin L. Combs III

Southern Regional Council Formed in 1944, the Southern Regional Council (SRC) was a descendent of the **Commission on Interracial Cooperation,** and the brainchild of University of North Carolina sociologist **Howard W. Odum.** Composed of black and white moderates, the council's original mission was to work within the system of racial separation in the South to make "separate but equal more equal" and to promote economic development in the region. In 1949, as a result of an internal debate, the SRC publicly announced its opposition to segregation. Though its membership dropped dramatically after that decision, the SRC survived. The council, still in existence, has since worked to promote racial integration, voter registration, and increased public awareness of southern social and economic problems.

Selected Bibliography Guy B. Johnson, "Southern Offensive," *Common Ground* 4 (Summer 1944), 87–93; Anne C. Loveland, *Lillian Smith: A Southerner Confronting the South: A Biography* (1986); Julia A. McDonaugh, " Men and Women of Good Will: A History of the Commission on Interracial Cooperation and the Southern Regional Council, 1919–1954" (Ph.D. diss., University of Virginia, 1993); Morton Sosna, *In Search of the Silent South: Southern Liberals and the Race Issue* (1977); Web site: www.southerncouncil.org.

Randall L. Patton

Southern School News Published monthly by the **Southern Education Reporting Service** from September 1954 to June 1965, The *Southern School News* (SSN) aimed to provide factual, objective, unbiased coverage of school segregation-desegregation in 17 southern and border states and the District of Columbia. Drawing on correspondents who worked for newspapers across the South, each issue of *SSN* contained a major article on events in each state. It reached more than 10,000 educators, government officials, clergy, libraries, and interested layman in all 50 states and more than 40 foreign countries. *SSN* staff and correspondents also produced several books, including *With All Deliberate Speed* (1957) and *Southern Schools: Progress and Problems* (1959). *SSN* won a number of awards. In 1956 the National Newspaper Publishers Association awarded it its Russworm Award for outstanding achievement, and in 1962 Texas Southern University gave *SSN* its "layman's citation for distinguished service in the public journals." In 1965 the board of the Southern Education Reporting Service decided that the **Civil Rights Act of 1964** signaled the end of the transition from segregated to desegregated schools and ended publication of *SSN*. In the summer of 1965 *SSN* was replaced by the *Southern Education Report*, which concentrates on the education of socially and economically handicapped in the southern and border states.

Selected Bibliography *Race Relations Law Reporter; Southern Education Report; Southern School News.*

Charles W. Eagles

Southern Tenant Farmers' Union   In July 1934, two Socialists, **Harry Leland Mitchell** and Henry Clay East, helped a small band of economically displaced black and white farmers around Tyronza, Arkansas, organize the Southern Tenant Farmers Union (STFU). STFU leaders attempted to unite the disinherited of both races in Arkansas, Oklahoma, and Missouri in hopes of forcing more equitable treatment from the planters. They also tried to secure constructive changes in Agricultural Adjustment Administration policy. The strikes, protests, and propaganda of the union were never more than marginally successful. Although it eventually evolved into the National Farm Labor Union, ideological, interracial, and personal strife had enervated the STFU by the early 1940s. During the mid-1930s, however, this union represented a rare and courageous attempt at economic and interracial solidarity.

Selected Bibliography M. Langley Biegert, "Legacy of Resistance: Uncovering the History of Collective Action by Black Agricultural Workers in Central East Arkansas from the 1860s to the 1930s," *Journal of Social History* 32 (No. 1, 1998), 73–99; Donald H. Grubbs, *Cry from the Cotton: The Southern Tenant Farmers' Union and the New Deal* (1971); Howard A. Kester, *Revolt Among the Sharecroppers* (1936); H. L. Mitchell, *Mean Things Happening in This Land: The Life and Times of H. L. Mitchell, Co-founder of the Southern Tenant Farmers' Union* (1979); Elizabeth Ann Payne, "The Lady Was a Sharecropper: Myrtle Lawrence and the Southern Tenant Farmers' Union," *Southern Cultures* 4 (No. 2, 1998), 5–27; Southern Tenant Farmers' Union Papers, Southern Historical Collection, The University of North Carolina at Chapel Hill.

Robert F. Martin

Spencer, Anne   (8 February 1882, Henry County, Va.–27 July 1975, Lynchburg, Va.). An important African American **Harlem Renaissance** poet, her home in Lynchburg, Virginia, was a southern way-station for civil rights leaders and renowned African American artists denied public accommodations in the region. **James Weldon Johnson,** poet and, at the time, field secretary for the **NAACP,** not only opened the way for publishing her work but also helped her organize a NAACP chapter in the city. Spencer graduated from Virginia Theological Seminary and College and was a librarian at segregated Dunbar High School, both in Lynchburg. She was instrumental in making library facilities and materials accessible to black residents.

Selected Bibliography J. Lee Greene, "Anne Spencer of Lynchburg," *Virginia Cavalcade* (Spring 1987), 178–82; J. Lee Greene, *Time's Unfading Garden: Anne Spencer's Life and Poetry* (1977).

Nancy E. Fitch

Spingarn, Arthur Barnett (28 March 1878, New York, N.Y.–1 December 1971, New York, N.Y.). A leading civil rights attorney and one of the founders of the **NAACP,** Spingarn was involved in its operations for over half a century and was its president for 26 years (1940–66). He was born into a socially prominent and wealthy New York family on 28 March 1878 to Elias and Sarah Barnett Spingarn. Spingarn received a bachelor's degree in 1896, a master's degree in 1899 and his law degree in 1900 from Columbia University. He spent 35 years as the volunteer chairman of the National Legal Defense Committee and served as vice president of the NAACP from 1911 to 1940. Additionally Spingarn won a number of important civil rights court cases for African

Arthur Spingarn (center) with Roy Wilkins (left) and Hubert H. Humphrey, undated. © Library of Congress.

Americans in northern cities and southern state courts. He also was instrumental in defeating many presidential federal judge nominees who opposed civil rights legislation. Spingarn was one of the leading bibliophiles and collectors of African and African American works. In 1946 he incorporated his extensive personal collection of over five thousand books and pamphlets into the already impressive holdings at **Howard University**'s Negro Foundation Library, now called the Moorland-Spingarn Research Center.

Selected Bibliography "Arthur B. Spingarn" *Current Biography* 26 (June 1965), 34–35; Arthur Spingarn Papers, Manuscript Division, Moorland-Spingarn Research Center, Howard University, Washington, D.C.; Beverly Gray, "White Warrior," *Negro Digest* 41 (September 1962), 63–64.

Glenn O. Phillips

Spingarn Medal   Established in 1913 by Joel E. Spingarn, the Spingarn Medal is awarded annually by the **NAACP** to a man or woman of African descent for outstanding achievement. In offering the gold medal, which he endowed with a $20,000 bequest, Spingarn hoped to promote cultural awareness and black pride by honoring people whose achievements helped to preserve or enrich the unique black cultural heritage. Spingarn thought that the Negro was especially well endowed in the arts, but he did not stipulate that only black artists were eligible for the award. Indeed, the first recipient in 1915, Ernest E. Just, was a research biologist, and over the years those honored have come from the fields of law, religion, education, politics, and business along with the arts and sciences. Spingarn Medalists, which include such distinguished people as **W.E.B. Du Bois, James Weldon Johnson, Mary McLeod Bethune, Richard Wright, A. Philip Randolph, Thurgood Marshall, Martin Luther King, Jr., Leontyne Price,** and **Benjamin E. Mays,** constitute a veritable Who's Who of African Americans.

Selected Bibliography Harry A. Ploski and James Williams, eds., *The Negro Almanac: A Reference Work on the Afro- American* (1983); B. Joyce Ross, *J. E. Spingarn and the Rise of the NAACP, 1911–1939* (1972); Mabel M. Smythe, ed., *The Black American Reference Book* (1976).

Charles D. Lowery

Springfield, Illinois, Race Riot (1908)   The migration of blacks into urban areas of Illinois at the turn of the century threatened white dominance of jobs and the ballot box. In July 1908, a white man discovered a young black vagrant named Joe James in his 16-year-old daughter's bedroom and in the scuffle was killed. James was indicted for murder. Five weeks later, another black man allegedly raped a white woman, and, although he protested his innocence, he was arrested and placed in jail alongside James. A mob that quickly grew to four thousand people threatened the jail house. The sheriff, who had done nothing to disperse the crowd, now decided to move the prisoners, spiriting them away to the state prison in Bloomington. When the mob discovered it had no prisoners to punish, it went on a rampage against the community's blacks. Significant property damage was done; numerous individuals were beaten and injured; and two blacks, both elderly males, were lynched. The state militia had to be called in to restore order. Thousands of terrified blacks left the city permanently; white residents even refused to sell them any food. The horror of the situation was only increased by the fact that Springfield was preparing to celebrate the centennial of the birth of its most famous citizen, Abraham Lincoln. On 12 February 1909, reformers, horrified by the disaster, met in Springfield and founded the **NAACP.**

Selected Bibliography James L. Crouthamel, "The Springfield, Illinois Race Riot of 1908," *Journal of Negro History* 45 (July 1960), 164–81; *Illinois State Journal* (Springfield), July, August, 1908; Roberta Senechal, *The Sociogenesis of a Race Riot: Springfield, Illinois, in 1908* (1990); William E. Walling, "Race War in the North," *The Independent* 65 (3 September 1908), 529–34.

John F. Marszalek

Springfield, Massachusetts, Race Riot (1965) A few weeks before the worst race riot of 1965 took place in the Watts community of Los Angeles, California, a racial incident caused several weeks of unrest in the rifle manufacturing city of Springfield, Massachusetts. While not as destructive to life and property as the **Watts race riot,** the Springfield disturbance highlighted the serious racial discord that existed throughout the nation. The incident leading to the riot occurred in the early morning hours of 17 July when Springfield police attempted to break up a fight outside a black nightclub. According to the authorities, several hundred onlookers pelted police with rocks and bottles, forcing them to arrest 18 people. Black witnesses charged the police with excessive force in making the arrests. Springfield blacks protested for the next several weeks. Led by the local branches of the **Congress of Racial Equality** and the **NAACP,** they marched on City Hall and picketed downtown stores, demanding an official investigation of the incident. Mayor Charles V. Ryan, Jr., called out the National Guard, but he also promised an official probe. The demands of blacks were not met and the protests continued as the summer ended.

Selected Bibliography *New York Times,* 20, 22, 25 July, 11, 14, 15, 16, 17, 19, 22, 23, 24 August 1965; *Springfield Daily News,* 17, 21, 22 July 1965.

Dorothy A. Autrey

State Athletic Commission v. Dorsey, 359 U.S. 533 (1959) The decision in this case extended the principle of the unconstitutionality of racial segregation to public athletic contests. Joseph Dorsey, Jr., a black professional boxer, sought to compete against both black and white opponents. Louisiana law prohibited interracial contests. Dorsey sued to prohibit the Louisiana State Athletic Commission from enforcing this law on the grounds that it violated the equal protection clause of the **Fourteenth Amendment.** In the landmark school desegregation case of ***Brown v. Board of Education,*** the Supreme Court had ruled that classification based upon race in public education is inherently discriminatory and violates the equal protection clause of the Fourteenth Amendment. Through a series of unanimous opinions, the

Supreme Court summarily had extended this principle to segregation in any public facilities or functions. In *Dorsey*, the Supreme Court affirmed the lower court decision that concluded that the Louisiana law violated the equal protection clause by requiring racial segregation in a publicly regulated activity.

Selected Bibliography Henry J. Abraham, *Freedom and the Court, Civil Rights and Liberties in the United States* (1988); Derrick A. Bell, Jr., *Race, Racism, and American Law* (1980).

Frederick G. Slabach

Staupers, Mabel   (27 February 1898, Barbados, West Indies–5 October 1989, Washington, D.C.). While she was executive director (1934–46) and president (1949–51) of the National Association of Colored Graduate Nurses (NACGN), Staupers campaigned for the desegregation of the American nursing service. From 1945 to 1950, desegregation took place in the Army and

Mrs. Mabel Keaton Staupers (right), winner of the Spingarn Medal, being congratulated for outstanding work in the integration of African American nurses into the nursing profession. © Library of Congress.

Navy Nurse Corps, the American Nurses Association, most of the southern state nursing associations, and most of the formerly all-white nursing schools. As a result of these developments, Staupers believed that the NACGN was no longer necessary and helped disband it in 1951. The **NAACP** awarded her its **Spingarn Medal** in 1951. In 1996 she was inducted posthumously into the Nurses Hall of Fame.

Selected Bibliography Darlene Clark Hine, *Black Women in White: Racial Conflict and Cooperation in the Nursing Profession, 1890–1950* (1989); Darlene Clark Hine, "Mabel K. Staupers and the Integration of Black Nurses into the Armed Forces," in John Hope Franklin and August Meier, eds., *Black Leaders of the Twentieth Century* (1982); Obituary, *New York Times,* 6 October 1989; Mabel Keaton Staupers, *No Time for Prejudice: A Story of the Integration of Nurses in Nursing in the United States* (1961).

Gloria Waite

Steele, Charles Kenzie (7 February 1914, Gary, W. Va.–19 August 1980, Tallahassee, Fla.). A graduate of **Morehouse College** and an ordained minister, Steele was a leading civil rights activist, a charter member and first vice president of the **Southern Christian Leadership Conference,** and a friend and confidant of **Martin Luther King, Jr.** Steele pastored Baptist churches in Georgia and Alabama before assuming pastorship of the Bethel Baptist Church in Tallahassee, Florida, in 1951. In Tallahassee, as local president of the **NAACP** and president of the Inter-Civic Council, Steele attacked segregation through nonviolent means. In 1956 he led the ultimately successful **Tallahassee, Florida, bus boycott** against the City Transit Company.

Selected Bibliography Adam Fairclough, *To Redeem the Soul of America: The SCLC and Martin Luther King, Jr.* (1987); David J. Garrow, *Bearing the Cross: Martin Luther King and the SCLC* (1986); Gregory Padgett, "C. K. Steele: A Biography" (Ph.D. diss., Florida State University, 1994); Glenda A. Rabby, *The Pain and the Promise: The Struggle for Civil Rights in Tallahassee, Florida* (1999); Charles U. Smith, ed., *The Civil Rights Movement in Florida and the United States* (1989); Charles U. Smith and Lewis M. Killian, *The Tallahassee Bus Protest* (1958).

Maxine D. Jones

Stevens, Thaddeus (4 April 1792, Danville, Vt.–11 August 1868, Washington, D.C.). Thaddeus Stevens was born with a birth defect commonly known as clubfoot—a problem that is said to have affected his thinking as much as his lifestyle. It also channeled him into education and intellectual pursuits rather than physical ones. He graduated from Dartmouth College in Hanover, New Hampshire, in 1814. His unpopularity among his peers there would be a problem that would follow him throughout his life. He spent 1815 teaching at Pennsylvania's York Academy while studying law. When the local bar association ruled that a year of full-time study was a prerequisite for taking the bar exam, he went to Maryland and passed the examination there. He established his law practice in Gettysburg in 1816, and he earned a reputation as a sly lawyer. One of his victories ironically came before the State Supreme Court, when he represented a slaveowner against a slave claiming freedom as a result of six months' residence in Pennsylvania. He was also implicated in the death of a black woman, a murder that was never officially solved. Local voters apparently did not believe him guilty, however, for they elected and reelected him to state and national offices. Stevens served seven terms in the state legislature of Pennsylvania beginning in 1833. Moving to Lancaster in 1842, he was sent to Congress on the Whig ticket from 1849 to 1853 and from 1859 to 1868. Anti-Masonry and abolition were the two issues that Stevens rode to political prominence. Somewhat less passionately, he also promoted free public education and the equality of all men. His great ambitions were injured by his apparent concubinage with a free woman of color who kept his house. Stevens could be a ruthless and self-seeking politician. An ardent abolitionist, he was a humanitarian and one of the few politicians of his era who believed that equal rights should be granted to freedmen. As a key leader in the House during and after the Civil War, he helped pass much of the period's legislation. His mark is clearly visible on measures that supported the Union war effort, ranging from taxes to the **Emancipation Proclamation.** He was a principal architect of military and **radical Reconstruction** plans and a major force behind the **Thirteenth, Fourteenth,** and **Fifteenth Amendments**, which granted freedom to African Americans and lay the foundations for the twentieth-century civil rights movement. In spite of venality and personality quirks, Thaddeus Stevens, arguably, did more for American blacks than any other politician of his era.

Selected Bibliography Jean V. Berlin, Eric Foner, and Raymond W. Smock, Three Essays, *Pennsylvania History* 60 (No. 2, 1993); *Biographical Directory of the American Congress, 1774–1971* (1971); Fawn M. Brodie, *Thaddeus Stevens: Scourge of the South* (1959); Richard N. Current, *Old Thad Stevens: A Story of Ambition* (1942); Ralph Korngold, *Thaddeus Stevens: A Being Darkly Wise and Rudely Great* (1955); Beverly Wilson Palmer and Holly Byers Ochra, eds., *The Selected Papers of Thaddeus Stevens* (1997); Hans L. Trefousse, *Thaddeus Stevens, Nineteenth Century Egalitarian* (1997).

Gary B. Mills

Still, William Grant (11 May 1895, Woodville, Miss.–3 December 1978, Los Angeles, Calif.). The undisputed dean of African American composers, Still grew up in Arkansas, earned a baccalaureate degree from Wilberforce University, and studied at Oberlin Conservatory of Music before embarking upon a career in popular music. Working especially with the violin, cello, and oboe, playing and orchestrating, he worked during the 1920s for such notable musicians as W. C. Handy, Paul Whiteman, Sophie Tucker, and Artie Shaw. After studying briefly at the New England Conservatory in the mid-1920s, he moved to New York and successfully made the difficult transition from popular to classical music. His fame as arranger, composer, and orchestrator grew quickly. In 1924, while he was doing the orchestration for various musical shows, his composition *Darker America* won a publication prize at the Eastman School of Music. Three years later he completed his first ballet, *La Guiablesse*, which was later performed in New York and Chicago. In 1926 he wrote *Levee Land* and in 1927 *From the Black Belt*, pioneering pieces that drew upon his racial heritage and experience. In 1930 he wrote *Afro-American Symphony*, his first major success. In this and in a companion piece, *Africa* (1930), Still employed his new black idiom, incorporating Negro musical influences—spirituals, blues, work songs, and jazz—into his compositions.

As a black, Still had no chance of becoming resident composer for a large symphony orchestra. Only his exceptional talent gained for him access to areas of music normally open only to whites. He was among the few blacks who managed to obtain regular employment on radio, occasional work in Hollywood, where he wrote the score for *Pennies from Heaven* and other movies, and in television, where in the 1960s he wrote music for such popular series as *Perry Mason* and *Gunsmoke*. He was a man of many firsts whose extraordinary talent helped lower the racial barriers in the area of serious music. For example, he was the first African American to compose a symphony performed by a major orchestra; the first of his race to conduct a major symphony orchestra in the United States; and the first black to have an opera produced by a major company in the United States. His music, though inspired by black culture and experience, was universal in appeal.

Selected Bibliography Tilford Brooks, *America's Black Musical Heritage* (1984); Paul Elliot Cobbs, *William Grant Still's The Afro-American Symphony: A Culturally Inclusive Perspective* (1990); Robert Haas, ed., *William Grant Still and the Fusion of Cultures in American Music* (1972); James Haskins, *Black Music in America: A History Through Its People* (1987); Gayle Minetta Murchison, *Nationalism in William Grant Still and Aaron Copland between the Wars: Style and Ideology* (1993); Obituary, *New York Times*, 6 December 1978; Catherine Parsons Smith, *William Grant Still: A Study in Contradictions* (2000); Judith Anne Still, Michael J. Dabrishus, and Carolyn L. Quin, *William Grant Still: A Bio-Biography* (1996); Judith Anne Still, ed., *William Grant Still and the Fusion of Cultures in American Music* (1995).

Charles D. Lowery

Stokes, Carl B. (21 June 1927, Cleveland, Ohio–3 April 1996, Cleveland, Ohio). First African American to hold positions in all three branches of state government, Stokes was reared in poverty. A high school dropout and a self-described street hustler, he enlisted in the Army in July 1945. He then resumed his education, completed high school, and obtained a bachelor's degree from the University of Minnesota and a law degree from Cleveland's John Marshall School of Law. His election as the mayor of Cleveland in 1967 made him the first African American mayor of a major American city. In office he increased the number of African American officeholders and opened the door for African American entrepreneurs. He also served in the Ohio legislature and as a municipal court judge. In 1994, President Clinton appointed Stokes as ambassador to the Republic of Seychelles.

Selected Bibliography Carl B. Stokes, *Promises of Power, Then and Now* (1989); Kenneth G. Weinberg, *Black Victory: Carl Stokes and the Winning of Cleveland* (1968); Estelle Zannes, *Checkmate in Cleveland: The Rhetoric of Confrontation During the Stokes Years* (1972).

Lester S. Brooks and Leonne M. Hudson

Storey, Moorfield (19 March 1845, Roxbury, Mass.–24 October 1929, Lincoln, Mass.). Lawyer, author, reformer and civil rights advocate, Storey combined a highly successful corporate practice with a commitment to racial equality that culminated in his becoming the first president of the **NAACP.** Descended from New England Puritan stock, Storey's parents and grandparents moved in Boston's Brahmin society. Graduating from Harvard College in 1866, Storey attended the law school of that institution briefly before pursuing legal studies in a prominent Boston firm and being admitted to the bar in 1869.

In 1867 he went to Washington to become Senator **Charles Sumner's** personal secretary, playing, at the same time, an active behind-the-scenes role in the impeachment proceedings of President Andrew Johnson. As a reformer, Storey crusaded against political corruption, and he led the Anti-Imperialist League in opposition to American involvement in the Philippine Islands. He also defended the rights of the American Indian. As a staunch supporter of the struggle of African Americans, he brought his enormous personal influence and legal talents to bear on behalf of the NAACP's most important cases before the Supreme Court.

Selected Bibliography *Boston Transcript*, 25 October 1929; *Dictionary of American Biography*, vol. 20 (1937); William B. Hixon, Jr., *Moorfield Storey and the Abolitionist Tradition* (1972).

George E. Walker

Straker, Daniel A. (1842, Barbados–14 February 1908, Detroit, Mich.). Born and educated in Barbados, Straker was invited in 1868 by Benjamin B. Smith, an Episcopal minister, to teach in a school established for blacks in Kentucky. In 1869 he enrolled in Howard Law School, where he earned a law degree in 1871. Straker published a number of black perspective essays in *New National Era*, a newspaper that was owned and edited by **Frederick Douglass.** Straker moved to Charleston, South Carolina, as a customs service agent in 1875 and later practiced law there. He was elected to the House of Representatives of South Carolina in 1876, but he was removed from office in 1877 by former Confederates who now called themselves Redeemers. He also twice won elections for the state legislature; however, in both cases he was not allowed to take his seat. He later served as U.S. inspector of customs and a professor of law at Allen University between 1880 and 1882, both in Columbia, South Carolina. He and Robert B. Elliot led a group of blacks who met with President James A. Garfield in 1881 to protest the oppression of blacks in the South. Straker left South Carolina for Detroit in 1887 where he continued to be involved in black civil rights efforts. He won a case in 1890 on appeal before the Supreme Court of Michigan that involved a black man who had been discriminated against in a restaurant in Detroit. Straker became a judge in Wayne County, Michigan, in 1893. His civil rights activities helped prepare the way for the founding after his death of the **National Association for the Advancement of Colored People.**

Selected Bibliography Eric Foner, *Freedom's Lawmakers: A Dictionary of Black Officeholders during Reconstruction* (1993); Glenn O. Phillips, "The Response of a West Indian Activist: D. A. Straker, 1842–1908," *Journal of Negro History* 66 (1981), 128–39; Howard N. Rabinowith, ed.,

Southern Black Leaders of the Reconstruction Era (1982); Daniel A. Straker, *Negro Suffrage in the South* (1906); Daniel A. Straker, *The New South Investigated* (1888).

Amos A. Beyan

Strauder v. West Virginia, 100 U.S. 303 (1880) In 1874, a Wheeling, West Virginia, jury found a black carpenter named Taylor Strauder guilty of murdering his wife. The jury was composed entirely of whites; in fact, state law limited jury service to whites. Strauder petitioned to have his case moved into a federal court on the grounds that he could not receive a fair trial under West Virginia law. Although the motion was denied by the county court, the U.S. Supreme Court agreed to review the case in 1879. In *Strauder* the Court ruled that West Virginia's statutory exclusion of blacks from juries was unconstitutional under the **Fourteenth Amendment.** The court also held that the removing of a case like Strauder's from a state to federal court for trial was a proper way of enforcing rights under the Fourteenth Amendment. The *Strauder* case, however, was far from being a great civil rights victory; handed down at the same time was **Virginia v. Rives** in which the court displayed unconcern with all-white juries if the state statutes did not specifically limit jury service to whites.

Selected Bibliography Stephen Cresswell, "The Case of Taylor Strauder," *West Virginia History* 44 (Spring 1983), 193–211; Benno C. Schmidt, "Juries, Jurisdiction, and Race Discrimination: The Lost Promise of *Strauder v. West Virginia*," *Texas Law Review* (May 1983), 1402–99.

Stephen Cresswell

Stride Toward Freedom Subtitled *The Montgomery Story*, **Martin Luther King, Jr.**'s 1958 book depicted the use of collective mass action during the successful 1955–56 **Montgomery bus boycott.** A combination of autobiography, history, and philosophy, the study encompasses King's life, the protest tactic of **nonviolent resistance,** race relations in Montgomery, community mobilization, and the virulent opposition. King wrote the account while preoccupied with his other duties as the civil rights conflict intensified after Montgomery. Reviewers either lauded or condemned the work depending upon their perspective of the civil rights struggle. Although scholars have pointed to some factual and textual problems, this remains an informative book remarkably rich in content.

Selected Bibliography Taylor Branch, *Parting the Waters: America in the King Years, 1954–63* (1988); Adam Fairclough, *To Redeem the Soul of America: The Southern Christian Leadership Conference and Martin Luther King, Jr.* (1987); David J. Garrow, *Bearing the Cross: Martin Luther King, Jr. and the Southern Christian Leadership Conference* (1986); David J. Garrow, ed., *The Walking City: The Montgomery Bus Boycott, 1955–1956* (1990); David Levering Lewis, *King: A Critical Biography* (1970); Stephen B. Oates, *Let the Trumpet Sound: The Life of Martin Luther King, Jr.* (1982).

Bruce A. Glasrud

Student Nonviolent Coordinating Committee The Student Nonviolent Coordinating Committee (SNCC) resulted from the need to coordinate the widespread student protests following the **Greensboro, North Carolina, sit-**

Stokely Carmichael speaking with a group during an SNCC fund-raising event in Philadelphia, 1966. © Library of Congress.

in. At a conference at Shaw University in Raleigh, North Carolina, in April 1960, over 200 student delegates, after listening to **Martin Luther King, Jr.,** and other civil rights leaders urge them to affiliate with the **Southern Christian Leadership Conference** (SCLC), **NAACP,** or some other similar group, established a Temporary Coordinating Committee to provide communications among the campuses and student groups. A few months later with **Ella Baker** as an advisor and key leader, they organized as the Temporary Student Nonviolent Coordinating Committee, with **Marion Barry,** a leader of the student movement in Nashville, Tennessee, as chairman. **Robert Moses** left the SCLC to work for SNCC. At a conference in October, the delegates decided to drop the temporary from the organization's name. They also elected **Charles McDew** to replace Barry as chairman. McDew served until 1963, when **John Lewis** succeeded him. SNCC staff members and volunteers became involved with the **Freedom Rides** in 1961 and in other forms of protest throughout the South. In 1961, **James Forman,** a Chicago school teacher, became executive secretary and brought a measure of stability to the organization. When SNCC members could not agree on whether to concentrate on **direct action** or to place primary emphasis on voter registration, they compromised by agreeing to do both. SNCC led voter registration drives in

Mississippi and other southern states. As a part of the **Council of Federated Organizations** (COFO), SNCC sponsored the **Freedom Summer of 1964** project in Mississippi. Members also staged sit-ins at segregated lunch counters, wade-ins at segregated beaches, and pray-ins and kneel-ins at segregated churches. By late 1961 about 50 towns and cities in the South had experienced demonstrations. Over 70,000 white and black students had participated, and many of them had gone to jail. The demonstrations resulted in the desegregation of eating places in many southern and border-state cities. In 1966 SNCC members elected **Stokely Carmichael** chairman, and he became a leader and interpreter of the **Black Power** movement. Racial violence during the remaining years of the 1960s led to repression of student activities by law enforcement agencies and to the decline of SNCC.

Selected Bibliography Clayborne Carson, *In Struggle: SNCC and the Black Awakening of the 1960's* (1981); John Dittmer, *Local People: The Struggle for Civil Rights in Mississippi* (1994); James Forman, *The Making of Black Revolutionaries* (1972); Joanne Grant, *Ella Baker: Freedom Bound* (1998); Anne Moody, *Coming of Age in Mississippi* (1968); Howell Raines, *My Soul Is Rested: Movement Days in the Deep South Remembered* (1977); Cleveland Sellers, *The River of No Return: The Autobiography of a Black Militant and the Life and Death of SNCC* (1973).

Arvarh E. Strickland

Sullivan v. Little Hunting Park, 396 U.S. 229 (1969)   This case extended the application of the **Civil Rights Act of 1866** to prohibit discrimination in access to community facilities conveyed incident to a sale or lease of property. Paul E. Sullivan, a white homeowner in an unincorporated community known as Little Hunting Park in Virginia, rented his home to a black, T. R. Freeman, Jr., and assigned his membership in a community organization that operated recreation facilities for all community residents. The organization refused to admit Freeman; Sullivan and Freeman sued. The Supreme Court had ruled in **Jones v. Alfred H. Mayer Co.** (1968) that the **Civil Rights Act of 1866** prohibited racial discrimination by private individuals in the sale or rental of housing. In *Sullivan*, the Supreme Court reasoned that the right to sell or lease property enunciated in *Jones* would be impaired if an owner could not also assign membership rights in a neighborhood recreational facility to a black, and ruled that such discrimination violated the Civil Rights Act of 1866. As a result of the *Jones* and *Sullivan* cases, the Supreme Court significantly expanded the protection of minorities to enter into a broad range of commercial transactions involving property.

Selected Bibliography Henry J. Abraham, *Freedom and the Court: Civil Rights and Liberties in the United States* (1988); Chester J. Antieau, *Federal Civil Rights Acts, Civil Practice* (1980); Derrick A. Bell, Jr., *Race, Racism, and American Law* (1980); Theodore Eisenberg, *Civil Rights Legislation* (1981).

Frederick G. Slabach

Sumner, Charles (6 January 1811, Boston, Mass.–10 March 1874, Washington, D.C.). After graduating from Harvard Law School in 1833, working as a reporter for the United States Circuit Court, teaching for two years at his alma mater, and touring Europe extensively, Sumner began to practice law in Boston in 1840. An enthusiastic reformer, Sumner's hatred of slavery and of war led him to oppose the annexation of Texas and the Mexican War. Elected to the United States Senate as a Free Soiler in 1851, he fought against the enforcement of the 1850 fugitive slave law and the Kansas-Nebraska Act of 1854. His abolitionism and inflammatory rhetoric angered Southerners and Northerners alike; after his 1856 speech, "The Crime Against Kansas," Congressman Preston Brooks of South Carolina caned Sumner severely and made the New England senator an abolitionist martyr. During the Civil War, Sumner pressured Abraham Lincoln to emancipate the slaves, and after the war, he argued vehemently for an end to segregation and racial discrimination. He helped lead the congressional impeachment attempt against President Andrew Johnson and from 1870 until his death in early 1874, he unsuccessfully tried to force through Congress a broad-based civil rights act that would have outlawed most forms of segregation and guaranteed equal economic and legal rights. The **Civil Rights Act of 1875,** a watered-down version of Sumner's bill, was largely ignored in the South and in 1883 was ruled unconstitutional by the U.S. Supreme Court.

Selected Bibliography David Herbert Donald, *Charles Sumner and the Coming of the Civil War* (1960); David Herbert Donald, *Charles Sumner and the Rights of Man* (1970); Edward Pierce, *Memoirs and Letters of Charles Sumner,* 4 vols. (1878–93).

James Marten

Swann v. Charlotte-Mecklenburg Board of Education, 402 U.S. 1 (1971)

This decision upheld the first extensive court-ordered use of busing to achieve desegregation. In 1965 only two percent of black students in the Charlotte-Mecklenburg school system in North Carolina, attended school with whites. Black parents filed suit to establish the school district's affirmative obligation not merely to abolish its segregated system but also to create an integrated system. Judge J. Braxton Craven rejected the plaintiff's arguments, and the Fourth Circuit upheld his position a year later. The plaintiffs reopened *Swann* after the Supreme Court ruled, in **Green v. School Board of New Kent County, Virginia** (1968), that school districts had an "affirmative duty to take whatever steps" necessary to create a nonsegregated system. Judge James B. McMillan ruled that the school district did not meet the requirement established in *Green.* After the school district submitted several unsatisfactory desegregation plans, McMillan appointed a consultant to advise the court on how desegregation should be accomplished. The plan redrew school districts and bused about one thousand students solely for the purpose of desegregation. By a vote of four to two, the Fourth Circuit Court of Appeals upheld McMillan's use of busing in junior and senior high schools but overturned the extensive busing of elementary school children. The Supreme Court unanimously upheld McMillan's use of busing.

Selected Bibliography Davison M. Douglas, *Reading, Writing, and Race: The Desegregation of the Charlotte Schools* (1995); Owen M. Fiss, "The Charlotte-Macklenburg Case: Its Significance for Northern School Desegregation," *University of Chicago Law Review* 38 (1971), 699–709; Frye Gaillard, *The Dream Long Deferred* (1988); Robert I. Richter, "School Desegregation after

Swann: A Theory of Government Responsibility," *University of Chicago Law Review* 39 (1972), 421–47; Bernard Schwartz, *Swann's Way* (1986); J. Harvie Wilkinson III, *From Brown to Bakke: The Supreme Court and School Integration, 1954–1978* (1979).

Michael S. Mayer

Sweatt v. Painter, 339 U.S. 629 (1950)   On 5 June 1950, the U.S. Supreme Court ruled that the University of Texas Law School had to admit Herman Marion Sweatt, a postal worker from Houston, as a full time student. In 1946 Sweatt applied for admission to the University of Texas Law School, but the Texas State Board of Regents denied him admission on the basis of a state law that required segregation in Texas schools. The *Sweatt* case was unique because in 1947 the Regents also established a "separate but equal" Negro law school on the campus of Texas College for Negroes in Houston to prevent any further challenges to segregated education in Texas. The Regents were fully aware of the Supreme Court's decisions in the **Gaines** (1938) and **Sipuel v. Board of Regents of the University of Oklahoma** (1948) cases requiring state-assisted graduate and professional schools to admit African American students when no **separate-but-equal** institution existed for them. The Regents attempted to circumvent these precedents by establishing a Negro law school in Houston almost overnight to prevent the integration of the University of Texas. Despite their effort, the Supreme Court ruled that the Regents had denied Sweatt his individual rights under the equal protection clause because he would not have received as good an education at the hastily created Negro law school as he would have at the University of Texas with its prestigious faculty, larger library, and national accreditation. **Thurgood Marshall** of the **NAACP** and Dallas attorney William J. Durham won this landmark decision that became one of the precedents for overturning the 1896 *Plessy v. Ferguson* decision.

Selected Bibliography Margaret L. Butler, "The History of Texas Southern University, Thurgood Marshall School of Law: 'The House that Sweatt Built,'" *Thurgood Marshall Law Review* 23 (1997), 45–53; *Dallas Express,* 18 May 1946, 17 June 1950, 14 April 1956; Richard Kluger, *Simple Justice: The History of Brown v. Board of Education and Black America's Struggle for Equality* (1976).

W. Marvin Dulaney

Sweet Briar Institute v. Button, 280 F. Supp. 312 (1967)   When southern institutions of higher education went into court in the 1950s and 1960s, as a rule it was in an effort to prevent desegregation. Sweet Briar College, a private school in Virginia, was different. As early as November 1963, the college's board of directors determined to explore the possibility of contravening a trust-fund provision that restricted enrollment to "white girls and young women." Some months later, Sweet Briar felt itself compelled to act—and, in the end, found itself empowered to act—as a consequence of the **Civil Rights Act of 1964,** which barred federal aid to institutions of higher education that could not certify that they accepted students regardless of race. The school initiated legal action in both the state and federal courts. Eventually, in July

1967, the U.S. District Court for the Western District of Virginia ruled that judicial enforcement of the restriction would constitute "state action" in violation of the **Fourteenth Amendment.** The previous year, the college had enrolled its first African American student, Marshalyn Yeargin.

Selected Bibliography Richard Bardolph, ed., *The Civil Rights Record: Black Americans and the Law, 1849–1970* (1970); Richard Paul Chait, "The Desegregation of Higher Education: A Legal History" (Ph.D. diss., University of Wisconsin, 1972); *Richmond Times-Dispatch*, 31 August 1966.

Peter Wallenstein

Sweet, Ossian Hayes   (1895, Barstow, Fla.–21 March 1960, Detroit, Mich.). An African American physician and activist, Sweet was educated at Wilberforce University in Ohio (B.S. 1917) and **Howard University** (M.D. 1921). In 1926 Sweet purchased a home in a white neighborhood in Detroit, Michigan. An angry white mob attacked the house, and a shot rang out that killed one man. Police arrested Sweet, his wife, his brother, Henry, and nine other occupants of the house and charged them with murder. The case became a cause celebre for the **NAACP,** which hired Clarence Darrow for the defense. In a trial presided over by future U.S. Supreme Court Justice Frank Murphy, the trial ended in a hung jury.

Selected Bibliography Clarence S. Darrow, *Attorney for the Damned* (1957); Clarence Darrow, *The Story of My Life* (1932); Sidney Fine, *Frank Murphy: The Detroit Years* (1966); Irving Stone, *Clarence Darrow for the Defense* (1941); Thomas Sugrue, *The Origins of the Urban Crisis: Race and Inequality in Postwar Detroit* (1996); B. J. Widick, *Detroit: City of Race and Class Violence* (1972).

Brenda M. Brock

Symbionese Liberation Army   A Marxist, revolutionary group with a handful of members, the Symbionese Liberation Army (SLA) was founded in 1973 and led by Donald Defreeze. In Berkeley, California, on 5 February 1974, the SLA kidnapped Patricia Hearst, the 19-year-old scion of the Hearst newspaper family. The SLA demanded ransom in the form of food given to the poor. On 3 April Patricia denounced her father as a capitalist and announced that she had joined the SLA. She participated in a bank robbery for which she and other SLA members were convicted in 1976. Defreeze and five other SLA members died in a shoot-out with Los Angeles police on 17 May 1974. The publicity from the Hearst kidnapping gave the SLA visibility without which it would have been little noted. In 2001, President Bill Clinton pardoned Patty Hearst. That same year Sara Jane Olson, a former SLA member, was sentenced to jail for her involvement in some 1970 police car bombings.

Selected Bibliography Nathan M. Adams, "The Rise and Fall of the S.L.A.," *The Reader's Digest* (September 1974), 64–69; Vin McLellan and Paul Avery, *The Voices of the Guns: The Definitive and Dramatic Story of the Twenty-two Month Career of the Symbionese Liberation Army: One of the Most Bizarre Chapters in the History of the American Left* (1977); *New York Times*, 21 January, 14 December 2001; "The Politics of Terror," *Time* (4 March 1974), 11–15; John F. Stacks, "Patricia Hearst," *1975 Britannica Book of the Year* (1975).

Lorenzo Crowell

T

Taconic Foundation   Located in New York City, the foundation was created in 1958 by Stephen and Audrey Currier as a vehicle for opening the doors of opportunity to all Americans. Under the leadership of the Curriers, the foundation made grants to nonprofit organizations and to private and public institutions. During the civil rights era, the foundation financed several programs aimed at improving the status of blacks. The most important of these programs was its **Voter Education Project.** Established in 1962, the Voter Education Project distributed funds to major civil rights groups and local voters' leagues for voter registration drives. In addition, Taconic financed programs to improve southern race relations and to provide legal aid for minorities and the poor who could not afford an attorney. Taconic's most recent concerns have been with youth unemployment and urban housing in the New York City area.

Selected Bibliography Taylor Branch, *Parting the Waters: America in the King Years, 1954–63* (1988); David J. Garrow, *Bearing the Cross: Martin Luther King, Jr. and the Southern Christian Leadership Conference* (1986); Taconic Foundation, *Taconic Foundation: Twenty-five Years* (1983).

Dorothy A. Autrey

Tallahassee, Florida, Bus Boycott   The bus boycott was launched in May 1956 when Florida Agricultural and Mechanical University (FAMU) students Wilhemina Jakes and Carrie Patterson ignored the segregated seating policy of the City Transit Company and took the only remaining seats available in the white section of the bus. They were arrested for "inciting a riot." FAMU students then overwhelmingly agreed to boycott the bus company. Although it began as a student movement, the Reverend **Charles K. Steele** and the

Photograph taken during the Tallahassee bus boycott. © Bettmann/CORBIS.

Tallahassee Inter-Civic Council quickly assumed leadership of the boycott. By May 1958 the bus company had abolished its segregated seating policy.

Selected Bibliography Adam Fairclough, *To Redeem the Soul of America: The Southern Christian Leadership Conference and Martin Luther King, Jr.* (1987); David J. Garrow, *Bearing the Cross: Martin Luther King, Jr. and the Southern Christian Leadership Conference* (1986); Gregory Padgett, "C. K. Steele: A Biography" (Ph.D. diss., Florida State University, 1994); Glenda Alice Rabby, *The Pain and the Promise: The Struggle for Civil Rights in Tallahassee, Florida* (1999); Charles U. Smith, ed., *The Civil Rights Movement in Florida and the United States* (1989); Charles U. Smith and Lewis M. Killian, *The Tallahassee Bus Protest* (1958).

Maxine D. Jones

Tallahassee, Florida, Jail-In   On 20 February 1960, 11 Florida Agricultural and Mechanical University students, members of the **Congress of Racial Equality,** were arrested after staging a second sit-in at the Woolworth's counter. Charged on 17 March with disturbing the peace and assembling unlawfully, they were sentenced to pay $300 in fines or serve 60 days in the Leon County jail. Eight of the students chose the jail sentence. This militant tactic attracted national attention, encouraged other young activists to "fill the jails for equal rights," and contributed to the integration of Tallahassee.

Selected Bibliography Kenneth B. Clark, "The Civil Rights Movement: Momentum and Organization," *Daedalus* 95 (Winter 1966), 239–67; Glenda A. Rabby, "Fighting for Civil Rights: The Tallahassee Story," *Research in Review* (June 1985), 10–12; Glenda A. Rabby, *The Pain and the Promise: The Struggle for Civil Rights in Tallahassee, Florida* (1999); Ruth Searles and J. Allen Williams, Jr., "Negro College Students' Participation in Sit-Ins," *Social Forces* 40 (March 1962), 215–20; Harvard Sitkoff, *The Struggle for Black Equality, 1954–1980* (1981); Robert Melvin White, "The Tallahassee Sit-Ins and CORE: A Nonviolent Revolutionary Submovement" (Ph.D. diss., Florida State University, 1964).

Jane F. Lancaster

Tallahassee, Florida, Sit-Ins   On 13 February 1960, Florida A & M students and **CORE** members Patricia and Priscilla Stephens and eight other young blacks sat at a segregated lunch counter to protest discrimination in Tallahassee. The following weekend, CORE resumed the boycott, but police arrested 11 members for disturbing the peace and for unlawful assembly. On 5 March the sit-ins became interracial and more violent as police officers arrested numerous participants and fired tear gas into black crowds while armed whites patrolled the streets. The 11 individuals previously arrested were later tried, found guilty, and given $300 fines or 60 days in prison. They chose "jail over bail," and CORE used their imprisonment to gain support for the emerging civil rights struggle. On 20 March Florida Governor LeRoy Collins publicly declared segregation facilities "unfair and morally wrong" and asked communities to solve racial problems peacefully. Tallahassee merchants resisted initially, but they desegregated their lunch counters in January 1963.

Selected Bibliography August Meier and Elliot Rudwick, CORE: A study in the Civil Rights Movement, 1942–1968 (1975); Glenda Alice Rabby, The Pain and the Promise: The Struggle for Civil Rights in Tallahassee, Florida (1999); Harvard Sitkoff, The Struggle of Black Equality, 1954–1980 (1981).

Michael Butler

Tampa, Florida, Race Riot (1967)   During the early 1960s, many of Tampa's racial barriers had fallen without fanfare under the guidance of a biracial committee. However, discrimination persisted in subtle and powerful forms, especially with respect to the quality of housing, employment, and police protection. On Sunday, 11 June 1967, a major race riot erupted in the black section adjacent to the downtown business district. Triggered by a white policeman's fatal shooting of an unarmed black robbery suspect, rioting broke out in an area where over half of the families earned less than $3,000; the unemployment rate for black males was double that of whites; and 60 percent of the housing units were substandard. The riot lasted for four days and caused considerable property damage. No one was killed, though 16 people were injured and 111 were arrested. The riot ended after the city's Commission on Community Relations arranged for withdrawal of police and dispatched black youths wearing white helmets to patrol ghetto streets. With calm restored, business and civic leaders disbursed increased funds for recreational activities and job training programs. By the end of the decade, however, most of these projects had terminated, and many of the problems that had sparked the riot remained.

Selected Bibliography Gayle Everett Davis, "Riot in Tampa" (M.A. thesis, University of South Florida, 1976); Steven F. Lawson, "From Sit-In to Race Riot: Businessmen, Blacks, and the Pursuit of Racial Moderation in Tampa, 1960–1967," in Elizabeth Jacoway and David R. Colburn, eds., Southern Businessmen and Desegregation (1982); National Advisory Commission on Civil Disorders, Report (1968).

Steven P. Lawson

Tanner, Benjamin Tucker (25 December 1835, Pittsburgh, Pa.–15 January 1923, Philadelphia, Pa.). An editor and the eighteenth bishop of the African Methodist Episcopal (A.M.E.) Church, Tanner attended Avery College in Allegheny, Pennsylvania (1852–57), working as a barber to pay his expenses. He studied at Western Theological Seminary (1858–60) and was ordained a deacon and then an elder in the A.M.E. Church (1860). From 1868 to 1884 Tanner edited the *Christian Recorder*, the official organ of the A.M.E. Church, which emerged as an important newspaper whose columns focused on national political events as well as church affairs. In 1884 he launched the *A.M.E. Church Review*, a quarterly that soon became a leading periodical of African American literary and intellectual thought. During the post-Reconstruction era, Tanner urged racial solidarity as the most effective means to combat racial injustice and prodded African Americans to support the black press and black businesses. For a brief period in 1901, he served as dean of Payne Theological Seminary of Wilberforce University, in Wilberforce, Ohio.

Selected Bibliography *Christian Recorder* (21 June 1888); Lawrence S. Little, *Disciples of Liberty: The African Methodist Episcopal Church in the Age of Imperialism, 1884–1916* (2000); August Meier, *Negro Thought in America, 1880–1915; Racial Ideologies in the Age of Booker T. Washington* (1963); Obituary, *New York Times*, 16 January 1923; Charles Spencer Smith, *A History of the African Methodist Episcopal Church* (1922); Richard R. Wright, Jr., ed., *Encyclopedia of African Methodism* (1948).

George E. Walker

Tappan, Lewis (23 May 1788, Northampton, Mass.–21 June 1873, Brooklyn, N.Y.). Lewis Tappan served as the leader of the evangelical wing of the nineteenth-century abolition movement. In the early 1830s, he formulated the chief strategies of the fledgling crusade to free American slaves: raising of funds, growth of local and state antislavery societies, and creation of reading materials designed for special audiences, especially children, churchwomen, businessmen. The antislavery program in which he and coworkers engaged consisted of these propositions: It should begin at once; it should take place on American, not foreign, soil; and it should provide no compensation to slave owners. Without the New Yorker's expertise in finance, journalism, and organization, "immediate emancipation" would probably not have had the impact on northern society and national politics that it did.

Like most other abolitionists, Tappan and a brother had first adopted the colonization scheme. Then, William Lloyd Garrison convinced them that sending blacks to Africa stained its sponsors with sin and strengthened slavery at home. With Garrison and other reformers, the New York entrepreneurs founded the American Anti-Slavery Society, over which Arthur Tappan presided until 1840.

The abolitionist cause split apart on issues ranging from women's rights to the efficacy of reform partisanship. Though reluctant at first, the New York merchant eventually saw the value of political action. In 1843 he vainly tried to persuade the British government to recognize a Texas without slavery and

Engraved portrait of Lewis Tappan, 1875. © Library of Congress.

to prevent its American annexation. With greater success, he helped to form the Liberty and Free Soil parties but always mistrusted politicians as guardians of pure principle.

Tappan's real influence lay in evangelical circles in which he urged separation from the sin of slaveholding. Out of his work to free the *Amistad* prisoners from 1839 to 1841, he fashioned the **American Missionary Association.** This fast-growing agency united abolitionists in various evangelical faiths, but chiefly the Presbyterian and Congregational. As its chief supervisor, Tappan supported missions at home and abroad, most particularly in emancipated British Jamaica, Free Soil Kansas, and even slaveholding Kentucky where the Reverend John G. Fee was to found the future antiracist Berea College. In his declining years, Tappan helped the AMA to send to the South hundreds of Yankee teachers, male and female, black and white, for the instruction of the African Americans freed during and after the Civil War.

Far ahead of his time with regard to race relations, Tappan often spoke forcefully against the "spirit of caste," which he found displayed even in antislavery councils. Although Tappan's religious inspiration and his sternly paternalistic precepts for action might be regarded as outdated, he did more to further the cause of racial equality than all but a handful of his fellow white contemporaries.

Selected Bibliography Lawrence F. Friedman, *Gregarious Saints: Self and Community in American Abolitionism, 1830–1870* (1982); James Brewer Stewart, *Holy Warriors: The Abolitionists and American Slavery* (1976); Lewis Tappan, *The Life of Arthur Tappan* (1870); Bertram Wyatt-Brown, *Lewis Tappan and the Evangelical War against Slavery* (1969).

Bertram Wyatt-Brown

Taylor, Hobart, Jr. (17 December 1920, Texarkana, Tex.–3 April 1981, Washington, D.C.). Hobart Taylor, Jr., son of a successful African American businessman, grew up in Houston, Texas, and graduated from Prairie View State College in 1939. Two years later he earned a master's degree in economics from **Howard University** and then received a law degree at the University of Michigan in 1943. Although he was an established lawyer in Wayne County, Michigan, where he worked as both a prosecuting attorney and corporate counsel, Hobart Taylor, Jr., gained national prominence during the administrations of John F. Kennedy and Lyndon B. Johnson. In February 1961, Vice President Johnson appointed Taylor to be the special counsel for the President's Committee on Equal Employment Opportunity (PCEEO), which Johnson chaired. Following an internal dispute over the future direction of the committee, Johnson in 1962 named Taylor to be its executive vice chairman, a job that Taylor held until 1965. When the PCEEO was replaced by the **Equal Employment Opportunity Commission** in 1965, President Johnson appointed Taylor the director of the Export-Import Bank of the United States. In 1968 Taylor resigned to enter private law practice in Washington, D.C. In addition to his political successes, Taylor received achievement awards from the **National Urban League** (1965) and the **NAACP** (1975).

Selected Bibliography Hugh Davis Graham, *The Civil Rights Era* (1990); *Who's Who among Black Americans* (1976).

Dean K. Yates

***Taylor v. Georgia,* 315 U.S. 25 (1942)** James Taylor, a black citizen of Georgia, was indicted and convicted in 1940 of accepting an advance money payment for work he did not subsequently perform. He stood convicted of violating a Georgia statue that made breach of a labor contract prima facie evidence of intent to defraud the employer. In a nearly identical 1911 case, **Bailey v. Alabama,** the Supreme Court had ruled that state statutes that make it a crime to fail to perform the terms of a labor contract after receiving a cash advance violated both the **Thirteenth Amendment** and federal antipeonage laws. Despite this earlier ruling, Taylor was compelled to carry his case to the Supreme Court to secure justice. The Court was unanimous in reversing Taylor's conviction. The Georgia statute, it held, sanctioned coerced labor, which was prohibited by the Constitution and by federal antipeonage laws. Like a number of earlier rulings, *Taylor* struck a blow at forced labor statutes.

It was not until 1944, however, in **Pollock v. Williams,** that the Supreme
Court dealt the death blow to the **black peonage** system.

Selected Bibliography Pete Daniel, *The Shadow of Slavery: Peonage in the South, 1909–1969*
(1972); Loren Miller, *The Petitioners: The Story of the Supreme Court of the United States and the
Negro* (1966); "Recent Cases," *George Washington Law Review* 10 (1942), 748–50; Melvin I.
Urofsky, *A March of Liberty: A Constitutional History of the United States* (1988).

Charles D. Lowery

Terrell, Mary Church (9 September 1863, Memphis, Tenn.–24 July 1954,
Annapolis, Md.). An educator, writer, and lifelong activist against discrimination, Terrell received a B.A. and M.A. (1884, 1888) from Oberlin and then
taught the classics in Washington, D.C. The first black woman to be on the
District of Columbia Board of Education, she formed the Colored Women's
League of D.C., served as president of the **National Association of Colored
Women** (1896–1901), and was a charter member of the **NAACP.** As an
activist, she worked for women's suffrage, workers' rights, and black achievement, and against **lynching,** discrimination, and black disenfranchisement.

Mary Church Terrell, c. 1880. © Library of Congress.

She was eloquent and powerful as a writer and orator; she reached out to both whites and blacks.

Selected Bibliography Beverly W. Jones, *Quest for Equality: The Life and Writings of Mary Eliza Church Terrell, 1863–1954* (1990); Gladys B. Shepperd, *Mary Church Terrell: Respectable Person* (1959); Mary Church Terrell, *A Colored Woman in a White World* (1940).

Linda G. Ford

Terrell, Robert Herberton (27 November 1857, Charlottesville, Va.–20 December 1925, Washington, D.C.). Terrell attended public schools in Washington, D.C., and later graduated magna cum laude from Harvard College in June 1884. After teaching in Washington's public schools for five years, he attended Harvard Law School and received an LL.B. in 1889 and an LL.M. in 1893. While in law school, he married Mary E. Church of Memphis (See **Mary Church Terrell**). His public career was varied. He worked as a clerk in the U.S. Treasury in 1889 and was elected to the Board of Trade in the 1890s. He enjoyed a successful law partnership with **John R. Lynch,** former Mississippi congressman, from 1892 to 1898. After receiving an appointment as a municipal court judge in the District of Columbia from President William H. Taft in 1910, he served with distinction in that position until his death. While on the bench, he also served on the faculty of the **Howard University** Law School. Living most of their lives in Washington, D.C., Terrell and his wife participated in numerous black community organizations. The city recognized his contributions by naming an elementary school in his honor.

Selected Bibliography Rayford W. Logan and Michael R. Winston, eds., *Dictionary of American Negro Biography* (1982); Obituary, *The Journal of Negro History* 11 (January 1926), 223–25; Mary Church Terrell, *A Colored Woman in a White World* (1940).

Thomas D. Cockrell

Terry v. Adams*, 345 U.S. 461 (1953)** The Jaybird Democratic Association, organized in 1889 in Fort Bend County, Texas, restricted its membership to white citizens. Winners of the Jaybird's primary filed as candidates in the regular Democratic primary. With few exceptions, Jaybird candidates won every election. John Terry sought a declaratory judgment and injunction to permit black participation in the Jaybird primary. The federal district court ruled the Jaybird Association a political party and found for Terry. Defendants appealed, and the **United States Court of Appeals for the Fifth Judicial Circuit** reversed the decision. By writ of certiorari, the Supreme Court held the Jaybird "primary" in violation of the **Fifteenth Amendment** and existing civil rights laws. Citing ***United States v. Classic (1941), extending federal power to state primary elections, and ***Smith v. Allwright*** (1944), condemning discrimination when the primary was the only effective means of choice, the court ruled that the state was obliged to protect its citizens' voting privileges and to guarantee voters access to all phases of the election process. Justices Hugo Black, William Douglas, and Harold Burton charged the state's election process with denying blacks political influence and participation. Justice Felix Frankfurter concurred, arguing that county officials participated in and condoned efforts to exclude blacks from voting. Justices Tom Clark and Stanley Reed and Chief Justice Fred Vinson concurred, claiming that the Jaybird organization was a political party that excluded blacks. Justice Sherman Minton dissented: Jaybird activities were not state actions and, therefore, not forbidden.

Selected Bibliography "Terry v. Adams," *American Bar Association Journal* 39 (1953), 822–23; "Terry v. Adams," *Alabama Law Review* 6 (1954), 291–95; "Terry v. Adams," *Harvard Law Review* 67 (1953), 104–5; "Terry v. Adams," *Texas Law Review* 32 (1953), 223–25; "Terry v. Adams," *Washington and Lee Law Review* 11 (1954), 60–65.

William A. Paquette

They Shall Not Die   A play by John Wexley, loosely based on the **Scottsboro Trials,** *They Shall Not Die* was performed in New York on 23 February 1934. The play revolves around black **lynching, Jim Crow** restrictions, white supremacy, and economic oppression of both blacks and whites. It exposes the racial fears, hatred, and ignorance behind the Scottsboro case. It was barred after its 26 February 1934 performance in Washington, D.C., and again in 1947 in Trenton, New Jersey. The play has, however, been hailed as a disturbing yet important statement of racial prejudice in American society.

Selected Bibliography *Schomburg Center Clipping File, 1925–1974;* John Wexley, *They Shall Not Die* (1934).

Jessie M. Carter

Thirteenth Amendment   This amendment to the Constitution adopted in 1865 ended slavery or involuntary servitude in the United States or any place subject to its jurisdiction. It applies to individuals as well as to governments. The amendment is a guarantee against forced labor and, under recent Supreme Court rulings, gives Congress power to legislate against any acts that impose a "badge of slavery" on anyone. It capped a series of Civil War emancipation endeavors, including abolition of slavery in the District of Columbia and the territories, the **Confiscation Act** of 1862, and President Abraham Lincoln's **Emancipation Proclamation,** which freed the slaves in areas still in rebellion after 1862. In addition, three border states (West Virginia, Maryland, and Missouri) and three occupied Confederate states (Arkansas, Louisiana, and Tennessee) ended slavery during the war. When the Civil War ended, the institution legally existed in two border states and parts of two others under Union control, but many Republicans, including Lincoln, questioned whether these wartime actions had peacetime legal force. In 1864, therefore, Congress initiated the Thirteenth Amendment, which banned slavery and involuntary servitude (except as punishment for crime) in the nation and its territories. The measure passed the Senate on 8 April 1864, but lacked the necessary two-thirds vote in the House until 31 January 1865 when it passed under strong administration pressure. By 18 December 1865 the requisite three-fourths of the states had completed ratification. Three Union states (New Jersey, Kentucky, and Delaware) withheld support, but eight former Confederate states ratified the amendment in the fall of 1865 as a condition of restoration under President Andrew Johnson's Reconstruction program.

Selected Bibliography Herman Belz, *Emancipation and Equal Rights: Politics and Constitutionalism in the Civil War Era* (1978); John H. Cox and LaWanda Cox, *Politics, Principle, and Prejudice, 1865–1866: Dilemma of Reconstruction America* (1963); James M. McPherson, *Ordeal by Fire: The Civil War and Reconstruction* (1982); David M. Potter, *Division and the Stresses of Reunion, 1845–1876* (1973).

Marvin Thomas and James B. Potts

Thirty Years of Lynching in the United States, 1889–1918   Written as a part of the **NAACP** campaign to stop mob violence against black people in the United States, this work documented more than 2,500 lynchings during the time period covered. Additionally, researchers working on the project were able to demonstrate that the vast majority of lynchings were *not* due to rape accusations. Later this information was used to help support efforts in Congress to pass a federal antilynching law sponsored by Missouri Congressman L. C. Dyer. The act did not pass due to southern resistance and Republican party indifference.

Selected Bibliography NAACP, *Thirty Years of Lynching in the United States, 1889–1918* (1919); Robert L. Zangrando, *THE NAACP Crusade against Lynching 1909–1950* (1980).

Kenneth W. Goings

Till, Emmett Louis   (25 July 1941, near Chicago, Ill.–28 August 1955, near Glendora, Miss.). Till was the only child of Louis Till and Mamie Bradley Till, who had migrated to Chicago from Missouri and Tallahatchie County, Mississippi, respectively. Till had completed the seventh grade when his mother sent him in August 1955 to Mississippi for a vacation with relatives. Till and his cousin, Curtis Jones, stayed in Leflore County with Jones's grandfather, Mose Wright. On the evening of 24 August, Till and Jones went to Bryant's Grocery and Meat Market in Money. Mrs. Carolyn Bryant later claimed the black youth grabbed her at the waist and asked her for a date; and when he was pulled from the store by friends, Till allegedly said, "Bye, baby" and "wolf whistled." Late the following Saturday night, Roy Bryant and his half brother, J. W. Milam, took Till from Mose Wright's home, drove him to the Tallahatchie River, shot him in the head, tied a heavy cotton gin fan to his body, and threw him in the river. The body was found three days later. Till's murder and, especially, the pictures of his nearly unrecognizable body shocked black Americans. The acquittal on 23 September

Emmett Till, 1955. © Library of Congress.

501

of Bryant and Milam on murder charges prompted demonstrations in many northern cities.

Selected Bibliography William Bradford Huie, *Wolf Whistle* (1959); Stephen J. Whitfield, *A Death in the Delta: The Story of Emmett Till* (1988); Juan Williams, *Eyes on the Prize: America's Civil Rights Years, 1954–1965* (1987).

Charles W. Eagles

To Secure These Rights   President Harry S Truman, at the instigation of the **NAACP**'s **Walter Francis White,** appointed a special committee to investigate racial violence. In 1947 this interracial organization issued its report, *To Secure These Rights*, which became the Democrats' civil rights agenda for the next several decades. The agenda included the establishment of the permanent **United States Commission on Civil Rights,** the abolition of the **poll tax,** and an end to segregation in the armed forces. Based on the testimony of some 40 witnesses and information from 25 federal agencies, the report summed up past progress in the area of race relations but also warned that full equality was far from a reality.

Selected Bibliography William C. Berman, *The Politics of Civil Rights in the Truman Administration* (1970); Alonzo L. Hamby, *Beyond the New Deal: Harry S Truman and American Liberalism* (1973); Steven F. Lawson and Charles Payne, *Debating the Civil Rights Movement, 1945–1968* (1998); President's Committee on Civil Rights, *To Secure These Rights: The Report of the President's Committee on Civil Rights* (1947).

Carol Wilson

Tolson, Melvin Beaunorus   (6 February 1898, Moberly, Mo.–29 August 1966, Dallas Tex.). African American educator and writer of poetry, drama, and fiction, Tolson was especially noted for his work, *Harlem Gallery*, published after his death, which chronicled Harlem's "double consciousness." Tolson attended **Fisk University** and received his baccalaureate degree from Lincoln University in Pennsylvania. He did graduate work at Columbia University, taught at Wiley and Langston Colleges, and served four terms as mayor of historically black Langston, Oklahoma. He lectured for the **NAACP** and said he was often a "facer of mobs." Tolson's themes were democracy, universal brotherhood, the developing Third World, and the U.S. race problem, which he saw as economic exploitation.

Selected Bibliography *Book World, Washington Post,* 14 October 1984; Mariann Russell, *Melvin B. Tolson's Harlem Gallery: A Literary Analysis* (1980).

Nancy E. Fitch

Tonkins v. City of Greensboro, **171 F. Supp. 476 (M.D. N.C., 1959)** Decided on 13 August 1959, this U.S. district court case involved a decision made on a supplemental complaint by Deloris Tonkins and her colleagues against the City of Greensboro, North Carolina. The original complaint, filed in 1958, had sought to enjoin the city from refusing to permit African American citizens from using the Lindley Park Swimming Pool and from selling the pool for the sole purpose of denying these same citizens their constitutional rights. The original complaint had been dismissed, but the plaintiffs were allowed to file a supplemental complaint. One of the plaintiff's attorneys was **Thurgood Marshall.** After the first dismissal, the city sold the pool at a public sale to the Greensboro Pool Corporation. The supplemental complaint by Tonkins sought to show that the sale was not bona fide because there had been collusion between the city and the successful bidder regarding the future operation of the pool to the exclusion of nonwhites. The plaintiffs alleged that the Greensboro Pool Corporation would either default in its payments, be granted an extension of time to pay the annual installments, or that the city would repurchase the property at a subsequent foreclosure sale. These and other allegations were determined by the court to be unsupported theories and thus not sufficient evidence upon which to decide a legal issue. The plaintiffs' supplemental complaints were dismissed.

Selected Bibliography Richard Bardolph, ed., *The Civil Rights Record: Black Americans and the Law, 1849–1970* (1970); William H. Chafe, *Civilities and Civil Rights: Greensboro, North Carolina, and the Black Struggle for Freedom* (1980).

Charles A. Risher

Toomer, Jean (26 December 1894, Washington, D.C.–30 March 1967, Doylestown, Pa.). Poet, novelist, and short story writer, Jean Toomer was born in Washington, D.C., and attended the University of Wisconsin, the University of Chicago, and the City College of New York. Hailed by critics as the most promising and original voice of the **Harlem Renaissance,** Toomer launched a modernist revolution in African American writing that signaled "an awakening of black artistic expression." Boldly experimental in form, technique, language, and perception, *Cane* (1923), a collection of short fiction, poetry, and drama, presents an all-inclusive portrait of the black American experience: a fusion of past and present, pain and beauty, strength and failings. In this literary masterpiece, Jean Toomer established a precedent that liberated black writing.

Selected Bibliography Hurston Baker, "Journey Towards Black Art: Jean Toomer's *Cane*," in Henry Louis Gates, Jr., ed., *Singers of Daybreak: Shades in Black American Literature* (1977); Brian Benson and Mable Dillard, *Jean Toomer* (1980); Charles Davis, "Jean Toomer and the South: Region and Race as Elements within Literary Imagination," in *Black Is the Color of the Cosmos: Essays on Afro-American Literature and Culture, 1942–1981* (1982); Cynthia E. Kerman, *The Lives of Jean Toomer: A Hunger for Wholeness* (1987); Darwin Turner, *In a Minor Cord* (1971).

Jacquelyn Jackson

Tougaloo College Tougaloo College, established in 1869 by the **American Missionary Association,** is one of the nation's oldest predominantly black private colleges. The campus is located approximately eight miles north of Jackson, Mississippi. Initially a private institution, Tougaloo was chartered by the state in 1871 and remained state related until 1892 when it once again became private. After becoming a state institution, its name became Tougaloo University; in 1916, the original designation was restored. Tougaloo has an excellent academic reputation among both black and white educators. It has served Mississippi and the South well, producing some of Mississippi's most prominent black educational and business leaders. It played a major role in Mississippi in the civil rights movement of the 1960s. As metropolitan Jackson spreads out toward it in the early twenty-first century, Tougaloo College has continued to provide a high quality education in an increasingly urban setting.

Selected Bibliography Clarice T. Campbell and Oscar Allan Rogers, Jr., *Mississippi: The View from Tougaloo* (1979); W. Augustus Low and Virgil A. Clift, eds., *Encyclopedia of Black America* (1981); Web site: www.tougaloo.edu.

Allen Dennis

Townsend, Willard Saxby (4 December 1897, Cincinnati, Ohio–3 February 1957, Chicago, Ill.). Founder and president of the United Transport Service Employees (Redcaps), Townsend grew up in Cincinnati, Ohio, with his grandfather. After completing two years of high school he went to work as a Redcap and later served in an all-black stateside unit during World War I. Following the war Townsend completed his education in Canada and then returned to Chicago, where he turned his energy toward labor organization. He considered the unionization of black workers a prerequisite for first-class citizenship. Later he sat on the executive board of the American Federation of Labor and Congress of Industrial Organizations as one of the two highest-ranking black officers in the hierarchy of American labor.

Selected Bibliography Richard Bardolph, *The Negro Vanguard* (1959); Beth T. Bates, *Pullman Porters and the Rise of Protest Politics in Black America, 1925–1945* (2001); Obituary, *New York Times*, 5 February 1957.

Michael S. Downs

Trent, William Johnson, Jr. (8 March 1910, Asheville, N.C.– 27 November 1993, Greensboro, S.C.). The son of the fourth president of Livingstone College, in Salisbury, North Carolina, and a graduate of and later professor at that institution, he was appointed a member of Franklin D. Roosevelt's **Black Cabinet** in 1934. He served as advisor on Negro affairs for the Department of Interior (1938–39) and as a race relations officer in the Federal Works Agency (1934–44). In 1944, Trent became the first executive director of the newly formed **United Negro College Fund**—an organization of privately supported, generally church-related, African American colleges. He served until 1963 when he became the top African American executive for Time, Incorporated.

Selected Bibliography Editors of *Ebony, Negro Handbook* (1966), *Ebony Handbook* (1974); John Hope Franklin and August Meier, eds., *Black Leaders of the Twentieth Century* (1982); J. P. Guzman, ed., *Negro Year Book: 1947* (1947); William J. Trent, "Development of Negro Life Insurance Enterprises" (MBA thesis, University of Pennsylvania, 1932); United Negro College Fund Archives, *Papers of William J. Trent*, http://www.auc.edu/arch/uncf.htm.

Aingred G. Dunston

Trotter, (William) Monroe (7 April 1872, Chillicothe, Ohio–7 April 1934, Boston, Mass.). Monroe Trotter inherited a militant civil rights stance from his father, James Monroe Trotter (1842–92), who declared himself for "a great

Principle, that for the attainment of which we gladly peril our lives—Manhood and Equality." Monroe Trotter lived his life in that vein. He showed brilliance at Harvard (A.B., 1895; M.A., 1896), where he won election to Phi Beta Kappa in his junior year—the first black the college so honored. He employed his cutting intelligence in the *Boston Guardian,* the newspaper he began in 1902. Assailing what he considered to be the misguided leadership of **Booker T. Washington,** Trotter and his newspaper became primary antagonists of what was called "the Tuskegee Machine." Invoking "the spirit of protest, of independence, of revolt," Trotter lambasted Washington's accommodationism for demeaning black political rights and denigrating classical education. For a time Trotter allied himself with **W.E.B. Du Bois,** notably in the **Niagara Movement** of 1905. Trotter founded the **National Equal Rights League** (1908), which he described, in contrast to the **NAACP,** as "an organization of the colored people and for the colored people and led by the colored people."

Selected Bibliography Stephen R. Fox, *The Guardian of Boston: William Monroe Trotter* (1970); Rayford W. Logan and Michael R. Winston, eds., *The Dictionary of American Negro Biography* (1982); Christine A. Lunardini, "Standing Firm: William Monroe Trotter's Meetings with Woodrow Wilson, 1913–1914," *Journal of Negro Education* 64 (Summer 1979), 244–64; Charles W. Puttkammer and Ruth Worthy, "William Monroe Trotter, 1872–1934," *Journal of Negro History* 43 (October 1958), 298–316.

Thomas J. Davis

Tucker, Rosina C. (4 November 1881, Washington, D.C.–3 March 1987, Washington, D.C.). A music teacher, civic worker, organizer for the **Brotherhood of Sleeping Car Porters and Maids,** and president of a local chapter and international secretary-treasurer of the Ladies Auxiliary of the Brotherhood of Sleeping Car Porters, Tucker attended M Street High School but left in 1898 to marry James D. Corrothers, a literary figure and clergyman. Corrothers died in 1917, and in 1918 she married Berthea J. Tucker, a pullman porter. In 1928 she and other porters' wives formed the Ladies Auxiliary of the Brotherhood of Sleeping Car Porters. Believing that they could assist their husbands in the struggle against racism and unfair labor practices, Tucker and others held secret meetings (some at her home). They raised money and disseminated information about the union for **A. Philip Randolph.**

Selected Bibliography Melinda Chateauvert, *Marching Together: Women of the Brotherhood of Sleeping Car Porters* (1998); Obituary, *Washington Post,* 5 March 1987; Jack Santino, *Miles of Smiles, Years of Struggle Stories of Black Pullman Porters* (1989).

Betty L. Plummer

Tureaud, Alexander Pierre, Sr. (26 February 1899, New Orleans, La.–22 January 1972, New Orleans, La.). A civil rights attorney and legal counsel for the **NAACP** in Louisiana, Tureaud was educated in the public schools of New Orleans and Washington, D.C. In 1922 he entered the **Howard University** Law School, graduating in 1925. On returning to New Orleans in 1926, he began his long years of association with the New Orleans Branch of the

NAACP. After he spearheaded the ouster of the old leadership, the NAACP became the symbol of progressive action throughout Louisiana. He used the courts to transform the **Brown v. Board of Education** decision into reality for African Americans. Although his main efforts were made in the field of education, Tureaud also devoted time to securing voting rights and integration of public accommodations. From 1940 to 1943 he helped gain salary equalization for public schoolteachers in Orleans, Jefferson, East Baton Rouge, and Iberville parishes. *Hall v. Nagel* (1946) opened voter registration rolls to African Americans. In the 1950s he helped blacks gain equal access to higher education and the integration of the public schools. He filed *Garner v. Louisiana* in 1960, the first sit-in case decided by the U.S. Supreme Court.

Selected Bibliography Numan V. Bartley, *The Rise of Massive Resistance: Race and Politics in the South during the 1950s* (1969); Robert Carter and Thurgood Marshall, "The Meaning and Significance of the Supreme Court Decree," *Journal of Negro Education* 24 (Summer 1955), 397–404; Morton Inger, *Politics and Reality in an American City: The New Orleans School Crisis of 1960* (1960); August Meier and Elliott Rudwick, *CORE: A Study in the Civil Rights Movement, 1942–1968* (1973); J. W. Peltason, *Fifty-eight Lonely Men: Southern Federal Judges and School Desegregation* (1961); Frank T. Read and Lucy S. McGough, *Let Them Be Judged: The Judicial Integration of the Deep South* (1978); Barbara A. Worthy, "The Travail and Triumph of a Southern Black Civil Rights Lawyer: The Legal Career of Alexander Pierre Tureaud, 1899–1972" (Ph.D. diss., Tulane University, 1984).

Barbara A. Worthy

Tureaud v. Board of Supervisors, 347 U.S. 971 (1954)   This was the final decision arising out of a class action suit filed in 1953 by A. P. Tureaud, Jr., who wished to pursue a combined six-year arts and sciences and law curriculum at Louisiana State University. Tureaud was denied admission because a similar course of study was offered at Southern University, a predominantly African American institution. The suit contended that the Southern University course was not substantially equal to that offered by Louisiana State University. On 24 May 1954 the U.S. Supreme Court affirmed the judgment of the district court that had ordered Tureaud's admission to Louisiana State University.

Selected Bibliography *Board of Supervisors Louisiana State University et al. V. Tureaud*, 207 F.2d 807 (1953); *McLaurin v. Oklahoma*, 339 U.S. 637 (1950); Loren Miller, *The Petitioners: The Story of the Supreme Court of the United States and the Negro* (1966); *Missouri ex rel. Gaines v. Canada*, 305 U.S. 337 (1938); *Sweatt v. Painter*, 339 U.S. 629 (1950); *Tureaud v. Board of Supervisors Louisiana State University et al.*, 116 F. Supp. 248 (1953).

Barbara A. Worthy

Turner, Henry McNeal   (1 February 1834, Newberry Court House, S.C.–8 May 1915, Atlanta, Ga.). A bishop in the African Methodist Episcopal (A.M.E.) church, he was born a free person and served as a plantation laborer, porter, United States Army chaplain, political organizer, college chancellor, editor, emigrationist, black nationalist, preacher and minister, teacher, and political activist. The Civil War raised Turner's hopes, but Reconstruction put an end to his faith in white America's ability to trade its racism for equality and justice for all United States citizens. Expelled illegally from the Georgia legislature in 1868, he was reprimanded by the Republican party for organizing African Americans to be members of the A.M.E. Church and the Republican party. In 1876, he became the manager of the A.M.E. Book Concern. This position allowed Turner to voice the discontent he and the African American rural class had about life in the United States. In 1880 he became an A.M.E. bishop. In the 1890s, black violence escalated, and it led Turner and working-class African Americans to view emigration as the only alternative. Using his editorial control of the A.M.E. publication *Voice of Missions*, Turner diligently tried to facilitate African American migration to Africa by calling for payment of **reparations** to ex-slaves, working to establish a steamship company, and seeking middle-class African American financial support. He envisioned trade, guidance, independence, self-governance, and modernization for Africa. Turner combined religion and politics in an attempt to make African Americans full citizens. He was part of a century-old protest movement based in the African American religious-political tradition that spanned the Atlantic Ocean linking the resistance to racism and colonialism.

Selected Bibliography Stephen Ward Angell, *Bishop Henry McNeal Turner and African American Religion in the South* (1992); Edwin S. Redkey, *Black Exodus, Black Nationalist, and Back-to-Africa Movements 1890–1910* (1969); Edwin S. Redkey, ed., *The Writings and Speeches of Henry McNeal Turner* (1971); George Shepperson and Thomas Price, *Independent African, John Chilembwe and the Origins, Setting, and Significance of the Nyasaland Native Rising of 1915* (1958); Clarence E. Walker, *A Rock in a Weary Land: The African Methodist Episcopal Church during the Civil War and Reconstruction* (1982); Gayraud S. Wilmore, *Black Religion and Black Radicalism: An Interpretation of the Religious History of Afro-American People* (1983).

Gregory Mixon

Turner, James Milton (16 May 1840, St. Louis, Mo.–1 November 1915, Ardmore, Okla.). Born a slave but freed at an early age through purchase by his father, he attended Oberlin College before the Civil War. After the war, he rose to prominence in Missouri as the major spokesman for the Equal Rights League. He taught school and organized black schools across the state during 1869–70, while also getting out the black vote for **Radical Republican** candidates. As a reward, President Ulysses Grant appointed Turner minister resident and consul general to Liberia in 1871, a post he held until 1878. Returning to Missouri politics but also involving himself in the interests of black residents of the Indian Territory, Turner continued to serve his race until he was killed in an explosion.

Selected Bibliography Lawrence O. Christensen, "J. Milton Turner: An Appraisal," *Missouri Historical Review* 70 (October 1975), 1–19; Lawrence O. Christensen, "Schools for Blacks: J. Milton Turner in Reconstruction Missouri," *Missouri Historical Review* 76 (January 1982), 121–35; Gary R. Kremer, "Background to Apostasy: James Milton Turner and the Republican Party," *Missouri Historical Review* 71 (October 1976), 59–75; Gary R. Kremer, "For Justice and a Fee: James Milton Turner and the Cherokee Freedmen," *Chronicles of Oklahoma* 58 (July 1981), 376–91; Gary R. Kremer, *James Milton Turner and the Promise of America* (1991); Gary R.

Kremer, "The World of Make-Believe: James Milton Turner and Black Masonry," *Missouri Historical Review* 74 (October 1979), 50–71.

Lawrence O. Christensen

Tuskegee Airmen   The Tuskegee Airmen breached the color barrier in the U.S. Army Air Corps in 1941 and went on to compile a distinguished combat record during World War II, a record that served as an important source of pride for black Americans, who resented the dominant view of whites that blacks could not fight. In 1940 African Americans made up approximately 1.5 percent of the regular Army and Navy. Although law and tradition guaranteed the existence of four black army regiments (see **Buffalo Soldiers**), Negroes had been totally excluded from the Air Corps. Civil rights leaders such as **Walter F. White, A. Philip Randolph, William H. Hastie,** and others used America's preparation for and entry into the war to expand opportunities for their people and to attack **Jim Crow** in the armed services. The racial barrier in the glamorous air corps fell in January 1941 when the War Department announced formation of a black aviation pursuit squadron. It was a Pyrrhic victory, how-

Second Lt. Gabe C. Hawkins, second from right, an Army instruction teacher, with his students at Tuskegee, Alabama, 1942. The cadets are being trained to join the first black combat unit in the U.S. Army Air Corps. © AP/Wide World Photos.

ever, because the black pilots were to be trained at separate facilities in Tuskegee rather than at the white airbase in nearby Montgomery.

Initially the Tuskegee Airmen, who numbered almost 1,000 before war's end, were trained exclusively for difficult and dangerous pursuit flying. The first such unit to be organized, the **Ninety-ninth Pursuit Squadron,** was sent to the Mediterranean theater in April 1943. It was followed a year later by the 332nd Fighter Group. A black bomber group, the 447th, was organized in late 1943, but the overburdened training facility at Tuskegee was unable to train the bomber crews before the war was over. The "Black 99th" and the 332nd Fighter Group, commanded by Lieutenant Colonel **Benjamin O. Davis, Jr.,** son of the army's first black general, engaged in combat all over Europe, escorting bombers and flying other missions. Their record on escort duty was unparalleled. In more than 200 missions in the European theater, not a single bomber escorted by the Ninety-ninth was lost to enemy fighters. These all-black units were credited with destroying 111 enemy planes in the air and 150 others on the ground while flying a total of 15,533 sorties. The exceptional combat record of the Tuskegee Airmen, who during the war had been such a powerful symbol of armed forces segregation, contributed much to the ultimate demise of **Jim Crow** in the military.

Selected Bibliography Richard M. Dalfiume, *Desegregation of the U.S. Armed Forces: Fighting on Two Fronts, 1939–1953* (1969); Jack D. Foner, *Blacks and the Military in American History: A New Perspective* (1974); Alan L. Gropman, *The Air Force Integrates, 1945–1964* (1985); Morris J. MacGregor, Jr., *Integration of the Armed Forces, 1940–1965* (1981); Robert A. Rose, *The Lonely Eagles: The Story of America's Black Air Force in World War II* (1946); Stanley Sandler, *Segregated Skies: All-Black Combat Squadrons of World War II* (1992); Web site: www.tuskegeeairmen.org.

Charles D. Lowery

Tuskegee Civic Association Organized in 1941 by black professors at **Tuskegee Institute**—including sociology professor **Charles G. Gomillion**—and by black employees at the Veterans Hospital in the town, this group fought for the rights of blacks in Macon County, Alabama, for more than 25 years. Blacks outnumbered whites more than three to one in Macon County, yet whites deprived them of basic constitutional rights, particularly the right to vote. Beginning in the 1940s, working chiefly through the courts, the association began to challenge disenfranchisement in the county. Its most important victory came in *Gomillion v. Lightfoot* (1960) when the U.S. Supreme Court declared unconstitutional an Alabama gerrymandering law that excluded nearly all black votes from Tuskegee's city limits. By the 1960s, largely as a result of the organization's efforts and federal law, Justice Department suits, and the work of the other local civil rights groups, blacks had achieved full voting rights in the county. The association also acted to equalize city services for blacks and to desegregate the county's public schools.

Selected Bibliography Harry Holloway, *The Politics of the Southern Negro: From Exclusion to Big City Organization* (1969); Robert J. Norell, *Reaping the Whirlwind: The Civil Rights Movement in Tuskegee* (1985).

Dorothy A. Autrey

A class at the Tuskegee Institute, 1902. © Library of Congress.

Tuskegee Institute   (Tuskegee University). In 1880 a political deal was con-
summated between Lewis Adams, a black tinsmith, and two white Democrats
from Macon County, Alabama: William F. Foster, who was a candidate for the
state senate, and Arthur L. Brooks, who was running for a seat in the lower
house. They promised to secure in exchange for Adams's deliverance of the
black vote in Macon County, approval for a Negro normal school in Tuskegee.
Both men were elected, and in 1881 they used their influence to pass a bill
that secured an appropriation of $2,000 annually for Tuskegee. This act placed
the proposed school under the control of a three-member board of commissioners. The board's search for someone to organize the school led them to
Hampton Institute and General Samuel C. Armstrong, who recommended
his former pupil, **Booker T. Washington.** Washington came to Tuskegee on 14
June 1888 and on 4 July he opened the doors of Tuskegee Negro Normal
Institute. The school emphasized industrial education but did not neglect academic subjects. Under Washington's conservative leadership, Tuskegee grew
into one of the finest black schools in the country. Its students and faculty
remained aloof from local, state, and national politics—the key to its survival
in the white-controlled hill country of Macon County. Still, Washington lobbied against the disenfranchising clauses of Alabama's 1901 constitution and

surreptitiously supported the *Giles v. Harris* suit of 1903, the first test case challenging the constitutionality of the Alabama suffrage law. The Supreme Court ruled against the plaintiff. A second Washington-supported suit, *Giles v. Teasley* in 1904, suffered the same fate. The *Bailey v. Alabama* black peonage case, which received Washington's behind-the-scene support, resulted in the Supreme Court's invalidating an Alabama contract labor law in 1911. When Booker T. Washington died in 1915, he was replaced by **Robert Russa Moton,** Hampton Institute's commandant of cadets. Moton continued the school's apolitical policy and its tradition of industrial training. In 1930, during Moton's tenure, Tuskegee was rated a class "B" institution by the Southern Association of Colleges and Secondary Schools. Concern over the denial of the franchise to Alabama blacks did not die with Washington. **Charles G. Gomillion,** a black South Carolinian trained at Paine's College in Georgia, came to Tuskegee to teach in 1928. In 1941, he changed the Tuskegee men's club into the **Tuskegee Civic Association** and opened membership to women. Through this organization and the efforts of its founder, Tuskegee assumed a leading role in the civil rights struggle in Macon County. In the early twenty-first century, the university has an enrollment of three thousand students on a five-thousand-acre campus and offers a whole range of course offerings and degrees. The entire campus is a national historical site.

Selected Bibliography Addie Louise Joyner Butler, *The Distinctive Black College: Talladega, Tuskegee, and Morehouse* (1977); Louis R. Harlan, *Booker T. Washington: The Making of a Black Leader, 1856–1901* (1972); Louis R. Harlan, *Booker T. Washington: The Wizard of Tuskegee, 1901–1915* (1983); B. D. Mayberry, *A Century of Agriculture in the 1890 Land Grant Institutions and Tuskegee University 1890–1990* (1991); Robert J. Norrell, *Reaping the Whirlwind: The Civil Rights Movement in Tuskegee* (1985); Michael O. West, "The Tuskegee Model of Development in Africa: Another Dimension of the African/American Connection," *Diplomatic History* 16 (No. 3, 1992), 371–87.

Joe Louis Caldwell

Tuttle, Elbert Parr (17 July 1897, Pasadena, Calif.–24 June 1996, Atlanta, Ga.). Educated at Cornell University, where he earned both baccalaureate and law degrees, he practiced law in Atlanta, Georgia, and in Washington, D.C., from 1937 until 1955, when he was appointed to the **United States Court of Appeals for the Fifth Judicial Circuit.** He served as chief judge of the Fifth Circuit from 1961 to 1967, when he retired, only to return to the bench in 1981 when he was reassigned to the Eleventh Circuit Court of Appeals. During the late 1950s and 1960s, Judge Tuttle provided vigorous leadership for a court that, more than any other appeals court in the country, bore the burden of civil rights litigation. He, together with colleagues **John Minor Wisdom, John Robert Brown,** and **Richard Taylor Rives**—all of whom shared a strong commitment to racial justice—transformed the role of the federal judiciary in the Deep South by making the courts a major vehicle for social and political change. The judicial activism he promoted helped ensure the ultimate success of the civil rights revolution. Much of the Fifth's caseload after 1955 had to do with the desegregation of the public schools in the Deep South, but Tuttle and his colleagues expanded the mandate of **Brown v. Board of Education** for equality beyond education, issuing landmark decisions that swept away the barriers of discrimination in jury selection, voting, and employment. Tuttle led the court as it pioneered procedures, most notably the civil rights injunction, which transformed the **Fourteenth Amendment**'s neglected due process clause into a powerful instrument for racial justice. Under his leadership the United States Court of Appeals for the Fifth Circuit established standards and procedures designed not only to strike down the barriers of discrimination, but also to overcome the effects of past discrimination. He retired from active duty as a senior judge on the Eleventh Circuit Court in 1995. In 1980 President Jimmy Carter awarded Tuttle the Presidential Medal of Freedom. Nine years later he was awarded, jointly with Judge John Minor Wisdom, the Edward J. Devitt Distinguished Service to Justice Award, the most prestigious recognition given to a federal judge.

Selected Bibliography Jack Bass, *Unlikely Heroes* (1981); Harvey C. Couch, *A History of the Fifth Circuit, 1891–1981* (1984); J. W. Peltason, *Fifty-eight Lonely Men: Southern Federal Judges and School Desegregation* (1961).

Charles D. Lowery

U

Uncle Tom's Children   Awarded the best fiction prize in 1938 and critically acclaimed, **Richard Wright**'s novella firmly established his place as a major American writer and ushered in a powerful new voice and tradition in black literature. Direct, forceful, and starkly realistic, this seminal collection signaled something terrifyingly new: a refutation of the myths of the docile Negro. Its impact was resounding. In each story, the characters assert themselves, expressing racial hatred, stoic endurance, and at times mass action. *Uncle Tom's Children* sounded a warning that forced America's attention to the violent realities of race relations in the South and to the Negro's determination to survive and reclaim his rightful place.

Selected Bibliography Edwin B. Burgum, "The Art of Richard Wright's Short Stories," *Quarterly Review of Literature* 1 (Spring 1944), 198–211; Michael Fabre, *The Unfinished Quest of Richard Wright* (1973); James R. Giles, "Richard Wright's Successful Failure: A Look at *Uncle Tom's Children*," *Phylon* 34 (Fall 1973), 256–66; Edward Margolies, *The Art of Richard Wright* (1969).

Jacquelyn Jackson

Union League   Originating in the North during the Civil War, the Union League notion hitched a ride South in the political baggage of Union soldiers and so-called Carpetbaggers. It proved to be an effective tool for raising the political consciousness of ex-slaves and sowing the seeds of Republicanism among them. Although some local Union Leagues existed in the South before 1867, by 1 January 1868, nearly all eligible black voters had become League members. Interracial groups like the ones established in Tennessee and North Carolina were the exceptions. Union League members attempted to push the nation toward true republicanism by insisting upon equality before the law, full participation by blacks in the political and economic life of the South, the promotion of black education, and the elimination of racial barriers to social intercourse. Union League success among blacks was the result not only of the skill and zeal of its organizers, but also of the fact that its platform was identical with black ideals and aspirations. A short-lived phenomenon, Union League radicalism had succumbed to Republican moderation by the end of 1868.

Selected Bibliography Avery Craven, *Reconstruction: The Ending of the Civil War* (1969); Michael W. Fitzgerald, *The Union League Movement in the Deep South: Politics and Agricultural Changes During Reconstruction* (1989); Eric Foner, *Reconstruction: America's Unfinished Revolution, 1863–1877* (1988); Benyan H. Severance, "Loyalty's Political Vanguard: The Union League of Maryville Tennessee, 1867–1869," *Journal of East Tennessee History* 71 (1999), 25–46.

Joe Louis Caldwell

United Colored Socialists of America In 1928 Frank P. Crosswaith, the leading African American socialist spokesperson, the "black Eugene Debs," founded this organization in Harlem, New York, to recruit African Americans into the Socialist party. Eager to organize a socialist based black labor movement as well as achieve political and economic equality, the group attacked racism in organized labor; demanded more funding for education; and urged that blacks be allowed to serve on juries and be extended voting rights in all states. Black Harlemites Ethelred Brown, V.C. Gasper, Arther C. Parker, and Noah C.A. Walker led this group until 1934, when intraparty conflict split the local Socialist party.

Selected Bibliography Philip S. Foner, *American Socialism and Black Americans: From the Age of Jackson to World War II* (1977); Philip S. Foner, *Organized Labor and the Black Worker, 1619–1973* (1974); Mark Naison, *Communism in Harlem during the Depression* (1983).

Barbara L. Green

United Negro College Fund In 1944 Frederick D. Patterson, the president of **Tuskegee Institute,** met with 14 presidents from a consortium of 27 black colleges and universities and established the United Negro College Fund. Chartered in New York, the fund became the first cooperative fundraising venture in the history of higher education. Initial funding for the organization came, in part, from the **General Education Board** established by John D. Rockefeller and the Julius **Rosenwald Fund** founded by **Julius Rosenwald,** president of Sears, Roebuck and Company. In the early twenty-first century over 40 traditional black colleges and universities continued to benefit from the organization's financial support, public relations efforts, advocacy role, and overall self-help philosophy.

Selected Bibliography Antoine Garibaldi, *Black Colleges and Universities: Challenges for the Future* (1984); John H. Johnson, "Biggest Fundraiser Ever for Black Education," *Ebony* 36 (April 1981) 146–47; Lea Williams, "The United Negro College Fund in Retrospect: A Search for Its True Meaning," *Journal of Negro Education* 46 (Fall 1980) 363–72; Charles V. Willie and Ronald R. Edmonds, eds., *Black Colleges in America* (1978); Web site: www.uncf.org.

Barbara L. Green

The Civil Rights Commission investigated complaints made by demonstrators such as these in Raleigh, North Carolina, May 1963. © North Carolina Division of Archives and History. *The News Observor* of Raleigh, N.C.

United States Commission on Civil Rights   The Civil Rights Commission is a temporary independent bipartisan agency established by Congress in 1957. The commission's purpose is to investigate deprivation of voting rights complaints by citizens because of race, color, religion, or national origin, or due to fraudulent practices; to study and collect information on the denial of equal protection under law; to appraise federal laws and policies regarding equal protection enforcement; to serve as a national equal protection information clearinghouse; and to submit reports, findings and recommendations to the president and Congress. The commission comprises eight commissioners appointed by Congress and the president and in 2003 oversaw 50 state and District of Columbia advisory committees. It played a major role in investigating possible civil rights violations in Florida during the disputed 2000 presidential elections.

   Selected Bibliography *Civil Rights Update* (March 1984); Foster Rhea Dulles, *The Civil Rights Commission: 1957–1965* (1968); John Hope Franklin and Alfred A. Moss, Jr., *From Slavery to Freedom: A History of African Americans,* 8th ed. (2000); Robert Rankin Civil Rights Memorial Library, Washington D.C.; Web site: www.usccr.gov.

Donald Cunnigen

United States Court of Appeals for the Fifth Judicial Circuit   During the decade bracketed by the ***Brown v. Board of Education*** decision of 1954 and the **Voting Rights Act of 1965,** the Fifth Circuit Court, with headquarters in New Orleans, Louisiana, was a major legal battleground for the civil rights revolution. Because its jurisdiction included six states of the old Confederacy (Georgia, Florida, Alabama, Mississippi, Louisiana, and Texas), the Fifth had the heaviest civil rights case load of any of the federal circuit courts. This load, together with the failure of the Supreme Court after *Brown* to provide direction to the lower courts, created the opportunity for the Fifth Circuit Court to blaze a new trail in civil rights law. This it did, making law as well as following it.

As a result of the vigorous and imaginative leadership of a small group of liberal judges unequivocally committed to justice and equality under the law, the Fifth became one of the most active instruments for social and political change in the recalcitrant American South. The liberal judges were **Elbert Parr Tuttle, John Robert Brown, John Minor Wisdom,** and **Richard Taylor Rives.** By dominating three-judge panels that heard appeals from the 17 district courts comprising the circuit, these four jurists translated the Supreme Court's school desegregation decision into a broad mandate for justice and equality under the law. They vigorously worked to dismantle the dual school system. They led the Fifth Circuit Court to develop the civil rights injunction, which concentrated power in judges and thereby enabled them to restructure the school system. They led the Court beyond education to issue landmark decisions striking down barriers of discrimination in employment, voting, and jury selection. As Judge Tuttle explained, "We started to enforce *Brown* in the lower courts and then expanded it from the schools to everything else, long ahead of the Supreme Court, by adopting the same principles as *Brown*." The strong civil rights record of the Fifth Circuit Court during a period of social upheaval provided assurance to civil rights activists that the federal courts could serve as effective instruments of peaceful change. After 1968, when President Richard Nixon, as a part of his "Southern Strategy," began to appoint strict-constructionists to the federal bench, the Fifth began to backslide on school desegregation cases and ceased to offer judicial leadership in the area of civil rights.

Selected Bibliography Deborah J. Barrow and Thomas G. Walker, *A Court Divided: The Fifth Circuit Court of Appeals and the Politics of Judicial Reform* (1988); Jack Bass, *Unlikely Heroes* (1981); Harvey C. Couch, *A History of the Fifth Circuit, 1891–1981* (1984); J. W. Peltason, *Fifty-eight Lonely Men: Southern Federal Judges and School Desegregation* (1961); Frank T. Read and Lucy S. McGough, *Let Them Be Judged: The Judicial Integration of the Deep South* (1978); Web site: www.ca5.uscourts.gov.

Charles D. Lowery

United States ex rel. Goldsby v. Harpole, **263 F.2d 71 (5th Cir., 1959)**
Robert Lee Goldsby, a black resident of Carroll County, Mississippi, was indicted and convicted of the 1954 murder of a white couple. His jury was all-white even though 57 percent of Carroll County was black. Jury duty in the state was confined to registered voters, and since there were no registered

black voters in the county, there were no blacks eligible for jury duty. In what would become one of its landmark civil rights decisions, the **United States Court of Appeals for the Fifth Judicial Circuit** reversed Goldsby's conviction on the ground that blacks had been systematically excluded from jury duty. The court remanded the case to Mississippi with instructions that Goldsby be retried speedily by a jury from which blacks were not excluded. Although Goldsby was subsequently retried, adjudged guilty, and executed, his trial affirmed the fundamental constitutional right of the accused to a jury selected without discrimination by race. *Goldsby* provided the important basis for a number of juror discrimination cases that would come before the Fifth Circuit Court subsequently.

Selected Bibliography Jack Bass, *Unlikely Heroes* (1981); Harvey C. Couch, *A History of the Fifth Circuit, 1891–1981* (1984); Loren Miller, *The Petitioners: The Story of the Supreme Court of the United States and the Negro* (1966); Frank T. Read and Lucy S. McGough, *Let Them Be Judged: The Judicial Integration of the Deep South* (1978).

Charles D. Lowery

United States v. Alabama, 171 F. Supp. 720 (M. D. Ala., 1959) To thwart the enforcement of the **Civil Rights Act of 1957,** southern election officials sometimes resigned from office en masse, thereby leaving the U.S. Department of Justice without a proper party to sue. Shortly before a suit against an Alabama registrar was to begin, the offending official resigned. The Justice Department responded by amending its complaint to name as defendants the State of Alabama and the Board of Registrars. Holding that the resigned registrar could not be tried since he was no longer an official, and that the Board of Registrars and the State of Alabama were not suable, the lower courts dismissed the suit. The case was appealed, but before it reached the Supreme Court the **Civil Rights Act of 1960** was enacted. Under the new law action could be brought against a state, making it a suable entity. The Supreme Court thereupon remanded the case for retrial under the new statute.

Selected Bibliography Richard Bardolph, ed., *The Civil Rights Record, Black Americans, and the Law, 1849–1970* (1970); Jack Greenberg, *Race Relations and American Law* (1959); Charles V. Hamilton, *The Bench and the Ballot* (1973); Steven F. Lawson, *Black Ballots: Voting Rights in the South, 1944–1969* (1976).

Charles D. Lowery

United States v. Classic, 313 U.S. 299 (1941) Growing out of the federal government's prosecution of an election fraud case in New Orleans, Louisiana, *United States v. Classic* indirectly undermined the legal doctrine supporting the constitutionality of white primaries—that is, primaries restricting participation to whites. The case did not involve racial discrimination but rather the criminal prosecution of five election commissioners for violating the Civil Rights Act of 1870 (see **Enforcement Acts**) by altering ballots in favor of one of the candidates seeking the Democratic nomination for a seat in the United States House of Representatives. Reversing a lower court decision that

Congress lacked power to regulate primaries, the Supreme Court noted that primaries, which restricted voters' choices in the general election, were funded and regulated by the state. They were not private activities but rather a part of the electoral process. The Court held that Article I, Section 4 of the Constitution authorized Congress to regulate primaries to protect the people's constitutional right to elect their representatives. The Court's reasoning would later be extended to invalidate white primaries. If primaries were part of a state's electoral process, then the state was prohibited by the **Fifteenth Amendment** from denying participation to blacks.

Selected Bibliography Liva Baker, *The Second Battle of New Orleans: The Hundred-Year Struggle to Integrate the Schools* (1996); Theodore M. Berry, "*United States v. Classic,*" *National Bar Journal* 1 (October 1941), 149–56; Richard Claude, *The Supreme Court and the Electoral Process* (1970); V. O. Key, Jr., *Southern Politics in State and Nation* (1949); Note, "Primaries as Subjects of Congressional Regulation," *Brooklyn Law Review* 11 (October 1941), 90–97.

Patricia A. Behlar

United States v. Cruikshank, 92 U.S. 542 (1876), 25 F. Cas. 707 (C. C. D. La. 1874) (No. 14, 897) This case arose from perhaps the bloodiest violence of Reconstruction—the killing of 60 African Americans in Colfax, Louisiana, on Easter Sunday, 1873, in an election campaign struggle for control of the state government. Federal prosecutors indicted more than 100 whites under the Voting Rights Act of 31 May 1870 (see **Enforcement Acts**). U.S. Supreme Court Justice Joseph P. Bradley on circuit for the District of Louisiana held the indictments void, saying Congress lacked constitutional authority for "directly enforcing the privileges and immunities of U.S. citizens." The **Fourteenth Amendment** allowed Congress to remedy state action, not private actions, Bradley held. The **Thirteenth** and **Fifteenth Amendments** allowed federal action against private denial of rights, but only on the specified bases of race, color, or previous condition of servitude, which he ruled the indictments failed to show. The full U.S. Supreme Court affirmed this ruling and *Cruikshank* became one of two major reversals of federal protections of civil rights handed down on 27 March 1876. In it and **United States v. Reese** the Supreme Court advanced the state's primary jurisdiction and affirmed limited federal power in civil rights.

Selected Bibliography Michael L. Benedict, "Preserving Federalism: Reconstruction and the Waite Court," *Supreme Court Review* (1978), 39–79; William Gillette, *Retreat from Reconstruction, 1869–1879* (1979); Robert Kaczorowski, *The Politics of Judicial Interpretation: The Federal Courts, Department of Justice and Civil Rights, 1866–1876* (1985); John Anthony Scott, "Justice Bradley's Evolving Concept of the Fourteenth Amendment from the Slaughterhouse Cases to the Civil Rights Cases," *Rutgers Law Review* 25 (1971), 552–69; Everette Swinney, "Enforcing the Fifteenth Amendment, 1870–1877," *Journal of Southern History* 28 (1962), 202–18.

Thomas J. Davis

United States v. Guest, 383 U.S. 745 (1966) Defendant Herbert Guest, with five others, was indicted under 18 U.S.C., Section 241, for conspiracy to deprive black citizens in the vicinity of Athens, Georgia, of the free exercise and enjoyment of rights secured to them by the Constitution and laws of the United States, viz., the right to use state facilities without discrimination on the basis of race, the right freely to engage in interstate travel, and the right to equal enjoyment of privately owned places of public accommodation. The defendants contended that the indictment was invalid because Section 241 protected only against interference with the exercise of the right to equal utilization of state facilities, which was not a right "secured" by the **Fourteenth Amendment.** The district court dismissed the indictment on the ground that it did not involve national citizenship rights to which it deemed Section 241 solely applicable. The Supreme Court, upon appeal, ruled that it had no jurisdiction over that portion of the indictment dealing with interference with the right to use public accommodations. The Court did, however, claim jurisdiction over other parts of the indictment and reversed the lower court and remanded the case to it for further adjudication.

Selected Bibliography John E. Moye, "Fourteenth Amendment Congressional Power to Legislate Against Private Discriminations: The Guest Case," *Cornell Law Quarterly* 52 (1967), 586–99; Harvard Sitkoff, *The Struggle for Black Equality, 1954–1980* (1981); C. Vann Woodward, *The Strange Career of Jim Crow,* 3rd rev. ed. (1974).

Michael S. Downs

United States v. Harris, 106 U.S. 629 (1882)   In 1876 R. G. Harris and 19 other whites violently attacked 4 black suspects in the custody of a Tennessee deputy sheriff. A federal prosecution charged them with conspiracy to deprive their victims of the equal protection of the laws, in violation of the Third **Enforcement Act** (Ku Klux Klan Act) of 1871. In addition to prohibiting the use of disguises on public or private property for purposes of intimidation, this act also punished attempts to prevent state authorities from according equal protection of the laws. Justice William Woods's opinion for the Supreme Court majority struck down the law as being broader than either the **Thirteenth** or **Fourteenth Amendments** would allow, and irrelevant to the **Fifteenth Amendment.** The statute punished private actions of individuals, whereas the Fourteenth Amendment prohibited only discriminatory actions by states. In this case there had been no wrongful state action to correct. The doctrine of "state action" was a central pillar of the Court's reasoning in cases involving interpretation of the postwar amendments, and also the area of greatest criticism on the part of scholars. This case saw the first of several dissents by Justice **John Marshall Harlan,** objecting to what he perceived as disregard for the legal rights of blacks.

Selected Bibliography Alfred Avins, "The Ku Klux Klan Act of 1871: Some Reflected Light on State Action and the Fourteenth Amendment," *St. Louis University Law Journal* 11 (Spring 1967), 331–73; Charles Fairman, *Reconstruction and Reunion, 1864–1888* (1987).

James E. Sefton

United States v. Jefferson County Board of Education, 372 F. 2d 836 (5th Cir., 1966)   This decision by the **United States Court of Appeals for the**

Fifth Judicial Circuit clarified the 1954 *Brown v. Board of Education* ruling by ordering compulsory integration to achieve a racially nondiscriminatory school system. The decision, which combined cases from the Northern Alabama and Western Louisiana U.S. District Courts, ordered **affirmative action** to eliminate the effects of **de jure segregation** and to achieve and shift to unitary, nonracial public school systems. The **Civil Rights Act of 1964** had mandated that the United States Office of Education, Department of Health Education and Welfare (HEW), establish "Guidelines" for school integration. With the Jefferson County decree, the Fifth Circuit adopted the 1966 HEW Guidelines as its uniform plan, which strengthened the government's ability to withhold federal funds and, thus, forced recalcitrant districts to comply with the court-ordered integration. In effect, the opinion, written by Judge **John Minor Wisdom,** invalidated for the Fifth Circuit the largely unsuccessful free choice method of school desegregation set forth by the *Briggs v. Elliot* decision of 1955. The **NAACP** called the *Jefferson County* opinion the most significant since *Brown.* The U.S. Supreme Court would later uphold compulsory integration over free choice in its 1968 ruling in *Green v. County School Board of New Kent County, Virginia.*

Selected Bibliography George R. Metcalf, *From Little Rock to Boston* (1983); "Recent Cases: Constitutional Law," *Harvard Law Review* 81 (December 1967), 474–79; Frank T. Spindel, "Constitutional Law," *Texas Law Review* 46 (December 1967), 266–74; Raymond Wolters, *The Burden of Brown: Thirty Years of School Desegregation* (1984).

Glenn T. Eskew

United States v. Lynd, 349 F.2d 785 (5th Cir., 1965)   Soon after the passage of the **Voting Rights Act of 1965,** federal authorities began to investigate the activities of Theron C. Lynd, registrar of voters for Forrest County, Mississippi. Less than 3 percent of the county's black voting-age population was registered at that time. Acting under provisions of the new Voting Rights Act, federal officials asked Lynd for permission to examine registration records. When he refused, they filed suit. Federal District Court Judge W. Harold Cox, a staunch segregationist, allowed the case to drag on for years, granting the defendants numerous postponements. Exasperated Justice Department officials asked the **United States Court of Appeals for the Fifth Judicial Circuit** for relief. The appellate court responded with an injunction enjoining Lynd from continuing his discriminatory registration practices. This action was a sharp departure from standard appellant procedure. Ordinarily the appeals court only reviewed final decisions of district courts. In *Lynd,* Judge Cox had postponed action and had rendered no final decision. The Fifth blazed a new trail in legal procedure by issuing an injunction, pending appeal, that did more than preserve the status quo. The decision put recalcitrant district judges such as Cox on notice that attempts to delay justice by inaction or postponement would not be tolerated. The "injunction pending appeal" became a legal procedure widely employed by civil rights lawyers in voter registration and school desegregation cases.

Selected Bibliography Jack Bass, *Unlikely Heroes* (1981); Harvey C. Couch, *A History of the Fifth Circuit, 1891–1981* (1984); Frank T. Read and Lucy S. McGough, *Let Them Be Judged: The Judicial Integration of the Deep South* (1978).

Charles D. Lowery

United States v. Montgomery County School Board, 395 U.S. 225 (1969)

The public schools of Montgomery County, Alabama, had failed to desegregate 10 years after the 1954 **Brown v. Board of Education** decision in defiance of repeated federal court decisions that such actions were unconstitutional and despite court orders to expedite integration. The school board's failure forced the federal district court to order desegregation of faculty and staff on a three-to-two ratio of white to black faculty in each school to reflect the county's population and fixed the ratio of substitute, student, and night school teachers in the same ratio as the number of white to black teachers for the entire school system. In addition, the court required schools with fewer than 12 full-time teachers to have at least 1 teacher whose race was different from the faculty racial majority and required schools with more than 12 full-time teachers to have at least 1 teacher of a minority race for every 6 faculty and staff. **The United States Court of Appeals for the Fifth Judicial Circuit** reversed the decision. On certiorari, the Supreme Court reversed the Appeals Court. Writing for a unanimous court, Justice Hugo Black held that the goal of faculty and staff desegregation was important to end the county's history of desegregation and that the District Court's action was appropriate and necessary given the school board's intransigence.

Selected Bibliography Lino A. Graglia, *Disaster by Degree, the Supreme Court Decisions on Race and the Schools* (1976); E. Edmund Reutter, Jr., *The Supreme Court's Impact on Public Education* (1982); Roland L. Young, "Review of Recent Supreme Court Decisions: Schools," *American Bar Association Journal* 55 (September 1969) 876.

William A. Paquette

United States v. Northwest Louisiana Restaurant Club, 256 F. Supp. 151 (W.D. LA. 1966)

This and similar cases prohibited sham private organizations from utilizing the "private club" exemption of the antidiscrimination in public accommodations section of the **Civil Rights Act of 1964.** The U.S. attorney general sued the Northwest Louisiana Restaurant Club to prohibit its member restaurants from refusing to serve blacks. The club's voting members consisted of approximately one hundred restaurant owners in Shreveport and Lake Charles, Louisiana. Nonvoting membership cards were routinely issued to any white customer who sought admission to a member restaurant. Blacks were denied membership cards and then were denied admission to the restaurants on the basis of nonmembership. Club officers admitted the club was formed for the express purpose of circumventing the 1964 Civil Rights Act by claiming the statutory exemption of a "private club." The court ruled that only bona fide private clubs that based exclusive membership on some identifiable nonracial requirement or condition could claim exemption from the public accommodation section of the 1964 Civil Rights Act. This decision and others like it prevented businesses providing public accommodations from circumventing the 1964 Civil Rights Act by forming sham private clubs that continued to operate on a racially discriminatory basis.

Selected Bibliography Henry J. Abraham, *Freedom and the Court: Civil Rights and Liberties in the United States* (1988); Chester J. Antieau, *Federal Civil Rights Act: Civil Practice* (1980); Derrick A. Bell, Jr., *Race, Racism, and American Law* (1980); Theodore Eisenberg, *Civil Rights Legislation* (1981).

Frederick G. Slabach

United States v. Raines, 362 U.S. 17 (1960)   Reversing a decision of Judge T. Hoyt Davis of the Middle District of Georgia, the Supreme Court upheld the constitutionality of the **Civil Rights Act of 1957.** The legislation had authorized the attorney general to seek an injunction in federal court against persons who had deprived others of the right to vote based upon race. Although the defendants were public officials accused of voter discrimination, Judge Davis accepted their argument that because the legislation did not refer to persons acting "under color of law," it unconstitutionally authorized the attorney general to act in cases in which there was only private discrimination and thus was beyond the reach of the **Fifteenth Amendment.** In reversing Judge Davis, the Court noted that the defendants were indeed acting "under color of law" and could not challenge the law on the basis of how it might affect others. Moreover, Justice William Brennan stated that it was within the power of Congress to protect private constitutional rights. A contrary decision would have meant that victims of voter discrimination would have had to bear the financial burden of bringing suit themselves rather than relying upon the attorney general to defend their rights.

Selected Bibliography Richard Claude, *The Supreme Court and the Electoral Process* (1970); Note, "Civil Rights-Elections-Federal Injunction against Racial Discrimination," *Michigan Law Review* 58 (April 1960), 925–29; Donald S. Strong, *Negroes, Ballots and Judges: National Voting Rights Legislation in the Federal Courts* (1968).

Patricia A. Behlar

United States v. Reese, 92 U.S. 214 (1876)   This Supreme Court decision undercut the protection of African Americans' voting rights. Reese and another municipal election inspector refused to receive and count the vote of William Garner, a black man, thus denying his suffrage. Federal prosecutors charged violation of the Voting Rights Act of 31 May 1870 (see **Enforcement Acts**). The U.S. Circuit Court for the District of Kentucky dismissed the indictments as invalid. The Supreme Court affirmed the ruling, holding that in providing penalties for obstructing *any* person's right to vote, Congress had overreached its constitutional powers. States held primary control of suffrage and were restricted only by the specific prohibitions in the **Fifteenth Amendment,** wrote Chief Justice Morrison R. Waite. As neither the indictment against Reese nor the Voting Rights Act restricted itself to offenses based on "race, color, or previous condition of servitude," both the indictment and statute were unlawful. Congress has no power for comprehensive proscriptions, the Court ruled. *United States v. Reese* was one of two major reversals of federal protections of civil rights handed down by the U.S. Supreme Court on 27 March 1876; the other was **United States v. Cruikshank.**

Selected Bibliography Richard Claude, "Constitutional Voting Rights and Early U.S. Supreme Court Doctrine," *Journal of Negro History* 52 (1966), 114–24; William Gillette, "Anatomy of a Failure: Federal Enforcement of the Right to Vote in the Border States during Reconstruction" in Richard L. Curry, ed., *Radicalism, Racism, and Party Realignment: the Border States during Reconstruction* (1969); William Gillette, *Retreat from Reconstruction, 1869–1879* (1979); Robert J. Harris, *The Quest for Equality: The Constitution, Congress, and the Supreme Court* (1960); Everette Swinney, "Enforcing the Fifteenth Amendment, 1870–1877," *Journal of Southern History* 28 (May 1962), 202–18.

Thomas J. Davis

United States v. Reynolds, 235 U.S. 133 (1914)   This case involved the constitutionality under the **Thirteenth Amendment** of an Alabama criminal-surety statute. The law provided that a convict who was unable to pay his fines and court costs could be confined to hard labor on a chain gang. Alternatively, he could be released into the custody of a surety who paid the convict's debt. Typically, the period of labor owed by the convict (usually black) to the surety far exceeded the convict's sentence to hard labor. In the case that generated *Reynolds*, a man convicted of petit larceny was fined $58 or 68 days on a chain gang. Instead, a local farmer paid the fine and the convict signed a contract that required him to work for over nine months to satisfy the debt. The U.S. Supreme Court found nothing objectionable with this part of the arrangement. The Thirteenth Amendment allowed involuntary servitude "as punishment for crime" and individuals were free to sell their labor for whatever price they chose.

The Alabama statute, however, provided that if the ex-convict broke his contract with the surety, he could be imprisoned again with an enhanced fine. A second surety could then pay the fine and employ the convict for an even longer period "thus keeping him chained to an ever turning wheel of servitude to discharge the obligation which he ha[d] incurred to his surety." The *Reynolds* majority reasoned that, though the ex-convict had a private contract with his surety, he worked under "the constant coercion and threat" of arrest if he broke his contract. This form of coercion, the Court found, "is as potent as it would have been had the law provided for the seizure and compulsory service of the convict." While the state could impose servitude "as punishment for crime," the ex-convict was being punished for breach of a labor contract. This arrangement, according to the Court, violated the Thirteenth Amendment prohibition against involuntary servitude and federal statutes prohibiting peonage (see also **black peonage**).

Selected Bibliography Alexander M. Bickel and Benno C. Schmidt, *History of the Supreme Court of the United States, vol. 9: The Judiciary and Responsible Government 1910–21* (1984); Pete Daniel, *The Shadow of Slavery: Peonage in the South, 1909–1969* (1972); Loren Miller, *The*

Petitioners: The Story of the Supreme Court of the United States and the Negro (1966); Daniel A. Novak, *The Wheel of Servitude: Black Forced Servitude after Slavery* (1978).

Kenneth DeVille

United States v. School District of Cook County,* 286 F. Supp. 786 (W.D. ILL. 1968)** This is one of several cases holding that affirmative policies of school systems to preserve segregation originally caused by housing patterns transforms permissible **de facto segregation** into unconstitutional de jure segregation. The U.S. attorney general sued to desegregate Illinois School District 151 in suburban Chicago. The school district contended natural ethnic housing choices resulted in the system's segregation and that such neighborhood schools were permissible pursuant to the landmark Supreme Court case of ***Brown v. Board of Education (1954). The district court ruled that the school district affirmatively constructed school buildings, drew attendance zones, and assigned teachers by race to preserve racial segregation in violation of the **Fourteenth Amendment** and the **Civil Rights Act of 1964.** Many lower federal courts had interpreted *Brown* as ruling that mere failure to correct a de facto racial imbalance is not de jure segregation. Thus, neighborhood schools that merely recognized natural ethnic housing patterns were not unconstitutional. This and other cases like it looked not only at the formal laws of the state, but at the policies and procedures of the school district to determine whether impermissible de jure segregation existed.

Selected Bibliography Derrick A. Bell, Jr., *Race, Racism and American Law* (1980); Paul R. Dimond, *Beyond Busing, Inside the Challenge to Urban Segregation* (1985); Note, "Demise of the Neighborhood School Plan," *Cornell Law Review* 55 (1970), 594.

Frederick G. Slabach

***United States v. Wallace,* 218 F. Supp. 290 (N.D., Ala., 1963)** This case grew out of efforts by the Department of Justice to prevent Governor George C. Wallace from interfering with the court-ordered desegregation of the University of Alabama. On 16 May 1963, a federal district court in Alabama had directed the university to admit two blacks during its summer session. Wallace publicly stated his intention to uphold his 1962 campaign pledge to oppose desegregation even if it required that he stand in the school house door. The Justice Department on 5 June requested and received a federal court injunction blocking the governor from carrying out his plans. But Wallace defied the injunction and on 11 June stood in the doorway of a university building barring Assistant Attorney General Nicholas Katzenbach from escorting the black students inside to register. Wallace's action was perhaps more a move to gain national attention than an attempt to impede the integration process in the state. Later that day, he vacated the university door and allowed the students to enter when ordered to do so by the commander of the federalized Alabama National Guard.

Selected Bibliography Michael R. Belknap, *Federal Law and Southern Order: Racial Violence and Constitutional Conflict in the Post-Brown South* (1987); Taylor Branch, *Parting the Waters:*

America in the King Years, 1954–63 (1988); Jody Carlson, *George C. Wallace and the Politics of Powerlessness: The Wallace Campaign for the Presidency, 1964–1970* (1981); Philip Crass, *The Wallace Factor* (1975); Donald S. Strong, "Alabama: Transition and Alienation," in William C. Harvard, ed., *The Changing Politics of the South* (1972).

Dorothy A. Autrey

United States v. Ward, 352 F.2d 329 (5th Cir. 1965)   The decision in this case recognized the codification and expansion of the "freeze" principle developed by federal courts in voting rights cases prior to the passage of the **Voting Rights Act of 1965.** The U.S. attorney general sued Katherine Ward, the Registrar of Voters of Madison Parish and the State of Louisiana, to stop discriminatory application of state registration requirements. The appeals court ordered a "freeze" on restrictive registration requirements for two years allowing all applicants to use the less restrictive methods applied to whites. After two years, the restrictive registration requirements could again be applied, but in a racially nondiscriminatory manner. Immediately after the effective date of the 1965 Voting Rights Act, the Court modified its ruling to extend the "freeze" to five years as authorized by the Act. The federal courts developed the "freeze" principle because merely to apply restrictive voting prerequisites uniformly to blacks *and* whites would perpetuate the effect of past discrimination by locking onto voter rolls whites already registered without restrictive requirements and prohibiting most blacks from registering to vote because of the onerous prerequisites. Passage of the 1965 Voting Rights Act and the Courts' application of the "freeze" principle attempted to treat all registrants equally.

Selected Bibliography Chester J. Antieau, *Federal Civil Rights Acts, Civil Practice* (1980); Jack Bass, *Unlikely Heroes* (1990); Derrick A. Bell, Jr., *Race, Racism and American Law* (1980).

Frederick G. Slabach

United Steelworkers v. Weber, 443 U.S. 193 (1979)   In this case, the Supreme Court upheld the legality of an **affirmative action** training program in the skilled crafts over a challenge that it violated the **Civil Rights Act of 1964** by reserving 50 percent of the positions in the program for blacks. Brian Weber, a white man, challenged the program, instituted voluntarily by a collective bargaining agreement, because he had been denied admission while blacks with less seniority had not. The Court based its decision on statutory interpretation, stating that the act's ban on discrimination in hiring and training was not intended to prohibit voluntary race-conscious programs having the same objective as the legislation—that is, the elimination of the last vestiges of job discrimination. The majority stressed that the program was temporary, until the percentage of blacks in skilled positions approximated their percentage in the local labor force, and it cost no whites their jobs. But the dissenters considered the program a violation of the clear language of the Civil Rights Act, which prohibited discrimination based upon race. Such race-conscious programs, called affirmative action by supporters and reverse dis-

525

crimination by opponents, continued to be controversial into the twenty-first century.

Selected Bibliography Robert K. Fullinwider, *The Reverse Discrimination Controversy: A Moral and Legal Analysis* (1980); Edmund W. Kitch, "The Return of Color-Consciousness to the Constitution: Weber, Dayton, and Columbus," *Supreme Court Review* (1979), 1–15; Terry Leap and Irving Kovarsky, "What is the Impact of Weber on Collective Bargaining?" *Labor Law Journal* 31 (June 1980), 323–27; Edward Tivnan, *The Moral Imagination: Confronting the Ethical Issues of Our Day* (1996).

Patricia A. Behlar

Universal African Legion   One of the many uniformed auxiliary units to **Marcus Mosiah Garvey's Universal Negro Improvement Association,** the African Legion's spit-and-polish military appearance and physical conditioning were intended to promote race pride and brotherhood. The unit, dressed in dark blue uniforms with narrow red trouser stripes, officers outfitted with dress sabres, appeared at public functions both on horseback and foot. The African Legion also frequently served as Garvey's personal bodyguard.

Selected Bibliography Edmund David Cronon, *Black Moses* (1955); Elton C. Fox, *Garvey* (1972); Dixie C. Hicks, "Marcus Garvey and Pan-Africanism" (Ph.D. diss., University of Memphis, 1992); Tony Martin, *Marcus Garvey, Hero* (1983).

Michael S. Downs

Universal Negro Improvement Association   Established in 1914 by Jamaican **Marcus Mosiah Garvey,** the Universal Negro Improvement Association (UNIA) became the prototype for future black nationalist organizations in the United States. The organization's aim was to improve the lives of African peoples and their descendants. In 1916 Garvey established a branch office (destined to become international headquarters) in New York City and within months enlisted 1,000 members in Harlem. By 1919 the Universal Negro Improvement Association had 30 branch offices throughout the United States and claimed two million members. The UNIA operated as an independent nation. The organization's motto was: "One God! One Aim! One Destiny!" It also adopted a flag with the colors red, black and green; published **Negro World,** a weekly newspaper; established "Liberty Halls" (auditoriums) as meeting places; operated the **Black Star Steamship Line,** a steamship company; and incorporated a Negro Factories Corporation. In addition, the UNIA organized the Black Cross Nurses, the African Orthodox Church, and paramilitary units such as the **Universal African Legion,** the Universal Africa Motor Corps, and the Black Eagle Flying Corps. At the First International Convention in 1920, Garvey was elected Provisional President of Africa and President General and Administrator of the UNIA. A Declaration of Rights of the Negro Peoples of the World was drafted, and titles such as Knight of the Nile, Earl of the Congo, Viscount of the Niger, and Baron Zambesi were created. Integrationists attacked the UNIA for its black nationalist and separatist ideas. These critics included **William Monroe Trotter, W.E.B. Du Bois,** and prominent **NAACP** members. The associa-

Marcus Garvey, third from left, and UNIA associates at his deportation from the United States, 1927. © Arthur P. Bedou Photographs, Xavier University Archives, New Orleans.

tion's downfall, however, was Garvey's 1923 federal court conviction for sell-ing Black Star Line stock when the company was insolvent. He was fined $1000 and sentenced to five years in prison. The UNIA never recovered. By 1930 it was defunct.

Selected Bibliography Adolph Edwards, *Marcus Garvey: 1887–1940* (1967); Robert A. Hill and Barbara Bair, eds., *Marcus Garvey Life and Lessons: A Centennial Companion to the Marcus Garvey and Universal Negro Improvement Association Papers* (1987); Robert A. Hill, ed., *The Marcus Garvey and Universal Negro Improvement Association Papers,* 7 vols. (1983–90); Rupert Lewis, *Marcus Garvey: Anti-Colonial Champion* (1988); Tony Martin, *Race First: The Ideological and Organizational Struggles of Marcus Garvey and the Universal Negro Improvement Association* (1986).

Wali Rashash Kharif

***University of California Regents v. Bakke,* 438 U.S. 265 (1978)** This popularly labeled "reverse discrimination" case led to a split decision by the U.S. Supreme Court. The University of California at Davis medical school twice rejected Alan Bakke's application for admission, leading him to file suit on the grounds that the school's affirmative action policy denied him admis-sion because he was white and in so doing violated his constitutional right to equal protection of the law. The medical school had mandated that 16 seats be reserved for minority applicants in each class of 100 students to insure a diverse medical student body. Bakke contended that, had this **affirmative**

action policy not been in operation, he would have gained admission to the school, since several minority applicants who were admitted allegedly had inferior qualifications. The Supreme Court voted five-to-four that no state university could establish a quota system setting aside a number of spots for minorities because that process would deny nonminorities fair access. To complicate matters, the Court added a second and different five-to-four opinion, arguing that a university policy could include race as one variable among others in its admissions criteria, if it was attempting to rectify past instances of discrimination that were not present in the *Bakke* case. The issues raised by this case represent an ongoing dilemma in American society. The *Bakke* case has served as a precedent for several other related cases and state actions affecting civil rights.

Selected Bibliography Howard Ball, *The Bakke Case: Race, Education, and Affirmative Action* (2000); John Brigham, *Civil Liberties and American Democracy* (1984); Frank Brown, "Equal Educational Opportunity, the Law, and the Courts," *Urban Education* 11 (July 1976), 135–50; Martin D. Carcieri, "The Wages of Taking Bakke Seriously: The Untenable Denial of the Primacy of the Individual," *Tennessee Law Review* 67 (2000), 949–69; Lee Epstein, "Piercing the Veil: William J. Brennan's Account of Regents of the University of California v. Bakke," *Yale Law and Policy Review* 19 (2000), 341–79; Reynolds Farley, "Trends in Racial Inequalities: Have the Gains of the 1960s Disappeared in the 1970s?" *American Sociological Review* 42 (April 1977), 189–208; Richard Kluger, *Simple Justice: The History of Brown v. The Board of Education and Black America's Struggle for Equality* (1976); Carol M. Swain, et al., "Life after Bakke: Where Whites and Blacks Agree: Public Support for Fairness in Educational Opportunities," *Harvard Blackletter Law Journal* 16 (2000), 147–84; Finis Welch, "Affirmative Action and Its Enforcement," *American Economic Review* 71 (May 1981), 127–33; J. Harvie Wilkerson, *From Brown to Bakke: The Supreme Court and School Integration, 1954–1978* (1979).

Marshall Hyatt

University of Maryland v. Murray, **165 Md. 478 (1935)** In 1935 Donald Gaines Murray, an African American resident of Baltimore and a graduate of Amherst College, was refused admission to the University of Maryland School of Law in Baltimore. Murray sued, and was represented by **Charles H. Houston,** special counsel for the **NAACP,** and his assistant, **Thurgood Marshall.** On 15 January 1936, the Maryland Court of Appeals affirmed a Baltimore City Court decision admitting Murray. The Court of Appeals ruled that the state's failure to provide a separate law school for black Marylanders violated the equal protection clause of the **Fourteenth Amendment.** The court also ruled that Maryland's policy of providing $200 toward the cost of an out-of-state education when in-state facilities were not available to African Americans placed an undue hardship on Murray. The state's tuition scheme, said the court, "falls short of providing for students of the colored race facilities substantially equal to those furnished to the whites in the law school maintained in Baltimore." The state had a choice between opening a new law school for blacks or admitting Murray to the existing school. Since Murray was entitled to immediate relief, he had to be admitted. *Maryland v. Murray* was one of many landmark cases handled by the NAACP in the decades before

Brown v. Board of Education that helped erase the color line.

Selected Bibliography "The Admission of Negroes to the University of Maryland," *School and Society* 46 (11 September 1937); *Baltimore Evening Sun*, 22 April 1935; Richard Bardolph, ed., *The Civil Rights Record: Black Americans and the Law, 1849–1970* (1970); Mark Tushnet, *The NAACP's Legal Strategy Against Segregated Education, 1925–1950* (1987).

Stephen P. Labash

Up from Slavery **Booker T. Washington**'s autobiography written in 1901 recounts his life from childhood as a slave in Franklin County, Virginia, through the early days of freedom, his struggle for literacy and then a higher education at **Hampton Institute,** the founding of **Tuskegee Institute,** and the establishment of the **National Negro Business League.** It contains an account of and the text of the **Atlanta Exposition Speech** of 1895 as well as commentary on the philosophy underlying his national program. A nationwide best seller that has been translated into many languages, the narrative has been praised by literary critics and hailed as an account of human triumph over adversity.

Selected Bibliography Louis R. Harlan, *Booker T. Washington: The Making of a Black Leader, 1856–1901* (1989); Louis R. Harlan, *Booker T. Washington: The Wizard of Tuskegee, 1901–1915* (1983); Kevern J. Verney, *The Art of the Possible: Booker T. Washington and Black Leadership in the United States, 1881–1925* (2001); Booker T. Washington, *Up from Slavery* (1901).

Suzanne Ellery Greene Chapelle

V

Vann, Robert (27 August 1879, Hertford County, N.C.–24 October 1940, Philadelphia, Pa.). Throughout the 1920s Robert Vann, editor of the *Pittsburgh Courier,* was the head of the "colored division" of the Republican party, which sought to gain patronage and rights for African Americans. Seeing little prospect for himself as a Republican leader, he defected to the Democratic party. In his newspaper during the 1932 elections, he told his readers that it was time to turn Lincoln's portrait to the wall. In many black homes there was a picture of the Great Emancipator and most African Americans continued to vote Republican because of Lincoln. While Vann's now famous editorial did not have a great impact on the 1932 election, by 1934 and 1936 many African Americans abandoned the Republican party for the Democratic party. This set into motion a process that would greatly aid the Democratic party, its candidates, and the black leaders themselves. In other ways, Vann used the *Courier,* the largest-selling Negro newspaper in the United States, to champion the political, economic, and social interests of his race and to champion racial equality. During the New Deal he served as a special adviser to the U.S. attorney general and a member of Franklin D. Roosevelt's **Black Cabinet,** which advised the president on various matters affecting the African American community.

Selected Bibliography Andrew A. Buni, *Robert L. Vann of the Pittsburgh Courier: Politics and Black Journalism* (1974); Harvard Sitkoff, *A New Deal for Blacks. The Emergence of Civil Rights as a National Issue,vol. 1: The Depression Decade* (1978); Nancy J. Weiss, *Farewell to the Party of Lincoln* (1983).

Charles T. Pete Banner-Haley

Villard, Oswald Garrison (13 March 1872, Wiesbaden, Germany–1 October 1949, New York, N.Y.). Born to railroad and newspaper wealth, the grandson of famed abolitionist William Lloyd Garrison, Villard took seriously his family's passion for social justice. After earning two Harvard degrees in history by 1896, Villard embraced virtually every liberal cause, particularly black civil rights and pacifism. He was particularly well equipped to pursue liberal causes because of his impeccable pedigree, his social connections, and his ownership of the *New York Evening Post* and *The Nation*, the latter of which he turned into a muckraking journal. On Lincoln's birthday in 1909, Villard joined **Mary White Ovington,** William English Walling, and others to protest the recent **Springfield, Illinois, race riot** and to create the interracial **National Association for the Advancement of Colored People** (NAACP). Under Villard's chairmanship, the NAACP gathered data on racial crimes and established a legal defense arm to take discrimination cases to court. The NAACP quickly became and would remain the most important civil rights organization in American history, but Villard withdrew from the organization's leadership when the fiery black editor of the NAACP's the **Crisis, W.E.B. Du Bois,** challenged him. Despite this conflict, Villard worked tirelessly to remove racial discrimination. Villard never moderated his invariably unpopular beliefs, and this "aristocrat of liberalism" paid a price for his convictions. His editorials against World War I and the American invasion of Siberia scandalized subscribers and forced the sale of the *Post* and *The Nation*. Villard himself was vilified as a Bolshevik traitor, and his family suffered social ostracism.

Selected Bibliography Dollena Humes, *Oswald Garrison Villard: Liberal of the 1920's* (1977); Flint Kellogg, "Villard and the NAACP," *The Nation* 81 (14 February 1959), 137–40; Mary White Ovington, *How the National Association for the Advancement of Colored People Began* (1914); Oswald Garrison Villard, *Fighting Years: Memoirs of a Liberal Editor* (1939); Michael Wreszin, *Oswald Garrison Villard: Pacifist at War* (1965).

Bruce J. Dierenfield

Virginia School Closing Experiment In 1956 in response to the **Brown v. Board of Education** decision, the Virginia General Assembly passed a law that provided for the closing of any school or schools that the federal courts had ordered integrated. In 1959 the Virginia Supreme Court declared this law unconstitutional. In response, the Virginia Assembly repealed the state's compulsory school attendance laws. With school attendance now a matter of local choice, several school boards closed their schools. In cities such as Norfolk, Charlottesville, and Front Royal, local citizens sought to accommodate the needs of students through private education. These efforts, however, were an inadequate substitute for public schooling. Many white parents and businessmen, consequently, came to believe that public education was more important than maintaining segregation. This shift in public opinion, together with a series of federal court orders, forced the opening of integrated schools in most of the cities and counties that previously had been closed. By 1962, only

Prince Edward County schools remained closed. With tuition grants from the Virginia Assembly and tax credits from the Board of Supervisors, white citizens opened a private school system in the county. In **Griffin v. Prince Edward School Board** (1964), the Supreme Court struck down the county's system of subsidization of private white schools. In the fall of that same year, Prince Edward County Schools reopened.

Selected Bibliography Earl Black and Merle Black, *Politics and Society in the South* (1987); Robbins L. Gates, *The Making of Massive Resistance: Virginia's Politics of Public School Desegregation, 1954–1956* (1964); Dewey W. Grantham, *The Life and Death of the Solid South: A Political History* (1988); J. Harvie Wilkinson III, *From Brown to Bakke: The Supreme Court and School Integration, 1954–1978* (1979).

Phillip A. Gibbs

Virginia v. Rives, 100 U.S. 545 (1880)   On 1 March 1880 the U.S. Supreme Court handed down a trio of decisions dealing with black jury rights. In **Strauder v. West Virginia** the Court overturned a state law that limited jury service to whites, in **Ex parte Virginia** the Court went so far as to approve the indictment and arrest of a state judge who had excluded blacks from juries. The third case, *Virginia v. Rives,* was not a victory for American blacks. In this case, two black citizens of Virginia were charged with murdering a white man. When an all-white jury pool was summoned, the defendants asked that a new pool including black citizens be ordered. The state court denied the defendants' petition, pointing out that the jury had been summoned according to Virginia's jury law, which did not exclude blacks. The Supreme Court upheld the action of the state court, since Virginia's law did not bar blacks from the jury box. Black jury service in the South became a rarity, as state leaders passed laws allowing black jury service, then appointed state officials who would not choose blacks for the jury panels.

Selected Bibliography Stephen Cresswell, "The Case of Taylor Strauder," *West Virginia History* 44 (Spring 1983), 193–211; Benno C. Schmidt, "Juries, Jurisdiction, and Race Discrimination: The Lost Promise of *Strauder v. West Virginia,*" *Texas Law Review* (1983), 1402–99.

Stephen Cresswell

Voice of the Negro   Edited in Atlanta by John Wesley Edward Brown and later in Chicago by Jesse Max Barber, this monthly journal first appeared in January 1904. Topics included church life, **lynching,** family values, business, politics, and international affairs. In September 1905 the editors endorsed the **Niagara Movement,** precursor of the **NAACP,** and applauded demands for an unfettered press, which **Booker T. Washington** had attempted to subvert to his accommodationist views. After the brutal **Atlanta race riot (1906),** in which Brown was badly injured, the magazine found a new home in Chicago. Circulation, once 12,000, dropped off, and in October 1907 the last issue, a skimpy 30 pages, was published. An important primary source, *Voice of the Negro* reflected competing African American ideologies in the early twentieth century. It was the first substantial journal edited by southern blacks for a national audience.

Selected Bibliography Louis R. Harlan, ed., *The Booker T. Washington Papers* (1972–79); Bethany Johnson, "Freedom and Slavery in the *Voice of the Negro*: Historical Memory and African-American Identity, 1904–1907," *Georgia Historical Quarterly* 84 (2000), 29–71; August Meier, *Negro Thought in America 1880–1915: Racial Ideologies in the Age of Booker T. Washington* (1963); Alfred A. Moss, Jr., *The American Negro Academy: Voice of the Talented Tenth* (1981).

Richard W. Resh

Voter Education Project   In 1960 and 1961, as the sit-ins and activities of the **Freedom Riders** began to meet with success in desegregating lunch counters and interstate travel facilities, black civil rights leaders sought new goals for their movement. In September 1961, following months of debate and wrangling, the **Congress of Racial Equality** (CORE), the **Student Nonviolent Coordinating Committee** (SNCC), the **National Urban League,** and the **NAACP** joined together to launch the Voter Education Project (VEP). The project had the full blessing of the Kennedy administration, which was willing to provide federal protection for civil rights workers engaged in registering voters, but not for protestors participating in **direct action** activities. Scheduled to last for two and one-half years and financed by $870,000 in grants from the **Taconic Foundation** and other northern foundations, VEP got underway in April 1962. The campaign targeted southern blacks in the rural black belt and Mississippi delta regions, where white election officials had manipulated literacy tests and complex registration forms to prevent even literate blacks from voting. At the beginning of the project only about 25 percent of voting age southern blacks were registered; in Mississippi the figure stood at 5 percent.

Student activists working for CORE, SNCC, or one of the other organizations canvassed blacks throughout the rural South, conducted literacy and citizenship clinics, and encouraged blacks to register and vote. In Mississippi SNCC workers led by **Robert Moses** encountered determined opposition from inveterate white racists. There and elsewhere student volunteers were threatened, jailed, beaten, bombed, and killed, but they persisted in their effort. Attorney General Robert Kennedy assisted them by enlarging the **Civil Rights Section of the Justice Department** and directing it to begin wholesale prosecution of voting rights cases. The results of VEP were mixed. The percentage of southern adult blacks who were registered to vote rose from 25 to 40 percent between 1962 and 1964, but the educational and political process was laborious, difficult, and dangerous. The frustrations and dangers involved in the voter registration campaign ultimately contributed to the passage of the **Civil Rights Act of 1964** and the **Voting Rights Act of 1965.**

Selected Bibliography Taylor Branch, *Parting the Waters: America in the King Years, 1954–63* (1988); David J. Garrow, *Bearing the Cross: Martin Luther King, Jr., and the Southern Christian Leadership Conference* (1968); Donald G. Nieman, *Promises to Keep, African-Americans and the Constitutional Order, 1776 to the Present* (1991); Harvard Sitkoff, *The Struggle for Black Equality, 1954–1980* (1981).

Charles D. Lowery

NAACP head Roy Wilkins and President Lyndon B. Johnson confer on strategies to secure passage of the 1965 Voting Rights Act. © Library of Congress.

Voting Rights Act of 1965   In 1964 the Lyndon B. Johnson administration began planning voting rights legislation, and the president called for legislation in his 1965 State of the Union address. Meanwhile, **Martin Luther King, Jr.**'s, voting rights campaign in Selma, Alabama, prompted the administration to act more quickly. In a 15 March address to Congress at the height of the Selma demonstrations that climaxed with the **Selma to Montgomery March,** the president employed the phrase "we shall overcome" to call for voting rights legislation. On 25 May, the Senate invoked cloture and the next day passed (78–18) the bill. Six weeks later the House of Representatives also passed (333–85) a voting rights bill. A conference quickly approved a bill very similar to the administration's proposal, and Congress easily approved it early in August. On 6 August the president signed it.

The main provisions of the Voting Rights Act outlawed educational requirements for voting in states or counties where less than half of the voting age population had been registered on 1 November 1964, or voted in the 1964 presidential election and empowered the attorney general to have the Civil Service Commission assign federal registrars to enroll voters. Other parts of the bill required a federal district court in Washington, D.C., to approve all changes in voting procedures in the affected jurisdictions for the next 10 years, and permitted the same court to lift the provisions when a state proved it had not discriminated for 10 years.

Implementation began on 10 August when, at the direction of Attorney General Nicholas Katzenbach, federal registrars began registering voters in nine southern counties. By the end of 1965, federal examiners had registered nearly eighty thousand new voters. Many of the affected southern states attempted to use a variety of devices—gerrymandering, at-large elections, more appointive offices, higher qualifications for candidates—to dilute or negate the effect of black voters.

Largely as a result of enforcement of the Voting Rights Act, black registration soared in the South. In Mississippi, for example, black registrants went from 28,500 in 1964 to 251,000 in 1968. The percentage of voting-age blacks registered to vote in the South grew from 43 percent in 1964 to 62 percent in 1968. The larger number of black voters produced more black officeholders and white officials more receptive to black constituents.

In 1966 the U.S. Supreme Court upheld the Voting Rights Act in *South Carolina v. Katzenbach* and *Katzenbach v. Morgan.* Congress renewed the Voting Rights Act in 1970, 1975, and 1982.

Selected Bibliography Chandler Davidson and Bernard Grofman, eds. *Quiet Revolution in the South: The Impact of the Voting Rights Act, 1965–1990* (1994); David J. Garrow, *Protest at Selma: Martin Luther King, Jr., and the Voting Rights Act of 1965* (1978); Steven F. Lawson, *Black Ballots: Voting Rights in the South, 1944–1969* (1976); Frank R. Parker, *Black Votes Count: Political Empowerment in Mississippi after 1965* (1990).

Charles W. Eagles

W

Wagner-Gavagan Anti-Lynching Bill (1940) In their continuing fight against mob violence directed against black Americans, the **NAACP** supported the Wagner-Gavagan antilynching bill, the third such major bill to come before the Congress. In 1921 the NAACP had supported the Dyer antilynching bill and, although it passed the House, the bill was defeated in the Senate by a combination of southern resistance and Republican indifference. In 1935 the NAACP supported the **Costigan-Wagner Antilynching Bill.** In its support the NAACP released a pamphlet on the **Claude Neal** lynching, which had taken place in 1934. The pamphlet detailed Neal's castration, his mutilation with hot irons, and finally his death. Although this publication aroused some passion in Congress and around the nation, the Costigan-Wagner Bill met the same fate as the Dyer Bill—southern resistance and Republican indifference in the Senate. Again in 1940 the NAACP supported a bill, this time the Wagner-Gavagan Bill. The bill would ensure that, if the state did not take action against the perpetrators of lynchings, the federal government would intervene. The bill received widespread support in the North. However, President Franklin D. Roosevelt gave the bill only lukewarm support. Southern resistance together with Democratic indifference meant a defeat for the bill.

Selected Bibliography Charles F. Kellogg, *NAACP: A History of the National Association for the Advancement of Colored People* (1967); Robert L. Zangrando, *The NAACP Crusade against Lynching, 1909–1950* (1980).

Kenneth W. Goings

Walker, Alice (9 February 1944, Eatonton, Ga.–). Since 1968 this poet, novelist, essayist, editor, biographer, social activist, and "womanist" has won critical acclaim as a major American writer, was awarded both the Pulitzer Prize and the American Book Award for *The Color Purple*, and honored with numerous other fellowships and awards. As a student in the 1960s at Spelman College in Atlanta, Georgia, where she was actively involved in the civil rights movement and later at Sarah Lawrence College, in Bronxville, New York (B.A., 1965), she came to poetic maturity in the climate of civil rights activism. This period was vital to Walker's personal and artistic growth, for it allowed her to find her artistic, spiritual, and political identity: a commitment to and strong identification with the South and the whole survival of her people. Alice Walker's insistence that the writer be actively involved and politically committed gives her works a depth of understanding of the human condition and of the spiritual significance of the black experience.

Selected Bibliography Harold Bloom, ed., *Alice Walker* (1989); Elliott Butler-Evans, "History and Genealogy in Alice Walker's, *The Third Life of Grange Copeland*," in *Race, Gender, and Desire* (1989); Klaus Enssler, "Collective Experience and Individual Responsibility in Alice Walker, *The Third Life of Grange Copeland*," in *The Afro-American Novel Since 1960* (1982); Trudier Harris, "Folklore in the Fiction of Alice Walker: A Perpetuation of Historical and Literary Tradition," *Black American Literature Forum* 2 (Spring 1977), 3–8; Mary Helen Washington, "Black Women: Myth and Image Maker," *Black World* 23 (August 1974), 10–18.

Jacquelyn Jackson

Walker, Madame C. J. (23 December 1867, Delta, La.–25 May 1919, Irvington, N.Y.). Sarah Breedlove was born to sharecroppers in 1867. She was orphaned at 6, married at 14, and widowed at 20 with one daughter, A'Leila. In 1905, working as a washerwoman in St. Louis, Missouri, she created hair growers and straighteners for African Americans. She then moved to Denver, Colorado, where she married newspaperman Charles Walker and established a mail order business, which flourished. Calling herself Madame C. J. Walker, she established an office in Pittsburgh, Pennsylvania, and in Indianapolis, Indiana, and founded labs and training schools for "Walker agents" who sold her products across the United States. She employed over 3,000 people, mostly women, and supported philanthropic and educational efforts. She founded scholarships for women at **Tuskegee Institute** and elsewhere, and supported the **NAACP** and black philanthropies. In 1914 she moved to New York. In 1917 she built Villa Lewaro on the Hudson River, designed by black architect Vertner Tandy. Her house in Harlem, known as the "Dark Tower," became after her death a meeting place for black and white artists and intellectuals, presided over by her daughter. She died in Irvington in 1919, leaving the bulk of her million dollar estate to her daughter, with generous bequests to several educational and philanthropic causes.

Selected Bibliography *Crisis* 18 (July 1919), 131; *Dictionary of American Biography* (1936); Walter Fisher, "Madame C. J. Walker," in *Notable American Women* (1971), 533–35; Rayford W. Logan and Michael R. Winston, eds., *Dictionary of American Negro Biography* (1982);"Madame C. J. Walker," in *The 100 Most Influential Women of all Time* (1996); "Madame C. J. Walker," in Henry Louis Gates and Cornel West, eds., *The African-American Century: How Black Americans Have Shaped Our Country* (2000); Obituary, *New York Times*, 26 May 1919.

Cheryl Greenberg

Walker, Margaret. See Alexander, Margaret Walker.

Walker v. City of Birmingham, **388 U.S. 307 (1967)** In this decision, a divided U.S. Supreme Court ruled that injunctions against protests were to be challenged in the courts and not defied in the streets. The case stemmed from the arrests of the Reverends **Martin Luther King, Jr., Alfred Daniel Williams King, Ralph David Abernathy,** and **Wyatt Tee Walker** in Birmingham, Alabama, on Good Friday, 12 April 1963. Unlike the **Albany, Georgia, sit-ins** in which King had obeyed a federal court injunction that prohibited marches—and by doing so ended the protests and lost the creative tension necessary for reform—in Birmingham he violated state circuit Judge William A. Jenkins's ex parte temporary injunction against "unlawful street parades, unlawful processions, unlawful demonstrations, unlawful boycotts, unlawful trespasses, and unlawful picketing or other like unlawful conduct." This marked a turning point in King's life. Henceforth he decided to violate unjust laws and risk arrest. While incarcerated, King wrote **"Letter from Birmingham Jail,"** and President John F. Kennedy intervened on his behalf. Disobeying the injunction, the **Birmingham confrontation** continued as the **Southern Christian Leadership Conference** led demonstrations that ultimately forced the federal government to support the movement. As a result, the Kennedy administration proposed the civil rights bill of 1963. Sustaining the Alabama Supreme Court ruling in *Walker v. City of Birmingham,* the U.S. Supreme Court diminished greatly the constitutional protection afforded protestors under the Bill of Rights. Five of the justices ruled that petitioners must appeal the issuance of the injunction and not a contempt conviction. Thus until properly challenged, a court injunction remained the law. Chief Justice Earl Warren and Justices William J. Brennan, William O. Douglas and Abe Fortas dissented, arguing that the delay created by the appeals process against a clearly unconstitutional injunction violated the petitioners' First Amendment rights. The Walker ruling was immediately used to stifle student protest, and it ushered in a new era of law and order.

Selected Bibliography *The American University Law Review* 17 (1967), 113–19; David J. Garrow, *Bearing the Cross: Martin Luther King, Jr., and the Southern Christian Leadership Conference* (1986); David B. Oppenheimer, "Martin Luther King, *Walker v. City of Birmingham* and the Letter from the Birmingham Jail," *U.C. Davis Law Review* 26 (1993), 791–833; "The Supreme Court, 166 Term: Civil Rights," *Harvard Law Review* 81 (1967), 141–46; Alan F. Westin and Barry Mahoney, *The Trial of Martin Luther King* (1974).

Glenn T. Eskew

Walker, Wyatt Tee (16 August 1929, Brockton, Mass.–). As first permanent executive director of the **Southern Christian Leadership Conference** (SCLC), Walker assumed the task of turning the new movement, based on **nonviolent resistance**, which was under the leadership of **Martin Luther King, Jr.,** into a prominent and permanent civil rights organization. During his tenure (1960–64), Walker developed an effective civil rights bureaucracy and hired a talented staff, including Walter Fauntroy, who became director of the Washington, D.C. bureau. After graduating from Virginia Union University with B.S. and M. Div. degrees, Walker had pastored the historic Gillfield Baptist Church in Petersburg, Virginia, had served as the chairman of the local **NAACP** and as the Virginia director of the **Congress of Racial Equality**, and had been an SCLC board member. Under Walker's no-nonsense direction, the SCLC became one of the leading civil rights organizations of the 1960s. However, Walker's greatest asset also proved to be a liability. His heavy-handed leadership caused staff tensions and morale problems. After a series of impasses, Walker resigned to help publish a black history series for the Negro History Library. In 1975 he received the D.Min. degree from Colgate Rochester School of Divinity and published "*Somebody's Calling My Name*": *Black Sacred Music and Social Change*. During the 1980s he was World Commissioner of the Programme to Combat Racism of the World Council of Churches and also a special assistant to **Jesse Jackson** in the **People United to Save Humanity** (PUSH)/Rainbow Coalition. In 1993, *Ebony* magazine named him one of the 15 greatest black preachers in the nation. In 1996 he was elected president of the American Committee on Africa. In 2001 he served as chairman of **Al Sharpton**'s National Action Network and pastor of Harlem's Canaan Baptist Church. He condemned Jesse Jackson upon hearing Jackson had fathered an illegitimate child.

Selected Bibliography Lerone Bennett, Jr., *What Manner of Man: A Biography of Martin Luther King, Jr.* (1976); Chicago Citizen, 17 April 1996; Adam Fairclough, *To Redeem the Soul of America: The Southern Christian Leadership Conference and Martin Luther King, Jr.* (1987); David J. Garrow, *Bearing the Cross: Martin Luther King, Jr. and the Southern Christian Leadership Conference* (1986); David Levering Lewis, *King: A Critical Biography* (1970); Willie C. Matney, ed., *Who's Who among Black Americans, 1977–1978*, 2d ed. (1978); *New Pittsburgh Courier*, 16 May 2001; Stephen B. Oates, *Let the Trumpet Sound: The Life of Martin Luther King, Jr.* (1982).

Lawrence H. Williams

Walters, Alexander (1 August 1858, Bardstown, Ky.–2 February 1917, New York, N.Y.). Twenty-fourth bishop of the African Methodist Episcopal Zion (A.M.E.) Church, Walters, the sixth of eight children, was born of slave parents. He studied at private schools, including a church theological seminary, and graduated in 1875 as valedictorian of his class. Licensed to preach in 1877, he pastored a number of churches, including the famed Mother A.M.E. Zion Church in New York City. Rising rapidly in church ranks, he became one of the leaders of his denomination, contributing much to the administration of its affairs and to the extension of its bounds.

The widespread lynchings and other racially repressive acts directed against his people in the South prompted Bishop Walters to sign the call for the formation of the **Afro-American League** in 1889. In 1898 the league was merged with the **Afro-American Council** under his presidency. Later, Walters joined the **Niagara Movement,** which had been organized by **W.E.B. Du Bois** in 1909 to fight racial segregation and disenfranchisement. He also helped to

Bishop Alexander Walters. © Library of Congress.

found the National Negro Committee in 1909, which a year later changed its name to the **National Association for the Advancement of Colored People.**

Selected Bibliography *New York Age* (11 October 1890); Emma L .Thornbrough, *T. Thomas Fortune; Militant Journalist* (1972); William Jacob Walls, *The African Methodist Episcopal Zion Church: Reality of the Black Church* (1974); Alexander Walters, *My Life and Work* (1917); Carter G. Woodson, *Negro Orators and Their Orations* (1925).

George E. Walker

War on Poverty   In January 1964 President Lyndon Johnson announced that his administration "declares unconditional war on poverty." The Economic Opportunity Act followed by other legislation created such programs as Community Action Programs (CAP), Operation **Head Start,** the Job Corps, and Volunteers in Service to America (VISTA) to conduct a multifront assault on poverty entrenched amid plenty in America. To win this war Johnson appointed Sargent Schriver to head the Office of Economic Opportunity. President Johnson linked the abolition of poverty with the civil rights movement to provide the full benefits of citizenship to African Americans. The war on poverty helped millions while expanding the scope and changing the nature of federal spending on social welfare, but it failed to eliminate poverty.

Selected Bibliography Theodore Howard Andrews, "John F. Kennedy, Lyndon Johnson, and the Politics of Poverty, 1960–1987" (Ph.D. diss., Stanford University, 1998); Carl M. Brauer,

"Kennedy, Jackson, and the War on Poverty," *Journal of American History* 69 (1982), 98–119; Roger Friedland, "Class Power and Social Control: The War on Poverty," *Politics and Society* 6 (1976), 459–89; Sar A. Levitan and Robert Taggart, *The Promise of Greatness* (1976); Allen J. Matusow, *The Unraveling of America: A History of Liberalism in the 1960s* (1984); Charles Murray, "The War on Poverty, 1965–1980," *The Wilson Quarterly* 8 (Autumn 1984), 95–136; John E. Schwarz, *America's Hidden Success: A Reassessment of Twenty Years of Public Policy* (1983).

Lorenzo Crowell

Ward v. Regents of the University System of Georgia, 191 F. Supp. 491 (1957) In 1950 Horace Ward, an African American, was denied admission to the Law School of the University of Georgia. After unsuccessful appeals to the Law School and the Board of Regents, he sought an injunction in 1952 to prevent the Regents from denying his admission on the basis of race. The case was continued when Ward was drafted into the armed forces; it was not taken up until December 1956. University officials asserted that Ward had not been denied admission for racial reasons but because he had failed to file for readmission for later school terms as required by school regulations. Besides, he was presently a student at the Northwestern University Law School. In February 1957 the court declared itself unable to rule on Ward's claim. He had not made any new application since 1950, so the Board of Regents had thus been unable to review his qualifications and make an admission decision. Ward had further refused to submit character references as required by new Board regulations promulgated in 1952. Finally, he had become a law student at Northwestern, thus abandoning his application for admission to the Georgia Law School as a first year student. Ward then asked the Court to retain jurisdiction because he planned to seek admission to the Georgia Law School as a transfer student. In March 1957, the Court denied the motion insisting it had already declared its lack of jurisdiction. Since Ward now planned to reapply, this fact indicated that his position in the original motion in refusing to reapply had indeed been proper reason for the Court to dismiss his case. There was no longer an issue over which the Court had jurisdiction. Ward, therefore, was kept out of the Georgia Law School on administrative procedural grounds; the true segregation reasons did not have to be utilized.

Selected Bibliography Jack Greenberg, *Race Relations and American Law* (1959); Lexis-Nexis Database, Number 4410; R.R.L.R. 369, 599 (1957) .

John F. Marszalek

Ward v. Texas, 316 U.S. 547 (1942) This U.S. Supreme Court case helped clarify the conditions under which a confession becomes involuntary and its admission into evidence becomes a violation of the due process clause of the **Fourteenth Amendment.** In January 1941, on the basis of his confession alone, William Ward, a black house servant residing in Titus County, Texas, was convicted in State District Court of the murder without malice of Levi Brown, an elderly white man, and sentenced to three years confinement in the state penitentiary in January 1941. In May 1942 Ward's appeal reached the Supreme Court. An uneducated man, Ward had been arrested at night without a warrant, driven for three days from county to county under continuous interrogation, jailed more than 100 miles from home, and warned of alleged threats of mob violence against him. He finally said that although he was innocent, he would make any statement desired of him. The Court ruled that ample precedent had established the involuntary character of confessions elicited from ignorant persons who are subjected to protracted questioning, or held incommunicado, or threatened with mob violence, or taken at night to isolated places for interrogation, and that on any one of these grounds Ward's conviction was reversible.

Selected Bibliography Jack Greenberg, *Race Relations and American Law* (1959); *New York Times*, 2 June 1942; "Recent Decisions," *Virginia Law Review* 29 (1942), 115–16.

Robert A. Calvert

Waring, J. Waties (27 July 1880, Charleston, S.C.–11 January 1968, New York, N.Y.). An eighth-generation Charlestonian, Waring stands with **Richard Taylor Rives, Frank Minis Johnson,** and a few other contemporary southern federal judges who spoke the accent but not the language of segregation. After earning a baccalaureate degree from the College of Charleston in 1900, he studied law on his own, passed the state bar exam, and joined a prominent Charleston law firm. His practice flourished. As an assistant U.S. attorney during Woodrow Wilson's presidency he developed expertise in federal litigation, and in 1942 Franklin D. Roosevelt appointed him to the position of U.S. District Judge for the Eastern District of South Carolina. During his controversial tenure on the federal bench, Waring ended such racially discriminatory practices within his court as white-only jury lists; ruled in favor of equal pay for the state's black and white teachers; and struck down the political basis of white supremacy in South Carolina by ruling, in *Rice v. Elmore* (1947), that the **white primary** was unconstitutional. The *Rice* ruling was a major victory for blacks whose **Fifteenth Amendment** rights had effectively been thwarted by the white primary. When South Carolina Democratic party officials subsequently tried to get around the ruling by organizing the party by counties into private clubs open only to white Democrats, Judge Waring was incensed. In *Brown v. Baskin* (1948) he issued an injunction on the grounds that the party's actions were "a clear and flagrant evasion of the law." He went on to admonish Democratic officials that his court would not tolerate "further evasions, subterfuges or attempts to get around" the law.

Waring was as great an enemy of segregated schools as he was of the white primary. He encouraged **NAACP** officials such as **Thurgood Marshall** to make a direct frontal assault on the **separate-but-equal** doctrine in the public schools. When fellow jurists on a three-judge panel upheld the state's segregated school system, Waring vigorously dissented, saying that "Segregation is per se inequality." Waring's controversial rulings, together with his numerous public speeches and statements from the bench criticizing southern bigotry, alienated and isolated him from South Carolina's white society. In 1952 he retired from the bench and lived out his life as an "exile" in New York City. Upon his death in 1968, journalist Carl Rowan wrote that "the judge's indestructible monument is the army of Americans who walk a bit more proudly because of the courage he had in interpreting the rules of justice."

Selected Bibliography Derrick A. Bell, Jr., *Race, Racism, and American Law* (1980); J. W. Peltason, *Fifty-eight Lonely Men: Southern Federal Judges and School Desegregation* (1961); Mark V. Tushnet, *The NAACP's Legal Strategy against Segregated Education, 1925–1950* (1987); Tinsley E. Yarbrough, *A Passion for Justice: J. Waties Waring and Civil Rights* (1987).

Charles D. Lowery

Washington Bee   See Chase, W. Calvin.

Washington, Booker Taliaferro   (5 April 1856, Franklin County, Va.–14 November 1915, Tuskegee, Ala.). Educator, founder, and first president of **Tuskegee Normal School,** he was, after the death of **Frederick Douglass** in 1895, the most famous black man in America and indisputably the spokesman for his race until his own death in 1915.

Born of a slave mother and white father, Washington received only an informal education before entering **Hampton Institute.** There he came under the influence of General Samuel C. Armstrong, who became his mentor and guiding light. There, too, he caught the spirit of helping blacks help them-

Booker T. Washington seated at his desk. © Library of Congress.

selves, a spirit that remained with him for the rest of his life. After graduating from Hampton in 1875, Washington taught school for three years and then enrolled at Wayland Seminary in Washington, D.C. Unimpressed by its liberal arts emphasis, he became convinced that Hampton had the best solution for blacks who were taking their first steps as free citizens.

In 1881 Washington was offered the principalship of a normal school to be founded at Tuskegee, Alabama. He shrewdly nurtured the support of the white Alabamians for his school, which he modeled after Hampton. By investing power in the trustees, he kept his school free from direct state intervention. He also relied on sources outside of the state for financial support. During his first year he had an average of 37 students and 3 faculty members. By 1915 Tuskegee had 1,500 students, 180 faculty—many of them distinguished such as George Washington Carver—and an endowment of $2,000,000.

As early as 1884, Washington indicated his acceptance of the **separate-but-equal** doctrine. When he announced it before the Cotton States and International Exhibition in Atlanta in 1895, he became famous. Frederick Douglass, long the voice of black Americans, had just died. Southern Populists had raised the question of black voting in recent elections. All eyes were on Washington, the one black man who had been invited by southern whites to give an address. When Washington announced, "In all things that are purely social we can be as separate as the fingers, yet one as the hand in all things essential to mutual progress," the applause from all sections was deafening. Praise for the speech was universal and included praise from later critics such as **T. Thomas Fortune** and **W.E.B. Du Bois.** By his stance Washington traded away hard-won civil rights for the promise of economic gain. Popular among whites, his position became increasingly controversial among blacks. Du Bois soon referred to the speech as the "Atlanta Compromise." For the next 12 years, however, Washington was the unchallenged black spokesman. No African American was appointed to federal office without his consent or recommendation. His bases of power were the "Tuskegee Machine," a large network of influential blacks with whom he kept in touch, and the **National Negro Business League,** which he controlled from its founding in 1900. His dinner with President Teddy Roosevelt in 1901 raised a storm of protest in the South, but it only gained him further national fame.

At the apogee of his popularity, Washington wrote his own story, **_Up from Slavery_** (1901), which has become one of the classic American autobiographies and established him as an international figure. Washington remained the undisputed spokesman of his race until the **Brownsville, Texas, affray** of 1906. Washington feared loss of his influence over federal appointments and offered little protest to President Roosevelt's action against the black soldiers involved in the incident. He had always placed his trust in white authority figures and could not reverse his practice at this time. Black voices of protest, heretofore known as the **Niagara Movement,** reached a crescendo at Washington's failure, and they soon found a more effective voice in the **NAACP.**

Washington fought segregation and discriminatory practices by secretly financing court cases and by writing articles. Some cases were successful, particularly **Rogers vs. Alabama** (1904) and **Bailey v. Alabama** (1911), which struck down Alabama black peonage laws. Washington also fought a long but losing battle for equality in black public education in the South.

Selected Bibliography Tunde Adeleke, ed., *Booker T. Washington: Interpretive Essays* (1998); Houston A. Baker, *Turning South Again: Rethinking Modernism, Rereading Booker T.* (2001); W. E. B. Du Bois, *Dusk of Dawn* (1941); Louis R. Harlan, *Booker T. Washington*, 2 vols. (1972, 1983); *The Booker T. Washington Papers*, 14 vols. (1972–89); Hugh Hawkins, *Booker T. Washington and His Critics* (1962); Samuel R. Spencer, Jr., *Booker T. Washington* (1955); Booker T. Washington, *Up from Slavery* (1901).

James G. Smart

Washington (Colored) American   This paper, edited and owned by Edward E. Cooper and published during the years from 1893 to 1904, received sustained financial support from **Booker T. Washington.** It espoused a philosophy for African Americans that encouraged economic development, self-help, racial solidarity, civil rights, and political enfranchisement. Washington secretly subsidized the paper to use as a weapon against those who criticized him. He used it to send out **Tuskegee Institute** news releases, paying for the cost of their printing. The paper also received Republican party campaign patronage and advertisements from friends of Washington.

Selected Bibliography Frederick Detweiler, *The Negro Press in the United States* (1922); August Meier, *Negro Thought in America 1880–1915: Racial Ideologies in the Age of Booker T. Washington* (1963).

Jessie M. Carter

Washington, D.C., Race Riot (1919)   In late June and early July of 1919, rumors, fanned by a sensationalist press and general antiblack attitudes, spread throughout the city that white women were under attack by black males. This alleged violence included something as trivial as a black man accidentally bumping into a white woman. On Friday, 18 July, two black men jostled a white woman, the wife of a sailor. This incident set off a riot that saw sailors and marines, quickly joined by other whites, attacking blacks almost at the very door of the White House. The violence spread into black neighborhoods, and some blacks tried to fight back. The **NAACP** and the U.S. Congress bemoaned the rioting, and preparations were begun to bring in federal troops to put down the violence. Blacks grew increasingly frightened and began to arm themselves; there were sporadic attacks on men in uniform. Monday night, July 21, was a horrible night of white-on-black and black-on-white violence. President Woodrow Wilson called in the Secretary of War and made arrangements to call up additional troops. Meanwhile the NAACP worked to calm matters and protect the besieged black citizens. On Tuesday all this activity paid dividends; the level of rioting lessened considerably. On Wednesday morning Secretary of War Newton D. Baker announced that matters were under control. In the aftermath of the riot, there were calls for a stronger police force. Black leaders wanted, instead, a neutral police. The riots showed the depth of the antiblack feeling that existed in the nation's capital and demonstrated that blacks were willing and able to fight back when they found themselves unprotected by the legal authorities.

Selected Bibliography Joseph Boskin, ed., *Urban Racial Violence in the Twentieth Century*, 2nd ed. (1976); Robert T. Kerlin, *The Voice of the Negro, 1919* (1920); *Washington Post*, June and July 1919; Arthur I. Waskow, *From Race Riot to Sit-In, 1919 and the 1960s: A Study in the Connections between Conflict and Violence* (1966).

John F. Marszalek

Washington, Forrester   (24 September 1887, Salem, Mass.–24 August 1963, New York, N.Y.). Born in Massachusetts and educated at Tufts, Harvard, and Columbia universities, Washington's career reflected some of the important changes in the twentieth century black American experience. In 1917, Washington earned his M.A. degree in social work from Columbia while assuming a role in the growth of the **National Urban League** (NUL). Executive secretary of the Detroit Urban League prior to World War I, he was later a league organizer in Michigan and Illinois. During the twenties, he maintained his NUL ties while serving both local and national government in various capacities. In 1927, he became head of the **Atlanta University** School of Social Work where he came in contact with **Will W. Alexander** of the **Commission on Interracial Cooperation.** Due in part to Alexander, Washington joined the Roosevelt administration in 1934 as a race relations adviser to the Federal Emergency Relief Administration and as a participant in an informal group of white and black New Dealers who sought the inclusion of blacks in the New Deal's social and economic programs. Washington left government service after six months because he believed that the Roosevelt administration's policies failed to address the root causes of black economic and social inequality. Although a political moderate, he called for an expanded federal involvement to assure jobs for skilled and unskilled black workers. Fearful of black dependency on federal relief and welfare, a notion later expressed by more radical critics in the 1960s and 1970s, Washington returned to Atlanta where he felt he could be "of the most service to the needy of my race."

Selected Bibliography Thomas Lee Green, "Black Cabinet Members in the Franklin Delano Roosevelt Administration" (Ph.D. diss., University of Colorado, 1981); Allen Kifer, "The Negro Under the New Deal, 1933–1941" (Ph.D. diss., University of Wisconsin, 1961); John B. Kirby, *Black Americans in the Roosevelt Era* (1980); Arvarh E. Strickland, *History of the Chicago Urban League* (1966).

John B. Kirby

***Watson v. City of Memphis*, 373 U.S. 526 (1963)**   I. A. Watson, Jr., and other black residents of Memphis, Tennessee, sought declaratory and injunctive relief from the continued segregation of municipal parks and other city owned recreational facilities. Two-thirds of the 61 city playgrounds, 30 of 56 recreational areas, 8 of 12 community centers, and 5 of 7 golf courses were reserved for whites while the remainder were set aside for black use. While acknowledging that continued segregation of the Memphis municipal facilities was unconstitutional since the **Brown v. Board of Education** decision in 1954, the Tennessee courts agreed to allow Memphis a six-month extension to submit a desegregation plan. On certiorari, Justice Arthur Goldberg, writing for a unanimous Supreme Court, reversed the Tennessee decision. City claims that a proposed slower desegregation process would avert race conflicts, would promote peace, and would enable planning for potential problems were inadequate justifications for invoking the 1955 **Brown** decision, which allowed a "step by step" desegregation of schools to facilitate a smooth transition in a complex environment. With the zoo, art gallery, and boating areas desegregated without incident, constitutional rights under the **Fourteenth Amendment** could not be denied simply out of fear of their exercise.

Selected Bibliography Richard Bardolph, ed., *The Civil Rights Record, Black Americans, and the Law, 1849–1970* (1970); George Rossman, "Review of Recent Supreme Court Cases: Segregation," *American Bar Association Journal* 49 (1963) 1124; David A. Strauss, "The Myth of Colorblindness," *Supreme Court Review Annual, 1986* (1986), 99–134.

William A. Paquette

Watts Race Riot (1965) Watts, a small neighborhood in south-central Los Angeles, has become symbolic for a series of massive African American urban uprisings that occurred in the mid-1960s. In terms of magnitude, the **Newark, New Jersey, race riot** and the **Detroit race riot,** both of which occurred in 1967, were greater in intensity, but the sudden explosion that took place in Los Angeles between 11–16 August 1965 remains the significant episode precisely because it was not supposed to have happened in America's paradise city. The oppressive quality of black life, visible in many eastern and midwestern cities by thickly compacted housing projects in deteriorating neighborhoods with poor quality schools, high unemployment, low-paying jobs and law enforcement bias, was obscured in Los Angeles by an urban horizontal spread, stuccoed houses with grass lawns, a freeway system that bypassed the section, and the state's self-image of fulfilling the American Dream.

Similar to other urban protests of the period, the event in Watts began inauspiciously during a heat wave with the arrest by white officers of two black men for a minor vehicle violation. Within minutes, however, the police car was surrounded, and reinforcements were subsequently attacked with stones and bottles. The riot then spread to virtually the entire south-central region of the city. After several days of skirmishes between the residents and police and fire departments, the area came under total control of the community, whose people proceeded to loot and fire bomb those businesses and professional groups long known for their exploitative practices. Surveys taken after the riot pointed to a high degree of resident participation, paralleling that of the other riots as well, and indicating the development of a nationwide ghetto urban consciousness. Approximately 15 percent of the inhabitants (teenagers and older), were active at some point during the week; an additional 35–40 percent looked on as lively spectators. Significantly, all of the actions took place *within* the perimeters of the black community.

The riot eventually ended as hundreds of law enforcement personnel from throughout the state and the National Guard surrounded the area. Thirty-four people were killed, mainly blacks, and property damage was estimated at $35 to $40 million dollars. The revolt fused a powerful identity within the black community, but the factors that caused the uprising nonetheless persisted.

Selected Bibliography Kenneth B. Clark, *Dark Ghetto: Dilemmas of Social Power* (1965); Robert Conot, *Rivers of Blood, Years of Darkness* (1967); Hugh David Graham and Ted Robert Gurr, *The History of Violence in America* (1969); U.S. Riot Commission, *Report of the National Advisory Commission on Civil Disorders* (1968).

Joseph Boskin

Watts v. Indiana, 338 U.S. 49 (1949) On 12 November 1947 Robert A. Watts, a black man, was arrested and held for an alleged criminal assault that had occurred earlier that day. Later that same day, a woman's body was found in the vicinity of Watts's alleged crime. Taken to the Indiana State Police headquarters and kept there for several days in solitary confinement, Watts was interrogated by six to eight officers in relays for eight to nine hours a day for six days. He confessed. He had not been given a prompt preliminary hearing, had been without friendly or professional aid, had not been advised of his constitutional rights, and had not been given proper food or rest. Watts was convicted and his appeals were rejected by the Indiana courts. He appealed on a writ of certiorari to the United States Supreme Court. Justice Felix Frankfurter, joined by Justices Frank Murphy and Wiley Rutledge, wrote the majority opinion. The Court held that in a murder trial in a state court the use of a confession obtained by relentless police interrogation violated "due process" under the **Fourteenth Amendment,** a decision that allowed the federal courts to severely restrict the states in their administration of criminal justice. Concurring opinions were written by Justices Hugo Black, William O. Douglas, and Robert Jackson. Chief Justice Fred Vinson and Justices Stanley Reed and Harold Burton dissented without comment. Petitioner Watts was represented by attorney **Thurgood Marshall.**

Selected Bibliography William V. Batchelder, "Notes and Comments," *Journal of Criminal Law* 40 (1950), 671–72; "Recent Decisions," *Syracuse Law Review* 1 (1949), 313–15.

William A. Paquette

"We Shall Overcome" The anthem, slogan, and philosophy of the 1960s civil rights movement, and certainly the best known of the freedom songs, "We Shall Overcome" was based on an old black church hymn. It began as a labor song in the 1940s, spreading from black tobacco workers in South Carolina to the **Highlander Folk School** in Tennessee. There future **Student Nonviolent Coordinating Committee** activists learned a version whose words and music were copyrighted in 1960 by Zelphia Horton, Frank Hamilton, Guy Carawan, and Pete Seegar. In the early 1960s—first at Nashville, Tennessee,

Four young marchers singing during the 1963 March on Washington. © National Archives.

and then at Raleigh, North Carolina—black student demonstrators participating in the sit-in movement ritualized the song with spirited resolve and emotion as a serious and resonant affirmation of their goals. It was an oath of mutual determination and courage. From that spirit, this song became the theme song of the 1963 **March on Washington** and the concluding song of all black sit-ins, marches, demonstrations, church meetings, and racial confrontations throughout the South and later the North. A moving and majestic song, "We Shall Overcome" was "the 'Marseillaise' of the movement."

Selected Bibliography Frank Adams with Myles Horton, *Unearthing Seeds of Fire: The Idea of Highlander* (1975); Taylor Branch, *Parting the Waters: America in the King Years, 1954–63* (1988); Guy Carawan and Candie Carawan, compilers, *Songs of the Southern Freedom Movement: We Shall Overcome!* (1963); Josh Dunson, *Freedom in the Air: Song Movements of the 1960's* (1965); Mary King, *Freedom Journey* (1987); Pete Seegar and Robert S. Reiser, *Everyone Knows Freedom: The Civil Rights Movement in Words, Pictures, and Song* (1990).

Jacquelyn Jackson

Weaver, Robert C. (29 December 1907, Washington, D.C.–17 July 1997, New York, N.Y.). Raised by middle class parents in Washington D.C. Weaver was taught the value of an education and racial self respect. He earned a schol-

Dr. Robert C. Weaver speaking at the Ebenezer AME Church in Detroit, about 1944.
© Library of Congress.

arship to Harvard, where he came to know black students **Ralph Johnson Bunche** and **William Henry Hastie** who remained his friends and allies throughout his career. After graduating cum laude, he earned his Ph.D. in economics from Harvard. At the start of the New Deal, Weaver joined Harvard colleague, **John P. Davis,** in establishing the **Joint Committee on National Recovery,** which represented black concerns before Congress and the Roosevelt administration. In 1933 **Clark H. Foreman,** race relations adviser to Secretary of Interior **Harold L. Ickes,** selected Weaver as his assistant. Two years later he succeeded Foreman and in 1937 assumed a similar position with the U.S. Housing Authority. During World War II, Weaver worked for a number of government agencies, principally as an expert on black labor and racial issues. From the thirties on, Weaver's public and professional career focused on black employment, housing, and urban conditions and the need for more enlightened public and private responses to these circumstances. With **Mary McLeod Bethune,** he was a key figure in the Roosevelt administration's **Black Cabinet** and in encouraging black involvement in the federal government. A prolific scholar, his two most important works are *Negro Labor* (1946) and *The Negro Ghetto* (1948).

Weaver left the Roosevelt administration during World War II but returned to government service in 1961 as an administrator for the U.S. Housing and Finance Agency during the Kennedy years. In 1966 he became the first black to head a federal cabinet post when Lyndon B. Johnson appointed him Secretary of Housing and Urban Development. Following the Johnson years, Weaver served for two years as president of Baruch College, in New York City. In 2000, the HUD headquarters was named after him.

Selected Bibliography John B. Kirby, *Black Americans in the Roosevelt Era* (1980); New York *Amsterdam News*, 16 August 2000; Nancy J. Weiss, *Farewell to the Party of Lincoln* (1983); Alma Rene Williams, "Robert C. Weaver: From the Black Cabinet to the President's Cabinet" (Ph.D. diss., Washington University, 1978); Raymond Wolters, *Negroes and the Great Depression* (1970).

John B. Kirby

Western Freedmen's Aid Commission The Western Freedmen's Aid Commission evolved from the Cincinnati Contraband Relief Association (1862), one of the earliest private societies committed to providing for future freedmen. A group dominated by evangelical clergymen withdrew from the latter and organized the Commission when their proposal to expand the Association's efforts to include educating the freedmen met with opposition. Following the Civil War the Commission entered into a close association with the American Methodist Association and maintained its own identity until 1870, when it merged with the Methodist organization.

Selected Bibliography G. K. Eggleston, "The Works of Relief Societies During the Civil War," *Journal of Negro History* 14 (July 1929), 272–99; Joseph E. Holliday, "Freedmen's Aid Societies in Cincinnati, 1862–1870," *Cincinnati Historical Society Bulletin* 22 (July 1964), 169–85.

Michael S. Downs

Wharton, Clifton Reginald (13 September 1926, Boston, Mass.–). Son of the first African American career diplomat, Wharton entered Harvard at the age of 16, graduating with a B.A. in history in 1947. He went on to earn an M.A. at Johns Hopkins in 1948. He worked five years at the American Institute of International Social Development before entering the University of Chicago where he earned M.A. and Ph.D. degrees in economics. Wharton became the first African American to head a major, predominantly white, university when he was appointed president of Michigan State University in 1970. Eight years later he became the first black chancellor of the State University of New York, the largest university complex in the U.S. From 1987 to 1994 Wharton held the presidency of Teachers' Insurance and Annuity Association (TIAA), the nation's largest independent pension fund. In 1993–94 he was deputy secretary of state in the Bill Clinton administration. At the beginning of the twenty-first century, he remained one of the nation's leading economic thinkers.

Selected Bibliography *Detroit News Sunday Magazine*, 14 December 1969; "A New Boss Takes Over at Michigan State," *Ebony*, July 1970, February 1987.

Clarence Hooker

What the Negro Thinks   Robert Russa Moton, Booker T. Washington's successor at the **Tuskegee Institute** and longtime president of the **National Negro Business League,** wrote *What the Negro Thinks* in 1928. In it, he addressed white America, citing black advances in education, business, and income and summarized the many forms of discrimination that had made blacks "the most underprivileged group in American Life." Moton struck a conciliatory posture, chiding rather then condemning society. Like his mentor, Washington, he appealed to decency and fair play from the more educated and progressive whites, especially in the South. Segregation, increasingly unacceptable to more radical blacks, might continue "if [it were] equitable and voluntary following the natural lines of social cleavage . . . and [was] the most favorable condition for the development of [black] latent capacities." *What the Negro Thinks* showed practically none of the **New Negro movement**'s greater militancy. The work revealed the depth of white racism that existed in the 1920s and remains a disturbing document.

Selected Bibliography Robert L. Clayton, *Robert Russa Moton: Successor to Booker T. Washington and a Strong Black Presence from 1916 until 1940, "The Early Years"* (1988); August Meier, "Booker T. Washington and the Rise of the N.A.A.C.P.," in August Meier and Elliot Rudwick, *Along the Color Line* (1976); August Meier, *Negro Thought in America, 1880–1915: Racial Ideologies in the Age of Booker T. Washington* (1963).

Richard W. Resh

Wheeler, John W.   (1847, Lexington, Ky.–5 January 1912, St. Louis, Mo.). A free-born African American, Wheeler made his contribution to civil rights by representing the interests of his race as a St. Louis politician and newspaper publisher from the 1870s until 1911. A Republican stalwart, Wheeler mobilized black votes for the party but always made it clear he expected protection of black rights and patronage in return. As publisher of the *St. Louis Palladium*, he consistently echoed the racial philosophy of **Booker T. Washington,** while preaching a doctrine of racial solidarity. It is through extant copies of his newspaper (1903–7) that researchers have an excellent window into the black life of St. Louis.

Selected Bibliography Lawrence O. Christensen, "The Racial Views of John W. Wheeler," *Missouri Historical Review* 67 (July 1973), 535–47; *St. Louis Palladium*, 10 January 1903–5 October 1907, copies available on microfilm, the State Historical Society of Missouri, Columbia, Missouri.

Lawrence O. Christensen

White House Conference "To Fulfill These Rights"   In June 1965, with most of the legal barriers to racial equality tumbling, President Lyndon B. Johnson proposed a White House Conference on Civil Rights to find affirmative ways to combat the remaining social and economic problems hampering blacks. Scheduled for the fall, it was postponed when a controversial agenda item, based on a report written by Assistant Secretary of Labor Daniel Patrick Moynihan on the pathology of the black family, nearly wrecked the effort. After the subject was scrapped at the insistence of black leaders and a planning session held in November, Johnson appointed Ben Heineman, a railway executive, to ensure that the conference came off smoothly. The planners drew up a detailed document, "To Fulfill These Rights," and carefully selected the 2500 participants from across the nation. The militant **Student Nonviolent Coordinating Committee** boycotted the proceedings in protest of Johnson's domestic and foreign policies. On 1 and 2 June 1966, the delegates hotly debated the topics of housing, welfare, education, and the administration of justice, but they were not permitted to change the specific contents of the report drawn up in advance. Increasingly stung by criticism from black activists, upset by urban race riots, and preoccupied with the Vietnam War, the president did not give the conference report high priority. Nevertheless, several of the recommendations did become the basis for the **Civil Rights Act of 1968.**

Selected Bibliography Steven F. Lawson, *In Pursuit of Power: Southern Blacks and Electoral Politics, 1965–1982* (1985); Harry McPherson, *A Political Education* (1972); Lee Rainwater and William L. Yancey, *The Moynihan Report and the Politics of Controversy* (1967).

Steven F. Lawson

White Primary   The white primary was one of several devices used by southern states to disenfranchise blacks after Reconstruction. Across the South, where impotent Republican parties gave Democrats a monopoly, the white primary excluded blacks from the only elections that mattered, the Democratic primaries. It was justified by the argument that political parties and primaries were private institutions. The first suit challenging the white primary was brought in Texas in 1923 by black physician, Dr. Lawrence A. Nixon. It was not until 1944, however, after years of litigation and evasive action by legislatures, that the Supreme Court ruled in **Smith v. Allwright** that a primary was an election and, therefore, the white primary violated the **Fifteenth Amendment.**

Selected Bibliography Conrey Bryson, *Dr. Lawrence A. Nixon and the White Primary* (1993); V. O. Key, Jr., *Southern Politics in State and Nation* (1949); Paul Lewinson, *Race, Class and Party: A History of Negro Suffrage and White Politics in the South* (1932).

Allen Kifer

White v. Texas, 309 U.S. 631 (1940)   This case originated in Livingston, Texas in 1937 when a white female reported that a black man had raped her. Police in Livingston arrested 16 black men. The police chief noticed that Robert White, an uneducated farmhand, did not eat well and appeared withdrawn. He decided White committed the crime. On the sixth night of interrogation, White confessed at 3:30 A.M. An all-white jury convicted him, and the court sentenced him to death. Appellant courts affirmed his conviction. Ultimately, the U.S. Supreme Court overturned the conviction under the coerced confession rule. Justice William Douglas explained that "Due process of law, preserved for all by our Constitution, commands that no such practice as that disclosed by this record shall send any accused to his death."

Selected Bibliography William D. Good, "Burden of Admissibility of Confessions [Federal]," *Journal of Criminal Law and Criminology* 31 (1941), 598–600; Jack Greenberg, *Race Relations and American Law* (1959); Mark V. Tushnet, *Making Civil Rights Law: Thurgood Marshall and the Supreme Court, 1936–1961* (1994); Juan Williams, *Thurgood Marshall: American Revolutionary* (1988).

Stephen Middleton

White, Walter Francis (1 July 1893, Atlanta, Ga.–21 March 1955, New York, N.Y.). Reared in a middle-class, African American family, he graduated from **Atlanta University** in 1916. Two years later, the **NAACP** appointed him assistant executive secretary at its national headquarters in New York City. Until his fatal coronary 37 years later, he, the NAACP, and the civil rights movement were inseparable. White investigated 41 **lynchings** and 8 race riots. His widely publicized findings fueled the Association's campaign for federal antilynching legislation from 1918 to the 1950s. His book, ***Rope and Faggot: A Biography of Judge Lynch*** (1929), became a standard. He achieved further

Walter White with the widow of a lynch victim during the 1940s. © Library of Congress.

recognition through the **Harlem Renaissance,** when he published two novels, *The Fire in the Flint* (1924) and *Flight* (1926), and worked unselfishly to promote the careers of young African American authors, performers, and artists.

In 1931 White became NAACP Executive Secretary. He placed the Association at the center of an emerging civil rights coalition of civil libertarian, labor, ethnic, church, and women's groups, a coalition with close ties to the New Deal. During the presidential campaign of 1948, the Truman administration embraced the coalition's agenda: antilynching and anti–poll tax legislation, military desegregation, and a **Fair Employment Practice Committee.** White and his associates had made interracial justice a fixture on the national landscape.

Walter White possessed a world vision. He attended the 1921 Pan-African Congress in London and Paris, campaigned for an end to American domination in Haiti, and championed economic development throughout the Caribbean. As a war correspondent, he visited England, North Africa, and Italy in 1944, and the South Pacific in 1945, to monitor the treatment accorded black troops. Serving as advisor to the American delegation to the United Nations, in April 1945 at San Francisco and in autumn 1948 at Paris, White urged the decolonization of Italy's former territories in Africa.

Three of White's six books appeared in the last decade of his life: *A Rising Wind* (1945), *A Man Called White* (his autobiography, 1948), and *How Far the Promised Land?* (published posthumously in 1955). His influence and his health both declined after 1949, the former in part because of a controversial divorce and remarriage that year. More importantly, Cold War hysteria and the conservative posture of the Eisenhower presidency diverted public attention from civil rights. Still, White remained head of the NAACP, wrote his weekly newspaper columns, hosted a public affairs radio show in New York City, and maintained an exhausting speaking schedule. Nonetheless, a series of NAACP Supreme Court victories from 1944 to 1955 allowed **Thurgood Marshall**'s reputation to eclipse White's; and by the end of 1955 the public had found a new hero in **Martin Luther King, Jr.**

Selected Bibliography Poppy Cannon, *A Gentle Knight: My Husband, Walter White* (1956); Edward E. Waldron, *Walter White and the Harlem Renaissance* (1978); Robert L. Zangrando, *The NAACP Crusade against Lynching, 1909–1950* (1980).

Robert L. Zangrando

Whitsett, Daniel Cleveland (12 July 1909, Milry, Ala.–21 March 1984, Montgomery, Ala.). Born the son of a Methodist minister in a rural section of Alabama, Whitsett attended a Methodist-affiliated college, Birmingham-Southern, and earned his divinity degree from Duke University in 1933. During the 1930s and '40s he pastored Methodist churches in Alabama and Florida. His liberal racial views prompted church authorities to transfer him northward, to Sylacauga First (United) Methodist Church, where it was hoped his beliefs would be more acceptable. While he was there during the years

1947–58, the African American civil rights movement gained momentum, and he worked diligently to promote its goals. He invited blacks to present special services at his church, and he served as president of the **Alabama Council on Human Relations.** The Ku Klux Klan turned its enmity against Whitsett. Klan motorcades circled his home, it burned crosses on his front lawn, and threatened injury to his family, including the three Whitsett children. Whitsett refused to be intimidated. By the late 1950s, however, he had become persona non grata in the North Alabama Conference of the Methodist Church. His liberal racial views made him unacceptable to most of its churches in Alabama. In 1958 Harvard University's Epworth Methodist Church invited Whitsett to become its minister. Though loath to leave Alabama, he decided that he could no longer risk his family's well-being. His ministry at Epworth was successful. As a resident of the Cambridge Council of Churches, he challenged the city to address its own racial problems. He returned to his roots in Alabama in 1963, but the Alabama–West Florida bishop assigned him to a small church in the Florida panhandle, the type of appointment that would normally go to a young minister not long out of seminary. Without complaint or bitterness, Whitsett served that and several other churches before retiring from the ministry to become director of church relations at Huntingdon College, a Methodist-affiliated institution. Resolute in his belief that the Christian faith was color blind, he devoted his life and ministry to the effort to achieve racial equality and justice. From the pulpit his was a courageous and persistent voice calling for an end to **Jim Crow.** Mississippi's **Will Campbell,** like Whitsett, helped prepare the way for a new era in race relations.

Selected Bibliography Cambridge (Massachusetts) *Chronicle,* 5 February 1959; Powers McLeod, *Southern Accents . . . Different Voices* (1993); *The Methodist Christian Advocate* 93 (27 November 1973); "Zion's Herald," *New England Methodist Monthly* (October 1958), 7–13; Jan Gregory Thompson, "The History of the Alabama Council of Human Relations from Roots to Redirection, 1920–1968" (Ph.D. diss., Auburn University, 1983).

Charles D. Lowery

Whittaker, Johnson C.   (August 23, 1858, Camden, S.C.–January 14, 1931, Orangeburg, S.C.).   Born a slave on the plantation of the senior James Chesnut, he attended the then integrated University of South Carolina (1874–76). He was admitted to the United States Military Academy, at West Point, in 1876. Briefly a roommate of the first black West Point graduate, **Henry Ossian Flipper,** Whittaker was ostracized by white cadets because of his race. The morning of 6 April 1880, he was found unconscious and bleeding, the result, he said, of the visit of three masked men. Authorities decided he had mutilated himself to escape the following June examinations. To clear himself, he demanded a court of inquiry and later a court martial, both of which found him guilty. The U.S. Army Judge Advocate General reversed the decision, but military authorities separated him from the Academy in March 1882 for alleged deficiencies in the June 1880 examination. Whittaker later

West Point cadet Johnson C. Whittaker's first trial for allegedly mutilating himself, 1880. © Library of Congress.

became a lawyer and a school principal in South Carolina and Oklahoma. His courtroom battles were among the most sensational and widely publicized trials in American history and in them was exemplified the depth of prejudice against black Americans in the post–Civil War era. In 1995, President Bill Clinton awarded a posthumous U.S. Army commission to Whittaker, a presentation accepted by his descendents in the first of a number of White House ceremonies righting wrongs against African American military men.

Selected Bibliography "Assault at West Point," Showtime Television film (1994); John F. Marszalek, *Assault at West Point*, paperback ed. (1994); John F. Marszalek, "A Black Cadet at West Point," *American Heritage* 12 (August 1971), 30–37, 104–6; John F. Marszalek, *Court Martial: A Black Man in America* (1972).

John F. Marszalek

Whitus v. Georgia, 385 U.S. 545 (1967) Petitioners Phil Whitus and Leon Davis, convicted of a crime, filed a writ of certiorari with the United States Supreme Court charging racial discrimination in the grand and petit jury selection process in Mitchell County, Georgia. They sought redress under the "equal protection clause" of the **Fourteenth Amendment.** In 1962 on certiorari, the Supreme Court in *Whitus v. Balkcom* vacated an earlier judgment and remanded the case to district court for reconsideration. *Whitus v. Georgia* was a reappeal. Prior to 1965 Georgia county commissioners used white tax return sheets for white taxpayers and yellow ones for blacks to compile the jury list. Although blacks comprised 45 percent of Mitchell County's population, none had ever been chosen for jury duty. After 1965, tax returns were still segregated, but commissioners selected jurors whom they knew personally. In 1966, of the 2,004 black males in the county, only 3 of 33 prospective grand jurors were black. One was selected to serve with 18 whites. Of the 90 chosen for petit jury selection, 7 were black; however, none of them was selected. Justice Thomas Clark wrote a unanimous Supreme Court opinion that reversed earlier decisions and confirmed racial discrimination when Georgia could offer no explanation for the disparity between the number of blacks on the tax lists and those called. However, the Supreme Court did not order that petitioners be set free, but rather that they be properly retried.

Selected Bibliography Derrick A. Bell, Jr., *Race, Racism, and American Law* (1980); George Rossman and Rowland L. Young, "Review of Recent Supreme Court Decisions: Juries," *American Bar Association Journal* 53 (1967), 361.

William A. Paquette

Wilder, Lawrence Douglas (31 January 1931, Richmond, Va.–). **P.B.S. Pinchback** served as acting governor of Louisiana for six weeks in 1872–73, but he had been elected only to the state senate. William **Henry Hastie** served as governor in the late 1940s, but that was an appointive post and in the Virgin Islands. Thus, until 1989, when L. Douglas Wilder won in Virginia, no African American had ever won a popular election to be governor of any state. That he did so by only the slenderest of margins masked the fact that, in a state fully 80 percent white, a substantial majority of his support came from white voters. Wilder had earned his undergraduate degree from Virginia Union University in 1951 and his law degree (J.D.) at **Howard University** in 1959. In between, he had been awarded a Bronze Star in the Korean War. After a decade of law practice in Richmond, he ran for a seat in the state senate in 1969. The first black candidate to win election to that body in the twentieth century, he won reelection in 1973, 1977, and 1981, and by 1976 he had gained the first of three committee chairmanships. Then, in 1985, elected to the office of lieutenant governor, he became the first successful black candidate in a statewide popular election for any legislative or executive post in a southern state since the 1870s. That victory, followed by his gubernatorial win four years later, epitomized the transformation of southern life that the civil rights movement had fostered. After he left office, he remained active in politics, the law, race relations, and even hosted a radio talk show. In 1998, at the last moment, he decided against becoming president of historically black Virginia Union University.

Selected Bibliography Donald P. Baker, *Wilder: Hold Fast to Dreams, A Biography of L. Douglas Wilder* (1989); Margaret Edds, *Claiming the Dream: The Victorious Campaign of Douglas Wilder of Virginia* (1990); "News and Views: Douglas Wilder Withdraws from the Presidency of His Alma Mater, Virginia Union University," *Journal of Blacks in Higher Education* 20 (December 31, 1998), 49; Dwayne Yancey, *When Hell Froze Over: The Untold Story of Doug Wilder, A Black Politician's Rise to Power in the South* (1988).

Peter Wallenstein

Roy Wilkins displays a hangman's noose from Florida, of the kind used for lynching. © Library of Congress.

Wilkins, Roy   (30 August 1901, St. Louis, Mo.–9 September 1981, New York, N.Y.). An African American civil rights activist, he served as executive director of **NAACP** from 1955 until his retirement in 1977. He strongly opposed violence and rejected the concepts of black power and black nationalism. He also opposed student demands for all black departments on college campuses as a "return to segregation and **Jim Crow.**" Wilkins graduated from the University of Minnesota in 1923 with a degree in sociology. He also was a talented journalist, having served as night editor of the university newspaper—Minnesota *Daily,* and editor of the St. Paul *Appeal,* a black weekly. After graduation he worked as a newspaperman with the *Kansas City Call,* in Kansas City, Missouri. Life in Kansas City introduced him to rigid segregation. Wilkins was active in the St. Paul and Kansas City chapters of the NAACP. He later became assistant secretary under **Walter Francis White** and from 1931 to 1934 took investigative assignments in the Deep South that placed his life in jeopardy. When **W.E.B. Du Bois,** editor of *Crisis,* left the NAACP in 1934, the versatile Wilkins replaced him. He jointly held the assistant secretary and editor positions until 1949. Following the death of White in 1955, Wilkins became executive secretary of the NAACP, only the third black to hold that position. Wilkins was a strong proponent of desegregation, protection of voting rights, and equality in jobs, housing and public accommodations. He participated in the 1963 **March on Washington,** the **Selma to Montgomery March** (1965), and the James **Meredith March** against Fear (1966) among others. His judgment and opinions were often solicited by American presidents. Wilkins's tenure as NAACP executive secretary (executive director) parallels significant gains in black civil rights: school desegregation, federal antilynching, fair housing, and voting rights legislation. In January 2001, the United States Postal Service issued a commemorative stamp in his honor.

Selected Bibliography Joan M. Burke, *A Current Guide to the People, Organization, and Events* (1970); Elton C. Fax, *Contemporary Black Leaders* (1970); Edgar A. Toppin, *A Biographical History of Blacks in America since 1528* (1971); Roy Wilkins, *Standing Fast: The Autobiography of Roy Wilkins* (1982); Sondra Kathryn Wilson, *In Search of Democracy: The NAACP Writings of James Weldon Johnson, Walker White, and Roy Wilkins (1920–1977)* (1999).

Wali Rashash Kharif

Williams, Aubrey (23 August 1890, Springville, Ala.–3 March 1965, Washington, D.C.). Born in Alabama and educated as a social worker at the University of Cincinnati, Williams became head of the University of Wisconsin Conference of Social Work in 1922. Ten years later he joined the staff of the American Public Welfare Association where he worked on behalf of impoverished blacks and whites in Mississippi. In 1933, Harry Hopkins selected Williams to head the southwestern district for the Federal Emergency Relief Administration. In 1935 he was appointed first head of the National Youth Administration (NYA) where he remained until 1943, when the agency was closed by Congress.

Under Williams, the NYA created the Division of Negro Affairs, led by **Mary McLeod Bethune.** Working with Bethune, Williams saw that blacks were hired to NYA supervisory positions at national and state levels and that NYA educational funds went to black students and institutions. Increasingly militant in the cause of civil rights, Williams was a major influence during the 1930s in fostering greater racial understanding among New Deal liberals. He had a particularly strong impact on the racial ideas of **Eleanor Roosevelt.** Unlike some white interracialists, his commitment to race equality increased during and after the war years. In 1947 he became president of the Southern Conference Educational Fund (SCEF), one of the few organizations during the Cold War era that opposed segregation and discrimination in the South. Because of his activities, Williams was often branded a "Communist sympathizer" by racist white politicians. Undaunted, he supported the emerging southern civil rights movement and the leadership of **Martin Luther King, Jr.,** during the 1950s and 1960s.

Selected Bibliography Irwin Kilbaner, "The Southern Conference Educational Fund: A History" (Ph.D. diss., University of Wisconsin, 1971); Thomas A. Krueger, *And Promises to Keep* (1967); Richard A. Reiman, *The New Deal and American Youth: Ideas and Ideals in a Depression*

Decade (1992); John Salmond, *A Southern Rebel* (1983); Morton Sosna, *In Search of the Silent South* (1977); Patricia Sullivan, *Days of Hope: Race and Democracy in the New Deal Era* (1996).

John B. Kirby

Williams, George Washington (16 October 1849, Bedford Springs, Pa.–2 August 1891, Blackpool, England). From his humble upbringing in the backwoods of western Pennsylvania, Williams became a soldier, theologian, journalist, lawyer, politician, and scholar. He was the first historian committed to a serious, scientific investigation of African and African American history. His life epitomized the African American struggle for individual and community achievement. Following five years of military service, Williams graduated from **Howard University**'s theological department in 1874 and became the minister of Baptist churches in Boston, the District of Columbia, and Cincinnati. He served as editor and columnist for two newspapers between 1875 and 1878. He studied law in 1878, entered Ohio politics in 1879, and frequently traveled in Europe and Africa from 1884 until his death in England in 1891. In all his careers, Williams was committed to the study of African American history. A prodigious researcher and prolific writer of books, speeches, newspaper columns, pamphlets, and articles, Williams's illumination of African American history has earned him the title, "Grandfather of Afro-American History."

Selected Bibliography John Hope Franklin, *George Washington Williams: A Biography* (1985); John Hope Franklin, *George Washington Williams: The Massachusetts Year* (1983); John Hope Franklin, "Stalking George W. Williams," *American Visions* 4 (No. 2, 1989), 28–31; George Washington Williams, *History of the Negro Race in America from 1619 to 1880,* 2 vols. (1883); George Washington Williams, *A History of the Negro Troops in the War of the Rebellion, 1861–1865* (1887).

Lillie Johnson Edwards

Williams, Hosea Lorenzo (5 January 1926, Attapulgus, Ga.–16 November 2000, Atlanta, Ga.). The son of blind African American parents, he survived a troubled, violent youth and military service in World War II. Educated at Morris Brown College and **Atlanta University,** both in Atlanta, Georgia, he was employed by the U.S. Department of Agriculture as a research chemist in Savannah. By 1961 he was a controversial activist in the local **NAACP** chapter. In 1963, Williams moved to Atlanta to join the staff of **Martin Luther King, Jr.,** at the **Southern Christian Leadership Conference.** Because of his ability to organize and embolden constituencies at the grassroots with his fiery rhetoric and forceful personality, and because of his supervision of voter registration efforts in the South, he was arrested on 124 occasions. He led marchers who were brutally assaulted by state troopers near the Edmund Pettus Bridge outside Selma, Alabama, on 7 March 1965 (see **Selma to Montgomery March**). Williams was elected to the Georgia General Assembly in 1974. He publicly endorsed Ronald Reagan for U.S. President in 1980; was elected to the Atlanta City Council in 1985 and led a march in Forsyth County, Georgia, which led to a violent confrontation with the Ku Klux Klan in 1987. Though he lost a bid to become mayor of Atlanta in 1989, he was a DeKalb County commissioner from 1991 to 1996. In his later years, arrests for drunken driving, numerous traffic violations, and financial mismanagement tarnished his reputation. For many years until his death from cancer, he operated a chemical manufacturing and distribution company and headed a charitable group that fed tens of thousands of Atlanta's poor on Thanksgiving and Christmas.

Selected Bibliography *Atlanta Journal*, 24 May 1981; Shirelle Phelps, ed., *Contemporary Black Biography* vol. 15 (1997); Ashyia N. Henderson, ed., *Who's Who among Black Americans* (2000); Obituary, *Atlanta Journal and Constitution*, 17 November 2000.

Robert Fikes, Jr.

Williams, Robert F. (1925, Monroe, N.C.–15 October 1996, Grand Rapids, Mich.). A United States Marine veteran, Williams became president of the Union County, North Carolina, **NAACP** in 1956. An advocate of armed self-defense, he recruited and drilled his membership. Faced with an discriminatory county judicial system, he began urging the use of violence against violence. The national NAACP suspended him for this call. Falsely accused of kidnapping a white couple, Williams and his wife fled to Cuba in 1961. From there he published the monthly newsletter, *The Crusader,* and became chairman of the **Revolutionary Action Movement,** a small militant group of college educated youth. In 1969 he returned to the United States but charges were not dropped until 1976. He spent his last years as a lecturer and activist for the Michigan based, People's Association for Human Rights. In 2000, a memorial was dedicated to Williams in Baldwin, Michigan.

Selected Bibliography James Forman, *The Making of Black Revolutionaries* (1985); James A. Geschwender, ed., *The Black Revolt* (1971); Michigan *Citizen*, 20 May 2000; Timothy B. Tyson, *Radio Free Dixie: Robert F. Williams and the Roots of Black Power* (1999); Robert F. Williams, *Negroes with Guns* (1962).

Ray Branch

Williams v. Mississippi, 170 U.S. 213 (1897) In the late nineteenth century, political leaders in Mississippi tried to find a way to circumvent black voting without violating the **Fifteenth Amendment.** The result was the state's constitution of 1890, soon widely imitated across the South. The new constitution and subsequent statutes provided that the would-be voter must have paid a **poll tax** for at least the previous two years. Further, a voter had to be literate or else show his ability to interpret a section of the state constitution when it was read to him. White registration officials had full power to decide whether a black applicant's performance on the literacy or understanding test was sufficient. *Williams v. Mississippi* was the Supreme Court's first major ruling on the constitutionality of the legal devices used to effect black disfranchisement in the late nineteenth century. The court ruled that because the Mississippi constitution did not mention race, and because the poll tax and literacy test on their face applied equally to blacks and whites, Mississippi's constitution and statutes were not in conflict with the Fifteenth Amendment. The court's decision made it clear that the Fifteenth Amendment would be a dead letter in the South for many years to come.

Selected Bibliography Richard Bardolph, ed., *The Civil Rights Record: Black Americans and the Law, 1849–1970* (1970); John Braeman, *Before the Civil Rights Revolution: The Old Court and Individual Rights* (1988).

Stephen Cresswell

Willis and Kennedy v. Pickrick Restaurant, **243 F. Supp. 179 (N.D. Ga. 1964)** After three African American citizens were refused service at a restaurant in Atlanta, Georgia, they filed suit seeking an injunction restraining Pickrick Restaurant from violating the provisions of the **Civil Rights Act of 1964.** Deeming the case one of "general public importance," Attorney General Robert Kennedy, under Section 204 of the Civil Rights Act, intervened in the case on the side of the plaintiffs. Lester Maddox, the owner of Pickrick Corporation and later governor of Georgia, contended that the Civil Rights Act of 1964 was unconstitutional. When the constitutionality of the act was upheld in *Heart of Atlanta Motel Inc. v. United States,* the court ordered Maddox to desegregate his restaurant. He closed the restaurant for a brief period of time and then reopened it as the Lester Maddox Cafeteria. On 5 February 1965 the court found Lester Maddox bound by the original court order to desegregate. He was found guilty of civic contempt for refusing to serve African American customers. Future contempt charges would result in a $200 fine per day from the date the court order was entered. Choosing not to desegregate, Lester Maddox closed his establishment. This case showed that the judicial system and the federal government were willing to intervene to uphold the provisions of the Civil Rights Act of 1964.

Selected Bibliography *Atlanta Constitution*, 6 February 1965; Ronald H. Bayor, *Race and the Shaping of Twentieth-Century Atlanta* (1996); Bruce Galphin, *The Riddle of Lester Maddox* (1968); David Andrew Harmon, *Beneath the Image of the Civil Rights Movement and Race Relations: Atlanta Georgia, 1946–1981* (1996); Lester Maddox, *Speaking Out: The Autobiography of Lester Maddox* (1975); *Race Relations Law Reporter* 9 (1964), 912–18, 1434–38.

David A. Harmon

Wilson, August (27 April 1945, Pittsburgh, Pa.–). Poet and playwright, Wilson was born Frederick August Kittel, one of six children of a German father and African American mother. Wilson grew up in a multicultural neighborhood in the poor section of Pittsburgh. He dropped out of high school at age 14 but continued to study on his own, focusing on writings about African American culture and history, but also drawing influences from European traditions. In 1965 Wilson discovered blues music for the first time and was drawn to the writings of Amiri Baraka. In 1968 he cofounded the Black Horizons Theater Company (Pittsburgh, Pa.), added the **Black Power** and the Black Arts movements to his creative inventory, and published his first poem, "For Malcolm X and Others." By the early 1970s, Wilson had turned to theater.

After a series of small productions—including *The Homecoming, Black Bart and the Sacred Hills,* and *Jitney*—Wilson had his first major hit, *Ma Rainey's Black Bottom,* based on the singer's life. Wilson brought black culture, history, and the blues tradition to the American theater with other critically acclaimed plays: *Fences* (1983); *Joe Turner's Come and Gone* (1988); *The Piano Lesson* (1987); and *Two Trains Running* (1989). Wilson was awarded the Pulitzer Prize for *Fences* and *The Piano Lesson,* which also won a Tony Award. In 2003 he received a Lifetime Achievement Award from the New Dramatists.

Selected Bibliography Chip Brown, "The Light in August," *Esquire* (April 1989), 116–25; Elizabeth H. Heard, interviewer, "August Wilson in Playwriting: An Interview," *African American Review* 35 (No. 1, 2001), 93–102; Mark Rocha, "A Conversation with August Wilson," *Diversity: A Journal of Multicultural Issues* 1 (Fall 1992), 24–42; New York *Amsterdam News,* 7 May 2003.

Eric Love

Wilson, Butler Roland (22 July 1860, Greensboro, Ga.–31 October 1939, Boston, Mass.). Lawyer and civil rights leader, Wilson was educated in the public schools of his small hometown near Atlanta and at **Atlanta University,** where he excelled in public speaking. In 1881 he moved to Boston and enrolled in the Boston University School of Law. He became a close friend of Harvard University Law School's second black graduate, **Archibald Grimke.** Together they edited the local black newspaper, *The Hub,* during the mid-1880s. After graduating from law school in 1884, Wilson established a successful private criminal law practice in Boston. He soon was involved with Grimke as joint counsel for an African American who had been denied admission to a local skating rink because of his race. They won their discrimination suit in the lower court only to have it lost by dismissal in the higher court. This defeat intensified Wilson's lifelong mission to protect and extend the civil rights of blacks. In 1893 he initiated action that resulted in the passage of a Massachusetts statute enlarging these rights by giving blacks access to public facilities and businesses that had previously been closed to them.

A vocal member of the Boston "radicals," which included Grimke and **William Monroe Trotter,** Wilson was a sharp critic of the accommodationist philosophy espoused by **Booker T. Washington.** He was one of the originators of the **Niagara Movement** and a founder of the Boston branch of the **NAACP,** which he served first as executive secretary and then as president from its founding in 1912 until a few short years before his death. As the leader of this organization his voice could be heard far beyond Boston as he denounced racial discrimination of every type and championed the civil rights of blacks. In 1912 Wilson was one of the first two African Americans to gain admission to the American Bar Association.

Selected Bibliography Clarence G. Contee, "Butler R. Wilson and the Boston NAACP Branch," *The Crisis* 81 (December 1974), 346–48; John Daniels, *In Freedom's Birthplace* (1941); Stephen R. Fox, *The Guardian of Boston, William Monroe Trotter* (1970).

Charles D. Lowery

Winston-Salem, (N.C.) Sit-in Carl Matthews, Jr., "beat the students to the punch" and sat-in at the S. H. Kress Company lunch counter on 8 February 1960. Sit-ins had been planned by Winston-Salem State University students. Within hours, 25 students had joined Matthews who stated that he wanted "to test the authority of the All-American City." By 9 February, lunch counter sit-ins were being staged all over the city. Mass meetings in the African American community began the evening of 12 February. By the end of February, the demonstrators were joined in protests and arrests by sympathetic youths from Wake Forest University. By April all the city's lunch counters were closed and did not reopen on a desegregated basis until 25 May 1960.

Selected Bibliography Aingred G. Dunston, "Black Struggle for Equality in Winston-Salem, North Carolina: 1947–1977" (Ph.D. diss., Duke University, 1981); Aldon D. Morris, *Origins of the Civil Rights Movement: Black Communities Organizing for Change* (1984); Wake Forest University, *Leadership and Civil Rights Symposium*, http://civilrights.wfu.edu.

Aingred G. Dunston

Wisdom, John Minor (17 May 1905, New Orleans, La.–15 May 1999, New Orleans, La.). Born into a prominent New Orleans family, Wisdom was educated at Washington and Lee University (A.B. 1925) and Tulane University (LL.B. 1929). After graduating first in his law class, he established a successful private practice in his home town, specializing in trusts and estates and teaching part-time at the Tulane law school. Convinced that the South would never enjoy a robust, democratic political and social order without a two-party system, he devoted much time in the 1940s and 1950s trying to organize a viable Republican party in Louisiana. This effort brought him into association with like-minded men such as **Elbert P. Tuttle** of Georgia and attracted the attention of national Republican leaders. In 1957 President Dwight D. Eisenhower appointed him to the **United States Fifth Circuit Court of Appeals.**

Widely read in history, literature, and political philosophy, Wisdom was the intellectual leader of the Fifth Circuit Court. He quickly aligned himself with the court's liberal integrationist bloc, which included his old friend Elbert P. Tuttle, **Richard T. Rives,** and **John Robert Brown.** These four men, irrevocably committed to justice and equality for all under the law, made the Fifth Circuit Court one of the most effective instruments for social change in the embattled South of the 1950s and 60s. With Wisdom providing much of the intellectual context, the Court blazed a new trail in civil rights law. It translated the Supreme Court's 1954 *Brown v. Board of Education* decision into a broad mandate not just to dismantle the dual school system, but also to strike down barriers of discrimination in voting, employment, and jury selection. Many of the landmark civil rights decisions handed down by the Appeals Court bear Wisdom's strong imprint—careful craftsmanship, intellectual vigor, and scholarly opinions rich in historical and legal analyses. Wisdom wrote the opinion that enabled James Meredith to enroll at the University of Mississippi. In 1966 he wrote the opinion in *United States v. Jefferson County* that laid the philosophical foundation for affirmative action. Judge Wisdom considered this case to be perhaps the most important of his career. In the area of race relations law, Wisdom was the voice of the Fifth Circuit Court of Appeals, and that voice resonated throughout the South and nation. In 1977 Wisdom assumed senior judge status and relinquished his administrative duties on the court. He remained active in civil and professional matters, and in 1989 was honored jointly with fellow Judge Elbert P. Tuttle with the prestigious Edward J. Divitt Distinguished Service to Justice Award. In 1993 President Bill Clinton conferred on him the Presidential Medal of Freedom and a year later the Court of Appeals building for the Fifth Circuit located in New Orleans was named for him.

Selected Bibliography "A Dedication to Judge John Minor Wisdom," *Washington and Lee Law Review* 53 (1996), 3–262; Deborah J. Barrow and Thomas G. Walker, *A Court Divided: the Fifth Circuit Court of Appeals and the Politics of Judicial Reform* (1988); Jack Bass, *Unlikely Heroes* (1981); Harvey C. Couch, *A History of the Fifth Circuit, 1891–1981* (1984); Joel William Friedman, "John Minor Wisdom: The Noblest Tulanian of Them All," *Tulane Law Review* 74 (No.1, 1999), 1–38; Henry T. Greely, "Quantitative Analysis of a Judicial Career: A Case Study of Judge John Minor Wisdom," *Washington and Lee Law Review* 53 (1996), 99–157; J. W. Peltason, *Fifty-eight Lonely Men: Southern Federal Judges and School Desegregation* (1961); Frank T. Read and Lucy S. McGough, *Let Them Be Judged: The Judicial Integration of the Deep South* (1978); "Tributes in Remembrance of Judges Frank M. Johnson and John Minor Wisdom," *Yale Law Journal* 109 (No. 6, 2000), 1207–78.

Charles D. Lowery

The Woman's Era This was the first periodical to be owned and published by African American women. Edited by Josephine St. Pierre Ruffin of Boston, the first issue was dated March 24, 1894. Referred to both as a newspaper and magazine, *The Woman's Era* focused on the activities of black women's clubs and organizations with particular emphasis on racial advancement, civil rights, and the vote for women. By 1896, with the creation of a national network of black women's clubs, *The Woman's Era* expanded beyond the Northeast and included states of the far West and the Deep South, but by the end of the century it had ceased publication.

Selected Bibliography Robert L. Allen, *Reluctant Reformers: Racism and Social Reform Movements in the United States* (1975); Penelope L. Bullock, *The Afro-American Periodical Press: 1838–1900* (1981); Paula Giddings, *When And Where I Enter: The Impact of Black Women on Race and Sex in America* (1984); Gerda Lerner, ed., *Black Women in White America: A Documentary History* (1973); Wilson Jermiah Moses, *The Golden Age of Black Nationalism* (1978).

Willi Coleman

Woodson, Carter Godwin (19 December 1875, New Canton, Va.–3 April 1950, Washington, D.C.). An African American educator and historian, Woodson received his secondary education at Layette, Virginia. He earned his B.A. and M.A. degrees at the University of Chicago, and his Ph.D. at Harvard in 1912. Woodson traveled to North Africa, Europe, and Asia before completing his doctorate. His travel, study, and research experience taught him that American historians ignored black contributions to America's development. He and others decided to form the **Association for the Study of Afro-American Life and History** in 1915. The Association published its first issue, *The Journal of Negro History,* in 1916. While Woodson served as chief editor of the journal, he was also the Dean of the College of Arts and Sciences at **Howard University.** In 1920 he left Howard to become dean of West Virginia Collegiate Institute. While in West Virginia, Woodson founded the Associated Publishers to help young black scholars publish their works. Woodson decided to resign his deanship at West Virginia to concentrate on black-related research in 1922. His important works on blacks included: *Education of the Negro Prior to 1861* (1915); *A Century of Negro Migration,* (1918); *The Negro in Our History* (1922); and *The Mind of the Negro as Reflected in Letters Written during the Crisis* (1926). It is not surprising that Woodson is called the father of black history.

Selected Bibliography Lorenza J. Greene, *Working with Carter G. Woodson, the Father of Black History: A Diary, 1928–1930* (1989); Mary Anthony Scally, *Carter G. Woodson: A Bio-Bibliography* (1985); Mary Anthony Scally, *Walking Proud, the Story of Dr. Carter G. Woodson* (1989); Earl E. Thorpe, *Black Historians* (1971).

Amos J. Beyan

Work, Monroe Nathan (15 August 1866, Iredell County, N.C.–2 May 1945, Tuskegee, Ala.). An African American sociologist who collected and disseminated information on the history of black peoples in order to empower them, Work received baccalaureate and master's degrees from the University of Chicago. As Director of the Department of Records and Research at **Tuskegee Institute,** Work kept annual tabulations on lynchings of African Americans and edited *The Negro Year Book.* In 1928 he published the *Bibliography of the Negro,* a seminal reference book. In 1945 Work began research on his most ambitious project, unpublished due to his death, entitled "A Bibliography of European Colonization, and the Resulting Contacts of Peoples, Races, Nations and Culture."

Selected Bibliography Linda O. McMurry, *Recorder of the Black Experience: A Biography of Monroe Nathan Work* (1985); Robert J. Norrell, *Reaping the Whirlwind. The Civil Rights Movement in Tuskegee* (1985); Anne Kendrick Walker, *Tuskegee and the Black Belt. A Portrait of A Race* (1944); *Who Was Who in America, 1943–1950* (1950).

Nancy E. Fitch

Wright, J. Skelly (14 January 1911, New Orleans, La.–6 August 1988, Westmorland Hills, Md.). A self-acknowledged judicial activist, educated at Loyola University in New Orleans, J. Skelly Wright was appointed to the federal bench in 1949. As a district judge he ordered the admission of black students to the Louisiana State University School of Law on the grounds that the law facilities the state provided for blacks at Southern University were not equal. Soon afterward he ordered LSU to admit a black undergraduate for the same reason. These rulings, both of which preceded ***Brown v. Board of***

Education, made Wright unpopular with white Louisianans. In 1956 he was part of a three-judge panel that, in **Bush v. Orleans Parish School Board,** struck down Louisiana's public school segregation laws. Then, in what was the first such action undertaken by a federal judge in the Fifth Circuit, he instructed the New Orleans school board to desegregate all of its public schools "with deliberate speed." Delays followed. Finally in May of 1960 Wright set a specific date in September for desegregation of the public schools to begin. A major confrontation followed between Wright and state officials, who were determined to maintain segregated schools. With the support of the **United States Court of Appeals for the Fifth Judicial Circuit** and the U.S. Justice Department, Wright faced down the state officials and successfully integrated New Orleans public schools. In addition to abolishing the dual school system, he desegregated the parks and city buses of New Orleans and championed voting rights for blacks. Because of his unwavering enforcement of *Brown v. Board of Education* in Louisiana, including the issuance of numerous injunctions against the state legislature's obstructive efforts, Senator Russell Long prevented his elevation from federal district judge to the Court of Appeals for the Fifth Circuit. He was then appointed to the Court of Appeals for the District of Columbia Circuit where he held de facto segregation in Washington, D.C. schools to be unconstitutional. In Louisiana and Washington, he rendered numerous decisions protecting voting rights.

Selected Bibliography Liva Baker, *The Second Battle of New Orleans: The Hundred-Year Struggle to Integrate the Schools* (1996); Jack Bass, *Unlikely Heroes* (1981); Michael S. Bernick, "The Unusual Odyssey of J. Skelly Wright," *Hastings Constitutional Law Quarterly* 7 (1980), 971–99; Arthur Selwyn Miller, *A "Capacity for Outrage": The Judicial Odyssey of J. Skelly Wright* (1984); J. W. Peltason, *Fifty-eight Lonely Men: Southern Federal Judges and School Desegregation* (1961); Geoffrey R. Stone, "A Passion for Justice," *Yale Law Journal* 98 (1988), 207–19; J. Skelly Wright, "The Judicial Right and the Rhetoric of Restraint: A Defense of Judicial Activism in an Age of Conservative Judges," *Hastings Constitutional Law Quarterly* 14 (1987), 487–523.

Patricia A. Behlar

Wright, Richard (4 September 1908, Roxie, Miss.–28 November 1960, Paris, France). From his birth on a Mississippi plantation to his death in Paris, Richard Wright was a man plagued by hunger for the acceptance and recognition of one's humanity that a racist society seeks desperately to deny. After a deprived childhood that included minimal formal education, Wright migrated to Chicago in 1927. In the Depression years he worked at various odd jobs until he found employment with the Federal Theater Project and the Federal Writers Project. He also became a member of the John Reed Club, which promoted the publication of his proletarian poetry in such magazines as *Left Front,* *The Anvil,* and *New Masses.* His association with left-wing literary circles led him to become a member of the **Communist Party,** but Wright was too independent to adhere to the party's regimentation, and he broke with it in 1942. Wright's experiment with Marxism, however, did sharpen his perspective on how to write about racial discrimination and class problems. In 1937 he moved

Richard Wright, 1951. © Library of Congress.

to New York to work as a journalist with the Harlem bureau of the *Daily Worker*. In 1938, he won the *Story Magazine* prize for "Fire and Cloud" and published **Uncle Tom's Children,** a collection of stories about racial tensions and black resistance in the rural South. The success of his first book enabled Wright to write **Native Son** (1940), a portrait of the life of a black youth in the Chicago ghettoes, for which he was awarded the **Spingarn Medal** in 1941. He followed this overwhelmingly successful novel with *Twelve Million Black Voices* (1941), a folk history, and **Black Boy,** the autobiography that made him the spokesman for an entire generation of black Americans. With a passion matched only in the classic slave narratives, Wright sought to alert the world to the deepest feelings of people shaped and mangled by racist oppression. Ironically, American racism was more than Wright could endure, and he chose to exile himself to France in 1947. In the 1950s, Wright was often criticized for having lost any perspective on the development of civil rights in the United States, especially in *The Long Dream* (1958), the last book published before his death. Nevertheless, one could argue that Wright developed a broader view of the struggle for human rights in the work produced during his European exile. In *The Outsider* (1953), *Black Power* (1954), *The Color Curtain* (1956), *Pagan Spain* (1957) and the essays in *White Man, Listen!* (1957), Wright projects a prophetic vision of the global issues that eventually changed the nature of civil rights activities in the United States. His hometown of

Natchez, Mississippi, began giving a literary award in his name in the late 1990s.

Selected Bibliography Margaret Walker Alexander, "Natchez and Richard Wright in Southern American Literature," *Southern Quarterly* 29 (No.4, 1991), 171–75; Russell C. Brignano, *Richard Wright: An Introduction to the Man and His Works* (1970); Michel Fabre, *The Unfinished Quest of Richard Wright* (1973); Addison Gayle, *Richard Wright: Ordeal of a Native Son* (1980); Yoshinobu Hakutani, ed., *Critical Essays on Richard Wright* (1982); Yoshinobu Hakutani, *Richard Wright and Racial Discourse* (1996); Keneth Kinnamom, *The Emergence of Richard Wright* (1972); Hazel Rowley, "Framing Richard Wright," *Yale University Library Gazette* 73 (Nos. 1–2, 1998), 56–63; Margaret Walker, *Richard Wright, Daemonic Genius: A Portrait of the Man, A Critical Look at His Works* (1988); Constance Webb, *Richard Wright: A Biography* (1968).

Jerry Ward

Wright, Richard Robert, Jr. (16 April 1878 Cuthbert, Ga.–12 December 1967 Philadelphia, Pa.). Wright conducted some very significant studies of black northern workers before World War I. His social scientific writings, especially *The Negro in Pennsylvania* (1912), were influenced by **W.E.B. Du Bois,** who actively guided his scholarly career. After studying theology and sociology at University of Chicago (B.D., 1901; A.M. 1904) he earned a doctorate in sociology from the University of Pennsylvania in 1911 but then turned away from full-time scholarship to a career as an editor and minister in the African Methodist Episcopal (A.M.E.) Church. A political moderate, Wright used his editorship of the African Methodist Episcopal (A.M.E.) Church's *Christian Recorder* (1909–28) to champion the **Great Migration** and to promote a more active role for the church in social reform, as well as an increased awareness of black history. A long time promoter of black businesses and property ownership, Wright was an officer of the Citizens and Southern Bank and Trust founded by his father in 1921. He was president of Wilberforce College (1932–36, 1941–42) and was elected 57th A.M.E. Bishop in 1936, serving in South Africa, the West Indies, and the United States.

Selected Bibliography Robert Gregg, *Sparks from the Anvil of Oppression: Philadelphia's African Methodists and Southern Migrants, 1890–1940* (1993); Francille R. Wilson, *The Segregated Scholars: Black Labor Historians, 1895–1950* (2002); R.R. Wright, Jr., *Eighty-seven Years Behind the Black Curtain* (1965); R. R. Wright, Jr., "The Negro in Times of Industrial Unrest," *Charities* 15 (7 October 1905), 69–73; Milton C. Sternett, *Bound for the Promised Land: African American Religion and the Great Migration* (1997).

Francille Rusan Wilson

Wright, Richard Robert, Sr. (16 May 1855? Dalton, Ga.–2 July 1947, Philadelphia, Pa.). Slave-born educator and businessman, Wright was a member of **Atlanta University**'s first graduating class. A popular symbol of the capabilities and courage of the freedmen, he was the boy in John Greenleaf Whittier's 1869 poem, "Howard at Atlanta," who called out "tell 'em we're rising," when General **O. O. Howard** requested a message from the black children in a boxcar schoolhouse to their friends in the North. Wright became the principal of Georgia's first black public high school (1880–90) and the president of Georgia State Industrial College for Negroes (1890–1921). A Republican party activist in the 1880s and 1890s, Wright was appointed as an army paymaster with the rank of major during the Spanish American War, but he was simultaneously forced out of state politics by segregationists. Wright thereafter publicly aligned himself and his college with **Booker T. Washington,** but as an alumni trustee, he cofounded the **Atlanta University Conference for the Study of Negro Problems** in 1895, and urged the hiring of **W.E.B. Du Bois.** In 1921 Wright and his family established Citizens and Southern Bank and Trust in Philadelphia, which was the third-largest bank in the United States by the end of his presidency of the National Negro Bankers Association (1926–42). He successfully lobbied for a postage stamp honoring Booker T. Washington (1940) and the establishment of 1 February, the day Lincoln signed the **Thirteenth Amendment** into law, as National Freedom Day (1948).

Selected Bibliography James D. Anderson, *The Education of Blacks in the South, 1860–1935* (1988); Elizabeth Ross Haynes, *Black Boy of Atlanta* (1952, 1997); Alexa Benson Henderson, "Richard R. Wright and the National Negro Bankers Association: Early Organizing Efforts Among Black Bankers, 1924–1942," *Pennsylvania Magazine of History and Biography* (January–April 1993), 51–81; June O. Patton, "Major Richard R. Wright" (Ph.D. diss., University of Chicago, 1980); Francille Rusan Wilson, "Introduction," to Elizabeth Ross Haynes, *Unsung Heroes*, "*Negroes in Domestic Service in the United States*," *The Black Boy of Atlanta* (1997); R. R. Wright, Sr., "Negro Companions of the Spanish Explorers," *American Anthropologist* (1902).

Francille Rusan Wilson

Y

Young, Andrew (12 March 1932, New Orleans, La.–). A dynamic clergy-man and civil rights leader with an outstanding record as a public official, Andrew Young attended Dillard University, in New Orleans, Louisiana, before he earned a B.S. degree at **Howard University** in 1951 and a B.D. degree from Hartford Theological Seminary in 1955. Active in interracial and civil rights projects since his seminary days, Young joined the staff of the **Southern Christian Leadership Conference** (SCLC) in 1961. A skillful strategist and negotiator, Young soon gained prominence as one of **Martin Luther King, Jr.**'s lieutenants. From 1964 to 1970 Young served as the executive director of SCLC and between 1967 and 1970 as the organization's executive vice president as well. He now sits on its board of directors and on the board of the Martin Luther King, Jr., Center for Social Change. In 1972 Andrew Young became the first African American from Georgia to be elected to the United States House of Representatives since Reconstruction. In 1977 President Jimmy Carter appointed him the first black United States ambassador to the United Nations. Between 1982 and 1990 he served as mayor of Atlanta, but, in 1990, Young lost his bid to become Georgia's first African American governor. In 1994, President Bill Clinton appointed him chair of the Southern Africa Enterprise Development Fund. He played a major role in Atlanta's successful bid to host the 1996 Olympics. In the early twenty-first century, he remained a major national and international leader while continuing to serve as one of the pastors of the First Congregational Church in Atlanta. In 2000–2001 he served as president of the National Council of Churches. In 2003 he was board chair of that year's Leon Howard Sullivan Summit in Nigeria.

Andrew Young (center) with President Jimmy Carter and Rosalynn Carter, Martin Luther King, Sr. and Coretta Scott King at Atlanta's Ebenezer Baptist Church, January 14, 1979. © Jimmy Carter Library.

Selected Bibliography Hamilton Bims, "A Southern Activist Goes to the House: King Lieutenant Andrew Young Is Declared Winner in Georgia," *Ebony* 28 (February 1973), 83; David J. Garrow, *Bearing the Cross: Martin Luther King, Jr., and the Southern Leadership Conference* (1986); W. Augustus Low and Virgil A Clift, eds., *Encyclopedia of Black America* (1981); Stephen B. Oates, *Let the Trumpet Sound: The Life of Martin Luther King, Jr.* (1982); Eleanora W. Schoenebaum, ed., *Political Profiles*, vol. 5 (1979); Andrew Young, *A Way Out of No Way: The Spiritual Memories of Andrew Young* (1994); Andrew Young, *An Easy Burden: The Civil Rights Movement and the Transformation of America* (1996); New York *Amsterdam News*, 9 July 2003.

Barbara L. Green

Young, Charles (12 March 1864, Mays Lick, Ky.–8 January 1922, Lagos, Nigeria). An army officer and cartographer, Charles Young was the third African American graduate (1884–89) from the United States Military Academy at West Point. His military career included duty in Haiti, Mexico, the Philippines, and Liberia. In 1916 Young received the **NAACP**'s annual **Spingarn Medal** for his exceptional work in Liberia. In 1917 the army medical board found him unfit for service because of high blood pressure and retired him with the rank of colonel. He rode horseback from Columbus, Ohio to Washington, D.C. to disprove this contention. On 6 November 1918, the army returned him to active duty and shortly thereafter sent him to Liberia. On 8 January 1922, Young died of nephritis in Lagos, Nigeria. He is buried in Arlington National Cemetery.

Selected Bibliography Abraham Chew, *A Biography of Colonel Charles Young* (1923); Robert E. Greene *Black Defenders of America, 1775–1973* (1974) in Rayford W. Logan and Michael R. Winston, eds., *Dictionary of American Negro Biography* (1982).

Barbara L. Green

Young, P(lummer) B(ernard) (27 July 1884, Littleton, N.C.–9 October 1962, Norfolk, Va.). Editor and publisher of the largest black newspaper in the South during the first half of the twentieth century, a member of the **Fair Employment Practice Committee,** and a black higher education leader, P. B. Young attended St. Augustine College, in Raleigh, North Carolina, from 1900 to 1906. In 1907 he moved to Norfolk, Virginia, to become a foreman for the **Norfolk Journal and Guide,** the newspaper of the Knights of Gideon. He soon became a part of the city's black elite, and he established a relationship with **Booker T. Washington.** In 1910 he bought the *Journal and Guide* from the Gideons. Despite a disastrous fire in 1913, the newspaper grew in circulation and influence. It reflected Booker T. Washington's accommodationist philosophy, which was expressed in Young's slogan, "Build Up, Don't Tear Down." He maintained his conservative approach to race relations all his life. Before and after the **Brown v. Board of Education** decision in 1954 he supported the "equal" in **separate but equal** when he spoke to whites and talked of integration to blacks. Politically, he changed from being a fervent Republican to a New Deal Democrat. He was the epitome of the black bourgeoisie, a pillar of the African American press, and a key spokesman to white society for Norfolk blacks.

Selected Bibliography Rayford W. Logan and Michael R. Winston, eds., *Dictionary of American Negro Biography* (1982); Henry Lewis Suggs, "Black Strategy and Ideology in the Segregation Era: P. B. Young and the *Norfolk Journal and Guide*, 1910–1954," *Virginia Magazine of History and Biography* 91 (April 1983), 161–90; Henry Lewis Suggs, *P. B. Young Newspaperman: Race, Politics, and Journalism in the New South* (1988); Henry Lewis Suggs, "P. B. Young of the *Norfolk Journal and Guide*: A Booker T. Washington Militant, 1904–1928," *Journal of Negro History* 64 (Fall 1979), 365–76.

John F. Marszalek

Young, Whitney Moore, Jr. (31 July 1921, Lincoln Ridge, Ky.–11 March 1971, Lagos, Nigeria). Often called the nation's most creative civil rights leader, Whitney Young led the **National Urban League** during the height of the civil rights movement. After completing high school at Lincoln Institute, Young attended Kentucky State College and taught briefly before joining the U.S. Army during World War II. He spent 1942–43 studying engineering at Massachusetts Institute of Technology. His experiences of working with people in the military caused him to decide on a career in the field of race relations. He earned a master's degree from the University of Minnesota in 1947 and spent the next seven years with the Urban League branch offices in Saint Paul, Minnesota, and Omaha, Nebraska. Then, in 1954, he accepted the deanship of the **Atlanta University** School of Social Work. Under his leadership, Atlanta became one of the leading schools of social work in the South. He interrupted his work there in 1960 to accept a Rockefeller grant to study at Harvard. The following year he succeeded **Lester B. Granger** as executive director of the National Urban League. During the militant protests of the 1960s, when faced with a choice, business executives preferred to talk to Young rather than to those black leaders they considered more militant. Young took advantage of these opportunities to open jobs for black workers and to build financial support for his organization, By the mid-1960s, the National Urban League's budget had increased from $270,000 to $3 million, and the number of branches had risen from 62 to 82. Young realized that this was not enough. In 1963 he proposed that the nation undertake a domestic Marshall Plan to help black Americans catch up. He presented a full discussion of his plan in *To Be Equal*. President Lyndon B. Johnson's **War on Poverty** owed much to Young's proposal. Young was aware that he and his organization must not lose credibility among black Americans. He insisted that the Urban League participate in the **March on Washington** in 1963 and in the other major civil rights events. Although he was reluctant to bring his organization into the **Meredith March** in 1966, he did participate in its final phase. He, along with **Roy Wilkins** of the **NAACP** and **Martin Luther King, Jr.,** was slow to embrace the new **Black Power** philosophy. When he realized that aspects of this philosophy reflected the mood of black Americans, he came to see its positive possibilities. In his book *Beyond Racism: Building an Open Society*, he explained how black power could move the nation toward a more democratic society. Young's brilliant career as a civil rights leader was cut short when he died on 11 March 1971 while attending a conference of American and African leaders in Lagos, Nigeria.

Selected Bibliography L. E. Lomax, *Negro Revolt* (1963); George R. Metcalf, *Black Profiles* (1968); Guichard Parris and Lester Brooks, *Blacks in the City: A History of the National Black Urban League* (1971); Edgar A Toppin, *A Biographical History of Blacks in America since 1528* (1971); *Who Was Who in America* (1973); Nancy J. Weiss, *Whitney M. Young, Jr., and the Struggle for Civil Rights* (1989).

Arvarh E. Strickland

Younge, Samuel, Jr. (17 November 1944, Tuskegee, Ala.–3 January 1966, Tuskegee, Ala.). This 21-year-old **Tuskegee Institute** student and civil rights activist spent 3 January 1966 (the day of his death) working as a voter registration volunteer at the Macon County, Alabama, courthouse. That night he stopped at a service station in town to buy some cigarettes and use the restroom. When attendant Marvin Segrest directed him to a rear restroom, which Younge believed was a **Jim Crow** facility, an argument ensued. Younge armed himself with a golf club and Segrest picked up his pistol. Segrest fatally shot Younge as the latter ran away from him. The death of the fifth civil rights worker in Alabama since the beginning of the voter registration campaign just a year earlier sparked immediate protest. Tuskegee blacks marched through the rain to the site of Younge's murder. Segrest was arrested, and Mayor Charles Kever promised justice would be done "regardless of race." These words seemed empty when an all-white jury in nearby Lee County determined that Segrest had acted in self-defense and acquitted him.

Selected Bibliography James Forman. *Sammy Younge, Jr.: The First Black College Student to Die in the Black Liberation Movement* (1968); *Montgomery Advertiser*, 5–6 January 1966; Robert J. Norell, *Reaping the Whirlwind: The Civil Rights Movement in Tuskegee* (1985); *Tuskegee News*, 6 January 1966.

William Warren Rogers, Jr.

Z

Zinn, Howard (24 August 1922, New York, N.Y.–). Historian and social activist, Zinn attended New York University (B.A. 1951) and Columbia University (M.A. 1952; Ph.D. 1958) on the GI Bill. Prior to Zinn completing his graduate work, the president of Spelman College offered him the chairmanship of the department of history and social science. While at Spelman (1956–63) he joined his students in protesting racial segregation. Zinn's first published article, "A Fate Worse than Integration," appeared in *Harper's Magazine* in 1959. For recognition of his involvement in the civil rights struggle, Zinn was invited to join the executive board of the **Student Nonviolent Coordinating Committee** (SNCC) as one of its two "adult advisors." The other invitee was **Ella Baker.** By his own account, Zinn became an "observer-participant" in civil rights demonstrations across the South, and played a part in events in Atlanta and Albany, Georgia; Selma, Alabama; and Hattiesburg, Mississippi. The author of more than a dozen books (including the best-selling *A People's History of the United States*), Zinn wrote *SNCC: The New Abolitionists* (1964), a history of that organization, and the *Southern Mystique* (1964) a study of black-white relations in the South. In 1994 he wrote a play about anarchist Emma Goldman entitled *Emma.* Since 1988 Zinn has been professor emeritus of political science at Boston University. In the early twenty-first century, he continued to be active in radical politics.

Selected Bibliography Howard Zinn, *Declaration of Independence: Cross Examining American Ideology* (1990); Howard Zinn, *SNCC: The New Abolitionists* (1964); Howard Zinn, *The Howard Zinn Reader* (1997); Howard Zinn, *The Southern Mystique* (1964); Howard Zinn, *You Can't Be Neutral on a Moving Train* (1994).

Eric Love

CHRONOLOGY

Compiled and Arranged by Anthony J. Iacono

1859   First American Missionary Association (AMA) school for blacks established at Fortress Monroe, Virginia. The AMA was created as a result of the *Amistad* case, which sought to provide freedom for a group of slaves who took over a Spanish slave ship on the open seas and were captured by a U.S. naval vessel.

1859   John Greg Fee founded Berea College in Kentucky. Berea, although closed soon after opening in the wake of John Brown's raid at Harper's Ferry, became a model for future AMA schools. The success of AMA schools could be seen by 1870, when nearly half of the black teachers in the South were graduates of AMA schools.

1861   First Confiscation Act, a forerunner of the Emancipation Proclamation, empowered the federal government to free slaves used by the South during the war. It was one of many attempts by Congress to use political and economic, instead of military, means to quell the rebellion.

1862   Second Confiscation Act passed. More comprehensive than its predecessor, the Second Confiscation Act gave secessionist Southerners 60 days to end their hostilities against the federal government. Following the initial 60-day period, the federal government was authorized to confiscate slaves and other property. The act also gave President Lincoln the right to enlist free slaves into the Union army and navy.

     The National Freedmen's Relief Association, inspired by the American Missionary Association, was established by abolitionists in New York City with the purpose of educating freed slaves on the South Carolina Sea Islands. In 1863, the National Freedmen's Relief Association joined with other like-minded organizations to help create the Freedmen's Bureau.

1863   The Emancipation Proclamation expanded upon earlier confiscation acts by declaring that the federal government would confiscate slaves in states still in rebellion by 1 January 1863. The proclamation was an economic and political attempt to end the rebellion. It originated, in part, because of immense pressure placed upon Lincoln by Radical Republicans who sought to elevate the war to a moral cause. In spite of its wording, the Emancipation Proclamation did not lead to an instant end of slavery. Freedom usually depended upon arrival of the Union army or owner abandonment. The Thirteenth Amendment formally abolished slavery in the United States in 1865.

New York City Draft Riots occurred as a result of the Federal Enrollment Act. Protesting their forced entry into the Union military, some fifty thousand people rioted at the New York draft office. Rioting mobs set fire to the office, a black orphanage, and other structures. Anger was also directed toward black New Yorkers, who were beaten, robbed, and murdered. Recently arrived troops from Gettysburg were used to end the riot but not before 1,000 people were injured or killed in what is considered the worst race riot in American history.

1864 National Equal Rights League formed under the direction of John Mercer Langston, the organization's first president, to advance black Americans' civil rights. A second league was formed in the early 1900s under the direction of William Monroe Trotter. Although it was initially an integrationist organization, Trotter, in the 1920s, tried to connect the league to Marcus Garvey's segregationist movement. The league disbanded before Trotter could attain his goal.

President Lincoln pocket vetoed the Wade-Davis Bill. The bill sought to punish the South for its role in the Civil War. In response to its passage, Lincoln vetoed the bill in the interest of more moderate Reconstruction policies.

1865 Thirteenth Amendment outlawing slavery ratified. The amendment formally ended slavery in the United States and can be viewed as the completion of a series of legislative measures aimed at emancipation, including the 1861 and 1862 Confiscation Acts and Lincoln's Emancipation Proclamation.

Black Codes passed to restrict freedmen. Passed by southern states during Presidential Reconstruction, the Black Codes were laws that restricted the amount of freedom and mobility freedmen could enjoy. Enforced until the 1950s, the codes often conflicted with the Fourteenth and Fifteenth Amendments by not allowing black Americans to enjoy their constitutional rights, including serving on juries, testifying against white men, voting under the same conditions as white males, refusing forced labor conditions, and more.

Freedmen's Bank chartered by Congress. Located in every southern state, New York, and Philadelphia, the Freedmen's Bank was established to provide economic security for its black customers, who confidently deposited a total of 56 million dollars. The bank failed in 1874 as a result of national economic conditions and the financial mismanagement of its officers.

Congress created the Freedmen's Bureau. Formally established as the Bureau of Refugees, Freedmen, and Abandoned Lands, the bureau, headed by army officer General Oliver Otis Howard, initially helped more whites than blacks until Congress instructed its officers to devote more attention to the freedmen. The bureau provided shelter, food, and medical attention to those who qualified. Created with tremendous enthusiasm, it lost its effectiveness after 1868 when public support for black equality waned.

Black Conventions meet in the interest of promoting more African American participation in society. Voting, legal rights, and schools were the main issues at such conventions. The popularity of these meetings remained high throughout much of the Reconstruction years, when black Americans actively participated in nearly all levels of government.

President Andrew Johnson announced restoration of the Union on 10 May. Johnson made the announcement when all but a few Confederate units had surrendered.

Congressional Joint Committee of Fifteen was created to examine the reconstruction issue. The committee examined and rejected President Johnson's reconstruction announcement. In turn, the committee refused to recognize congressmen and senators elected by the former Confederates states. Without southern representation, Congress passed the Thirteenth Amendment.

1866   Civil Rights Act of 1866 passed by Congress. The 1866 Civil Rights Act states that, with the exception of Native Americans not taxed, all persons born in the United States are citizens regardless of race, color, or other conditions. Anyone who denied these rights to others, in particular, to former slaves, would be charged with a misdemeanor punishable by fine or imprisonment.

Congress passed the Fourteenth Amendment, granting citizenship to freedmen. Although this amendment was not ratified until 1868, it built on the Civil Rights Act of 1866 by focusing specifically on the freedmen. The Fourteenth Amendment also repudiated the Confederate war debt, guaranteed the federal war debt, and banned high-ranking Confederate officials from holding political office.

Fisk University founded in Nashville, Tennessee, by the American Missionary Association. The university, plagued with financial and racial setbacks, established itself as a first-rate educational institution when it became the first black school to earn an A rating from the Southern Association of Colleges and Secondary Schools.

Memphis race riot occured between 1–4 May. The riot was the result of tension between Irish police and black federal soldiers. During the three days of rioting, 48 people died, dozens more were injured, and more than 100 structures were destroyed. A congressional committee concluded that a corrupt local government caused the riot.

Southern Homestead Act passed by Congress as an extension of the 1862 Homestead Act. The law was created to help freedmen make the transition to independent farming by opening lands in five Confederate states, including Alabama, Arkansas, Florida, Louisiana, and Mississippi. Much of 46 million acres provided by the federal government consisted of swamps and was thus unusable. Poor-quality land and corrupt local governments caused the Southern Homestead Act to fail.

First Reconstruction Act stated that although the Fourteenth Amendment restricted former high-ranking Confederate officials from participating in politics, including the ratification of new state constitutions, they could reenter the political arena after the ratification process had been completed.

President Johnson vetoed the bill on 2 March 1866, but the House and Senate overrode the veto.

Atlanta University established by American Missionary Association with assistance from the Freedmen's Bureau. Atlanta University is one of the oldest African American universities in the nation. The school's initial success, seen as early as the 1870s, was producing teachers for black schools throughout the South. In the late 1920s, Atlanta University began offering graduate degrees in various disciplines, at the same time merging with Morehouse and Spelman colleges to create the Atlanta University System. In 1988, after a merger with Clark University, it became Clark Atlanta University.

Howard University established by Radical Republicans and former Union officers who sought to advance the freedmen through educational opportunities. Although then considered a "Negro College," more than one-third of its student body was white. One of the leaders in the founding of Howard University, and its namesake, was Oliver Otis Howard, a Union general and commissioner of the Freedmen's Bureau. Howard served as the school's third president and then served as a trustee for more than 30 years after his presidency.

Morehouse College established as the Augusta Institute. Relocated to Atlanta in 1879, it became known as the Atlanta Baptist Seminary and later the Atlanta Baptist College. In 1913, its name was again changed, this time to Morehouse College, after the secretary of the American Baptist Home Mission Society. Morehouse is best known for its black leaders such as John Hope and its alumni including Dr. Martin Luther King, Jr. Today, it is affiliated with Clark Atlanta University.

Peabody Education Fund established by George Peabody, a banker and merchant. Peabody was a philanthropist who desired to help disadvantaged young black and white Americans in the southern and southwestern states. The fund provided more than $3.5 million, primarily for the building of schools.

1869   W.E.B. Du Bois born in Great Barrington, Massachusetts. Du Bois, one of the few black Americans who held a graduate degree in this period, received a Ph.D. from Harvard in 1895 and dedicated his life to scholarship and civil rights. Unlike Booker T. Washington, Du Bois advocated immediate equal rights for black Americans. Du Bois was a founder of the NAACP, an editor of its political magazine *Crisis*, a professor at Atlanta University, and the author of six books. Late in life, Du Bois advocated voluntary segregation, became a member of the American Communist Party, and eventually denounced his American citizenship.

Hampton Institute admitted its first students. Founded by Union General Samuel C. Armstrong and the American Missionary Association, it sought to provide greater freedom to freedmen by teaching black students how to teach other freedmen. This concept, known as the "Hampton Idea," was popular and was adopted by Booker T. Washington's Tuskegee Institute.

1869   Congress passed the Fifteenth Amendment, granting black males the right to vote. Black political participation led to a rise in black office holders. White southerners effectively nullified the Fifteenth Amendment by passing state and local laws, intimidating black voters, and committing violent acts against black Republicans. The 1965 Voting Rights Act, passed under President Lyndon Johnson, proved far more successful in enfranchising black voters.

Tougaloo College founded in Mississippi by the American Missionary Association. The college is one of America's oldest private black colleges. Located outside of the state capital of Jackson, Tougaloo gained an excellent reputation for its education and business programs. It was active during the civil rights movement of the 1960s.

1870   Enforcement Acts passed to protect freedmen in exercising Fourteenth and Fifteenth Amendment rights. To deal more effectively with racial crimes and to disband the Ku Klux Klan, Congress passed a series of laws stating specific punishments for crimes committed against those trying to exercise their rights as stated in the Fourteenth and Fifteenth Amendments. The laws had mixed success. When the accused was convicted, the sentencing was generally mild. The Enforcement Acts did little to improve voting conditions in the South.

Great Migration of blacks from rural South to urban North begins. Between 1870–90, 80,000 black Southerners relocated to the urban North in search of better jobs and living conditions. During the World War I–era another 500,000 black southerners moved into northern cities. An additional 750,000 black southerners made the North their home in the decade following the war. The impact of the migrations was profound. Prior to 1870, nine-tenths of all African Americans lived in the rural South. Following the migrations, three-fourths lived in urban areas outside of the South.

Hiram R. Revels elected to United States Senate from Mississippi. Revels, a freeborn black Mississippian, was elected to fill Jefferson Davis's unexpired seat in the U.S. Senate. Revels was the first African American to hold a seat in the Senate. In the age of Radical Reconstruction, Revels was a moderate who called for amnesty for ex-Confederates and fairness for black Americans as they were assimilated into American society after remaining loyal to the federal government during the Civil War.

1871   Fisk University's Jubilee Singers conducted fund-raising tour. In 1871, Fisk had accumulated a debt in excess of $2,000 with no foreseeable way to pay it. To prevent the closure of Fisk, George L. White, the school's treasurer and music teacher, organized his best students and went on a fund-raising tour of the North. The Jubilee Singers raised more than $20,000 while on tour. They paid the school debt and had enough money left to buy Fort Gillem, where the university in now located.

1873   Supreme Court's *Slaughterhouse Cases* ruling limited the scope of the Fourteenth Amendment. In spite of Congress's efforts to provide civil rights for African Americans, the Supreme Court's interpretation of the Thirteenth and Fourteenth Amendments slowed the progress of equality when deciding that the amendments had only procedural meaning. The *Slaughterhouse Cases* came to the attention of the Court when the state of Louisiana gave a 25-year monopoly on cattle slaughtering to one local company.

1874   New Orleans race riot occurred when Louisiana Governor James Madison Wells organized a convention on black suffrage. The city's mayor responded by organizing a protest in which New Orleans police and white citizens attacked the black and white Republican convention delegates, killing 35 while losing one of their own. Federal troops were eventually used to end the rioting.

1875   Congress passed the Civil Rights Act of 1875. The bill was first introduced in 1870 by Massachusetts Senator Charles Sumner, who died in 1874, before the bill passed. The Fourteenth Amendment restricted discrimination imposed by the states but lacked jurisdiction over cases of private discrimination. The Civil Rights Act of 1875 sought to desegregate all public facilities, including theaters, schools, hospitals, and railroad cars. Advocates of the act argued that these were not private enterprises because they were licensed public services. Although the Supreme Court voided the act, it established a basis for civil rights legislation since 1964.

1876   Hamburg, South Carolina, race riot occurred. One of the last significant riots of the Reconstruction era, the Hamburg, South Carolina, race riot began when "Doc" Adams, commander to the town's Negro militia company, refused to allow a carriage carrying local white residents use of the main street. Adams, upon request, refused to apologize for his actions and did not appear in court as scheduled three days after the incident. His refusal to apologize and appear before a judge led General Butler, attorney for the those who filed the suit, to demand that the Negro militia surrender its weapons. When black militiamen, taking refuge in their armory, refused and opened fire on a white mob, they were forced from the armory and executed by white vigilantes. South Carolina's governor never brought the murderers to justice but instead called in federal troops to restore order.

1877   Compromise of 1877 led to the end of Reconstruction. The election of 1876 was the third time in American history that the U.S. Congress was forced to select a president. After creating a committee made up of select members of the House, Senate, and Supreme Court, Congress proclaimed Republican candidate Rutherford B. Hayes of Ohio president over Democrat, and southern favorite, Samuel J. Tilden of New York. Fearing the South might again attempt to secede, a behind-the-scenes compromise was effected to solidify the agreement. The major parts of the compromise include removal of federal troops from the South, the appointment of a southerner to a presidential cabinet position, and financial support in the construction of southern railroads. With the removal of federal troops from the South, black southerners were left unprotected. It is generally agreed that the act effectively ended Reconstruction and the progress of the civil rights struggle.

1878   Chicago's first black newspaper, the *Chicago Conservator*, established by Ferdinand L. Barnett. The paper reflected the views and values of the city's black professionals while emphasizing self-improvement. The focus of the *Chicago Conservator* changed after 1900, when it shifted to the struggle between Booker T. Washington and his black critics in Chicago.

1879   Exodus of southern blacks to Kansas and the Southwest began for reasons similar to those that led to the Great Migration in 1870.

1882   Slater Fund established to aid education for blacks. John Fox Slater, a Connecticut industrialist, sought to help black southerners improve themselves through education. Initially, the Slater funds were granted primarily to black colleges such as Tuskegee and Hampton Institute, but after 1911 local teacher-training schools also became recipients. Whether given to black colleges or training schools, the Slater Fund increased the number of teachers for black elementary schools in the rural South.

1883   Supreme Court's Civil Rights Cases struck down the Civil Rights Act of 1875.

1886   Colored Farmers' National Alliance and Cooperative Union established. Created in 1886 in Houston County, Texas, the alliance sought to educate black farmers in agricultural sciences. The alliance also provided some communal support for black farming families such as the use of warehouses and cooperative buying. Essentially, the Colored National Alliance served black farming families in the same ways the white alliance served whites. The two alliance groups were also similar in that they were both led by white southerners. Suffering the paternalistic views and practices of their white organizational leaders, the Colored Farmers' Alliance disbanded in 1892 as a result of violence and racial discrimination.

T. Thomas Fortune founded *New York Age*. Fortune began life as a slave but in the post–Civil War years became one of the nation's premier black newspaper owners. He started his career as a printer and quickly became a highly skilled compositor. In 1879, he became part owner of the *Rumor*. He later became sole owner of the *New York Freeman*, which became known as the *New York Age* in 1887. Through his newspapers, Fortune became a recognized opponent of racial discrimination. In the 1920s Fortune became the editor of Marcus Garvey's *Negro World*.

1887   The all-black town of Mound Bayou founded in Mississippi by freemen Isaiah T. Montgomery and Benjamin T. Green. The town, praised by Booker T. Washington and patronized by philanthropists like Andrew Carnegie, was the most celebrated of any of the all-black towns in the United States. At its peak in the early twentieth century, the town featured a bank, a cottonseed oil mill, schools, a newspaper, a railroad depot, and communications services. It was created as a haven from Jim Crow discrimination. The town began failing in the early 1940s as a result of discrimination, the inability to compete in a modern economy, and the Great Migration.

1888   *Indianapolis Freeman* began publication. Edward Elder Cooper's newspaper distinguished itself from other black newspapers by being the first black illustrated publication in the United States. Unlike white publications that included stereotypical illustrations of black Americans, Cooper's newspaper depicted its subjects with reality and dignity. The paper relied on black journalists and covered such topics as history, literature, and politics.

Booker T. Washington opened doors of Tuskegee Institute. Created in 1881 after a political deal had been made between black and white politicians, it was originally known as Tuskegee Negro Normal Institute. The school, known simultaneously for its purpose and its first president, focused on both industrial skills and academic subjects and is important not only for its educational qualities but also for the high level of pride and accomplishment it instilled in its students. Robert Russa Morton became president of Tuskegee when his predecessor died in 1915. Under Washington,

Tuskegee distinguished itself as one of the finest and best-known black colleges in the nation.

1890 T. Thomas Fortune founded Afro-American League. Fortune, one of the nation's premier newspaper editor-owners, created the League to battle racial discrimination. This organization merged with the Afro-American Council in 1898.

Force Bill passed to protect black suffrage. Created by Massachusetts Republican Senator Henry Cabot Lodge, and formally known as the Federal Elections Bill, it proposed to enforce the Fifteenth Amendment militarily. Democrats, opposing the bill, called it the "Force Bill." The bill is important because it was the last federal attempt to protect voting rights for black Americans between Reconstruction and the Civil Rights Act of 1957. It is also significant in that it was the last African American civil rights legislation sponsored by the Republican party.

Lake Mohonk Conference held. Quaker Philanthropist Albert K. Smiley organized the conference to deal with the "Negro question." Inviting hundreds of men and women from around the nation, Smiley did not include any blacks, as he feared it would discourage white southerners from attending. Topics discussed included the impact and opportunity of religion, industrialism, family relations, and public education upon black Americans.

Second Morrill Act passed, creating black land-grant colleges. The Second Morrill Act, also known as the Morrill-McComas Act, increased the amount of funding provided by the First Morrill Act. The second act sought to ensure more educational opportunity for black students, but because of the wording used in the document, it actually restricted black students from being admitted to colleges throughout the South.

New Mississippi state constitution became a model for other southern states. In 1890, the Democratic party began "redeeming" the South when it excluded black Mississippians from voting by requiring the payment of poll taxes and literacy tests. Following the passage of the 1890 constitution, seven other southern states followed suit by writing similar discriminatory state constitutions.

1891 Second Mohonk Conference meets.

1894 Hampton Conference met to discuss the future of black Americans. The conference gave notoriety to Booker T. Washington and inspired W. E. B. Du Bois. It also led to the Atlanta University Conference which further examined the plight of black Americans.

1895 Booker T. Washington delivered Atlanta Compromise Speech. Washington, openly accepting segregation, proclaimed in Atlanta that "in all things that are purely social we can be as separate as the fingers, yet one as the hand in all things essential to mutual progress." White Southerners appreciated his views, but soon after the address he gained many black critics, including W.E.B. Du Bois, who called his speech the "Atlanta Compromise." Critics argued that Washington's views were regressive and even destructive to the progress made in civil rights. Washington argued that economic freedom would bring greater equality in due time.

Frederick Douglass died. Born into slavery but escaping to the North at the age of 20, Douglas became an abolitionist and speaker for the Massachusetts Anti-Slavery Society. In the post–Civil War years, Douglass became a leading civil rights advocate, pushing political figures, including President Andrew Johnson, to extend greater equality and rights to freedmen. Later in life he served the United States as minister-resident and consul-general to the Republic of Haiti and chargé d'affaires of the Dominican Republic.

1896   Supreme Court's *Plessy v. Ferguson* decision enunciated separate-but-equal doctrine. The Supreme Court, in this landmark case, ruled that "separate but equal" was acceptable. The case began when Homer A. Plessy, a black American, refused to surrender his seat on a Louisiana train. The *Plessy* decision effectively sanctioned Jim Crow and made segregation the law of the land until the 1954 Supreme Court case of *Brown v. the Board of Education* overturned the decision.

W.E.B. Du Bois establishes the Atlanta University Conference for the Study of Negro Problems. Although the conference was initiated by R. R. Wright, Sr., Du Bois made the conference an annual event and used comprehensive studies to understand black life in America and the dilemmas unknown to white Americans. Du Bois used the conference and its studies to foster social reform for black Americans.

Kowaliga Industrial Community began. William Benson founded the community to stop black migration to the North. His community, intended to promote black self-sufficiency, boasted a saw mill, a shingle mill, a turpentine plant, a plantation store, and a school that operated on the principles advocated by Booker T. Washington.

National Association of Colored Women founded. Created to demonstrate the importance of black women's efforts to improve the lives of black Americans, NACW was a powerful organization that owed much of its strength to the more than 100 similar organizations that it had merged with, including the National League of Colored Women and the National Federation of Afro-American Women.

1897   T. Thomas Fortune founded the Afro-American Council. With the help of African Methodist Episcopal Bishop Alexander Walters, Fortune revitalized the Afro-American League, which had ceased to exist by 1893. The council proved less belligerent than its predecessor due to the influence of leaders such as Booker T. Washington. W.E.B. Du Bois's aggressive Niagara Movement, however, limited the influence of the council. By 1908, the Afro-American Council ceased to exist.

Alexander Crummel founded American Negro Academy, which was the first major African American intellectual organization. It consisted of the black elite and focused on scholarly work concerning African American culture, history, and accomplishments.

1898   Grandfather clause written into new Louisiana constitution restricted black suffrage. Following Reconstruction, southern Democrats actively worked to restrict black southerners from voting. The grandfather clause formalized the restrictions on black voters yet made it possible for poor whites to continue voting. By grandfathering in whites, they did not have to take literacy tests or adhere to other restrictions placed on black voters.

Blacks fought in the Spanish American War. Demonstrating their patriotism and continuing their quest for equality and acceptance, African American men, including the 9th and 10th Cavalry units—better known as the Buffalo Soldiers—volunteered to serve the U.S. military once again. The war did little to advance the rights of black Americans or even to change the way society as a whole viewed them. Black soldiers who fought at the Battle of San Juan Hill were given no recognition, but instead their participation in the famed battle was clouded by the more popular story that contributed to making Theodore Roosevelt one of America's great heroes.

1899   Capon Springs Conference promoted industrial education for southern blacks. Not unlike the Lake Mohonk and Hampton conferences, the Capon Springs Conference sought to provide more opportunities for black southerners while encouraging independence. Those who participated in the conference called for additional industrial education and the advancement of southern secondary schools.

Sam Hose lynching in Georgia. During a series of racial murders in Georgia, Sam Hose, a black American agricultural worker, was lynched for his self-defense killing of his employer and plantation owner Alfred Cranford. The lynchings drew protests from around the nation, but President William McKinley declared that lynching was a local and not federal issue.

1900   National Negro Business League formed by Booker T. Washington. The organization worked to create more economic independence for black Americans. The NNBL was supported by as many as 40,000 members who hailed from 36 states and West Africa. Significant financing for the group came from northern philanthropists such as Julius Rosenwald and Andrew Carnegie.

New Orleans race riot occurred. Following the Sam Hose lynching in Georgia, racial tensions around the South increased. In anger, Robert Charles, an African American man from New Orleans, engaged in a scuffle with a police officer. That initial confrontation resulted in Charles killing 9 whites, including 3 police officers, and wounding 20 others, some seriously. White mobs responded by lynching and beating local blacks and destroying the best school in the state. To end the rioting, Mayor Paul Capdeville called in the state militia.

Norfolk Journal and Guide began publication. Sharing the ideals of leaders such as Booker T. Washington, P. B. Young, the newspaper's owner and editor, created one of the most recognized black newspapers in the nation. Although the paper changed its name a number of times over the years, it remained conservative and is still in print today. It is currently entitled *New Journal and Guide*.

1901   The African American protest newspaper *Boston Guardian* established. As one of the leading protest newspapers of the period, its owners and editors William Monroe Trotter and George W. Forbes used the paper to demand full equality and to denounce more compromising civil rights leaders such as Booker T. Washington.

Southern Education Board founded to promote education. Created with a grant from George F. Peabody, the Southern Education Board favored a tax-supported southern school system in the belief that terminating ignorance would lead to improvements in race relations.

Booker T. Washington's *Up from Slavery* was published. This autobiographical account of one of America's best-known and most successful civil rights leaders tells the story of how hard work and perseverance elevated Washington from just another poor black sharecropper to an important American. It is generally viewed as a classic American success story.

Booker T. Washington dined with President Theodore Roosevelt at the White House. Already known as a civil rights leader through his Atlanta Compromise and as the builder of the Tuskegee Institute, Washington was one of the first black Americans invited by an American president to dine at the White House. The occasion brought swift and strong criticism from southern whites, but it did not hamper Roosevelt's success as a president or his ability to win reelection. Washington gained increased recognition from the dinner.

1902   John D. Rockefeller established the General Education Board to aid education for blacks. Rockefeller began the board with a $1 million gift. By the time the organization concluded its work in 1960, it had given some $325 million to improve education, with roughly 20 percent of that money specifically designated for the education of southern blacks.

1903   The all-black town of Boley, Oklahoma, founded. Formed through land grants of the Oklahoma territory, Boley was named for the president of the Fort Smith and Western Railroad, who encouraged its settlement. Boley represents the type of limited success that black Americans often experienced in the post-Reconstruction years. Black migrants created a town populated by more than 2,000 people, yet white Oklahomans, who controlled the election process, bypassed this well-populated town for county seat and then disenfranchised black Oklahomans. In time, the Great Migration caused many black residents to leave Boley in search of a better life in the industrial North.

1904   At a Carnegie Hall Meeting, W.E.B. Du Bois and Booker T. Washington parted ways. They had worked to create a unified civil rights movement that included a significant number of black intellectuals and were secretly funded by Andrew Carnegie. In spite of their efforts, a compromise could not be found when the organization became largely controlled by Washington. In opposition, Du Bois distinguished himself as the leader of the anti-Bookerites. The Carnegie Hall Meeting was the last time that Du Bois and Washington worked together.

1905   Anna T. Jeanes Fund established to improve educational opportunities for southern blacks. Philadelphia Quaker Anna T. Jeanes gave an initial gift of $200,000 to improve education for southern blacks. She later gave the majority of her estate to continue her mission of providing additional education, particularly in the industrial arts and the training of teachers.

Chicago Defender was launched. Started under humble conditions and with a limited readership, the *Defender* quickly became the nation's leading black newspaper, with more than 18,000 readers. The paper's owner, Robert S. Abbott, generated his success by combining exaggerated news stories, racial protest, and unique business practices. He employed both blacks and whites. It remains a major black newspaper today.

Niagara Movement launched by W.E.B. Du Bois and others. Following the Carnegie Meeting, where Du Bois and his supports found they could not compromise with the Washington camp, Du Bois created the militant Niagara Movement. Unlike Booker T. Washington's organizations, it did not favor compromise but instead called for immediate economic and educational equality and full civil rights, among other demands. It further advocated the duties of African Americans, including voting, working, and obeying the laws.

1906   Brownsville, Texas, affray occurred. President Roosevelt discharged 167 African American soldiers from the 25th Infantry after they were accused, without evidence, of wounding a policeman and murdering a citizen of Brownsville, Texas, where they were stationed. Booker T. Washington did not protest Theodore Roosevelt's decision. The event is a reminder of how little power black Americans had during America's Progressive Era.

1907   *Horizon*, journal of the Niagara Movement, began publication in an attempt to attract black Americans to the Niagara Movement. Owners W.E.B. Du Bois, Freeman Murray, and Lafayette M. Henshaw used the paper to advance their ideas on economics, politics, and civil rights.

1908   Springfield, Illinois, race riot broke out. Mounting racial tensions resulting from job competition between whites and a growing number of black immigrants from the South led to an outburst of violence in which two black men were lynched and many others injured. The riot served as a catalyst for the formation of the NAACP.

1909   New York weekly newspaper *Amsterdam News* began publication. Founded by James H. Anderson and bought by Philip Savory and Clelan B. Powell, the *Amsterdam News* is one of the nation's oldest black newspapers. Beginning in 1936, the focus of the paper shifted from a protest tone to one of accomplishment, reporting the success of African Americans. It remains an important and widely read newspaper today.

1910   NAACP formally established by W.E.B. Du Bois and others. Organizing in protest against Booker T. Washington's accommodation methods, Du Bois and other civil rights advocates, including Mary Ovington, a third-generation abolitionist, and Oswald Garrison Villard, grandson of William Lloyd Garrison, met on President Lincoln's birthday to discuss more aggressive methods of bringing forth full and uncompromising equality for African Americans. The National Association for the Advancement of Colored People relied on a three-pronged approach to complete their goals. They sought to use publicity, protest, and the courts to champion civil rights. Such methods produced success. The lynching rate dropped from 70 per year in 1910 to 4 per year in 1940. More widespread success was found through the creation of the NAACP Legal Defense and Educational Fund, which fought against all-white juries, segregation of public facilities, and other discriminatory practices. One of their more successful legal battles included blocking the

Supreme Court nominations of four would-be judges. Their participation in the 1963 March on Washington helped pass the 1964 Civil Rights Act. The NAACP remains a leading vehicle for civil rights today.

NAACP journal, the *Crisis*, launched. Using publicity to strike against civil inequities and bring equality to African Americans, the NAACP created the *Crisis*. NAACP organizer W.E.B. Du Bois served as its editor until 1934. The paper, still in publication, addresses all issues relevant to black Americans and their struggle to gain civil rights. The journal also includes articles on influential black Americans, cultural issues, and events.

1911 National Urban League founded by George E. Haynes and Eugene Kinkle Jones. The League sought to end discrimination in the workplace and in federal programs. The League also worked to end segregation in the military. In the radical 1960s, the League broadened its role in the civil rights movement to include helping redevelop black communities, increase the number of black high school graduates, and register black voters. For its many methods in improving civil rights, the National Urban League is considered the most diverse organization of its type.

Phelps-Stokes Fund established by Carolina Phelps-Stokes to promote education for Africans, African Americans, Native Americans, and poor whites. The fund also provided housing for women working in New York City. Its best-known accomplishment was the creation of the United Negro College Fund, which not only provides funding to educate African and Native Americans but also monitors court cases in which minorities are accused of committing crimes.

1915 Carter G. Woodson established the Association for the Study of Afro-American Life and History. The organization received significant financial support from several major philanthropic groups, including the Carnegie Corporation and the Rockefeller Foundation. To promote black history, the organization founded the *Journal of Negro History* and the *Negro History Bulletin*. They further promoted their cause by publishing black-history textbooks. The Association for the Study of Afro-American Life and History is still an active organization based in Silver Springs, Maryland.

1916 The *Journal of Negro History* founded by Carter G. Woodson. The *Journal* quickly became recognized as a publication for black scholars and one of the few history journals where they could publish without discrimination. It also published white authors who were considered too liberal for more mainstream journals. Both black and white authors used the journal to champion black rights and challenge racist ideas about black Americans and their place in society. The *Journal of Negro History* was successful in becoming the premier publication for such topics, but it also caused the historical profession at large to reconsider the way it studied slavery. Previous to the *Journal*, most historians focused on slavery from a slave owner's perspective, but after the *Journal*, the profession began to look at slavery from a slave's viewpoint.

1917 In the landmark *Buchanon v. Warley* decision, Supreme Court struck down residential segregation ordinance. In 1914, black Louisville, Kentuckian William Warley and white realtor Charles Buchanan tested local segregation ordinances when Buchanan sued Warley for breach of contract. Warley offered to purchase property in an all-white neighborhood contingent upon his ability to occupy the property. When he refused to pay realtor Charles Buchanan because he could not occupy the land, Buchanan sued. State courts upheld residential segregation laws, but when the NAACP joined the suit and the Supreme Court heard the case, the decision was overturned on the ground that residential segregation laws violate the Fourteenth Amendment. The case is considered a major success for the NAACP.

East St. Louis race riot and Houston race riot occurred. With some 39 blacks and 9 whites killed, the St. Louis race riot is considered the deadliest urban race riot in twentieth-century American history. The riot occurred as a result of increased tensions brought forth from the Great Migration and a poor job climate mixed with corruption, fear, and prejudice. In Houston, black soldiers returning from World War I responded violently to traditional mistreatment of black citizens, including assaults upon black soldiers and the arrest of a black woman. In anger and protest, the soldiers, after securing weapons and ammunition, marched on the city and incited a riot that lasted several hours and left 15 whites and 4 black soldiers dead. After the riot the U.S. Army began court-martial proceedings of all 118 black soldiers. Eighty-two of the men were found guilty. The riot brought the NAACP to Houston, where the organization established a chapter and began work on gaining pardons for the accused.

Marcus Garvey established a Universal Negro Improvement Association branch in the United States and launched "Back to Africa" movement. Born in Jamaica, Garvey moved to England in 1911, where African scholars convinced him to dedicate his life to spreading information about Africa and its people. In 1914, Garvey returned to Jamaica and organized the Universal Negro Improvement and Conservation Association and African Communities League. In 1916, Marcus Garvey came to the United States and embarked on a speaking tour that lasted a year and took him to 38 states. While in the United States, Garvey began publishing the *Negro World* to further spread his ideas. A black nationalist, Garvey attempted to convince African Americans to leave the country and make a new life for themselves in Africa. He viewed Liberia as an ideal relocation destination. Relatively few African Americans shared Garvey's vision. In 1925, Garvey was found guilty of mail fraud and sentenced to prison. President Coolidge interrupted Garvey's sentence at midpoint and deported him. Garvey temporarily returned to Jamaica but after some difficulties moved to England, where he spent the remainder of his life.

The radical black newspaper *The Messenger* began publication. Founded by A. Philip Randolph and Chandler Owen, the newspaper's owners referred to their publication as the "Only Radical Newspaper in America." Randolph and Owen denounced more established civil rights leaders such as W.E.B. Du Bois and others while endorsing women's suffrage, black labor unions, and even the Russian Revolution. More radical than most publications, the newspaper lasted only slightly more than a decade due to financial problems.

Julius Rosenwald Fund established to aid black education. Created by the president of the Sears, Roebuck and Company, the Julius Rosenwald Fund provided money for the building of schools, various educational programs, health services, and other causes related to bettering black Americans and fostering improvements between black and white Americans. The fund operated until 1948.

Blacks fought in World War I. W.E.B. Du Bois best expressed the reason that black Americans living in an age of Jim Crow eagerly sought to serve their nation by saying that " if this is our country, then this is our war." Even while striving to serve their country, black Americans faced discrimination. In general, the U.S. military considered blacks lacking in courage and skill to serve as soldiers. Nevertheless, black Americans did fight as the 92nd Division. Poorly trained, the 92nd Division performed less than effectively, but its willingness to serve demonstrated the commitment of black Americans to contribute to their nation. Upon returning to the United States after the war, black veterans found an America that did not value their efforts. World War I failed to bring any significant advancements in civil rights.

1918   The monthly magazine *The Crusader* was launched. Founded by Cyril Briggs, *The Crusader*, lasting only until 1922, featured articles from a wide array of black American writers, including socialists, businessmen, and entertainers. It served as a voice for militant black American views.

1919   Associated Negro Press established. Claude Barnett founded the press to serve black newspapers as the Associated Press served white newspapers. By 1919, nearly every black newspaper subscribed to the Associated Negro Press. With the declining popularity of black newspapers, the ANP went out of business in 1964.

During Red Summer, major race riots occurred in Charleston, South Carolina; Chicago, Illinois; Knoxville, Tennessee; Omaha, Nebraska; Washington, D.C.; and elsewhere. Because of the civil unrest that followed World War I, fears of Communist infiltration after the rise of Bolshevism in Russia, and xenophobia, the year saw some 25 racial conflicts. Among the worst in American history was the riot in Chicago that left 38 dead after a week of conflict. Other areas throughout the United States also saw tremendous violence, including the mass murder of more than 200 black sharecroppers in Arkansas.

Houston Informer began publication. Under the direction of Carter W. Wesley, the *Houston Informer* merged with a number of other newspapers and became a part of one of the largest African American newspapers in the nation. Wesley used his newspaper as a voice of protest and supported a number of important civil rights cases.

1920   Harlem Renaissance flourished. In the 1920s, black American writers, poets, painters, and musicians expressed their pride by revealing black culture and its contributions to the nation. The movement, which began in Harlem, New York, produced such creative talents as poets Langston Hughes and Claude McKay, writers such as Zora Neale Hurston, and jazz greats that included Louis Armstrong, among others. Renaissance artists focused on common black American workers, musicians, gamblers, shopkeepers, and more, and in doing so they attracted the attention of white enthusiasts.

James Weldon Johnson became the executive secretary of the NAACP. A poet, lawyer, diplomat, and civil right activist, Johnson enjoyed a long and successful career. In 1906, Johnson, recommended by Booker T. Washington, served as the U.S. consul to Venezuela. While serving, he wrote *The Autobiography of an Ex-Colored Man*, his only novel. Johnson later edited the *New York Age* and served as executive secretary of the NAACP. As a leader of the NAACP Johnson organized peaceful protests against lynching and investigated the deaths during the Red Summer of 1919. Johnson spent much of his later years editing poetry and history books.

1921   Marcus Garvey established the Black Star Steamship Line. Between 1919–22, this Jamaican-born black nationalist, with support from his Universal Negro Improvement Association, operated this steamship line. Funding came through the sale of stock. Garvey envisioned this business venture to link black businesses around the world with one another and to serve as transportation for his "Back to Africa" movement. The steamship line closed after Garvey experienced serious financial problems but not before the U.S. government charged him with mail fraud. He served jail time for his conviction. President Coolidge deported him in 1927.

Antilynching bill introduced in Congress. Missouri Republican Leonidas D. Dyer introduced a bill in the House of Representatives to stop lynchings in the United States. Dyer's bill called for harsh punishment of anyone involved in a lynching, including government officials who refused to protect victims. The bill passed the House of Representatives.

1922   Dyer Antilynching Bill failed in Congress. Although Leonidas D. Dyer's antilynching bill passed the House of Representatives, it failed in the Senate after a southern filibuster. Although it failed to become law, the Dyer Antilynching Bill did influence future bills on the same matter.

1923   National Urban League began publication of *Opportunity*. This magazine, as initiated by Charles S. Johnson, sought to encourage professional interracial relationships and ease discrimination. Articles ranged from the labor market to cultural events. Contributors included black Americans such as Claude McKay and Langston Hughes and white writers including H. L. Mencken and Clarence Darrow. Because of poor sales, and the drain it became on the National Urban League, *Opportunity* went out of business in 1949.

1925   A. Philip Randolph founded Brotherhood of Sleeping Car Porters and Maids. Beginning in 1867, the Pullman Company employed black men and women as porters and maids at low wages. In 1925, workers invited A. Philip Randolph to help them secure more rights. In response to worker demands, Randolph organized this union. The Pullman Company refused to recognize it until 1937 when the Brotherhood received assistance from President Roosevelt's New Deal. Randolph strengthened his union by affiliating it with the American Federation of Labor.

Alain Locke's *New Negro Movement* was a precursor of black pride. Shunning Booker T. Washington's accommodationist methods, African American scholars, artists, and militants worked together to promote the cultural values and pride in black America while pledging to use violence if necessary to defend themselves. Such attitudes could be found in newspaper-owner and activist Alain Locke's publication *The New Negro*.

1926   Negro History Week launched. A creation of Carter G. Woodson, Negro History Week was created to honor and celebrate past accomplishments of African Americans while promoting a more positive image of black Americans in the 1920s. The holiday was held during the same week in February as Frederick Douglass's and President Lincoln's birthdays to further honor and associate the occasion with two of the nation's most-recognized abolitionist leaders.

1929   Martin Luther King, Jr., born 15 January in Atlanta, Georgia, the son of a Baptist minister. King, Jr., received a formal education at Booker T. Washington High School and at Morehouse College, where he received a bachelor's degree. He later attended Boston College, where he earned a Ph.D. in theology. While seeking his education, he became an ordained minister in his father's church. King earned national attention as the minister at the Dexter Avenue Baptist Church when senior members of the church selected him to lead the Montgomery Improvement Association. In this position, he led the Montgomery bus boycott which began when Rosa Parks refused to relinquish her seat. The success of the boycott made Dr. King, Jr., the premier civil rights leader in the nation. His method of peaceful protest met with significant success. He was assassinated while organizing a march in Memphis, Tennessee, in 1968.

Oscar DePriest was elected to Congress, the first black to be elected in the twentieth century. Born in the South but raised in the North as a result of the Great Migration, DePriest entered politics first as a local Republican party boss in Chicago, Illinois. In 1915, he became the first black member of Chicago's city council. In 1929, he won a seat in the U.S. House of Representatives. As a House member, he fought for equality in the federal workplace and for an antilynching bill. He lost his seat to an African American Democrat, Arthur W. Mitchell, in 1934.

"Don't Buy Where You Can't Work" movement launched. Using economics to gain greater equality, the "Don't Buy Where You Can't Work" movement began as a grassroots movement in Chicago, Illinois. Initiated by local black churches and area residents and supported by black newspapers and the NAACP, the movement spread into 35 cities by the time World War II had begun. The organization had some success in securing better jobs for black Americans, but its greatest success was in causing other black groups to organize at the grassroots to achieve their goals.

"Jobs for Negroes" movement began. Closely affiliated with the "Don't Buy Where You Can't Work" movement, the "Jobs for Negroes" movement was also a grassroots movement that began in Chicago. Organized by Bill Tate, an ex–prize fighter, and A. C. O'Neal, editor of the black Chicago newspaper the *Whip*, the organization encouraged black consumers to boycott businesses that did not employ black workers. By the 1930s, the "Jobs for Negroes" movement quickly spread into other major cities across the nation. Successful in that it forced several major companies, including Edison Bell Telephone and New York Bus Company, among others, into hiring black workers, the movement also contributed to racial tensions and riots. Like the "Don't Buy

Where You Can't Work" movement, it inspired similar boycotts, including Dr. King's marches in the 1950s.

1931   Scottsboro Trials began. In a highly controversial, politicized, and publicized trail, nine African Americans, aged 12–19, were tried for the alleged rape of two white girls in Alabama. The first trial resulted in a guilty verdict, but the verdict was overturned when the International Labor Defense Committee appealed the decision. The ILD's interest took the case all the way to the Supreme Court, *Powell v. Alabama*, where it was overturned. In a second trial, *Norris v. Alabama*, the Supreme Court set aside the conviction on the grounds that the trial was in violation of the Fourteenth Amendment since black Americans did not serve on the jury. Joining the ILD, the NAACP and other related organizations created the Scottsboro Defense Committee. The SDC helped four of the accused win an acquittal and helped win pardons for the other defendants.

1932   *Journal of Negro Education* established at Howard University. This publication was created by its first editor, Charles H. Thompson, Howard University Professor of Education. The *Journal of Negro Education* studies dilemmas in African American education and serves as a resource for scholars working on related topics. It remains an important publication.

Black voters began moving into the Democratic party. Since the end of Reconstruction in 1877, and the "redeeming" of the South by white Democrats, black Republicans found that their party failed to adequately represent, or even include, them in any significant manner. In the 1920s, under three Republican presidents, the nation witnessed a rise in racial tension fueled by xenophobia and an influential Ku Klux Klan that differed from its predecessor in that it was not limited to the South but was a national organization with immense popularity in the Midwest. The 1932 presidential election of New York Democrat Franklin Roosevelt introduced a "new" Democratic party. In the midst of the Great Depression, Roosevelt's New Deal was offered to all Americans, regardless of race. Work programs such as the Civilian Conservation Corps employed black and white men but in segregated camps. Nevertheless, Roosevelt did include black Americans in these relief programs. Roosevelt also appointed black Americans to various federal positions.

1933   Black Cabinet advised President Franklin Roosevelt on African American issues. Recognizing that President Roosevelt took an interest in black Americans and their needs, influential black Americans began meeting informally, and sporadically, to assess the current state of black Americans during the Great Depression and advise President Roosevelt of their findings. The group included such recognizable individuals as Mary McLeod Bethune, the head of the Negro Division of the National Youth Administration, and Robert Weaver, an adviser for the Interior Department. Bethune and Weaver, generally considered the primary leaders within the group, called the meetings to order and established an agenda. The real importance of the group was that it served to inform Roosevelt's policy makers on racial issues and demonstrated inclusion of black Americans in the federal government.

Joint Committee on National Recovery established to help blacks. Supported by 20 different groups, the Joint Committee on National Recovery represented black Americans during Franklin Roosevelt's First Hundred Days. It focused on educating black Americans on New Deal programs and advising the Roosevelt administration on the living conditions and needs of African Americans.

1934   Eleanor Roosevelt entertained Mary McLeod Bethune at the White House. Actively supporting her husband, the first lady concerned herself with the nation's social problems, including poverty and the plight of African Americans. Eleanor Roosevelt met Mary McLeod Bethune in the late 1920s. The two remained lifelong friends. Bethune advised the first lady on racial issues. Eleanor Roosevelt played a significant role in Mary McLeod Bethune's appointment as the leader of the Negro Division of the National Youth Administration.

Claude Neal lynching in Florida. Accused on circumstantial evidence of raping and murdering a white woman, Neal, a resident of Jackson County, Florida, was lynched by a mob after enduring grotesque bodily mutilation.

Elijah Muhammad (Elijah Poole) assumed command of the Nation of Islam. Born in Sandersville, Georgia, in 1897 and relocated to Detroit, Michigan, in 1923, Poole came under the influence of W. D. Fard, who claimed to be Allah. Upon Fard's unexplained disappearance, Elijah Poole changed his name to Elijah Muhammad to reflect his new identity and standing and took control of the struggling Nation of Islam. Under Elijah Muhammad's direction, membership in the Nation of Islam swelled to include 50,000–250,000 believers. The Nation of Islam, also known as the Black Muslims, became recognized as a northern militant organization that denounced white Americans. Elijah Muhammad did not advocate integration but rather segregation.

Arthur W. Mitchell, a black Democrat, was elected to Congress. A black Chicagoan, Mitchell won election after narrowly defeating black Republican Oscar DePriest. Serving two terms as a U.S. congressman, Mitchell is best remembered as a New Deal Democrat and staunch supporter of President Franklin D. Roosevelt. As a civil rights advocate, Mitchell successfully sued the Pullman Company when railroad officials denied him a seat in the white section of the train.

1935   Harlem race riot occurred. Following rumors that police officers had murdered a black youth for shoplifting, crowds protested by destroying more than 600 storefront windows and quarreling with law officials. Police arrested some 75 people; dozens more were injured. Following the riot, the government strengthened programs to increase opportunities for African Americans and improve race relations.

National Negro Congress established. Led by its first president, A. Philip Randolph, the National Negro Congress attempted, but failed, to create racial solidarity. The organization called for unionization of black workers and improvements in society for black Americans, including increased educational opportunities. The group later came under the control of the Communist Party.

1936   Jesse Owens won four gold medals at Olympic games in Berlin. Born to Alabama sharecroppers, Jesse Owens was raised in Cleveland, Ohio, after his parents relocated there during the Great Migration. In Ohio, Owens came under the direction of a white coach who recognized Owens's remarkable talent and worked closely with him to develop it further. Owens went on to participate in the Olympics and won gold medals for individual and team competitions.

1936   *Negro History Bulletin* founded by Carter G. Woodson. Created as a magazine aimed at a popular audience, Woodson's publication proved highly successful until very recent years, when it became plagued by financial problems. At its best, the *Negro History Bulletin* supplemented American history textbooks, which rarely focused on the national contributions and personal accomplishments of African Americans. In the mid 1980s, more than 7,000 people subscribed to the magazine.

1938   Supreme Court's *Missouri ex rel. Gaines v. Canada* decision eroded *Plessy* doctrine. An indirect predecessor to the *Brown v. Board of Education* case in 1954, the *Gaines* case redefined the *Plessy* decision when Supreme Court Chief Justice Charles Evans Hughes decided that black Missourian Lloyd Gaines could not be denied admission to a state law school solely because of his race because there were no black law schools in the state.

NAACP Legal Defense and Educational Fund established to challenge segregated education. This fund has contributed enormously to the success of the NAACP. Initially, two individuals staffed the organization, but today more than 400 individuals, black and white, work for the fund to improve education, employment, and civil rights for black Americans.

Southern Conference for Human Welfare founded to promote civil rights. The SCHW was created to deal with civil injustice and poverty throughout the South. Closely related to New Deal ideals, it worked specifically to create more black political involvement and economic opportunity for both poor blacks and whites.

1939   Civil Liberties Unit (subsequently retitled the Civil Rights Section) was created in the U.S. Department of Justice by Franklin Roosevelt's Attorney General Frank Murphy. The Civil Liberties Unit worked within the Criminal Division of the Department of Justice to offer solutions to civil rights cases.

Thurgood Marshall became director of NAACP Legal Defense and Educational Fund. One of the most important figures in the civil rights movement, Marshall held this appointment for more than two decades and experienced enormous success as a civil rights leader, including the 1954 Supreme Court case *Brown v. Board of Education*, which overturned the 1896 Supreme Court decision of *Plessy v. Ferguson*.

1940   Wagner-Gavagan Antilynching Bill failed in Congress. In the NAACP's third major attempt to secure passage of a federal antilynching bill, the Wagner-Gavagan bill suffered the same fate as the previously introduced Dyer and Costigan-Wagner bills. The Wagner-Gavagan bill stipulated that if states did not punish those involved in lynchings, the federal government would intercede. The bill failed because it did not receive support from President Roosevelt and met serious hostility from the South.

Phylon founded by W.E.B. Du Bois. Recognized as one of the "best university journals in the nation," *Phylon* was an important publication focusing on

African American thought. It demanded meticulous research and writing. Although created as a scholarly journal with a highly specialized interest, it enjoyed a large public audience.

1941   Supreme Court decision *Taylor v. Georgia* struck a blow against black peonage. James Taylor, a black man, was convicted by the state of Georgia for breach of contract. Taylor accepted payment for work he allegedly did not complete. Taylor took his case to the Supreme Court, which ruled in Taylor's favor on the ground that the Georgia court's decision violated the Constitution's Thirteenth Amendment.

A. Philip Randolph launched a March on Washington movement. Protesting labor discrimination in federal workplaces, civil rights leader A. Philip Randolph organized a march on Washington to demand "equal participation in National Defense." Randolph realized his success when President Roosevelt mandated that discrimination in the defense industry was no longer acceptable. Those guilty of violating Roosevelt's executive order would be punished by the federal government.

National Committee to Abolish the Poll Tax was formed by Joseph Gelders and Virginia Foster Durr as an outgrowth of the Southern Conference for Human Welfare. The NCAPT enjoyed the support of the NAACP and other civil rights groups yet failed to accomplish its primary objective. Although the National Committee to Abolish the Poll Tax concluded its business in 1948, its efforts did see the end of poll taxes in Georgia, Tennessee, and Alabama.

1942   Congress of Racial Equality (CORE) founded. Formed by pacifists George Houser, James Farmer, and Bayard Rustin, CORE and its founders spread the idea of peaceful protests around the nation. CORE gained major attention in the 1960s with its sit-ins, Freedom Riders, and boycotts of major department stores such as Woolworth's. CORE played a significant role in the success of the modern civil rights movement.

President Franklin D. Roosevelt Executive Order 8802 created Fair Employment Practices Committee (FEPC). Responding to A. Philip Randolph's March on Washington movement, President Roosevelt ordered that discrimination in the defense industry be stopped immediately. The FEPC monitored federal workplaces to ensure that Roosevelt's executive order was obeyed.

1943   Detroit race riot occurred. The 1943 Detroit race riot is considered the worst of the World War II riots. It lasted 48 hours and was sparked by long-standing racial discrimination, economic oppression, and the arrival of tens of thousands of newly arrived black Americans who came to Detroit as part of the Great Migration. The newly arrived migrants joined previously settled local blacks in the "Double V" campaign. After two days of rioting, the riots concluded after police killed 17 blacks. No whites were killed. Local government officials later created agencies to prevent future riots. Their success was limited, and sizable riots returned to Detroit in the 1960s.

Harlem race riot occurred. The Harlem race riot was caused by social and economic discrimination against blacks. On 1 August, local residents erupted into violence for some twelve hours. The rioting took 6 lives, caused more than 100 injuries, and more than $200,000 in property damage. Harlem's race riots reflected the changing pace of civil rights from Booker T. Washington's accommodationist approach to the use of violent protest.

1944   Supreme Court's *Pollock v. Williams* decision dealt a death blow to black peonage. Closely related to previous Supreme Court cases including *Taylor v. Georgia* and *Bailey v. Alabama*, *Pollock v. Williams* was yet another case in which the Court ruled that peonage was unconstitutional. The Court's ruling was strong enough that black peonage effectively ended after the *Pollock* decision.

Southern Regional Council founded to improve educational and economic opportunities in the South. Founded by North Carolina sociologist Howard W. Odum, the Southern Region Council was an interracial organization that worked to bring forth more civil equality and greater economic activity in the South. The council still exists.

United Negro College Fund established. Tuskegee Institute President Frederick D. Patterson organized a consortium of 27 other black colleges and universities to establish a fund that would allow African Americans a greater opportunity to earn a higher education. The organization remains vital and important today.

The Supreme Court in *Smith v. Allwright* struck down the white primary. NAACP chief legal counsel Thurgood Marshall represented black Texan Lonnie E. Smith when the latter had been denied his right to vote in the Texas Democratic primary election because of his race. The Supreme Court ruled that Texas's white-only primary was in violation of the Fifteenth Amendment.

1945   Adam Clayton Powell, Jr., began his long congressional career. Enjoying 11 successive terms in the U.S. House of Representatives, Powell proved to be an effective congressman and champion of civil rights. Because of his efforts, black journalists were allowed into the congressional press galleries. He also fought to prevent federal money from being used to support public projects that discriminated against black Americans.

1946   President Harry S Truman's Executive Order 9808 created the Presidential Committee on Civil Rights. Truman ordered the creation of this committee to examine how existing federal, state, and local governments could be improved in the interest of protecting and promoting civil rights. Although little legislation was passed because of the order, it did bring more attention to civil rights while allowing President Truman to demonstrate his interest in the cause.

1947   CORE sponsored the Journey of Reconciliation. Testing new laws that prohibited segregation in interstate transportation, an interracial group of 16 men traveled throughout the upper South on public transportation. The journey caused four of the men to get arrested and sentenced to labor on a chain gang. The Journey of Reconciliation was a predecessor to the 1961 Freedom Rides.

Jackie Robinson broke the color barrier in major league baseball. He was a recognized athlete at UCLA where he excelled in four sports before he came to national attention when he joined the Brooklyn Dodgers. In spite of death threats, and enduring Jim Crow laws when the Dodgers played in the South, Robinson persevered and won the hearts of many black and white fans. For his outstanding athletic ability, Robinson became the first black American inducted into the Baseball Hall of Fame. In his postathletic life, he became a civil rights advocate who urged peaceful protest.

Special report *To Secure These Rights* was released. Initiated by NAACP's Walter F. White, President Truman created a civil rights agenda detailed in this report. Chief among its objectives were ending the poll tax, establishing a permanent civil rights commission, and desegregating the military.

1948 President Truman unsuccessfully sought strong civil rights legislation abolishing the poll tax. As part of his agenda stated in *To Secure These Rights*, the president tried to convince Congress to pass a federal bill against poll taxes. The bill failed because Truman could not generate enough southern support.

President Truman's Executive Order 9981 integrated the armed forces. In *To Secure These Rights*, President Truman declared his intent to desegregate the military. Executive Order 9981 prevented discrimination in the military on the basis of race, color, religion, or national origin.

President Truman appointed the Fahy Committee. The Fahy Committee supported Executive Order 9981 by ensuring that the Order was upheld and by searching for ways to improve racial conditions in the armed forces. In less than a year and a half, the committee helped create American military nondiscrimination policies.

1949 The Supreme Court in *Sweatt v. Painter* declared unequal educational facilities for blacks unconstitutional. Recognized as another landmark victory for Thurgood Marshall, the Supreme Court upheld the *Gaines* decision when it ordered the University of Texas Law School to admit Heman Marion Sweatt, a black postal worker, as a full-time student. The board of regents attempted to block his admission by quickly creating a law school for African Americans, but the Court argued that because of its speedy creation it could not offer an education equal to that at the University of Texas. Sweatt was admitted, yet like *Gaines*, the case is generally not considered as furthering desegregation as much as honoring the *Plessy* decision.

1954 *Brown v. Board of Education* abolished the separate-but-equal doctrine. Under Chief Justice Earl Warren, the Supreme Court came to agree with Thurgood Marshall's argument that separate but equal in educational institutions was unequal. The Fourteenth Amendment, Marshall further argued, was not being upheld in the case of academic segregation. Agreeing with Marshall, Chief Justice Warren decided that "in the field of public education the doctrine of separate but equal has no place." The Court's decision reversed the *Plessy* decision and initiated major changes in the United States.

Brown v. Board of Education II called for desegregation of public schools with "all deliberate speed." Often known as *Brown II*, the second decision dealt with the methods in which desegregation would be conducted. In spite of the declaration of "all deliberate speed," *Brown II* recognized the complexity of desegregating the nation and that it could not be done as quickly in some areas as in others. The Supreme Court entrusted lower court judges to determine the course and even the amount of time it might take to honor the

Brown decision. Effectively, *Brown II* recognized that desegregating the nation would be gradual.

Montgomery bus boycott catapulted Martin Luther King, Jr., into national prominence. When Rosa Parks, a black seamstress from Alabama, refused to give up her seat to a white passenger, the modern civil rights movement made a giant leap forward. At the forefront of the protest was Dr. Martin Luther King, Jr. King called for peaceful protest and led black Montgomerians in a boycott of Montgomery public transportation. Montgomery's buses ran nearly empty for a year before transit officials announced that black passengers could sit anywhere they chose. African Americans throughout the South took note not only of the method and success of the boycott but its young leader. Dr. King became recognized as the premier civil rights leader in the United States.

Montgomery Improvement Association founded. Prominent black Montgomerians organized this association one day after the Montgomery bus boycott began. With Martin Luther King, Jr., as president of the organization, the MIA provided free transportation to thousands of black workers who agreed not to ride Montgomery's segregated buses. After the boycott ended, the MIA continued to participate in the civil rights movement.

Emmett Louis Till murdered in Mississippi. Raised in Chicago, Till was visiting relatives in Mississippi in the summer when he was killed for allegedly asking a white woman for a date. The acquittal of his murderers sparked protests in many northern cities.

Roy Wilkins became executive secretary of the NAACP. Wilkins earned a degree in sociology from the University of Minnesota and took a keen interest in civil rights and integration. He rejected all forms of segregation, including those sought by black activists. For his involvement with local chapters of the NAACP, Wilkins became the assistant secretary of the organization from 1931–34. In 1955, the NAACP appointed him its new executive secretary, in which capacity he continued his fight for desegregation, participated in the March on Washington, and joined protest marches in a number of other cities.

Autherine Juanita Lucy enrolled as the first black student at the University of Alabama. After earning a bachelor's degree from Miles College, a black institution in Birmingham, Lucy decided to pursue a master's degree in library science at the University of Alabama. Although Lucy, after a lengthy battle, was permitted to enroll in the program, the board of regents expelled her as a result of white segregationist pressure and her allegation that the university encouraged such behavior. She returned in 1992 and earned a master's degree.

Tallahassee, Florida, bus boycott launched. When the Tallahassee City Transit Company denied Florida Agricultural and Mechanical University students integrated seating on their buses, it sparked a bus boycott not unlike that seen earlier in Montgomery, Alabama. The boycott lasted until 1958 when the bus company desegregated its vehicles.

Civil Rights Act of 1957 passed by Congress. Recognized as the first piece of civil rights legislation Congress passed since Reconstruction, the act established a federal Civil Rights Commission with power to investigate discriminatory practices. It worked to protect black Americans' voting rights and served as a significant morale booster for African Americans. The bill was passed under President Eisenhower but was the work of Texas Senator Lyndon B. Johnson.

United States Commission on Civil Rights created to ensure that Americans, regardless of race, religion, color, or national origin were not denied their voting rights. It also examined cases where the Fourteenth Amendment had been violated and in general worked to ensure the success of desegregation. It most recently investigated the 2000 presidential election in Florida.

Martin Luther King, Jr., formed the Southern Christian Leadership Conference (SCLC). Dr. King created this organization after the success of the Montgomery bus boycott to keep the spirit of the civil rights movement alive. More specifically, the SCLC was organized to create local awareness and participation in nonviolent protest throughout the South. The SCLC was led primarily by King and other Baptist ministers whose admiration of Jesus Christ and Mohandas K. Gandhi led them to use peaceful protest methods. More assertive than Booker T. Washington's organizations, and less militant than those of Marcus Garvey or Elijah Muhammad, the SCLC led marches around the South, gaining national attention for its methods and success alike. The Southern Christian Leadership Conference played a key role in the passage of the 1964 Civil Rights Act.

President Dwight D. Eisenhower called on the National Guard to handle the Little Rock desegregation crisis. When nine black students attempted to attend Little Rock, Arkansas' Central High School, the state's governor, Orval Faubus, reacted by calling on the Arkansas Guard to prevent their admittance. President Eisenhower sent in 1,000 men from the 101st Airborne division and nationalized the Arkansas Guard to take it out of Faubus's control. Military troops remained with the students until the end of the school year.

Durham, North Carolina, sit-ins began. In August, Reverend Douglas E. Moore of Asbury Temple led a small group of black students from North Carolina College into the Royal Ice Cream Company store. The group, having requested service at the white-only lunch counter, was arrested for trespassing. Although a similar attempt would not be made until 1960, the movement is still important as it initiated sit-ins in North Carolina and other parts of the South.

1958 Martin Luther King, Jr.'s, *Stride toward Freedom* published. King wrote this book while working on race relations in Montgomery, Alabama. It is a combination of autobiography, history, and philosophy that because of its content remains important today in understanding civil rights.

Greensboro, North Carolina, sit-in began. On 1 February, four black students from nearby North Carolina Agricultural and Technical College staged a sit-in protest at the local Woolworth's lunch counter. Denied service and arrested, the four men returned the next day with a larger group of white and black students. The Woolworth's sit-in concept quickly spread around the state. By July 1960, the protests succeeded in desegregating lunch counters.

Student Nonviolent Coordinating Committee (SNCC) founded. A major civil rights group that advocated peaceful protest, SNCC drew large support from white northern college students. The organization was first created after a group of some two hundred students heard Martin Luther King, Jr., and other civil rights leaders speak at Shaw University in North Carolina. SNCC was affiliated with Dr. King's Southern Christian Leadership Conference, the Congress of Racial Equality, and other similar organizations. SNCC members worked on voter registration, Freedom Rides, sit-ins, and other forms of nonviolent protest. SNCC contributed enormously to desegregating the South.

Supreme Court's *Boynton v. Virginia* decision declared segregation in railway and bus terminals unconstitutional. The Supreme court ruled that restaurants and facilities connected with bus companies could not deny service to customers on the basis of race or other discriminatory factors even if the bus company did not own the restaurants. Not serving customers because of their race, the Court ruled, was a violation of the earlier decision in *Morgan v. Virginia*.

Nashville sit-ins began. On 12 February, local college students under the guidance of Vanderbilt University student James Lawson staged a series of sit-ins at the Nashville Woolworth's lunch counter. In May, lunch counters in Nashville began to desegregate.

Tallahassee, Florida, sit-ins began. More violent than many sit-ins in the South, the Tallahassee sit-in began in February and did not end until January 1963. The sit-in began when Florida A & M students, supported by members of the Congress of Racial Equality, along with several young black residents, staged a sit-in. Police officers routinely arrested and tear-gassed protestors, but after more than two years of such behavior, the state governor denounced segregated facilities.

1961 Freedom Riders assaulted in Alabama and Mississippi. On May 4, a group of CORE activists were attacked. Their bus was destroyed in Anniston, Alabama. In Mississippi, students riding on a separate bus were beaten by angry segregationists.

Martin Luther King, Jr., launched Albany, Georgia, sit-in. Over the Thanksgiving weekend a group of African American civil rights activists began a sit-in in a whites-only section of a Trailways bus depot. Organized by Charles Sherrod and Cordell Reagon, both workers for the Student Nonviolent Coordinating Committee, the sit-in attracted the participation of Dr. King. King, however, later referred to the protest in Albany as his greatest public defeat.

Northern Student Movement launched at Yale University. The NSM was founded by Yale student Peter Countryman and was initially a civil rights organization populated by white college students. NSM members promoted civil rights first by tutoring black students in inner-city neighborhoods and later by recruiting black Americans living in northern slums to serve in leadership capacities. A popular organization, NSM became a national organization that fought against poverty and police brutality and that worked to desegregate public schools.

Leontyne Price debuted at the New York Metropolitan Opera. Price did her part for civil rights by pursuing her dream as an opera singer. She dreamed of singing at the Met but was initially denied the opportunity because of her race. She was eventually offered secondary parts but refused them on the basis that her talent merited a leading role. In 1961, Leontyne Price became the first African American woman to sing at the Met in a major role. She starred as Leonora in *Ill Trovatore*.

1962   Council of Federated Organizations (COFO) established. This organization was founded by Robert Moses of the Student Nonviolent Coordinating Committee and David Dennis of the Congress of Racial Equality. Through combined efforts, Moses and Dennis sought to create a statewide coalition of civil rights organizations in Mississippi. COFO workers demonstrated their strength by registering voters, casting protest votes, and even nominating candidates for the Mississippi gubernatorial election. An interracial organization, COFO chose Aaron Henry of the NAACP and R. Edwin King, Jr., a white minister from Tougaloo College, as candidates for governor and lieutenant governor, respectively. The organization was also supported by white college students from the North. COFO paved the way for 1964's Freedom Summer.

Voter Education Project launched. With support of the Kennedy administration evident, the Congress of Racial Equality, the Student Nonviolent Coordinating Committee, the National Urban League, and the National Advancement for the Association of Colored People united in an effort to champion civil rights through voting. Volunteers were given federal protection and worked tirelessly throughout the South's black belt to teach illiterate black southerners how to read and write. They contributed further by registering black southerners to vote. Volunteers associated with these organizations were frequently arrested, beaten, and even killed. Their success, however, can be measured in the increased number of registered voters. In 1962, only 25 percent of adult black southerners were registered to vote. By 1964 that number had increased to 40 percent.

James Meredith integrated the University of Mississippi. On 30 September, James Howard Meredith captured national attention when a federal court ordered the University of Mississippi to accept him. Meredith was a 28-year-old Air Force veteran and had previously attended Jackson State College. Mississippi Governor Ross Barnett vowed he would not desegregate the University of Mississippi. President Kennedy ordered federal troops to Mississippi to protect Meredith and ensure that his civil rights were not violated by denial of his entrance to the university. Meredith graduated one year later without further major incident after the initial riot.

1963   Birmingham confrontation began with the Southern Christian Leadership Conference leading demonstrations against racial injustice and organizing black boycotts against white merchants in this industrial city. Public Safety Commissioner Eugene "Bull" Connor ordered police officers and firefighters to respond against the marchers by beating demonstrators; having police dogs attack men, women, and children; and hitting them with high-pressure fire hoses. For his involvement in the protest, Dr. Martin Luther King, Jr., among others, was arrested. While in jail, King wrote the "Letter from Birmingham Jail." President Kennedy telephoned King's wife to express his concern. After King and other incarcerated demonstrators were released from jail, the protest grew increasingly violent. White segregationists bombed a local motel and the house of the Reverend A. D. King. Riots followed.

March on Washington for Jobs and Freedom began. Organized by accomplished civil rights leader A. Philip Randolph, who led the March on Washington movement in 1941, the 1963 march included such recognized leaders as Martin Luther King, Jr., of the Southern Christian Leadership Conference, Roy Wilkins of the NAACP, James Farmer of the Congress of Racial Equality, Whitney M. Young, Jr., from the National Urban League, and John Lewis of the Student Nonviolent Coordinating Committee. Demonstrators held this march in an effort to bring more attention to civil rights injustices, specifically substandard housing and lack of job opportunities for black Americans. The march is best remembered for Dr. King's "I Have a Dream" speech. It is one of the most remembered events in the modern civil rights movement.

Martin Luther King, Jr., delivered "I Have a Dream" speech at the Lincoln Memorial in Washington, while participating in the March on Washington for Jobs and Freedom. In his speech, King enlightened the nation on the deprived conditions black Americans suffered under. King immortalized his dream for a better and more inclusive America when he proclaimed "I have a dream that one day this nation will rise up and live out the true meaning of its creed: 'We hold these truths to be self-evident, that all men are created equal . . .'" The speech established King as the premier spokesman for the civil rights movement.

Medgar W. Evers assassinated in Mississippi. A recognized civil rights leader in Mississippi, Evers committed himself to improving life for black Mississippians. A graduate of Alcorn Agricultural and Mechanical College, Evers revitalized the state's nearly defunct NAACP by creating new chapters, publicizing civil rights violations, and campaigning against injustice. For his efforts, opponents frequently threatened his life. On 11 June, an assassin murdered Evers. Even in death, Evers remained important to the struggle for civil rights.

Governor George Wallace "stood in school house door" to block admission of blacks students to the University of Alabama. "Segregation Now, Segregation Tomorrow, Segregation Forever," proclaimed Alabama's segregationist governor. He stepped aside, however, to allow admittance of black students. He later vowed to block integration in Alabama's public schools but obeyed court orders and did not uphold segregation.

Martin Luther King, Jr., wrote "Letter from Birmingham Jail." Incarcerated for violating a court injunction against protest marches in Birmingham, King wrote his most famous letter while in jail. The letter was a response to Christian and Jewish religious leaders who criticized King for his actions. King informed these individuals why he was acting now and not waiting any longer for justice.

Chattanooga Freedom Walk took place. William L. Moore, a white postman from Baltimore, initiated a one-man protest when he began walking from Chattanooga, Tennessee, to Jackson, Mississippi, to personally deliver a letter to the Magnolia State's segregationist governor Ross Barnett. Wearing a sign reading "Equal Rights for All—Mississippi or Bust," Moore was murdered two days into his journey. Like-minded civil rights demonstrators attempted to finish his walk but were arrested by Alabama police officers.

1964   President Lyndon B. Johnson declared War on Poverty. Johnson viewed the war on poverty as part of the war on civil injustice. Under the Economic Opportunity Act, and follow-up legislation, Johnson conducted a multi-pronged attack on poverty in America.

Economic Opportunity Act passed. The Economic Opportunity Act was the cornerstone of President Lyndon B. Johnson's War on Poverty.

Civil Rights Act of 1964 passed by Congress. One of the key measuring sticks of the success of the civil rights movement, the 1964 Civil Rights Act prohibited segregation of gas stations, restaurants, hotels, and entertainment venues. It further outlawed discrimination in the workplace, including union membership, hiring, promoting, and firing. Violators of the law could be fined, sued, and denied federal economic assistance.

Ratification of Twenty-fourth Amendment abolishes poll tax. In the immediate post–Civil War years, southern states adopted the poll tax, a tax each voter had to pay in order to vote, to prevent African Americans from voting. The poll tax was abolished for federal elections with the passage of the Twenty-fourth Amendment. Because it did not abolish the tax in state and local elections, it was largely ineffective.

Martin Luther King, Jr., received the Nobel Peace Prize. For his nonviolent protest method in the struggle for civil rights, Dr. King received the Nobel Peace Prize. The award came in the wake of his participating in the 1963 March on Washington and his "I Have a Dream" speech.

Equal Employment Opportunity Commission established. A part of the 1964 Civil Rights Act, the Equal Employment Opportunity Commission enforced nondiscrimination in nonpublic workplaces. Initially, the commission could not bring lawsuits against those in violation. Instead, it used conciliation to force employers to comply.

Harlem race riot and race riots in other northern cities occurred. Initiated when an off-duty police officer shot a young black male on 16 July, Harlem erupted into violence after Congress of Racial Equality leaders led a march on the police station. For some four days, rioters and police clashed violently with a mixture of bullets, bricks, firebombs, and projectiles. Major civil rights leaders such as A. Philip Randolph and President Johnson alike called for an end of hostilities but to no avail. The riot was the first of many riots that characterized the 1960s.

Freedom Summer of 1964 launched in Mississippi. In a biracial effort some one thousand, mostly white, college students joined in the civil rights movement with black protesters in the South. Freedom volunteers worked to register black voters and provide education and health services. The especially violent murders of two white northern volunteers, however, brought the violence previously directed at black southerners to the attention of white northerners, transforming the civil rights movement from being viewed as a regional movement of black concerns into a national issue.

Three young civil rights workers—James Earl Chaney, Andrew Goodman, Michael Henry Schwerner—were murdered near Philadelphia, Mississippi.

Serving with the Council of Federated Organizations through the Congress of Racial Equality, Chaney, a black student, and Goodman and Schwerner, white students from New York, joined the protest movement during Freedom Summer. Arrested in Neshoba County, Mississippi, the three men were released from jail only to be beaten and murdered by Klansmen. Their bodies were found in a dam on 9 August. The deaths of Goodman and Schwerner brought the violence committed against black southerners into the homes of white northerners.

Selma to Montgomery March accompanied by violence and murder of Viola Liuzzo and the Reverend James J. Reeb. Viola Fauver Gregg Liuzzo joined the civil rights movement after watching events in Selma, Alabama, on her television. Angered by what she saw and eager to do her part for civil rights, Liuzzo drove to Alabama, where she was murdered by Klansmen for shuttling protesters between Montgomery and Selma. James Reeb, a white Unitarian minister, was murdered in Selma, Alabama, for participating in the desegregation movement. Because Liuzzo and Reeb were white, the deaths sparked a national outcry.

Voting Rights Act of 1965 passed by Congress in response to Dr. King's campaign in Selma, Alabama. It forbade educational requirements for voting in states or counties where less than half of the voting-age population had been registered on 1 November 1964 or had voted in the 1964 presidential election. The act also allowed federal officials, appointed by the Civil Service Commission, to register voters. Following the Voting Rights Act of 1965, black voters in the South increased by nearly 20 percent between 1964 and 1968.

The Watts race riot, in California, is the worst racial riot in the nation's history. In the middle 1960s the Watts community, located in south-central Los Angeles, was unique in that it did not mirror the urban slums of the eastern United States. Instead of tenements, Watts residents lived in houses with lawns. Nevertheless, when Los Angeles police arrested two black men in Watts for a minor traffic violation, they sparked the tensions and anger brewing in the neighborhood over America's civil rights movement. The violence lasted several days and resulted in nearly three dozen deaths and millions of dollars in property damage.

Chicago race riot occurred. On the same weekend as the Watts riot, Chicago's black residents responded violently when a fire truck accidentally hit and killed a black woman. Three hundred black Chicagoans immediately protested. By the time the riot had ended the next day, police arrested more than 100 people. Sixty others were hospitalized. The riots occurred as Dr. King launched his campaign in Chicago.

Malcolm X was assassinated. Refusing to accept Martin Luther King, Jr.'s pacifistic protest, X proclaimed "By Any Means Necessary." Rising quickly within the Nation of Islam under Elijah Muhammad, X offered civil rights activists another route to accomplish their goals. Estranged from the Nation of Islam after he made a controversial remark concerning President Kennedy's assassination, Malcolm X created the Organization of Afro-American Unity. While he was making a speech, opponents murdered him in New York on 21 February.

President Johnson created the Federal Office of Grant Compliance to supervise affirmative action in awarding government contracts. By creating this office, also known as Executive Order 11246, President Johnson established the basis for affirmative action, a term introduced in Kennedy legislation. The Federal Office of Grant Compliance forced federal contractors to comply with antidiscrimination orders by investigating complaints, conducting compliance reviews, holding hearings, and imposing sanctions on companies in violation. Contractors were forbidden to discriminate on the basis of race, color, religion, or national origin. Gender was added through Executive Order 11375.

Mississippi Freedom Democratic Party founded. In opposition to the state regular Democratic party, the MFDP was created by participants in the 1964 Freedom Summer project. The MFDP challenged the national Democratic party after the latter rejected civil rights on its platform.

1966 James Meredith shot during the Meredith March, "the March against Fear." After helping to desegregate the University of Mississippi, Meredith attended Columbia University as a law student. On a protest walk from Memphis, Tennessee, to Jackson, Mississippi, to promote voter registration for black southerners, Meredith was wounded by a shotgun blast. He was unable to complete his mission, but Martin Luther, King, Jr., of the Southern Christian Leadership Conference, Floyd McKissick of the Congress of Racial Equality, and Stokely Carmichael of the Student Nonviolent Coordinating Committee completed it with some one thousand demonstrators who arrived in Jackson, Mississippi, on 26 June. It is estimated that between 2,000 and 3,000 black Mississippians registered to vote as a result of Meredith's March against Fear.

Stokely Carmichael coined *Black Power* phrase during the Meredith March. Carmichael introduced the phrase *Black Power* while speaking in Greenwood, Mississippi. Although the term caused many to associate Black Power with violence, Carmichael argued that he intended the term to mean unity and serve as a call for black Americans to build a sense of community among one another. The Southern Christian Leadership Conference and the NAACP both rejected the concept of Black Power because they believed it promoted black racism.

Black Panther party organized by Bobby Seale and others. A militant group that protested oppressed living conditions and police brutality, among other things, the Black Panthers followed Oakland, California, police to ensure that black Oaklanders were treated fairly. The Black Panthers called for black Americans to have more freedom in their neighborhoods, better housing, improved education, exemption from their military, and a separate judicial system free from white control. In spite of their militant reputation, members of the Black Panthers worked to create community programs, including a free breakfast program for public school students.

Widespread racial rioting occurred during the summer in the northern cities of Chicago, Cleveland, New York, and elsewhere.

Edward William Brooke elected by Massachusetts as first black to serve in the U.S. Senate since Reconstruction. Serving two terms, Brooke worked to desegregate housing while also pushing for low- and moderate-income housing projects.

Chicago Freedom Movement led by Martin Luther King, Jr., began. By merging the Southern Christian Leadership Conference with the Coordinating Council of Community Organizations, King hoped to desegregate Chicago. The movement failed because of disunity between the civil rights organizations involved.

Robert C. Weaver became the first black to hold a cabinet post in the federal government. After earning a Ph.D. in economics from Harvard University, Weaver became a noted adviser to Harold Ickes, President Roosevelt's Secretary of the Interior. Having spent his adult life in federal politics, Weaver was appointed by President Johnson as the Secretary of Housing and Urban Development.

1967   Black college students rioted on campuses of Fisk, Jackson State, Southern University, and elsewhere.

Atlanta race riot occurs. On 18 June, Atlanta police wounded a black man during a disagreement. Civil rights advocate Stokely Carmichael encouraged those who witnessed the action to protest in the streets. More than 1,000 black protesters responded by throwing bottles and rocks at police cars. Local law enforcement quickly ended the protest and immediately acceded to some of the demands of Atlanta's black residents.

Detroit race riot and Newark, New Jersey, race riot occurred in the summer. After police raided a nightclub in the black section of Detroit, onlookers ignited a riot. Lasting some five days, the riot did not end until President Johnson sent in the 82nd and 101st Airborne units, a total of 4,700 troops. The riot proved to be the most costly of the 59 riots that occurred that year. Forty-three people died. In Newark, New Jersey, black residents of this predominantly black city protested the police beating of a cab driver by rioting outside the police station. Lasting for four days, the riot ended when more than 1,000 police officers were supported by hundreds of state troops and more than 4,000 National Guardsmen. Twenty-four people died.

President Lyndon B. Johnson established the Commission on Civil Disorders (Kerner Commission) to study disorder. After an extensive study of civil rights relations, an 11-member panel, chaired by Illinois Governor Otto Kerner, informed President Johnson that the problem was worsening rapidly. To improve civil rights and end rioting that characterized many American cities, the panel recommended that the government initiate massive spending to improve housing, poverty, and unemployment. Distracted by Vietnam, President Johnson did not act on the advice of the Kerner Commission.

Thurgood Marshall became the first black Supreme Court justice. On 13 June, President Lyndon Johnson nominated Marshall, a longtime civil rights crusader and federal judge, to the Supreme Court. Although many southern senators opposed Marshall, the Senate confirmed him on 1 September. Marshall served until 27 June 1991.

1968   Civil Rights Act of 1968 passed with provisions for open housing. Building on a succession of civil rights acts passed throughout the decade, the 1968 Civil Rights Act forbade discrimination in housing rentals and sales. Open housing was one of the last major steps in the process of desegregating the nation. The act further prohibited interfering with or harming individuals involved in exercising their civil rights, including voting and the use of public facilities.

Shirley Chisholm elected to Congress. Elected to the New York state assembly in 1964, Chisholm gave up her seat four years later to run for the U.S. House of Representatives. In the election, she ran against James Farmer, the former director of the Congress of Racial Equality. Two major strengths for Chisholm during the election included her district's large number of registered women voters and the fact that Farmer was not a native of the area. Chisholm served in the House until 1983.

Martin Luther King, Jr., assassinated in Memphis on 4 April. Less than 15 years after coming to the nation's attention as a civil rights leader, King was murdered in Memphis, Tennessee, while supporting a strike on behalf of black sanitation workers. White segregationist James Earl Ray was convicted of the murder.

Poor People's March on Washington occurred. The last major demonstration planned by Martin Luther King, Jr., was conducted by King's successor in the Southern Christian Leadership Conference, Ralph Abernathy. King organized the march calling for full employment, a guaranteed income, and construction funds for low-cost housing for black Americans. Such things, King argued, would improve the daily lives of African Americans more than the right to vote or the desegregation of eating establishments.

Eldridge Cleaver published best-selling *Soul on Ice*. Cleaver's first book discussed black militant ideology and his opposition to traditional means of accomplishing civil justice. It quickly became a best seller.

Knoxville riot occurred. Tensions increased substantially in Tennessee when National Guard units began training for urban riots. Among the four state cities where the Guard trained was Knoxville. In an unrelated incident police arrested a black student for public intoxication and a black man for criminal trespass. The arrests sparked a riot that resulted in one death.

Resurrection City erected in Washington, D.C. Located near the Lincoln Memorial, the "city" consisted of plywood and tarpaper shacks that symbolized the living conditions of black Americans. The city was built under the leadership of Ralph Abernathy, King's successor in the Southern Christian Leadership Conference.

1969 Office of Minority Business Enterprise established. Created by President Richard Nixon to increase minority businesses, the OMBE, through other organizations that it created, offered venture capital and long-term credit to minority business owners.

1971 Congressional Black Caucus founded. As the number of black congressmen increased from six to nine, an organization was created known as the Congressional Black Caucus. Caucus members demonstrated their existence and strength by boycotting President Nixon's State of the Union address on the ground that he refused to grant them an audience. Nixon later met with the CBC. Other accomplishments of the CBC include the creation of the Martin Luther King, Jr., national holiday in 1982 and the Anti-Apartheid Act of 1986, among a number of other notable successes.

Jesse Jackson ran for mayor of Chicago. Jackson became a recognized civil rights activist under Martin Luther King, Jr., and ran unsuccessfully for mayor against Richard Daly.

Jesse Jackson founded People United to Save Humanity. PUSH is a Chicago economic/civil rights organization based on the idea that civil rights cannot be accomplished without economic progress. Through the use of boycotts against them, companies such as Coca-Cola, Burger King, and others have been forced to hire more black employees and use more black banks.

Public school busing to achieve integration began. Under President Nixon the government fostered integration by busing students into neighborhoods they would not have previously been educated in. Nixon advocated the redesignation of school districts to end segregation in education. In 1974, Boston gained national attention for white protests against busing. By the late 1970s and the 1980s, the Supreme Court rejected the use of busing to promote integration.

1972   Equal Employment Opportunity Act of 1972 passed. The EEOA provides enforcement of the Equal Employment Opportunity Commission. Under the EEOA, employers in violation of the EEOA can be sued in federal court. Local and state employers and educational institutions are subject to the restrictions of the EEOA.

Barbara C. Jordan elected to Congress from Texas. After escaping a life of poverty through education, Jordan began her political career organizing a voter registration drive for John Kennedy's bid for the presidency in 1960. In 1966, she became the first black person elected to the Texas State Senate. Five years later, Jordan won a seat in the U.S. House of Representatives.

Andrew Young elected to Congress from Georgia. Serving under Martin Luther King, Jr., during the early 1960s and as the executive vice president of the Southern Christian Leadership Conference from 1967–70, Young became the first African American from Georgia to win a seat in the U.S. House of Representatives.

1973   Maynard Jackson elected first black mayor of Atlanta. After losing an election bid to the U.S. Senate in 1968, Jackson defeated a white opponent and won the office of Atlanta's vice-mayor. Five years later, he became the city's mayor after defeating Sam Massell, Atlanta's first Jewish mayor.

1976   Alex Haley's *Roots: The Saga of an American Family* became a best seller. Written from his memories of his grandmother's stories of their family's beginnings from Africa to slavery and freedom, Haley became a household name with this popular novel. *Roots* made a strong impact as a book but more so as a television miniseries. *Roots*, in spite of its factual errors, is important for raising Americans awareness of African American history.

1977   Benjamin Hooks became executive director of the NAACP. After an accomplished career dedicated to civil rights, including a presidential appointment from Nixon, Hook, who holds a J.D. degree from De Paul University in Chicago, Illinois, accepted the position of executive director of the NAACP. He served in this capacity until 1992.

Ernest N. Morial elected first black mayor of New Orleans. Louisiana State University's first black law graduate, Morial led a remarkable, trailblazing life.

His election as the first black mayor of New Orleans came after he made a name for himself as an NAACP attorney, the first African American to serve as assistant U.S. attorney in Louisiana, and the first African American to serve in the Louisiana House of Representatives since the end of the nineteenth century.

Andrew Young appointed the first black U.S. ambassador to the United Nations. After a remarkable list of accomplishments, including being the first African American from Georgia to serve in the U.S. House of Representatives, Andrew Young, appointed by President Jimmy Carter, became the first black American to serve as America's ambassador to the United Nations.

1978   U.S. Supreme Court in *University of California Regents v. Bakke* rejected racial quotas. When the University of California at Davis medical school refused to admit Alan Bakke, a white student, on the ground that they had no more openings for white male candidates, Bakke sued on the ground of reverse discrimination. The medical school held 16 seats for minority students. Bakke argued that had a quota not existed, he would have been admitted. The Supreme Court ruled that a quota system was unacceptable since it denied nonminorities their rights.

1982   Voting Rights Act of 1965 renewed for another 25 years. This landmark piece of legislation that forbade educational requirements for voting had earlier been renewed in 1970 and 1975.

1983   Harold Washington elected first black mayor of Chicago, defeating incumbent mayor Jane Byrne. He won reelection in 1987 but died seven months later from a massive heart attack.

1984   Jesse Jackson sought the Democratic party nomination for president after helping Harold Washington win election as Chicago's first African American mayor. Jackson's Rainbow Coalition encouraged black voters to support his bid for the Democratic nomination. Although he did not succeed in his goal, he did win the third-highest number of delegates and thus carried significant influence in the 1984 Democratic party platform.

1985   Antiapartheid rallies were held throughout the world. Protesting South Africa's apartheid policies, political groups around the world held protest rallies calling for boycotts and other methods to promote desegregation.

1986   Martin Luther King, Jr's. birthday declared a national holiday. In reaction to the idea of King's birthday being recognized as a national holiday, some Americans protested against the economic expense of shutting down federal offices. To such concerns Kansas Senator Bob Dole replied, "I suggest they hurry back to their pocket calculators and estimate the cost of three hundred years of slavery, followed by another century or more of economic, political, social exclusion and discrimination." Congress declared the slain civil rights leader's birthday a national holiday to be held the third Monday of each January. President Reagan signed the bill. Biracial support for the bill reflected how far the nation had come since first becoming aware of Dr. King in 1955.

1988   Jesse Jackson sought Democratic party nomination for president. Having lost his bid for the nomination in 1983, Jackson ran again. Although he continued to enjoy the support of African American voters, the party did not nominate him. His influence within the Democratic party, however, continued to increase.

1989   Lawrence Douglas Wilder became governor of Virginia, the first black to be elected by popular vote to the governorship in any state. Elected by a narrow margin, Wilder's victory, in a state with 80 percent white voters, indicates the progress of the civil rights movement.

1990   Civil Rights Bill of 1990 vetoed by President George Bush. The bill worked to end discrimination against minorities in the workplace. Supported by Senator Edward Kennedy and Congressman Augustus Hawkins, President Bush vetoed the bill because he believed it was "destructive" in its use of quotas. Bush and Reagan are the only two presidents to reject civil rights legislation since the early 1950s.

1991   Clarence Thomas became the second black appointed to the U.S. Supreme Court. After a controversial and highly publicized confirmation hearing, in which Thomas was accused of sexual harassment by his former assistant Anita Hill, the U.S. Senate approved Clarence Thomas.

Mae Jamison became the first black female astronaut on a NASA space mission. She earned her medical degree from Cornell University before being contacted by NASA. After extensive training, Jamison traveled into orbit on 12 September 1992 as part of the crew on the space shuttle Endeavor. She later became a professor of environmental studies at Dartmouth College.

Rodney King beaten by Los Angeles police, sparking debate over police brutality toward minorities. When L.A. resident Rodney King, a black man, was brutally beaten by four police officers, and CNN televised a videotape of the beating, the nation recoiled in shock. Black residents of Los Angeles responded by destroying and looting area businesses, particularly those owned by Koreans. As ordered by President Bush, the Justice Department launched an investigation and charged the police officers involved with violating King's civil rights. King was awarded a $3.8 million settlement. The police were found not guilty, and a massive riot resulted.

1992   Carol Moseley Braun became the first black woman elected to U.S. Senate. She became the second African American in the twentieth century to win a seat in the Senate.

1993   Joycelyn Elders became the first black female appointed U.S. Surgeon General. President Clinton first appointed Elders as the director of Arkansas's Department of Health when he was that state's governor. Because of Elders's success in Arkansas, where she doubled the immunization rate for two-year-olds and increased early childhood screening by ten times its original levels, President Clinton, on 8 September 1993, appointed Elders U.S. Surgeon General. In that position, Elders called for universal health care and health care reforms. Her controversial views on sex education forced her resignation only 15 months into the job. After resigning she accepted a position at the University of Arkansas Medical Center as a professor of pediatrics.

1994   African American Religious Leaders Summit on HIV/AIDS held. Realizing the devastating impact the AIDS virus had on black communities, where the rates of infection significantly surpassed white communities, religious leaders met to discuss ways to deal with the problem.

O. J. Simpson trial, considered the trial of the century was held. After being charged with murdering his ex-wife Nicole Brown Simpson and her friend Ronald Goldman, former football great and actor O. J. Simpson was found not guilty in a highly publicized trial. Simpson's legal team represented some of the best-known attorneys in the nation, including F. Lee Bailey, Robert Shapiro, and Johnny Cockran.

Tiger Woods broke the de facto color line in the sport of golf, becoming the first black and the youngest person of any race to win the U.S. Amateur golf championship. Woods did for golf what Arthur Ashe did for tennis and Michael Jordan did for basketball in the 1990s.

1995   The Million Man March was organized by Louis Farrakhan of the Nation of Islam. The march's purpose was to inspire black men to take an active role in their communities and families. It had its critics, but it proved to be a spectacular event, not unlike those of the earlier Civil Rights years.

1996   Welfare Reform Act passed. Also known as the Work Opportunity Reconciliation Act of 1996, the act overhauled the welfare system in an effort to better serve recipients and reduce the number of people on welfare. The average time a recipient spent on welfare was reduced due to educational and employment assistance and opportunities.

Franklin Raines became the first black appointed director of the Office of Management and Budget for the U.S. government. Previously he had served as that agency's associate director, and previous to that office he served as the assistant director of White House Domestic Policy Staff from 1977–79. He later became the chief executive officer of Fannie Mae.

California voters passed Proposition 209, forbidding racial quotas in hiring. Highly controversial, Proposition 209 prohibits the use of quotas by federal, state, and locals government agencies, including schools and universities. Violators can be punished under federal law.

In *Hopwood v. Texas*, the Fifth Circuit Court prohibited the University of Texas from using race in order to insure a diverse student body. This court, which had led in the desegregation of the South, was now unwilling to expand on its judicial heritage.

1997   Advisory Board to the President's Initiative on Race established. Created under President Bill Clinton, the board, chaired by noted historian John Hope Franklin, made recommendations to the president on race relations in America.

1999   Guinean immigrant Amadou Diallo killed by New York City police in another case of racial profiling. NYPD special forces acted aggressively when they shot Diallo 19 times because he fit the description of a serial rapist. When he reached for his wallet, police said they though he was reaching for a weapon. Special forces fired 41 shots at Diallo but were not charged with a crime.

Representatives John Conyers and Tony Hall each introduced resolutions in the House of Representatives calling for national action to right the wrongs of slavery. These resolutions were part of a past movement, seemingly growing in importance in modern times, to have the nation pay reparations to the descendants of the slaves for the unrequited labor that black people had been forced to give in slavery and the wrongs of segregation. Several famous black attorneys have promised a law suit against the United States for the wrongs of slavery and Jim Crow segregation.

2000   Cincinnati race riots erupted over the killing of a black teenager by city police in another case of racial profiling. When Cincinnati police shot Timothy Thomas, a young black man with 14 outstanding warrants, including one for failure to wear a seat belt, it marked the fifth incident in some seven months in which a young black man was shot by police after fleeing from authorities. Thomas's death sparked a riot. Sixty-five people were injured before the riot ended.

2000–2001   The presidential election of 2000 ended with the outcome depending on the vote count in the state of Florida. Many African Americans believed that they had been improperly excluded from the vote in this state. The United States Commission on Civil Rights held hearings and concluded that the vote in Florida had indeed been affected by major violations of the Voting Rights Act. The U.S. Supreme Court blocked a recount, and the result was the controversial election of Republican George W. Bush over Democrat Al Gore. Whichever candidate they supported, Americans were shocked that, at the beginning of the twenty-first century, the greatest democracy in the world could suffer such suffrage irregularities and that race was still a factor in ensuring a fair vote.

2001   As he prepared to complete his eight years as president, Bill Clinton, frequently referred to in the black community as the nation's "first black president," published a set of reflections and recommendations to the next president and Congress on ways to bridge the nation's continuing racial divide.

2003   A black woman and a black man, Carol Moseley Braun and Al Sharpton, are candidates for the 2004 Democratic presidential nomination.

The U.S. Supreme Court in *Gutter v. Bollinger* and *Gratz v. Bollinger* issued decisions on the highly controversial issue of affirmative action. The former dealt with admission into the law school and the latter with admission to undergraduate education at the University of Michigan. The Court ruled that the University of Michigan's use of race as one factor in determining admission into the law school was constitutional, but the use of a point system that gave a set number of points to minority candidates was not. Advocates of affirmative action saw the decisions as victories for the idea that affirmative action was a legitimate tool for ensuring a diverse student body and a diverse population.

SELECTED
BIBLIOGRAPHY

Abraham, Henry J., and Barbara A. Perry. *Freedom and the Court: Civil Rights and Liberties in the United States*, 6th ed. (1994).

Ackerman, Peter, and Jack Duvall. *A Force More Powerful: A Century of Nonviolent Conflict* (2000).

America, Richard F. *Paying the Social Debt: What White America Owes Black America* (1993).

Anderson, James D. *The Education of Blacks in the South: 1860–1935* (1988).

Aptheker, Bettina. *The Morning Breaks: The Trial of Angela Davis* (1999).

Armor, David J. *Forced Justice: School Desegregation and the Law* (1995).

Ashmore, Harry. *Civil Rights and Wrongs: A Memoir of Race and Politics, 1944–1994* (1994).

Ball, Howard. *A Defiant Life: Thurgood Marshall and the Persistence of Racism in America* (1998).

Bardolph, Richard, ed. *The Civil Rights Record: Black Americans and the Law, 1849–1970* (1970).

Barnes, Catherine A. *Journey from Jim Crow: The Desegregation of Southern Transit* (1983).

Bartley, Numan V. *The Rise of Massive Resistance: Race and Politics in the South during the 1950s* (1969).

Bates, Berth T. *Pullman Porters and the Rise of Protest Politics in Black America, 1925–1945* (2001).

Bayor, Ronald H. *Race and the Shaping of Twentieth Century Atlanta* (1996).

Bean, Annemarie, ed. *A Sourcebook of African-American Performances: Plays, People, Movements* (1999).

Belknap, Michael R. *Federal Law and Southern Order: Racial Violence and Constitutional Conflict in the Post-Brown South* (1987).

Bell, Derrick A., Jr. *Race, Racism, and American Law*, 2nd ed. (1980).

Belz, Herman. *Emancipation and Equal Rights: Politics and Constitutionalism in the Civil War Era* (1978).

Berman, William C. *The Politics of Civil Rights in the Truman Administration* (1970).

Berry, Mary Francis. *The Pig Farmer's Daughter and Other Tales of American Justice: Episodes of Racism and Sexism in the Courts from 1865 to the Present* (2000).

Blumberg, Rhoda Lois. *Civil Rights: The 1960s Freedom Struggle* (1991).

Bond, James E. *No Easy Walk to Freedom: Reconstruction and the Ratification of the Fourteenth Amendment* (1997).

Branch, Taylor. *Parting the Waters: America in the King Years, 1954–1963* (1989).

———. *Pillar of Fire: America in the King Years, 1963–1965* (1998).

Brauer, Carl M. *John F. Kennedy and the Second Reconstruction* (1977).

Brinkley, Douglas. *Mine Eyes Have Seen the Glory: The Life of Rosa Parks* (2000).

Brisbane, Robert H. *Black Activism: Radical Revolution in the United States, 1954–1970* (1974).

———. *The Black Vanguard: Origins of the Negro Social Revolution, 1900–1960* (1970).

Brooks, Thomas R. *Walls Came Tumbling Down: A History of the Civil Rights Movement, 1940–1970* (1974).

Brown, Mary J. *Eradicating this Evil: Women in the American Anti-Lynching Movement, 1892–1940* (2000).

Brundage, W. Fitzhugh, ed. *Under Sentence of Death: Lynching in the South* (1997).

Bullock, Henry Allen. *The History of Negro Education in the South from 1619 to the Present* (1967).

Bullock, Penelope L. *The Afro-American Periodical Press: 1838–1900* (1981).

Bunche, Ralph J. *The Political Status of the Negro in the Age of FDR* (1973).

Burk, Robert Frederick. *The Eisenhower Administration and Black Civil Rights* (1984).

Burstein, Paul. *Discrimination, Jobs, and Politics: The Struggle for Equal Employment Opportunity in the United States since the New Deal* (1985).

Carson, Clayborne. *In Struggle: SNCC and the Black Awakening of the 1960s* (1981).

Chateauvert, Melinda. *Marching Together: Women of the Brotherhood of Sleeping Car Porters* (1998).

Clay, William L. *Just Permanent Interests: Black Americans in Congress, 1870–1992* (1993).

Cleaver, Kathleeen, and George Katsiaficas, eds. *Liberation, Imagination, and the Black Panther Party: A New Look at the Black Panthers and Their Legacy* (2001).

Collier-Thomas, Bettye, and V. P. Franklin, eds. *Sisters in the Struggle: African American Women in the Civil Rights–Black Power Movements* (2001).

Combs, Michael W., and John Gruhl, eds. *Affirmative Action Theories, Analysis and Prospects* (1986).

Cortner, Richard C. *The Supreme Court and the Second Bill of Rights: The Fourteenth Amendment and the Nationalization of Civil Liberties* (1981).

Couch, Harvey C. *A History of the Fifth Circuit, 1891–1981* (1984).

Cripps, Thomas. *Slow Fade to Black: The Negro in American Film, 1900–1946* (1977).

Cruden, Robert. *The Negro in Reconstruction* (1969).

Dalfiume, Richard M. *Desegregation of the U.S. Armed Forces: Fighting on Two Fronts, 1939–1953* (1969).

Daniel, Pete. *The Shadow of Slavery: Peonage in the South, 1901–1969* (1972).

Daniel, Walter C. *Black Journals of the United States* (1982).

Darling, Marsha J. Tyson, ed. *Race, Voting, Redistricting, and the Constitution: Sources and Explorations on the Fifteenth Amerndment, vol. 3: Alternate Redistricting, Registering and Voting Systems* (2001).

Davis, Arthur P. *From the Black Tower: Afro-American Writers, 1900 to 1960* (1974).

Davis, Cyprian. *The History of Black Catholics in the United States* (1995).

Davis, George, and Gregg Watson. *Black Life in Corporate America* (1982).

Davis, Marianna W., ed. *Contributions of Black Women to America, vol. 1: The Arts, Media, Business, Law, Sports* (1982).

Davison, Chandler, and Bernard Grofman, eds. *Quiet Revolution in the South: The Impact of the Voting Rights Act, 1965–1990* (1994).

De Santis, Christopher C., ed. *Langston Hughes and the Chicago Defender: Essays on Race, Politics, and Culture, 1942–62* (1995).

Dittmer, John. *Local People: The Struggle for Civil Rights in Mississippi* (1994).

Du Bois, W.E.B. *Black Reconstruction in America* (1935).

Entman, Robert M., and Andrew Rojecki. *The Black Image in the White Mind: Media and Race in America* (2001).

Eskew, Glenn T. *But for Birmingham: The Local and National Movements in the Civil Rights Struggle* (1997).

Fairclough, Adam. *To Redeem the Soul of America: The Southern Christian Leadership Conference and Martin Luther King, Jr.* (1987).

Fairman, Charles. *History of the Supreme Court of the United States, vol. 7: Reconstruction and Reunion, 1864–1888, Part 2* (1986).

Findlay, James F., Jr. *Church People in the Struggle: The National Council of Churches and the Black Freedom Movement, 1950–1970* (1993).

Fletcher, Marvin E. *The Black Soldier and Officer in the United States Army* (1974).

Foner, Eric. *Freedom's Lawmakers: A Dictionary of Black Officeholders during Reconstruction* (1993).

———. *Reconstruction: America's Unfinished Revolution, 1863–1877* (1988).

Foner, Philip S. *American Socialism and Black Americans: From the Age of Jackson to World War II* (1977).

———. *Organized Labor and the Black Worker, 1619–1981* (1982).

Foner, Philip S., and Ronald L. Lewis, eds. *The Black Worker: A Documentary History from Colonial Times to the Present, vol. 5: The Black Worker from 1900 to 1919* (1980).

Foner, Philip S., and George E. Walker, eds. *Proceedings of the Black National and State Conventions, 1865–1900* (1986).

Fowler, Virginia. *Nikki Giovanni* (1992).

Franklin, John Hope. *The Emancipation Proclamation* (1963).

Franklin, John Hope, and August Meier, eds. *Black Leaders of the Twentieth Century* (1982).

Franklin, John Hope, and Alfred A. Moss, Jr. *From Slavery to Freedom: A History of Negro Americans*, 8th ed. (2000).

Friedman, Leon, and Fred L. Israel, eds. *The Justices of the United States Supreme Court, 1789–1969: Their Lives and Major Opinions*, 5 vols. (1969–78).

Fullinwider, S. P. *The Mind and Mood of Black America* (1969).

Garrow, David J. *Bearing the Cross: Martin Luther King, Jr., and the Southern Christian Leadership Conference* (1986).

―――. *Protest at Selma: Martin Luther King, Jr., and the Voting Rights Act of 1965* (1978).

Gillette, William. *Retreat from Reconstruction, 1869–1879* (1979).

Gillon, Steven M. *Politics and Vision: The ADA and American Liberalism, 1947–1985* (1987).

Goings, Kenneth W. *The NAACP Comes of Age: The Defeat of Judge John J. Parker* (1990).

Goldfied, David R., Jr. *Black, White, and Southern: Race Relations and Southern Culture, 1940 to the Present* (1990).

Goldman, Robert M. *Reconstruction and Black Suffrage: Losing the Vote in Reese and Cruikshank* (2000).

Gordon, Ann D., et al. *African American Women and the Vote, 1837–1965* (1997).

Graham, Hugh Davis. *The Civil Rights Era* (1990).

Grant, Donald B. *The Anti-Lynching Movement, 1883–1932* (1975).

Greenberg, Cheryl Lynn, ed. *A Circle of Trust: Remembering SNCC* (1998).

Greenberg, Jack. *Race Relations and American Law* (1959).

Greene, Kathanne W. *Affirmative Action and Principles of Justice* (1989).

Grossman, James R. *Land of Hope: Chicago, Black Southerners, and the Great Migration* (1989).

Gutman, Herbert G. *The Family in Slavery and Freedom, 1750–1925* (1976).

Habenstreit, Barbara. *Eternal Vigilance: The American Civil Liberties Union in Action* (1971).

Hampton, Henry, and Steve Fayer. *Voices of Freedom: An Oral History of the Civil Rights Movement from the 1950s through the 1980s* (1990).

Harlan, Louis R. *Booker T. Washington: The Making of a Black Leader, 1856–1901* (1972).

―――. *Booker T. Washington: The Wizard of Tuskegee, 1901–1915* (1983).

Harmon, David Andrew. *Beneath the Image of the Civil Rights Movement and Race Relations: Atlanta, Georgia, 1946–1981* (1996).

Harris, Fred, and Roger W. Wilkins, eds. *Quiet Riots: Race and Poverty in the United States, The Kerner Report Twenty Years Later* (1988).

Harris, Jacqueline L. *History and Achievement of the NAACP* (1992).

Henry, Charles P. *Ralph Bunche: Model Negro or American Other?* (1999).

Higginbotham, A. Leon. *Shades of Freedom: Racial Politics and Presumptions of the American Legal Process* (1996).

Higginbotham, Evelyn Brooks, Leon F. Litwack, Darlene Clark Hine, Henry Louis Gates, Jr., and Randall K. Burkett, eds. *The Harvard Guide to African-American History* (2001).

Hine, Darlene Clark, et al., eds. *Black Women in America: An Historical Encyclopedia* (1993).

Hogan, Lawrence D. *A Black National News Service, the Associated Press and Claude Barnett, 1919–1945* (1984).

Huggins, Nathan Irvin. *Harlem Renaissance* (1977).

Irons, Peter, and Stephanie Guitton, eds. *May It Please the Court: The Most Significant Arguments Made before the Supreme Court Since 1955* (1994).

Jenkins, Robert L., and Mfanya D. Tryman. *Malcolm X Encyclopedia* (2002).

Kaczorowski, Robert. *The Politics of Judicial Interpretation: The Federal Courts, Department of Justice and Civil Rights, 1866–1876* (1985).

Kellner, Bruce, ed. *The Harlem Renaissance: A Historical Dictionary for the Era* (1984).

Kellogg, Charles Flint. *NAACP: A History of the National Association for the Advancement of Colored People* (1967).

Kennedy, Randall. *Race, Crime, and the Law* (1997).

Kirby, John B. *Black Americans in the Roosevelt Era* (1980).

Kluger, Richard. *Simple Justice: The History of Brown v. Board of Education and Black America's Struggle for Equality* (1976).

Kousser, J. Morgan. *Colorblind Justice: Minority Voting Rights and the Undoing of the Second Reconstruction* (1999).

Krenn, Michael. *Black Diplomacy: African Americans and the State Department, 1945–1965* (1999).

Kulik, Gerhard. *Africa and the Blues* (1999).

Lawson, Steven F. *Black Ballots: Voting Rights in the South, 1944–1969* (1976).

———. *In Pursuit of Power: Southern Blacks and Electoral Politics, 1965–1982* (1985).

———. *Running for Freedom: Civil Rights and Black Politics in America since 1941* (1991).

Lawson, Steven F., and Charles Payne. *Debating the Civil Rights Movement, 1945–1968* (1998).

Levine, Robert S. *Martin Delany, Frederick Douglass, and the Politics of Representative Identity* (1997).

Lewis, David Levering. *King: A Critical Biography* (1970).

———. *W.E.B. Du Bois: Biography of a Race, 1868–1919* (1993).

———. *W.E.B. Du Bois: The Fight for Equality and the American Century* (2000).

Lewis, John, with Michael D'Orso. *Walking with the Wind: A Memoir of the Movement* (1998).

Lichtenstein, Nelson. *The Most Dangerous Man in Detroit: Walter Reuther and the Fate of American Labor* (1995).

Lincoln, C. Eric. *The Black Muslims in America* (1973).

———. *Race, Religion, and the Continuing American Dilemma* (1984).

Little, Lawrence S. *Disciples of Liberty: The African Methodist Episcopal Church in the Age of Imperialism, 1884–1916* (2000).

Litwack, Leon, and August Meier, eds. *Black Leaders of the Nineteenth Century* (1988).

Lofgren, Charles A. *The Plessy Case: A Legal-Historical Interpretation* (1987).

Logan, Rayford W., and Michael R. Winston, eds. *Dictionary of American Negro Biography* (1982).

Love, Spencie. *One Blood: The Death and Resurrection of Charles R. Drew* (1996).

MacGregor, Morris J. *Integration of the Armed Forces, 1940–1965* (1981).

McMillen, Neil R. *Dark Journey: Black Mississippians in the Age of Jim Crow* (1989).

McPherson, James M. *The Abolitionist Legacy: From Reconstruction to the NAACP* (1975).

———. *The Struggle for Equality: Abolitionists and the Negro in the Civil War and Reconstruction* (1964).

Manis, Andrew M. *A Fire You Can't Put Out: The Civil Rights Life of Birmingham's Reverend Fred Shuttlesworth* (1999).

Marks, Carole, and Diana Edkins. *The Power of Pride: Stylemakers and Rulebreakers of the Harlem Renaissance* (1999).

Mayberry, B. D. *A Century of Agriculture in the 1890 Land Grant Institutions and Tuskegee University, 1890–1990* (1991).

Mayer, Kenneth R. *With the Stroke of a Pen: Executive Orders and Presidential Power* (2001).

Meier, August. *Negro Thought in America, 1880–1915: Racial Ideologies in the Age of Booker T. Washington* (1963).

Meier, August, and Elliott Rudwick. *Black History and the Historical Profession, 1915–1980* (1986).

———. *CORE: A Study in the Civil Rights Movement, 1942–1968* (1973).

Melnick, Jeffrey P. *A Right to Sing the Blues: African Americans, Jews, and American Popular Song* (1999).

Mendelsohn, Jack. *The Martyrs: Sixteen Who Gave Their Lives for Racial Justice* (1966).

Meyer, Stephen Grant. *As Long as They Don't Move Next Door: Segregation and Racial Conflict in American Neighborhoods* (2000).

Miller, Loren. *The Petitioners: The Story of the Supreme Court of the United States and the Negro* (1966).

Moore, Jesse Thomas, Jr. *A Search for Equality: The National Urban League, 1910–1961* (1981).

Morris, Aldon D. *The Origins of the Civil Rights Movement: Black Communities Organizing for Change* (1984).

Moses, Wilson J. *The Golden Age of Black Nationalism, 1850–1925* (1978).

Muse, Benjamin. *The American Negro Revolution: From Nonviolence to Black Power, 1963–1967* (1968).

Myrdal, Gunnar. *An American Dilemma: The Negro Problem and Modern Democracy* (1944).

Nalty, Bernard C. *Strength for the Fight: A History of Black Americans in the Military* (1986).

National Advisory Commission on Civil Disorders, *Report* (1968).

Nelson, William E. *The Fourteenth Amendment: From Political Principle to Judicial Doctrine* (1988).

Nieman, Donald G. *Promises to Keep: African-Americans and the Constitutional Order, 1776 to the Present* (1991).

Norrell, Robert J. *Reaping the Whirlwind: The Civil Rights Movement in Tuskegee* (1985).

Oates, Stephen B. *Let the Trumpet Sound: The Life of Martin Luther King, Jr.* (1982).

Olson, Lynne. *Freedom's Daughters: The Unsung Heroines of the Civil Rights Movement from 1830–1970* (2001).

Oppenheimer, Martin. *The Sit-In Movement of 1960* (1989).

Parks, Rosa, with Jim Haskins. *Rosa Parks: My Story* (1992).

Patterson, James T. *Brown v. Board of Education: A Civil Rights Milestone and Its Troubled Legacy* (2001).

Payne, Charles M. *I've Got the Light of Freedom. The Organizing Tradition and the Mississippi Freedom Struggle* (1995).

Peltason, J. W. *Fifty-eight Lonely Men: Southern Federal Judges and School Desegregation* (1961).

Perry, Michael J. *We the People: The Fourteenth Amendment and the Supreme Court* (1999).

Pfeffer, Paula F. *A. Philip Randolph: Pioneer of the Civil Rights Movement* (1996).

Ploski, Harry A., and James Williams, eds. *The Negro Almanac: A Reference Work on the African American*, 5th ed. (1989).

Polsgrove, Carol. *Divided Minds: Intellectuals and the Civil Rights Movement* (2001).

Powers, Roger, and William Vogele, eds. *Protest and Change: An Encyclopedia of Nonviolent Action from ACT-UP to Women's Suffrage* (1997).

Pride, Armstead S., and Clint C. Wilson II. *A History of the Black Press* (1997).

Rabinowitz, Howard N. *Race Relations in the Urban South, 1865–1890* (1978).

Read, Frank T., and Lucy S. McGough. *Let Them Be Judged: The Judicial Integration of the Deep South* (1978).

Robinson, Randall. *The Debt: What America Owes to Blacks* (2001).

Rogers, Mary Beth. *Barbara Jordan: American Hero* (2000).

Rubino, Phil A. *A History of Affirmative Action, 1619–2000.* (2000).

Salem, Dorothy C., ed. *African American Women* (1993).

Shapiro, Herbert. *White Violence and Black Response from Reconstruction to Montgomery* (1988).

Shattuck, Gardiner H. *Episcopalians and Race: Civil War to Civil Rights* (2000).

Singh, Robert. *The Congressional Black Caucus: Racial Politics in the U.S. Congress* (1997).

Sitkoff, Harvard. *A New Deal for Blacks: The Emergence of Civil Rights as a National Issue, The Depression Decade* (1978).

———. *The Struggle for Black Equality, 1954–1980* (1981).

Smith, John C. *Emancipation: The Making of the Black Lawyer, 1844–1944* (1993).

Solomon, Mark I. *The Cry Was Unity: Communists and African Americans, 1917–1936* (1998).

Southern, David W. *Gunnar Myrdal and Black-White Relations: The Use and Abuse of an American Dilemma, 1944–1969* (1987).

Southern, Eileen. *Biographical Dictionary of Afro-American and African Musicians* (1982).

Sternett, Milton C. *Bound for the Promised Land: African American Religion and the Great Migration* (1997).

Stoper, Emily. *The Student Nonviolent Coordinating Committee* (1989).

Strickland, Arvarh E., and Robert E. Weems, Jr., eds. *The African-American Experience: An Historiographical and Bibliographical Guide* (2000).

Sudarshan, Kapur. *Raising Up a Prophet: The African American Encounter with Gandhi* (1992).

Suggs, Henry Lewis, ed. *The Black Press in the South, 1865–1979* (1983).

Sullivan, Patricia. *Days of Hope: Race and Democracy in the New Deal Era* (1996).

Swain, Carol M. *Black Faces, Black Interests: The Representation of African Americans in Congress* (1993).

Thomas, Brooks, ed. *Plessy v. Ferguson: A Brief History with Documents* (1997).

Thompson, Julius. *The Black Press in Mississippi, 1865–1985* (1993).

Thurber, Timothy. *The Politics of Equality: Hubert H. Humphrey and the African American Freedom Struggle* (1999).

Toppin, Edgar A. *A Biographical History of Blacks in America since 1528* (1971).

Trefousse, Hans L. *Lincoln's Decision for Emancipation* (1975).

———. *The Radical Republicans: Lincoln's Vanguard for Racial Justice* (1969).

Tushnet, Mark V. *Making Civil Rights Law: Thurgood Marshall and the Supreme Court, 1936–1961* (1994).

———. *The NAACP's Legal Strategy against Segregated Education, 1925–1950* (1987).

Urquhart, Brian. *Ralph Bunche: An American Life* (1993).

U.S. Equal Employment Opportunity Commission. *A History of the Equal Employment Opportunity Commission, 1965–1984* (1984).

Verney, Kavern J. *The Art of the Possible: Booker T. Washington and Black Leadership in the United States, 1881–1925* (2001).

Walker, Juliet E. K. *The History of Black Business in America: Capitalism, Race, and Entrepreneurship* (1998).

Wallenstein, Peter. *Tell the Court I Love My Wife: Race, Marriage, and the Law—An American History* (2002).

Waskow, Arthur I. *From Race Riot to Sit-In, 1919 and the 1960s: A Study in the Connections between Conflict and Violence* (1966).

Watts, Jerry G. *Heroism and the Black Intellectual: Ralph Ellison, Politics, and Afro-American Intellectual Life* (1994).

Watts, Jill. *God, Harlem U.S.A.: The Father Divine Story* (1992).

Wedin, Carolyn. *Inheritors of the Spirit: Mary White Ovington and the Founding of the NAACP* (1998).

Weisbrot, Robert. *Freedom Bound: A History of America's Civil Rights Movement* (1990).

Weiss, Nancy J. *Farewell to the Party of Lincoln* (1983).

———. *The National Urban League, 1910–1940* (1974).

White, Marjorie L. *A Walk to Freedom: The Reverend Fred Shuttlesworth and the Alabama Christian Movement for Human Rights, 1954–1964* (1998).

Wilkinson, J. Harvie, III. *From Brown to Bakke: The Supreme Court and School Integration, 1954–1978* (1979).

Williams, Juan. *Eyes on the Prize: America's Civil Rights Years, 1954–1965* (1987).

———. *Thurgood Marshall: American Revolutionary* (1998).

Williamson, Joel. *The Crucible of Race: Black-White Relations in the American South since Emancipation* (1984).

Wilmore, Gayraud S. *Black Religion and Black Radicalism: An Interpretation of the Religious History of Afro-American People* (1983).

Wilson Francille R. *The Segregated Scholars: Black Social Scientists and the Development of Black Labor Studies, 1890–1950* (2002).

Wolters, Raymond. *The Burden of Brown: Thirty Years of School Desegregation* (1984).

———. *Negroes and the Great Depression* (1970).

Woodward, C. Vann. *The Strange Career of Jim Crow*, 2nd ed. (1974).

Wright, Roberta Hughes. *The Birth of the Montgomery Bus Boycott* (1991).

Young, Andrew. *An Easy Burden: The Civil Rights Movement and the Transformation of America* (1996).

———. *A Way Out of No Way: The Spiritual Memoirs of Andrew Young* (1994).

Zangrando, Robert L. *The NAACP Crusade against Lynching, 1909–1950* (1980).

Zigler, Edward, and Susan Muenchow. *Head Start: The Inside Story of America's Most Successful Education Experiment* (1992).

Zinn, Howard. *SNCC: The New Abolitionists* (1964).

PREFACE TO PRIMARY DOCUMENTS

Assembling this collection of documents for the expanded and revised edition of *The Greenwood Encyclopedia of African American Civil Rights* has been a challenging but enjoyable task. I am indebted to the editors, Charles Lowery and John Marszalek, and to Cynthia Harris of Greenwood Press, for the opportunity.

In preparing this collection, I have tried to cover a wide spectrum of time, issues, and voices—so wide in fact that it has proven impossible to give every era, issue, and voice the amount of space each deserves in this volume. I have thus made difficult choices about which sources to include, how much of each source to include, and what to omit altogether. As a rule, I have included only those documents that show a clear promotion of African American civil rights or that otherwise represent steps of progress in the continuing struggle. I have deliberately omitted those documents that represent setbacks in the struggle. If certain important documents, influential leaders, or pivotal events in the civil rights movement seem to be conspicuously absent, I can only assure readers that I made every effort to be as inclusive as possible. In order to show graphically the attitudes of earlier years, I left standing insulting words that grate on the modern ear.

I believe that the selections of primary source documents will help bring to life many of the individuals, organizations, acts of Congress, court cases, literary works, and miscellaneous contributions to the civil rights movement that are listed in the alphabetical section of this encyclopedia. Above all, I hope readers will find this collection to be, like the rest of the encyclopedia, educational and inspirational.

Thomas Adams Upchurch

PRIMARY
DOCUMENTS

Compiled, Arranged, and Edited by Thomas Adams Upchurch

1.

FREDERICK DOUGLASS ON THE FUTURE OF THE NEGRO PEOPLE IN THE SLAVE STATES
(1862)

Easily the most renowned abolitionist-turned-civil rights advocate of his age, Douglass had a way with words that would have complemented any reform movement in any age. As an orator and writer, he was unsurpassed in the late nineteenth century. Below is a sample of one of his many forceful speeches. It was delivered to the Emancipation League in Boston in early 1862, before President Lincoln issued the Emancipation Proclamation.

At the opening session of the present Congress there was a marked, decided, and emphatic expression against slavery as the great motive power of the present slaveholding war. Many petitions, numerously and influentially signed, were duly sent in and presented to that body, praying, first, for the entire abolition of slavery in all the slaveholding States; secondly, that a just award be made by Congress to loyal slaveholders; and thirdly, that the slaves of rebels be wholly confiscated. The vigor, earnestness, and power with which these objects were advocated, as war measures . . . inspired the loyal friends of Freedom all over the North with renewed confidence and hope, both for the country and for the slave. The conviction was general that at last the country was to have a policy, and that that policy would bring freedom and safety to the Republic.

Thus far, however, this hope, this confidence, this conviction has not been justified. The country is without a known policy. The enemies of the Abolition cause, taking alarm from these early efforts, have earnestly set themselves to the work of producing a reaction in favor of slavery, and have succeeded beyond what they themselves must have expected at the first.

Among other old, and threadbare, and worn out objections which they have raised against the Emancipation policy, is the question as to what shall be done with the four million slaves of the South, if they are emancipated? Or in other words, what shall be the future of the four million slaves?

I am sensible, deeply sensible, of the importance of this subject, and of the many difficulties which are supposed to surround it.

If there is any one great, pressing, and all-commanding problem for this nation to solve, and to solve without delay, that problem is slavery. Its claims are urgent, palpable, and powerful. The issue involves the whole question of life and death to the nation. . . .

It is now or never with us.

The field is ripe for the harvest. God forbid that when the smoke and thunder of this slaveholding war shall have rolled from the troubled face of the country it shall be said that the harvest is past, the summer is ended and we are not saved. . . .

But why, O why should we not abolish slavery now? All admit that it must be abolished at some time. What better time than now can be assigned for that great work?—Why should it longer live? What good thing has it done that it should be given further lease of life? What evil thing has it left undone? Behold its dreadful history! Saying nothing of the rivers of tears and streams of blood poured out by its 4,000,000 victims—saying nothing of the leprous poison it has diffused through the life blood of our morals and our religion—saying nothing of the many humiliating concessions already made to it—saying nothing of the deep and scandalous reproach it has brought upon our national good name—saying nothing of all this, and more the simple fact that this monster Slavery has eaten up and devoured the patriotism of the whole South, kindled the lurid flames of a bloody rebellion in our midst, invited the armies of hostile nations to desolate our soil, and break down our Government, is good and all-sufficient cause of smiting it as with a bolt from the heaven. If it is possible for any system of barbarism to sign its own death warrant, Slavery, by its own natural working, is that system. All the arguments of conscience, sound expediency, national honor and safety unite in the fiat—let it die the death of its own election. . . .

I rejoice therefore in the formation of the Emancipation league. May its work be quick, certain and complete. . . .

But I come now to the more immediate subject of my lecture, namely: What shall be done with the four million slaves if they are emancipated? . . .

My answer to the question . . . shall be short and simple: Do nothing with them, but leave them like you have left other men, to do with and for themselves. . . .

Let us alone. Do nothing with us, for us, or by us as a particular class. What you have done with us thus far has only worked to our disadvantage. We now simply ask to be allowed to do for ourselves. . . .

What shall be done with the four million slaves, if emancipated. I answer, deal justly with them; pay them honest wages for honest work; dispense with the biting lash, and pay them the ready cash; awaken a new class of motives in them; remove those old motives of shriveling fear of punishment which benumb and degrade the soul, and supplant them by the higher and better motives of hope, of self-respect, of honor, and of personal responsibility. Reverse the whole current of feeling in regard to them. They have been compelled hitherto to regard the white man as a cruel, selfish, and remorseless tyrant, thirsting for wealth, greedy of gain, and caring nothing as to the means by which he obtains it. Now, let him see that the white man has a nobler and better side to his character, and he will love, honor, esteem the white man. . . .

Again, it is affirmed that the Negro, if emancipated, could not take care of himself. My answer to this is, let him have a fair chance to try it. For 200 years he has taken care of himself and his master in the bargain. I see no reason to believe that he could not take care, and very excellent care, of himself when having only himself to support. . . .

We are asked if we would turn the slaves all loose. I answer, Yes. Why not? . . .

But would you have them stay here? Why should they not? . . .

Will they occupy more room in freedom than slavery? If you could bear them as objects of your injustice, can they be more offensive as objects of your justice and humanity? Why send them away? . . .

My friends, the destiny of the colored American, however this mighty war shall terminate, is the destiny of America. We shall never leave you. . . .

See Philip S. Foner, ed., *The Life and Writings of Frederick Douglass, vol. 3: The Civil War, 1861–1865* (New York: International Publishers, 1952), 211–25.

2.

THE EMANCIPATION PROCLAMATION
(1863)

Abraham Lincoln wrote this document over a period of time in early 1862, presented it to his cabinet in July, and issued it on 22 September after the Union army victory at Antietam. It went into effect on 1 January 1863. Although it represented a limited assault on slavery, the Proclamation had an important psychological effect on both sides in the conflict as well as on nations in Europe. Even though the slaves were already freeing themselves, Lincoln's action gained him the reputation as the "Great Emancipator."

By the President of the United States of America:

A Proclamation

Whereas on the 22nd day of September, A.D. 1862, a proclamation was issued by the President of the United States, containing, among other things, the following, to wit:

"That on the 1st day of January, A.D. 1863, all persons held as slaves within any State or designated part of a State the people whereof shall then be in rebellion against the United States shall be then, thenceforward, and forever free; and the executive government of the United States, including the military and naval authority thereof, will recognize and maintain the freedom of such persons and will do no act or acts to repress such persons, or any of them, in any efforts they may make for their actual freedom.

"That the executive will on the 1st day of January aforesaid, by proclamation, designate the States and parts of States, if any, in which the people thereof, respectively, shall then be in rebellion against the United States; and the fact that any State or the people thereof shall on that day be in good faith represented in the Congress of the United States by members chosen thereto at elections wherein a majority of the qualified voters of such States shall have participated shall, in the absence of strong countervailing testimony, be deemed conclusive evidence that such State and the people thereof are not then in rebellion against the United States."

Now, therefore, I, Abraham Lincoln, President of the United States, by virtue of the power in me vested as Commander-In-Chief of the Army and Navy of the United States in time of actual armed rebellion against the authority and government of the United States, and as a fit and necessary war measure for suppressing said rebellion, do, on this 1st day of January, A.D. 1863, and in accordance with my purpose so to do, publicly proclaimed for the full period of one hundred days from the first day above mentioned, order and designate as the States and parts of States wherein the people thereof, respectively, are this day in rebellion against the United States the following, to wit:

Arkansas, Texas, Louisiana (except the parishes of St. Bernard, Palquemines, Jefferson, St. John, St. Charles, St. James, Ascension, Assumption, Terrebone, Lafourche, St. Mary, St. Martin, and Orleans, including the city of New Orleans), Mississippi, Alabama, Florida, Georgia, South Carolina, North Carolina, and Virginia (except the forty-eight counties designated as West Virginia, and also the counties of Berkeley, Accomac, Northampton, Elizabeth City, York, Princess Anne, and Norfolk, including the cities of Norfolk and Portsmouth), and which excepted parts are for the present left precisely as if this proclamation were not issued.

And by virtue of the power and for the purpose aforesaid, I do order and declare that all persons held as slaves within said designated States and parts of States are, and henceforward shall be, free; and that the Executive Government of the United States, including the military and naval authorities thereof, will recognize and maintain the freedom of said persons.

And I hereby enjoin upon the people so declared to be free to abstain from all violence, unless in necessary self-defense; and I recommend to them that, in all case when allowed, they labor faithfully for reasonable wages.

And I further declare and make known that such persons of suitable condition will be received into the armed service of the United States to garrison forts, positions, stations, and other places, and to man vessels of all sorts in said service.

And upon this act, sincerely believed to be an act of justice, warranted by the Constitution upon military necessity, I invoke the considerate judgment of mankind and the gracious favor of Almighty God.

See 12 *Statutes at Large*, 1268.

3.

ABOLITIONISTS CONTINUE THE ANTISLAVERY CRUSADE (1864)

William Wells Brown, for many years a leading black abolitionist, spoke at the New England Anti-Slavery Convention in Boston in May 1864 while the Civil War was in progress. Despite the Emancipation Proclamation, he, like many of his fellow abolitionists, feared that slavery might yet survive the war. Motivated by this fear, he urged his fellow abolitionists not to grow complacent, but to continue pressing for the liberation of all slaves.

Slavery has received a severe, it may be a fatal blow. Yet the colored man has everything to fear. Even when Grant's army shall be successful, we, the colored people, will be yet in danger. The advantages we have so far received have come as much through Jeff. Davis as through President Lincoln. The war was begun with the purpose of restoring the nation as it was, and leaving the black man where he was. Now the time has come when you must recognize the black man as on the same footing with the white man. If not, the mission of this war is not ended, and we must have yet more disasters to scourge us into the right way.

See William Edward Farrison, *William Wells Brown: Author and Reformer* (Chicago: The University of Chicago Press, 1969), 390.

4.

THIRTEENTH AMENDMENT TO THE UNITED STATES CONSTITUTION (1865)

The Republican Congress passed this self-explanatory amendment almost immediately after the Civil War to ensure that no African Americans would be re-enslaved in coming days or years.

Section 1. Neither slavery nor involuntary servitude, except as a punishment for crime whereof the party shall have been duly convicted, shall exist within the United States, or any place subject to their jurisdiction.
Section 2. Congress shall have power to enforce this article by appropriate legislation.

See *U.S. Code*, Amendment 13.

5.

FIRST RECONSTRUCTION ACT (1867)

The Republican Congress, unhappy with the progress of Presidential Reconstruction, especially the treatment of the freedmen, wrested control of national policy away from President Andrew Johnson and passed this act, thus initiating the three-year phase of military Reconstruction.

March 2, 1867
An Act to provide for the more efficient Government of the Rebel States

WHEREAS no legal State governments or adequate protection for life or property now exists in the rebel States of Virginia, North Carolina, South Carolina, Georgia, Mississippi, Alabama, Louisiana, Florida, Texas, and Arkansas; and whereas it is necessary that peace and good order should be enforced in said States until loyal and republican State governments can be legally established: Therefore,

Be it enacted by the Senate and the House of Representatives of the United States of America in Congress assembled, That said rebel States shall be divided into military districts and made subject to the military authority of the United States as hereinafter prescribed, and for that purpose Virginia shall constitute the first district; North Carolina and South Carolina the second district; Georgia, Alabama, and Florida the third district; Mississippi and Arkansas the fourth district; and Louisiana and Texas the fifth district.

Section 2. And be it further enacted, That it shall be the duty of the President to assign to the command of each of said districts an officer of the army, not below the rank of brigadier-general, and to detail a sufficient military force to enable such officer to perform his duties and enforce his authority within the district to which he is assigned.

Section 3. And be it further enacted, That it shall be the duty of each officer assigned as aforesaid, to protect all persons in their rights of person and property, to suppress insurrection, disorder, and violence, and to punish, or cause to be punished, all disturbers of the public peace and criminals; and to this end he may allow local civil tribunals to take jurisdiction of and to try offenders, or, when in his judgment it may be necessary for the trial of offenders, he shall have power to organize military commissions or tribunals for that purpose, and all interference under color of State authority with the exercise of military authority under this act, shall be null and void.

Section 4. And be it further enacted, That all persons put under military arrest by virtue of this act shall be tried without unnecessary delay, and no cruel or unusual punishment shall be inflicted, and no sentence of any military commission or tribunal hereby authorized, affecting the life or liberty of any person, shall be executed until it is approved by the officer in command of the district, and the laws and regulations for the government of the army shall not be affected by this act, except in so far as they conflict with its provisions: Provided, That no sentence of death under the provisions of this act shall be carried into effect without the approval of the President.

Section 5. And be it further enacted, That when the people of any one of said rebel States shall have formed a constitution of government in conformity with the Constitution of the United States in all respects, framed by a convention of delegates elected by the male citizens of said State, twenty-one years old and upward, of whatever race, color, or previous condition, who have been resident in said State for one year previous to the day of such election, except such as may be disfranchised for participation in the rebellion or for felony at common law, and when such constitution shall provide that the elective franchise shall be enjoyed by all persons as have the qualifications herein stated for electors of delegates, and when such constitution shall be ratified by a majority of the persons voting on the question of ratification who are qualified as electors for delegates, and when such constitution shall have been submitted to Congress for examination and approval, and Congress shall have approved the same, and when said State, by a vote of its legislature elected under said constitution, shall have adopted the amendment to the Constitution of the United States, proposed by the Thirty-ninth Congress, and known as article fourteen and when said article shall have become a part of the Constitution of the United States said State shall be declared entitled to representation in Congress, and senators and representatives shall be admitted therefrom on their taking the oath prescribed by law, and then and thereafter the preceding sections of this act shall be inoperative in said State: Provided, That no person excluded from the privilege of holding office by said proposed amendment to the Constitution of the United States, shall be eligible to election as a member of the convention to frame a constitution for any of said rebel States, nor shall any person vote for members of such convention.

Section 6. And be it further enacted, That, until the people of said rebel States shall be by law admitted to representation in the Congress of the United States, any civil governments which may exist there in shall be deemed provisional only, and in all respects subject to the paramount authority of the United States at any time to abolish, modify, control, or supersede the same; and in all elections to any office under such provisional governments all persons shall be entitled to vote, and none others, who are entitled to vote, under the provisions of the fifth section of this act; and no persons shall be eligible to any office under any such provisional government who would be disqualified from holding office under the provisions of the third article of said constitutional amendment.

See 14 *Statutes at Large*, 428.

6.

SECOND RECONSTRUCTION ACT (1867)

This act provided for the reorganization of state governments in the Confederate states, under the watchful eye of U.S. military supervisors.

March 23, 1867

SUPPLEMENTARY RECONSTRUCTION ACT OF THE FORTIETH CONGRESS

An Act supplementary to an act entitled "An act to provide for the more efficient government of the rebel states," passed March second, eighteen hundred and sixty-seven, and to facilitate restoration.

Be it enacted by the Senate and the House of Representatives of the United States of America in Congress assembled, That before the first day of September, eighteen hundred and sixty-seven, the commanding general in each district defined by an act entitled "An Act to provide for the more efficient government of the rebel States," passed March second, eighteen hundred and sixty-seven, shall cause a registration to be made of the male citizens of the United States, twenty-one years of age and upwards, resident in each county or parish in the State or States included in his district, which registration shall include only those persons who are qualified to vote for delegates by the act aforesaid, and who shall have taken and subscribed the following oath or affirmation: "I, _____, do solemnly swear, (or affirm,) in the presence of Almighty God, that I am a citizen of the State of _____; that I have resided in said State for _____ months next preceding this day, and now reside in the county of _____, or the parish of _____, in said State, (as the case may be;) that I am twenty-one years old; that I have not been disfranchised for participation in any rebellion or civil war against the United States, nor for felony committed against the laws of any State or of the United States; that I have never been a member of any State legislature, nor held any executive or judicial office in any State and afterwards engaged in insurrection or rebellion against the United States, or given aid or comfort to the enemies thereof; that I have never taken an oath as a member of Congress of the United States, or as an officer of the United States, or as a member of any State legislature, or as an executive or judicial officer of any State, to support the Constitution of the United States, and afterwards engaged in insurrection or rebellion against the United States or given aid or comfort to the enemies thereof; that I will faithfully support the Constitution and obey the laws of the United States, and will, to the best of my ability, encourage others so to do, so help me God;" which oath or affirmation may be administered by any registering officer.

Section 2. That after the completion of the registration hereby provided for in any State, at such time and places therein as the commanding general shall appoint and direct, of which at least thirty days' public notice shall be given, an election shall be held of delegates to a convention for the purpose of establishing a constitution and civil government for such state loyal to the Union, said convention in each State, except Virginia, to consist of the same number of members as the most numerous branch of the State legislature of such State in the year eighteen hundred and sixty, to be apportioned among the several

districts, counties, or parishes of such State by the commanding general, giving to each representation in the ratio of voters registered as aforesaid, as
nearly as may be. The convention in Virginia shall consist of the same number of members as represented the territory now constituting Virginia in the
most numerous branch of the legislature of said State in the year eighteen hundred and sixty, to be apportioned as aforesaid.

Section 3. That at said election the registered voters of each State shall vote
for or against a convention to form a constitution therefor under this act.
Those voting in favor of such a convention shall have written or printed on
the ballots by which they vote for delegates, as aforesaid, the words "For a convention," and those voting against such a convention shall have written or
printed on such ballots the words "Against a convention." The person appointed to superintend said election, and to make return of the votes given
thereat, as herein provided, shall count and make return of the votes given for
and against a convention; and the commanding general to whom the same
shall have been returned shall ascertain and declare the total vote in each
State for and against a convention. If a majority of the votes given on that
question shall be for a convention, then such convention shall be held as hereinafter provided; but if a majority of said votes shall be against a convention,
then no such convention shall be held under this act: Provided, That such
convention shall not be held unless a majority of all such registered voters
shall have voted on the question of holding such convention.

Section 4. That the commanding general of each district shall appoint as
many boards of registration as may be necessary, consisting of three loyal officers or persons, to make and complete the registration, superintend the election, and make return to him of the votes, lists of voters, and of the persons
elected as delegates by a plurality of the votes cast at said election; and upon
receiving said returns he shall open the same, ascertain the persons elected as
delegates according to the returns of the officers who conducted said election,
and make proclamation thereof; and if a majority of the votes given on that
question shall be for a convention, the commanding general, within sixty days
from the date of election, shall notify the delegates to assemble in convention,
at a time and place to be mentioned in the notification, and said convention,
when organized, shall proceed to frame a constitution and civil government
according to the provisions of this act and the act to which is it supplementary; and when the same shall have been so framed, said constitution shall be
submitted by the convention for ratification to the persons registered under
the provisions of this act at an election to be conducted by the officers or persons appointed or to be appointed by the commanding general, as hereinbefore provided, and to be held after the expiration of thirty days from the date
of notice thereof, to be given by said convention; and the returns thereof shall
be made to the commanding general of the district.

Section 5. That if, according to said returns, the constitution shall be ratified
by a majority of the votes of the registered electors qualified as herein specified,
cast at said election, (at least one half of all the registered voters voting upon the

question of such ratification), the president of the convention shall transmit a copy of the same, duly certified, to the President of the United States, who shall forthwith transmit the same to Congress, if then in session, and if not in session, then immediately upon its next assembling; and if it shall, moreover, appear to Congress that the election was one at which all the registered and qualified electors in the State had an opportunity to vote freely and without restraint, fear, or the influence of fraud, and if the Congress shall be satisfied that such constitution meets the approval of a majority of all the qualified electors in the State, and if the said constitution shall be declared by Congress to be in conformity with the provisions of the act to which this is supplementary, and the other provisions of said act shall have been complied with, and the said constitution shall be approved by Congress, the State shall be declared entitled to representation, and Senators and Representatives shall be admitted therefrom as therein provided.

Section 6. That all elections in the States mentioned in the said "Act to provide for the more efficient government of the rebel States," shall, during the operation of said act, be by ballot; and all officers making the said registration of voters and conducting said elections shall, before entering upon the discharge of their duties, take and subscribe the oath prescribed by the act approved July second, eighteen hundred and sixty-two, entitled "An act to prescribe an oath of office:" Provided, That if any person shall knowingly and falsely take and subscribe any oath in this act prescribed, such person so offending and being thereof duly convicted, shall be subject to the pains, penalties, and disabilities which by law are provided for the punishment of the crime of wilful and corrupt perjury.

Section 7. That all expenses incurred by the several commanding generals, or by virtue of any orders issued, or appointments made, by them, under or by virtue of this act, shall be paid out of any moneys in the treasury not otherwise appropriated.

Section 8. That the convention for each State shall prescribe the fees, salary, and compensation to be paid to all delegates and other officers and agents herein authorized or necessary to carry into effect the purposes of this act not herein otherwise provided for, and shall provide for the levy and collection of such taxes on the property in such State as may be necessary to pay the same.

Section 9. That the word article, in the sixth section of the act to which this is supplementary, shall be construed to mean section.

See 15 *Statutes at Large*, 2.

7.

THIRD RECONSTRUCTION ACT (1867)

When southern states continued their opposition to the incorporation of the freedmen into the mainstream of southern society, the Republican Congress passed this act to clarify the meaning and expound the true intent of the Second Reconstruction Act.

July 19, 1867

An Act supplementary to an Act entitled "An Act to provide for the more efficient Government of the Rebel States," passed on the second day of March, eighteen hundred and sixty-seven, and the Act supplementary thereto, passed on the twenty-third day of March, eighteen hundred and sixty-seven.

Be it enacted by the Senate and House of Representatives of the United States of America in Congress assembled, That it is hereby declared to have been the true intent and meaning of the act of the second day of March, one thousand eight hundred and sixty-seven, entitled "An act to provide for the more efficient government of the rebel States," and of the act supplementary thereto, passed on the twenty-third day of March, in the year one thousand eight hundred and sixty-seven, that the governments then existing in the rebel States of Virginia, North Carolina, South Carolina, Georgia, Mississippi, Alabama, Louisiana, Florida, Texas, and Arkansas were not legal State governments; and that thereafter said governments, if continued, were to be continued subject in all respects to the military commanders of the respective districts, and to the paramount authority of Congress.

Section 2. And be it further enacted, That the commander of any district named in said act shall have power, subject to the disapproval of the General of the army of the United States, and to have effect till disapproved, whenever in the opinion of such commander the proper administration of said act shall require it, to suspend or remove from office, or from the performance of official duties and the exercise of official powers, any officer or person holding or exercising, or professing to hold or exercise, any civil or military office or duty in such district under any power, election, appointment or authority derived from, or granted by, or claimed under, any so-called State or the government thereof, or any municipal or other division thereof, and upon such suspension or removal such commander, subject to the disapproval of the General as aforesaid, shall have power to provide from time to time for the performance of the said duties of such officer or person so suspended or removed, by the detail of some competent officer or soldier of the army, or by the appointment of some other person, to perform the same, and to fill vacancies occasioned by death, resignation, or otherwise.

Section 3. And be it further enacted, That the General of the army of the United Sates shall be invested with all the powers of suspension, removal, appointment, and detail granted in the preceding section to district commanders.

Section 4. And be it further enacted, That the acts of the officers of the army already done in removing in said districts persons exercising the functions of civil officers, and appointing others in their stead, are hereby confirmed: Provided, That any person heretofore or hereafter appointed by any district commander to exercise the functions of any civil office, may be removed either by the military officer in command of the district, or by the General of the army. And it shall be the duty of such commander to remove from office as aforesaid all persons who are disloyal to the government of the United States, or who use their official influence in any manner to hinder, delay, prevent, or obstruct the due and proper administration of this act and the acts to which it is supplementary.

Section 5. And be it further enacted, That the boards of registration provided for in the act entitled "An act supplementary to an act entitled 'An act to provide for the more efficient government of the rebel States,' passed March two, eighteen hundred and sixty-seven, and to facilitate restoration," passed March twenty-three, eighteen hundred and sixty-seven, shall have power, and it shall be their duty before allowing the registration of any person, to ascertain, upon such facts or information as they can obtain, whether such person is entitled to be registered under said act, and the oath required by said act shall not be conclusive on such question, and no person shall be registered unless such board shall decide that he is entitled thereto; and such board shall also have power to examine, under oath, (to be administered by any member of such board,) any one touching the qualification of any person claiming registration; but in every case of refusal by the board to register an applicant, and in every case of striking his name from the list as hereinafter provided, the board shall make a note or memorandum, which shall be returned with the registration list to the commanding general of the district, setting forth the grounds of such refusal or such striking from the list: Provided, That no person shall be disqualified as member of any board of registration by reason of race or color.

Section 6. And be it further enacted, That the true intent and meaning of the oath prescribed in said supplementary act is, (among other things,) that no person who has been a member of the legislature of any State, or who has held any executive or judicial office in any State, whether he has taken an oath to support the Constitution of the United Sates or not, and whether he was holding such office at the commencement of the rebellion, or had held it before, and who has afterwards engaged in insurrection or rebellion against the United States, or given aid or comfort to the enemies thereof, is entitled to be registered or to vote; and the words "executive or judicial office in any State" in said oath mentioned shall be construed to include all civil offices created by law for the administration of any general law of a State, or for the administration of justice.

Section 7. And be it further enacted, That the time for completing the original registration provided for in said act may, in the discretion of the commander of any district be extended to the first day of October, eighteen hundred and sixty-seven; and the boards of registration shall have power, and it shall be their duty, commencing fourteen days prior to any election under said act, and upon reasonable public notice of the time and place thereof, to revise, for a period of five days, the registration lists, and upon being satisfied that any person not entitled thereto has been registered, to strike the name of such person from the list, and such person shall not be allowed to vote. And such board shall also, during the same period, add to such registry the names of all persons who at that time possess the qualifications required by said act who have not been already registered; and no person shall, at any time, be entitled to be registered or to vote by reason of any executive pardon or amnesty for any act or thing which, without such pardon or amnesty, would disqualify him from registration or voting.

Section 8. And be it further enacted, That section four of said last-named act shall be construed to authorize the commanding general named therein, whenever he shall deem it needful, to remove any member of a board of registration and to appoint another in his stead, and to fill any vacancy in such board.

Section 9. And be it further enacted, That all members of said boards of registration and all persons hereafter elected or appointed to office in said military districts, under any so-called State or municipal authority, or by detail or appointment of the district commanders, shall be required to take and to subscribe the oath of office prescribed by law for officers of the United States.

Section 10. And be it further enacted, That no district commander or member of the board of registration, or any of the officers or appointees acting under them shall be bound in his action by any opinion of any civil officer of the United States.

Section 11. And be it further enacted, That all the provisions of this act and of the acts to which this is supplementary shall be construed liberally, to the end that all intents thereof may be fully and perfectly carried out.

See 15 *Statutes at Large*, 14.

8.

FOURTH RECONSTRUCTION ACT (1868)

This act further explained the purpose and intent of the Second and Third Reconstruction Acts.

March 11, 1868

An Act to amend the Act passed March twenty-third, eighteen hundred and sixty-seven, entitled "An act supplementary to 'An act to provide for the more efficient Government of the Rebel States,' passed March second, eighteen hundred and sixty-seven, and to facilitate their restoration."

Be it enacted by the Senate and the House of Representatives of the United States of America in Congress assembled, That hereafter any election authorized by the act passed March twenty- three, eighteen hundred and sixty-seven, entitled "An act supplementary to 'An act to provide for the more efficient government of the rebel States,' passed March two, eighteen hundred and sixty-seven, and to facilitate their restoration," shall be decided by a majority of the votes actually cast; and at the election in which the question of the adoption or rejection of any constitution is submitted, any person duly registered in the State may vote in the election district where he offers to vote when he has resided therein for ten days next preceding such election, upon presentation of his certificate of registration, his affidavit, or other satisfactory evidence, under such regulations as the district commanders may prescribe.

Section 2. And be it further enacted, That the constitutional convention of any of the States mentioned in the acts to which this amendatory may provide that at the time of voting upon the ratification of the constitution the registered voters may vote also for members of the House of Representatives of the United States, and for all elective officers provided for by the said constitution; and the same election officers who shall make the return of the votes cast on the ratification or rejection of the constitution shall enumerate and certify the votes cast for members of Congress.

See 15 *Statutes at Large*, 14.

9.

FOURTEENTH AMENDMENT TO THE UNITED STATES CONSTITUTION (1868)

The intent of the Republican Congress in proposing the Fourteenth Amendment was to grant citizenship to the former slaves and to provide them with all the concomitant rights of citizenship, including the right to vote and hold office. Over time, however, the amendment's meaning underwent change at the hands of lawyers and judges in a variety of court cases, including most notably the *Slaughterhouse Cases*. The amendment became a protector for corporations against government regulation, while the intended protection for the freedmen was eliminated.

Section 1. All persons born or naturalized in the United States, and subject to the jurisdiction thereof, are citizens of the United States and of the state wherein they reside. No state shall make or enforce any law which shall abridge the privileges or immunities of citizens of the United States; nor shall any state deprive any person of life, liberty, or property, without due process of law; nor deny to any person within its jurisdiction the equal protection of the laws.

Section 2. Representatives shall be apportioned among the several states according to their respective numbers, counting the whole number of persons in each state, excluding Indians not taxed. But when the right to vote at any election for the choice of electors for President and Vice President of the United States, Representatives in Congress, the executive and judicial officers of a state, or the members of the legislature thereof, is denied to any of the male inhabitants of such state, being twenty-one years of age , and citizens of the United States, or in any way abridged, except for participation in rebellion, or other crime, the basis of representation therein shall be reduced in the proportion which the number of such male citizens shall bear to the whole number of male citizens twenty-one years of age in such state.

Section 3. No person shall be a Senator or Representative in Congress, or elector of President and Vice President, or hold any office, civil or military, under the United States, or under any state, who, having previously taken an oath, as a member of Congress, or as an officer of the United States, or as a member of any state legislature, or as an executive or judicial officer of any state, to support the Constitution of the United States, shall have engaged in insurrection or rebellion against the same, or given aid or comfort to the enemies thereof. But Congress may by a vote of two-thirds of each House, remove such disability.

Section 4. The validity of the public debt of the United States, authorized by law, including debts incurred for payment of pensions and bounties for services in suppressing insurrection or rebellion, shall not be questioned. But neither the United States nor any state shall assume or pay any debt or obligation incurred in aid of insurrection or rebellion against the United States, or any claim for the loss or emancipation of any slave; but all such debts, obligations and claims shall be held illegal and void.

Section 5. The Congress shall have power to enforce, by appropriate legislation, the provisions of this article.

See *U.S. Code*, Amendment 14.

10.

INSCRIPTION ON THADDEUS STEVENS'S TOMBSTONE (1868)

Stevens, one of the foremost proponents of emancipation, citizenship, and equality for African Americans, died and was buried in 1868 in a black cemetery in Lancaster, Pennsylvania. The inscription above his grave explains his choice of cemeteries.

I repose in this quiet and secluded spot
Not from any natural preference for solitude
But, finding other Cemeteries limited as to Race
by Charter Rules,
I have chosen this that I might illustrate
in my death
The Principles which I advocated
Through my long life
EQUALITY OF MAN BEFORE HIS CREATOR

See Hans Trefousse, *Thaddeus Stevens: Nineteenth-Century Egalitarian* (Mechanicsburg, PA: Stockpole, 2001), xi.

11.

FIFTEENTH AMENDMENT TO THE UNITED
STATES CONSTITUTION (1870)

As antiblack state legislatures used ambiguities in the Fourteenth Amendment to keep the freedmen from voting, the Republican Congress and President Ulysses S. Grant supported this amendment to remove all doubt about their suffrage rights.

Section 1. The right of citizens of the United States to vote shall not be denied or abridged by the United States or by any state on account of race, color, or previous condition of servitude.

Section 2. The Congress shall have power to enforce this article by appropriate legislation.

See *U.S.Code*, Amendment 15.

12.

FIRST ENFORCEMENT ACT (1870)

This act was designed to enforce the Fourteenth and Fifteenth Amendments by, among other things, prescribing the penalties for violating them.

An Act to enforce the Right of Citizens of the United States to vote in the several States of this Union, and for other Purposes.

Be it enacted by the Senate and House of Representatives of the United States of America in Congress assembled, That all citizens of the United States who are or shall be otherwise qualified by law to vote at any election by the people in any State, Territory, district, county, city, parish, township, school district, municipality, or other territorial subdivision, shall be entitled and allowed to vote at all such elections, without distinction of race, color, or previous condition of servitude; any constitution, law, custom, usage, or regulation of any State or Territory, or by or under its authority, to the contrary notwithstanding.

Section 2. And be it further enacted That if by or under the authority of the constitution or laws of any State, or the laws of any Territory, any act is or shall be required to be done as a prerequisite or qualification for voting, and by such constitution or laws persons or officers are or shall be charged with the performance of duties in furnishing to citizens an opportunity to perform such prerequisite, or to become qualified to vote, it shall be the duty of every such person and officer to give to all citizens of the United States the same and equal opportunity to perform such prerequisite, and to become qualified to vote without distinction of race, color, or previous condition of servitude; and if any such person or officer shall refuse or knowingly omit to give full effect to this section, he shall, for every such offence, forfeit and pay the sum of five hundred dollars to the person aggrieved thereby, to be recovered by an action on the case, with full costs, and such allowance for counsel fees as the court shall deem just, and shall also, for every such offence, be deemed guilty of a misdemeanor, and shall, on conviction thereof, be fined not less than five hundred dollars, or be imprisoned not less than one month and not more than one year, or both, at the discretion of the court.

Section 3. And be it further enacted, That whenever, by or under the authority of the constitution or laws of any State, or the laws of any Territory, any act is or shall be required to [be] done by any citizen as a prerequisite to qualify or entitle him to vote, the offer of any such citizen to perform the act required to be done as aforesaid shall, if it fail to be carried into execution by reason of the wrongful act or omission aforesaid of the person or officer charged with the duty of receiving or permitting such performance or offer to perform, or acting thereon, be deemed and held as a performance in law of such act; and the person so offering and failing as aforesaid, and being otherwise qualified, shall be entitled to vote in the same manner and to the same extent as if he had in fact performed such act; and any judge, inspector, or other officer of election whose duty it is or shall be to receive, count, certify, register, report, or give effect to the vote of any such citizen who shall wrongfully refuse or omit to receive, count, certify, register, report, or give effect to the vote of such citizen upon the presentation by him of his affidavit stating such offer and the time and place thereof, and the name of the officer or person whose duty it was to act thereon, and that he was wrongfully prevented by such person or officer from performing such act, shall for every such offence forfeit and pay the sum of five hundred dollars to the person aggrieved thereby, to be recovered by an action on the case, with full costs, and such allowance for counsel fees as the court shall deem just, and shall also for every such offence be guilty of a misdemeanor, and shall, on conviction thereof, be fined not less than five hundred dollars, or be imprisoned not less than one month and not more than one year, or both, at the discretion of the court.

Section 4. And be it further enacted, That if any person, by force, bribery, threats, intimidation, or other unlawful means, shall hinder, delay, prevent, or obstruct, or shall combine and confederate with others to hinder, delay, prevent, or obstruct, any citizen from doing any act required to be done to qualify him to vote or from voting at any election as aforesaid, such person shall for every such offence forfeit and pay the sum of five hundred dollars to the person aggrieved thereby, to be recovered by an action on the case, with full costs, and such allowance for counsel fees as the court shall deem just, and shall also for every such offence be guilty of a misdemeanor, and shall, on conviction thereof, be fined not less than five hundred dollars, or be imprisoned not less than one month and not more than one year, or both, at the discretion of the court.

Section 5. And be it further enacted, That if any person shall prevent, hinder, control, or intimidate, or shall attempt to prevent, hinder, control, or intimidate, any person from exercising or in exercising the right of suffrage, to whom the right of suffrage is secured or guaranteed by the fifteenth amendment to the Constitution of the United States, by means of bribery, threats, or threats of depriving such person of employment or occupation, or of ejecting such person from rented house, lands, or other property, or by threats of refusing to renew leases or contracts for labor, or by threats of violence to himself or family, such person so offending shall be deemed guilty of a misdemeanor, and shall, on conviction thereof, be fined not less than five hundred dollars, or be imprisoned not less than one month and not more than one year, or both, at the discretion of the court.

Section 6. And be it further enacted, That if two or more persons shall band or conspire together, or go in disguise upon the public highway, or upon the premises of another, with intent to violate any provision of this act, or to injure, oppress, threaten, or intimidate any citizen with intent to prevent or hinder his free exercise and enjoyment of any right or privilege granted or secured to him by the Constitution or laws of the United States, or because of his having exercised the same, such persons shall be held guilty of felony, and, on conviction thereof, shall be fined or imprisoned, or both, at the discretion of the court, the fine not to exceed five thousand dollars, and the imprisonment not to exceed ten years, and shall, moreover, be thereafter ineligible to, and disabled from holding, any office or place of honor, profit, or trust created by the Constitution or laws of the United States.

Section 7. And be it further enacted, That if in the act of violating any provision in either of the two preceding sections, any other felony, crime, or misdemeanor shall be committed, the offender, on conviction of such violation of said sections, shall be punished for the same with such punishments as are attached to the said felonies, crimes, and misdemeanors by the laws of the State in which the offence may be committed.

Section 8. And be it further enacted, That the district courts of the United States, within their respective districts, shall have, exclusively of the courts of the several States, cognizance of all crimes and offences committed against the provisions of this act, and also, concurrently with the circuit courts of the United States, of all causes, civil and criminal, arising under this act, except as herein otherwise provided, and the jurisdiction hereby conferred shall be exercised in conformity with the laws and practice governing United States courts; and all crimes and offences committed against the provisions of this act may be prosecuted by the indictment of a grand jury, or, in cases of crimes and offences not infamous, the prosecution may be either by indictment or information filed by the district attorney in a court having jurisdiction.

Section 9. And be it further enacted, That the district attorneys, marshals, and deputy marshals of the United States, the commissioners appointed by the circuit and territorial courts of the United States, with powers of arresting, imprisoning, or bailing offenders against the laws of the United States, and every other officer who may be specially empowered by the President of the

United States, shall be, and they are hereby, specially authorized and required, at the expense of the United States, to institute proceedings against all and every person who shall violate the provisions of this act, and cause him or them to be arrested and imprisoned, or bailed. as the case may be, for trial before such court of the United States or territorial court as has cognizance of the offense. And with a view to afford reasonable protection to all persons in their constitutional right to vote without distinction of race, color, or previous condition of servitude, and to the prompt discharge of the duties of this act, it shall be the duty of the circuit courts of the United States, and the superior courts of the Territories of the United States, from time to time, to increase the number of commissioners, so as to afford a speedy and convenient means for the arrest and examination of persons charged with a violation of this act; and such commissioners are hereby authorized and required to exercise and discharge all the powers and duties conferred on them by this act, and the same duties with regard to offences created by this act as they are authorized by law to exercise with regard to other offences against the laws of the United States.

Section 10. And be it further enacted, That it shall be the duty of all mar-shals and deputy marshals to obey and execute all warrants and precepts issued under the provisions of this act, when to them directed; and should any mar-shal or deputy marshal refuse to receive such warrant or other process when tendered, or to use all proper means diligently to execute the same, he shall, on conviction thereof, be fined in the sum of one thousand dollars, to the use of the person deprived of the rights conferred by this act. And the better to enable the said commissioners to execute their duties faithfully and efficiently, in conformity with the Constitution of the United States and the require-ments of this act, they are hereby authorized and empowered, within their dis-tricts respectively, to appoint, in writing, under their bands, any one or more suitable persons, from time to time, to execute all such warrants and other process as may be issued by them in the lawful performance of their respective duties, and the persons so appointed to execute any warrant or process as afore-said shall have authority to summon and call to their aid the bystander or posse comitatus of the proper county, or such portion of the land or naval forces of the United States, or of the militia, as may be necessary to the per-formance of the duty with which they are charged, and to insure a faithful observance of the fifteenth amendment to the Constitution of the United States; and such warrants shall run and be executed by said officers anywhere in the State or Territory within which they are issued.

Section 11. And be it further enacted, That any person who shall knowingly and wilfully obstruct, hinder, or prevent any officer or other person charged with the execution of any warrant or process issued under the provisions of this act, or any person or persons lawfully assisting him or them from arresting any person for whose apprehension such warrant or process may have been issued, or shall rescue or attempt to rescue such person from the custody of the officer or other person or persons, or those lawfully assisting as aforesaid, when so arrested pursuant to the authority herein given and declared, or shall aid, abet, or assist any person so arrested as aforesaid, directly or indirectly, to escape from the custody of the officer or other person legally authorized as aforesaid, or shall harbor or conceal any person for whose arrest a warrant or process shall have been issued as aforesaid, so as to prevent his discovery and arrest after notice or knowledge of the fact that a Warrant has been issued for the apprehension of such person, shall, for either of said offences, be subject to a fine not exceeding one thousand dollars, or imprisonment not exceeding six months, or both, at the discretion of the court, on conviction before the district or circuit court of the United States for the district or circuit in which said offence may have been committed, or before the proper court of criminal jurisdiction, if committed within any one of the organized Territories of the United States.

Section 12. And be it further enacted, That the commissioners, district attorneys, the marshals, their deputies, and the clerks of the said district, circuit, and territorial courts shall be paid for their services the like fees as may be allowed to them for similar services in other cases. The person or persons authorized to execute the process to be issued by such commissioners for the arrest of offenders against the provisions of this act shall be entitled to the usual fees allowed to the marshal for an arrest for each person be or they may arrest and take before any such commissioner as aforesaid, with such other fees as may be deemed reasonable by such commissioner for such other additional services as may be necessarily performed by him or them, such as attending at the examination, keeping the prisoner in custody, and providing him with food and lodging during his detention and until the final determination of such commissioner, and in general for performing such other duties as may be required in the premises; such fees to be made up in conformity with the fees usually charged by the officers of the courts of justice within the proper district or county as near as may be practicable, and paid out of the treasury of the United States on the certificate of the judge of the district within which the arrest is made, and to be recoverable from the defendant as part of the judgment in case of conviction.

Section 13. And be it further enacted, That it shall be lawful for the President of the United States to employ such part of the land or naval forces of the United States, or of the militia, as shall be necessary to aid in the execution of judicial process issued under this act.

Section 14. And be it further enacted, That whenever any person shall hold office, except as a member of Congress or of some State legislature, contrary to the provisions of the third section of the fourteenth article of amendment of the Constitution of the United States, it shall be the duty of the district attorney of the United States for the district in which such person shall hold office, as aforesaid, to proceed against such person, by writ of quo warranto, returnable to the circuit or district court of the United States in such district, and to prosecute the same to the removal of such person from office; and any writ of quo warranto so brought, as aforesaid, shall take precedence of all other cases on the docket of the court to which it is made returnable, and shall not be continued unless for cause proved to the satisfaction of the court.

Section 15. And be it further enacted, That any person who shall hereafter knowingly accept or hold any office under the United States, or any State to which he is ineligible under the third section of the fourteenth article of amendment of the Constitution of the United States, or who shall attempt to hold or exercise the duties of any such office, shall be deemed guilty of a misdemeanor against the United States, and, upon conviction thereof before the circuit or district court of the United States, shall be imprisoned not more than one year, or fined not exceeding one thousand dollars, or both, at the discretion of the court.

Section 16. And be it further enacted, That all persons within the jurisdiction of the United States shall have the same right in every State and Territory in the United States to make and enforce contracts, to sue, be parties, give evidence, and to the full and equal benefit of all laws and proceedings for the security of person and property as is enjoyed by white citizens, and shall be subject to like punishment, pains, penalties, taxes, licenses, and exactions of every kind, and none other, any law, statute, ordinance, regulation, or custom to the contrary notwithstanding. No tax or charge shall be imposed or enforced by any State upon any person immigrating thereto from a foreign country which is not equally imposed and enforced upon every person immigrating to such State from any other foreign country; and any law of any State in conflict with this provision is hereby declared null and void.

Section 17. And be it further enacted, That any person who, under color of any law, statute, ordinance, regulation, or custom, shall subject, or cause to be subjected, any inhabitant of any State or Territory to the deprivation of any right secured or protected by the last preceding section of this act, or to different punishment, pains, or penalties on account of such person being an alien, or by reason of his color or race, than is prescribed for the punishment of citizens, shall be deemed guilty of a misdemeanor, and, on conviction, shall be punished by fine not exceeding one thousand dollars, or imprisonment not exceeding one year, or both, in the discretion of the court.

Section 18. And be it further enacted, That the act to protect all persons in the United States in their civil rights, and furnish the means of their vindication, passed April nine, eighteen hundred and sixty six, is hereby reenacted; and sections sixteen and seventeen hereof shall be enforced according to the provisions of said act.

Section 19. And be it further enacted, That if at any election for representative or delegate in the Congress of the United States any person shall knowingly personate and vote, or attempt to vote, in the name of any other person, whether living, dead, or fictitious; or vote more than once at the same election for any candidate for the same office; or vote at a place where he may not be lawfully entitled to vote; or vote without having a lawful right to vote; or do any unlawful act to secure a right or an opportunity to vote for himself or any other person; or by force, threat, menace, intimidation, bribery, reward, or offer, or promise thereof, or otherwise unlawfully prevent any qualified voter of any State of the United States of America, or of any Territory thereof, from freely exercising the right of suffrage, or by any such means induce any voter to refuse to exercise such right; or compel or induce by any such means, or otherwise, any officer of an election in any such State or Territory to receive a vote from a person not legally qualified or entitled to vote; or interfere in any manner with any officer of said elections in the discharge of his duties; or by any of such means, or other unlawful means, induce any officer of an election, or officer whose duty it is to ascertain, announce, or declare the result of any such election, or give or make any certificate, document, or evidence in relation thereto, to violate or refuse to comply with his duty, or any law regulating the same; or knowingly and wilfully receive the vote of any person not entitled to vote, or refuse to receive the vote of any person entitled to vote; or aid, counsel, procure, or advise any such voter, person, or officer to do any act hereby made a crime, or to omit to do any duty the omission of which is hereby made a crime, or attempt to do so, every such person shall be deemed guilty of a crime, and shall for such crime be liable to prosecution in any court of the United States of competent jurisdiction, and, on conviction thereof, shall be punished by a fine not exceeding five hundred dollars, or by imprisonment for a term not exceeding three years, or both, in the discretion of the court, and shall pay the costs of prosecution.

Section 20. And be it further enacted, That if, at any registration of voters for an election for representative or delegate in the Congress of the United States, any person shall knowingly personate and register, or attempt to register, in the name of any other person, whether living, dead, or fictitious, or fraudulently register, or fraudulently attempt to register, not having a lawful right so to do; or do any unlawful act to secure registration for himself or any other person; or by force, threat, menace, intimidation, bribery, reward, or offer, or promise thereof, or other unlawful means, prevent or hinder any person having a lawful right to register from duly exercising such right; or compel or induce, by any of such means, or other unlawful means, any officer of registration to admit to registration any person not legally entitled thereto, or interfere in any manner with any officer of registration in the discharge of his duties, or by any such means, or other unlawful means, induce any officer of registration to violate or refuse to comply with his duty, or any law regulating the same; or knowingly and wilfully receive the vote of any person not entitled to vote, or refuse to receive the vote of any person entitled to vote, or aid, counsel, procure, or advise any such voter, person, or officer to do any act hereby made a crime, or to omit any act, the omission of which is hereby made a crime, every such person shall be deemed guilty of a crime, and shall be liable to prosecution and punishment therefor, as provided in section nineteen of this act for persons guilty of any of the crimes therein specified: Provided, that every registration made under the laws of any State or Territory, for any State or other election at which such representative or delegate in Congress shall be chosen, shall be deemed to be a registration within the meaning of this act, notwithstanding the same shall also be made for the purposes of any State, territorial, or municipal election.

Section 21. And be it further enacted, That whenever, by the laws of any State or Territory, the name of any candidate or person to be voted for as representative or delegate in Congress shall be required to be printed, written, or contained in any ticket or ballot with other candidates or persons to be voted for at the same election for State, territorial, municipal, or local officers, it shall be sufficient prima facie evidence, either for the purpose of indicting or convicting any person charged with voting, or attempting or offering to vote, unlawfully under the provisions of the preceding sections, or for committing either of the offenses thereby created, to prove that the person so charged or indicted, voted, or attempted or offered to vote, such ballot or ticket, or committed either of the offenses named in the preceding sections of this act with reference to such ballot. And the proof and establishment of such facts shall be taken, held, and deemed to be presumptive evidence that such person voted, or attempted or offered to vote, for such representative or delegate, as the case may be, or that such offense was committed with reference to the election of such representative or delegate, and shall be sufficient to warrant his conviction, unless it shall be shown that any such ballot, when cast, or attempted or offered to be cast, by him, did not contain the name of any candidate for the office of representative or delegate in the Congress of the United States, or that such offense was not committed with reference to the election of such representative or delegate.

Section 22. And be it further enacted That any officer of any election at which any representative or delegate in the Congress of the United States shall be voted for, whether such officer of election be appointed or created by or under any law or authority of the United States, or by or under any State, territorial, district, or municipal law or authority, who shall neglect or refuse to perform any duty in regard to such election required of him by any law of the United States, or of any State or Territory thereof; or violate any duty so imposed, or knowingly do any act thereby unauthorized, with intent to affect any such election, or the result thereof; or fraudulently make any false certificate of the result of such election in regard to such representative or delegate; or withhold, conceal, or destroy any certificate of record so required by law respecting, concerning, or pertaining to the election of any such representative or delegate; or neglect or refuse to make and return the same as so required by law; or aid, counsel, procure, or advise any voter, person, or officer to do any act by this or any of the preceding sections made a crime; or to omit to do any duty the omission of which is by this or any of said sections made a crime, or attempt to do so, shall be deemed guilty of a crime and shall be liable to prosecution and punishment therefor, as provided in the nineteenth section of this act for persons guilty of any of the crimes therein specified.

Section 23. And be it further enacted, That whenever any person shall be defeated or deprived of his election to any office, except elector of President or Vice-President, representative or delegate in Congress, or member of a State legislature, by reason of the denial to any citizen or citizens who shall offer to vote, of the right to vote, on account of race, color, or previous condition of servitude, his right to hold and enjoy such office, and the emoluments thereof, shall not be impaired by such denial; and such person may bring any appropriate suit or proceeding to recover possession of such office, and in cases where it shall appear that the sole question touching the title to such office arises out of the denial of the right to vote to citizens who so offered to vote, on account of race, color, or previous condition of servitude, such suit or proceeding may be instituted in the circuit or district court of the United States of the circuit or district in which such person resides. And said circuit or district court shall have, concurrently with the State courts, jurisdiction thereof so far as to determine the rights of the parties to such office by reason of the denial of the right guaranteed by the fifteenth article of amendment to the Constitution of the United States, and secured by this act.

See 16 *Statutes at Large*, 140.

13.

THIRD ENFORCEMENT ACT (1871)

Better known as the "Ku Klux Act," this measure was designed to ensure that no illegal or undesirable organizations such as the Ku Klux Klan would be allowed to operate openly in the southern states, mainly by prescribing the penalties for such subversive activities.

An Act to enforce the Provisions of the Fourteenth Amendment to the Constitution of the United States, and for other Purposes.

Be it enacted by the Senate and House of Representatives of the United States of America in Congress assembled, That any person who, under color of any law, statute, ordinance, regulation, custom, or usage of any State, shall subject, or cause to be subjected, any person within the jurisdiction of the United States to the deprivation of any rights, privileges, or immunities secured by the Constitution of the United States, shall, any such law, statute, ordinance, regulation, custom, or usage of the State to the contrary notwithstanding, be liable to the party injured in any action at law, suit in equity, or other proper proceeding for redress; such proceeding to be prosecuted in the several district or circuit courts of the United States, with and subject to the same rights of appeal, review upon error, and other remedies provided in like cases in such courts, under the provisions of the act of the ninth of April, eighteen hundred and sixty six, entitled "An act to protect all persons in the

United States in their civil rights, and to furnish the means of their vindication"; and the other remedial laws of the United States which are in their nature applicable in such cases.

Section 2. That if two or more persons within any State or Territory of the United States shall conspire together to overthrow, or to put down, or to destroy by force the government of the United States, or to levy war against the United States, or to oppose by force the authority of the government of the United States, or by force, intimidation, or threat to prevent, hinder, or delay the execution of any law of the United States, or by force to seize, take, or possess any property of the United States, contrary to the authority thereof, or by force, intimidation, or threat to prevent any person from accepting or holding any office or trust or place of confidence under the United States, or from discharging the duties thereof, or by force, intimidation, or threat to induce any officer of the United States to leave any State, district, or place where his duties as such officer might lawfully be performed, or to injure him in his person or property on account of his lawful discharge of the duties of his office, or to injure his person while engaged in the lawful discharge of the duties of his office, or to injure his property so as to molest, interrupt, hinder, or impede him in the discharge of his official duty, or by force, intimidation, or threat to deter any party or witness in any court of the United States from attending such court, or from testifying in any matter pending in such court fully, freely, and truthfully, or to injure any such party or witness in his person or property on account of his having so attended or testified, or by force, intimidation, or threat to influence the verdict, presentment, or indictment, of any juror or grand juror in any court of the United States, or to injure such juror in his person or property on account of any verdict, presentment, or indictment lawfully assented to by him, or on account of his being or having been such juror, or shall conspire together, or go in disguise upon the public highway or upon the premises of another for the purpose, either directly or indirectly, of depriving any person or any class of persons of the equal protection of the laws, or of equal privileges or immunities under the laws, or for the purpose of preventing or hindering the constituted authorities of any State from giving or securing to all persons within such State the equal protection of the laws, or shall conspire together for the purpose of in any manner impeding, hindering, obstructing, or defeating the due course of justice in any State or Territory, with intent to deny to any citizen of the United States the due and equal protection of the laws, or to injure any person in his person or his property for lawfully enforcing the right of any person or class of persons to the equal protection of the laws, or by force, intimidation, or threat to prevent any citizen of the United States lawfully entitled to vote from giving his support or advocacy in a lawful manner towards or in favor of the election of any lawfully qualified person as an elector of President or Vice President of the United States, or as a member of the Congress of the United States, or to injure any such citizen in his person or property on account of such support or advocacy, each and every person so offending shall be deemed guilty of a high crime, and, upon conviction thereof in any district or circuit court of the United States or district or supreme court of any Territory of the United States having jurisdiction of similar offences, shall be punished by a fine not less than five hundred nor more than five thousand dollars, or by imprisonment, with or without hard labor, as the court may determine, for a period of not less than six months nor more than six years, as the court may determine, or by both such fine and imprisonment as the court shall determine. And if any one or more persons engaged in any such conspiracy shall do, or cause to be done, any act in furtherance of the object of such conspiracy, whereby any person shall be injured in his person or property, or deprived of having and exercising any right or privilege of a citizen of the United States, the person so injured or deprived of such rights and privileges may have and maintain an action for the recovery of damages occasioned by such injury or deprivation of rights and privileges against any one or more of the persons engaged in such conspiracy, such action to be prosecuted in the proper district or circuit court of the United States, with and subject to the same rights of appeal, review upon error, and other remedies provided in like cases in such courts under the provisions of the act of April ninth, eighteen hundred and sixty six, entitled "An act to protect all persons in the United States in their civil rights, and to furnish the means of their vindication."

Section 3. That in all cases where insurrection, domestic violence, unlawful combinations, or conspiracies in any State shall so obstruct or hinder the execution of the laws thereof, and of the United States, as to deprive any portion or class of the people of such State of any of the rights, privileges, or immunities, or protection, named in the Constitution and secured by this act, and the constituted authorities of such State shall either be unable to protect, or shall, from any cause, fail in or refuse protection of the people in such rights, such facts shall be deemed a denial by such State of the equal protection of the laws to which they are entitled under the Constitution of the United States; and in all such cases, or whenever any such insurrection, violence, unlawful combination, or conspiracy shall oppose or obstruct the laws of the United States or the due execution thereof, or impede or obstruct the due course of justice under the same, it shall be lawful for the President, and it shall be his duty to take such measures, by the employment of the militia or the land and naval forces of the United States, or of either, or by other means, as he may deem necessary for the suppression of such insurrection, domestic violence, or combinations; and any person who shall be arrested under the provisions of this and the preceding section shall be delivered to the marshal of the proper district, to be dealt with according to law.

Section 4. That whenever in any State or part of a State the unlawful combinations named in the preceding section of this act shall be organized and armed, and so numerous and powerful as to be able, by violence, to either overthrow or set at defiance the constituted authorities of such State, and of the

United States within such State, or when the constituted authorities are in complicity with, or shall connive at the unlawful purposes of, such powerful and armed combinations; and whenever, by reason of either or all of the causes aforesaid, the conviction of such offenders and the preservation of the public safety shall become in such district impracticable, in every such case such combinations shall be deemed a rebellion against the government of the United States, and during the continuance of such rebellion, and within the limits of the district which shall be so under the sway thereof, such limits to be prescribed by proclamation, it shall be lawful for the President of the United States, when in his judgment the public safety shall require it, to suspend the privileges of the writ of habeas corpus, to the end that such rebellion may be overthrown: Provided, That all the provisions of the second section of an act entitled "An act relating to habeas corpus, and regulating judicial proceedings in certain cases," approved March third, eighteen hundred and sixty three, which relate to the discharge of prisoners other than prisoners of war, and to the penalty for refusing to obey the order of the court, shall be in full force so far as the same are applicable to the provisions of this section: Provided further, That the President shall first have made proclamation, as now provided by law, commanding such insurgents to disperse: And provided also, That the provisions of this section shall not be in force after the end of the next regular session of Congress.

Section 5. That no person shall be a grand or petit juror in any court of the United States upon any inquiry, hearing, or trial of any suit, proceedings or prosecution based upon or arising under the provisions of this act who shall, in the judgment of the court, be in complicity with any such combination or conspiracy; and every such juror shall, before entering upon any such inquiry, hearing, or trial, take and subscribe an oath in open court that he has never, directly or indirectly, counseled, advised, or voluntarily aided any such combination or conspiracy; and each and every person who shall take this oath, and shall therein swear falsely, shall be guilty of perjury, and shall be subject to the pains and penalties declared against that crime and the first section of the act entitled "An act defining, additional causes of challenge and prescribing an additional oath for grand and petit jurors in the United States courts," approved June seventeenth, eighteen hundred and sixty two, be, and the same is hereby, repealed.

Section 6. That any person or persons, having knowledge that any of the wrongs conspired to be done and mentioned in the second section of this act are about to be committed, and having power to prevent or aid in preventing the same, shall neglect or refuse so to do, and such wrongful act shall be committed, such person or persons shall be liable to the person injured, or his legal representatives, for all damages caused by any such wrongful act which such first named person or persons by reasonable diligence could have prevented; and such damages may be recovered in an action on the case in the proper circuit court of the United States, and any number of persons guilty of such wrongful neglect or refusal may be joined as defendants in such action: Provided, That such action shall be commenced within one year after such cause of action shall have accrued; and if the death of any person shall be caused by any such wrongful act and neglect, the legal representatives of such deceased person shall have such action therefor, and may recover not exceeding five thousand dollars damages therein, for the benefit of the widow of such deceased person, if any there be, or if there be no widow, for the benefit of the next of kin of such deceased person.

Section 7. That nothing herein contained shall be construed to supersede or repeal any former act or law except so far as the same may be repugnant thereto; and any offences heretofore committed against the tenor of any former act shall be prosecuted, and any proceeding already commenced for the prosecution thereof shall be continued and completed, the same as if this act had not been passed, except so far as the provisions of this act may go to sustain and validate such proceedings.

See 18 *Statutes at Large*, 336, 337.

14.

A DISSENTING OPINION IN THE *SLAUGHTERHOUSE CASES* (1873)

A landmark set of cases ruled upon jointly, the *Slaughterhouse Cases* revealed the elasticity and inadequacy of the wording of the Fourteenth Amendment, as the rights of citizenship intended solely for the freedmen were applied to corporations. Because the ruling limited civil rights for African Americans, the majority opinion of the court is not included here. Instead, the dissenting opinion of Justice Noah H. Swayne, who clearly thought the Court's ruling was not only wrong but an absolute travesty, is presented.

83 U.S. 36

Mr. Justice SWAYNE, dissenting.

I concur in the dissent in these cases and in the views expressed by my brethren, Mr. Justice [Stephen J.] Field and Mr. Justice [Joseph P.] Bradley. I desire, however, to submit a few additional remarks.

The first eleven amendments to the Constitution were intended to be checks and limitations upon the government which that instrument called into existence. They had their origin in a spirit of jealousy on the part of the States which existed when the Constitution was adopted. The first ten were proposed in 1789 by the first Congress at its first session after the organization of the government. The eleventh was proposed in 1794, and the twelfth in 1803. The one last mentioned regulates the mode of electing the President and Vice-President. It neither increased nor diminished the power of the General Government, and may be said in that respect to occupy neutral ground. No further amendments were made until 1865, a period of more than sixty years. The thirteenth amendment was proposed by Congress on the 1st of February, 1865, the fourteenth on the 16th of June, 1866, and the fifteenth on the 27th of February, 1869. These amendments are a new departure, and mark an important epoch in the constitutional history of the country. They trench [touch?] directly upon the power of the States, and deeply affect those bodies. They are, in this respect, at the opposite pole from the first eleven.

Fairly construed, these amendments may be said to rise to the dignity of a new Magna Charta. The thirteenth blotted out slavery and forbade forever its restoration. It struck the fetters from four millions of human beings, and raised them at once to the sphere of freemen. This was an act of grace and justice performed by the Nation. Before the war, it could have been done only by the States where the institution existed, acting severally and separately from each other. The power then rested wholly with them. In that way, apparently, such a result could never have occurred. The power of Congress did not extend to the subject, except in the Territories.

. . . .

The first section of the fourteenth amendment is alone involved in the consideration of these cases. No searching analysis is necessary to eliminate [illuminate?] its meaning. Its language is intelligible and direct. Nothing can be more transparent. Every word employed has an established signification. There is no room for construction. There is nothing to construe. Elaboration may obscure, but cannot make clearer, the intent and purpose sought to be carried out.

(1) Citizens of the States and of the United States are defined.

(2) It is declared that no State shall, by law, abridge the privileges or immunities of citizens of the United States.

(3) That no State shall deprive any person, whether a citizen or not, of life, liberty, or property, without due process of law, nor deny to any person within its jurisdiction the equal protection of the laws.

A citizen of a State is ipso facto a citizen of the United States. No one can be the former without being also the latter; but the latter, by losing his residence in one State without acquiring it in another, although he continues to be the latter, ceases for the time to be the former. "The privileges and immunities" of a citizen of the United States include, among other things, the fundamental rights of life, liberty, and property, and also the rights which pertain to him by reason of his membership of the Nation. The citizen of a State has the same fundamental rights as a citizen of the United States, and also certain others, local in their character, arising from his relation to the State, and, in addition, those which belong to the citizen of the United States, he being in that relation also. There may thus be a double citizenship, each having some rights peculiar to itself. It is only over those which belong to the citizen of the United States that the category here in question throws the shield of its protection. All those which belong to the citizen of a State, except as a bills of attainder, ex post facto laws, and laws impairing the obligation of contracts, are left to the guardianship of the bills of rights, constitutions, and laws of the States respectively. Those rights may all be enjoyed in every State by the citizens of every other State by virtue of clause 2, section 4, article 1, of the Constitution of the United States as it was originally framed. This section does not in anywise affect them; such was not its purpose.

In the next category, obviously ex industria, to prevent, as far as may be, the possibility of misinterpretation, either as to persons or things, the phrases "citizens of the United States" and "privileges and immunities" are dropped, and more simple and comprehensive terms are substituted. The substitutes are "any person," and "life," "liberty," and "property," and "the equal protection of the laws." Life, liberty, and property are forbidden to be taken "without due process of law," and "equal protection of the laws" is guaranteed to all. Life is the gift of God, and the right to preserve it is the most sacred of the rights of man. Liberty is freedom from all restraints but such as are justly imposed by law. Beyond that line lies the domain of usurpation and tyranny. Property is everything which has an exchangeable value, and the right of property includes the power to dispose of it according to the will of the owner. Labor is property, and as such merits protection. The right to make it available is next in importance to the rights of life and liberty. It lies to a large extent at the foundation of most other forms of property, and of all solid individual and national prosperity. "Due process of law" is the application of the law as it exists in the fair and regular course of administrative procedure. "The equal protection of the laws" places all upon a footing of legal equality and gives the same protection to all for the preservation of life, liberty, and property, and the pursuit of happiness.

It is admitted that the plaintiffs in error are citizens of the United States, and persons within the jurisdiction of Louisiana. The cases before us, therefore, present but two questions.

(1) Does the act of the legislature creating the monopoly in question abridge the privileges and immunities of the plaintiffs in error as citizens of the United States?

(2) Does it deprive them of liberty or property without due process of law, or deny them the equal protection of the laws of the State, they being persons "within its jurisdiction?"

Both these inquiries I remit for their answer as to the facts to the opinions of my brethren, Mr. Justice Field and Mr. Justice Bradley. They are full and conclusive upon the subject. A more flagrant and indefensible invasion of the rights of many for the benefit of a few has not occurred in the legislative history of the country. The response to both inquiries should be in the affirmative. In my opinion, the cases, as presented in the record, are clearly within the letter and meaning of both the negative categories of the sixth section. The judgments before us should, therefore, be reversed.

These amendments are all consequences of the late civil war. The prejudices and apprehension as to the central government which prevailed when the Constitution was adopted were dispelled by the light of experience. The public mind became satisfied that there was less danger of tyranny in the head than of anarchy and tyranny in the members. The provisions of this section are all eminently conservative in their character. They are a bulwark of defense, and can never be made an engine of oppression. The language employed is unqualified in its scope. There is no exception in its terms, and there can be properly none in their application. By the language "citizens of the United States" was meant all such citizens; and by "any person" was meant all persons within the jurisdiction of the State. No distinction is intimated on account of race or color. This court has no authority to interpolate a limitation that is neither expressed nor implied. Our duty is to execute the law, not to make it. The protection provided was not intended to be confined to those of any particular race or class, but to embrace equally all races, classes, and conditions of men. It is objected that the power conferred is novel and large. The answer is that the novelty was known, and the measure deliberately adopted. The power is beneficent in its nature, and cannot be abused. It is such as should exist in every well-ordered system of polity. Where could it be more appropriately lodged than in the hands to which it is confided? It is necessary to enable the government of the nation to secure to everyone within its jurisdiction the rights and privileges enumerated, which, according to the plainest considerations of reason and justice and the fundamental principles of the social compact all are entitled to enjoy. Without such authority, any government claiming to be national is glaringly defective. The construction adopted by the majority of my brethren is, in my judgment, much too narrow. It defeats, by a limitation not anticipated, the intent of those by whom the instrument was framed and of those by whom it was adopted. To the extent of that limitation, it turns, as it were, what was meant for bread into a stone. By the Constitution as it stood before the war, ample protection was given against oppression by the Union, but little was given against wrong and oppression by the States. That want was intended to be supplied by this amendment. Against the former, this court has been called upon more than once to interpose. Authority of the same amplitude was intended to be conferred as to the latter. But this arm of our jurisdiction is, in these cases, stricken down by the judgment just given. Nowhere than in this court ought the will of the nation, as thus expressed, to be more liberally construed or more cordially executed. This determination of the majority seems to me to lie far in the other direction.

I earnestly hope that the consequences to follow may prove less serious and far-reaching than the minority fear they will be.

See 83 U.S. 36.

15.

A SOUTHERN ARISTOCRAT APPRAISES CHARLES SUMNER, THE CIVIL RIGHTS SENATOR (1874)

Richard Taylor, a planter and former Confederate officer from Louisiana, and the son of President Zachary Taylor, visited Washington, D.C., in 1874–75, making the rounds on Capitol Hill and at the White House to socialize with the leaders of the American government and discuss the policies of Reconstruction. Charles Sumner, the great civil rights advocate from Massachusetts, entertained Taylor as a distinguished guest. He would not live long after their meeting. Here are some of Taylor's impressions of Sumner in the closing hours of his life.

I visited Mr. Charles Sumner, Senator from Massachusetts, who received me pleasantly. A rebel, a slave-driver, and without the culture of Boston, ignorant, I was an admirable vessel into which he could pour the inexhaustible stream of his acquired eloquence. . . . Negro suffrage . . . he thought should be accompanied by education. I ventured to suggest that negro education should precede suffrage, observing that some held the opinion that the capacity of the white race for government was limited, although accumulated and transmitted through many centuries. He replied that the "ignorance of the negro was due to the tyranny of the whites," which appeared in his view to dispose of the question of the former's incapacity. He seemed over-educated—had retained, not digested his learning; . . . Hence he failed to understand the force of language, and became the victim of his own metaphors, mistaking them for facts. . . . Yet I hold him to have been the purest and most sincere man of his party. A lover, nay, a devotee of liberty, he thoroughly understood that it could only be preserved by upholding the supremacy of civil law. . . .

See Richard Taylor, *Destruction and Reconstruction: Personal Experiences of the Late War* (D. Appleton & Company, 1879; reprint, Nashville: J. S. Sanders & Company, 1998), 252–53.

16.

JAMES RAPIER ON THE CIVIL RIGHTS BILL (1875)

Rapier, a mulatto congressman from Alabama, eloquently explained in a speech in the House of Representatives on 4 February 1875 why the Civil Rights Bill—initiated by the then-deceased Senator Charles Sumner of Massachusetts—was such a necessity for African Americans. At the time, Reconstruction was drawing to an unceremonious close, although neither Rapier nor anyone else knew it. Nor did they know that the U.S. Supreme Court would soon nullify this very Civil Rights

Bill. In the excerpts below, Rapier lashes out at the ignorant and debased white men of the South who were determined to hold the black race down.

I must confess it is somewhat embarrassing for a colored man to urge the passage of this bill, because if he exhibits an earnestness in the matter and expresses a desire for its immediate passage, straightway he is charged with a desire for social equality, as explained by the demagogue and understood by the ignorant white man. But then it is just as embarrassing for him not to do so, for if he remains silent while the struggle is being carried on around, and for him, he is liable to be charged with a want of interest in a matter that concerns him more than any one else, which is enough to make his friends desert his cause. . . .

Sir, I submit that I am degraded as long as I am denied the public privileges common to other men, and that the members of this House are correspondingly degraded by recognizing my political equality while I occupy such a humiliating position. What a singular attitude for lawmakers of this great nation to assume, rather come down to me than allow me to go up to them. Sir, did you ever reflect that this is the only Christian country where poor, finite man is held responsible for the crimes of the infinite God whom you profess to worship? But it is; I am held to answer for the crime of color, when I was not consulted in the matter. Had I been consulted, and my future fully described, I think I should have objected to being born in this Gospel land. The excuse offered for all this inhuman treatment is that they consider the negro inferior to the white man, intellectually and morally. This reason might have been offered and probably accepted as truth some years ago, but not one now believes him incapable of the high order of culture, except someone who is himself below the average of mankind in natural endowments. . . .

Sir, there is a cowardly propensity in the human heart that delights in oppressing somebody else, and in the gratification of this base desire we always select a victim that can be outraged with safety. . . . And the smaller the caliber of the white man the more frantically has he fought to prevent the intellectual and moral progress of the Negro, for a simple but good reason that he has most to fear from such a result. . . .

See the *Congressional Record*, 43rd Cong., 1st sess., vol. 2, pt. 1, 565–67.

17.

THE CIVIL RIGHTS ACT (1875)

Initiated by Charles Sumner, the Civil Rights Bill was finally enacted into law after Sumner's death. Its purpose was to guard against racial discrimination in public places—the very threat that eventually materialized and gave rise to the Jim Crow era, after the U.S. Supreme Court struck down the act as unconstitutional in 1883. Here are some of the more salient excerpts from the act.

An Act to Protect All Citizens in the Civil and Legal Rights

Whereas, it is essential to just government that we recognize the equality of all men before the law, and hold that it is the duty of government in its dealings with the people to mete out equal and exact justice to all, of whatever nativity, race, color, or persuasion, religious or political; and it being the appropriate object of legislation to enact great fundamental principles into law: Therefore,

Be it enacted by the Senate and House of Representatives of the United States of America in Congress assembled, That all persons within the jurisdiction of the United States shall be entitled to the full and equal enjoyment of the accommodations, advantages, facilities, and privileges of inns, public conveyances on land or water, theaters, and other places of public amusement; subject only to the conditions and limitations established by law, and applicable alike to citizens of every race and color, regardless of any previous condition of servitude.

Section 2. That any person who shall violate the foregoing section by denying to any citizen, except for reasons by law applicable to citizens of every race and color, and regardless of any previous condition of servitude, the full enjoyment of any of the accommodations, advantages, facilities, or privileges in said section enumerated, or by aiding or inciting such denial, shall for every such offense, forfeit and pay the sum of five hundred dollars to the person aggrieved thereby, to be recovered in an action of debt, with full costs; and shall also, for every such offense, be deemed guilty of a misdemeanor. . . .

Section 3. That the district and circuit courts of the United States . . . are hereby specially authorized and required to institute proceedings against every person who shall violate the provisions of this act. . . .

Section 4. That no citizen possessing all other qualifications which are or may be prescribed by law shall be disqualified for service as grand or petit juror in any court of the United States, or of any State, on account of race, color, or previous condition of servitude. . . .

See 18 *Statutes at Large*, 336.

18.

SENATOR BLANCHE K. BRUCE ON THE OUTRAGE OF THE "REDEMPTION" OF MISSISSIPPI (1876)

Bruce was one of only two African Americans to serve in the U.S. Senate during Reconstruction. As a representative of Mississippi, he expressed dire concern for the events of the so-called Redemption of his home state by radical white Democrats. Here he pleads for the federal government to live up to this nation's creed and enforce the law in the southern states before it was too late. Unfortunately, by the time he made his appeal, it was already too late; Reconstruction would soon meet its demise, falling victim to war and postwar weariness within the federal government and, more importantly, the American public.

I had hoped that no occasion would arise to make it necessary for me again to claim the attention of the Senate until at least I had acquired a larger acquaintance with the methods of business and a fuller experience in public affairs; but silence at this time would be infidelity to my senatorial trust and unjust to both the people and the State I have the honor in part to represent. . . .

Lawless outbreaks have not been confined to any particular section of the country, but have prevailed in nearly every State at some period in its history. But the violence complained of and exhibited in Mississippi and other Southern States, pending a political canvass, is exceptional and peculiar. . . . Violence so unprovoked, inspired by such motives, and looking to such ends, is a spectacle not only discreditable to the country, but dangerous to the integrity of our free institutions.

I beg Senators to believe that I refer to this painful and reproachful condition of affairs in my own State not in resentment, but with sentiments of profound regret and humiliation. . . .

It will not accord with the laws of nature or history to brand the colored people as a race of cowards. On more than one historic field, beginning in 1776 and coming down to this centennial year of the Republic, they have attested in blood their courage as well as love of liberty. I ask Senators to believe that no consideration of fear or personal danger has kept us quiet and forbearing under the provocations and wrongs that have so sorely tried our souls. But feeling kindly toward our white fellow-citizens, appreciating the good purposes and offices of the better classes, and, above all, abhorring a war of races, we determined to wait until such time as an appeal to the good sense and justice of the American people could be made.

A notable feature of the outrages alleged is that they have referred almost exclusively to the colored citizens of the State. Why is the colored voter to be proscribed? Why direct the attack upon him? While the methods of violence, resorted to for political purposes in the south, are foreign to the genius of our institutions as applied to citizens generally—and so much is conceded by even the opposition—yet they seem to think we are an exceptional class and citizens, rather by sufferance than right; and when pressed to account for their bitterness and proscription toward us they, with more or less boldness, alleged incompetent and bad government as their justification before the public opinion of the country. Now, I declare that neither political incapacity nor venality are qualities of the masses of colored citizens. The emancipation of the colored race during the late civil strife was an expression alike of the magnanimity and needs of the nation; and the subsequent and early subtraction of millions of the industrial values from the resources of the insurrectionary States and the presence of many thousand additional brave hearts and strong hands around the flag of the country vindicated the justice and wisdom of the measure.

The close of the war found four millions of freedmen, without homes or property, charged with the duty of self-support and with the oversight of their personal freedom, yet without civil and political rights! The problem presented by this condition of things was one of the gravest that has ever been submitted to the American people. Shall these liberated millions of a separate race, while retaining personal liberty, be deprived of political rights? The practical sense of the American people definitely settled this delicate and difficult question, and the demand for a more pronounced loyal element in the work of reconstruction in the lately rebellious States furnished an opportunity for the recognition of the political rights of the race, both in the interest of justice and good government. . . .

We want peace and good order at the South; but it can only come by the fullest recognition of the rights of all classes. The opposition must concede the necessity of change, not only in the temper but in the philosophy of their party organization and management. The sober American judgment must obtain in the South as elsewhere in the Republic, that the only distinctions upon which parties can be safely organized and in harmony with our institutions are differences of opinions relative to principles and policy of government, and that differences of religion, nationality, or race can neither with safety nor propriety be permitted for a moment to enter into the party contests of the day. The unanimity with which the colored voters act with a party is not referable to any race prejudice on their part. On the contrary, they invite the political cooperation of their white brethren, and vote as a unit because proscribed as such. . . .

We simply demand the practical recognition of the rights given us in the Constitution and laws, and ask from our white fellow-citizens only the consideration and fairness that we so willingly extend to them. . . .

It has been suggested, as the popular sentiment of the country, that the colored citizens must no longer expect special legislation for their benefit, nor exceptional interference by the National Government for their protection. . . . We do not ask the enactment of new laws, but only the enforcement of those that already exist. . . .

The South has neither the means nor the ability to resist the authority of the Government. It needs the protection of the law, the security which its enforcement gives. If there have been violations of the law, if colored voters have been prevented from voting by fraud, intimidation, or violence, let the violators of the law be punished. The judiciary of the State of Mississippi, State and Federal, belongs to the party defeated in the late election in that State. If the laws have been so flagrantly broken, why sit these judges idle? . . .

See the *Congressional Record*, 44th Cong., 1st sess., pt. 2, 2101–3.

19.

EX PARTE SIEBOLD (1879)

The ruling in this case upheld the right of Congress to supervise federal elections through the Enforcement Act of 1870. Although this ruling was ignored throughout the coming Jim Crow era, it served as a legal precedent for federal control of the electoral process in America, which was effected during the Civil Rights Movement some eight decades later.

MR. JUSTICE [Joseph P.] BRADLEY delivered the opinion of the court.

The petitioners in this case, Albert Siebold, Walter Tucker, Martin C. Burns, Lewis Coleman, and Henry Bowers, were judges of election at different voting precincts in the city of Baltimore, at the election held in that city, and in the State of Maryland, on the fifth day of November, 1878, at which representatives to the Forty-sixth Congress were voted for.

At the November Term of the Circuit Court of the United States for the District of Maryland, an indictment against each of the petitioners was found in said court, for offences alleged to have been committed by them respectively at their respective precincts whilst being such judges of election; upon which indictments they were severally tried, convicted, and sentenced by said court to fine and imprisonment. They now apply to this court for a writ of habeas corpus to be relieved from imprisonment. . . .

Without attempting to decide how far this case may be regarded as law for the guidance of this court, we are clearly of opinion that the question raised in the cases before us is proper for consideration on habeas corpus. The validity of the judgments is assailed on the ground that the acts of Congress under which the indictments were found are unconstitutional. If this position is well taken, it affects the foundation of the whole proceedings. An unconstitutional law is void, and is as no law. An offence created by it is not a crime. A conviction under it is not merely erroneous, but is illegal and void, and cannot be a legal cause of imprisonment. It is true, if no writ of error lies, the judgment may be final, in the sense that there may be no means of reversing it. But personal liberty is of so great moment in the eye of the law that the judgment of an inferior court affecting it is not deemed so conclusive but that, as we have seen, the question of the court's authority to try and imprison the party may be reviewed on habeas corpus by a superior court or judge having authority to award the writ. We are satisfied that the present is one of the cases in which this court is authorized to take such jurisdiction. We think so, because, if the laws are unconstitutional and void, the Circuit Court acquired no jurisdiction of the causes. Its authority to indict and try the petitioners arose solely upon these laws. . . .

The indictments commence with an introductory statement that, on the 5th of November, 1878, at the Fourth [or other] Congressional District of the State of Maryland, a lawful election was held, whereat a representative for that congressional district in the Forty-sixth Congress of the United States was voted for; that a certain person [naming him] was then and there a supervisor of election of the United States, duly appointed by the Circuit Court aforesaid, pursuant to sect. 2012 of the Revised Statutes, for the third [or other] voting precinct of the fifteenth [or other] ward of the city of Baltimore, in the said congressional district, for and in respect of the election aforesaid, thereat; that a certain person [naming him] was then and there a special deputy marshal of the United States, duly appointed by the United States marshal for the Maryland district, pursuant to sect. 2021 of the Revised Statutes, and assigned for such duty as is provided by that and the following section, to the said precinct of said ward of said city, at the congressional election aforesaid, thereat. Then come the various counts.

The petitioner, Bowers, was convicted on the second count of the indictment against him, which was as follows:—

> That the said Henry Bowers, afterwards, to wit, on the day and year aforesaid, at the said voting precinct within the district aforesaid, unlawfully did obstruct, hinder, and, by the use of his power and authority as such judge as aforesaid (which judge he then and there was), interfere with and prevent the said supervisor of election in the performance of a certain duty in respect to said election required of him, and which he was then and there authorized to perform by the law of the United States, in such case made and provided, to wit, that of personally inspecting and scrutinizing, at the beginning of said day of election, and of the said election, the manner in which the voting was done at the said poll of election, by examining and seeing whether the ballot first voted at said poll of election was put and placed in a ballot-box containing no ballots whatever, contrary to sect. 5522 of said statutes, and against the peace, government, and dignity of the United States.

Tucker, who was indicted jointly with one Gude, was convicted upon the second and fifth counts of the indictment against them, which were as follows:—

> (2d.) That the said Justus J. Gude and the said Walter Tucker afterwards, to wit, on the day and year aforesaid, at the said voting precinct of said ward of said city, unlawfully and by exercise of their power and authority as such judges as afore-

said, did prevent and hinder the free attendance and presence of the said James N. Schofield (who was then and there such deputy marshal as aforesaid, in the due execution of his said office), at the poll of said election of and for the said voting precinct, and the full and free access of the same deputy marshal to the same poll of election, contrary to the said last-mentioned section of said statutes (sect. 5522), and against the peace, government, and dignity of the United States.

(5th.) That the said Justus J. Gude and the said Walter Tucker, on the day and year aforesaid, at the precinct aforesaid, within the district aforesaid (they being then and there such officers of said election as aforesaid), knowingly and unlawfully at the said election did a certain act, not then and there authorized by any law of the State of Maryland, and not authorized then and there by any law of the United States, by then and there fraudulently and clandestinely putting and placing in the ballot-box of the said precinct twenty (and more) ballots (within the intent and meaning of sect. 5514 of said statutes), which had not been voted at said election in said precinct before the ballots, then and there lawfully deposited in the same ballot-box, had been counted, with intent thereby to affect said election and the result thereof, contrary to sect. 5515 of said statutes, and against the peace, government, and dignity of the United States.

This charge, it will be observed, is for the offence commonly known as "stuffing the ballot-box."

The counts on which the petitioners, Burns and Coleman, were convicted were similar to those above specified. Burns was charged with refusing to allow the supervisor of elections to inspect the ballot-box, or even to enter the room where the polls were held, and with violently resisting the deputy marshal who attempted to arrest him, as required by sect. 2022 of the Revised Statutes. The charges against Coleman were similar to those against Burns, with the addition of a charge for stuffing the ballot-box. Siebold was only convicted on one count of the indictment against him, which was likewise a charge of stuffing the ballot-box. . . .

In the light of recent history, and of the violence, fraud, corruption, and irregularity which have frequently prevailed at such elections, it may easily be conceived that the exertion of the power [of Congress to regulate federal elections], if it exists, may be necessary to the stability of our frame of government.

The counsel for the petitioners, however, do not deny that Congress may, if it chooses, assume the entire regulation of the elections of representatives; but they contend that it has no constitutional power to make partial regulations intended to be carried out in conjunction with regulations made by the States. . . .

We are unable to see why it necessarily follows that, if Congress makes any regulations on the subject, it must assume exclusive control of the whole subject. The Constitution does not say so.

The clause of Constitution under which the power of Congress, as well as that of the State legislatures, to regulate the election of senators and representatives arises, is as follows: "The times, places, and manner of holding elections for senators and representatives shall be prescribed in each State by the Legislature thereof; but the Congress may at any time, by law, make or alter such regulations, except as to the place of choosing Senators."

It seems to us that the natural sense of these words is the contrary of that assumed by the counsel of the petitioners. After first authorizing the States to prescribe the regulations, it is added, "The Congress may at any time, by law, make or alter such regulations." "Make or alter": What is the plain meaning of these words? If not under the prepossession of some abstract theory of the relations between the State and national governments, we should not have any difficulty in understanding them. There is no declaration that the regulations shall be made either wholly by the State legislatures or wholly by Congress. If Congress does not interfere, of course they may be made wholly by the State; but if it chooses to interfere, there is nothing in the words to prevent its doing so, either wholly or partially. On the contrary, their necessary implication is that it may do either. It may either make the regulations, or it may alter them. If it only alters, leaving, as manifest convenience requires, the general organization of the polls to the State, there results a necessary co-operation of the two governments in regulating the subject. But no repugnance in the system of regulations can arise thence; for the power of Congress over the subject is paramount. It may be exercised as and when Congress sees fit to exercise it. When exercised, the action of Congress, so far as it extends and conflicts with the regulations of the State, necessarily supersedes them. This is implied in the power to "make or alter."

Suppose the Constitution of a State should say, "The first legislature elected under this Constitution may by law regulate the election of members of the two Houses; but any subsequent legislature may make or alter such regulations,"—could not a subsequent legislature modify the regulations made by the first legislature without making an entirely new set? Would it be obliged to go over the whole subject anew? Manifestly not: it could alter or modify, add or subtract, in its discretion. The greater power, of making wholly new regulations, would include the lesser, of only altering or modifying the old. The new law, if contrary or repugnant to the old, would so far, and so far only, take its place. If consistent with it, both would stand. The objection, so often repeated, that such an application of congressional regulations to those previously made by a State would produce a clashing of jurisdictions and a conflict of rules, loses sight of the fact that the regulations made by Congress are paramount to those made by the State legislature; and if they conflict therewith, the latter, so far as the conflict extends, ceases to be operative. No clashing can possibly arise. There is not the slightest difficulty in a harmonious combination into one system of the regulations made by the two sovereignties, any more than there is in the case of prior and subsequent enactments of the same legislature.

Congress has partially regulated the subject heretofore. In 1842, it passed a law for the election of representatives by separate districts; and, subsequently, other laws fixing the time of election, and directing that the elections shall be by ballot. No one will pretend, at least at the present day, that these laws were unconstitutional because they only partially covered the subject.

The peculiarity of the case consists in the concurrent authority of the two sovereignties, State and National, over the same subject-matter. This, however, is not entirely without a parallel. The regulation of foreign and inter-state commerce is conferred by the Constitution upon Congress. It is not expressly taken away from the States. But where the subject-matter is one of a national character, or one that requires a uniform rule, it has been held that the power of Congress is exclusive. On the contrary, where neither of these circumstances exist, it has been held that State regulations are not unconstitutional. In the absence of congressional regulation, which would be of paramount authority when adopted, they are valid and binding. . . . In 1789, Congress had passed a law declaring that all pilots should continue to be regulated in conformity with the laws of the States respectively wherein they should be. Hence, each State continued to administer its own laws, or passed new laws for the regulation of pilots in its harbors. Pennsylvania passed the law then in question in 1803. Yet the Supreme Court held that this was clearly a regulation of commerce; and that the State laws could not be upheld without supposing that, in cases like that of pilotage, not requiring a national and uniform regulation, the power of the States to make regulations of commerce, in the absence of congressional regulation, still remained. The court held that the power did so remain, subject to those qualifications; and the State law was sustained under that view.

Here, then, is a case of concurrent authority of the State and national governments, in which that of the latter is paramount. In 1837, Congress interfered with the State regulations on the subject of pilotage, so far as to authorize the pilots of adjoining States, separated only by navigable waters, to pilot ships and vessels into the ports of either State located on such waters. It has since made various regulations respecting pilots taking charge of steam vessels, imposing upon them peculiar duties and requiring of them peculiar qualifications. It seems to us that there can be no doubt of the power of Congress to impose any regulations it sees fit upon pilots, and to subject them to such penalties for breach of duty as it may deem expedient. The States continue in the exercise of the power to regulate pilotage subject to the paramount right of the national government. If dissatisfied with congressional interference, should such interference at any time be imposed, any State might, if it chose, withdraw its regulations altogether, and leave the whole subject to be regulated by Congress. But so long as it continues its pilotage system, it must acquiesce in such additional regulations as Congress may see fit to make.

So in the case of laws for regulating the elections of representatives to Congress. The State may make regulations on the subject; Congress may make regulations on the same subject, or may alter or add to those already made. The paramount character of those made by Congress has the effect to supersede those made by the State, so far as the two are inconsistent, and no farther. There is no such conflict between them as to prevent their forming a harmonious system perfectly capable of being administered and carried out as such.

As to the supposed conflict that may arise between the officers appointed by the State and national governments for superintending the election, no more insuperable difficulty need arise than in the application of the regulations adopted by each respectively. The regulations of Congress being constitutionally paramount, the duties imposed thereby upon the officers of the United States, so far as they have respect to the same matters, must necessarily be paramount to those to be performed by the officers of the State. If both cannot be performed, the latter are pro tanto superseded and cease to be duties. If the power of Congress over the subject is supervisory and paramount, as we have seen it to be, and if officers or agents are created for carrying out its regulations, it follows as a necessary consequence that such officers and agents must have the requisite authority to act without obstruction or interference from the officers of the State. No greater subordination, in kind or degree, exists in this case than in any other. It exists to the same extent between the different officers appointed by the State, when the State alone regulates the election. One officer cannot interfere with the duties of another, or obstruct or hinder him in the performance of them. Where there is a disposition to act harmoniously, there is no danger of disturbance between those who have different duties to perform. When the rightful authority of the general government is once conceded and acquiesced in, the apprehended difficulties will disappear. Let a spirit of national as well as local patriotism once prevail, let unfounded jealousies cease, and we shall hear no more about the impossibility of harmonious action between the national and State governments in a matter in which they have a mutual interest.

As to the supposed incompatibility of independent sanctions and punishments imposed by the two governments, for the enforcement of the duties required of the officers of election, and for their protection in the performance of those duties, the same considerations apply. While the State will retain the power of enforcing such of its own regulations as are not superseded by those adopted by Congress, it cannot be disputed that if Congress has power to make regulations it must have the power to enforce them, not only by punishing the delinquency of officers appointed by the United States, but by restraining and punishing those who attempt to interfere with them in the performance of their duties; and if, as we have shown, Congress may revise existing regulations, and add to or alter the same as far as it deems expedient, there can be as little question that it may impose additional penalties for the prevention of frauds committed by the State officers in the elections, or for their violation of any duty relating thereto, whether arising from the common law or from any other law, State or national. Why not? Penalties for fraud and delinquency are part of the regulations belonging to the subject. If Congress, by its power to make or alter the regulations, has a general supervisory power over the whole subject, what is there to preclude it from imposing additional sanctions and penalties to prevent such fraud and delinquency?

It is objected that Congress has no power to enforce State laws or to punish State officers, and especially has no power to punish them for violating the laws of their own State. As a general proposition, this is undoubtedly true; but when, in the performance of their functions, State officers are called upon to fulfil duties which they owe to the United States as well as to the State, has the former no means of compelling such fulfilment? Yet that is the case here. It is the duty of the States to elect representatives to Congress. The due and fair election of these representatives is of vital importance to the United States. The government of the United States is no less concerned in the transaction than the State government is. It certainly is not bound to stand by as a passive spectator, when duties are violated and outrageous frauds are committed. It is directly interested in the faithful performance, by the officers of election, of their respective duties. Those duties are owed as well to the United States as to the State. This necessarily follows from the mixed character of the transaction, State and national. A violation of duty is an offence against the United States, for which the offender is justly amenable to that government. No official position can shelter him from this responsibility. In view of the fact that Congress has plenary and paramount jurisdiction over the whole subject, it seems almost absurd to say that an officer who receives or has custody of the ballots given for a representative owes no duty to the national government which Congress can enforce; or that an officer who stuffs the ballot-box cannot be made amenable to the United States. If Congress has not, prior to the passage of the present laws, imposed any penalties to prevent and punish frauds and violations of duty committed by officers of election, it has been because the exigency has not been deemed sufficient to require it, and not because Congress had not the requisite power.

The objection that the laws and regulations, the violation of which is made punishable by the acts of Congress, are State laws and have not been adopted by Congress, is no sufficient answer to the power of Congress to impose punishment. It is true that Congress has not deemed it necessary to interfere with the duties of the ordinary officers of election, but has been content to leave them as prescribed by State laws. It has only created additional sanctions for their performance, and provided means of supervision in order more effectually to secure such performance. The imposition of punishment implies a prohibition of the act punished. The State laws which Congress sees no occasion to alter, but which it allows to stand, are in effect adopted by Congress. It simply demands their fulfilment. Content to leave the laws as they are, it is not content with the means provided for their enforcement. It provides additional means for that purpose; and we think it is entirely within its constitutional power to do so. It is simply the exercise of the power to make additional regulations.

That the duties devolved on the officers of election are duties which they owe to the United States as well as to the State, is further evinced by the fact that they have always been so regarded by the House of Representatives itself. In most cases of contested elections, the conduct of these officers is examined and scrutinized by that body as a matter of right; and their failure to perform their duties is often made the ground of decision. Their conduct is justly regarded as subject to the fullest exposure; and the right to examine them personally, and to inspect all their proceedings and papers, has always been maintained. This could not be done, if the officers were amenable only to the supervision of the State government which appointed them.

Another objection made is, that, if Congress can impose penalties for violation of State laws, the officer will be made liable to double punishment for delinquency, at the suit of the State, and at the suit of the United States. But the answer to this is, that each government punishes for violation of duty to itself only. Where a person owes a duty to two sovereigns, he is amenable to both for its performance; and either may call him to account. Whether punishment inflicted by one can be pleaded in bar to a charge by the other for the same identical act, need not now be decided; although considerable discussion bearing upon the subject has taken place in this court, tending to the conclusion that such a plea cannot be sustained.

In reference to a conviction under a State law for passing counterfeit coin, which was sought to be reversed on the ground that Congress had jurisdiction over that subject, and might inflict punishment for the same offence, Mr. Justice [Peter V.] Daniel, speaking for the court, said: "It is almost certain that, in the benignant spirit in which the institutions both of the State and Federal systems are administered, an offender who should have suffered the penalties denounced by the one would not be subjected a second time to punishment by the other for acts essentially the same, unless, indeed, this might occur in instances of peculiar enormity, or where the public safety demanded extraordinary rigor. But, were a contrary course of policy or action either probable or usual, this would by no means justify the conclusion that offences falling within the competency of different authorities to restrain or punish them would not properly be subjected to the consequences which those authorities might ordain and affix to their perpetration." . . . The same judge, delivering the opinion of the court in the case of United States v. Marigold . . . , where a conviction was had under an act of Congress for bringing counterfeit coin into the country, said, in reference to Fox's Case: "With the view of avoiding conflict between the State and Federal jurisdictions, this court, in the case of Fox v. State of Ohio, have taken care to point out that the same act might, as to its character and tendencies, and the consequences it involved, constitute an offence against both the State and Federal governments, and might draw to its commission the penalties denounced by either, as appropriate to its character in reference to each. We hold this distinction sound;" and the conviction was sustained. The subject came up again for discussion in the case of Moore v. State of Illinois . . . , in which the plaintiff in error had been convicted under a State law for harboring and secreting a negro slave, which was contended to be properly an offence against the United States under the fugitive-slave law of 1793, and not an offence against the State. The objection of double punishment was again raised. Mr. Justice [Robert C.] Grier, for the court, said: "Every citizen of the United States is also a citizen of a State or Territory. He may be said to owe allegiance to two sovereigns, and may be liable to punishment for an infraction of the laws of either. The same act may be an offence or transgression of the laws of both." Substantially the same views are expressed in United States v. Cruikshank . . . , referring to these cases; and we do not well see how the doctrine they contain can be controverted. A variety of instances may be readily suggested, in which it would be necessary or proper to apply it. Suppose, for example, a State judge having power under the naturalization laws to admit aliens to citizenship should utter false certificates of naturalization, can it be doubted that he could be indicted under the act of Congress providing penalties for that offence, even though he might also, under the State laws, be indictable for forgery as well as liable to impeachment? So, if Congress, as it might, should pass a law fixing the standard of weights and measures, and imposing a penalty for sealing false weights and false measures, but leaving to the States the matter of inspecting and sealing those used by the people, would not an offender, filling the office of sealer under a State law, be amenable to the United States as well as to the State?

If the officers of election, in elections for representatives, owe a duty to the United States, and are amenable to that government as well as to the State, as we think they are, then, according to the cases just cited, there is no reason why each should not establish sanctions for the performance of the duty owed to itself, though referring to the same act.

To maintain the contrary proposition, the case of Commonwealth of Kentucky v. Dennison . . . is confidently relied on by the petitioners' counsel. But there, Congress had imposed a duty upon the governor of the State which it had no authority to impose. The enforcement of the clause in the Constitution requiring the delivery of fugitives from justice was held not to belong to the United States. It is a purely executive duty, and Congress had no authority to require the governor of a State to execute this duty.

We have thus gone over the principal reasons of a special character relied on by the petitioners for maintaining the general proposition for which they contend; namely, that in the regulation of elections for representatives the national and State governments cannot co-operate, but must act exclusively of each other; so that, if Congress assumes to regulate the subject at all, it must assume exclusive control of the whole subject. The more general reason assigned, to wit, that the nature of sovereignty is such as to preclude the joint co-operation of two sovereigns, even in a matter in which they are mutually concerned, is not, in our judgment, of sufficient force to prevent concurrent and harmonious action on the part of the national and State governments in the election of representatives. It is at most an argument ab inconveniente. There is nothing in the Constitution to forbid such co-operation in this case. On the contrary, as already said, we think it clear that the clause of the Constitution relating to the regulation of such elections contemplates such co-operation whenever Congress deems it expedient to interfere merely to alter or add to existing regulations of the State. If the two governments had an entire equality of jurisdiction, there might be an intrinsic difficulty in such co-operation. Then the adoption by the State government of a system of regulations might exclude the action of Congress. By first taking jurisdiction of the subject, the State would acquire exclusive jurisdiction in virtue of a well-known principle applicable to courts having co-ordinate jurisdiction over the same matter. But no such equality exists in the present case. The power of Congress, as we have seen, is paramount, and may be exercised at any time, and to any extent which it deems expedient; and so far as it is exercised, and no farther, the regulations effected supersede those of the State which are inconsistent therewith.

As a general rule, it is no doubt expedient and wise that the operations of the State and national governments should, as far as practicable, be conducted separately, in order to avoid undue jealousies and jars and conflicts of jurisdiction and power. But there is no reason for laying this down as a rule of universal application. It should never be made to override the plain and manifest dictates of the Constitution itself. We cannot yield to such a transcendental view of state sovereignty. The Constitution and laws of the United States are the supreme law of the land, and to these every citizen of every State owes obedience, whether in his individual or official capacity. There are very few subjects, it is true, in which our system of government, complicated as it is, requires or gives room for conjoint action between the State and national sovereignties. Generally, the powers given by the Constitution to the government of the United States are given over distinct branches of sovereignty from which the State governments, either expressly or by necessary implication, are excluded. But in this case, expressly, and in some others, by implication, as we have seen in the case of pilotage, a concurrent jurisdiction is contemplated, that of the State, however, being subordinate to that of the United States, whereby all question of precedency is eliminated.

In what we have said, it must be remembered that we are dealing only with the subject of elections of representatives to Congress. If for its own convenience a State sees fit to elect State and county officers at the same time and in conjunction with the election of representatives, Congress will not be thereby deprived of the right to make regulations in reference to the latter. We do not mean to say, however, that for any acts of the officers of election, having exclusive reference to the election of State or county officers, they will be amenable to Federal jurisdiction; nor do we understand that the enactments of Congress now under consideration have any application to such acts.

It must also be remembered that we are dealing with the question of power, not of the expediency of any regulations which Congress has made. That is not within the pale of our jurisdiction. In exercising the power, however, we are bound to presume that Congress has done so in a judicious manner; that it has endeavored to guard as far as possible against any unnecessary interference with State laws and regulations, with the duties of State officers, or with local prejudices. It could not act at all so as to accomplish any beneficial object in preventing frauds and violence, and securing the faithful performance of duty at the elections, without providing for the presence of officers and agents to carry its regulations into effect. It is also difficult to see how it could attain these objects without imposing proper sanctions and penalties against offenders.

The views we have expressed seem to us to be founded on such plain and practical principles as hardly to need any labored argument in their support. We may mystify any thing. But if we take a plain view of the words of the Constitution, and give to them a fair and obvious interpretation, we cannot fail in most cases of coming to a clear understanding of its meaning. We shall not have far to seek. We shall find it on the surface, and not in the profound depths of speculation.

The greatest difficulty in coming to a just conclusion arises from mistaken notions with regard to the relations which subsist between the State and national governments. It seems to be often overlooked that a national constitution has been adopted in this country, establishing a real government therein, operating upon persons and territory and things; and which, moreover, is, or should be, as dear to every American citizen as his State government is. Whenever the true conception of the nature of this government is once conceded, no real difficulty will arise in the just interpretation of its powers. But if we allow ourselves to regard it as a hostile organization, opposed to the proper sovereignty and dignity of the State governments, we shall continue to be vexed with difficulties as to its jurisdiction and authority. No greater jealousy is required to be exercised towards this government in reference to the preservation of our liberties, than is proper to be exercised towards the State governments. Its powers are limited in number, and clearly defined; and its action within the scope of those powers is restrained by a sufficiently rigid bill of rights for the protection of its citizens from oppression. The true interest of the people of this country requires that both the national and State governments should be allowed, without jealous interference on either side, to exercise all the powers which respectively belong to them according to a fair and practical construction of the Constitution. State rights and the rights of the United States should be equally respected. Both are essential to the preservation of our liberties and the perpetuity of our institutions. But, in endeavoring to vindicate the one, we should not allow our zeal to nullify or impair the other.

Several other questions bearing upon the present controversy have been raised by the counsel of the petitioners. Somewhat akin to the argument which has been considered is the objection that the deputy marshals authorized by the act of Congress to be created and to attend the elections are authorized to keep the peace; and that this is a duty which belongs to the State authorities alone. It is argued that the preservation of peace and good order in society is not within the powers confided to the government of the United States, but belongs exclusively to the States. Here again we are met with the theory that the government of the United States does not rest upon the soil and territory of the country. We think that this theory is founded on an entire misconception of the nature and powers of that government. We hold it to be an incontrovertible principle, that the government of the United States may, by means of physical force, exercised through its official agents, execute on every foot of American soil the powers and functions that belong to it. This necessarily involves the power to command obedience to its laws, and hence the power to keep the peace to that extent.

This power to enforce its laws and to execute its functions in all places does not derogate from the power of the State to execute its laws at the same time and in the same places. The one does not exclude the other, except where both cannot be executed at the same time. In that case, the words of the Constitution itself show which is to yield. "This Constitution, and all laws which shall be made in pursuance thereof, . . . shall be the supreme law of the land."

This concurrent jurisdiction which the national government necessarily possesses to exercise its powers of sovereignty in all parts of the United States is distinct from that exclusive power which, by the first article of the Constitution, it is authorized to exercise over the District of Columbia, and over those places within a State which are purchased by consent of the legislature thereof, for the erection of forts, magazines, arsenals, dock-yards, and other needful buildings. There its jurisdiction is absolutely exclusive of that of the State, unless, as is sometimes stipulated, power is given to the latter to serve the ordinary process of its courts in the precinct acquired.

Without the concurrent sovereignty referred to, the national government would be nothing but an advisory government. Its executive power would be absolutely nullified.

Why do we have marshals at all, if they cannot physically lay their hands on persons and things in the performance of their proper duties? What functions can they perform, if they cannot use force? In executing the processes of the courts, must they call on the nearest constable for protection? must they rely on him to use the requisite compulsion, and to keep the peace whilst they are soliciting and entreating the parties and bystanders to allow the law to take its course? This is the necessary consequence of the positions that are assumed. If we indulge in such impracticable views as these, and keep on refining and re-refining, we shall drive the national government out of the United States, and relegate it to the District of Columbia, or perhaps to some foreign soil. We shall bring it back to a condition of greater helplessness than that of the old confederation.

The argument is based on a strained and impracticable view of the nature and powers of the national government. It must execute its powers, or it is no government. It must execute them on the land as well as on the sea, on things as well as on persons. And, to do this, it must necessarily have power to command obedience, preserve order, and keep the peace; and no person or power in this land has the right to resist or question its authority, so long as it keeps within the bounds of its jurisdiction. Without specifying other instances in which this power to preserve order and keep the peace unquestionably exists, take the very case in hand. The counsel for the petitioners concede that Congress may, if it sees fit, assume the entire control and regulation of the election of representatives. This would necessarily involve the appointment of the places for holding the polls, the times of voting, and the officers for holding the election; it would require the regulation of the duties to be performed, the custody of the ballots, the mode of ascertaining the result, and every other matter relating to the subject. Is it possible that Congress could not, in that case, provide for keeping the peace at such elections, and for arresting and punishing those guilty of breaking it? If it could not, its power would be but a shadow and a name. But, if Congress can do this, where is the difference in principle in its making provision for securing the preservation of the peace, so as to give to every citizen his free right to vote without molestation or injury, when it assumes only to supervise the regulations made by the State, and not to supersede them entirely? In our judgment, there is no difference; and, if the power exists in the one case, it exists in the other.

The next point raised is, that the act of Congress proposes to operate on officers or persons authorized by State laws to perform certain duties under them, and to require them to disobey and disregard State laws when they come in conflict with the act of Congress; that it thereby of necessity produces collision, and is therefore void. This point has been already fully considered. We have shown, as we think, that, where the regulations of Congress conflict with those of the State, it is the latter which are void, and not the regulations of Congress; and that the laws of the State, in so far as they are inconsistent with the laws of Congress on the same subject, cease to have effect as laws.

Finally, it is objected that the act of Congress imposes upon the Circuit Court duties not judicial, in requiring them to appoint the supervisors of election, whose duties, it is alleged, are entirely executive in their character. It is contended that no power can be conferred upon the courts of the United States to appoint officers whose duties are not connected with the judicial department of the government.

The Constitution declares that "the Congress may, by law, vest the appointment of such inferior officers as they think proper, in the President alone, in the courts of law, or in the heads of departments." It is no doubt usual and proper to vest the appointment of inferior officers in that department of the government, executive or judicial, or in that particular executive department to which the duties of such officers appertain. But there is no absolute requirement to this effect in the Constitution; and, if there were, it would be difficult in many cases to determine to which department an office properly belonged. Take that of marshal, for instance. He is an executive officer, whose appointment, in ordinary cases, is left to the President and Senate. But if Congress should, as it might, vest the appointment elsewhere, it would be questionable whether it should be in the President alone, in the Department of Justice, or in the courts. The marshal is pre-eminently the officer of the courts; and, in case of a vacancy, Congress has in fact passed a law bestowing the temporary appointment of the marshal upon the justice of the circuit in which the district where the vacancy occurs is situated.

But as the Constitution stands, the selection of the appointing power, as between the functionaries named, is a matter resting in the discretion of Congress. And, looking at the subject in a practical light, it is perhaps better that it should rest there, than that the country should be harassed by the endless controversies to which a more specific direction on this subject might have given rise. The observation . . . that the appointing power . . . "was no doubt intended to be exercised by the department of the government to which the official to be appointed most appropriately belonged," was not intended to define the constitutional power of Congress in this regard, but rather to express the law or rule by which it should be governed. The cases in which the courts have declined to exercise certain duties imposed by Congress, stand upon a different consideration from that which applies in the present case. The law of 1792, which required the circuit courts to examine claims to revolutionary pensions, and the law of 1849, authorizing the district judge of Florida to examine and adjudicate upon claims for injuries suffered by the inhabitants of Florida from the American army in 1812, were rightfully held to impose upon the courts powers not judicial, and were, therefore, void. But the duty to appoint inferior officers, when required thereto by law, is a constitutional duty of the courts; and in the present case there is no such incongruity in the duty required as to excuse the courts from its performance, or to render their acts void. It cannot be affirmed that the appointment of the officers in question could, with any greater propriety, and certainly not with equal regard to convenience, have been assigned to any other depositary of official power capable of exercising it. Neither the President, nor any head of department, could have been equally competent to the task.

In our judgment, Congress had the power to vest the appointment of the supervisors in question in the circuit courts.

The doctrine laid down at the close of counsel's brief, that the State and national governments are co-ordinate and altogether equal, on which their whole argument, indeed, is based, is only partially true.

The true doctrine, as we conceive, is this, that whilst the States are really sovereign as to all matters which have not been granted to the jurisdiction and control of the United States, the Constitution and constitutional laws of the latter are, as we have already said, the supreme law of the land; and, when they conflict with the laws of the States, they are of paramount authority and obligation. This is the fundamental principle on which the authority of the Constitution is based; and unless it be conceded in practice, as well as theory, the fabric of our institutions, as it was contemplated by its founders, cannot stand. The questions involved have respect not more to the autonomy and existence of the States, than to the continued existence of the United States as a government to which every American citizen may look for security and protection in every part of the land.

We think that the cause of commitment in these cases was lawful, and that the application for the writ of habeas corpus must be denied.

Application denied.

See 100 U.S. 371.

20.

GEORGE WASHINGTON WILLIAMS AND *THE HISTORY OF THE NEGRO RACE IN AMERICA* (1882)

Williams, the first great African American historian, wrote, as he explains here, this mammoth 584-page treatise because of the dearth of recorded history about his race.

I became convinced that a history of the Colored people in America was required, because of the ample historically trustworthy material at hand; because the Colored people themselves had been the most vexatious problem in North America, from the time of its discovery down to the present day; because that in every attempt upon the life of the nation, whether by foes from without or within, the Colored people had always displayed a matchless patriotism and an incomparable heroism in the cause of Americans; and because such a history would give the world more correct ideas of the Colored people, and incite the latter to greater effort in the struggle for citizenship and manhood. The single reason that there was no history of the Negro race would have been a sufficient reason for writing one. . . .

Not as the blind panegyrist of my race, nor as the partisan apologist, but from a love for "*the truth of history*," have I striven to record the truth, the whole truth, and nothing but the truth. I have not striven to revive the sectional animosities or race prejudices. I have avoided comment so far as it was consistent with a clear exposition of the truth. My whole aim has been to write a thoroughly trustworthy history; and what I have written, if it have no other merit, is reliable.

I commit this work to the public, white and black, to the friends and foes of the Negro, in the hope that the obsolete antagonisms which grew out of the relation of master and slave may speedily sink as storms beneath the horizon;

and that the day will hasten when there shall be no North, no South, no Black, no White,—but all be American citizens, with equal duties and rights. George W. Williams.

New York, November, 1882.

See George W. Williams, *The History of the Negro Race in America, 1619–1880* (New York: G. P. Putnam's Sons, 1883), v–vi, x.

21.

T. THOMAS FORTUNE ON THE PLIGHT OF BLACK SHARECROPPERS IN THE POST-RECONSTRUCTION SOUTH (1884)

Fortune, the mulatto editor of the *New York Age*, was an outspoken civil rights advocate at a time when there was little audience for his egalitarian rhetoric. Here he chastises the critics of his day who blamed black southerners for causing their own poverty and thus deserving their second-class citizenship.

Herein lies the great social wrong which has turned the beautiful roses of freedom into thorns to prick the hands of the black men of the South; which made slavery a blessing, paradoxical as it may appear, and freedom a curse. . . . To tell a man he is free when he has neither money nor the opportunity to make it, is simply to mock him. To tell him he has no master when he cannot live except by permission of the man who, under favorable conditions, monopolizes all the land, is to deal in the most tantalizing contradiction of terms. But this is just what the United States did for the black man. And yet because he has not grown learned and wealthy in twenty years, because he does not own broad acres and a large bank account, people are not wanting who declare he has no capacity, that he is improvident by nature and mendacious from inclination.

See T. Thomas Fortune, *Black and White: Land, Labor, and Politics in the South* (1884; reprint, New York: Arno Press, 1968), 36.

22.

EX PARTE YARBROUGH (1884)

The ruling in this case set a fundamental legal precedent for upholding black voting rights and punishing violators of the Fourteenth and Fifteenth Amendments and the Enforcement Acts. Although largely ignored during the Jim Crow era, this ruling provided a basis upon which to begin the arduous process of restoring black voting rights during the Civil Rights Movement of the mid-twentieth century.

MILLER, [Samuel F.]

This case originates in this court by an application for a writ of habeas corpus on the part of Jasper Yarbrough and seven other persons, who allege that they are confined by the jailer of Fulton county in the custody of the United States marshal for the Northern district of Georgia, and that the trial, conviction, and sentence in the circuit court of the United States for that district, under which they are held, were illegal, null, and void. The court, on the filing of this petition, issued a rule on the marshal, or on any person in whose custody the prisoners might be found, to show cause why the writ of habeas corpus should not issue for their release. It appears, by the returns made to this rule, that the sentence of the court, which ordered their imprisonment in the Albany penitentiary, in the state of New York, at hard labor for the term of two years, has been so far executed that they are now in that prison. The rule having been served on John McEwan, superintendent of the penitentiary, he makes return that he holds the prisoners by virtue of the sentence of the circuit court for the Northern district of Georgia, and annexes to his return a transcript of the proceeding in that court. As this return is precisely the same that the superintendent would make if the writ of habeas corpus had been served on him, the court here can determine the right of the prisoners to be released on this rule to show cause as correctly and with more convenience in the administration of justice, than if the prisoners were present under the writ in the custody of the superintendent; and such is the practice of this court. That this court has no general authority to review on error or appeal the judgments of the circuit courts of the United States in cases within their criminal jurisdiction is beyond question; but it is equally well settled that when a prisoner is held under the sentence of any court of the United States in regard to a matter wholly beyond or without the jurisdiction of that court, it is not only within the authority of the supreme court, but it is its duty, to inquire into the cause of commitment when the matter is properly brought to its attention, and if found to be as charged, a matter of which such court had no jurisdiction, to discharge the prisoner from confinement.

It is, however, to be carefully observed that this latter principle does not authorize the court to convert the writ of habeas corpus into a writ of error, by which the errors of law committed by the court that passed the sentence can be reviewed here; for if that court had jurisdiction of the party, and of the offense for which he was tried, and has not exceeded its powers in the sentence which it pronounced, this court can inquire no further. This principle disposes of the argument made before us on the insufficiency of the indictments under which the prisoners in this case were tried. Whether the indictment sets forth in comprehensive terms the offense which the statute describes and forbids, and for which it prescribes a punishment, is in every case a question of law which must necessarily be decided by the court in which the case originates, and is therefore clearly within its jurisdiction. Its decision on the conformity of the indictment to the provisions of the statute may be erroneous; but, if so, it is an error of law made by a court acting within its jurisdiction, which could be corrected on a writ of error, if such writ was allowed, but which cannot be looked into on a writ of habeas corpus limited to an inquiry into the existence of jurisdiction on the part of that court. . . .

This, however, leaves for consideration the more important question—the one mainly relied on by counsel for petitioners—whether the law of congress, as found in the Revised Statutes of the United States, under which the prisoners are held, is warranted by the constitution, or, being without such warrant, is null and void. If the law which defines the offense and prescribes its punishment is void, the court was without jurisdiction, and the prisoners must be discharged. Though several different sections of the Revised Statutes are brought into the discussion as the foundation of the indictments found in the record, we think only two of them demand our attention here, namely, sections 5508 and 5520. They are in the following language:

Sec. 5508. If two or more persons conspire to injure, oppress, threaten, or intimidate any citizen in the free exercise or enjoyment of any right or privilege secured to him by the constitution or laws of the United States, or because of his having so exercised the same or if two or more persons go in disguise on the highway, or on the premises of another, with intent to prevent or hinder his free exercise or enjoyment of any right or privilege so secured, they shall be fined not more than five thousand dollars and imprisoned not more than ten years; and shall, moreover, be thereafter ineligible to any office or place of honor, profit, or trust created by the constitution or laws of the United States.

Sec. 5520. If two or more persons in any state or territory conspire to prevent, by force, intimidation, or threat, any citizen who is lawfully entitled to vote from giving his support or advocacy, in a legal manner, towards or in favor of the election of any lawfully qualified person as an elector for president or vice-president, or as a member of the congress of the United States, or to injure any citizen in person or property on account of such support or advocacy, each of such persons shall be punished by a fine of not less than five hundred nor more than five thousand dollars, or by imprisonment, with or without hard labor, not less than six months nor more than six years, or by both such fine and imprisonment.

The indictments, four in number, on which petitioners were tried, charge in each one all of the defendants with a conspiracy under these sections, directed against a different person in each indictment. On the trial the cases were consolidated, and as each indictment is in the identical language of all the others, except as to the name of the person assaulted and the date of the transaction, the copy which is here presented will answer for all of them:

We, the grand jurors of the United States, chosen, selected, and sworn in and for the Northern district of Georgia, upon our oaths, present: That . . . Jasper Yarbrough, [et al. did] combine, conspire, and confederate together, by force, to injure, oppress, threaten, and intimidate Berry Saunders, a person of color, and a citizen of the United States of America of African descent, on account of his race, color, and previous condition of servitude, in the full exercise and enjoyment of the right and privilege of suffrage in the election of a lawfully qualified person as a member of the congress of the United States of America, and because the said Berry Saunders had so exercised the same, and on account of such exercise, which said right and privilege of suffrage was secured to the said Berry Saunders by the constitution and laws of the United States of America, the said Berry Saunders being then and there lawfully entitled to vote in said election; and, having so then and there conspired, the said Jasper Yarbrough, [et al.] . . . did unlawfully, feloniously, and willfully beat, bruise, wound, and maltreat the said Berry Saunders, contrary to the form of the statute in such case made and provided, and against the peace and dignity of the United States of America.

Second Count. And the jurors aforesaid, upon their oaths aforesaid, do further present: That Jasper Yarbrough, [et al.] . . . did commit the offense of conspiracy, for that the said Jasper Yarbrough, [et al.], having then and there conspired together, by force, to injure, oppress, threaten, and intimidate Berry Saunders, a person of color, and a citizen of the United States of America of African descent, on account of his race, color, and previous condition of servitude, did then and there unlawfully, willfully, and feloniously go in disguise on the highway, and on the premises of Berry Saunders, with the intent to prevent and hinder his free exercise and enjoyment of the right to vote at an election for a lawfully qualified person as a member of the congress of the United States of America, which said right had then and there been guarantied to the said Berry Saunders by the constitution and laws of the United States of America, the said Berry Saunders being then and there lawfully qualified to vote at said election; and having so conspired, with intent as aforesaid, the said Jasper Yarbrough, [et al.] did then and there beat, bruise, wound, and maltreat the said Berry Saunders, contrary to the form of the statute in such case made and provided, and against the peace and dignity of the United States of America.

Stripped of its technical verbiage, the offense charged in this indictment is that the defendants conspired to intimidate Berry Saunders, a citizen of African descent, in the exercise of his right to vote for a member of the congress of the United States, and in the execution of that conspiracy they beat, bruised, wounded, and otherwise maltreated him; and in the second count that they did this on account of his race, color, and previous condition of servitude, by going in disguise and assaulting him on the public highway and on his own premises. If the question were not concluded in this court, as we have already seen that it is by the decision of the circuit court, we entertain no doubt that the conspiracy here described is one which is embraced within the provisions of the Revised Statutes which we have cited. That a government whose essential character is republican, whose executive head and legislative body are both elective, whose numerous and powerful branch of the legislature is elected by the people directly, has no power by appropriate laws to secure this election from the influence of violence, of corruption, and of fraud, is a proposition so startling as to arrest attention and demand the gravest consideration. If this government is anything more than a mere aggregation of delegated agents of other states and governments, each of which is superior to the general government, it must have the power to protect the elections on which its existence depends, from violence and corruption. If it has not this power, it is left helpless before the two great natural and historical enemies of all republics, open violence and insidious corruption.

The proposition that it has no such power is supported by the old argument often heard, often repeated, and in this court never assented to, that when a question of the power of congress arises the advocate of the power must be able to place his finger on words which expressly grant it. The brief of counsel before us, though directed to the authority of that body to pass criminal laws, uses the same language. Because there is no express power to provide for preventing violence exercised on the voter as a means of controlling his vote, no such law can be enacted. It destroys at one blow, in construing the constitution of the United States, the doctrine universally applied to all instruments of writing, that what is implied is as much a part of the instrument as what is expressed. This principle, in its application to the constitution of the United States, more than to almost any other writing, is a necessity, by reason of the inherent inability to put into words all derivative powers,—a difficulty which the instrument itself recognizes by conferring on congress the authority to pass all laws necessary and proper to carry into execution the powers expressly granted, and all other powers vested in the government or any branch of it by the constitution. . . .

We know of no express authority to pass laws to punish theft or burglary of the treasury of the United States. Is there therefore no power in congress to protect the treasury by punishing such theft and burglary? Are the mails of the United States, and the money carried in them, to be left at the mercy of robbers and of thieves who may handle the mail, because the constitution contains no express words of power in congress to enact laws for the punishment of those offenses? The principle, if sound, would abolish the entire criminal jurisdiction of the courts of the United States, and the laws which confer that jurisdiction. It is said that the states can pass the necessary law on this subject, and no necessity exists for such action by congress. But the existence of state laws punishing the counterfeiting of the coin of the United States has never been held to supersede the acts of congress passed for that purpose, or to justify the United States in failing to enforce its own laws to protect the circulation of the coin which it issues. It is very true that while congress at an early day passed criminal laws to punish piracy with death. and for punishing all ordinary offenses against person and property committed within the District of Columbia, and in forts, arsenals, and other places within the exclusive jurisdiction of the United States, it was slow to pass laws protecting officers of the government from personal injuries inflicted while in discharge of their official

685

duties within the states. This was not for want of power, but because no occasion had arisen which required such legislation, the remedies in the state courts for personal violence having proved sufficient.

Perhaps the earliest attempt of congress to protect government officers while in the exercise of their duty in a hostile community, grew out of the nullification ordinance of South Carolina, and is found in the "Act further to provide for the collection of duties on imports." That act gave a right of action in the courts of the United States to any officer engaged in the collection of customs who should receive any injury to his person or property for or on account of any act done by him under any law of the United States for the protection of the revenues. And where any suit or prosecution should be commenced against him in a state court on account of any act done under the revenue laws of the United States or under color thereof, the case might, on his petition, at any time before trial, be removed into the circuit court of the United States. . . .

When early in the late civil war the enforcement of the acts of congress for obtaining soldiers by draft, brought the officers engaged in it into hostile neighborhoods, it was found necessary to pass laws for their protection. Accordingly, in 1863, an act was passed making it a criminal offense to assault or obstruct any officer while engaged in making the draft, or in any service in relation thereto. . . . And the next year the act was amended by making it applicable to the enrollment and resistance made thereto, and adding that if any assault on any officer or other person engaged in making such enrollment shall result in death, it shall be murder and punished accordingly. . . . Under this statute Scott was found guilty of murder in the circuit court of the United States for the district of Indiana, and the case was brought here by a certificate of division of opinion. It was not doubted for a moment by court or counsel that congress had the power to pass these statutes, but it was held that serving notice of a draft, in doing which the man was killed, was not a service in the enrollment, as charged in the indictment. . . .

In the case of U.S. v. Gleason, . . . , the defendant was convicted and sentenced to death for the murder of an enrolling officer while engaged in making the enrollment, and his sentence being commuted to imprisonment for life, he died in the Iowa penitentiary while undergoing the modified sentence. It was never suggested that congress had no power to pass the law under which he was convicted.

So, also, has the congress been slow to exercise the powers expressly conferred upon it in relation to elections by the fourth section of the first article of the constitution. This section declares that "the times, places, and manner of holding elections for senators and representatives shall be prescribed in each state by the legislature thereof; but the congress may at any time make or alter such regulations, except as to the place of choosing senators." It was not until 1842 that congress took any action under the power here conferred, when, conceiving that the system of electing all the members of the house of representatives from a state by general ticket, as it was called, that is, every elector voting for as many names as the state was entitled to representatives in that house, worked injustice to other states which did not adopt that system, and gave an undue preponderance of power to the political party which had a majority of votes in the state, however small, enacted that each member should be elected by a separate district, composed of contiguous territory. . . . And to remedy more than one evil arising from the election of members of congress occurring at different times in the different states, congress, by the act of February 2, 1872, 30 years later, required all the elections for such members to be held on the Tuesday after the first Monday in November in 1876, and on the same day of every second year thereafter.

The frequent failures of the legislatures of the states to elect senators at the proper time, by one branch of the legislature voting for one person and the other branch for another person, and refusing in any manner to reconcile their differences, led congress to pass an act which compelled the two bodies to meet in joint convention, and fixing the day when this should be done, and requiring them so to meet on every day thereafter and vote for a senator until one was elected. In like manner congress has fixed a day, which is to be the same in all the states, when the electors for president and vice-president shall be appointed.

Now, the day fixed for electing members of congress has been established by congress without regard to the time set for election of state officers in each state, and but for the fact that the state legislatures have, for their own accommodation, required state elections to be held at the same time, these elections would be held for congressmen alone at the same time fixed by the act of congress. Will it be denied that it is in the power of that body to provide laws for the proper conduct of those elections? To provide, if necessary, the officers who shall conduct them and make return of the result? And especially to provide, in an election held under its own authority, for security of life and limb to the voter while in the exercise of this function? Can it be doubted that congress can, by law, protect the act of voting, the place where it is done, and the man who votes from personal violence or intimidation, and the election itself from corruption or fraud? If this be so, and it is not doubted, are such powers annulled because an election for state officers is held at the same time and place? Is it any less important that the election of members of congress should be the free choice of all the electors, because state officers are to be elected at the same time? . . . These questions answer themselves; and it is only because the congress of the United States, through long habit and long years of forbearance, has, in deference and respect to the states, refrained from the exercise of these powers that they are now doubted. But when, in the pursuance of a new demand for action, that body, as it did in the cases just enumerated, finds it necessary to make additional laws for the free, the pure, and the safe exercise of this right of voting, they stand upon the same ground, and are to be upheld for the same reasons.

It is said that the parties assaulted in these cases are not officers of the United States, and their protection in exercising the right to vote by congress does not stand on the same ground. But the distinction is not well taken. The power in either case arises out of the circumstance that the function in which the party is engaged or the right which he is about to exercise is dependent on the laws of the United States. In both cases it is the duty of that government to see that he may exercise this right freely, and to protect him from violence while so doing, or on account of so doing. This duty does not arise solely from the interest of the party concerned, but from the necessity of the government itself that its service shall be free from the adverse influence of force and fraud practiced on its agents, and that the votes by which its members of congress and its president are elected shall be the free votes of the electors, and the officers thus chosen the free and uncorrupted choice of those who have the right to take part in that choice.

This proposition answers, also, another objection to the constitutionality of the laws under consideration, namely, that the right to vote for a member of congress is not dependent upon the constitution or laws of the United States, but is governed by the law of each state respectively. If this were conceded, the importance to the general government of having the actual election-the voting for those members-free from force and fraud is not diminished by the circumstance that the qualification of the voter is determined by the law of the state where he votes. It equally affects the government; it is as indispensable to the proper discharge of the great function of legislating for that government, that those who are to control this legislation shall not owe their election to bribery or violence, whether the class of persons who shall vote is determined by the law of the state, or by the laws of the United States, or by their united result. But it is not correct to say that the right to vote for a member of congress does not depend on the constitution of the United States. The office, if it be properly called an office, is created by that constitution, and by that alone. It also declares how it shall be filled, namely, by election. Its language is: "The house of representatives shall be composed of members chosen every second year by the people of the several states; and the electors in each state shall have the same qualifications requisite for electors of the most numerous branch of the state legislature." . . . The states, in prescribing the qualifications of voters for the most numerous branch of their own legislatures, do not do this with reference to the election for members of congress. Nor can they prescribe the qualification for voters. . . . They define who are to vote for the popular branch of their own legislature, and the constitution of the United States says the same persons shall vote for members of congress in that state. It adopts the qualification thus furnished as the qualification of its own electors for members of congress. It is not true, therefore, that electors for members of congress owe their right to vote to the state law, in any sense which makes the exercise of the right to depend exclusively on the law of the state.

Counsel for petitioners, seizing upon the expression found in the opinion of the court in the case of Minor v. Happersett, . . . that "the constitution of the United States does not confer the right of suffrage upon any one," without reference to the connection in which it is used, insists that the voters in this case do not owe their right to vote in any sense to that instrument. But the court was combating the argument that this right was conferred on all citizens, and therefore upon women as well as men. In opposition to that idea, it was said the constitution adopts as the qualification for voters of members of congress that which prevails in the state where the voting is to be done; therefore, said the opinion, the right is not definitely conferred on any person or class of persons by the constitution alone, because you have to look to the law of the state for the description of the class. But the court did not intend to say that when the class or the person is thus ascertained, his right to vote for a member of congress was not fundamentally based upon the constitution, which created the office of member of congress, and declared it should be elective, and pointed to the means of ascertaining who should be electors. The fifteenth amendment of the constitution, by its limitation on the power of the states in the exercise of their right to prescribe the qualifications of voters in their own elections, and by its limitation of the power of the United States over that subject, clearly shows that the right of suffrage was considered to be of supreme importance to the national government, and was not intended to be left within the exclusive control of the states. . . .

While it is quite true, as was said by this court in U.S. v. Reese, . . . , that this article gives no affirmative right to the colored man to vote, and is designed primarily to prevent discrimination against him whenever the right to vote may be granted to others it is easy to see that under some circumstances it may operate as the immediate source of a right to vote. In all cases where the former slave-holding states had not removed from their constitutions the words "white man" as a qualification for voting, this provision did, in effect, confer on him the right to vote, because, being paramount to the state law, and a part of the state law, it annulled the discriminating word "white," and thus left him in the enjoyment of the same right as white persons. And such would be the effect of any future constitutional provision of a state which should give the right of voting exclusively to white people, whether they be men or women. . . . In such cases this fifteenth article of amendment does . . . substantially confer on the negro the right to vote, and congress has the power to protect and enforce that right.

In the case of U.S. v. Reese, so much relied on by counsel, this court said, in regard to the fifteenth amendment, that "it has invested the citizens of the United States with a new constitutional right which is within the protecting power of congress. That right is an exemption from discrimination in the exercise of the elective franchise on account of race, color, or previous condition of servitude." This new constitutional right was mainly designed for citizens of African descent. The principle, however, that the protection of the exercise of this right is within the power of congress, is as necessary to the right of other citizens to vote as to the colored citizen, and to the right to vote in general as to the right to be protected against discrimination. The exercise of the right in both instances is guarantied by the constitution, and should be kept free and pure by congressional enactments whenever that is necessary.

The reference to cases in this court in which the power of congress under the first section of the fourteenth amendment has been held to relate alone to acts done under state authority can afford petitioners no aid in the present case. For, while it may be true that acts which are mere invasions of private rights, which acts have no sanction in the statutes of a state, or which are not committed by any one exercising its authority, are not within the scope of that amendment, it is quite a different matter when congress undertakes to protect the citizen in the exercise of rights conferred by the constitution of the United States, essential to the healthy organization of the government itself. But it is a waste of time to seek for specific sources of the power to pass these laws. Chancellor [James] KENT, in the opening words of that part of his Commentaries which treats of the government and constitutional jurisprudence of the United States, says: "The government of the United States was created by the free voice and joint will of the people of American for their common defense and general welfare. Its powers apply to those great interests which relate to this country in its national capacity, and which depend for their protection on the consolidation of the Union. It is clothed with the principal attributes of political sovereignty, and it is justly deemed the guardian of our best rights, the source of our highest civil and political duties, and the sure means of national greatness." . . .

It is as essential to the successful working of this government that the great organisms of its executive and legislative branches should be the free choice of the people, as that the original form of it should be so. In absolute governments, where the monarch is the source of all power, it is still held to be important that the exercise of that power shall be free from the influence of extraneous violence and internal corruption. In a republican government, like ours, where political power is reposed in representatives of the entire body of the people, chosen at short intervals by popular elections, the temptations to control these elections by violence and by corruption is a constant source of danger. Such has been the history of all republics, and, though ours has been comparatively free from both these evils in the past, no lover of his country can shut his eyes to the fear of future danger from both sources. If the recurrence of such acts as these prisoners stand convicted of are too common in one quarter of the country, and give omen of danger from lawless violence, the free use of money in elections, arising from the vast growth of recent wealth in other quarters, presents equal cause for anxiety. If the government of the United States has within its constitutional domain no authority to provide against these evils,—if the very sources of power may be poisoned by corruption or controlled by violence and outrage, without legal restraint,—then, indeed, is the country in danger, and its best powers, its highest purposes, the hopes which it inspires, and the love which enshrines it, are at the mercy of the combinations of those who respect no right but brute force on the one hand, and unprincipled corruptionists on the other.

The rule to show cause in this case is discharged, and the writ of habeas corpus denied.

See 110 U.S. 65.

23.

GEORGE WASHINGTON CABLE CONDEMNS RACIAL SEGREGATION (1885)

Cable was one of the few white southerners to speak out against the new type of racism that began taking shape in the South after Reconstruction. Here he makes a strong argument against segregation of the races. It is important to note that when he penned these words in 1885, it was not a foregone conclusion that full-blown Jim Crowism would overtake the South. Clearly, he feared that it would, and thus he made this urgent appeal to fellow southerners to stop the madness of both segregation itself and the tacit acceptance of segregation before it was too late.

Any colored man gains unquestioned admission into innumerable places the moment he appears as the menial attendant of some white person, where he could not cross the threshold in his own right as a well-dressed and well-behaved master of himself. The contrast is even greater in the case of colored women. There could not be a system which when put into practice would more offensively condemn itself. It does more: it actually creates the confusion it pretends to prevent. It blunts the sensibilities of the ruling class themselves. It waives all strict demand for painstaking in either manners or dress or either master or menial, and, for one result, makes the average Southern railway coach more uncomfortable than the average of railway coaches elsewhere. It prompts the average Southern white passenger to find less offense in the presence of a profane, boisterous, or unclean white person than in that of a quiet, well-behaved colored man or woman attempting to travel on an equal footing with him without a white master or mistress. The holders of the old sentiments hold the opposite choice in scorn. It is only when we go on to say that there are regions where the riotous expulsion of a decent and peaceable colored person is preferred to his inoffensive company, that it may seem necessary to bring in evidence. And yet here again it is *prima facie* evidence; for the following extract was printed in the Selma (Alabama) "Times" not six months ago [in the summer of 1884], and not as a complaint, but as a boast:

A few days since, a negro minister, of this city, boarded the east-bound passenger train . . . and took a seat in the coach occupied by white passengers. Some of the passengers complained to the conductor and brakeman, and expressed considerable dissatisfaction that they were forced to ride alongside a negro. The railroad officials informed the complainants that they were not authorized to force the colored passenger into the coach set apart for the negroes, and they would lay themselves liable should they do so. The white passengers then took the matter in their own hands and ordered the ebony-hued minister to take a seat in the next coach. He positively refused to obey orders, whereupon the white men gave him a sound flogging and forced him to a seat among his own color and equals. We learned yesterday that the vanquished preacher was unable to fill his pulpit on account of the severe chastisement inflicted upon him. . . .

. . . . Must such men, such acts, such sentiments, stand alone to represent us of the South before an enlightened world? No. I say, as a citizen of an extreme Southern State, a native of Louisiana, an ex-Confederate soldier, and a lover of my home, my city, and my State, as well as of my country, that this is not the best sentiment in the South, nor the sentiment of her best intelligence; and that it would not ride up and down that beautiful land dominating and domineering were it not for its tremendous power as the *traditional* sentiment of a conservative people. But is not silent endurance criminal? I cannot but repeat my own words, spoken near the scene and about the time of the event. Speech may be silvern and silence golden; but if a lump of gold is only big enough, it can drag us to the bottom of the sea and hold us there while the world sails over us.

See George Washington Cable, "The Freedmen's Case in Equity," *Century Magazine* (1885); reprinted in Arlin Turner, ed., *The Silent South* (Montclair, New Jersey: Patterson Smith, 1969), 23–26.

24.

CALVIN W. CHASE OF THE *WASHINGTON BEE* URGES BLACKS TO DIVORCE THE REPUBLICAN PARTY (1887)

The *Washington Bee* was among the foremost African American newspapers in the nation in the late 1800s. Its editor, Calvin Chase, agreed with several other prominent black leaders, including T. Thomas Fortune and Henry M. Turner, that black voters owed no allegiance to the Republican party, in light of the GOP's abandonment of their race in the post-Reconstruction period. Here Chase argues that the best hope for the black man's voice to be heard in America lay in political independence.

The time has now arrived in the politics of this country for the Negro to think and act for himself. Too long, for his best interests, has he been the subservient tool of men who had no further use for him than to count on, in advance, his vote to serve their party interest. With no compensating results other than a few minor offices grudgingly given, the Negro has steadily and solidly for years, voted the republican ticket, without even availing himself of the privileges accorded the meanest, lowest, and most ignorant white man, viz. "to scratch a ticket." The reading and thinking portion of them were first aroused from their political apathy by the concerted action of the republican governors of several southern states, recommending to President Grant the disarming of the colored militia in the several states, thereby placing the Negro at the tender mercy of a bitter and unrelenting foe. . . .

See Martin E. Dann, ed., *The Black Press, 1827–1890: The Quest for National Identity* (New York: G. P. Putnam's Sons, 1971), 174.

25.

THE REPUBLICAN PRESS ON THE DEFEAT OF THE "FORCE BILL" (1890)

The Federal Elections Bill of 1890, otherwise called the "Force Bill," was the last meaningful legislation that the Republican party offered for the benefit of African Americans before abandoning the ideals of Reconstruction entirely. While Democrats rejoiced at its defeat, partisan Republicans found the defeat difficult to accept. Herein are articles from three northern newspapers, all of which were partisan Republican in their ideology and all denouncing the defeat and the party defectors who caused it.

There never was a better test of genuine Republicanism than the elections bill. If its agitation has served no other purpose, it has at least developed the base metal in the party and prepared the way for casting it out. There is no meaning in Republicanism which will not stand up for fair elections [in the] South as well as North. It is the logical sequence of what the party has always stood for and fought for. Slavery restriction, emancipation, negro suffrage, civil rights, and fair elections are but the basic pillars of one political faith, and the stand men take upon them, independent of their personal interest, is the measure of their Republicanism.

—*Philadelphia Press*, 17 January 1891

The rebel victory yesterday was unexpected and discouraging. But Grant did not put down the armed rebellion without encountering many and trying discouragements. He never knew how to let up his grip on Lee's army, and a saved Nation and restored Union were the rewards of his tenacity. We do not believe that Republicanism is going to be fatally betrayed in the Senate and beaten by a combination of reconstructed rebels and weak-kneed or demoralized and traitorous Republicans. There are enough Republican Senators who have been tried and proved faithful, to pass the elections bill, peaceably if possible, of course, but to pass it over any revolutionary resistance. Since the war closed, no such noble opportunity for fearless Republican statesmanship has been offered as that which exists in the Senate today. Thanks to a conspiracy of mendacity, a bill that is no more entitled to the prefix of "force" than any of the existing statutes of the United States has been so put before the people that a large proportion really believe the reiterated lies. . . .

—*New York Mail and Express*, 7 January 1891

Between Republican Senators who are busy trying to be their own successors, those who have silver bullion they want to unload on the Government at more than the market value, and those who speculate in silver pools, the elections bill is in a fair way to be strangled. It makes but little difference to these Senators whether the pledges of the party are fulfilled or not, so personal ends may be subserved. It would be well for them to remember that the eyes of the Republicans of the country are upon them and there must be an accounting sooner or later for a plain dereliction of duty. Enemies outside the camp can be tolerated, but traitors inside the lines deserve, and will be accorded, political death. The faith of the Republican party is pledged to the enactment of a measure similar to the elections bill, and the Senators who seek to block the wheels of the party chariot will be crushed beneath its wheels.

—*Ohio State Journal*, 27 January 1891

26.

FREDERICK DOUGLASS ON "THE NEGRO PROBLEM" (1890)

Here Douglass addresses the Bethel Literary and Historical Association in Washington, D.C., on the most politically charged topic of 1890, the southern race problem. White politicians and writers often called it "The Negro Problem," but as this speech clearly reveals, Douglass took strong exception to that terminology.

I shall endeavor to say only what I believe to be the truth upon what is popularly called "The Negro problem."

My first thought respects the importance of calling things by their true names. . . . I object to characterizing the relation subsisting between the white and colored people of this country as the negro problem, as if the negro precipitated that problem, and as if he were in any way responsible for the problem. . . .

The true problem in not the negro, but the nation. Not the law-abiding blacks of the South, but the white men of that section, who by fraud, violence, and persecution, are breaking the law, trampling on the Constitution, corrupting the ballot-box, and defeating the ends of justice. The true problem is whether these white ruffians shall be allowed by the nation to go on in their lawless and nefarious career, dishonoring the Government and making its very name a mockery. It is whether this nation has in itself sufficient moral stamina to maintain its honor and integrity by vindicating its own Constitution and fulfilling its own pledges, or whether it has already touched that dry rot of moral depravity by which nations decline and fall, and governments fade and vanish . . .

See John W. Blassingame and John R. McKivigan, eds., *The Frederick Douglass Papers: Series One: Speeches, Debates, and Interviews, Vol. 5: 1881–95* (New Haven: Yale University Press, 1992), 436–44.

27.

J. C. PRICE: EDUCATION WILL SOLVE THE RACE PROBLEM (1890)

Price, the founder and president of Livingstone College in North Carolina, was widely considered the heir apparent to Frederick Douglass as the foremost spokesman for the rights of African Americans in the late 1880s and early 1890s. His untimely death in 1893, however, allowed Booker T. Washington to gain that distinction. Price was a devout Christian, a proponent of education for all, and an uncompromising critic of Jim Crowism. His address to the National Education Association's annual convention, held in Minneapolis in 1890, is excerpted below.

The real question implied in this subject, as I understand it, is, Will education solve the race problem? With such an idea in view, it is but proper that we have some conception of what the problem is, in order that we may select the best means for its solution. . . .

The race problem, as now understood, had its beginning in 1620, when the negroes were forced to accept this country as their home. So, in one form or another, the negro question has been before the country for two hundred and seventy years, and this question, with its constant and incident dangers, has been a source of anxiety and vexation, and rock of offense, during all those years. . . .

The "peculiar institution" continued to grow, with all its attendant evils, until it threatened the very life of the republic; so much so, until it was declared by one of the wisest men the country ever produced, that the nation could not live half free and half slave. . . .

Slavery, as a system, degraded the negro to the level of the brute, because it denied him the untrammeled exercise of all the instincts of a higher and better manhood. . . .

The feeling against the negro, which helps to make our race problem is called prejudice, and is not without some grounds. For two hundred and fifty years the white man of the South saw only the animal, or mechanical, side of the negro. Wherever he looked, there was degradation, ignorance, superstition, darkness there, and nothing more, as he thought. . . .

I do not argue that increased intelligence, or multiplied facilities for education, will, by some magic spell, transform the negro into the . . . embodiment of excellence . . . [or] in a day, or a decade, or a century, rid the black man of all physical peculiarities and deformities, moral perversions and intellectual distortions which are the debasing and logical heritage of more than two and a half centuries of enslavement. . . .

Now the question that at once presents itself, is this: Does education help improve the moral condition of a people? If this be granted, it is not hard to conclude that such a means will be a long step toward the removal of this element of the problem. . . .

The great work of education among negroes consists in leading them out of the errors which centuries of a debasing servitude fastened upon them; but even when this is done, the negro will not be an embodiment of every moral excellence, but he will at least stand on the same plane of morals with the other representatives of our common and fallen humanity, and whatever is the possibility and hope of one will be the possibility and hope of the other . . .

See National Education Association, *Journal of Proceedings and Addresses* (Topeka: Kansas Publishing, 1890), 267–76.

28.

A CONTEMPORARY NEWSPAPER PRAISES VIRGINIA CONGRESSMAN JOHN MERCER LANGSTON (1891)

Langston's contested election to Congress, along with several other contested elections and some controversial Republican legislation such as the Federal Elections Bill, produced extremely bitter partisan, sectional, and racial animosities in the so-called Billion Dollar Congress, of which Langston was a member. On the day Langston was seated, the Democrats in unison walked out of the chamber to show their contempt for their new colleague of color. Langston then had the dubious task of winning the respect of his antagonists, which he ultimately and incredibly did, as shown in this article from the 17 January 1891 edition of the *Cleveland Leader.*

Washington, January 16—The sensation which relieved the tedium of an otherwise dull day in the House was a speech by Mr. Langston, the colored member from Virginia, whose admission was so long fiercely contested by the Democrats in the last session. Evidently Mr. Langston had some things in his mind that he wanted to say on the race question. . . . Mr. Langston made a speech that was eloquent and effective. It would not be an exaggeration to say it was brilliant. No sooner had he warmed to his theme than members on both sides laid aside newspapers and pens and turned their chairs around to look and listen. No higher compliment can be paid him than to state the fact that he commanded the close attention of all in the chamber, Democrats and Republicans alike.

There are not five men in the House who can talk as well as Langston. He speaks extemporaneously, without even notes, and his command of language is masterly. No doubt there are scores of Democrats in that body who would give a year's salary for half as good a gift of oratory. When he began the Democrats showed a disposition to ignore him, but he compelled them to hear him, and before he had finished a dozen . . . were over on the Republican side listening intently to his every word. It is scarcely credible, but it is true that he caused the eyes of some of these case-hardened Democrats to moisten by his impassioned appeals for justice to the black men and the white men of the South who are proscribed because they are Republicans.

See John Mercer Langston, *From the Virginia Plantation to the National Capitol* (Hartford: American Publishing Company, 1894; reprint, New York: Kraus Reprint Co., 1969), 514–15.

29.

THE SECOND MOHONK CONFERENCE'S PLATFORM: RECOMMENDATIONS TO CONGRESS (1891)

One of the major developments in African American history in the late 1800s was the rise of the "convention movement." Counted among the many conventions held to discuss the "Negro Question" were the Mohonk Conferences held in Ulster, New York, in 1890 and 1891. Speakers included former President Rutherford B. Hayes, "Judge" Albion Tourgee, General O. O. Howard, and General S. C. Armstrong—all white proponents of civil rights for black Americans. The conferences were significant in that they showed how a small but vocal contingent of white political and social leaders continued the vigil of the abolitionists and Reconstructionists to make the United States a land of equality of opportunity for all people, even in the midst of overwhelming public opinion to the contrary.

THE PLATFORM

1. The accomplishing of the primary education of the Negro by the States themselves, and the further development of means and methods to this end, till all Negroes are creditably trained in primary schools.

2. The largely increased support of schools aided by private benevolence, which shall supply teachers and preachers for the Negro race.

3. The grounding of the vast majority of these teachers and preachers in common English studies and in the English Bible, with the further opportunity for any of them to carry on their studies as far as they may desire.

4. The great extension of industrial education for both men and women.

5. The encouragement of secondary schools established, maintained, and conducted by Negroes.

6. The purchase of homesteads by as many Negro households as possible, with an increased number of decent houses to replace the old one-room cabin.

7. The establishment by the government of postal savings-banks, in which Negroes can be encouraged to save their earnings until they can purchase homes.

8. The aid of public education by the national government, for the special benefit of those sections in which illiteracy most prevails.

9. The removal of all disabilities under which Negroes labor, by the sure forces of education, thrift, and religion.

See *Second Mohonk Conference on the Negro Question* (New York: Negro Universities Press, 1892; reprint, 1969), 109.

30.

BOOKER T. WASHINGTON'S "ATLANTA COMPROMISE" (1895)

Washington was already considered one of the most prominent African Americans of his generation before he made this address, but the tremendous media coverage generated by the event increased his notoriety tenfold. He thereafter became the recognized black leader in the United States well into the twentieth century.

Mr. President and Gentlemen of the Board of Directors and Citizens.

One-third of the population of the South is of the Negro race. No enterprise seeking the material, civil, or moral welfare of this section can disregard this element of our population and reach the highest success. I but convey to you, Mr. President and Directors, the sentiment of the masses of my race when I say that in no way have the value and manhood of the American Negro been more fittingly and generously recognized than by the managers of this magnificent Exposition at every stage of its progress. It is a recognition that will do more to cement the friendship of the two races than any occurrence since the dawn of our freedom.

Not only this, but the opportunity here afforded will awaken among us a new era of industrial progress. Ignorant and inexperienced, it is not strange that in the first years of our new life we began at the top instead of at the bottom; that a seat in Congress or the state legislature was more sought than real estate or industrial skill; that the political convention or stump speaking had more attractions that starting a dairy farm or truck garden. . . .

To those of my race who depend on bettering their condition in a foreign land or who underestimate the importance of cultivating friendly relations with the Southern white man, who is their next-door neighbour, I say: "Cast down your bucket where you are"—cast it down in making friends in every manly way of the people of all races by whom we are surrounded.

Cast it down in agriculture, mechanics, in commerce, in domestic service, and in the professions. And in this connection it is well to bear in mind that whatever other sins the South may be called to bear, when it comes to business, pure and simple, it is in the South that the Negro is given a man's chance in the commercial world, and in nothing is this Exposition more eloquent than in emphasizing this chance. Our greatest danger is that in the great leap from slavery to freedom we may overlook the fact that the masses of us are to live by the productions of our hands, and fail to keep that we shall prosper in proportion as we learn to dignify and glorify labour and put brains and skill into the common occupations of life. . . . No race can prosper till it learns that there is as much dignity in tilling a field as in writing a poem. It is at the bottom of life we must begin, and not at the top. Nor should we permit our grievances to overshadow our opportunities.

To those of the white race who look to the incoming of those of foreign birth and strange tongue and habits for the prosperity of the South, were I permitted I would repeat what I say to my own race, "Cast down your bucket where you are." Cast it down among the eight millions of Negroes whose habits you know, whose fidelity and love you have tested in days when to have proved treacherous meant the ruin of your firesides. Cast down your bucket among these people who have, without strikes and labour wars, tilled your fields, cleared your forests, builded your railroads and cities, and brought forth treasures from the bowels of the earth, and helped make possible this magnificent representation of the progress of the South. . . . We shall stand by you with a devotion that no foreigner can approach, ready to lay down our lives, if need be, in defence of yours, interlacing our industrial, commercial, civil, and religious life with yours in a way that shall make the interests of both races one. In all things that are purely social we can be as separate as the fingers, yet one as the hand in all things essential to mutual progress. . . .

The wisest among my race understand that the agitation of questions of social equality is the extremest folly, and that progress in the enjoyment of all privileges that will come to us must be the result of severe and constant struggle rather than of artificial forcing. . . . The opportunity to earn a dollar in a factory just now is worth infinitely more than the opportunity to spend a dollar in an opera-house.

See Booker T. Washington, *Up from Slavery* (New York: A. L. Burt Company, 1901), 18–25.

31.

A *NEW YORK WORLD* REPORTER ON BOOKER T. WASHINGTON'S ATLANTA SPEECH (1895)

Washington's speech at the Atlanta Cotton States Exposition in 1895 made national headlines, because it seemed to many observers to present the long-overdue final solution to the southern race problem. Here is a typical newspaper report on the speech and the man who delivered it.

All eyes were turned on a tall tawny Negro sitting in the front row of the platform. . . . As Professor Washington strode to the edge of the stage, the low descending sun shot fiery rays through the window into his face. A great shout greeted him. He turned his head to avoid the blinding light, and moved about the platform for relief. Then he turned his wonderful countenance to the sun without a blink of the eyelids, and began to talk. There was a remarkable figure; tall, bony, straight as a Sioux chief, high forehead, straight nose, heavy jaws, and strong, determined mouth, with big white teeth, piercing eyes, and a commanding manner. . . . His voice rang out clear and true, and he paused impressively as he made each point. . . . And when he held his dusky hand high above his head with the fingers stretched wide apart, and said to the white people of the South on behalf of his race, "In all things that are purely social we can be as separate as the fingers, yet as one hand in all things essential to mutual progress," the great wave of sound dashed itself against the walls, and the whole audience was on its feet in a delirium of applause. It was as if the orator had bewitched them.

See Ridgely Torrence, *The Story of John Hope* (New York: The MacMillan Company, 1948), 113–14.

32.

A DISSENTING OPINION IN *PLESSY V. FERGUSON* (1896)

This landmark case established the doctrine of "separate but equal" and served as the foundation upon which the whole Jim Crow segregation system was built and maintained for more than a half-century. This ruling, which had such a devastating impact upon African Americans, did not represent a unanimous decision of the court. Here the dissenting opinion of Justice John Marshall Harlan is presented.

May 18, 1896.
Mr. Justice [John Marshall] HARLAN dissenting.

By the Louisiana statute the validity of which is here involved, all railway companies (other than street-railroad companies) that carry passengers in that state are required to have separate but equal accommodations for white and colored persons, "by providing two or more passenger coaches for each passenger train, or by dividing the passenger coaches by a partition so as to secure separate accommodations." Under this statute, no colored person is permitted to occupy a seat in a coach assigned to white persons; nor any white person to occupy a seat in a coach assigned to colored persons. The managers of the railroad are not allowed to exercise any discretion in the premises, but are required to assign each passenger to some coach or compartment set apart for the exclusive use of his race. If a passenger insists upon going into a coach or compartment not set apart for persons of his race, he is subject to be fined, or to be imprisoned in the parish jail. Penalties are prescribed for the refusal or neglect of the officers, directors, conductors, and employees of railroad companies to comply with the provisions of the act.

Only "nurses attending children of the other race" are excepted from the operation of the statute. No exception is made of colored attendants traveling with adults. A white man is not permitted to have his colored servant with him in the same coach, even if his condition of health requires the constant personal assistance of such servant. If a colored maid insists upon riding in the same coach with a white woman whom she has been employed to serve, and who may need her personal attention while traveling, she is subject to be fined or imprisoned for such an exhibition of zeal in the discharge of duty.

While there may be in Louisiana persons of different races who are not citizens of the United States, the words in the act "white and colored races" necessarily include all citizens of the United States of both races residing in that state. So that we have before us a state enactment that compels, under penalties, the separation of the two races in railroad passenger coaches, and makes it a crime for a citizen of either race to enter a coach that has been assigned to citizens of the other race.

Thus, the state regulates the use of a public highway by citizens of the United States solely upon the basis of race.

However apparent the injustice of such legislation may be, we have only to consider whether it is consistent with the constitution of the United States.

That a railroad is a public highway, and that the corporation which owns or operates it is in the exercise of public functions, is not, at this day, to be disputed. Mr. Justice [Samuel] Nelson, speaking for this court in New Jersey Steam Nav. Co. v. Merchants' Bank, . . . , said that a common carrier was in the exercise "of a sort of public office, and has public duties to perform, from which he should not be permitted to exonerate himself without the assent of the parties concerned." Mr. Justice Strong, delivering the judgment of this court in Olcott v. Supervisors, . . . , said: "That railroads, though constructed by private corporations, and owned by them, are public highways, has been the doctrine of nearly all the courts ever since such conveniences for passage and transportation have had any existence. Very early the question arose whether a state's right of eminent domain could be exercised by a private corporation created for the purpose of constructing a railroad. Clearly, it could not, unless taking land for such a purpose by such an agency is taking land for public use. The right of eminent domain nowhere justifies taking property for a private use. Yet it is a doctrine universally accepted that a state legislature may author-ize a private corporation to take land for the construction of such a road, mak-ing compensation to the owner. What else does this doctrine mean if not that building a railroad, though it be built by a private corporation, is an act done for a public use?" So, in Township of Pine Grove v. Talcott, . . . : "Though the corporation [a railroad company] was private, its work was public, as much so as if it were to be constructed by the state." So, in Inhabitants of Worcester v. Western R. Corp., . . . : "The establishment of that great thoroughfare is regarded as a public work, established by public authority, intended for the public use and benefit, the use of which is secured to the whole community, and constitutes, therefore, like a canal, turnpike, or highway, a public ease-ment." "It is true that the real and personal property, necessary to the estab-lishment and management of the railroad, is vested in the corporation; but it is in trust for the public."

In respect of civil rights, common to all citizens, the constitution of the United States does not, I think, permit any public authority to know the race of those entitled to be protected in the enjoyment of such rights. Every true man has pride of race, and under appropriate circumstances, when the rights of others, his equals before the law, are not to be affected, it is his privilege to express such pride and to take such action based upon it as to him seems proper. But I deny that any legislative body or judicial tribunal may have regard to the race of citizens when the civil rights of those citizens are involved. Indeed, such legislation as that here in question is inconsistent not only with that equality of rights which pertains to citizenship, national and state, but with the personal liberty enjoyed by every one within the United States.

The thirteenth amendment does not permit the withholding or the depri-vation of any right necessarily inhering in freedom. It not only struck down the institution of slavery as previously existing in the United States, but it pre-vents the imposition of any burdens or disabilities that constitute badges of slavery or servitude. It decreed universal civil freedom in this country. This court has so adjudged. But, that amendment having been found inadequate to the protection of the rights of those who had been in slavery, it was followed by the fourteenth amendment, which added greatly to the dignity and glory of

American citizenship, and to the security of personal liberty, by declaring that "all persons born or naturalized in the United States, and subject to the jurisdiction thereof, are citizens of the United States and of the state wherein they reside," and that "no state shall make or enforce any law which shall abridge the privileges or immunities of citizens of the United States; nor shall any state deprive any person of life, liberty or property without due process of law, nor deny to any person within its jurisdiction the equal protection of the laws." These two amendments, if enforced according to their true intent and meaning, will protect all the civil rights that pertain to freedom and citizenship. Finally, and to the end that no citizen should be denied, on account of his race, the privilege of participating in the political control of his country, it was declared by the fifteenth amendment that "the right of citizens of the United States to vote shall not be denied or abridged by the United States or by any state on account of race, color or previous condition of servitude."

These notable additions to the fundamental law were welcomed by the friends of liberty throughout the world. They removed the race line from our governmental systems. They had, as this court has said, a common purpose, namely, to secure "to a race recently emancipated, a race that through many generations have been held in slavery, all the civil rights that the superior race enjoy." They declared, in legal effect, this court has further said, "that the law in the states shall be the same for the black as for the white; that all persons, whether colored or white, shall stand equal before the laws of the states; and in regard to the colored race, for whose protection the amendment was primarily designed, that no discrimination shall be made against them by law because of their color." We also said: "The words of the amendment, it is true, are prohibitory, but they contain a necessary implication of a positive immunity or right, most valuable to the colored race, the right to exemption from unfriendly legislation against them distinctively as colored; exemption from legal discriminations, implying inferiority in civil society, lessening the security of their enjoyment of the rights which others enjoy; and discriminations which are steps towards reducing them to the condition of a subject race." It was, consequently, adjudged that a state law that excluded citizens of the colored race from juries, because of their race, however well qualified in other respects to discharge the duties of jurymen, was repugnant to the fourteenth amendment. . . . At the present term, referring to the previous adjudications, this court declared that "underlying all of those decisions is the principle that the constitution of the United States, in its present form, forbids, so far as civil and political rights are concerned, discrimination by the general government or the states against any citizen because of his race. All citizens are equal before the law." . . .

The decisions referred to show the scope of the recent amendments of the constitution. They also show that it is not within the power of a state to prohibit colored citizens, because of their race, from participating as jurors in the administration of justice.

It was said in argument that the statute of Louisiana does not discriminate against either race, but prescribes a rule applicable alike to white and colored citizens. But this argument does not meet the difficulty. Every one knows that the statute in question had its origin in the purpose, not so much to exclude white persons from railroad cars occupied by blacks, as to exclude colored people from coaches occupied by or assigned to white persons. Railroad corporations of Louisiana did not make discrimination among whites in the matter of accommodation for travelers. The thing to accomplish was, under the guise of giving equal accommodation for whites and blacks, to compel the latter to keep to themselves while traveling in railroad passenger coaches. No one would be so wanting in candor as to assert the contrary. The fundamental objection, therefore, to the statute, is that it interferes with the personal freedom of citizens. "Personal liberty," it has been well said, "consists in the power of locomotion, of changing situation, or removing one's person to whatsoever places one's own inclination may direct, without imprisonment or restraint, unless by due course of law." . . . If a white man and a black man choose to occupy the same public conveyance on a public highway, it is their right to do so; and no government, proceeding alone on grounds of race, can prevent it without infringing the personal liberty of each.

It is one thing for railroad carriers to furnish, or to be required by law to furnish, equal accommodations for all whom they are under a legal duty to carry. It is quite another thing for government to forbid citizens of the white and black races from traveling in the same public conveyance, and to punish officers of railroad companies for permitting persons of the two races to occupy the same passenger coach. If a state can prescribe, as a rule of civil conduct, that whites and blacks shall not travel as passengers in the same railroad coach, why may it not so regulate the use of the streets of its cities and towns as to compel white citizens to keep on one side of a street, and black citizens to keep on the other? Why may it not, upon like grounds, punish whites and blacks who ride together in street cars or in open vehicles on a public road or street? Why may it not require sheriffs to assign whites to one side of a court room, and blacks to the other? And why may it not also prohibit the commingling of the two races in the galleries of legislative halls or in public assemblages convened for the consideration of the political questions of the day? Further, if this statute of Louisiana is consistent with the personal liberty of citizens, why may not the state require the separation in railroad coaches of native and naturalized citizens of the United States, or of Protestants and Roman Catholics?

The answer given at the argument to these questions was that regulations of the kind they suggest would be unreasonable, and could not, therefore, stand before the law. Is it meant that the determination of questions of legislative power depends upon the inquiry whether the statute whose validity is questioned is, in the judgment of the courts, a reasonable one, taking all the circumstances into consideration? A statute may be unreasonable merely because a sound public policy forbade its enactment. But I do not understand that the courts have anything to do with the policy or expediency of legislation. A statute may be valid, and yet, upon grounds of public policy, may well be characterized as unreasonable. Mr. Sedgwick correctly states the rule when he says that, the legislative intention being clearly ascertained, "the courts have no other duty to perform than to execute the legislative will, without any regard to their views as to the wisdom or justice of the particular enactment." . . . There is a dangerous tendency in these latter days to enlarge the functions of the courts, by means of judicial interference with the will of the people as expressed by the legislature. Our institutions have the distinguishing characteristic that the three departments of government are co-ordinate and separate. Each must keep within the limits defined by the constitution. And the courts best discharge their duty by executing the will of the law-making power, constitutionally expressed, leaving the results of legislation to be dealt with by the people through their representatives. Statutes must always have a reasonable construction. Sometimes they are to be construed strictly, sometimes literally, in order to carry out the legislative will. But, however construed, the intent of the legislature is to be respected if the particular statute in question is valid, although the courts, looking at the public interests, may conceive the statute to be both unreasonable and impolitic. If the power exists to enact a statute, that ends the matter so far as the courts are concerned. The adjudged cases in which statutes have been held to be void, because unreasonable, are those in which the means employed by the legislature were not at all germane to the end to which the legislature was competent.

The white race deems itself to be the dominant race in this country. And so it is, in prestige, in achievements, in education, in wealth, and in power. So, I doubt not, it will continue to be for all time, if it remains true to its great heritage, and holds fast to the principles of constitutional liberty. But in view of the constitution, in the eye of the law, there is in this country no superior, dominant, ruling class of citizens. There is no caste here. Our constitution is color-blind, and neither knows nor tolerates classes among citizens. In respect of civil rights, all citizens are equal before the law. The humblest is the peer of the most powerful. The law regards man as man, and takes no account of his surroundings or of his color when his civil rights as guaranteed by the supreme law of the land are involved. It is therefore to be regretted that this high tribunal, the final expositor of the fundamental law of the land, has reached the conclusion that it is competent for a state to regulate the enjoyment by citizens of their civil rights solely upon the basis of race.

In my opinion, the judgment this day rendered will, in time, prove to be quite as pernicious as the decision made by this tribunal in the Dred Scott Case.

It was adjudged in that case that the descendants of Africans who were imported into this country, and sold as slaves, were not included nor intended to be included under the word "citizens" in the constitution, and could not claim any of the rights and privileges which that instrument provided for and secured to citizens of the United States; that, at time of the adoption of the constitution, they were "considered as a subordinate and inferior class of beings, who had been subjugated by the dominant race, and, whether emancipated or not, yet remained subject to their authority, and had no rights or privileges but such as those who held the power and the government might choose to grant them." . . . The recent amendments of the constitution, it was supposed, had eradicated these principles from our institutions. But it seems that we have yet, in some of the states, a dominant race, a superior class of citizens, which assumes to regulate the enjoyment of civil rights, common to all citizens, upon the basis of race. The present decision, it may well be apprehended, will not only stimulate aggressions, more or less brutal and irritating, upon the admitted rights of colored citizens, but will encourage the belief that it is possible, by means of state enactments, to defeat the beneficent purposes which the people of the United States had in view when they adopted the recent amendments of the constitution, by one of which the blacks of this country were made citizens of the United States and of the states in which they respectively reside, and whose privileges and immunities, as citizens, the states are forbidden to abridge. Sixty millions of whites are in no danger from the presence here of eight millions of blacks. The destinies of the two races, in this country, are indissolubly linked together, and the interests of both require that the common government of all shall not permit the seeds of race hate to be planted under the sanction of law. What can more certainly arouse race hate, what more certainly create and perpetuate a feeling of distrust between these races, than state enactments which, in fact, proceed on the ground that colored citizens are so inferior and degraded that they cannot be allowed to sit in public coaches occupied by white citizens? That, as all will admit, is the real meaning of such legislation as was enacted in Louisiana.

The sure guaranty of the peace and security of each race is the clear, distinct, unconditional recognition by our governments, national and state, of every right that inheres in civil freedom, and of the equality before the law of all citizens of the United States, without regard to race. State enactments regulating the enjoyment of civil rights upon the basis of race, and cunningly devised to defeat legitimate results of the war, under the pretense of recognizing equality of rights, can have no other result than to render permanent peace impossible, and to keep alive a conflict of races, the continuance of which must do harm to all concerned. This question is not met by the suggestion that social equality cannot exist between the white and black races in this country. That argument, if it can be properly regarded as one, is scarcely worthy of consideration; for social equality no more exists between two races when traveling in a passenger coach or a public highway than when members of the same races sit by each other in a street car or in the jury box, or stand or sit with each other in a political assembly, or when they use in common the streets of a city or town, or when they are in the same room for the purpose of having their names placed on the registry of voters, or when they approach the ballot box in order to exercise the high privilege of voting.

There is a race so different from our own that we do not permit those belonging to it to become citizens of the United States. Persons belonging to it are, with few exceptions, absolutely excluded from our country. I allude to the Chinese race. But, by the statute in question, a Chinaman can ride in the same passenger coach with white citizens of the United States, while citizens of the black race in Louisiana, many of whom, perhaps, risked their lives for the preservation of the Union, who are entitled, by law, to participate in the political control of the state and nation, who are not excluded, by law or by reason of their race, from public stations of any kind, and who have all the legal rights that belong to white citizens, are yet declared to be criminals, liable to imprisonment, if they ride in a public coach occupied by citizens of the white race. It is scarcely just to say that a colored citizen should not object to occupying a public coach assigned to his own race. He does not object, nor, perhaps, would he object to separate coaches for his race if his rights under the law were recognized. But he does object, and he ought never to cease objecting, that citizens of the white and black races can be adjudged criminals because they sit, or claim the right to sit, in the same public coach on a public highway. The arbitrary separation of citizens, on the basis of race, while they are on a public highway, is a badge of servitude wholly inconsistent with the civil freedom and the equality before the law established by the constitution. It cannot be justified upon any legal grounds.

If evils will result from the commingling of the two races upon public highways established for the benefit of all, they will be infinitely less than those that will surely come from state legislation regulating the enjoyment of civil rights upon the basis of race. We boast of the freedom enjoyed by our people above all other peoples. But it is difficult to reconcile that boast with a state of the law which, practically, puts the brand of servitude and degradation upon a large class of our fellow citizens, our equals before the law. The thin disguise of "equal" accommodations for passengers in railroad coaches will not mislead any one, nor atone for the wrong this day done.

The result of the whole matter is that while this court has frequently adjudged, and at the present term has recognized the doctrine, that a state cannot, consistently with the constitution of the United States, prevent white and black citizens, having the required qualifications for jury service, from sitting in the same jury box, it is now solemnly held that a state may prohibit white and black citizens from sitting in the same passenger coach on a public highway, or may require that they be separated by a "partition" when in the same passenger coach. May it not now be reasonably expected that astute men of the dominant race, who affect to be disturbed at the possibility that the integrity of the white race may be corrupted, or that its supremacy will be imperiled, by contact on public highways with black people, will endeavor to procure statutes requiring white and black jurors to be separated in the jury box by a "partition," and that, upon retiring from the court room to consult as to their verdict, such partition, if it be a movable one, shall be taken to their consultation room, and set up in such way as to prevent black jurors from coming too close to their brother jurors of the white race. If the "partition" used in the court room happens to be stationary, provision could be made for screens with openings through which jurors of the two races could confer as to their verdict without coming into personal contact with each other. I cannot see but that, according to the principles this day announced, such state legislation, although conceived in hostility to, and enacted for the purpose of humiliating, citizens of the United States of a particular race, would be held to be consistent with the constitution.

I do not deem it necessary to review the decisions of state courts to which reference was made in argument. Some, and the most important, of them, are wholly inapplicable, because rendered prior to the adoption of the last amendments of the constitution, when colored people had very few rights which the dominant race felt obliged to respect. Others were made at a time when public opinion, in many localities, was dominated by the institution of slavery; when it would not have been safe to do justice to the black man; and when, so far as the rights of blacks were concerned, race prejudice was, practically, the supreme law of the land. Those decisions cannot be guides in the era introduced by the recent amendments of the supreme law, which established universal civil freedom, gave citizenship to all born or naturalized in the United States, and residing ere, obliterated the race line from our systems of governments, national and state, and placed our free institutions upon the broad and sure foundation of the equality of all men before the law.

I am of opinion that the state of Louisiana is inconsistent with the personal liberty of citizens, white and black, in that state, and hostile to both the spirit and letter of the constitution of the United States. If laws of like character should be enacted in the several states of the Union, the effect would be in the highest degree mischievous. Slavery, as an institution tolerated by law, would, it is true, have disappeared from our country; but there would remain a power in the states, by sinister legislation, to interfere with the full enjoyment of the blessings of freedom, to regulate civil rights, common to all citizens, upon the basis of race, and to place in a condition of legal inferiority a large body of American citizens, now constituting a part of the political community, called the "People of the United States," for whom, and by whom through representatives, our government is administered. Such a system is inconsistent with the guaranty given by the constitution to each state of a republican form of government, and may be stricken down by congressional action, or by the courts in the discharge of their solemn duty to maintain the supreme law of the land, anything in the constitution or laws of any state to the contrary notwithstanding.

For the reason stated, I am constrained to withhold my assent from the opinion and judgment of the majority.

See 163 U.S. 537.

33.

BOOKER T. WASHINGTON'S ADDRESS AT
THE NATIONAL PEACE JUBILEE (1898)

Washington's Atlanta Compromise speech in 1895 set the standard by which all of his later speeches would be judged. This speech, delivered in Chicago three years later—after the U.S. victory in the Spanish-American War—shows that Washington wanted to push further and faster for civil rights for his people than was evident in the Atlanta Compromise. In the following excerpts, he pleads for fairness and recognition for African Americans, who had been just as loyal to their country as white Americans in both war and peace.

When a few months ago, the safety and honor of the Republic were threatened by a foreign foe, when the wail and anguish of the oppressed from a distant isle reached his ears, we find the Negro forgetting his own wrongs, forgetting the laws and customs that discriminate against him in his own country. . . . And if you would know how he deported himself in the field at Santiago. . . the Negro faced death and laid down his life in defense of honor and humanity, and when you have gotten the full story of the heroic conduct of the Negro in the Spanish-American war—heard it from the lips of Northern soldiers and Southern soldiers, from ex-abolitionist and ex-master, then decide within yourselves whether a race that is thus willing to die for its country, should not be given the highest opportunity to live for its country.

In the midst of all the complaints of suffering in the camp and field, suffering from fever and hunger, where is the official or citizen that has heard a word of complaint from the lips of a black soldier? The only request that has come from the Negro soldier has been that he might be permitted to replace the white soldier when heat and malaria began to decimate the ranks of the white regiment, and to occupy at the same time the post of greatest danger. . . .

We can celebrate the era of peace in no more effectual way than by a firm resolve on the part of the Northern men and Southern men, black men and white men, that the trench which we together dug around Santiago, shall be the eternal burial place of all that which separates us in our business and civil relations. Let us be as generous in peace as we have been brave in battle. Until we thus conquer ourselves, I make no empty statement when I say that we shall have, especially in the Southern part of the country, a cancer gnawing at the heart of the Republic, that shall one day prove as dangerous as an attack from an army without or within. . . .

You know us; you are not afraid of us. When the crucial test comes, you are not ashamed of us. We have never betrayed or deceived you. You know that as it has been, so it will be. Whether in war or in peace, whether in slavery or in freedom, we have always been loyal to the Stars and Stripes.

See Louis R. Harlan, ed., *The Booker T. Washington Papers, 1895–98* (Urbana: University of Illinois Press, 1975), 4: 491–92.

34.

IDA B. WELLS BARNETT INVESTIGATES AND CONDEMNS THE SAM HOSE LYNCHING (1899)

Wells Barnett was the foremost champion of the cause of antilynching laws. She spent her career documenting cases such as this one, informing the public about the atrocities of lynching, and lobbying for reform. The Sam Hose lynching was perhaps the most notable and notorious single episode of its kind in American history. Wells Barnett hoped that by keeping such atrocities constantly before the public eye, she could bring about the same revulsion against this injustice as fellow Progressives were beginning to cause toward various other types of corruption in America.

CONSIDER THE FACTS

During six weeks of the months of March and April just past, twelve colored men were lynched in Georgia, the reign of outlawry culminating in the torture and hanging of the colored preacher, Elijah Strickland, and the burning alive of Samuel Wilkes, alias Hose, Sunday, April 23, 1899.

The real purpose of these savage demonstrations is to teach the Negro that in the South he has no rights that the law will enforce. Samuel Hose was burned to teach the Negroes that no matter what a white man does to them, they must not resist. Hose, a servant, had killed Cranford, his employer. An example must be made. Ordinary punishment was deemed inadequate. This Negro must be burned alive. To make the burning a certainty the charge of outrage was invented, and added to the charge of murder. The daily press offered reward for the capture of Hose and then openly incited the people to burn him as soon as caught. The mob carried out the plan in every savage detail. . . .

The burning of Samuel Hose, or, to give his right name, Samuel Wilkes, gave to the United States the distinction of having burned alive seven human beings during the past ten years. The details of this deed of unspeakable barbarism have shocked the civilized world, for it is conceded universally that no other nation on earth, civilized or savage, has put to death any human being with such atrocious cruelty as that inflicted upon Samuel Hose by the Christian white people of Georgia.

The charge is generally made that lynch law is condemned by the best white people of the South, and that lynching is the work of the lowest and lawless class. Those who seek the truth know the fact to be, that all classes are equally guilty, for what the one class does the other encourages, excuses and condones.

This was clearly shown in the burning of Hose. This awful deed was suggested, encouraged and made possible by the daily press of Atlanta, Georgia, until the burning actually occurred, and then it immediately condoned the burning by a hysterical plea to "consider the facts."

Samuel Hose killed Alfred Cranford Wednesday afternoon, April 12, 1899, in a dispute over the wages due Hose. The dispatch which announced the killing of Cranford stated that Hose had assaulted Mrs. Cranford and that bloodhounds had been put on his track.

The next day the Atlanta Constitution, in glaring double headlines, predicted a lynching and suggested burning at the stake. This it repeated in the body of the dispatch in the following language: "When Hose is caught he will either be lynched and his body riddled with bullets or he will be burned at the stake." And further in the same issue the Constitution suggests torture in these words: "There have been whisperings of burning at the stake and of torturing the fellow low, and so great is the excitement, and so high the indignation, that this is among the possibilities."

In the issue of the 15th, in another double-column display heading, the Constitution announces: "Negro will probably be burned," and in the body of the dispatch burning and torture is confidently predicted in these words: "Several modes of death have been suggested for him, but it seems to be the universal opinion that he will be burned at the stake and probably tortured before burned."

The next day, April 16th, the double-column head still does its inflammatory work. Never a word for law and order, but daily encouragement for burning. The headlines read: "Excitement still continues intense, and it is openly declared that if Sam Hose is brought in alive he will be burned," and in the dispatch it is said: "The residents have shown no disposition to abandon the search in the immediate neighborhood of Palmetto; their ardor has in no degree cooled, and if Sam Hose is brought here by his captors he will be publicly burned at the stake as an example to members of his race who are said to have been causing the residents of this vicinity trouble for some time."

On the 19th the Constitution assures the public that interest in the pursuit of Hose does not lag, and in proof of the zeal of the pursuers said: "'If Hose is on earth I'll never rest easy until he's caught and burned alive. And that's the way all of us feel,' said one of them last night."

Clark Howell, editor, and W. A. Hemphill, business manager, of the Constitution, had offered through their paper a reward of five hundred dollars for the arrest of the fugitive. This reward, together with the persistent suggestion that the Negro be burned as soon as caught, make it plain as day that the purpose to burn Hose at the stake was formed by the leading citizens of Georgia. The Constitution offered the reward to capture him, and then day after day suggested and predicted that he be burned when caught. . . .

Hose was caught Saturday night, April 23, and let the Constitution tell the story of his torture and death.

From the issue of April 24th the following account is condensed: Newnan, Ga., April 23.—(Special.)—Sam Hose, the Negro murderer of Alfred Cranford and the assailant of Cranford's wife, was burned at the stake one mile and a quarter from this place this afternoon at 2:30 o'clock. Fully 2,000 people surrounded the small sapling to which he was fastened and watched the flames eat away his flesh, saw his body mutilated by knives and witnessed the contortions of his body in his extreme agony.

Such suffering has seldom been witnessed, and through it all the Negro uttered hardly a cry. During the contortions of his body several blood vessels bursted. The spot selected was an ideal one for such an affair, and the stake was in full view of those who stood about and with unfeigned satisfaction saw the Negro meet his death and saw him tortured before the flames killed him.

A few smoldering ashes scattered about the place, a blackened stake, are all that is left to tell the story. Not even the bones of the Negro were left in the place, but were eagerly snatched by a crowd of people drawn here from all directions, who almost fought over the burning body of the man, carving it with knives and seeking souvenirs of the occurrence.

Preparations for the execution were not necessarily elaborate, and it required only a few minutes to arrange to make Sam Hose pay the penalty of his crime. To the sapling Sam Hose was tied, and he watched the cool, determined men who went about arranging to burn him.

First he was made to remove his clothing, and when the flames began to eat into his body it was almost nude. Before the fire was lighted his left ear was severed from his body. Then his right ear was cut away. During this proceeding he uttered not a groan. Other portions of his body were mutilated by the knives of those who gathered about him, but he was not wounded to such an extent that he was not fully conscious and could feel the excruciating pain. Oil was poured over the wood that was placed about him and this was ignited.

The scene that followed is one that never will be forgotten by those who saw it, and while Sam Hose writhed and performed contortions in his agony, many of those present turned away from the sickening sight, and others could hardly look at it. Not a sound but the crackling of the flames broke the stillness of the place, and the situation grew more sickening as it proceeded.

The stake bent under the strains of the Negro in his agony and his sufferings cannot be described, although he uttered not a sound. After his ears had been cut off he was asked about the crime, and then it was he made a full confession. At one juncture, before the flames had begun to get in their work well, the fastenings that held him to the stake broke and he fell forward partially out of the fire.

He writhed in agony and his sufferings can be imagined when it is said that several blood vessels burst during the contortions of his body. When he fell from the stake he was kicked back and the flames renewed. Then it was that the flames consumed his body and in a few minutes only a few bones and a small part of the body was all that was left of Sam Hose.

One of the most sickening sights of the day was the eagerness with which the people grabbed after souvenirs, and they almost fought over the ashes of the dead criminal. Large pieces of his flesh were carried away, and persons were seen walking through the streets carrying bones in their hands.

When all the larger bones, together with the flesh, had been carried away by the early comers, others scraped in the ashes, and for a great length of time a crowd was about the place scraping in the ashes. Not even the stake to which the Negro was tied when burned was left, but it was promptly chopped down and carried away as the largest souvenir of the burning.

. . . .

REPORT OF DETECTIVE LOUIS P. LE VIN

The colored citizens of Chicago sent a detective to Georgia, and his report shows that Samuel Hose, who was brutally tortured at Newnan, Ga., and then burned to death, never assaulted Mrs. Cranford and that he killed Alfred Cranford in self-defense.

The full test of the report is as follows:

About three weeks ago I was asked to make an impartial and thorough investigation of the lynchings which occurred near Atlanta, Ga., not long since. I left Chicago for Atlanta, and spent over a week in the investigation. The facts herein were gathered from interviews with persons I met in Griffin, Newnan, Atlanta and in the vicinity of these places.

I found no difficulty in securing interviews from white people. There was no disposition on their part to conceal any part they took in the lynchings. They discussed the details of the burning of Sam Hose with the freedom which one would talk about an afternoon's advertisement in which he had very pleasantly participated.

Who was Sam Hose? His true name was Samuel Wilkes. He was born in Macon, Ga., where he lived until his father died. The family, then consisting of his mother, brother and sister, moved to Marshall, where all worked and made the reputation of hard-working, honest people. Sam studied and was soon able to read and write, and was considered a bright, capable man. His mother became an invalid, and as his brother was considered almost an imbecile, Sam was the mainstay of the family. He worked on different farms, and among the men he worked for was B. Jones, who afterward captured him and delivered him over to the mob at Newnan.

Sam's mother partly recovered, and as his sister married, Sam left and went to Atlanta to better his condition. He secured work near Palmetto for a man named Alfred Cranford, and worked for him for about two years, up to the time of the tragedy. I will not call it a murder, for Samuel Wilkes killed Alfred Cranford in self-defense. The story you have read about a Negro stealing into the house and murdering the unfortunate man at his supper has no foundation in fact. Equally untrue is the charge that after murdering the husband he assaulted the wife. The reports indicated that the murderer was a stranger, who had to be identified. The fact is he had worked for Cranford for over a year.

Was there a murder? That Wilkes killed Cranford there is no doubt, but under what circumstances can never be proven. I asked many white people of Palmetto what was the motive. They considered it a useless question. A "nigger" had killed a white man, and that was enough. Some said it was because the young "niggers" did not know their places, others that they were getting too much education, while others declared that it was all due to the influence of the Northern "niggers." W. W. Jackson, of Newnan, said: "If I had my way about it I would lynch every Northern "nigger" that comes this way. They are at the bottom of this." John Low of Lincoln, Ala., said: "My negroes would die for me simply because I keep a strict hand on them and allow no Northern negroes to associate with them."

Upon the question of motive there was no answer except that which was made by Wilkes himself. The dispatches said that Wilkes confessed both to the murder and the alleged assault upon Mrs. Cranford. But neither of these reports is true. Wilkes did say that he killed Mr. Cranford, but he did not at any time admit that he assaulted Mrs. Cranford. This he denied as long as he had breath.

After the capture Wilkes told his story. He said that his trouble began with Mr. Cranford a week before. He said that he had word that his mother was much worse at home, and that he wanted to go home to visit his mother. He told Mr. Cranford and asked for some money. Cranford refused to pay Wilkes, and that provoked hard words. Cranford was known to be a man of quick temper, but nothing had occurred that day. The next day Cranford borrowed a revolver and said that if Sam started any more trouble he would kill him.

Sam, continuing his story, said that on the day Cranford was killed he (Sam) was out in the yard cutting up wood; that Cranford came out into the yard, and that he and Cranford began talking about the subject of the former trouble; that Cranford became enraged and drew his gun to shoot, and then Sam threw the ax at Cranford and ran. He knew the ax struck Cranford, but did not know Cranford had been killed by the blow for several days. At the time of the encounter in the yard, Sam said that Mrs. Cranford was in the house, and that after he threw the ax at Cranford he never saw Mrs. Cranford, for he immediately went to the woods and kept in hiding until he reached the vicinity of his mother's home, where he was captured. During all the time Sam was on the train going to the scene of the burning, Sam is said by all I talked with to have been free from excitement or terror. He told his story in a straightforward way, said he was sorry he had killed Cranford and always denied that he had attacked Mrs. Cranford.

I did not see Mrs. Cranford. She was still suffering from the awful shock. As soon as her husband was killed she ran to the home of his father and told him that Sam had killed her husband. She did not then say that Sam had assaulted her. She was completely overcome and was soon unconscious and remained so for most of the next two days. So that at the time when the story was started that Sam had added the crime of outrage to murder, Mrs. Cranford, the only one who could have told about it, was lying either unconscious or delirious at the home of her father-in-law, G. E. Cranford.

The burning of Wilkes was fully premeditated. It was no sudden outburst of a furious, maddened mob. It was known long before Wilkes was caught that he would be burned. The Cranfords are an old, wealthy and aristocratic family, and it was intended to make an example of the Negro who killed him. What exasperation the killing lacked was supplied by the report of the alleged attack on Mrs. Cranford. And it was not the irresponsible rabble that urged the burning, for it was openly advocated by some of the leading men of Palmetto. E. D. Sharkey, Superintendent Atlanta Bagging Mills, was one of the most persistent advocates of the burning. He claimed that he saw Mrs. Cranford the day after the killing and that she told him that she was assaulted. As a matter of fact, Mrs. Cranford was unconscious at that time. He persistently told the story and urged the burning of Sam as soon as caught.

John Haas, President of the Capitol Bank, was particularly prominent in advocating the burning. People doing business at his bank, and coming from Newnan and Griffin, were urged to make an example of Sam by burning him.

W. A. Hemphill, President and business manager, and Clark Howell, editor of the Atlanta Constitution, contributed more to the burning than any other men and all other forces in Georgia. Through the columns of their paper they exaggerated every detail of the killing, invented and published inflammatory descriptions of a crime that was never committed, and by glaring head lines continually suggested the burning of the man when caught. They offered a reward of $500 blood money for the capture of the fugitive, and during all the time of the manhunt they never made one suggestion that the law should have its course.

The Governor of the State acquiesced in the burning by refusing to prevent it. Sam Wilkes was captured at 9 o'clock Saturday night. He was in Griffin by 9 o'clock Sunday morning. It was first proposed to burn him in Griffin, but the program was changed, and it was decided to take him to Newnan to burn him. Governor Candler had ordered that Wilkes should be taken to the Fulton county jail when he was caught. That would have placed him in Atlanta. When Wilkes reached Griffin he was in custody of J. B. Jones, J. L. Jones, R.A. Gordon, William Mattews, P. F. Phelps, Charles Thomas and A. Rogowski. They would not take the prisoner to Atlanta, where the Governor had ordered him to be taken, but arranged to take him to Newnan, where they knew a mob of six thousand were waiting to burn him. It is nearer to Atlanta from Griffin than Newnan. Besides, there was no train going to Newnan that Sunday morning, so the captors of Wilkes were obliged to secure a special train to take the prisoner to the place of burning. This required over two hour's time to arrange so that the special train did not leave Griffin for Newnan until 11:40 am.

Meanwhile the news of the capture of Wilkes was known all over Georgia. It was known in Atlanta in the early morning that the prisoner would not be brought to Atlanta, but that he would be taken to Newnan to be burned. As soon as this was settled, a special train was engaged as an excursion train, to take people to the burning. It was soon filled by the criers, who cried out, "Special train to Newnan! All aboard for the burning!" After this special moved out, another was made up to accommodate the late comers and those who were at church. In this way more than two thousand citizens of Atlanta were taken to the burning, while the Governor, with all the power of the State at his command, allowed all preparations for the burning to be made during ten hours of daylight, and did not turn his hand to prevent it.

I do not need to give the details of the burning. I mention only one fact, and that is the disappointment which the crowd felt when it could not make Wilkes beg for mercy. During all the time of his torture he never uttered one cry. They cut off both ears, skinned his face, cut off his fingers, gashed his legs, cut open his stomach and pulled out his entrails, then when his contortions broke the iron chain, they pushed his burning body back into the fire. But through it all Wilkes never once uttered a cry or beg for mercy. Only once in a particularly fiendish torture did he speak, then he simply groaned, "Oh Lord Jesus."

Among the prominent men at the burning, and whose identity was disclosed to me, ... [were] gentlemen of eminent respectability [who] could give the authorities valuable information about the burning if called upon.

While Wilkes was being burned the colored people fled terror-stricken to the woods, for none knew where the fury would strike. I talked with many colored people, but all will understand why I can give no names. . . .

With these facts I made my way home, thoroughly convinced that a Negro's life is a very cheap thing in Georgia . . .

—Louis P. Le Vin

See Ida B. Wells Barnett, "Lynch Law in Georgia" (Washington, D.C.: Library of Congress, Daniel A. P. Murray Collection).

35.

BOOKER T. WASHINGTON EXPLAINS HIS "ATLANTA COMPROMISE" (1901)

Washington's speech became controversial within the black community soon after he delivered it, and here, in his autobiography *Up from Slavery,* he feels compelled to explain his intentions and clarify his philosophy about African American civil rights. Notice that he emphatically expresses his support for black voting rights.

I now come to that one of the incidents in my life which seems to have excited the greatest amount of interest, and which perhaps went farther than anything else in giving me a reputation that in a sense might be called National. I refer to the address which I delivered at the opening of the Atlanta Cotton states and International Exposition, at Atlanta, Ga., September 18, 1895.

So much has been said and written about this incident, and so many questions have been asked me concerning the address, that perhaps I may be excused for taking up the matter with some detail. . . .

The receiving of this invitation [to speak in Atlanta] brought to me a sense of responsibility that it would be hard for any one not placed in my position to appreciate. What were my feelings when this invitation came to me? I remembered that I had been a slave; that my early years had been spent in the lowest depths of poverty and ignorance, and that I had had little opportunity to prepare me for such a responsibility as this. It was only a few years before that time that any white man in the audience might have claimed me as this slave; and it was easily possible that some of my former owners might be present to hear me speak.

I knew, too, that this was the first time in the entire history of the Negro that a member of my race had been asked to speak from the same platform with white Southern men and women on any important National occasion. I was asked now to speak to an audience composed of the wealth and culture of the white South, the representatives of my former masters. I knew, too, that while the greater part of my audience would be composed of Southern people, yet there would be present a large number of Northern whites, as well as a great many men and women of my own race.

I was determined to say nothing that I did not feel from the bottom of my heart to be true and right. When the invitation came to me, there was not one word of intimation as to what I should say or as to what I should omit. In this I felt that the Board of Directors had paid a tribute to me. They knew that by one sentence I could have blasted, in a large degree, the success of the Exposition. I was also painfully conscious of the fact that, while I must be true to my own race in my utterances, I had it in my power to make such an ill-timed address as would result in preventing any similar invitation being extended to a black man again for years to come. I was equally determined to be true to the North, as well as to the best element of the South, in what I had to say. . . .

The coloured people and the coloured newspapers at first seemed to be greatly pleased with the character of my Atlanta address, as well as with its reception. But after the first burst of enthusiasm began to die away, and the coloured people began reading the speech in cold type, some of them seemed to feel that they had been hypnotized. They seemed to feel that I had been too liberal in my remarks toward the Southern whites, and that I had not spoken out strongly enough for what they termed the "rights" of the race. For a while there was a reaction, so far as a certain element of my own race was concerned, but later these reactionary ones seemed to have been won over to my way of believing and acting. . . .

I believe it is the duty of the Negro—as the greater part of the race is already doing—to deport himself modestly in regard to political claims, depending upon the slow but sure influences that proceed from the possession of property, intelligence, and high character for the full recognition of his political rights. I think that the according of the full exercise of political rights is going to be a matter of natural, slow growth, not an over-night, gourd-vine affair. I do not believe that the Negro should cease voting, for a man cannot learn the exercise of self-government by ceasing to vote any more than a boy can learn to swim by keeping out of the water, but I do believe that in his voting he should more and more be influenced by those of intelligence and character who are his next-door neighbours.

I know coloured men who, through the encouragement, help, and advice of Southern white people, have accumulated thousands of dollars' worth of property, but who, at the same time, would never think of going to those same persons for advice concerning the casting of their ballots. This, it seems to me, is unwise and unreasonable, and should cease. In saying this I do not mean that the Negro should truckle, or not vote from principle, for the instant he ceases to vote from principle he loses the confidence and respect of the Southern white man even.

I do not believe that any state should make a law that permits an ignorant and poverty-stricken white man to vote, and prevents a black man in the same condition from voting. Such a law is not only unjust, but it will react, as all unjust laws do, in time; for the effect of such a law is to encourage the Negro to secure education and property, and at the same time it encourages the white man to remain in ignorance and poverty. I believe that in time, through the operation of intelligence and friendly race relations, all cheating at the ballot box in the South will cease. It will become apparent that the white man who begins by cheating a Negro out of his ballot soon learns to cheat a white man out of his, and that the man who does this ends his career of dishonesty by the theft of property or by some equally serious crime. In my opinion, the time will come when the South will encourage all of its citizens to vote. It will see that it pays better, from every standpoint, to have healthy, vigorous life than to have that political stagnation which always results when one-half of the population has no share and no interest in the Government.

As a rule, I believe in universal, free suffrage, but I believe that in the South we are confronted with peculiar conditions that justify the protection of the ballot in many of the states, for a while at least, either by an educational test, or by both combined; but whatever tests are required, they should be made to apply with equal and exact justice to both races.

See Booker T. Washington, *Up from Slavery* (New York: A. L. Burt Company, 1901), 206–37.

36.

W.E.B. DU BOIS'S "FORETHOUGHT" TO *THE SOULS OF BLACK FOLK* (1903)

Du Bois's genius lay as much in the poetic flair with which he articulated his ideas as in his ideology. Here is an example of his lyrical prose. It shows the humble and happy side of a man who would later become famous for writing bitter attacks on the Jim Crow system that consigned his race to second-class citizenship.

Herein lie buried many things which if read with patience may show the strange meaning of being black here in the dawning of the Twentieth Century. This meaning is not without interest to you, Gentle Reader; for the problem of the Twentieth Century is the problem of the color line.

I pray you, then, receive my little book in all charity, studying my words with me, forgiving mistake and foible for sake of the faith and passion that is in me, and seeking the grain of truth hidden there. . . .

Leaving, then, the world of the white man, I have stepped with the Veil, raising it that you may view faintly its deeper recesses,—the meaning of its religion, the passion of its human sorrow, and the struggle of its greater souls. . . .

And, finally, need I add that I who speak here am bone of the bone and flesh of the flesh of them that live within the Veil?
W. E. B. Du B.
Atlanta, Ga., Feb. 1, 1903.

See W.E.B. Du Bois, *Souls of Black Folk* (1903; reprint, New York: The Modern Library, 1996), xxiii–xxiv.

37.

W.E.B. DU BOIS ON THE "TALENTED TENTH" (1903)

Du Bois was a relatively obscure black leader until he began formulating and articulating his theory of the "talented tenth," which seemed, superficially, to contradict Booker T. Washington's ideology that vocational education carried the best hope for the advancement of the next generation of African Americans. Here are excerpts from an article called "The Talented Tenth," which explains the theory that Du Bois propounded.

The Negro race, like all races, is going to be saved by its exceptional men. The problem of education, then, among Negroes must first of all deal with the Talented Tenth; it is the problem of developing the Best of this race that they may guide the mass away from the contamination and death of the Worst, in their own and other races. Now the training of men is a difficult and intricate task. Its technique is a matter for educational experts, but its object is for the vision of seers. If we make money the object of man-training, we shall develop money-makers but not necessarily men; if we make technical skill the object of education, we may possess artisans but not, in nature, men. Men we shall have only as we make manhood the object of the work of the schools—

intelligence, broad sympathy, knowledge of the world that was and is, and of the relation of men to it—this is the curriculum of that Higher Education which must underlie true life. On this foundation we may build bread winning, skill of hand and quickness of brain, with never a fear lest the child and man mistake the means of living for the object of life. . . .

Too little notice has been taken of the work which the Talented Tenth among Negroes took in the great abolition crusade. From the very day that a Philadelphia colored man became the first subscriber to Garrison's "Liberator," to the day when Negro soldiers made the Emancipation Proclamation possible, black leaders worked shoulder to shoulder with white men in a movement, the success of which would have been impossible without them. There was Purvis and Remond, Pennington and Highland Garnett, Sojourner Truth and Alexander Crummel, and above all, Frederick Douglass—what would the abolition movement have been without them? They stood as living examples of the possibilities of the Negro race, their own hard experiences and well wrought culture said silently more than all the drawn periods of orators—they were the men who made American slavery impossible. . . .

The Talented Tenth rises and pulls all that are worth the saving up to their vantage ground. . . .

Education and work are the levers to uplift a people. Work alone will not do it unless inspired by the right ideals and guided by intelligence. Education must not simply teach work—it must teach Life. The Talented Tenth of the Negro race must be made leaders of thought and missionaries of culture among their people. No others can do this work and Negro colleges must train men for it. The Negro race, like all other races, is going to be saved by its exceptional men.

See Booker T. Washington et al., *The Negro Problem: A Series of Articles by Representative American Negroes of To-Day* (New York: AMS Press, 1903), 33–34, 40–41, 45, 75.

38.

MARY McLEOD BETHUNE'S INSPIRATION FOR BUILDING HER SCHOOL (CIRCA 1904)

Bethune founded her school in 1904 under the name the Daytona Normal and Industrial Institute of Daytona Beach Florida. Her inspiration to launch this experimental school came from Booker T. Washington and Tuskegee Institute, as she explains below. This passage shows that Bethune's unshakable Christian faith undergirded her life and career. She saw her life's work as a high calling and a ministry. When recounting her "dreams," she means prophetic dreams or visions, which she believed were God's way of leading her.

When I got to Daytona I had only one dollar and a half left in cash. I got a little rented house. . . . I couldn't pay the rent. The house belonged to a Negro man named John Williams; he rented the house to me for eleven dollars a month. I told him I had no money but he said he would trust me. I had no furniture. I begged dry good boxes and made benches and stools; begged a basin and other things I needed and in 1904 five little girls there started school.

Before starting school I had three significant dreams. You see, I still believe in dreams. . . .

My third dream: . . . I was . . . praying for help and for the way to build my school. I thought as I looked up that I saw a man galloping down the street on a beautiful horse. He was dressed in a uniform suit, and when he got near me he jumped off his horse and approached me and said, "What are you sitting here for?" I said to him, "I am just trying to see my way clear to build my school." He said "I am Booker T. Washington," and he placed his hand back in his hip pocket and pulled out a parcel in a seemingly soiled handkerchief . . . that had evidently been used for mopping off the perspiration . . . and gave me a large diamond and said "Here, take this and build your school." And again he remounted his horse and galloped away. That was my first contact with Booker T. Washington. But oh, I had been a worshiper at his shrine when I read of what he was doing in the building of Tuskegee. I felt that this diamond represented confidence, will power, stick-to-it-iveness, work, suffering, friends, doubt, wisdom, common sense—everything necessary for the building of a beautiful Bethune-Cookman [school].

See Audrey Thomas McCluskey and Elaine M. Smith, eds., *Mary McLeod Bethune: Building a Better World, Essays and Selected Documents* (Bloomington: Indiana University Press, 1999), 48–49, 55.

39.

W.E.B. DU BOIS: VOCATIONAL EDUCATION v. *THE TALENTED TENTH* (CIRCA 1905)

In this excerpt, Du Bois reflects upon his well-publicized difference of opinion with the "Wizard of Tuskegee" about the best course for the uplift of African Americans in the midst of the Jim Crow era.

Since the controversy between me and Washington has become historic, it deserves more careful statement than it has had hitherto, both as to the matters and the motives involved. . . . I believed in the higher education of a Talented Tenth who through their knowledge of modern culture could guide the American Negro into a higher civilization. I knew that without this the Negro would have to accept white leadership. . . . Mr. Washington, on the other hand, believed that the Negro as an efficient worker could gain wealth and that eventually through his ownership of capital he would be able to achieve a recognized place in American culture and could then educate his children as he might wish and develop their possibilities. For this reason he proposed to put the emphasis at present upon training in the skilled trades and encouragement in industry and common labor.

These two theories of Negro progress were not absolutely contradictory. I recognized the importance of the Negro gaining a foothold in trades and his encouragement in industry and common labor. Mr. Washington was not absolutely opposed to college training and sent his own children to college. But he did minimize its importance, and discouraged the philanthropic support of higher education. He thought employers "gave" laborers work, thus opening the door to acquiring wealth. I openly and repeatedly criticized what seemed to me the poor work and small accomplishment of the Negro industrial school, but did not attack the fundamental wrong of giving the laborer less than he earned. It was characteristic of the Washington statesmanship that whatever he or anybody believed or wanted must be subordinated to dominant public opinion and that opinion deferred to and cajoled until it allowed a deviation toward better ways. It was my theory to guide and force public opinion by leadership.

See *The Autobiography of W. E. B. Du Bois* (International Publishers, 1968), 236–37.

40.

W.E.B. DU BOIS ON THE ORIGINS OF THE NIAGARA MOVEMENT (1905–6)

The Niagara Movement was the precursor of the NAACP. Here Du Bois shows the important first step he took on the road to the eventual multiracial founding of that most influential civil rights organization.

I sent out from Atlanta in June, 1905, a call to a few selected persons "for organized determination and aggressive action on the part of men who believe in Negro freedom and growth." . . .

I went to Buffalo and hired a little hotel on the Canada side of the river at Fort Erie, and waited for the men to attend the meeting. . . . [T]wenty-nine men, representing fourteen states, came. The "Niagara Movement" was organized January 31, 1906, and was incorporated in the District of Columbia.

Its particular business and objects are to advocated and promote the following principles:

1. Freedom of speech and criticism.
2. Unfettered and unsubsidized press.
3. Manhood suffrage.
4. The abolition of all caste distinctions based simply on race and color.
5. The recognition of the principles of human brotherhood as a practical present creed.
6. The recognition of the highest and best human training as the monopoly of no class or race.
7. A belief in the dignity of labor.
8. United effort to realize these ideals under wise and courageous leadership.

The Niagara Movement raised a furor of the most disconcerting criticism. I was accused of acting from motives of envy of a great leader and being ashamed of the fact that I was a member of the Negro race. . . . But the movement went on. The next year, 1906, instead of meeting in secret, we met openly at Harper's Ferry, the scene of John Brown's raid, and had in significance if not numbers one of the greatest meetings that American Negroes have ever held. We made pilgrimage at dawn bare-footed to the scene of Brown's martyrdom and we talked some of the plainest English that has been given voice to by black men in America.

See W.E.B. Du Bois, *Dusk of Dawn*; reprinted in Nathan Huggins, ed., *W. E. B. Du Bois: Writings* (New York: The Library of America), 617–21.

41.

BOOKER T. WASHINGTON AND JAMES WELDON JOHNSON ON THE COMPLEXITY OF SEGREGATING MULATTOES IN THE JIM CROW ERA (1901, 1912)

Light-skinned individuals of mixed racial lineage encountered difficulties with the Jim Crow system that their darker-skinned neighbors did not experience. As the passage that Washington relates shows, in many cases they could have "passed" for white, but because of the nebulous nature of segregation laws, they still may have been required to use the facilities designated for blacks. The *Plessy v. Ferguson* suit was brought by such an individual, Homer Plessy, who was "seven-eights white."

In one part of our country, where the law demands the separation of the races on the railroad trains, I saw at one time a rather amusing instance which showed how difficult it sometimes is to know where the black begins and the white ends.

There was a man who was well known in his community as a Negro, but who was so white that even an expert would have hard work to classify him as a black man. This man was riding in the part of the train set aside for the coloured passengers. When the train conductor reached him, he showed at once that he was perplexed. If the man was a Negro, the conductor did not want to send him into the white people's coach; at the same time, if he was a white man, the conductor did not want to insult him by asking him if he was a Negro. The official looked him over carefully, examining his hair, eyes, nose, and hands, but still seemed puzzled. Finally, to solve the difficulty, he stooped over and peeped at the man's feet. When I saw the conductor examining the feet of the man in question, I said to myself, "That will settle it"; and so it did, for the trainman promptly decided that the passenger was a Negro, and let him remain where he was. I congratulated myself that my race was fortunate in not losing one of its members.

See Booker T. Washington, *Up from Slavery* (New York: Doubleday & Company, 1901; reprinted in John Hope Franklin, ed., *Three Negro Classics*, New York: Avon Books, 1965), p. 82.

Although looking white had advantages in many cases, light-skinned African Americans often lacked a sense of belonging to either race and thus bore a cross of confusion about their identity which was unique to them. The passage from Johnson's fictionalized account shows that such people had to, at some point as a child, first discover that they were different from other children.

One day . . . at school the principal came into our room and . . . for some reason said: "I wish all of the white scholars to stand for a moment." I rose with the others. The teacher looked at me and, calling my name, said: "You sit down for the present, and rise with the others." I did not quite understand her, and questioned: "Ma'am?" She repeated, with a softer tone in her voice: "You sit down now, and rise with the others." I sat down dazed. . . . A few of the white boys jeered me, saying: "Oh, you're a nigger. . . ."

I . . . rushed to where my mother was sitting. . . . I buried my head in her lap and blurted out: "Mother, mother, tell me, am I a nigger?". . . . I looked up into her face and repeated: "Tell me, mother, am I a nigger?" There were tears in her eyes and I could see that she was suffering for me. And then it was that I looked at her critically for the first time. . . . I looked at her searching for defects. I could see that her skin was almost brown, that her hair was not so soft as mine, and that she did differ in some ways from the other ladies who came to the house; . . . She must have felt that I was examining her, for she hid her face in my hair and said with difficulty: "No, my darling, you are not a nigger." She went on: "You are as good as anybody; if anyone calls you a nigger, don't notice them." But the more she talked, the less was I reassured, and I stopped her by asking: "Well, mother am I white? Are you white?" She answered tremblingly: "No, I am not white, but you—

your father is. . . ." This suddenly opened up in my heart a fresh chasm of misgiving and fear. . . .

James Weldon Johnson, *The Autobiography of an Ex-Colored Man* [written 1912] (New York: Alfred A. Knopf, 1927; reprinted in John Hope Franklin, ed., *Three Negro Classics*, New York: Avon Books, 1965), 400–2.

42.

PREAMBLE TO THE CONSTITUTION OF MARCUS GARVEY'S UNIVERSAL NEGRO IMPROVEMENT ASSOCIATION (1914)

Marcus Garvey was an early leader in what later became the Black Is Beautiful movement. Despite the emphasis that he placed upon black nationalism and racial separation throughout his career as leader of the UNIA, in this preamble to the UNIA's constitution, he stressed, ironically, unity among all peoples.

The Universal Negro Improvement Association and African Communities' League is a social, friendly, humanitarian, charitable, educational, institutional, constructive and expansive society, and is founded by persons, desiring to the utmost, to work for the general uplift of the Negro peoples of the world. And the members pledge themselves to do all in their power to conserve the rights of their noble race to respect the rights of all mankind, believing always in the Brotherhood of Man and the Fatherhood of God. The motto of the organization is: "One God! One Aim! One Destiny!" Therefore, let justice be done to all mankind, realizing that if the strong oppresses the weak confusion and discontent will ever mark the path of man, but with love, faith and charity towards all the reign of peace and plenty will be heralded into the world and the generations of men shall be called Blessed.

See Amy Jacques Garvey, ed., *Philosophy and Opinions of Marcus Garvey, vol. 1* (reprint, New York: Arno Press, 1968), 102.

43.

RICHARD WRIGHT ON GROWING UP BLACK, POOR, FATHERLESS, AND HUNGRY IN MISSISSIPPI (CIRCA 1910s)

Wright's *Black Boy*, a quasi autobiography, describes his tortured childhood, confused adolescence, and self-assured adult conversion to communism. This passage reveals the meaning of the book's subtitle, *American Hunger*. In the years before government assistance to needy families, such situations as the one Wright describes were unfortunately all too common.

Hunger stole upon me so slowly that at first I was not aware of what hunger really meant. Hunger had always been more or less at my elbow when I played, but now I began to wake up at night to find hunger standing at my bedside, staring at me gauntly. . . . Whenever I begged for food now my mother would pour me a cup of tea which would still the clamor in my stomach for a moment or two; but a little later I would feel hunger nudging my ribs, twisting my empty guts until they ached. I would grow dizzy and my vision would dim. . . .

My mother finally went to work as a cook and left me and my brother alone in the flat each day with a loaf of bread and a pot of tea. . . .

My mother often took my brother and me with her to her cooking job. . . . I always loved to stand in the white folks' kitchen when my mother cooked, for it meant that I got occasional scraps of bread and meat; but many times I regretted having come, for my nostrils would be assailed with the scent of food that did not belong to me and which I was forbidden to eat. . . . If the white people left anything, my brother and I would eat well; but if they did not, we would have our usual bread and tea.

Watching the white people eat would make my empty stomach churn and I would grow vaguely angry. Why could I not eat when I was hungry? Why did I always have to wait until others were through? I could not understand why some people had enough food and others did not.

See Richard Wright, *Black Boy (American Hunger): A Record of Childhood and Youth* (New York: Harper & Brothers, 1945; reprint, Harper Perennial, 1993), 16, 18, 22, 27.

———————

44.

ROBERT R. MOTON ON THE MISSION OF TUSKEGEE INSTITUTE (CIRCA 1916)

Moton, a former student of Booker T. Washington at Tuskegee, was, upon the death of Washington in 1915, the choice of the college's trustees to become the second principal of the school. Here are excerpts from Moton's inaugural address in 1916, in which he stresses the importance of education for African Americans, and particularly the type of education provided by Tuskegee.

No greater or more serious responsibility was ever placed upon the Negro than is left us here at Tuskegee. The importance of the work and the gravity of the duty that has been assigned the principal, the officers, and the teachers in forwarding this work cannot be overestimated. But along with the respon-

sibility and difficulties we have a rare opportunity, one almost to be envied—
an opportunity to help in the solution of the great problem, the human problem of race, not merely changing the modes of life and the ideals of a race but
of almost equal importance, changing the ideas of other races regarding that
race. Let us keep in mind the fact that while the outlook was never more hope-
ful, the Negro problem is not yet solved. True, there are many people who
thoroughly believe in Negro education, but we must remember that there are
also many honest, sincere white people who are still doubtful as to the wisdom
of educating the coloured man. We can and we must convince that class of
people that Negro education from every point of view is worth while. . . .

See Robert Russa Moton, *Finding a Way Out: An Autobiography* (New York:
Doubleday, Page & Company, 1920; reprint, College Park, Maryland:
McGrath Publishing Company, 1969), 210–17.

45.

MOORFIELD STOREY ON "THE NEGRO PROBLEM" (1918)

Here in the midst of the Jim Crow era just before the terrible Red Summer of
1919, Storey (a white man) explains that the so-called Negro problem was really the
"White man's problem."

This is the situation which confronts this country. We call it "The Negro
problem," but it is not. The Negroes did not come to this country as voluntary emigrants. We white men took them from their homes and brought
them here to be our slaves. We held them in slavery for more than two centuries. We called them "chattels," we refused them all the rights of men and
did our best to make them brutes. We were afraid to let them learn and we
kept them ignorant. Their patience, their kindness, their gentleness made all
this possible. . . .

It is a white man's problem which confronts us. The fault is in us, not in our
colored neighbors. It is our senseless and wicked prejudice against our fellow-
men which is the root of all our troubles. The question is, how can we make
the white people of this country recognize the rights which they themselves
have given to the Negro, how can we induce them to enforce the laws which
they themselves have made for his protection, how persuade them to do him
simple justice, how lead them to allow him equal opportunity, to educate the
men of whose ignorance we complain, to set the Negro up and not to beat him
down. We can blame him for nothing, for we are responsible for him and his
situation. Can we not make the American people feel how cruel, how wicked,
how cowardly is their treatment of men who have never injured them, and

who are in numbers and resources so much weaker? This is the question on the answer to which the future of this country in no small measure depends.

See Moorfield Storey, *The Negro Question: An Address Delivered before the Wisconsin Bar Association* (self-published, 1918), 14, 17.

46.

A. PHILIP RANDOLPH: *THE MESSENGER* AND THE MESSAGE (1919)

Randolph, later famous as the head of the black labor union known as the Brotherhood of Sleeping Car Porters and Maids, and the leader of the March on Washington Movement, was in 1919 the young socialist editor of *The Messenger* magazine. The magazine's message was essentially that African Americans should embrace socialism as the solution to the problems of racism and discrimination that plagued them. Here Randolph urges his people to divorce the Republican party and join the Socialist Party.

The Negro has had a pathetic and unpromising history in American politics. . . .

The old Negro leaders have been factors in producing and perpetuating a patent contradiction in American politics: the alliance of a race of poverty, the Negro, with a party of wealth, the Republican party.

The Republican party has been the instrumentality in American politics of abolishing agricultural feudalism of the South for the establishment of industrial capitalism of the North. Industrial slavery has been substituted for human slavery.

But how is the Negro to know which party to support? . . .

Since the Socialist Party has always . . . opposed all forms of race prejudice . . . the Negro should no longer look upon voting the Republican ticket as the lesser of two evils, but . . . reject both evils, the Republican and Democratic parties and select a positive good—Socialism.

The Negro, like any other class, should support that party which represents his chief interests. Who could imagine a brewer or saloon-keeper supporting the Prohibition party?

It is like an undertaker seeking the adoption of a law, if possible, to abolish death.

Such is not less ludicrous, however, than that of a Negro, living in virtual poverty, children without education, wife driven to the kitchen or wash-tub: continually dispossessed on account of high rents, eating poor food on account of high cost of food, working 10, 12 and 14 hours a day, and sometimes compelled to become sycophant and clownish for a favor, a "tip," supporting the party of Rockefeller, the party of his employer, whose chief interests are to overwork and underpay him. Let us abolish these contradictions and support our logical party—the Socialist Party.

See Sondra Kathryn Wilson, ed., *The Messenger Reader: Stories, Poetry, and Essays from* The Messenger *Magazine* (New York: The Modern Library, 2000), 338, 346–47.

47.

CLAUDE McKAY'S "IF WE MUST DIE" (1919)

Writing this poem in the midst of the Red Summer of 1919, McKay, who soon became one of the foremost writers of the Harlem Renaissance, protested the lynching and persecution of African Americans stemming from the many race riots that rocked the nation in the immediate aftermath of World War I.

If we must die, let it not be like hogs
Hunted and penned in an inglorious spot,
While round us bark the mad and hungry dogs,
Making their mock at our accursed lot.
If we must die, Oh let us nobly die,
So that our precious blood may not be shed
In vain; then even the monsters we defy
Shall be constrained to honor us though dead!
Oh, kinsmen! we must meet the common foe!
Though far outnumbered let us show us brave,
And for their thousand blows deal one death-blow!
What though before us lies the open grave?
Like men we'll face the murderous cowardly pack,
Pressed to the wall, dying, but fighting back!

See Jervis Anderson, *A. Philip Randolph: A Biographical Portrait* (New York: Harcourt Brace Jovanovich, Inc., 1972), 113.

48.

MARCUS GARVEY EXPLAINS THE MISSION OF THE UNIA (1920)

Outspoken, controversial, and enigmatic, Marcus Garvey created the largest mass movement of African Americans prior to the civil rights movement. In the wake of World War I, his plan of organizing Africa and the black peoples of the world into a giant, unified nation captured the attention of the U.S. State Department, as well as governments throughout the world. Here, in a speech he made in Washington, D.C., in 1920, he simultaneously explains his vision and vents his frustrations.

Now what is this Universal Negro Improvement Association? It is a worldwide movement of Negroes having as its purpose the drawing together of every colored man, woman, and child into one great huge body in preparation for a day that is sure to come, a day when the various races of black men will be in one common battleground to settle their differences and to maintain their respective rights. That day threatens as sure as the sun shines every day. . . .

We are asking you to lend your sympathy and your moral and financial and physical support to the building of Africa and the making of Africa a great republic. Make it a first-class nation, a first-rate power, and when Africa becomes a first-rate power, if you live in Georgia, if you live in Mississippi, if you live in Texas, as a black man I will dare them to lynch you, because you are an African citizen and you will have a great army and a great navy to protect your rights.

In concluding I want you to realize this: I am not talking for an untried organization. I am here representing an organization that is a power in the world. The Universal Negro Improvement Association is the only movement among Negroes now that is striking fear in the breast of the nations of the world, and it is no secret. Everybody knows it. They know it in Washington. If you doubt it, go up to the State Department and ask, and they tell you that that movement of Garvey's is hell. They have spent thousands, thousands of dollars already, following me all over the country, and who can tell that some stool pigeon is not in here tonight. . . .

See Robert A. Hill, ed., *The Marcus Garvey and Universal Negro Improvement Association Papers, vol. 3: September 1920–August 1921* (Berkeley: University of California Press, 1984), 15–17.

49.

WALTER WHITE DESCRIBES THE WRITING AND PUBLICATION OF *THE FIRE IN THE FLINT* (1922)

White, who was renowned as the president of the NAACP and of Atlanta University, here describes the beginnings of his long, distinguished career as a writer, as he sought to have his first novel published.

I wrote feverishly and incessantly for twelve days and parts of twelve nights, stopping only when complete fatigue made it physically and mentally impossible to write another word. On the twelfth day the novel was finished . . .

I sent the novel to John's Office [John Farrar, an editor at George H. Doran and Company] the next morning.

Not long afterward I received from Mr. Doran the most exciting—the most deliriously exciting—letter I had ever received in my life. We like your novel, he wrote, and will publish it after a few changes have been made which we wish to discuss with you.

To say that I walked on air between the receipt of the letter and the day of my appointment with Mr. Doran is a gross understatement. . . .

"Your novel has great drama and power," Mr. Doran told me. "But there are some changes we want you to make. Your Negro characters—uh, uh—are not what readers expect. I'm sure you will be willing to make the necessary changes," he added somewhat lamely, as he noticed my expression.

Disheartened and disillusioned, I sent the manuscript to Mencken [H. L. Mencken, the foremost literary critic and social commentator of the 1920s], who replied almost by return mail, "I have read *The Fire in the Flint*. There is not one episode in it which has not been duplicated in real life over and over again. I suggest that you send it to Alfred Knopf."

Knopf published the novel in 1924, and reaction to it was gratifyingly prompt and vigorous. . . .

The novel was catapulted into . . . a modest best seller. . . . It received the honor of being one of the books burned in Germany after Hitler came into power.

See Walter White, *A Man Called White: The Autobiography of Walter White* (New York: The Viking Press, 1948), 66–67.

50.

CARTER G. WOODSON ON THE NEED FOR NEGRO HISTORY (1922)

Woodson, the founder of the *Journal of Negro History*—the first scholarly history journal devoted to African Americans and racial issues—here explains why there was need for a vigorous pursuit of "Negro history." In taking up this cause, Woodson became heir to George Washington Williams as the most prominent black historian of his generation.

You have a history, a record, behind you. If you are unable to demonstrate to the world that you have this record, the world will say to you, "You are not worthy to enjoy the blessings of democracy or anything else." They will say to you, "Who are you, anyway? Your ancestors have never controlled empires or kingdoms and most of your race have contributed little or nothing to science and philosophy and mathematics." So far as you know, they have not; but if you will read the history of Africa, the history of your ancestors—people of whom you should feel proud—you will realize that they have a history that is worth while. They have traditions that have value of which you can boast and upon which you can base a claim for a right to a share in the blessings of democracy.

Let us, then, study this history, and study it with the understanding that we are not, after all, an inferior people, but simply a people who have been set back, a people whose progress has been impeded. We are going back to that beautiful history and it is going to inspire us to greater achievements. It is not going to be long before we can so sing the story to the outside world as to convince it of the value of our history and our traditions, and then we are going to be recognized as men.

See "Some Things Negroes Need to Do," *Southern Workman* 51 (1922), 33–36.

51.

CHARLES S. JOHNSON ON THE DAMAGING
EFFECTS OF RACIAL STEREOTYPING (1923)

In 1921, social scientist Dr. Charles S. Johnson became the National Urban League's director of research and investigation. In 1923, he became editor of the League's *Opportunity* magazine. This selection is taken from Johnson's address to the National Conference of Social Work, held in Washington, D.C., in 1923. His address was published in its entirety in the July 1923 edition of *Opportunity*.

Some of the familiar . . . stereotypes of the Negro will be quickly recognized. For example, that they are boisterous, over-assertive, lacking in civic consciousness, that they usually carry razors, shoot craps habitually, are inordinately fond of red, and of watermelon, are afraid of ghosts and graveyards. . . .

It is this mass of ideas about the Negro, accumulated through experience, passed on through tradition, embedded in the mores and absorbed even without conscious attention . . . [that] determine our attitudes. . . .

False notions, if believed . . . may control conduct as effectively as true ones. . . .

Now, what of the Negro themselves? What are the effects of all these beliefs upon them? They cannot escape being assailed on every hand from early childhood to the end of their lives, with a pervading intimation of their own inferiority. From the beginning they are "saturated in a tradition of their own incompetence." This is a poison. . . . They grow up in the system inferior not only to the other race, but to their potential selves. . . . Opinions and feelings on general questions must always be filtered through this narrow screen that separates them from their neighbors. Their opinions are therefore largely a negative product—either disparagement of difficulties or protest. This enforced self-consciousness has developed strange distortions of conduct, in many, increasing sensitiveness to sights and fabricating compensations for their inferior station. Natural impulses and desires are balked. Their conduct becomes unintelligible. The processes of thought by which opinions are reached and translated into action are as a result of their isolation. . . .

This distortion provokes in turn a sterner application of these beliefs and so on indefinitely, and with each step the isolation increases, each group building up its own myths and stiffening its own group morale. If the myths can be dissolved . . . many of our inhibitions to normal, rational and ethical conduct will be removed.

See Sondra Kathryn Wilson, ed., *The Opportunity Reader: Stories, Poetry, and Essays from the Urban League's Opportunity Magazine* (New York: The Modern Library, 1999), 438.

52.

ALAIN LOCKE AND JAMES WELDON JOHNSON ON THE UNIQUENESS OF HARLEM (1925)

Here two of the foremost writers of the Harlem Renaissance discuss the great black migration to the northern cities during World War I and explain why Harlem in particular was becoming such an attraction for African Americans in the 1920s.

The tide of Negro migration, northward and city-ward . . . is to be explained primarily in terms of a new vision of opportunity, of social and economic freedom, of a spirit to seize . . . a chance for improvement of conditions. . . .

Take Harlem as an instance of this. Here in Manhattan is not merely the largest Negro community in the world, but the first concentration in history of so many diverse elements of Negro life. It has attracted the African, the West Indian, the Negro American; has brought together the Negro of the North and the Negro of the South; the man from the city and the man from the town and village; the peasant, the student, the business man, the professional man, artist, poet, musician, adventurer and worker, preacher and criminal, exploiter and social outcast. Each group has come with its own separate motives and for its own special ends, but their greatest experience has been the finding of one another. Proscription and prejudice have thrown these dissimilar elements into a common area of contact and interaction. Within this area, race sympathy and unity have determined a further fusing of sentiment and experience. So what began in terms of segregation becomes more and more, as its elements mix and react, the laboratory of a great race-welding. . . . In Harlem, Negro life is seizing upon its first chances for group expression and self-determination. It is—or promises at least to be—a race capital.

—Locke

To my mind, Harlem is more than a Negro community; it is a large scale laboratory experiment in the race problem. . . .

I believe that the Negro's advantages and opportunities are greater in Harlem than in any other place in the country, and that Harlem will become the intellectual, the cultural and the financial center for Negroes of the United States, and will exert a vital influence upon all Negro peoples.

—Johnson

See Alain Locke, *The New Negro: An Interpretation* (New York: Albert and Charles Boni, 1925; reprint, New York: Arno Press, 1968) 6–7, 310–11.

53.

JAMES WELDON JOHNSON'S ADDRESS AT THE NAACP'S EIGHTEENTH ANNUAL CONFERENCE (1927)

Johnson, then Executive Secretary of the NAACP, delivered this address at the organization's annual conference in 1927. In it, he encouraged members to take heart, for the growth and prosperity of the NAACP during its first eighteen years testified to the fact that progress was being made in advancing the cause of civil rights for African Americans, despite appearances to the contrary in American society in the 1920s.

This organization began as an organization almost exclusively of agitation. When the National Association for the Advancement of Colored People was founded . . . the fundamental citizenship rights of the Negro and the estimation in which the Negro was held by the general American public had reached the lowest point possible. In fact, America in general was not concerned about the Negro . . . as a man and a citizen. . . . So the first job of this organization was the awakening, a quickening, a pricking, of the American conscience, of public opinion and we began with the only weapon which we had at hand and that weapon was intelligent and persistent agitation about the right and the wrong. . . .

We have got a big job; but we are going at it. When I sat with Miss Ovington and watched this great crowd filing in I wondered what must have been her thoughts when she remembered the two or three people who gathered together in a little room in New York City eighteen years ago and conceived the idea of this organization. At that time we could get only a few people together and here we have these ten thousand people this afternoon. But we have got to go on further. . . . We get discouraged sometimes, but after all it is such a big fight . . . that I could not do anything else but want to be in it. I want to do my part, at least, because I know that what this Association stands for and is working for will some day come to pass. The Negro fighting for his citizenship rights knows . . . that he is right. He has right on his side and he has his enemy at a great disadvantage in that respect. And so we are going to win. We cannot help but win. . . .

See Sondra Kathryn Wilson, ed., *The Crisis Reader: Stories, Poetry, and Essays from the N.A.A.C.P.'s Crisis Magazine* (New York: The Modern Library, 1999), 385, 393.

54.

EXCERPT FROM WALTER WHITE'S *ROPE AND FAGGOT* (1929)

White's book took the work of Ida B. Wells Barnett and the NAACP's 1918 study *Thirty Years of Lynching* a step further, seeking to educate the American public about the crime of vigilantism which had long plagued the South while being largely ignored by national political leaders. In this excerpt, White tries to explain the mentality of mob "justice" by blaming it on the conditioning of southern whites from early childhood.

Pavlov, the Russian psychologist, found that each succeeding generation of the rats he was observing went with fewer lessons at the sound of a bell to a fixed feeding place. Culturally, something of the same reaction to the use of mobbism affects certain Americans as, genetically, affected Pavlov's rats. Approximately similar conditioned responses actuate the human beings and the animals—the bell acted as an excitant for the latter; for the former a crime, real or fancied, by a Negro against a white person served and yet serves as a stimulus to lynching.

Generation after generation of Southern whites have been handicapped and stunted in their mental and moral growth by such a situation. They have had it constantly dinned into their ears from pulpit and press, in the home and school and on the street, that Negroes are given to sex crimes, that only lynching can protect white women, that unmentionably horrible deeds can be prevented only through the use of extreme brutality. Added to this is the belief that any white man, no matter how inept, criminal, or depraved, is infinitely superior to the "best Negro who ever lived." It is a well-known fact that any idea, no matter how unsound, if repeated often enough and in a sufficiently assured manner, is eventually adopted by the mob as its own. One can estimate the long and difficult climb the Southern white child, living in an atmosphere where dissenting opinion is ruthlessly suppressed, must make to attain even a reasonably intelligent attitude towards lynching and the Negro.

See Walter White, *Rope and Faggot: A Biography of Judge Lynch* (New York: Alfred A. Knopf, 1929; reprint, New York: Arno Press, 1969), 5–6.

55.

LANGSTON HUGHES'S *NOT WITHOUT LAUGHTER* (1930)

Hughes's novel follows the daily life of a black family in fictional Stanton, Kansas, during the years of the Great Migration and World War I. Here we see the family having a humorous discussion about "White Folks."

"Now, talking about white folks' religion, said Annjee, emerging from the house with a fresh white dress on, "why, Mis' Rice where I work don't think no more about playing bridge on Sunday than she does about praying—and I ain't never seen her pray yet."

"You're nuts," said Jimboy behind her. "People's due to have a little fun on Sundays. That's what's the matter with colored folks now—work all week and then set up in church all day Sunday, and don't even know what's goin' on in the rest of the world."

. . . .

"Jimboy's right," said Harriet. "Darkies do like the church too much, but white folks don't care nothing about it at all. They're too busy getting theirs out of this world, not from God. And I don't blame 'em, except that they're so mean to niggers. They're right, though, looking out for themselves . . . and yet I hate 'em for it. They don't have to mistreat us besides, do they?"

"Honey, don't talk that way," broke in Hager. "It ain't Christian, chile. If you don't like 'em, pray for 'em, but don't feel evil against 'em. I was in slavery, Harrie, an' I been knowin' white folks all ma life, an' they's good as far as they can see—but when it comes to po' niggers, they just can't see far, that's all."

Harriet opened her mouth to reply, but Jimboy, who left Annjee at the corner and had returned to the porch, beat her to it. "We too dark for 'em, ma," he laughed. "How they gonna see in the dark? You colored folks oughta get lighter, that's what!"

"Shut up yo' mouth, you yaller rooster!" said Sister Johnson. "White folks is white folks, an' dey's mean!". . . .

See Langston Hughes, *Not without Laughter* (New York: Alfred A. Knopf, 1930; 1968 reprint), 75–76.

56.

ANGELO HERNDON DISCOVERS COMMUNISM (1930)

Herndon was 17 years old when he attended his first communist meeting, which he describes below. The Unemployment Council he describes was a New York–based communist organization that had set up an office in his hometown of Birmingham, Alabama, to organize both black and white workers for their own economic betterment in the midst of the Great Depression. Note what a racially unifying force communism was to Herndon and, no doubt, many others in that era, even to the extent that it obliterated the most sacred of all white supremacy doctrines—opposition to miscegenation.

Wherever I went I bubbled over with my enthusiasm and discovery of the Unemployment Council. I talked to my relatives about the meeting and told them what the speakers said about Negroes and whites fighting together against their bosses so that they might live like human beings. They looked aghast and warned me very solemnly that I had better stay away from those Reds who were wicked people blaspheming against God.

I began to attend all of the meetings of the Unemployment Council regularly. Never was my mind stimulated to such an extent before! I eagerly listened to the ideas on social, economic, and political problems that the various speakers talked to us about. I felt like a man from Mars entering into a new world, a little bit puzzled, a whole lot confused, but tremendously thrilled with the sheer adventure of it. I felt like a Columbus sailing an uncharted sea of ideas, each day lured on by some new and exciting discovery. I heard Earl Browder, William Z. Foster and Bill Dunne speak about Communism as the only emancipating force for the workers. I was very anxious to understand all the fine things they were saying, so I began reading every piece of literature they wrote. . . .

I remember reading about a meeting in Southern Illinois at which Bill Dunne spoke. He had been asked by a white heckler the following question, designed to embarrass and floor him:

"Would you want a nigger to marry your daughter?"

Bill Dunne replied, "Listen, mister, my daughter will marry any man she likes whether white, Negro or Chinese. That will be her affair, not mine. But one thing you can rest assured of: I would rather that she jump into a lake than to marry such a yellow-bellied Negro-hater like you."

See Angelo Herndon, *Let Me Live* (New York: Random House, 1937; reprint, New York: Arno Press, 1969), 80–81.

57.

THEY SHALL NOT DIE: PARODY ON SCOTTSBORO (1934)

In 1932, during the depth of Great Depression, hoboes hopped freight trains from town to town and state to state looking for work. In Scottsboro, Alabama, that year, nine black male hoboes were arrested and charged with raping two white women. The trial set off a storm of controversy. Playwright John Wexley thereafter wrote a fictional play based loosely on the events in Scottsboro. The play was a powerful and emotionally charged depiction of the injustices to which African Americans were often subjected in the Jim Crow South. Here, in these excerpts from the play, we see two white females (Virginia and Lucy) arrested and brought to the county jail to be questioned by Deputy Sheriff Trent and County Solicitor (Attorney) Luther Mason about their alleged sexual relations with both black and white hoboes.

Trent:	These are the gals they tuk off the train at Rocky Point.
Mason:	That so? . . . Now what were you doin' on that train?
Virginia:	Just ridin'. . . .
Mason:	Well, girls . . . you know that I can arrest you for being travelling prostitutes? . . . what were you doing on that train with those boys and crossin' a state line? . . . I can prosecute you under the law . . . you and your boy friends. Understand?
Virginia:	Yes, suh, but we weren't doin' nothin' at atall. We were jest . . .
Trent:	Shut up. . . . [you] tramp whores have been crossin' the State line and lin' business on that train with these white hoboes.
Mason:	And the niggers . . . ?
Trent:	The niggers?
Mason:	Yes . . . ?
Trent:	. . . them black bastards seen 'em gals and got themselves together, outpopulated an' beat up them [white] hobo kids and threw 'em off the train. Then the niggers jumped the gals an' . . .
Mason:	. . . . These heah girls don't look to me like they've been attacked. . . . If these girls had been assaulted against their will, they wouldn't be acting the way they are. They would be crying all over the place. They would be hysterical and nervous. Their clothes would be torn. . . .
Trent:	You ain't sayin' Luther, that them niggers were left alone with these white gals and didn't try to . . . ?
Mason:	No! They didn't need to try. These whores just took them on for whatever they could get. . . .

Trent: Luther, you ain't goin' to let them black bastards get away with
            somethin' like that?
Mason: No. . . . I'm not letting them get away. . . .
Trent: I don't keer if they are whores . . . they're white women! You think
            I'm gonna let them stinkin' nigger lice get away from me? Like Hell
            I am! They're gonna git whut's comin' to 'em long as I'm the law
            round heah. . . theah's only one charge fo' that . . . Rape!

See John Wexley, *They Shall Not Die* (New York: Alfred A. Knopf, 1934),
17–20.

58.

JESSE OWENS: WHY WORRY ABOUT
HITLER? (1936)

Owens won four Gold Medals at the Berlin Olympics in 1936, despite the fact
that Adolph Hitler, a rabid racist, did not approve of blacks participating in the
games and did not welcome or congratulate him. Here he tells how he managed to
focus on his job rather than getting distracted by political and racial issues.

When I lined up in my lane for the finals of the 100 meters, I was looking
only at the finish line, and realizing that five of the world's fastest humans
wanted to beat me to it.

There were six of us finalists, all with gold medal ambitions. Yet there could
only be one winner. I thought of all the years of practice and competition, of
all who had believed in me, and of my state and university [Ohio, and the
Ohio State University.]

I saw the finish line, and knew that 10 seconds would climax the work of eight
years. One mistake could ruin those eight years. So, why worry about Hitler?

See William J. Baker, *Jesse Owens: An American Life* (New York: The Free
Press, 1986), 93–94.

59.

MARY WHITE OVINGTON AND THE
NAACP'S CRUSADE AGAINST LYNCHING
(CIRCA 1930s)

Ovington here describes the excruciatingly frustrating work of the NAACP, which
she helped found, as it sought incessantly in the late 1930s to get a federal anti-lynching bill passed in Congress. In referring to "the Association," she means the NAACP.

From January 1934, for six years, the Association made the passage of an Anti-Lynching Bill by Congress the first order of business.... Not only had we printed *Thirty Years of Lynching in the United States*, but we had secured a strong statement from ... Franklin D. Roosevelt in 1933.... We had tried for two years to pass the Dyer Anti-Lynching Bill. Now we were to enter upon a second battle ...

It was deemed wise to have the Bill next introduced in the House and by Representative Joseph A. Gavagan of New York....

Congressman Gavagan was not easily discouraged....

Walter White wrote ... "Congressman Gavagan remained on the floor at the head of his supporters and engineered his Bill by brilliant parliamentary strategy. He yielded no points and permitted no amendments."

Victory was made certain when a member arose in the House and read a press dispatch that read, "At Duck Hill, Mississippi, two colored men on sus-picion of having murdered a storekeeper, have been taken out of jail, chained to trees, and tortured with blow-torches. After this they were hanged." This story ... had its effect.... the Bill was carried 277 to 119.

In 1938, the Bill came ... before the Senate.... Again it was filibustered out of existence....

In one year, 1935, our annual report showed nineteen lynchings prevented. One argument used with the mobs was that, if they did not disperse, a federal anti-lynching bill would be passed that would destroy states' rights! ...

[Despite losing the legislative battle] "You have won your case," a friend told me in 1940. He was familiar with the history of lynching, and I had given him the number for 1939—two. Though this is in a large measure true, neverthe-less it rankles when, on the assumption that free speech means unlimited debate, it is possible to defeat a measure that has ... enough potential votes to pass the Senate.

See Mary White Ovington, *The Walls Came Tumbling Down* (New York: Harcourt, Brace and Company, 1947), 257–65.

60.

STATE OF MISSOURI EX REL. GAINES v. CANADA (1938)

The ruling in this case marked the first notable progress made in the desegrega-tion of education in America. It was a vitally important step on the road to *Brown v. Board of Education*.

Mr. Chief Justice [Charles Evans] HUGHES delivered the opinion of the court.

Petitioner Lloyd Gaines, a negro, was refused admission to the School of Law of the State University of Missouri. Asserting that this refusal constituted a denial by the State of the equal protection of the laws in violation of the Fourteenth Amendment of the Federal Constitution, U.S.C.A. Const. Amend. 14, petitioner brought this action for mandamus to compel the curators of the University to admit him. On final hearing, an alternative writ was quashed and a peremptory writ was denied by the Circuit Court. The Supreme Court of the State affirmed the judgment. 113 S. W.2d 783. We granted certiorari. . . .

Petitioner is a citizen of Missouri. In August , 1935, he was graduated with the degree of Bachelor of Arts at the Lincoln University, an institution maintained by the State of Missouri for the higher education of negroes. That University has no law school. Upon the filing of his application for admission to the law school of the University of Missouri, the registrar advised him to communicate with the president of Lincoln University and the latter directed petitioner's attention to Section 9622 of the Revised Statutes of Missouri (1929), . . . providing as follows:

> S. 9622. May arrange for attendance at university of any adjacent state-tuition fees. Pending the full development of the Lincoln university, the board of curators shall have the authority to arrange for the attendance of negro residents of the state of Missouri at the university of any adjacent state to take any course or to study any subjects provided for at the state university of Missouri, and which are not taught at the Lincoln university and to pay the reasonable tuition fees for such attendance; provided that whenever the board of curators deem it advisable they shall have the power to open any necessary school or department. . . .

Petitioner was advised to apply to the State Superintendent of Schools for aid under that statute. It was admitted on the trial that petitioner's "work and credits at the Lincoln University would qualify him for admission to the School of Law of the University of Missouri if he were found otherwise eligible." He was refused admission upon the ground that it was "contrary to the constitution, laws and public policy of the State to admit a negro as a student in the University of Missouri." It appears that there are schools of law in connection with the state universities of four adjacent States, Kansas, Nebraska, Iowa and Illinois, where non-resident negroes are admitted.

The clear and definite conclusions of the state court in construing the pertinent state legislation narrow the issue. The action of the curators, who are representatives of the State in the management of the state university . . . , must be regarded as state action. The state constitution provides that separate free public schools shall be established for the education of children of African descent . . . , and by statute separate high school facilities are supplied for colored students equal to those provided for white students. . . . While there is no express constitutional provision requiring that the white and negro races be separated for the purpose of higher education, the state court on a comprehensive review of the state statutes held that it was intended to separate the white and negro races for that purpose also. Referring in particular to Lincoln University, the court deemed it to be clear "that the Legislature intended to bring the Lincoln University up to the standard of the University of Missouri, and give to the whites and negroes an equal opportunity for higher education-the whites at the University of Missouri, and the negroes at Lincoln University". . . . Further, the court concluded that the provisions of Section 9622 (above quoted) to the effect that negro residents "may attend the university of any adjacent State with their tuition paid, pending the full development of Lincoln University," made it evident "that the Legislature did not intend that negroes and whites should attend the same university in this State." In that view it necessarily followed that the curators of the University of Missouri acted in accordance with the policy of the State in denying petitioner admission to its School of Law upon the sole ground of his race.

In answering petitioner's contention that this discrimination constituted a denial of his constitutional right, the state court has fully recognized the obligation of the State to provide negroes with advantages for higher education substantially equal to the advantages afforded to white students. The State has sought to fulfill that obligation by furnishing equal facilities in separate schools, a method the validity of which has been sustained by our decisions. . . . Respondents' counsel have appropriately emphasized the special solicitude of the State for the higher education of negroes as shown in the establishment of Lincoln University, a state institution well conducted on a plane with the University of Missouri so far as the offered courses are concerned. It is said that Missouri is a pioneer in that field and is the only State in the Union which has established a separate university for negroes on the same basis as the state university for white students. But, commendable as is that action, the fact remains that instruction in law for negroes is not now afforded by the State, either at Lincoln University or elsewhere within the State, and that the State excludes negroes from the advantages of the law school it has established at the University of Missouri.

It is manifest that this discrimination, if not relieved by the provisions we shall presently discuss, would constitute a denial of equal protection. That was the conclusion of the Court of Appeals of Maryland in circumstances substantially similar in that aspect. . . . It there appeared that the State of Maryland had "undertaken the function of education in the law" but had "omitted students of one race from the only adequate provision made for it, and omitted them solely because of their color"; that if those students were to be offered "equal treatment in the performance of the function, they must, at present, be admitted to the one school provided". . . . A provision for scholarships to enable negroes to attend colleges outside the State, mainly for the purpose of professional studies, was found to be inadequate . . . and the question, "whether with aid in any amount it is sufficient to send the negroes outside the

State for legal education," the Court of Appeals found it unnecessary to discuss. Accordingly, a writ of mandamus to admit the applicant was issued to the officers and regents of the University of Maryland as the agents of the State entrusted with the conduct of that institution.

The Supreme Court of Missouri in the instant case has distinguished the decision in Maryland upon the grounds (1) that in Missouri, but not in Maryland, there is "a legislative declaration of a purpose to establish a law school for negroes at Lincoln University whenever necessary or practical"; and (2) that, "pending the establishment of such a school, adequate provision has been made for the legal education of negro students in recognized schools outside of this State". . . .

As to the first ground, it appears that the policy of establishing a law school at Lincoln University has not yet ripened into an actual establishment, and it cannot be said that a mere declaration of purpose, still unfulfilled, is enough. The provision for legal education at Lincoln is at present entirely lacking. Respondents' counsel urge that if, on the date when petitioner applied for admission to the University of Missouri, he had instead applied to the curators of Lincoln University it would have been their duty to establish a law school; that this "agency of the State," to which he should have applied, was "specifically charged with the mandatory duty to furnish him what he seeks." We do not read the opinion of the Supreme Court as construing the state statute to impose such a "mandatory duty" as the argument seems to assert. The state court quoted the . . . mandatory duty of the board of curators to establish a law school in Lincoln University "whenever necessary and practicable in their opinion." This qualification of their duty, explicitly stated in the statute, manifestly leaves it to the judgment of the curators to decide when it will be necessary and practicable to establish a law school, and the state court so construed the statute. Emphasizing the discretion of the curators, the court said:

> The statute was enacted in 1921. Since its enactment no negro, not even appellant, has applied to Lincoln University for a law education. This fact demonstrates the wisdom of the Legislature in leaving it to the judgment of the board of curators to determine when it would be necessary or practicable to establish a law school for negroes at Lincoln University. Pending that time, adequate provision is made for the legal education of negroes in the university of some adjacent State, as heretofore pointed out. . . .

The state court has not held that it would have been the duty of the curators to establish a law school at Lincoln University for the petitioner on his application. Their duty, as the court defined it, would have been either to supply a law school at Lincoln University as provided in Section 9618 or to furnish him the opportunity to obtain his legal training in another State as provided in Section 9622. Thus the law left the curators free to adopt the latter course. The state court has not ruled or intimated that their failure or refusal to establish a law school for a very few students, still less for one student, would have been an abuse of the discretion with which the curators were entrusted. And, apparently, it was because of that discretion, and of the postponement which its exercise in accordance with the terms of the statute would entail until necessity and practicability appeared, that the state court considered and upheld as adequate the provision for the legal education of negroes, who were citizens of Missouri, in the universities of adjacent States. We may put on one side respondents' contention that there were funds available at Lincoln University for the creation of a law department and the suggestions with respect to the number of instructors who would be needed for that purpose and the cost of supplying them. The president of Lincoln University did not advert to the existence or prospective use of funds for that purpose when he advised petitioner to apply to the State Superintendent of Schools for aid under Section 9622. At best, the evidence to which argument as to available funds is addressed admits of conflicting inferences, and the decision of the state court did not hinge on any such matter. In the light of its ruling we must regard the question whether the provision for the legal education in other States of negroes resident in Missouri is sufficient to satisfy the constitutional requirement of equal protection, as the pivot upon which this case turns.

The state court stresses the advantages that are afforded by the law schools of the adjacent States, Kansas, Nebraska, Iowa and Illinois, which admit nonresident negroes. The court considered that these were schools of high standing where one desiring to practice law in Missouri can get "as sound, comprehensive, valuable legal education" as in the University of Missouri; that the system of education in the former is the same as that in the latter and is designed to give the students a basis for the practice of law in any State where the Anglo-American system of law obtains; that the law school of the University of Missouri does not specialize in Missouri law and that the course of study and the case books used in the five schools are substantially identical. Petitioner insists that for one intending to practice in Missouri there are special advantages in attending a law school there, both in relation to the opportunities for the particular study of Missouri law and for the observation of the local courts, and also in view of the prestige of the Missouri law school among the citizens of the State, his prospective clients. Proceeding with its examination of relative advantages, the state court found that the difference in distances to be traveled afforded no substantial ground of complaint and that there was an adequate appropriation to meet the full tuition fees which petitioner would have to pay.

We think that these matters are beside the point. The basic consideration is not as to what sort of opportunities, other States provide, or whether they are as good as those in Missouri, but as to what opportunities Missouri itself furnishes to white students and denies to negroes solely upon the ground of color. The admissibility of laws separating the races in the enjoyment of privileges afforded by the State rests wholly upon the equality of the privileges which the laws give to the separated groups within the State. The question here is not of a duty of the State to supply legal training, or of the quality of the training which it does supply, but of its duty when it provides such training to furnish it to the residents of the State upon the basis of an equality of right. By the operation of the laws of Missouri a privilege has been created for white law students which is denied to negroes by reason of their race. The white resident is afforded legal education within the State; the negro resident having the same qualifications is refused it there and must go outside the State to obtain it. That is a denial of the equality of legal right to the enjoyment of the privilege which the State has set up, and the provision for the payment of tuition fees in another State does not remove the discrimination.

The equal protection of the laws is "a pledge of the protection of equal laws". . . . Manifestly, the obligation of the State to give the protection of equal laws can be performed only where its laws operate, that is, within its own jurisdiction. It is there that the equality of legal right must be maintained. That obligation is imposed by the Constitution upon the States severally as governmental entities, each responsible for its own laws establishing the rights and duties of persons within its borders. It is an obligation the burden of which cannot be cast by one State upon another, and no State can be excused from performance by what another State may do or fail to do. That separate responsibility of each State within its own sphere is of the essence of statehood maintained under our dual system. It seems to be implicit in respondents' argument that if other States did not provide courses for legal education, it would nevertheless be the constitutional duty of Missouri when it supplied such courses for white students to make equivalent provision for negroes. But that plain duty would exist because it rested upon the State independently of the action of other States. We find it impossible to conclude that what otherwise would be an unconstitutional discrimination, with respect to the legal right to the enjoyment of opportunities within the State, can be justified by requiring resort to opportunities elsewhere. That resort may mitigate the inconvenience of the discrimination but cannot serve to validate it.

Nor can we regard the fact that there is but a limited demand in Missouri for the legal education of negroes as excusing the discrimination in favor of whites. We had occasion to consider a cognate question in the case of McCabe v. Atchison, Topeka & Santa Fe Railway Co., supra. There the argument was advanced, in relation to the provision by a carrier of sleeping cars, dining and chair cars, that the limited demand by negroes justified the State in permitting the furnishing of such accommodations exclusively for white persons. We found that argument to be without merit. It made, we said, the constitutional right "depend upon the number of persons who may be discriminated against, whereas the essence of the constitutional right is that it is a personal one. Whether or not particular facilities shall be provided may doubtless be conditioned upon there being a reasonable demand therefor; but, if facilities are provided, substantial equality of treatment of persons traveling under like conditions cannot be refused. It is the individual who is entitled to the equal protection of the laws, and if he is denied by a common carrier, acting in the matter under the authority of a state law, a facility or convenience in the course of his journey which, under substantially the same circumstances, is furnished to another traveler, he may properly complain that his constitutional privilege has been invaded". . . .

Here, petitioner's right was a personal one. It was as an individual that he was entitled to the equal protection of the laws, and the State was bound to furnish him within its borders facilities for legal education substantially equal to those which the State there afforded for persons of the white race, whether or not other negroes sought the same opportunity.

It is urged, however, that the provision for tuition outside the State is a temporary one, that it is intended to operate merely pending the establishment of a law department for negroes at Lincoln University. While in that sense the discrimination may be termed temporary, it may nevertheless continue for an indefinite period by reason of the discretion given to the curators of Lincoln University and the alternative of arranging for tuition in other States, as permitted by the state law as construed by the state court, so long as the curators find it unnecessary and impracticable to provide facilities for the legal instruction of negroes within the State. In that view, we cannot regard the discrimination as excused by what is called its temporary character.

We do not find that the decision of the state court turns on any procedural question. The action was for mandamus But it does not appear that the remedy would have been deemed inappropriate if the asserted federal right had been sustained. In that situation the remedy by mandamus was found to be a proper one in University of Maryland v. Murray, supra. In the instant case, the state court did note that petitioner had not applied to the management of Lincoln University for legal training. But, as we have said, the state court did not rule that it would have been the duty of the curators to grant such an application, but on the contrary took the view, as we understand it, that the curators were entitled under the state law to refuse such an application and in its stead to provide for petitioner's tuition in an adjacent State. That conclusion presented the federal question as to the constitutional adequacy of such a provision while equal opportunity for legal training within the State was not furnished, and this federal question the state court entertained and passed upon. We must conclude that in so doing the court denied the federal right which petitioner set up and the question as to the correctness of that decision is before us. We are of the opinion that the ruling was error, and that petitioner was entitled to be admitted to the law school of the State University in the absence of other and proper provision for his legal training within the State.

The judgment of the Supreme Court of Missouri is reversed and the cause is remanded for further proceedings not inconsistent with this opinion. It is so ordered.

Reversed and remanded.

See 305 U.S. 337.

61.

MARIAN ANDERSON ON THE CONSTITUTION HALL AFFAIR (1939)

Anderson was a world-renowned black opera singer who performed in the finest auditoriums in Europe and America in the 1930s. Yet she is best remembered for the infamous 1939 incident in which the Daughters of the American Revolution refused her permission to sing in Constitution Hall in Washington, D.C., which in turn prompted First Lady Eleanor Roosevelt to secure her a performance on the steps of the Lincoln Memorial. Here Anderson recalls her reaction to and feelings about the incident.

The excitement over the denial of Constitution Hall to me did not die down. It seemed to increase and to follow me wherever I went. . . . I could not escape it. . . . My friends wanted to discuss it, and even strangers went out of their way to express their strong feelings of sympathy and support.

What were my own feelings? I was saddened and ashamed. I was sorry for the people who had precipitated the affair. I felt that their behavior stemmed from a lack of understanding. They were not persecuting me personally or as a representative of my people so much as they were doing something that was neither sensible nor good. Could I have erased the bitterness, I would have done so gladly. . . . But . . . it would be fooling myself to think that I was meant to be a fearless fighter; I was not. . . .

Wherever we went I was met by reporters and photographers. The inevitable question was, "What about Washington?". . . .

I could see that my significance as an individual was small in this affair. I had become, whether I liked it or not, a symbol, representing my people.

See Marian Anderson, *My Lord, What a Morning* (New York: The Viking Press, 1966), 187–88.

62.

WILLIAM ATTAWAY'S *BLOOD ON THE FORGE* (1941)

Attaway's dark, tragic novel follows the lives of three black brothers from Kentucky who leave the sharecroppers' fields and migrate to the Pittsburgh area in the Great Migration to work in the high-paying but dangerous steel mills. The oldest brother, Big Mat, is a hulk of a man, a gentle giant who harbors pent-up rage against the racial system that has kept him down and disrespected all his life. He gets his big break in life—and his chance to get even—when, as the steel workers' union was organizing a strike, local law enforcement hired him to be a strike-breaking bouncer. Here we take up the story where the local sheriff is congratulating him on his new position.

"So long, pal. Just remember Monday that you're the boss in this here town. Anythin' you do is all right, 'cause you're the law. So don't take no back talk."

The nearer Big Mat got to his house the larger that thought loomed in his mind. The words began to take hold of him like a new green whisky, filling him with quick jubilation. All of his old hatreds came back and added flame to his feeling. He had been called "nigger" since childhood. "Nigger, nigger never die . . . " was the chant. The name that they gave to him had become a badge signifying poverty and filth. He had not been allowed to walk like a man. His food had been like the hog slops, and he had eaten. In the fields he had gone to the branch and gotten down on his belly. He had drunk his water like a dog left too long in the heat. They had taken his money and his women. They had made him run for his life. . . . And he had escaped the South. Now here in the North he was hated by his fellow workers. . . . The women covered their faces at sight of him; the men spat; the children threw rocks. Always within him was that instinctive knowledge that he was being turned to white men's uses. So always with him was a basic distrust of a white. But now he was a boss. He was the law. After all, what did right wrong matter in the case? Those thrilling new words were too much to resist. He was a boss, a boss over whites.

So Big Mat arrived at a kind of understanding. He would not be able to tell in words what it meant to be a deputy. But he could go home and strut before Anna.

See William Attaway, *Blood on the Forge* (New York: Doubleday, Doran & Company, 1941; reprint, Chatham, New Jersey: The Chatham Bookseller, 1969), 231–32.

63.

CALL FOR A MARCH ON WASHINGTON
(1941)

As World War II was well underway in Europe and American intervention was fast approaching, the Roosevelt administration led the way in the largest buildup of United States military equipment in the nation's history. This mass production created millions of jobs for American workers who had suffered from the effects of the Great Depression for more than a decade. A. Philip Randolph, the leader of the Brotherhood of Sleeping Car Porters and Maids, led the March on Washington Movement (MOWM) in 1941 in order to secure jobs for African Americans in the industries contracting with the federal government to build up the national defense. Here is a sample of the saber-rattling protest literature of Randolph, his union, and the MOWM. The threat produced the desired results, as President Roosevelt soon issued Executive Order 8802.

Negroes, by the mobilization and coordination of their mass power, can cause PRESIDENT ROOSEVELT TO ISSUE AN EXECUTIVE ORDER ABOLISHING DISCRIMINATION IN ALL GOVERNMENT DEPARTMENTS, ARMY, NAVY, AIR CORPS AND NATIONAL DEFENSE JOBS. . . .

The Negroes' stake in national defense is big. It consists of jobs, thousands of jobs. It may represent millions, yes, hundreds of millions of dollars in wages. It consists of new industrial opportunities and hope. This is worth fighting for. . . .

To this end, we propose that ten thousand Negroes MARCH ON WASHINGTON FOR JOBS IN NATIONAL DEFENSE AND EQUAL INTEGRATION IN THE FIGHTING FORCES OF THE UNITED STATES.

An "all-out" thundering march on Washington, ending in a monster and huge demonstration at Lincoln's Monument will shake up white America.

It will shake up official Washington.

It will give encouragement to our friends to fight all the harder by our side, with us, for our righteous cause.

It will gain respect for the Negro people.

It will create a new sense of self-respect among Negroes. . . .

To the hard, difficult and trying problem of securing equal participation in national defense, we summon all Negro Americans to march on Washington. We summon Negro Americans to form committees in various cities to recruit and register marchers and raise funds through the sale of buttons and other legitimate means for the expenses of marchers to Washington by buses, train, private automobiles, trucks, and on foot.

We summon Negro Americans to stage marches on their City Halls and Councils in their respective cities and urge them to memorialize the President to issue an executive order to abolish discrimination in the Government and national defense.

See *The Black Worker*, May 1941.

64.

EXECUTIVE ORDER 8802 (1941)

Franklin Roosevelt, under pressure from the MOWM, took a major step on the road to the civil rights movement when he issued this presidential decree. It guaranteed that no racial discrimination would be tolerated in hiring for national defense contract jobs. Roosevelt followed this order by creating the Fair Employment Practices Committee (FEPC) to ensure the enforcement of his executive order.

Reaffirming Policy Of Full Participation In The Defense Program By All Persons, Regardless Of Race, Creed, Color, Or National Origin, And Directing Certain Action In Furtherance Of Said Policy
June 25, 1941

WHEREAS it is the policy of the United States to encourage full participation in the national defense program by all citizens of the United States, regardless of race, creed, color, or national origin, in the firm belief that the democratic way of life within the Nation can be defended successfully only with the help and support of all groups within its borders; and

WHEREAS there is evidence that available and needed workers have been barred from employment in industries engaged in defense production solely because of considerations of race, creed, color, or national origin, to the detriment of workers' morale and of national unity:

NOW, THEREFORE, by virtue of the authority vested in me by the Constitution and the statutes, and as a prerequisite to the successful conduct of our national defense production effort, I do hereby reaffirm the policy of the United States that there shall be no discrimination in the employment of workers in defense industries or government because of race, creed, color, or national origin, and I do hereby declare that it is the duty of employers and of labor organizations, in furtherance of said policy and of this order, to provide for the full and equitable participation of all workers in defense industries, without discrimination because of race, creed, color, or national origin;

And it is hereby ordered as follows:

1. All departments and agencies of the Government of the United States concerned with vocational and training programs for defense production shall take special measures appropriate to assure that such programs are administered without discrimination because of race, creed, color, or national origin;

2. All contracting agencies of the Government of the United States shall include in all defense contracts hereafter negotiated by them a provision obligating the contractor not to discriminate against any worker because of race, creed, color, or national origin;

3. There is established in the Office of Production Management a Committee on Fair Employment Practice, which shall consist of a chairman and four other members to be appointed by the President. The Chairman and members of the Committee shall serve as such without compensation but shall be entitled to actual and necessary transportation, subsistence and other expenses incidental to performance of their duties. The Committee shall receive and investigate complaints of discrimination in violation of the provisions of this order and shall take appropriate steps to redress grievances which it finds to be valid. The Committee shall also recommend to the several departments and agencies of the Government of the United States and to the President all measures which may be deemed by it necessary or proper to effectuate the provisions of this order.

Franklin D. Roosevelt
The White House,
June 25, 1941.

See www.eeoc.gov/35th/theLaw/eo-8802.

65.

MELVILLE J. HERSKOVITS EXPLAINS *THE MYTH OF THE NEGRO PAST* (1941)

Herskovits's pioneering anthropological and historical study sought to refute some of the commonly held misconceptions about Africans and African Americans that undergirded the racial caste system which consigned the black race to the bottom rung of society. Here he lists five popular theses of the Jim Crow generation explaining alleged black inferiority, which he, through this study, proved false. Taken collectively, these false notions comprised the "myth of the Negro past."

The myth of the Negro past is one of the principal supports of race prejudice in this country. . . .

This myth of the Negro past, which validates the concept of Negro inferiority, may be outlined as follows:

1. *Negroes are naturally of a childlike character, and adjust easily to the most unsatisfactory social situations, which they accept readily and even happily, in contrast to the American Indians, who preferred extinction to slavery;*

2. *Only the poorer stock of Africa was enslaved, the more intelligent members of the African communities raided having been clever enough to elude the slavers' nets;*

3. *Since the Negroes were brought from all parts of the African continent, spoke diverse languages, represented greatly differing bodies of custom, and, as a matter of policy, were distributed in the New World so as to lose tribal identity, no least common denominator of understanding or behavior could have possibly been worked out by them;*

4. *Even granting enough Negroes of a given tribe had the opportunity to live together, and that they had the will and ability to continue their customary modes of behavior, the cultures of Africa were so savage and relatively so low in the scale of human civilization that the apparent superiority of European customs as observed in the behavior of their masters, would have caused and actually did cause them to give up such aboriginal traditions as they may otherwise have desired to preserve;*

5. *The Negro is thus a man without a past.*

See Melville J. Herskovits, *The Myth of the Negro Past* (Boston: Beacon Press, 1958), 1–2.

66.

"NO HALF-FREEDOMS" BY LANGSTON HUGHES, COLUMNIST FOR THE *CHICAGO DEFENDER* (1943)

This is an excerpt from one of Hughes's columns written for the *Defender* during World War II. Frustrated by the fact that black American soldiers were fighting for the four freedoms while being denied the same on the home front, Hughes here protests for the fullness of the four freedoms to be applied to his race in the United States. The column appeared on January 16, 1943.

Patrick Henry said: "Give me liberty or give me death." And his words have become one of America's great clarion calls down through the years. Suppose Patrick Henry had said, "Give me half-liberty and let me live half-dead." Nobody would have paid him any mind, nor would we remember his name today.

During the recent Spanish Civil War, Passionaria, the great woman leader and supporter of the Republican government, said: "It is better to die on your feet than to live on your knees." Suppose Passionaria had said, "It is better to exist on your knees than to die for liberty and freedom." Her words would have meant nothing then, nor would they have been a flame to the human spirit.

Christ drove the money changers from the temple. He didn't drive them to the vestibule and say, "You may sit here, half in and half out, and conduct your nefarious business."

The distinguished escaped slave, Frederick Douglass, in his speech at Faneuil Hall in Boston preceding the Civil War, said, "I shall always aim to be courteous and mild in my deportment towards all with whom I come in contact, at the same time firmly and constantly endeavoring to assert my equal rights as a man and a brother." Suppose Frederick Douglass had said instead, "weakly and occasionally endeavoring to half assert my half equal half rights as a half man and a half brother." Would his speech then have been remembered? Would it have acted as a spur to the anti-slavery movement?

Instead of "government of the people, by the people, and for the people," suppose Abraham Lincoln had said, "government of some of the people, by some of the people, for just some of the people." Who would have agreed with him, or paid any mind to his words except the exploiters and oppressors of people?

See Christopher C. De Santis, ed., *Langston Hughes and the Chicago Defender: Essays on Race, Politics, and Culture, 1942–62* (Urbana: University of Illinois Press, 1995), 25.

67.

THE "AMERICAN DILEMMA," ACCORDING
TO GUNNAR MYRDAL (1944)

Myrdal's work as a sociologist proved extremely important in setting the stage for the coming civil rights movement. Myrdal, a Swede, presented his study as that of a disinterested outsider. His international exposé awakened the slumbering United States to the deplorable condition of its race relations. The timing of its publication was crucial to its impact upon the American public and lawmakers. Coming at the same time that American soldiers were engaged in the liberation of Jewish prisoners of Nazi concentration camps, it reinforced the notion that, in its racial ideology, America was not so far removed from Nazism. This excerpt is a synopsis of Myrdal's conclusions about the "American Dilemma."

There is a "Negro problem in the United States and most Americans are aware of it . . . "

The American Negro problem is a problem in the heart of the American. It is there that the interracial tension has its focus. It is there that the decisive struggle goes on. This is the central view point of the treatise. . . . The "American Dilemma," referred to in the title of this book, is the ever-raging conflict between, on the one hand the valuations preserved on the general plane which we shall call the "American Creed," where the American thinks, talks, and acts under the influence of high national and Christian precepts, and, on the other hand, the valuations on specific planes of individual and group living, where personal and local interests; economic, social and sexual jealousies; considerations of community prestige and conformity; group prejudice against particular persons or types of people; and all sorts of miscellaneous wants, impulses, and habits dominate his outlook. . . .

Practically all the economic, social, and political power is held by whites. The Negroes do not by far have anything approaching a tenth of the things worth having in America.

It is thus the white majority group that naturally determines the Negro's "place." All our attempts to reach scientific explanations of why the Negroes are what they are and why they live as they do have regularly led to determinants on the white side of the race line. In the practical and political struggles of effecting changes, the views and attitudes of the white Americans are likewise strategic. The Negro's entire life and consequently, also his opinions on the Negro problem, are, in the main, to be considered as secondary reactions to more primary pressures from the side of the dominant white majority.

See Gunnar Myrdal, *An American Dilemma* (New York: Harper and Row, 1944), lxix–lxxv.

68.

"WHAT THE NEGRO WANTS," ACCORDING TO RAYFORD W. LOGAN (1944)

Penning this collection of essays near the end of World War II when an Allied victory seemed inevitable, African American leaders such as Logan demanded in advance that the same democratic ideals that the United States fought for abroad be instilled at home with regard to their race. Note how his demands, which were later spelled out in greater detail by Roy Wilkins in the same book on pages 116–17 and 126–28, read like a manifesto for the coming civil rights crusade of the 1950s and 1960s.

The Negro problem in the United States is especially acute today. In normal times the great masses of Negroes, North and South, accept more or less silently the not too violent disregard of what they more or less vaguely consider their constitutional and legal rights and the equally nebulous ideals of the Declaration of Independence. But when our nation goes to war to assure the victory of the "democracies" over the "fascist" nations, we naturally become more insistent that democracy, like charity, should begin at home. We want an equal share not only in the performance of responsibilities and obligations but also in the enjoyment of rights and opportunities. We want the same racial equality at the ballot-box that we have at the income-tax window; the same equality before a court of law that we have before an enemy's bullet; the same equality for getting a job, education, decent housing, and social security that American kinsmen of our nation's enemies possess. We want the Four Freedoms to apply to black Americans as well as to brutalized peoples of Europe and to the other underprivileged peoples of the world. We insist that insofar as the equality asserted in the Declaration of Independence is applicable to all men, it should include us. We declare that our presence in this country for more than three hundred years, our toil, our honorable service in all our nation's wars, our demonstrated capacity for progress warrant our aspirations for eventual first-class citizenship and eventual full integration into the public life of the American people.

See Rayford W. Logan, ed., *What the Negro Wants* (Chapel Hill: University of North Carolina Press, 1944), 7–8.

69.

SMITH v. ALLWRIGHT (1944)

This Supreme Court case resulted in the reversal of the *Grovey v. Townsend* decision, which in turn had been a reversal of the 1924 case *Nixon v. Herndon*. The

Grovey decision had previously allowed southern states to maintain separate primaries for white and black voters. In reexamining the issue in a new case, the court found that the so-called white primary used in the State of Texas violated the Fifteenth Amendment to the U.S. Constitution. Below is the case syllabus and decision of the court in this important case which helped set the legal precedent for the *Brown v. Board of Education* decision a decade later.

April 3, 1944
Syllabus

1. The right of a citizen of the United States to vote for the nomination of candidates for the United States Senate and House of Representatives in a primary which is an integral part of the elective process is a right secured by the Federal Constitution, and this right of the citizen may not be abridged by the State on account of his race or color.

2. Whether the exclusion of citizens from voting on account of their race or color has been effected by action of the State—rather than of individuals or of a political party—is a question upon which the decision of the courts of the State is not binding on the federal courts, but which the latter must determine for themselves.

3. Upon examination of the statutes of Texas regulating primaries, held: that the exclusion of Negroes from voting in a Democratic primary to select nominees for a general election—although, by resolution of a state convention of the party, its membership was limited to white citizens—was State action in violation of the Fifteenth Amendment.

   When, as here, primaries become a part of the machinery for choosing officials, state and federal, the same tests to determine the character of discrimination or abridgment should be applied to the primary as are applied to the general election.

4. While not unmindful of the desirability of its adhering to former decisions of constitutional questions, this Court is not constrained to follow a previous decision which, upon reexamination, is believed erroneous, particularly one which involves the application of a constitutional principle, rather than an interpretation of the Constitution to evolve the principle itself.

MR. JUSTICE [Stanley F.] REED delivered the opinion of the Court.

This writ of certiorari brings here for review a claim for damages in the sum of $5,000 on the part of petitioner, a Negro citizen of the 48th precinct of Harris County, Texas, for the refusal of respondents, election and associate election judges, respectively, of that precinct, to give petitioner a ballot or to permit him to cast a ballot in the primary election of July 27, 1940, for the nomination of Democratic candidates for the United States Senate and House of Representatives, and Governor and other state officers. The refusal is alleged to have been solely because of the race and color of the proposed voter. . . .

Texas is free to conduct her elections and limit her electorate as she may deem wise, save only as her action may be affected by the prohibitions of the United States Constitution or in conflict with powers delegated to and exercised by the National Government. The Fourteenth Amendment forbids a state from making or enforcing any law which abridges the privileges or immunities of citizens of the United States and the Fifteenth Amendment specifically interdicts any denial or abridgement by a state of the right of citizens to vote on account of color. Respondents appeared in the District Court and the Circuit Court of Appeals and defended on the ground that the Democratic party of Texas is a voluntary organization, with members banded together for the purpose of selecting individuals of the group representing the common political beliefs as candidates in the general election. As such a voluntary organization, it was claimed, the Democratic party is free to select its own membership and limit to whites participation in the party primary. Such action, the answer asserted, does not violate the Fourteenth, Fifteenth or Seventeenth Amendment, as officers of government cannot be chosen at primaries, and the Amendments are applicable only to general elections, where governmental officers are actually elected. Primaries, it is said, are political party affairs, handled by party, not governmental, officers. No appearance for respondents is made in this Court. Arguments presented here by the Attorney General of Texas and the Chairman of the State Democratic Executive Committee of Texas, as amici curiae, urged substantially the same grounds as those advanced by the respondents.

The right of a Negro to vote in the Texas primary has been considered heretofore by this Court. The first case was Nixon v. Herndon. . . . At that time, 1924, the Texas statute . . . declared "in no event shall a Negro be eligible to participate in a Democratic party primary election . . . in the State of Texas." Nixon was refused the right to vote in a Democratic primary, and brought a suit for damages against the election officers. . . . It was urged to this Court that the denial of the franchise the Nixon violated his Constitutional rights under the Fourteenth and Fifteenth Amendments. Without consideration of the Fifteenth, this Court held that the action of Texas in denying the ballot to Negroes by statute was in violation of the equal protection clause of the Fourteenth Amendment, and reversed the dismissal of the suit.

The legislature of Texas reenacted the article, but gave the State Executive Committee of a party the power to prescribe the qualifications of its members for voting or other participation. This article remains in the statutes. The State Executive Committee of the Democratic party adopted a resolution that white Democrats and none other might participate in the primaries of that party. Nixon was refused again the privilege of voting in a primary, and again brought suit for damages. . . . This Court again reversed the dismissal of the suit for the reason that the Committee action was deemed to be State action, and invalid as discriminatory under the Fourteenth Amendment. The test was said to be whether the Committee operated as representative of the State in the discharge of the State's authority. The question of the inherent power of a political party in Texas "without restraint by any law to determine its own membership" was left open.

In Grovey v. Townsend, . . . this Court had before it another suit for damages for the refusal in a primary of a county clerk, a Texas officer with only public functions to perform, to furnish petitioner, a Negro, an absentee ballot. The refusal was solely on the ground of race. This case differed from Nixon v. Condon, . . . in that a state convention of the Democratic party had passed the resolution of May 24, 1932, hereinbefore quoted. It was decided that the determination by the state convention of the membership of the Democratic party made a significant change from a determination by the Executive Committee. The former was party action, voluntary in character. The latter, as had been held in the Condon case, was action by authority of the State. The managers of the primary election were therefore declared not to be state officials in such sense that their action was state action. A state convention of a party was said not to be an organ of the state. This Court went on to announce that to deny a vote in a primary was a mere refusal of party membership, with which "the state need have no concern," . . . while for a state to deny a vote in a general election on the ground of race or color violated the Constitution. Consequently, there was found no ground for holding that the county clerk's refusal of a ballot because of racial ineligibility for party membership denied the petitioner any right under the Fourteenth or Fifteenth Amendments. . . .

The Nixon cases were decided under the equal protection clause of the Fourteenth Amendment without a determination of the status of the primary as a part of the electoral process. The exclusion of Negroes from the primaries by action of the State was held invalid under that Amendment. The fusing by the Classic case of the primary and general elections into a single instrumentality for choice of officers has a definite bearing on the permissibility under the Constitution of excluding Negroes from primaries. This is not to say that the Classic case cuts directly into the rationale of Grovey v. Townsend. This latter case was not mentioned in the opinion. Classic bears upon Grovey v. Townsend not because exclusion of Negroes from primaries is any more or less state action by reason of the unitary character of the electoral process, but because the recognition of the place of the primary in the electoral scheme makes clear that state delegation to a party of the power to fix the qualifications of primary elections is delegation of a state function that may make the party's action the action of the state. When Grovey v. Townsend was written, the Court looked upon the denial of a vote in a primary as a mere refusal by a party of party membership. As the Louisiana statutes for holding primaries are similar to those of Texas, our ruling in Classic as to the unitary character of the electoral process calls for a reexamination as to whether or not the exclusion of Negroes from a Texas party primary was state action.

The statutes of Texas relating to primaries and the resolution of the Democratic party of Texas extending the privileges of membership to white citizens only are the same in substance and effect today as they were when Grovey v. Townsend was decided by a unanimous Court. The question as to whether the exclusionary action of the party was the action of the State persists as the determinative factor. In again entering upon consideration of the inference to be drawn as to state action from a substantially similar factual situation, it should be noted that Grovey v. Townsend upheld exclusion of Negroes from primaries through the denial of party membership by a party convention. A few years before, this Court refused approval of exclusion by the State Executive Committee of the party. A different result was reached on the theory that the Committee action was state authorized, and the Convention action was unfettered by statutory control. Such a variation in the result from so slight a change in form influences us to consider anew the legal validity of the distinction which has resulted in barring Negroes from participating in the nominations of candidates of the Democratic party in Texas. Other precedents of this Court forbid the abridgement of the right to vote. . . .

It may now be taken as a postulate that the right to vote in such a primary for the nomination of candidates without discrimination by the State, like the right to vote in a general election, is a right secured by the Constitution. . . . By the terms of the Fifteenth Amendment, that right may not be abridged by any state on account of race. Under our Constitution, the great privilege of the ballot may not be denied a man by the State because of his color.

We are thus brought to an examination of the qualifications for Democratic primary electors in Texas, to determine whether state action or private action has excluded Negroes from participation. Despite Texas' decision that the exclusion is produced by private or party action, . . . , Federal courts must for themselves appraise the facts leading to that conclusion. It is only by the performance of this obligation that a final and uniform interpretation can be given to the Constitution, the "supreme Law of the Land." . . . Texas requires electors in a primary to pay a poll tax. Every person who does so pay and who has the qualifications of age and residence is an acceptable voter for the primary. . . . Texas requires by the law the election of the county officers of a party. These compose the county executive committee. The county chairmen so selected are members of the district executive committee and choose the chairman for the district. Precinct primary election officers are named by the county executive committee. Statutes provide for the election by the voters of precinct delegates to the county convention of a party and the selection of delegates to the district and state conventions by the county convention. The state convention selects the state executive committee. No convention may place in platform or resolution any demand for specific legislation without endorsement of such legislation by the voters in a primary. Texas thus directs the selection of all party officers.

Primary elections are conducted by the party under state statutory authority. The county executive committee selects precinct election officials and the county, district or state executive committees, respectively, canvass the returns. These party committees or the state convention certify the party's candidates to the appropriate officers for inclusion on the official ballot for the general election. No name which has not been so certified may appear upon the ballot for the general election as a candidate of a political party. No other name may be printed on the ballot which has not been placed in nomination by qualified voters who must take oath that they did not participate in a primary for the selection of a candidate for the office for which the nomination is made.

The state courts are given exclusive original jurisdiction of contested elections and of mandamus proceedings to compel party officers to perform their statutory duties.

We think that this statutory system for the selection of party nominees for inclusion on the general election ballot makes the party which is required to follow these legislative directions an agency of the state in so far as it determines the participants in a primary election. The party takes its character as a state agency from the duties imposed upon it by state statutes; the duties do not become matters of private law because they are performed by a political party. The plan of the Texas primary follows substantially that of Louisiana, with the exception that, in Louisiana, the state pays the cost of the primary, while Texas assesses the cost against candidates. In numerous instances, the Texas statutes fix or limit the fees to be charged. Whether paid directly by the state or through state requirements, it is state action which compels. When primaries become a part of the machinery for choosing officials, state and national, as they have here, the same tests to determine the character of discrimination or abridgement should be applied to the primary as are applied to the general election. If the state requires a certain electoral procedure, prescribes a general election ballot made up of party nominees so chosen and limits the choice of the electorate in general elections for state offices, practically speaking, to those whose names appear on such a ballot, it endorses, adopts and enforces the discrimination against Negroes, practiced by a party entrusted by Texas law with the determination of the qualifications of participants in the primary. This is state action within the meaning of the Fifteenth Amendment. . . .

The United States is a constitutional democracy. Its organic law grants to all citizens a right to participate in the choice of elected officials without restriction by any state because of race. This grant to the people of the opportunity for choice is not to be nullified by a state through casting its electoral process in a form which permits a private organization to practice racial discrimination in the election. Constitutional rights would be of little value if they could be thus indirectly denied. . . .

The privilege of membership in a party may be, as this Court said in Grovey v. Townsend, . . . no concern of a state. But when, as here, that privilege is also the essential qualification for voting in a primary to select nominees for a general election, the state makes the action of the party the action of the state. In

759

reaching this conclusion, we are not unmindful of the desirability of continuity of decision in constitutional questions. However, when convinced of former error, this Court has never felt constrained to follow precedent. In constitutional questions, where correction depends upon amendment, and not upon legislative action, this Court throughout its history has freely exercised its power to reexamine the basis of its constitutional decisions. This has long been accepted practice, and this practice has continued to this day. This is particularly true when the decision believed erroneous is the application of a constitutional principle, rather than an interpretation of the Constitution to extract the principle itself. Here, we are applying, contrary to the recent decision in Grovey v. Townsend, the well established principle of the Fifteenth Amendment, forbidding the abridgement by a state of a citizen's right to vote. Grovey v. Townsend is overruled.

Judgment reversed.

See 321 U.S. 649.

70.

WILL W. ALEXANDER ON THE EVILS OF SEGREGATION (1946)

In this essay entitled "Our Conflicting Racial Policies," Will W. Alexander, then vice president of the Julius Rosenwald Fund, decries the nationwide scourge of racial segregation and calls for its end.

Segregation is not only Southern, but national—it varies not so much in degree as in method in different sections of the country. In the South segregation . . . is maintained by law and by custom. In the North segregation is maintained by social pressure and by such quasi-legal arrangements as restrictive covenants. In connection with many public services, such as hotels and restaurants, segregation is as rigid in the North as in the South. Thus segregation is accepted in all sections of the country to about the same degree . . .

The fact that segregation exists is bad enough. To make matters worse, the patterns of segregation are so inconsistent as to be completely bewildering to Negroes. Often they cannot tell just what *is* expected of them. For example, in one railroad station in the South, Negro and white passengers have to board the railroad trains through separate gates; but leaving the trains in this station, they use the same gate. . . .

Much more important than these vagaries is the fact that segregation has meant inferior service to Negroes. . . .

In cities North and South, housing is far poorer for Negroes than for whites. Colored people are largely forced to live in slum areas which have been abandoned by other groups. . . .

The segregation of Negroes in jobs, their exclusion from free access to the ways in which other citizens earn their living, has meant permanent poverty, degradation, and defeat—not only for the majority of Negroes, but for other large sections of the American people. . . .

Segregation in the South not only separates the races but symbolizes the idea of the inevitable inferiority of Negroes. It "keeps the Negro in his place," not only on the streetcars and buses, but in the social and economic system. It is more effective as a symbol than as a means of preventing contact between the races. . . .

See Bucklin Moon, ed., *Primer for White Folks* (Garden City, New York: Doubleday & Company, Inc., 1946), 464–65, 470.

71.

JACKIE ROBINSON ON THE BURDEN OF BEING A CIVIL RIGHTS PIONEER AND A SPORTS HERO (1947)

Jackie Robinson's integration of "America's pastime" was both a symbolic and a substantive step on the road to civil rights reform. It opened an important economic and social door to African Americans that would never again be shut. But perhaps more significantly, it generated a sense of racial pride in the black community at a time when that was a rare commodity. Here Robinson reflects upon the enormous pressure he felt as he realized he was making history by tearing down the color bar in professional sports.

I guess if I could choose one of the most important moments in my life, I would go back to 1947, in the Yankee Stadium in New York City. It was the opening day of the world series and I was for the first time playing in the series as a member of the Brooklyn Dodgers team. It was a history-making day. It would be the first time that a black man would be allowed to participate in a world series. I had become the first black player in the major leagues.

I was proud of that and yet I was uneasy. I was proud to be in the hurricane eye of a significant breakthrough and to be used to prove that a sport can't be called national if blacks are barred from it. . . .

It hadn't been easy. Some of my own teammates refused to accept me because I was black. . . . It hadn't been that easy to fight the resentment expressed by players on other teams, by the team owners, or by bigoted fans screaming "nigger." . . .

[But] children from all races came to the stands. The very young seemed to have no hangup at all about my being black. They just wanted me to be good, to deliver, to win. The inspiration of their innocence is amazing. I don't think I'll ever forget the small, shrill voice of a tiny white kid who, in the midst of a racially tense atmosphere during an early game in a Dixie town, cried out, "Attaboy, Jackie." It broke the tension and it made me feel I had to succeed.

. . . .

There I was the black grandson of a slave, the son of a black sharecropper, part of a historic occasion, a symbolic hero to my people.

See Jackie Robinson and Alfred Duckett, *I Never Had It Made* (New York: G. P. Putnam's Sons, 1972), 9.

72.

ANNE MOODY DISCOVERS THE RACIAL DIVIDE (CIRCA 1940s)

Moody's book is considered one of the classics in civil rights literature, mainly because it contains a firsthand account of what it was like to be on the front lines of the 1960s civil rights movement. But Moody's life story begins before there was a civil rights movement. Here Moody tells about the moment in her childhood when she suddenly became aware of racial differences for the first time. It is very reminiscent of Richard Wright's racial awakening in *Black Boy*. Although she does not disclose her age or the year of these incidents, her description is one of southern race relations that was common in the 1940s and 1950s.

Every Saturday evening Mama would take us to the movies [in Centreville, Mississippi]. The Negroes sat upstairs in the balcony and the whites sat downstairs. One Saturday evening we arrived at the movies at the same time as the white children [playmates who lived next door]. When we saw each other, we ran and met. . . . Mama was talking to one of the white women and didn't notice that we had walked into the white lobby. I think she thought we were at the side entrance we had always used which led to the balcony. We were standing in the white lobby with our friends, when Mama came in and saw us. "C'mon! C'mon!" she yelled, . . . dragging me through the door. When we got outside, we stood there crying, and we could hear the white children crying inside the white lobby. After that, Mama didn't even let us stay at the movies. She carried us right home.

All the way back to our house, Mama kept telling us that we couldn't sit downstairs, we couldn't do this or that with white children. Up until that time I had never really thought about it. After all, we were playing together. I knew that we were going to separate schools and all, but I never knew why.

After the movie incident, the white children stopped playing in the front of our house. For about two weeks we didn't see them at all. Then one day they were there again and we started playing. But things were not the same. I had never really thought of them as white before. Now all of a sudden they were white, and their whiteness made them better than me. I now realized that not only were they better than me because they were white, but everything they owned and everything connected with them was better than what was available to me. . . .

See Anne Moody, *Coming of Age in Mississippi* (New York: Dial Press, Inc., 1968), 24–28.

73.

"TO SECURE THESE RIGHTS" (1947)

In 1947, President Truman created a Committee on Civil Rights to study the "American dilemma" of racial discrimination and determine its solutions. The committee emerged within the year with its "Report of the President's Committee on Civil Rights." Its conclusion was that the federal government of the United States should assume the responsibility for rectifying the situation.

GOVERNMENT'S RESPONSIBILITY: SECURING THE RIGHTS

The National Government of the United States must take the lead in safeguarding the civil rights of all Americans. We believe that this is one of the most important observations that can be made about the civil rights problem. . . .

Leadership by the federal government in safeguarding civil rights does not mean exclusive action by that government. There is much that the states and local communities can do in this field, and much that they alone can do. . . . Parallel state and local action supporting the national program is highly desirable. It is obvious that even though the federal government should take steps to stamp out the crime of lynching, the states cannot escape the responsibility to employ all of the powers and resources available to them for the same end. Or again, the enactment of a federal fair employment practice act will not render similar state legislation unnecessary.

In certain areas the states must do far more than parallel federal action. Either for constitutional or administrative reasons, they must remain the primary protectors of civil rights. This is true of governmental efforts to control or outlaw racial or religious discrimination practiced by privately supported public-service institutions such as schools and hospitals, and of places of public accommodation such as hotels, restaurants, theaters, and stores.

Furthermore, government action alone, whether federal, state, local, or all combined, cannot provide complete protection of civil rights. Everything that government does stems from and is conditioned by the state of public opinion. Civil rights in this country will never be adequately protected until the intelligent will of the American people approves and demands that protection. Great responsibility, therefore, will always rest upon private organizations, and private individuals who are in a position to educate and shape public opinion.

See "To Secure These Rights: Report of the President's Committee on Civil Rights" (New York, 1947).

74.

EXECUTIVE ORDER 9981 (1948)

President Harry Truman issued this presidential decree in response to notable contributions that African Americans made to the Allied war effort in World War II. It came just in time for the first integrated troops to serve together in the Cold War conflict in Korea (1950–1953).

ESTABLISHING THE PRESIDENT'S COMMITTEE ON EQUALITY OF TREATMENT AND OPPORTUNITY IN THE ARMED SERVICES

Whereas it is essential that there be maintained in the armed services of the United States the highest standards of democracy, with equality of treatment and opportunity for all those who serve in our country's defense:

Now therefore, by virtue of the authority vested in me as President of the United States, by the Constitution and the statutes of the United States, and as Commander in Chief of the armed services, it is hereby ordered as follows:

1. It is hereby declared to be the policy of the President that there shall be equality of treatment and opportunity for all persons in the armed services without regard to race, color, religion or national origin. This policy shall be put into effect as rapidly as possible, having due regard to the time required to effectuate any necessary changes without impairing efficiency or morale.

2. There shall be created in the National Military Establishment an advisory committee to be known as the President's Committee on Equality of Treatment and Opportunity in the Armed Services, which shall be composed of seven members to be designated by the President.

3. The Committee is authorized on behalf of the President to examine into the rules, procedures and practices of the armed services in order to determine in what respect such rules, procedures and practices may be altered or improved with a view to carrying out the policy of this order. The Committee shall confer and advise with the Secretary of the Air Force, and

shall make such recommendations to the President and to said Secretaries as in the judgement of the Committee will effectuate the policy hereof.

4. All executive departments and agencies of the Federal Government are authorized and directed to cooperate with the Committee in its work, and to furnish the Committee such information or the services of such persons as the Committee may require in the performance of its duties.

5. When requested by the Committee to do so, persons in the armed services or in any of the executive departments and agencies of the Federal Government shall testify before the Committee and shall make available for the use of the Committee such documents and other information as the Committee may require.

6. The Committee shall continue to exist until such time as the President shall terminate its existence by Executive Order.—Harry S. Truman

See www.trumanlibrary.org/998/a

75.

SIPUEL v. BOARD OF REGENTS OF UNIVERSITY OF OKLAHOMA ET AL. (1948)

Thurgood Marshall argued this case for the NAACP's Legal Defense and Educational Fund. In one of the most pithy rulings in the history of the Supreme Court, the state of Oklahoma was ordered to make available to the black plaintiff, Ada Sipuel, equal access to the state's public law school. The ruling affirmed the court's earlier decision in *Missouri ex rel. Gaines v. Canada.*

On January 14, 1946, the petitioner, a Negro, concededly qualified to receive the professional legal education offered by the State, applied for admission to the School of Law of the University of Oklahoma, the only institution for legal education supported and maintained by the taxpayers of the State of Oklahoma. Petitioner's application for admission was denied, solely because of her color.

Petitioner then made application for a writ of mandamus in the District Court of Cleveland County, Oklahoma. The writ of mandamus was refused, and the Supreme Court of the State of Oklahoma affirmed the judgment of the District Court. . . .

The petitioner is entitled to secure legal education afforded by a state institution. To this time, it has been denied her although during the same period many white applicants have been afforded legal education by the State. The State must provide it for her in conformity with the equal protection clause of the Fourteenth Amendment and provide it as soon as it does for applicants of any other group. . . .

The judgment of the Supreme Court of Oklahoma is reversed and the cause is remanded to that court for proceedings not inconsistent with this opinion.

The mandate shall issue forthwith.

Reversed.

See 332 U.S. 631.

76.

SWEATT v. PAINTER (1950)

This Supreme Court case, building upon the earlier similar cases of *Missouri ex rel. Gaines v. Canada, Sipuel v. University of Oklahoma et al.*, and *McLaurin v. Oklahoma State Regents*, among others, was another important step in the process of desegregating America's public education system. It effectively brought about the integration of the nation's public colleges and universities and helped establish legal precedents that would soon provide the rationale for integration of the nation's elementary and high schools as well. Below are the case syllabus and the decision of the court, with deletion of case citations and similar extraneous materials.

June 5, 1950.

Petitioner was denied admission to the state-supported University of Texas Law School, solely because he is a Negro and state law forbids the admission of Negroes to that Law School. He was offered, but he refused, enrollment in a separate law school newly established by the State for Negroes. The University of Texas Law School has 16 full-time and three part-time professors, 850 students, a library of 65,000 volumes, a law review, moot court facilities, scholarship funds, an Order of the Coif affiliation, many distinguished alumni, and much tradition and prestige. The separate law school for Negroes has five full-time professors, 23 students, a library of 16,500 volumes, a practice court, a legal aid association and one alumnus admitted to the Texas Bar; but it excludes from its student body members of racial groups which number 85% of the population of the State and which include most of the lawyers, witnesses, jurors, judges, and other officials with whom petitioner would deal as a member of the Texas Bar. Held: The legal education offered petitioner is not substantially equal to that which he would receive if admitted to the University of Texas Law School; and the Equal Protection Clause of the Fourteenth Amendment requires that he be admitted to the University of Texas Law School.

Reversed.

MR. CHIEF JUSTICE [Fred M.] VINSON delivered the opinion of the Court.

This case and McLaurin v. Oklahoma State Regents, . . . , present different aspects of this general question: To what extent does the Equal Protection Clause of the Fourteenth Amendment limit the power of a state to distinguish between students of different races in professional and graduate education in a state university? Broader issues have been urged for our consideration, but we adhere to the principle of deciding constitutional questions only in the context of the particular case before the Court. We have frequently reiterated that this Court will decide constitutional questions only when necessary to the disposition of the case at hand, and that such decisions will be drawn as narrowly as possible. . . . Because of this traditional reluctance to extend constitutional interpretations to situations or facts which are not before the Court, much of the excellent research and detailed argument presented in these cases is unnecessary to their disposition.

In the instant case, petitioner filed an application for admission to the University of Texas Law School for the February, 1946 term. His application was rejected solely because he is a Negro. Petitioner thereupon brought this suit for mandamus against the appropriate school officials, respondents here, to compel his admission. At that time, there was no law school in Texas which admitted Negroes.

The state trial court recognized that the action of the State in denying petitioner the opportunity to gain a legal education while granting it to others deprived him of the equal protection of the laws guaranteed by the Fourteenth Amendment. The court did not grant the relief requested, however, but continued the case for six months to allow the State to supply substantially equal facilities. At the expiration of the six months, in December, 1946, the court denied the writ on the showing that the authorized university officials had adopted an order calling for the opening of a law school for Negroes the following February. While petitioner's appeal was pending, such a school was made available, but petitioner refused to register therein. The Texas Court of Civil Appeals set aside the trial court's judgment and ordered the cause "remanded generally to the trial court for further proceedings without prejudice to the rights of any party to this suit."

On remand, a hearing was held on the issue of the equality of the educational facilities at the newly established school as compared with the University of Texas Law School. Finding that the new school offered petitioner "privileges, advantages, and opportunities for the study of law substantially equivalent to those offered by the State to white students at the University of Texas," the trial court denied mandamus. . . .

The University of Texas Law School, from which petitioner was excluded, was staffed by a faculty of sixteen full-time and three part-time professors, some of whom are nationally recognized authorities in their field. Its student body numbered 850. The library contained over 65,000 volumes. Among the other facilities available to the students were a law review, moot court facilities, scholarship funds, and Order of the Coif affiliation. The school's alumni occupy the most distinguished positions in the private practice of the law and in the public life of the State. It may properly be considered one of the nation's ranking law schools.

The law school for Negroes which was to have opened in February, 1947, would have had no independent faculty or library. The teaching was to be carried on by four members of the University of Texas Law School faculty, who were to maintain their offices at the University of Texas while teaching at both institutions. Few of the 10,000 volumes ordered for the library had arrived; nor was there any full-time librarian. The school lacked accreditation.

Since the trial of this case, respondents report the opening of a law school at the Texas State University for Negroes. It is apparently on the road to full accreditation. It has a faculty of five full-time professors; a student body of 23; a library of some 16,500 volumes serviced by a full-time staff; a practice court and legal aid association; and one alumnus who has become a member of the Texas Bar.

Whether the University of Texas Law School is compared with the original or the new law school for Negroes, we cannot find substantial equality in the educational opportunities offered white and Negro law students by the State. In terms of number of the faculty, variety of courses and opportunity for specialization, size of the student body, scope of the library, availability of law review and similar activities, the University of Texas Law School is superior. What is more important, the University of Texas Law School possesses to a far greater degree those qualities which are incapable of objective measurement but which make for greatness in a law school. Such qualities, to name but a few, include reputation of the faculty, experience of the administration, position and influence of the alumni, standing in the community, traditions and prestige. It is difficult to believe that one who had a free choice between these law schools would consider the question close.

Moreover, although the law is a highly learned profession, we are well aware that it is an intensely practical one. The law school, the proving ground for legal learning and practice, cannot be effective in isolation from the individuals and institutions with which the law interacts. Few students and no one who has practiced law would choose to study in an academic vacuum, removed from the interplay of ideas and the exchange of views with which the law is concerned. The law school to which Texas is willing to admit petitioner excludes from its student body members of the racial groups which number 85% of the population of the State and include most of the lawyers, witnesses, jurors, judges and other officials with whom petitioner will inevitably be dealing when he becomes a member of the Texas Bar. With such a substantial and significant segment of society excluded, we cannot conclude that the education offered petitioner is substantially equal to that which he would receive if admitted to the University of Texas Law School.

It may be argued that excluding petitioner from that school is no different from excluding white students from the new law school. This contention overlooks realities. It is unlikely that a member of a group so decisively in the majority, attending a school with rich traditions and prestige which only a history of consistently maintained excellence could command, would claim that the opportunities afforded him for legal education were unequal to those held open to petitioner. That such a claim, if made, would be dishonored by the State, is no answer. "Equal protection of the laws is not achieved through indiscriminate imposition of inequalities.". . .

It is fundamental that these cases concern rights which are personal and present. This Court has stated unanimously that "The State must provide [legal education] for [petitioner] in conformity with the equal protection clause of the Fourteenth Amendment and provide it as soon as it does for applicants of any other group.". . . That case "did not present the issue whether a state might not satisfy the equal protection clause of the Fourteenth Amendment by establishing a separate law school for Negroes.". . . In Missouri ex rel. Gaines v. Canada, . . . , the Court, speaking through Chief Justice Hughes, declared that "petitioner's right was a personal one. It was as an individual that he was entitled to the equal protection of the laws, and the State was bound to furnish him within its borders facilities for legal education substantially equal to those which the State there afforded for persons of the white race, whether or not other negroes sought the same opportunity." These are the only cases in this Court which present the issue of the constitutional validity of race distinctions in state-supported graduate and professional education.

In accordance with these cases, petitioner may claim his full constitutional right: legal education equivalent to that offered by the State to students of other races. Such education is not available to him in a separate law school as offered by the State. We cannot, therefore, agree with respondents that the doctrine of Plessy v. Ferguson, . . . , requires affirmance of the judgment below. Nor need we reach petitioner's contention that Plessy v. Ferguson should be reexamined in the light of contemporary knowledge respecting the purposes of the Fourteenth Amendment and the effects of racial segregation. . . .

We hold that the Equal Protection Clause of the Fourteenth Amendment requires that petitioner be admitted to the University of Texas Law School. The judgment is reversed and the cause is remanded for proceedings not inconsistent with this opinion.

Reversed.

See 339 U.S. 629.

77.

BROWN v. BOARD OF EDUCATION (1954)

Considered one of the most important Supreme Court cases in American history, the *Brown* case effectively reversed the course of American legal history on racial issues, and in the process likewise reversed the course of American society and race relations for future generations. It abolished the separate-but-equal doctrine established by *Plessy v. Ferguson* and *Cumming v. Richmond County Board of Education*, and opened all the nation's public schools to integration.

May 17, 1954

APPEAL FROM THE UNITED STATES DISTRICT COURT FOR THE DISTRICT OF KANSAS

Syllabus

Segregation of white and Negro children in the public schools of a State solely on the basis of race, pursuant to state laws permitting or requiring such segregation, denies to Negro children the equal protection of the laws guaranteed by the Fourteenth Amendment—even though the physical facilities and other "tangible" factors of white and Negro schools may be equal.

(a) The history of the Fourteenth Amendment is inconclusive as to its intended effect on public education.

(b) The question presented in these cases must be determined not on the basis of conditions existing when the Fourteenth Amendment was adopted, but in the light of the full development of public education and its present place in American life throughout the Nation.

(c) Where a State has undertaken to provide an opportunity for an education in its public schools, such an opportunity is a right which must be made available to all on equal terms.

(d) Segregation of children in public schools solely on the basis of race deprives children of the minority group of equal educational opportunities, even though the physical facilities and other "tangible" factors may be equal.

(e) The "separate but equal" doctrine adopted in Plessy v. Ferguson, . . . , has no place in the field of public education.

(f) The cases are restored to the docket for further argument on specified questions relating to the forms of the decrees.

MR. CHIEF JUSTICE [Earl] WARREN delivered the opinion of the Court.

These cases come to us from the States of Kansas, South Carolina, Virginia, and Delaware. They are premised on different facts and different local conditions, but a common legal question justifies their consideration together in this consolidated opinion.

In each of the cases, minors of the Negro race, through their legal representatives, seek the aid of the courts in obtaining admission to the public schools of their community on a nonsegregated basis. In each instance, they had been denied admission to schools attended by white children under laws requiring or permitting segregation according to race. This segregation was alleged to deprive the plaintiffs of the equal protection of the laws under the Fourteenth Amendment. In each of the cases other than the Delaware case, a three-judge federal district court denied relief to the plaintiffs on the so-called "separate but equal" doctrine announced by this Court in Plessy v. Ferguson. . . . Under that doctrine, equality of treatment is accorded when the races are provided substantially equal facilities, even though these facilities be separate. In the Delaware case, the Supreme Court of Delaware adhered to that doctrine, but ordered that the plaintiffs be admitted to the white schools because of their superiority to the Negro schools.

The plaintiffs contend that segregated public schools are not "equal" and cannot be made "equal," and that hence they are deprived of the equal protection of the laws. Because of the obvious importance of the question presented, the Court took jurisdiction. Argument was heard in the 1952 Term, and reargument was heard this Term on certain questions propounded by the Court.

Reargument was largely devoted to the circumstances surrounding the adoption of the Fourteenth Amendment in 1868. It covered exhaustively consideration of the Amendment in Congress, ratification by the states, then-existing practices in racial segregation, and the views of proponents and opponents of the Amendment. This discussion and our own investigation convince us that, although these sources cast some light, it is not enough to resolve the problem with which we are faced. At best, they are inconclusive. The most avid proponents of the post-War Amendments undoubtedly intended them to remove all legal distinctions among "all persons born or naturalized in the United States." Their opponents, just as certainly, were antagonistic to both the letter and the spirit of the Amendments and wished them to have the most limited effect. What others in Congress and the state legislatures had in mind cannot be determined with any degree of certainty.

An additional reason for the inconclusive nature of the Amendment's history with respect to segregated schools is the status of public education at that time. In the South, the movement toward free common schools, supported by general taxation, had not yet taken hold. Education of white children was largely in the hands of private groups. Education of Negroes was almost nonexistent, and practically all of the race were illiterate. In fact, any education of Negroes was forbidden by law in some states. Today, in contrast, many Negroes have achieved outstanding success in the arts and sciences, as well as in the business and professional world. It is true that public school education at the time of the Amendment had advanced further in the North, but the effect of the Amendment on Northern States was generally ignored in the congressional debates. Even in the North, the conditions of public education did not approximate those existing today. The curriculum was usually rudimentary; ungraded schools were common in rural areas; the school term was but three months a year in many states, and compulsory school attendance was virtually unknown. As a consequence, it is not surprising that there should be so little in the history of the Fourteenth Amendment relating to its intended effect on public education.

In the first cases in this Court construing the Fourteenth Amendment, decided shortly after its adoption, the Court interpreted it as proscribing all state-imposed discriminations against the Negro race. The doctrine of "separate but equal" did not make its appearance in this Court until 1896 in the case of Plessy v. Ferguson, . . . , involving not education but transportation. American courts have since labored with the doctrine for over half a century. In this Court, there have been six cases involving the "separate but equal" doctrine in the field of public education. In Cumming v. County Board of Education, . . . , and Gong Lum v. Rice, . . . , the validity of the doctrine itself was not challenged. In more recent cases, all on the graduate school level, inequality was found in that specific benefits enjoyed by white students were denied to Negro students of the same educational qualifications. . . . In none of these cases was it necessary to reexamine the doctrine to grant relief to the Negro plaintiff. And in Sweatt v. Painter, . . . , the Court expressly reserved decision on the question whether Plessy v. Ferguson should be held inapplicable to public education.

In the instant cases, that question is directly presented. Here, unlike Sweatt v. Painter, there are findings below that the Negro and white schools involved have been equalized, or are being equalized, with respect to buildings, curricula, qualifications and salaries of teachers, and other "tangible" factors. Our decision, therefore, cannot turn on merely a comparison of these tangible factors in the Negro and white schools involved in each of the cases. We must look instead to the effect of segregation itself on public education.

In approaching this problem, we cannot turn the clock back to 1868, when the Amendment was adopted, or even to 1896, when Plessy v. Ferguson was written. We must consider public education in the light of its full development and its present place in American life throughout the Nation. Only in this way can it be determined if segregation in public schools deprives these plaintiffs of the equal protection of the laws.

Today, education is perhaps the most important function of state and local governments. Compulsory school attendance laws and the great expenditures for education both demonstrate our recognition of the importance of education to our democratic society. It is required in the performance of our most basic public responsibilities, even service in the armed forces. It is the very foundation of good citizenship. Today it is a principal instrument in awakening the child to cultural values, in preparing him for later professional training, and in helping him to adjust normally to his environment. In these days, it is doubtful that any child may reasonably be expected to succeed in life if he is denied the opportunity of an education. Such an opportunity, where the state has undertaken to provide it, is a right which must be made available to all on equal terms.

We come then to the question presented: Does segregation of children in public schools solely on the basis of race, even though the physical facilities and other "tangible" factors may be equal, deprive the children of the minority group of equal educational opportunities? We believe that it does.

In Sweatt v. Painter, . . . , in finding that a segregated law school for Negroes could not provide them equal educational opportunities, this Court relied in large part on "those qualities which are incapable of objective measurement but which make for greatness in a law school." In McLaurin v. Oklahoma State Regents, . . . , the Court, in requiring that a Negro admitted to a white graduate school be treated like all other students, again resorted to intangible considerations: " . . . his ability to study, to engage in discussions and exchange views with other students, and, in general, to learn his profession." Such considerations apply with added force to children in grade and high schools. To separate them from others of similar age and qualifications solely because of their race generates a feeling of inferiority as to their status in the community that may affect their hearts and minds in a way unlikely ever to be undone. The effect of this separation on their educational opportunities was well stated by a finding in the Kansas case by a court which nevertheless felt compelled to rule against the Negro plaintiffs:

Segregation of white and colored children in public schools has a detrimental effect upon the colored children. The impact is greater when it has the sanction of the law, for the policy of separating the races is usually interpreted as denoting the inferiority of the negro group. A sense of inferiority affects the motivation of a child to learn. Segregation with the sanction of law, therefore, has a tendency to [retard] the educational and mental development of negro children and to deprive them of some of the benefits they would receive in a racial[ly] integrated school system.

Whatever may have been the extent of psychological knowledge at the time of Plessy v. Ferguson, this finding is amply supported by modern authority. Any language in Plessy v. Ferguson contrary to this finding is rejected.

We conclude that, in the field of public education, the doctrine of "separate but equal" has no place. Separate educational facilities are inherently unequal. Therefore, we hold that the plaintiffs and others similarly situated for whom the actions have been brought are, by reason of the segregation complained of, deprived of the equal protection of the laws guaranteed by the Fourteenth Amendment. This disposition makes unnecessary any discussion whether such segregation also violates the Due Process Clause of the Fourteenth Amendment.

Because these are class actions, because of the wide applicability of this decision, and because of the great variety of local conditions, the formulation of decrees in these cases presents problems of considerable complexity. On reargument, the consideration of appropriate relief was necessarily subordinated to the primary question—the constitutionality of segregation in public education. We have now announced that such segregation is a denial of the equal protection of the laws. In order that we may have the full assistance of the parties in formulating decrees, the cases will be restored to the docket, and the parties are requested to present further argument on Questions 4 and 5 previously propounded by the Court for the reargument this Term. The Attorney General of the United States is again invited to participate. The Attorneys General of the states requiring or permitting segregation in public education will also be permitted to appear as amici curiae upon request to do so by September 15, 1954, and submission of briefs by October 1, 1954.

It is so ordered.

See 347 U.S. 483.

78.

"WITH ALL DELIBERATE SPEED," ADDENDUM TO BROWN v. BOARD OF EDUCATION (1955)

After the initial *Brown* ruling of 1954, it immediately became apparent that some states would make no good faith effort to implement the decision in a timely manner. Hence, the court ordered that its earlier ruling now be enforced with "all deliberate speed." The ruling gave no specified time period for enforcement. Instead, to the dismay of civil rights advocates who favored immediate implementation, it allowed for a variety of factors and special circumstances to be taken into consideration that were unique to each state and school district.

May 31, 1955.

1. Racial discrimination in public education is unconstitutional and all provisions of federal, state or local law requiring or permitting such discrimination must yield to this principle.

2. The judgments below (except that in the Delaware case) are reversed and the cases are remanded to the District Courts to take such proceedings and enter such orders and decrees consistent with this opinion as are necessary and proper to admit the parties to these cases to public schools on a racially nondiscriminatory basis with all deliberate speed.

   (a) School authorities have the primary responsibility for elucidating, assessing and solving the varied local school problems which may require solution in fully implementing the governing constitutional principles.

   (b) Courts will have to consider whether the action of school authorities constitutes good faith implementation of the governing constitutional principles.

   (c) Because of their proximity to local conditions and the possible need for further hearings, the courts which originally heard these cases can best perform this judicial appraisal.

   (d) In fashioning and effectuating the decrees, the courts will be guided by equitable principles—characterized by a practical flexibility in shaping remedies and a facility for adjusting and reconciling public and private needs.

(e) At stake is the personal interest of the plaintiffs in admission to public schools as soon as practicable on a nondiscriminatory basis.

(f) Courts of equity may properly take into account the public interest in the elimination in a systematic and effective manner of a variety of obstacles in making the transition to school systems operated in accordance with the constitutional principles enunciated in 347 U.S. 483, 497; but the vitality of these constitutional principles cannot be allowed to yield simply because of disagreement with them.

(g) While giving weight to these public and private considerations, the courts will require that the defendants make a prompt and reasonable start toward full compliance with the ruling of this Court.

(h) Once such a start has been made, the courts may find that additional time is necessary to carry out the ruling in an effective manner.

(i) The burden rests on the defendants to establish that additional time is necessary in the public interest and is consistent with good faith compliance at the earliest practicable date.

(j) The courts may consider problems related to administration, arising from the physical condition of the school plant, the school transportation system, personnel, revision of school districts and attendance areas into compact units to achieve a system of determining admission to the public schools on a nonracial basis, and revision of local laws and regulations which may be necessary in solving the foregoing problems.

(k) The courts will also consider the adequacy of any plans the defendants may propose to meet these problems and to effectuate a transition to a racially nondiscriminatory school system.

(l) During the period of transition, the courts will retain jurisdiction of these cases.

3. The judgment in the Delaware case, ordering the immediate admission of the plaintiffs to schools previously attended only by white children, is affirmed on the basis of the principles stated by this Court in its opinion, 347 U.S. 483; but the case is remanded to the Supreme Court of Delaware for such further proceedings as that Court may deem necessary in the light of this opinion.

MR. CHIEF JUSTICE [Earl] WARREN delivered the opinion of the Court.

These cases were decided on May 17, 1954. The opinions of that date, declaring the fundamental principle that racial discrimination in public education is unconstitutional, are incorporated herein by reference. All provisions of federal, state, or local law requiring or permitting such discrimination must yield to this principle. There remains for consideration the manner in which relief is to be accorded.

Because these cases arose under different local conditions and their disposition will involve a variety of local problems, we requested further argument on the question of relief. In view of the nationwide importance of the decision, we invited the Attorney General of the United States and the Attorneys General of all states requiring or permitting racial discrimination in public education to present their views on that question. The parties, the United States, and the States of Florida, North Carolina, Arkansas, Oklahoma, Maryland, and Texas filed briefs and participated in the oral argument.

These presentations were informative and helpful to the Court in its consideration of the complexities arising from the transition to a system of public education freed of racial discrimination. The presentations also demonstrated that substantial steps to eliminate racial discrimination in public schools have already been taken, not only in some of the communities in which these cases arose, but in some of the states appearing as amici curiae, and in other states as well. Substantial progress has been made in the District of Columbia and in the communities in Kansas and Delaware involved in this litigation. The defendants in the cases coming to us from South Carolina and Virginia are awaiting the decision of this Court concerning relief.

Full implementation of these constitutional principles may require solution of varied local school problems. School authorities have the primary responsibility for elucidating, assessing, and solving these problems; courts will have to consider whether the action of school authorities constitutes good faith implementation of the governing constitutional principles. Because of their proximity to local conditions and the possible need for further hearings, the courts which originally heard these cases can best perform this judicial appraisal. Accordingly, we believe it appropriate to remand the cases to those courts.

In fashioning and effectuating the decrees, the courts will be guided by equitable principles. Traditionally, equity has been characterized by a practical flexibility in shaping its remedies and by a facility for adjusting and reconciling public and private needs. These cases call for the exercise of these traditional attributes of equity power. At stake is the personal interest of the plaintiffs in admission to public schools as soon as practicable on a nondiscriminatory basis. To effectuate this interest may call for elimination of a variety of obstacles in making the transition to school systems operated in accordance with the constitutional principles set forth in our May 17, 1954, decision. Courts of equity may properly take into account the public interest in the elimination of such obstacles in a systematic and effective manner. But it should go without saying that the vitality of these constitutional principles cannot be allowed to yield simply because of disagreement with them.

While giving weight to these public and private considerations, the courts will require that the defendants make a prompt and reasonable start toward full compliance with our May 17, 1954, ruling. Once such a start has been made, the courts may find that additional time is necessary to carry out the ruling in an effective manner. The burden rests upon the defendants to establish that such time is necessary in the public interest and is consistent with good faith compliance at the earliest practicable date. To that end, the courts may consider problems related to administration, arising from the physical condition of the school plant, the school transportation system, personnel, revision of school districts and attendance areas into compact units to achieve a system of determining admission to the public schools on a nonracial basis, and revision of local laws and regulations which may be necessary in solving the foregoing problems. They will also consider the adequacy of any plans the defendants may propose to meet these problems and to effectuate a transition to a racially nondiscriminatory school system. During this period of transition, the courts will retain jurisdiction of these cases.

The judgments below, except that in the Delaware case, are accordingly reversed and the cases are remanded to the District Courts to take such proceedings and enter such orders and decrees consistent with this opinion as are necessary and proper to admit to public schools on a racially nondiscriminatory basis with all deliberate speed the parties to these cases. The judgment in the Delaware case—ordering the immediate admission of the plaintiffs to schools previously attended only by white children—is affirmed on the basis of the principles stated in our May 17, 1954, opinion, but the case is remanded to the Supreme Court of Delaware for such further proceedings as that Court may deem necessary in light of this opinion.

It is so ordered.

See 349 U.S. 294.

79.

THURGOOD MARSHALL: THE MOST FAMOUS LAWYER IN AMERICA (1955)

After Marshall's leadership in getting the favorable *Brown v. Board of Education* decision from the U.S. Supreme Court, he became the most famous, although certainly not the most popular, attorney in the nation. A hero to African Americans in general, but especially black youth, his celebrity was captured in the following poem, which was set to the music of the popular children's song "The Ballad of Davy Crockett," and was published in the 9 July 1955 edition of the *Baltimore Afro-American*. The line about "Charlie" refers to Charles Houston, fellow NAACP lawyer and dean of Howard Law School.

Thurgood . . . Thurgood Marshall, Mr. Civil Rights.
Born in Maryland, the state of the free,
Went to Howard for his law degree,
Took his training at Charlie's knee,
Said, "it isn't so free, as you can see."
Thurgood . . . Thurgood Marshall, Mr. Civil Rights.
Fought for the teachers, fought for the schools,

Went down south where they broke all the rules,
Now he's working on the swimming pools,
Justice and right are his fighting tools.
Thurgood . . . Thurgood Marshall, Mr. Civil Rights.

See Juan Williams, *Thurgood Marshall: American Revolutionary* (New York: Times Books, 1998), 239–40.

80.

ROSA PARKS ON THE INCIDENT PRECIPITATING THE MONTGOMERY BUS BOYCOTT (1955)

Rosa Parks's bold stand against a common segregation ordinance in Montgomery, Alabama, in December 1955 set off a chain reaction of events, including a year-long boycott of the local bus system and the rise of Martin Luther King, Jr., as the leader of the civil rights movement. Here she recalls the day it all began.

When I got off from work that evening of December 1, I went to Court Square as usual to catch the Cleveland Avenue bus home. . . .

I saw a vacant seat in the middle section of the bus and took it. I didn't even question why there was a vacant seat even though there were quite a few people standing in the back. If I had thought about it at all, I would probably have figured maybe someone saw me get on and did not take the seat but left it vacant for me. There was a man sitting next to the window and two women across the aisle.

The next stop was the Empire Theater, and some whites got on. They filled up the white seats, and one man was left standing. The driver looked back and noticed the man standing. Then he looked back at us. He said, "Let me have those front seats," because they were the front seats of the black section. Didn't anybody move. We just sat right where we were, the four of us. Then he spoke a second time: "Ya'll better make it light on yourselves and let me have those seats." . . .

I could not see how standing up was going to "make it light" for me. . . .

As I sat there, I tried not to think about what might happen. I knew anything was possible. I could be manhandled or beaten. I could be arrested. People have asked me if it occurred to me then that I could be the test case the NAACP had been looking for. I did not think that at all. In fact if I had let myself think too deeply about what might happen to me, I might have gotten off the bus. But I chose to remain.

See Rosa Parks with Jim Haskins, *Rosa Parks: My Story* (New York: Dial Books, 1992), 113–16.

81.

ELIZABETH ECKFORD RECALLS HER
EXPERIENCE INTEGRATING LITTLE ROCK
HIGH SCHOOL (1957)

One of nine children to integrate the previously all-white public school in Little Rock, Arkansas, Eckford describes the gamut of emotions that swept through her as she made her way through the hateful mobs and armed guards surrounding the school on that fateful first day.

I caught the bus and got off a block from the school. I saw a large crowd of people standing across the street from the soldiers guarding Central. . . .

Then someone shouted, "Here she comes, get ready!" I moved away from the crowd on the sidewalk and into the street. If the mob came at me I could then cross back over so the guards could protect me.

The crowd moved in closer and then began to follow me, calling me names. I still wasn't afraid. Just a little bit nervous. Then my knees started to shake all of a sudden and I wondered whether I could make it to the center entrance a block away. It was the longest block I ever walked in my whole life. . . .

Somebody started yelling, "Lynch her! Lynch her!"

I tried to see a friendly face somewhere in the mob—someone who maybe would help. I looked into the face of an old woman and it seemed a kind face, but when I looked at her again, she spat on me.

They came closer, shouting, "No nigger bitch is going to get in our school! Get out of here!" . . .

Someone hollered, "Drag her over to this tree! Let's take care of that nigger." Just then a white man sat down beside me, put his arm around me and patted my shoulder. He raised my chin and said, "Don't let them see you cry."

See Chris Mayfield, ed., *Growing Up Southern: Southern Exposure Looks at Childhood, Then and Now* (New York: Random House, 1981), 258–61.

82.

WHY THE MONTGOMERY BUS BOYCOTT
WAS A "STRIDE TOWARD FREEDOM" (1958)

King prefaced his book *Stride toward Freedom*, which was essentially an autobiographical account of his role in leading the Montgomery bus boycott, with a gracious acknowledgment of the role played by the masses in uniting for a common cause. Here he praises the nameless and faceless thousands who persevered to the end of that long year 1956 and thus made a giant "stride toward freedom."

This is not a drama with only one actor. More precisely it is the chronicle of 50,000 Negroes who took to heart the principles of nonviolence, who learned to fight for their rights with the weapon of love, and who, in the process, acquired a new estimate of their own human worth. It is the story of Negro leaders of many faiths and divided allegiances, who came together in the bond of a cause they knew was right. And of the Negro followers, many of them beyond middle age, who walked to work and home again as much as twelve miles a day for over a year rather than submit to the discourtesies and humiliation of segregated buses. The majority of the Negroes who took part in the year-long boycott of Montgomery's buses were poor and untutored; but they understood the essence of the Montgomery movement. One elderly woman summed it up for the rest. When asked after several weeks of walking whether she was tired, she answered, "My feets is tired, but my soul is at rest."

See Martin Luther King, Jr., *Stride toward Freedom: The Montgomery Story* (New York: Harper & Row, 1958), 9–10.

83.

CORETTA SCOTT KING ON THE DUAL STRUGGLE OF RAISING FAMOUS CHILDREN/BLACK CHILDREN IN THE SEGREGATED SOUTH (CIRCA 1950s–1960s)

Too often, in remembering the sacrifices of the "leaders" of the civil rights movement, we forget that behind their public veneers lay ordinary people with spouses, children, and home lives. In the following autobiographical excerpts, Coretta Scott King gives us a glimpse inside the household of the King family and reveals the double difficulty of raising black children in the segregated South and in the spotlight of fame.

Martin and I, like any other young couple, were vitally absorbed with raising our children. However, we shared with our black brothers and sisters the especially demanding and often agonizing job of bringing our children up without fear or bitterness in their hearts. That is difficult enough in a segregated city, as Atlanta was, but our activities in the Movement made it doubly difficult.

. . . .

Marty was in the third grade when Yoki and Marty [the Kings's two oldest children] first attended an integrated school and on the second day of school, a boy in his class came up to him and said, " . . . Your father's that famous nigger." . . . More than anything, he [Marty] seemed to have been embarrassed at the use of the word "nigger . . . "

A new amusement park had been built in Atlanta, called Funtown, and it was advertised extensively. My children . . . would plead with us to take them, and we would keep making excuses, not wanting to tell them that the television invitations were not meant for black children. . . . finally Yoki, who was about six at the time, said, "You just don't want to take me to Funtown." . . . My daughter started crying, then I heard myself echoing those old words: "Yoki dear, this doesn't mean you are not as good as those people. You know, God made all of us and we are all His children. . . . Don't cry because it won't be long before you can go to Funtown. This is really what your daddy is doing in all his work. . . . " This was her first emotional realization and understanding of being black in a white world.

See Coretta Scott King, *My Life with Martin Luther King, Jr.* (New York: Holt, Rinehart and Winston, 1969), 210, 212–13.

84.

THE GREENSBORO SIT-INS: A PLEA FOR FAIRNESS (1960)

On 1 February 1960, four African American students from the North Carolina Agricultural and Technical College entered the racially segregated Woolworth's Department Store in Greensboro and asked for service. Their request was denied, but they were determined to persevere with their quest to end the injustice of racial segregation. On the night after the second day of the sit-in, they drafted a letter (ghost written by a white supporter) to send to the headquarters of F. W. Woolworth & Company in New York City. It was a plea for fairness, which they hoped the more racially moderate northern executives would honor. Below is their letter.

Dear Mr. President:

We the undersigned are students at the Negro college in the city of Greensboro. We have bought thousands of items at hundreds of the counters in your store. Our money being accepted without rancor or discrimination and with politeness toward us. When at a long counter just three feet away our money is not acceptable because of the color of our skins. This letter is not being written with resentment toward your company, but with a hope of understanding. . . .

We are asking that your company take a firm stand to eliminate discrimination. We firmly believe that God will give courage and guidance in the solving of this problem.

Sincerely yours,
Student Executive Committee
Ezell Blair Jr.
David Price
Joseph McNeil

David Richmond
Franklin McCain

See Miles Wolff, *Lunch at the Five and Ten: The Greensboro Sit-Ins* (New York: Stein and Day, 1970, 36–37.

85.

BOYNTON v. VIRGINIA (1960)

In this case, the Supreme Court ruled in favor of the black litigant who charged that a Virginia restaurant/bus terminal had discriminated against him based on his race. This case prompted CORE to stage the Freedom Rides in 1961 to test the decision in a much larger arena and under the spotlight of national media attention.

MR. JUSTICE [Hugo] BLACK delivered the opinion of the Court.

The basic question presented in this case is whether an interstate bus passenger is denied a federal statutory or constitutional right when a restaurant in a bus terminal used by the carrier along its route discriminates in serving food to the passenger solely because of his color.

Petitioner, a Negro law student, bought a Trailways bus ticket from Washington, D.C., to Montgomery, Alabama. He boarded a bus at 8 p.m. which arrived at Richmond, Virginia, about 10:40 p.m. When the bus pulled up at the Richmond "Trailways Bus Terminal," the bus driver announced a forty-minute stopover there. Petitioner got off the bus and went into the bus terminal to get something to eat. In the station, he found a restaurant in which one part was used to serve white people and one to serve Negroes. Disregarding this division, petitioner sat down on a stool in the white section. A waitress asked him to move over to the other section where there were "facilities" to serve colored people. Petitioner told her he was an interstate bus passenger, refused to move, and ordered a sandwich and tea. The waitress then brought the Assistant Manager, who "instructed" petitioner to "leave the white portion of the restaurant and advised him he could be served in the colored portion." Upon petitioner's refusal to leave, an officer was called and petitioner was arrested and later tried, convicted and fined ten dollars in the Police Justice's Court of Richmond on a charge that he "unlawfully did remain on the premises of the Bus Terminal Restaurant of Richmond, Inc. after having been forbidden to do so" by the Assistant Manager. The charge was based on . . . [the notion that] If any person shall without authority of law go upon or remain upon the lands or premises of another, after having been forbidden to do so by the owner, lessee, custodian or other person lawfully in charge of such land, . . . he shall be deemed guilty of a misdemeanor, and upon conviction thereof shall be punished by a fine of not more than one hundred dollars or by confinement in jail not exceeding thirty days, or by both such fine and imprisonment.

Petitioner appealed his conviction to the Hustings Court of Richmond, where, as in the Police Court, he admitted that he had remained in the white portion of the Terminal Restaurant although ordered not to do so. His defense in both courts was that he had a federal right as an interstate passenger of Trailways to be served without discrimination by this restaurant used by the bus carrier for the accommodation of its interstate passengers. On this basis, petitioner claimed he was on the restaurant premises lawfully, not "unlawfully" as charged, and that he remained there with, not "without authority of law." His federal claim to this effect was spelled out in a motion to dismiss the warrant in Hustings Court, which was overruled both before and after the evidence was heard. Pointing out that the restaurant was an integral part of the bus service for interstate passengers such as petitioner, and asserting that refusal to serve him was a discrimination based on color, the motion to dismiss charged that application of the Virginia law to petitioner violated the Interstate Commerce Act and the Equal Protection, Due Process, and Commerce Clauses of the Federal Constitution. On appeal, the Virginia Supreme Court held that the conviction was "plainly right," and affirmed without opinion, thereby rejecting petitioner's assignments of error based on the same grounds of discrimination set out in his motion to dismiss in Hustings Court, but not specifically charging that the discrimination violated the Interstate Commerce Act. We think, however, that the claims of discrimination previously made under the Act are sufficiently closely related to the assignments that were made to be considered within the scope of the issues presented to the State Supreme Court. We granted certiorari because of the serious federal questions raised concerning discrimination based on color.

The petition for certiorari we granted presented only two questions: first, whether the conviction of petitioner is invalid as a burden on commerce in violation of Article I, Section 8, Clause 3 of the Constitution, and, second, whether the conviction violates the Due Process and Equal Protection Clauses of the Fourteenth Amendment. Ordinarily we limit our review to the questions presented in an application for certiorari. We think there are persuasive reasons, however, why this case should be decided, if it can, on the Interstate Commerce Act contention raised in the Virginia courts. Discrimination because of color is the core of the two broad constitutional questions presented to us by petitioner, just as it is the core of the Interstate Commerce Act question presented to the Virginia courts. Under these circumstances, we think it appropriate not to reach the constitutional questions, but to proceed at once to the statutory issue.

The Interstate Commerce Act . . . uses language of the broadest type to bar discriminations of all kinds. We have held that the Act forbids railroad dining cars to discriminate in service to passengers on account of their color.

Section 216(d) of Part II of the Interstate Commerce Act, . . . , which applies to motor carriers, provides in part:

> It shall be unlawful for any common carrier by motor vehicle engaged in interstate or foreign commerce to make, give, or cause any undue or unreasonable preference or advantage to any particular person . . . in any respect whatsoever; or to subject any particular person . . . to any unjust discrimination or any unjust or unreasonable prejudice or disadvantage in any respect whatsoever. . . .

So far as relevant to our problem . . . it was an "undue or unreasonable prejudice" . . . for a railroad to divide its dining car by curtains, partitions and signs in order to separate passengers according to race. The Court said that, . . . where a dining car is available to passengers holding tickets entitling them to use it, each such passenger is equally entitled to its facilities in accordance with reasonable regulations.

The Henderson case largely rested on Mitchell v. United States, supra, which pointed out that, while the railroads might not be required by law to furnish dining car facilities, yet, if they did, substantial equality of treatment of persons traveling under like conditions could not be refused . . . It is also of relevance that both cases upset Interstate Commerce Commission holdings, the Court stating in Mitchell that, since the "discrimination shown was palpably unjust and forbidden by the Act," no room was left for administrative or expert judgment with reference to practical difficulties. . . .

Although this Court has not decided whether the same result would follow from a similar discrimination in service by a restaurant in a railroad or bus terminal, we have no doubt that the reasoning underlying the Mitchell and Henderson cases would compel the same decision as to the unlawfulness of discrimination in transportation services against interstate passengers in terminals and terminal restaurants owned or operated or controlled by interstate carriers. This is true as to railroad terminals because they are expressly made carriers . . . and as to bus terminals . . . specifically includes interstate transportation facilities and property operated or controlled by a motor carrier within the definition of the "services" and "transportation" to which the motor carrier provisions of the Act apply.

Respondent correctly points out, however, that whatever may be the facts, the evidence in this record does not show that the bus company owns or actively operates or directly controls the bus terminal or the restaurant in it. But the fact that . . . the protections of the motor carrier provisions of the Act extend to "include" facilities so operated or controlled by no means should be interpreted to exempt motor carriers from their statutory duty . . . not to discriminate should they choose to provide their interstate passengers with services that are an integral part of transportation through the use of facilities they neither own, control nor operate. The protections afforded by the Act against discriminatory transportation services are not so narrowly limited. We have held that a railroad cannot escape its statutory duty to treat its shippers alike either by use of facilities it does not own or by contractual arrangement with the owner of those facilities. United States v. Baltimore & Ohio R. Co., supra. And so here, without regard to contracts, if the bus carrier has volunteered to make terminal and restaurant facilities and services available to its interstate passengers as a regular part of their transportation, and the terminal and restaurant have acquiesced and cooperated in this undertaking, the terminal and restaurant must perform these services without discriminations prohibited by the Act. In the performance of these services under such conditions, the terminal and restaurant stand in the place of the bus company in the performance of its transportation obligations. . . . Although the courts below made no findings of fact, we think the evidence in this case shows such a relationship and situation here.

The manager of the restaurant testified that it was not affiliated in any way with the Trailways Bus Company, and that the bus company had no control over the operation of the restaurant, but that, while the restaurant had "quite a bit of business" from local people, it was primarily or partly for the service of the passengers on the Trailways bus. This last statement was perhaps much of an understatement, as shown by the lease agreement executed in writing and signed both by the "Trailways Bus Terminal, Inc.," as lessor, and the "Bus Terminal Restaurant of Richmond, Inc.," as lessee. The first part of the document showed that Trailways Terminal was then constructing a "bus station" with built-in facilities "for the operation of a restaurant, soda fountain, and news stand." Terminal covenanted to lease this space to Restaurant for its use; to grant Restaurant the exclusive right to sell foods and other things usually sold in restaurants, newsstands, soda fountains, and lunch counters; to keep the terminal building in good repair, and to furnish certain utilities. Restaurant, on its part, agreed to use its space for the sale of commodities agreed on at prices that are "just and reasonable"; to sell no commodities not usually sold or installed in a bus terminal concession without Terminal's permission; to discontinue the sale of any commodity objectionable to Terminal; to buy, maintain, and replace equipment subject to Terminal's approval in writing as to its quality; to make alterations and additions only after Terminal's written consent and approval; to make no "sales on buses operating in and out said bus station," but only "through the windows of said buses"; to keep its employees neat and clean; to perform no terminal service other than that pertaining to the operation of its restaurant as agreed on; and that neither Restaurant nor its employees were to sell transportation of any kind or give information pertaining to schedules, rates or transportation matters, but shall refer all such inquiries to the proper agents of Terminal. In short, as Terminal and Restaurant agreed, the operation of the restaurant and the said stands shall be in keeping with the character of service maintained in an up-to-date, modern bus terminal.

All of these things show that this terminal building, with its grounds, constituted one project for a single purpose, and that was to serve passengers of one or more bus companies—certainly Trailways' passengers. The restaurant area was specifically designed and built into the structure from the beginning to fill the needs of bus passengers in this "up-to-date, modern bus terminal." Whoever may have had technical title or immediate control of the details of the various activities in the terminal, such as waiting room seating, furnishing of schedule information, ticket sales, and restaurant service, they were all geared to the service of bus companies and their passengers, even though local people who might happen to come into the terminal or its restaurant might also be accommodated. Thus we have a well coordinated and smoothly functioning plan for continuous cooperative transportation services between the terminal, the restaurant, and buses like Trailways that made stopovers there. All of this evidence plus Trailways' use on this occasion shows that Trailways was not utilizing the terminal and restaurant services merely on a sporadic or occasional basis. This bus terminal plainly was just as essential and necessary, and as available, for that matter, to passengers and carriers like Trailways that used it, as though such carriers had legal title and complete control over all of its activities. Interstate passengers have to eat, and the very terms of the lease of the built-in restaurant space in this terminal constitute a recognition of the essential need of interstate passengers to be able to get food conveniently on their journey and an undertaking by the restaurant to fulfill that need. Such passengers in transit on a paid interstate Trailways journey had a right to expect that this essential transportation food service voluntarily provided for them under such circumstances would be rendered without discrimination prohibited by the Interstate Commerce Act. Under the circumstances of this case, therefore, petitioner had a federal right to remain in the white portion of the restaurant. He was there under "authority of law"—the Interstate Commerce Act—and it was error for the Supreme Court of Virginia to affirm his conviction.

Because of some of the arguments made here, it is necessary to say a word about what we are not deciding. We are not holding that, every time a bus stops at a wholly independent roadside restaurant, the Interstate Commerce Act requires that restaurant service be supplied in harmony with the provisions of that Act. We decide only this case, on its facts, where circumstances show that the terminal and restaurant operate as an integral part of the bus carrier's transportation service for interstate passengers. Under such circumstances, an interstate passenger need not inquire into documents of title or contractual arrangements in order to determine whether he has a right to be served without discrimination.

The judgment of the Supreme Court of Virginia is reversed, and the cause is remanded to that Court for proceedings not inconsistent with this opinion.

Reversed and remanded.

See 364 U.S. 454.

86.

JAMES FARMER, FREEDOM RIDER, DESCRIBES HIS EXPERIENCE IN A MISSISSIPPI JAIL (1961)

James Farmer, a founder of CORE and the chief instigator of the Freedom Rides, describes his group's incarceration first in the Hinds County jail and later the Parchman State Penitentiary for allegedly "Disturbing the peace, disobeying an officer, and inciting to riot." Actually, Farmer and his compatriots had done nothing more than ride into Mississippi on an integrated bus, then use the "whites only" facilities at the bus terminal in Jackson.

Our trial was perfunctory, and the verdict instantaneous: one year in jail for everyone. I urged all who could to remain in jail for forty days, the maximum one could serve and still file an appeal in Mississippi. We wanted to fill up the jails and place as great a burden on the state as possible, for as long as we could. Perhaps segregation would be seen as too heavy an albatross for the ship of state to bear.

All were aware of the jail-filling tactic of the Ride—a step beyond the lunch counter sit-ins of the year before, where the jailed were sprung as soon as bail could be arranged—and most eagerly agreed to stay in. The "forty days and forty nights" seemed somehow symbolic. . . .

We'd all heard of Parchman, of course, the most fabled state prison in the South. . . .

When we arrived, we were ordered out, under heavy guard, as dozens of red-necks stood by, staring. In a negative kind of way, we were celebrities and they had come to watch, some somber-faced and some grinning. It would be something to tell their children and grandchildren.

We were led into a large basement room and told to take all our clothes off, including shoes and socks. We stripped off our clothes, and with them a measure of dignity. The red-necks outside jostled for position at the barred windows, gawking. We were consumed by embarrassment. We stood for ages—uncomfortable, dehumanized. Our audience cackled with laughter and obscene comments. . . .

Each day, our numbers increased. We *were* filling up the jails.

Incoming freedom riders were put in our cell block—at the far end, only partially segregated. This fact did not escape our attention. . . .

For Mississippi, that was not a surrender of principle. It was simply an acknowledgment that they were fast running out of cell space.

See James Farmer, *Lay Bare the Heart: An Autobiography of the Civil Rights Movement* (New York: Arbor House, 1985), 6, 11–12, 22, 24–25.

87.

JAMES MEREDITH ON FEAR AND COURAGE
(1962)

Meredith, the first African American to integrate the University of Mississippi, here shares how he overcame his fear and determined to act on his belief that all races deserved equal educational opportunities.

During my first few weeks almost all of the focus was on the possibility of my being killed by the "White Supremacists." People have asked me if I was not terribly afraid. . . . My apprehensions had been faced a long time before that. The hardest thing in human nature is to decide to act. . . .

A quotation from Theodore Roosevelt was perhaps more important than anything else in helping me. . . . "It is not the critic who counts, not the man who points out how the strong man stumbles, where the doer of deeds could have done them better. The credit belongs to the man who is actually in the arena; whose face is marred by dust and sweat and blood; who strives valiantly; who errs and comes short again and again; who knows the great enthusiasm, the great devotion, and spends himself in a worthy cause: who, at the best, knows in the end the triumph of high achievement; and who, at the worst, if he fails, at least fails while daring greatly, so that his place shall never be with those cold and timid souls who know neither victory nor defeat." At various times different parts of that quotation have been important to me, but when I made the decision to return to Mississippi to try to gain admission to the university, the part I kept remembering was the "cold and timid souls who know neither victory nor defeat." I did not want to be one of those.

See James Meredith, *Three Years in Mississippi* (Bloomington: Indiana University Press, 1966), 216–17.

88.

AN OLE MISS PROFESSOR'S FIRST
IMPRESSIONS OF JAMES MEREDITH AS A
STUDENT (1962)

James Silver was chair of the history department at the University of Mississippi when James Meredith integrated that institution in 1962. He played a firsthand role in trying to open the "closed society" of Mississippi to the inevitability of integration. As part of his eye-witness account of the whole long Meredith affair, he published the following personal letter written to his daughter Betty, describing his first impressions of his first black student at Ole Miss.

October 10, 1962
University, Mississippi
Dear Betty:

.... I think that you will be interested in my first impressions of James Meredith. . . . We talked for over an hour, about everything from his professors and courses to his own daily problems.

It was already my opinion that he had handled himself magnificently, that he had said just the right things for the press, etc. Now I feel more than ever that here is a young man, solid in his conviction that this is what he has to do, with no thought of reward that will come to him. . . . When he says that all he wants to do is to sort of fade away from public attention and pursue his studies, I believe him. He says that in all honesty but with the knowledge that he will always be the center of attention, at least as long as he stays here. . . . He is a bit put out because he is in classes which he thinks are not advanced enough for him, but thinks this will be changed in time. . . . He is determined not to be exploited by the NAACP and I think he will have his way on this. His chances of ever being accepted here would be blasted if he started making speeches for the NAACP in other sections of the country, or anywhere. Personally, I think he has more judgment by far than those who are handling him. I think he could sell most of the students, even here, if he had a chance to talk with them. Maybe this will come to pass . . .

See James W. Silver, *Mississippi: The Closed Society* (New York: Harcourt, Brace & World, Inc., 1963), 173–74.

89.

JAMES BALDWIN ON ELIJAH MUHAMMAD AND THE NATION OF ISLAM (1963)

Baldwin, a black Christian, speaks here of the magnetism of the leader of the Nation of Islam and his message—a magnetism so great as to pull thousands of African American Christians away from their traditional faith and toward this peculiar brand of Islam. Baldwin himself felt attracted to this doctrine, which offered hope to his people. But in the end, he could only reject it, partly out of theological disagreement and partly out of practical considerations.

I had heard a great deal, long before I finally met him, of the Honorable Elijah Muhammad, and of the Nation of Islam movement, of which he is the leader. I paid very little attention to what I heard, because the burden of his message did not strike me as being very original; I had been hearing variations of it all my life. . . . Then two things caused me to begin to listen to the speeches, and one was the behavior of the police. . . . I had seen many crowds dispersed by policemen, with clubs or on horseback. But the policemen were doing nothing now. . . . because they were afraid. . . . The behavior of the crowd, its silent intensity, was the other thing that forced me to reassess the speakers and their message.

Power was the subject of the speeches I heard. We were offered, as Nation of Islam doctrine, historical and divine proof that all white people are cursed, and are devils, and are about to be brought down. . . .

The dream, the sentiment is old; only the color is new. And it is this dream, this sweet possibility, that thousands of oppressed black men and women in this country now carry away with them after the Muslim minister has spoken, through the dark, noisome ghetto streets, into the hovels where so many have perished. The white God has not delivered them; perhaps the Black God will. . . .

I felt very close to him, and really wished to be able to love and honor his as a witness, an ally, a father. . . . Yet . . . because of what he conceived as his responsibility and what I took to be mine—we would always be strangers, and possibly, one day, enemies. . . .

See James Baldwin, *The Fire Next Time* (New York: The Dial Press, 1963), 61–63, 92–93.

90.

MALCOLM X: WHAT'S IN A NAME? (1963)

Malcolm X was one of the many tragic figures of the civil rights movement. A fiery orator with a quick wit and a hot temper, he was simultaneously the most enigmatic and charismatic black leader of his generation. Challenging every convention of white American society, he inspired fear and hatred among many whites and blacks alike, as well as inspiring a devoted following of African American youth. Among civil rights leaders, none save Martin Luther King, Jr., has generated as much scholarly and popular attention as a historical figure. Below is an excerpt from the interview which first brought him into nationwide prominence. In it, Malcolm answers the age-old question "What's in a name?"

When I'm traveling around the country, I use my real Muslim name, Malik Shabazz. I make my hotel reservations under that name, and I always see the same thing. . . . I come to the desk and always see that "here-comes-a-Negro" look. It's kind of a reserved, coldly tolerant cordiality. But when I say "Malik Shabazz," their whole attitude changes: they snap to respect. They think I'm an African. People say what's in a name? There's a whole lot in a name. The

American black man is seeing the African respected as a human being. The African gets respect because he has an identity and cultural roots. But most of all because the African owns some land. For these reasons he has his human rights recognized, and that makes his civil rights automatic.

See the *Playboy* interview with Alex Haley, May 1963.

91.

MARTIN LUTHER KING, JR.'S "LETTER FROM BIRMINGHAM JAIL" (1963)

King arrived in Birmingham in April 1963 to lead demonstrations aimed at desegregating city government jobs. He was promptly thrown in jail for disturbing the peace. Local white clerics jointly authored a public letter denouncing King as an outside agitator and condemning the demonstrations as "untimely, unwise, unnecessary, and illegal." King's response was this letter written in the city jail, which explains his rationale for leading demonstrations in Birmingham and sets forth his long-term strategy for leading the civil rights movement in general. Here are excerpts from his letter.

April 16, 1963
MY DEAR FELLOW CLERGYMEN:
    While confined here in the Birmingham city jail, . . .
    I think I should indicate why I am here in Birmingham. . . .
    I am in Birmingham because injustice is here. . . .
    I am cognizant of the interrelatedness of all communities and states. I cannot sit idly by in Atlanta and not be concerned about what happens in Birmingham. Injustice anywhere is a threat to justice everywhere. We are caught in an inescapable network of mutuality, tied in a single garment of destiny. Whatever affects one directly, affects all indirectly. Never again can we afford to live with the narrow, provincial "outside agitator" idea. Anyone who lives inside the United States can never be considered an outsider anywhere within its bounds.
    . . . . It is unfortunate that demonstrations are taking place in Birmingham, but it is even more unfortunate that the city's white power structure left the Negro community with no alternative.
    In any nonviolent campaign there are four basic steps: collection of the facts to determine whether injustices exist; negotiation; self-purification; and direct action. We have gone through all these steps in Birmingham. There can be no gainsaying the fact that racial injustice engulfs this community. Birmingham is probably the most thoroughly segregated city in the United States. Its ugly record of brutality is widely known. Negroes have experienced grossly unjust

treatment in the courts. There have been more unsolved bombings of Negro homes and churches in Birmingham than in any other city in the nation. These are the hard, brutal facts of the case. On the basis of these conditions, Negro leaders sought to negotiate with the city fathers. But the latter consistently refused to engage in good-faith negotiation. . . .

You may well ask: "Why direct action? Why sit-ins, marches and so forth? Isn't negotiation a better path?" You are quite right in calling for negotiation. Indeed, this is the very purpose of direct action. Nonviolent direct action seeks to create such a crisis and foster such a tension that a community which has constantly refused to negotiate is forced to confront the issue. It seeks so to dramatize the issue that it can no longer be ignored. My citing the creation of tension as part of the work of the nonviolent-resister may sound rather shocking. But I must confess that I am not afraid of the word "tension." I have earnestly opposed violent tension, but there is a type of constructive, nonviolent tension which is necessary for growth. . . .

The purpose of our direct-action program is to create a situation so crisis-packed that it will inevitably open the door to negotiation. . . .

Oppressed people cannot remain oppressed forever. The yearning for freedom eventually manifests itself, and that is what has happened to the American Negro. . . .

Never before have I written so long a letter. . . .

. . . .

Yours for the cause of Peace and Brotherhood,
MARTIN LUTHER KING, JR.

See www.stanford.edu/group/king/frequentdocs/birmingham.

92.

MARTIN LUTHER KING, JR.'S "I HAVE A DREAM" SPEECH (1963)

King delivered this speech on the steps at the Lincoln Memorial in Washington, D.C., on 28 August 1963. It was the high point of the March on Washington. In this speech, King identified five particular points which would fulfill his dream of racial equality. Below, isolated from the rest of the speech, are those five points, along with his emotional conclusion which stirred the crowd into an eruption of wild cheering and applause.

I have a dream that one day this nation will . . . live out the true meaning of its creed " . . . that all men are created equal," . . . that . . . the sons of former slaves and the sons of former slaveowners will . . . sit down together at a table of brotherhood, . . . that . . . Mississippi . . . will be transformed into an oasis of freedom and justice, . . . that my four children will . . . live in a nation where they will not be judged by the color of their skin but by the content of their character, . . .

That . . . Alabama . . . will be transformed into a situation [*sic*] where little black boys and black girls will be able to join hands with little white boys and white girls and walk together as sisters and brothers. . . .

When we let freedom ring . . . we will be able to . . . join hands and sing . . . the old Negro spiritual, "Free at last! free at last! thank God Almighty, we are free at last!"

See www.extension.umn.edu/units/diversity/mlk.

93.

SNCC PREPARES FOR FREEDOM DAY IN SELMA (1963)

Zinn was a firsthand witness of the grassroots radicalism of the Student Nonviolent Coordinating Committee as well as a friend and mentor to some of its members. Here he describes SNCC's voter-registration drive in Selma, Alabama, from February to October 1963, which was to culminate in a "Freedom Day"—a final thrust to register voters in time to vote in the next election.

As Freedom Day approached, mass meetings were held every night, and the churches were packed.

On October 5, Dick Gregory came to Selma. His wife, Lillian, had been jailed in Selma while demonstrating. He spoke to a crowded church meeting that evening. It was an incredible performance. With armed deputies ringing the church outside, and three local officials sitting in the audience taking notes, Gregory lashed out at white Southern society with a steely wit and a passion that sent his Negro listeners into delighted applause again and again. Never in the history of this area had a black man stood like this on a public platform, ridiculing and denouncing white officials to their faces. It was a historic coming of age for Selma, Alabama. It was also something of a miracle that Gregory was able to leave town alive. The local newspaper said that a "wildly applauding crowd" listened that night to "the most scathing attack unleashed here in current radical demonstrations."

Gregory told the audience that the Southern white man had nothing he could call his own, no real identity, except "segregated drinking fountains, segregated toilets, and the right to call me a nigger.". . . .

Later, Jim Forman spoke to the crowd, making the last preparations for Freedom Day. "All right, let's go through the phone book. You'll know who's Negro, because they won't have a Mr. or Mrs. In front of their names! You got to get on the phone tonight and call these people and tell them to come down to the courthouse tomorrow, that it's Freedom Day. You take a baloney sandwich and a glass of cool water and go down there and stay all day. Now get on that phone tonight. Who'll take the letter "A"? . . . "

See Howard Zinn, SNCC: *The New Abolitionists* (Boston: Beacon Press, 1964), 150–51.

94.

MEMORIAL TO THREE MARTYRS IN MISSISSIPPI (CIRCA 1964)

The tragic murder of three civil rights activists in Neshoba County, Mississippi, captured the nation's attention in June 1964. The three young men, Michael Schwerner, James Chaney, and Andrew Goodman, had gone to Neshoba County, in the red clay hills of east-central Mississippi, to help register black voters during the Freedom Summer campaign of 1964. Using the Mt. Zion Methodist Church as a meeting place, they drew the ire of local whites, who burned the church down. Soon, the three civil rights workers were missing. Upon an FBI investigation, their bodies were found; they had been murdered. Later, the Mt. Zion Methodist Church was rebuilt, and in honor of the three young men who gave their lives for the cause of helping their black community, the church mounted the following memorial on the wall.

OUT OF ONE BLOOD GOD HATH MADE ALL MEN

This Plaque Is Dedicated
To The Memory Of
Michael Schwerner
James Chaney
Andrew Goodman
Whose concern for others, and more
particularly those of this community
led to their early martyrdom. Their
death quickened men's consciences
and more firmly established justice,
liberty and brotherhood in our land.

See Florence Mars, *Witness in Philadelphia* (Baton Rouge: Louisiana State University Press, 1977), 181.

95.

THE CIVIL RIGHTS ACT (1964)

President John F. Kennedy, before his assassination, had urged Congress to pass a civil rights bill that would once and for all enforce both the spirit and letter of the

U.S. Constitution and Declaration of Independence. Prompted to quick, vigorous action by the shock of Kennedy's death, by the leadership of new President Lyndon Johnson, and by the outbreak of increasingly intense civil rights demonstrations from Alabama to Washington, D.C., in 1963, Congress finally acted, reinforcing the Civil Rights Acts of 1957 and 1960, and producing the most notable piece of civil rights legislation since 1875. Herein are the most salient excerpts from the bill.

88th Congress, H. R. 7152
An Act

To enforce the constitutional right to vote, to confer jurisdiction upon the district courts of the United States to provide injunctive relief against discrimination in public accommodations, to authorize the Attorney General to institute suits to protect constitutional rights in public facilities and public education, to extend the Commission on Civil Rights, to prevent discrimination in federally assisted programs, to establish a Commission on Equal Employment Opportunity, and for other purposes.

Be it enacted by the Senate and House of Representatives of the United States of America in Congress assembled, That this Act may be cited as the "Civil Rights Act of 1964".

TITLE I: VOTING RIGHTS

Sec. 101.

. . . .

No person acting under color of law shall—

(A) in determining whether any individual is qualified under State law or laws to vote in any Federal election, apply any standard, practice, or procedure different from the standards, practices, or procedures applied under such law or laws to other individuals within the same county, parish, or similar political subdivision who have been found by State officials to be qualified to vote;

(B) deny the right of any individual to vote in any Federal election because of an error or omission on any record or paper relating to any application, registration, or other act requisite to voting, if such error or omission is not material in determining whether such individual is qualified under State law to vote in such election; or

(C) employ any literacy test as a qualification for voting in any Federal election unless (i) such test is administered to each individual and is conducted wholly in writing, and (ii) a certified copy of the test and of the answers given by the individual is furnished to him within twenty-five days of the submission of his request made within the period of time during which records and papers are required to be retained and preserved pursuant to title III of the Civil Rights Act of 1960 . . . : Provided, however, That the Attorney General may enter into agreements with appropriate State or local authorities that preparation, conduct, and maintenance of such tests in accordance with the provisions of applicable State or local law, including such special provisions as are necessary in the preparation, conduct, and maintenance of such tests for persons who are blind or otherwise physically handicapped, meet the purposes of this subparagraph and constitute compliance therewith. . . .

TITLE II: INJUNCTIVE RELIEF AGAINST DISCRIMINATION IN PLACES OF PUBLIC ACCOMMODATION

Sec. 201. (a) All persons shall be entitled to the full and equal enjoyment of the goods, services, facilities, and privileges, advantages, and accommodations of any place of public accommodation, as defined in this section, without discrimination or segregation on the ground of race, color, religion, or national origin.

(b) Each of the following establishments which serves the public is a place of public accommodation within the meaning of this title if its operations affect commerce, or if discrimination or segregation by it is supported by State action:

(1) any inn, hotel, motel, or other establishment which provides lodging to transient guests, other than an establishment located within a building which contains not more than five rooms for rent or hire and which is actually occupied by the proprietor of such establishment as his residence;

(2) any restaurant, cafeteria, lunchroom, lunch counter, soda fountain, or other facility principally engaged in selling food for consumption on the premises, including, but not limited to, any such facility located on the premises of any retail establishment; or any gasoline station;

(3) any motion picture house, theater, concert hall, sports arena, stadium or other place of exhibition or entertainment; and

(4) any establishment (A)(i) which is physically located within the premises of any establishment otherwise covered by this subsection, or (ii) within the premises of which is physically located any such covered establishment, and (B) which holds itself out as serving patrons of such covered establishment.

. . . .

(d) Discrimination or segregation by an establishment is supported by State action within the meaning of this title if such discrimination or segregation (1) is carried on under color of any law, statute, ordinance, or regulation; or (2) is carried on under color of any custom or usage required or enforced by officials of the State or political subdivision thereof; or (3) is required by action of the State or political subdivision thereof.

(e) The provisions of this title shall not apply to a private club or other establishment not in fact open to the public, except to the extent that the facilities of such establishment are made available to the customers or patrons of an establishment within the scope of subsection (b).

Sec. 202. All persons shall be entitled to be free, at any establishment or place, from discrimination or segregation of any kind on the ground of race, color, religion, or national origin, if such discrimination or segregation is or purports to be required by any law, statute, ordinance, regulation, rule, or order of a State or any agency or political subdivision thereof.

Sec. 203. No person shall (a) withhold, deny, or attempt to withhold or deny, or deprive or attempt to deprive, any person of any right or privilege secured by section 201 or 202, or (b) intimidate, threaten, or coerce, or attempt to intimidate, threaten, or coerce any person with the purpose of interfering with any right or privilege secured by section 201 or 202, or (c) punish or attempt to punish any person for exercising or attempting to exercise any right or privilege secured by section 201 or 202.

Sec. 204. (a) Whenever any person has engaged or there are reasonable grounds to believe that any person is about to engage in any act or practice prohibited by section 203, a civil action for preventive relief, including an application for a permanent or temporary injunction, restraining order, or other order, may be instituted by the person aggrieved and, upon timely application, the court may, in its discretion, permit the Attorney General to intervene in such civil action if he certifies that the case is of general public importance. Upon application by the complainant and in such circumstances as the court may deem just, the court may appoint an attorney for such complainant and may authorize the commencement of the civil action without the payment of fees, costs, or security. . . .

Sec. 205. The Service is authorized to make a full investigation of any complaint referred to it by the court under section 204(d) and may hold such hearings with respect thereto as may be necessary. The Service shall conduct any hearings with respect to any such complaint in executive session, and shall not release any testimony given therein except by agreement of all parties involved in the complaint with the permission of the court, and the Service shall endeavor to bring about a voluntary settlement between the parties.

Sec. 206. (a) Whenever the Attorney General has reasonable cause to believe that any person or group of persons is engaged in a pattern or practice of resistance to the full enjoyment of any of the rights secured by this title, and that the pattern or practice is of such a nature and is intended to deny the full exercise of the rights herein described, the Attorney General may bring a civil action in the appropriate district court of the United States by filing with it a complaint (1) signed by him (or in his absence the Acting Attorney General), (2) setting forth facts pertaining to such pattern or practice, and (3) requesting such preventive relief, including an application for a permanent or temporary injunction, restraining order or other order against the person or persons responsible for such pattern or practice, as he deems necessary to insure the full enjoyment of the rights herein described. . . .

Sec. 207. (a) The district courts of the United States shall have jurisdiction of proceedings instituted pursuant to this title and shall exercise the same without regard to whether the aggrieved party shall have exhausted any administrative or other remedies that may be provided by law. . . .

TITLE III: DESEGREGATION OF PUBLIC FACILITIES

Sec. 301. (a) Whenever the Attorney General receives a complaint in writing signed by an individual to the effect that he is being deprived of or threatened with the loss of his right to the equal protection of the laws, on account of his race, color, religion, or national origin, by being denied equal utilization of any public facility which is owned, operated, or managed by or on behalf of any State or subdivision thereof, other than a public school or public college as defined in section 401 of title IV hereof, and the Attorney General believes the complaint is meritorious and certifies that the signer or signers of such complaint are unable, in his judgment, to initiate and maintain appropriate legal proceedings for relief and that the institution of an action will materially further the orderly progress of desegregation in public facilities, the Attorney General is authorized to institute for or in the name of the United States a civil action in any appropriate district court of the United States against such parties and for such relief as may be appropriate, and such court shall have and shall exercise jurisdiction of proceedings instituted pursuant to this section. The Attorney General may implead as defendants such additional parties as are or become necessary to the grant of effective relief hereunder.

(b) The Attorney General may deem a person or persons unable to initiate and maintain appropriate legal proceedings within the meaning of subsection (a) of this section when such person or persons are unable, either directly or through other interested persons or organizations, to bear the expense of the litigation or to obtain effective legal representation; or whenever he is satisfied that the institution of such litigation would jeopardize the personal safety, employment, or economic standing of such person or persons, their families, or their property.

Sec. 302. In any action or proceeding under this title the United States shall be liable for costs, including a reasonable attorney's fee, the same as a private person.

Sec. 303. Nothing in this title shall affect adversely the right of any person to sue for or obtain relief in any court against discrimination in any facility covered by this title. . . .

TITLE IV: DESEGREGATION OF PUBLIC EDUCATION
DEFINITIONS

Survey and Report of Educational Opportunities

Sec. 402. The Commissioner shall conduct a survey and make a report to the President and the Congress, within two years of the enactment of this title,

concerning the lack of availability of equal educational opportunities for individuals by reason of race, color, religion, or national origin in public educational institutions at all levels in the United States, its territories and
possessions, and the District of Columbia.

Technical Assistance

Sec. 403. The Commissioner is authorized, upon the application of any
school board, State, municipality, school district, or other governmental unit
legally responsible for operating a public school or schools, to render technical
assistance to such applicant in the preparation, adoption, and implementation
of plans for the desegregation of public schools. Such technical assistance may,
among other activities, include making available to such agencies information
regarding effective methods of coping with special educational problems occasioned by desegregation, and making available to such agencies personnel of
the Office of Education or other persons specially equipped to advise and assist
them in coping with such problems.

Training Institutes

Sec. 404. The Commissioner is authorized to arrange, through grants or
contracts, with institutions of higher education for the operation of short-term
or regular session institutes for special training designed to improve the ability
of teachers, supervisors, counselors, and other elementary or secondary school
personnel to deal effectively with special educational problems occasioned by
desegregation. Individuals who attend such an institute on a full-time basis
may be paid stipends for the period of their attendance at such institute in
amounts specified by the Commissioner in regulations, including allowances
for travel to attend such institute.

Grants

Sec. 405. (a) The Commissioner is authorized, upon application of a school
board, to make grants to such board to pay, in whole or in part, the cost of—
(1) giving to teachers and other school personnel inservice training in dealing with problems incident to desegregation, and (2) employing specialists to
advise in problems incident to desegregation.

(b) In determining whether to make a grant, and in fixing the amount
thereof and the terms and conditions on which it will be made, the Commissioner shall take into consideration the amount available for grants under
this section and the other applications which are pending before him; the
financial condition of the applicant and the other resources available to it; the
nature, extent, and gravity of its problems incident to desegregation; and such
other factors as he finds relevant.

Payments

Sec. 406. Payments pursuant to a grant or contract under this title may be made (after necessary adjustments on account of previously made overpayments or underpayments) in advance or by way of reimbursement, and in such installments, as the Commissioner may determine.

Suits by the Attorney General

Sec. 407. (a) Whenever the Attorney General receives a complaint in writing—

(1) signed by a parent or group of parents to the effect that his or their minor children, as members of a class of persons similarly situated, are being deprived by a school board of the equal protection of the laws, or (2) signed by an individual, or his parent, to the effect that he has been denied admission to or not permitted to continue in attendance at a public college by reason of race, color, religion, or national origin, and the Attorney General believes the complaint is meritorious and certifies that the signer or signers of such complaint are unable, in his judgment, to initiate and maintain appropriate legal proceedings for relief and that the institution of an action will materially further the orderly achievement of desegregation in public education, the Attorney General is authorized, after giving notice of such complaint to the appropriate school board or college authority and after certifying that he is satisfied that such board or authority has had a reasonable time to adjust the conditions alleged in such complaint, to institute for or in the name of the United States a civil action in any appropriate district court of the United States against such parties and for such relief as may be appropriate, and such court shall have and shall exercise jurisdiction of proceedings instituted pursuant to this section, provided that nothing herein shall empower any official or court of the United States to issue any order seeking to achieve a racial balance in any school by requiring the transportation of pupils or students from one school to another or one school district to another in order to achieve such racial balance, or otherwise enlarge the existing power of the court to insure compliance with constitutional standards. The Attorney General may implead as defendants such additional parties as are or become necessary to the grant of effective relief hereunder.

(b) The Attorney General may deem a person or persons unable to initiate and maintain appropriate legal proceedings within the meaning of subsection (a) of this section when such person or persons are unable, either directly or through other interested persons or organizations, to bear the expense of the litigation or to obtain effective legal representation; or whenever he is satisfied that the institution of such litigation would jeopardize the personal safety, employment, or economic standing of such person or persons, their families, or their property. . . .

TITLE V: COMMISSION ON CIVIL RIGHTS

Rules of Procedure of the Commission Hearings

Sec. 102. (a) At least thirty days prior to the commencement of any hearing, the Commission shall cause to be published in the Federal Register notice of the date on which such hearing is to commence, the place at which it is to be held and the subject of the hearing. The Chairman, or one designated by him to act as Chairman at a hearing of the Commission, shall announce in an opening statement the subject of the hearing.

(b) A copy of the Commission's rules shall be made available to any witness before the Commission, and a witness compelled to appear before the Commission or required to produce written or other matter shall be served with a copy of the Commission's rules at the time of service of the subpoena.

(c) Any person compelled to appear in person before the Commission shall be accorded the right to be accompanied and advised by counsel, who shall have the right to subject his client to reasonable examination, and to make objections on the record and to argue briefly the basis for such objections. The Commission shall proceed with reasonable dispatch to conclude any hearing in which it is engaged. Due regard shall be had for the convenience and necessity of witnesses.

(d) The Chairman or Acting Chairman may punish breaches of order and decorum by censure and exclusion from the hearings.

(e) If the Commission determines that evidence or testimony at any hearing may tend to defame, degrade, or incriminate any person, it shall receive such evidence or testimony or summary of such evidence of testimony in executive session. The Commission shall afford any person defamed, degraded, or incriminated by such evidence or testimony an opportunity to appear and be heard in executive session, with a reasonable number of additional witnesses requested by him, before deciding to use such evidence or testimony. In the event the Commission determines to release or use such evidence or testimony in such manner as to reveal publicly the identity of the person defamed, degraded, or incriminated, such evidence or testimony, prior to such public release or use, shall be given at a public session, and the Commission shall afford such person an opportunity to appear as a voluntary witness or to file a sworn statement in his behalf and to submit brief and pertinent sworn statements of others. The Commission shall receive and dispose of requests from such person to subpoena additional witnesses.

(f) . . . the Chairman shall receive and the Commission shall dispose of requests to subpoena additional witnesses.

(g) No evidence or testimony or summary of evidence or testimony taken in executive session may be released or used in public sessions without the consent of the Commission. Whoever releases or uses in public without the consent of the Commission such evidence or testimony taken in executive session shall be fined not more than $1,000, or imprisoned for not more than one year.

"(h) In the discretion of the Commission, witnesses may submit brief and pertinent sworn statements in writing for inclusion in the record. The Commission shall determine the pertinency of testimony and evidence adduced at its hearings.

"(i) Every person who submits data or evidence shall be entitled to retain or, on payment of lawfully prescribed costs, procure a copy or transcript thereof, except that a witness in a hearing held in executive session may for good cause be limited to inspection of the official transcript of his testimony. Transcript copies of public sessions may be obtained by the public upon the payment of the cost thereof. An accurate transcript shall be made of the testimony of all witnesses at all hearings, either public or executive sessions, of the Commission or of any subcommittee thereof. . . .

(k) The Commission shall not issue any subpoena for the attendance and testimony of witnesses or for the production of written or other matter which would require the presence of the party subpoenaed at a hearing to be held outside of the State wherein the witness is found or resides or is domiciled or transacts business, or has appointed an agent for receipt of service of process except that, in any event, the Commission may issue subpoenas for the attendance and testimony of witnesses and the production of written or other matter at a hearing held within fifty miles of the place where the witness is found or resides or is domiciled or transacts business or has appointed an agent for receipt of service of process.

(l) The Commission shall separately state and currently publish in the Federal Register (1) descriptions of its central and field organization including the established places at which, and methods whereby, the public may secure information or make requests; (2) statements of the general course and method by which its functions are channeled and determined, and (3) rules adopted as authorized by law. No person shall in any manner be subject to or required to resort to rules, organization, or procedure not so published." . . .

Duties of the Commission

Sec. 104. (a) The Commission shall—

(1) investigate allegations in writing under oath or affirmation that certain citizens of the United States are being deprived of their right to vote and have

that vote counted by reason of their color, race, religion, or national origin; which writing, under oath or affirmation, shall set forth the facts upon which such belief or beliefs are based;

(2) study and collect information concerning legal developments constituting a denial of equal protection of the laws under the Constitution because of race, color, religion or national origin or in the administration of justice;

(3) appraise the laws and policies of the Federal Government with respect to denials of equal protection of the laws under the Constitution because of race, color, religion or national origin or in the administration of justice;

(4) serve as a national clearinghouse for information in respect to denials of equal protection of the laws because of race, color, religion or national origin, including but not limited to the fields of voting, education, housing, employment, the use of public facilities, and transportation, or in the administration of justice;

(5) investigate allegations, made in writing and under oath or affirmation, that citizens of the United States are unlawfully being accorded or denied the right to vote, or to have their votes properly counted, in any election of presidential electors, Members of the United States Senate, or of the House of Representatives, as a result of any patterns or practice of fraud or discrimination in the conduct of such election; and

(6) Nothing in this or any other Act shall be construed as authorizing the Commission, its Advisory Committees, or any person under its supervision or control to inquire into or investigate any membership practices or internal operations of any fraternal organization, any college or university fraternity or sorority, any private club or any religious organization. . . .

(f) The Commission, or on the authorization of the Commission any subcommittee of two or more members, at least one of whom shall be of each major political party, may, for the purpose of carrying out the provisions of this Act, hold such hearings and act at such times and places as the Commission or such authorized subcommittee may deem advisable. Subpoenas for the attendance and testimony of witnesses or the production of written or other matter may be issued in accordance with the rules of the Commission as contained in section 102 (j) and (k) of this Act, over the signature of the Chairman of the Commission or of such subcommittee, and may be served by any person designated by such Chairman. The holding of hearings by the Commission, or the appointment of a subcommittee to hold hearings pursuant to this subparagraph, must be approved by a majority of the Commission, or by a majority of the members present at a meeting at which at least a quorum of four members is present.

(g) In case of contumacy or refusal to obey a subpoena, any district court of the United States or the United States court of any territory or possession, or the District Court of the United States for the District of Columbia, within the jurisdiction of which the inquiry is carried on or within the jurisdiction of which said person guilty of contumacy or refusal to obey is found or resides or is domiciled or transacts business, or has appointed an agent for receipt of service of process, upon application by the Attorney General of the United States shall have jurisdiction to issue to such person an order requiring such person to appear before the Commission or a subcommittee thereof, there to produce pertinent, relevant and nonprivileged evidence if so ordered, or there to give testimony touching the matter under investigation; and any failure to obey such order of the court may be punished by said court as a contempt thereof. . . .

TITLE VI: NONDISCRIMINATION IN FEDERALLY ASSISTED PROGRAMS

Sec. 601. No person in the United States shall, on the ground of race, color, or national origin, be excluded from participation in, be denied the benefits of, or be subjected to discrimination under any program or activity receiving Federal financial assistance.

Sec. 602. Each Federal department and agency which is empowered to extend Federal financial assistance to any program or activity, by way of grant, loan, or contract other than a contract of insurance or guaranty, is authorized and directed to effectuate the provisions of section 601 with respect to such program or activity by issuing rules, regulations, or orders of general applicability which shall be consistent with achievement of the objectives of the statute authorizing the financial assistance in connection with which the action is taken. No such rule, regulation, or order shall become effective unless and until approved by the President. Compliance with any requirement adopted pursuant to this section may be effected (1) by the termination of or refusal to grant or to continue assistance under such program or activity to any recipient as to whom there has been an express finding on the record, after opportunity for hearing, of a failure to comply with such requirement, but such termination or refusal shall be limited to the particular political entity, or part thereof, or other recipient as to whom such a finding has been made and, shall be limited in its effect to the particular program, or part thereof, in which such non-compliance has been so found, or (2) by any other means authorized by law: Provided, however, That no such action shall be taken until the department or agency concerned has advised the appropriate person or persons of the failure to comply with the requirement and has determined that compliance cannot be secured by voluntary means. In the case of any action terminating, or refusing to grant or continue, assistance because of failure to comply with a requirement imposed pursuant to this section, the head of the federal department or agency shall file with the committees of the House and Senate having legislative jurisdiction over the program or activity involved a full written report of the circumstances and the grounds for such action. No such action shall become effective until thirty days have elapsed after the filing of such report.

Sec. 603. Any department or agency action taken pursuant to section 602 shall be subject to such judicial review as may otherwise be provided by law for similar action taken by such department or agency on other grounds. In the case of action, not otherwise subject to judicial review, terminating or refusing to grant or to continue financial assistance upon a finding of failure to comply with any requirement imposed pursuant to section 602, any person aggrieved (including any State or political subdivision thereof and any agency of either) may obtain judicial review of such action in accordance with section 10 of the Administrative Procedure Act, and such action shall not be deemed committed to unreviewable agency discretion within the meaning of that section.

Sec. 604. Nothing contained in this title shall be construed to authorize action under this title by any department or agency with respect to any employment practice of any employer, employment agency, or labor organization except where a primary objective of the Federal financial assistance is to provide employment.

Sec. 605. Nothing in this title shall add to or detract from any existing authority with respect to any program or activity under which Federal financial assistance is extended by way of a contract of insurance or guaranty.

TITLE VII: EQUAL EMPLOYMENT OPPORTUNITY

Discrimination Because of Race, Color, Religion, Sex, or National Origin

Sec. 703. (a) It shall be an unlawful employment practice for an employer—

(1) to fail or refuse to hire or to discharge any individual, or otherwise to discriminate against any individual with respect to his compensation, terms, conditions, or privileges of employment, because of such individual's race, color, religion, sex, or national origin; or

(2) to limit, segregate, or classify his employees in any way which would deprive or tend to deprive any individual of employment opportunities or otherwise adversely affect his status as an employee, because of such individual's race, color, religion, sex, or national origin.

(b) It shall be an unlawful employment practice for an employment agency to fail or refuse to refer for employment, or otherwise to discriminate against, any individual because of his race, color, religion, sex, or national origin, or to classify or refer for employment any individual on the basis of his race, color, religion, sex, or national origin.

(c) It shall be an unlawful employment practice for a labor organization—

(1) to exclude or to expel from its membership, or otherwise to discriminate against, any individual because of his race, color, religion, sex, or national origin;

(2) to limit, segregate, or classify its membership, or to classify or fail or refuse to refer for employment any individual, in any way which would deprive or tend to deprive any individual of employment opportunities, or would limit such employment opportunities or otherwise adversely affect his status as an employee or as an applicant for employment, because of such individual's race, color, religion, sex, or national origin; or

(3) to cause or attempt to cause an employer to discriminate against an individual in violation of this section.

(d) It shall be an unlawful employment practice for any employer, labor organization, or joint labor-management committee controlling apprenticeship or other training or retraining, including on-the-job training programs to discriminate against any individual because of his race, color, religion, sex, or national origin in admission to, or employment in, any program established to provide apprenticeship or other training.

(e) Notwithstanding any other provision of this title, (1) it shall not be an unlawful employment practice for an employer to hire and employ employees, for an employment agency to classify, or refer for employment any individual, for a labor organization to classify its membership or to classify or refer for employment any individual, or for an employer, labor organization, or joint labor-management committee controlling apprenticeship or other training or retraining programs to admit or employ any individual in any such program, on the basis of his religion, sex, or national origin in those certain instances where religion, sex, or national origin is a bona fide occupational qualification reasonably necessary to the normal operation of that particular business or enterprise, and (2) it shall not be an unlawful employment practice for a school, college, university, or other educational institution or institution of learning to hire and employ employees of a particular religion if such school, college, university, or other educational institution or institution of learning is, in whole or in substantial part, owned, supported, controlled, or managed by a particular religion or by a particular religious corporation, association, or society, or if the curriculum of such school, college, university, or other educational institution or institution of learning is directed toward the propagation of a particular religion.

(f) As used in this title, the phrase "unlawful employment practice" shall not be deemed to include any action or measure taken by an employer, labor organization, joint labor-management committee, or employment agency with respect to an individual who is a member of the Communist Party of the United States or of any other organization required to register as a Communist-action or Communist-front organization by final order of the Subversive Activities Control Board pursuant to the Subversive Activities Control Act of 1950.

(g) Notwithstanding any other provision of this title, it shall not be an unlawful employment practice for an employer to fail or refuse to hire and employ any individual for any position, for an employer to discharge any individual from any position, or for an employment agency to fail or refuse to refer any individual for employment in any position, or for a labor organization to fail or refuse to refer any individual for employment in any position, if—

(1) the occupancy of such position, or access to the premises in or upon which any part of the duties of such position is performed or is to be performed, is subject to any requirement imposed in the interest of the national security of the United States under any security program in effect pursuant to or administered under any statute of the United States or any Executive order of the President; and (2) such individual has not fulfilled or has ceased to fulfill that requirement.

(h) Notwithstanding any other provision of this title, it shall not be an unlawful employment practice for an employer to apply different standards of compensation, or different terms, conditions, or privileges of employment pursuant to a bona fide seniority or merit system, or a system which measures earnings by quantity or quality of production or to employees who work in different locations, provided that such differences are not the result of an intention to discriminate because of race, color, religion, sex, or national origin, nor shall it be an unlawful employment practice for an employer to give and to act upon the results of any professionally developed ability test provided that such test, its administration or action upon the results is not designed, intended or used to discriminate because of race, color, religion, sex or national origin. It shall not be an unlawful employment practice under this title for any employer to differentiate upon the basis of sex in determining the amount of the wages or compensation paid or to be paid to employees of such employer if such differentiation is authorized by the provisions of section 6(d) of the Fair Labor Standards Act of 1938, as amended.

(i) Nothing contained in this title shall apply to any business or enterprise on or near an Indian reservation with respect to any publicly announced employment practice of such business or enterprise under which a preferential treatment is given to any individual because he is an Indian living on or near a reservation.

(j) Nothing contained in this title shall be interpreted to require any employer, employment agency, labor organization, or joint labor-management committee subject to this title to grant preferential treatment to any individual or to any group because of the race, color, religion, sex, or national origin of such individual or group on account of an imbalance which may exist with respect to the total number or percentage of persons of any race, color, religion, sex, or national origin employed by any employer, referred or classified for employment by any employment agency or labor organization, admitted to membership or classified by any labor organization, or admitted to, or employed in, any apprenticeship or other training program, in comparison with the total number or percentage of persons of such race, color, religion, sex, or national origin in any community, State, section, or other area, or in the available work force in any community, State, section, or other area.

Other Unlawful Employment Practices

Sec. 704. (a) It shall be an unlawful employment practice for an employer to discriminate against any of his employees or applicants for employment, for an employment agency to discriminate against any individual, or for a labor organization to discriminate against any member thereof or applicant for membership, because he has opposed any practice made an unlawful employment practice by this title, or because he has made a charge, testified, assisted, or participated in any manner in an investigation, proceeding, or hearing under this title.

(b) It shall be an unlawful employment practice for an employer, labor organization, or employment agency to print or publish or cause to be printed or published any notice or advertisement relating to employment by such an employer or membership in or any classification or referral for employment by such a labor organization, or relating to any classification or referral for employment by such an employment agency, indicating any preference, limitation, specification, or discrimination, based on race, color, religion, sex, or national origin, except that such a notice or advertisement may indicate a preference, limitation, specification, or discrimination based on religion, sex, or national origin when religion, sex, or national origin is a bona fide occupational qualification for employment.

Equal Employment Opportunity Commission

Sec. 705. (a) There is hereby created a Commission to be known as the Equal Employment Opportunity Commission, which shall be composed of five members, not more than three of whom shall be members of the same political party, who shall be appointed by the President by and with the advice and consent of the Senate. One of the original members shall be appointed for a term of one year, one for a term of two years, one for a term of three years, one for a term of four years, and one for a term of five years, beginning from the date of enactment of this title, but their successors shall be appointed for terms of five years each, except that any individual chosen to fill a vacancy shall be appointed only for the unexpired term of the member whom he shall succeed. The President shall designate one member to serve as Chairman of the Commission, and one member to serve as Vice Chairman. The Chairman shall be responsible on behalf of the Commission for the administrative operations of the Commission, and shall appoint, in accordance with the civil service laws, such officers, agents, attorneys, and employees as it deems necessary to assist it in the performance of its functions and to fix their compensation in accordance with the Classification Act of 1949, as amended. The Vice Chairman shall act as Chairman in the absence or disability of the Chairman or in the event of a vacancy in that office. . . .

(d) The Commission shall at the close of each fiscal year report to the Congress and to the President concerning the action it has taken; the names, salaries, and duties of all individuals in its employ and the moneys it has disbursed; and shall make such further reports on the cause of and means of eliminating discrimination and such recommendations for further legislation as may appear desirable. . . .

(f) The principal office of the Commission shall be in or near the District of Columbia, but it may meet or exercise any or all its powers at any other place. The Commission may establish such regional or State offices as it deems necessary to accomplish the purpose of this title.

(g) The Commission shall have power—

(1) to cooperate with and, with their consent, utilize regional, State, local, and other agencies, both public and private, and individuals;

(2) to pay to witnesses whose depositions are taken or who are summoned before the Commission or any of its agents the same witness and mileage fees as are paid to witnesses in the courts of the United States;

(3) to furnish to persons subject to this title such technical assistance as they may request to further their compliance with this title or an order issued thereunder;

(4) upon the request of (i) any employer, whose employees or some of them, or (ii) any labor organization, whose members or some of them, refuse or threaten to refuse to cooperate in effectuating the provisions of this title, to assist in such effectuation by conciliation or such other remedial action as is provided by this title;

(5) to make such technical studies as are appropriate to effectuate the purposes and policies of this title and to make the results of such studies available to the public;

(6) to refer matters to the Attorney General with recommendations for intervention in a civil action brought by an aggrieved party under section 706, or for the institution of a civil action by the Attorney General under section 707, and to advise, consult, and assist the Attorney General on such matters.

(h) Attorneys appointed under this section may, at the direction of the Commission, appear for and represent the Commission in any case in court.

(i) The Commission shall, in any of its educational or promotional activities, cooperate with other departments and agencies in the performance of such educational and promotional activities.

(j) All officers, agents, attorneys, and employees of the Commission shall be subject to the provisions of section 9 of the Act of August 2, 1939, as amended (the Hatch Act), notwithstanding any exemption contained in such section.

Prevention of Unlawful Employment Practices

Sec. 706. (a) Whenever it is charged in writing under oath by a person claiming to be aggrieved, or a written charge has been filed by a member of the Commission where he has reasonable cause to believe a violation of this title has occurred (and such charge sets forth the facts upon which it is based) that an employer, employment agency, or labor organization has engaged in an unlawful employment practice, the Commission shall furnish such employer, employment agency, or labor organization (hereinafter referred to as the "respondent") with a copy of such charge and shall make an investigation of such charge, provided that such charge shall not be made public by the Commission. If the Commission shall determine, after such investigation, that there is reasonable cause to believe that the charge is true, the Commission shall endeavor to eliminate any such alleged unlawful employment practice by informal methods of conference, conciliation, and persuasion. Nothing said or done during and as a part of such endeavors may be made public by the Commission without the written consent of the parties, or used as evidence in a subsequent proceeding. Any officer or employee of the Commission, who shall make public in any manner whatever any information in violation of this subsection shall be deemed guilty of a misdemeanor . . .

(b) In the case of an alleged unlawful employment practice occurring in a State, or political subdivision of a State, which has a State or local law prohibiting the unlawful employment practice alleged and establishing or authorizing a State or local authority to grant or seek relief from such practice or to institute criminal proceedings with respect thereto upon receiving notice thereof, no charge may be filed under subsection (a) by the person aggrieved before the expiration of sixty days after proceedings have been commenced under the State or local law, unless such proceedings have been earlier terminated, provided that such sixty-day period shall be extended to one hundred and twenty days during the first year after the effective date of such State or local law. If any requirement for the commencement of such proceedings is imposed by a State or local authority other than a requirement of the filing of a written and signed statement of the facts upon which the proceeding is based, the proceeding shall be deemed to have been commenced for the purposes of this subsection at the time such statement is sent by registered mail to the appropriate State or local authority.

(c) In the case of any charge filed by a member of the Commission alleging an unlawful employment practice occurring in a State or political subdivision of a State, which has a State or local law prohibiting the practice alleged and establishing or authorizing a State or local authority to grant or seek relief from such practice or to institute criminal proceedings with respect thereto upon receiving notice thereof, the Commission shall, before taking any action with respect to such charge, notify the appropriate State or local officials and, upon request, afford them a reasonable time, but not less than sixty days (provided that such sixty-day period shall be extended to one hundred and twenty days during the first year after the effective day of such State or local law), unless a shorter period is requested, to act under such State or local law to remedy the practice alleged. . . .

(e) If within thirty days after a charge is filed with the Commission or within thirty days after expiration of any period of reference under subsection (c) (except that in either case such period may be extended to not more than sixty days upon a determination by the Commission that further efforts to secure voluntary compliance are warranted), the Commission has been unable to obtain voluntary compliance with this title, the Commission shall so notify the person aggrieved and a civil action may, within thirty days thereafter, be brought against the respondent named in the charge (1) by the person claiming to be aggrieved, or (2) if such charge was filed by a member of the Commission, by any person whom the charge alleges was aggrieved by the alleged unlawful employment practice. Upon application by the complainant and in such circumstances as the court may deem just, the court may appoint an attorney for such complainant and may authorize the commencement of the action without the payment of fees, costs, or security. Upon timely application, the court may, in its discretion, permit the Attorney General to intervene in such civil action if he certifies that the case is of general public importance. Upon request, the court may, in its discretion, stay further proceedings. . . .

(g) If the court finds that the respondent has intentionally engaged in or is intentionally engaging in an unlawful employment practice charged in the complaint, the court may enjoin the respondent from engaging in such unlawful employment practice, and order such affirmative action as may be appropriate, which may include reinstatement or hiring of employees, with or without back pay (payable by the employer, employment agency, or labor organization, as the case may be, responsible for the unlawful employment practice). Interim earnings or amounts earnable with reasonable diligence by the person or persons discriminated against shall operate to reduce the back pay otherwise allowable. No order of the court shall require the admission or reinstatement of an individual as a member of a union or the hiring, reinstatement, or promotion of an individual as an employee, or the payment to him of any back pay, if such individual was refused admission, suspended, or expelled or was refused employment or advancement or was suspended or discharged for any reason other than discrimination on account of race, color, religion, sex or national origin or in violation of section 704(a). . . .

Sec. 707. (a) Whenever the Attorney General has reasonable cause to believe that any person or group of persons is engaged in a pattern or practice of resistance to the full enjoyment of any of the rights secured by this title, and that the pattern or practice is of such a nature and is intended to deny the full exercise of the rights herein described, the Attorney General may bring a civil action in the appropriate district court of the United States by filing with it a complaint (1) signed by him (or in his absence the Acting Attorney General), (2) setting forth facts pertaining to such pattern or practice, and (3) requesting such relief, including an application for a permanent or temporary injunction, restraining order or other order against the person or persons responsible for such pattern or practice, as he deems necessary to insure the full enjoyment of the rights herein described. . . .

Effect on State Laws

Sec. 708. Nothing in this title shall be deemed to exempt or relieve any person from any liability, duty, penalty, or punishment provided by any present or future law of any State or political subdivision of a State, other than any such law which purports to require or permit the doing of any act which would be an unlawful employment practice under this title.

Investigations, Inspections, Records, State Agencies

(b) The Commission may cooperate with State and local agencies charged with the administration of State fair employment practices laws and, with the consent of such agencies, may for the purpose of carrying out its functions and duties under this title and within the limitation of funds appropriated specifically for such purpose, utilize the services of such agencies and their employees and, notwithstanding any other provision of law, may reimburse such agencies and their employees for services rendered to assist the Commission in carrying out this title. In furtherance of such cooperative efforts, the Commission may enter into written agreements with such State or local agencies and such agreements may include provisions under which the Commission shall refrain from processing a charge in any cases or class of cases specified in such agreements and under which no person may bring a civil action under section 706 in any cases or class of cases so specified, or under which the Commission shall relieve any person or class of persons in such State or locality from requirements imposed under this section. The Commission shall rescind any such agreement whenever it determines that the agreement no longer serves the interest of effective enforcement of this title.

(c) Except as provided in subsection (d), every employer, employment agency, and labor organization subject to this title shall (1) make and keep such records relevant to the determinations of whether unlawful employment practices have been or are being committed, (2) preserve such records for such periods, and (3) make such reports therefrom, as the Commission shall prescribe by regulation or order, after public hearing, as reasonable, necessary, or appropriate for the enforcement of this title or the regulations or orders thereunder. The Commission shall, by regulation, require each employer, labor organization, and joint labor-management committee subject to this title which controls an apprenticeship or other training program to maintain such records as are reasonably necessary to carry out the purpose of this title, including, but not limited to, a list of applicants who wish to participate in such program, including the chronological order in which such applications were received, and shall furnish to the Commission, upon request, a detailed description of the manner in which persons are selected to participate in the apprenticeship or other training program. Any employer, employment agency, labor organization, or joint labor-management committee which believes that the application to it of any regulation or order issued under this section would result in undue hardship may (1) apply to the Commission for an exemption from the application of such regulation or order, or (2) bring a civil action in the United States district court for the district where such records are kept. If the Commission or the court, as the case may be, finds that the application of the regulation or order to the employer, employment agency, or labor organization in question would impose an undue hardship, the Commission or the court, as the case may be, may grant appropriate relief.

(d) The provisions of subsection (c) shall not apply to any employer, employment agency, labor organization, or joint labor-management committee with respect to matters occurring in any State or political subdivision thereof which has a fair employment practice law during any period in which such employer, employment agency, labor organization, or joint labor-management committee is subject to such law, except that the Commission may require such notations on records which such employer, employment agency, labor organization, or joint labor-management committee keeps or is required to keep as are necessary because of differences in coverage or methods of enforcement between the State or local law and the provisions of this title. . . .

Investigatory Powers

Sec. 710. (a) For the purposes of any investigation of a charge filed under the authority contained in section 706, the Commission shall have authority to examine witnesses under oath and to require the production of documentary evidence relevant or material to the charge under investigation.

(b) If the respondent named in a charge filed under section 706 fails or refuses to comply with a demand of the Commission for permission to examine or to copy evidence in conformity with the provisions of section 709(a), or if any person required to comply with the provisions of section 709 (c) or (d) fails or refuses to do so, or if any person fails or refuses to comply with a demand by the Commission to give testimony under oath, the United States district court for the district in which such person is found, resides, or transacts business, shall, upon application of the Commission, have jurisdiction to issue to such person an order requiring him to comply with the provisions of section 709 (c) or (d) or to comply with the demand of the Commission, but the attendance of a witness may not be required outside the State where he is found, resides, or transacts business and the production of evidence may not be required outside the State where such evidence is kept.

(c) Within twenty days after the service upon any person charged under section 706 of a demand by the Commission for the production of documentary evidence or for permission to examine or to copy evidence in conformity with the provisions of section 709(a), such person may file in the district court of the United States for the judicial district in which he resides, is found, or transacts business, and serve upon the Commission a petition for an order of such court modifying or setting aside such demand. The time allowed for compliance with the demand in whole or in part as deemed proper and ordered by the court shall not run during the pendency of such petition in the court. Such petition shall specify each ground upon which the petitioner relies in seeking such relief, and may be based upon any failure of such demand to comply with the provisions of this title or with the limitations generally applicable to compulsory process or upon any constitutional or other legal right or privilege of such person. No objection which is not raised by such a petition may be urged in the defense to a proceeding initiated by the Commission under subsection (b) for enforcement of such a demand unless such proceeding is commenced by the Commission prior to the expiration of the twenty-day period, or unless the court determines that the defendant could not reasonably have been aware of the availability of such ground of objection.

(d) In any proceeding brought by the Commission under subsection (b), except as provided in subsection (c) of this section, the defendant may petition the court for an order modifying or setting aside the demand of the Commission.

Sec. 711. (a) Every employer, employment agency, and labor organization, as the case may be, shall post and keep posted in conspicuous places upon its premises where notices to employees, applicants for employment, and members are customarily posted a notice to be prepared or approved by the Commission setting forth excerpts from or, summaries of, the pertinent provisions of this title and information pertinent to the filing of a complaint. . . .

Veterans' Preference

Sec. 712. Nothing contained in this title shall be construed to repeal or modify any Federal, State, territorial, or local law creating special rights or preference for veterans.

Rules and Regulations

(b) In any action or proceeding based on any alleged unlawful employment practice, no person shall be subject to any liability or punishment for or on account of (1) the commission by such person of an unlawful employment practice if he pleads and proves that the act or omission complained of was in good faith, in conformity with, and in reliance on any written interpretation or opinion of the Commission, or (2) the failure of such person to publish and file any information required by any provision of this title if he pleads and proves that he failed to publish and file such information in good faith, in conformity with the instructions of the Commission issued under this title regarding the filing of such information. Such a defense, if established, shall be a bar to the action or proceeding, notwithstanding that (A) after such act or omission, such interpretation or opinion is modified or rescinded or is determined by judicial authority to be invalid or of no legal effect, or (B) after publishing or filing the description and annual reports, such publication or filing is determined by judicial authority not to be in conformity with the requirements of this title.

Forcibly Resisting the Commission or Its Representatives

. . . .

Special Study by Secretary of Labor

Sec. 715. The Secretary of Labor shall make a full and complete study of the factors which might tend to result in discrimination in employment because of age and of the consequences of such discrimination on the economy and individuals affected. The Secretary of Labor shall make a report to the Congress . . . containing the results of such study and shall include in such report such recommendations for legislation to prevent arbitrary discrimination in employment because of age as he determines advisable.

Effective Date

(c) The President shall, as soon as feasible after the enactment of this title, convene one or more conferences for the purpose of enabling the leaders of groups whose members will be affected by this title to become familiar with the rights afforded and obligations imposed by its provisions, and for the purpose of making plans which will result in the fair and effective administration of this title when all of its provisions become effective. The President shall invite the participation in such conference or conferences of (1) the members of the President's Committee on Equal Employment Opportunity, (2) the members of the Commission on Civil Rights, (3) representatives of State and local agencies engaged in furthering equal employment opportunity, (4) representatives of private agencies engaged in furthering equal employment opportunity, and (5) representatives of employers, labor organizations, and employment agencies who will be subject to this title.

TITLE VIII: REGISTRATION AND VOTING STATISTICS

Sec. 801. The Secretary of Commerce shall promptly conduct a survey to compile registration and voting statistics in such geographic areas as may be recommended by the Commission on Civil Rights. Such a survey and compilation shall, to the extent recommended by the Commission on Civil Rights, only include a count of persons of voting age by race, color, and national origin, and determination of the extent to which such persons are registered to vote, and have voted in any statewide primary or general election in which the Members of the United States House of Representatives are nominated or elected, since January 1, 1960. Such information shall also be collected and compiled in connection with the Nineteenth Decennial Census, and at such other times as the Congress may prescribe. . . . No person shall be compelled to disclose his race, color, national origin, or questioned about his political party affiliation, how he voted, or the reasons therefore, nor shall any penalty be imposed for his failure or refusal to make such disclosure. Every person interrogated orally, by written survey or questionnaire or by any other means with respect to such information shall be fully advised with respect to his right to fail or refuse to furnish such information.

TITLE IX: INTERVENTION AND PROCEDURE AFTER REMOVAL IN CIVIL RIGHTS CASES

. . . Sec. 902. Whenever an action has been commenced in any court of the United States seeking relief from the denial of equal protection of the laws under the fourteenth amendment to the Constitution on account of race, color, religion, or national origin, the Attorney General for or in the name of the United States may intervene in such action upon timely application if the Attorney General certifies that the case is of general public importance. In such action the United States shall be entitled to the same relief as if it had instituted the action.

TITLE X: ESTABLISHMENT OF COMMUNITY RELATIONS SERVICE

Sec. 1001. (a) There is hereby established in and as a part of the Department of Commerce a Community Relations Service (hereinafter referred to as the "Service"), which shall be headed by a Director who shall be appointed by the President with the advice and consent of the Senate for a term of four years. The Director is authorized to appoint, subject to the civil service laws and regulations, such other personnel as may be necessary to enable the Service to carry out its functions and duties, and to fix their compensation . . .

Sec. 1002. It shall be the function of the Service to provide assistance to communities and persons therein in resolving disputes, disagreements, or difficulties relating to discriminatory practices based on race, color, or national origin which impair the rights of persons in such communities under the Constitution or laws of the United States or which affect or may affect interstate commerce. The Service may offer its services in cases of such disputes, disagreements, or difficulties whenever, in its judgment, peaceful relations among the citizens of the community involved are threatened thereby, and it may offer its services either upon its own motion or upon the request of an appropriate State or local official or other interested person.

Sec. 1003. (a) The Service shall, whenever possible, in performing its functions, seek and utilize the cooperation of appropriate State or local, public, or private agencies.

(b) The activities of all officers and employees of the Service in providing conciliation assistance shall be conducted in confidence and without publicity, and the Service shall hold confidential any information acquired in the regular performance of its duties upon the understanding that it would be so held. No officer or employee of the Service shall engage in the performance of investigative or prosecuting functions of any department or agency in any litigation arising out of a dispute in which he acted on behalf of the Service. Any officer or other employee of the Service, who shall make public in any manner whatever any information in violation of this subsection, shall be deemed guilty of a misdemeanor . . .

Sec. 1004. . . . the Director shall, on or before January 31 of each year, submit to the Congress a report of the activities of the Service during the preceding fiscal year.

TITLE XI: MISCELLANEOUS

Sec. 1101. In any proceeding for criminal contempt arising under title II, III, IV, V, VI, or VII of this Act, the accused, upon demand therefor, shall be entitled to a trial by jury . . .

Sec. 1103. Nothing in this Act shall be construed to deny, impair, or otherwise affect any right or authority of the Attorney General or of the United States or any agency or officer thereof under existing law to institute or intervene in any action or proceeding.

Sec. 1104. Nothing contained in any title of this Act shall be construed as indicating an intent on the part of Congress to occupy the field in which any such title operates to the exclusion of State laws on the same subject matter, nor shall any provision of this Act be construed as invalidating any provision of State law unless such provision is inconsistent with any of the purposes of this Act, or any provision thereof. . . .

Approved July 2, 1964.

See 78 *Statues at Large*, 241.

96.

FANNIE LOU HAMER SPEAKS FOR THE MISSISSIPPI FREEDOM DEMOCRATIC PARTY AT THE DEMOCRATIC NATIONAL CONVENTION (1964)

Despite the passage of the Civil Rights Act of 1964, most black southerners were still excluded from the American political process as election day 1964 approached, and many were determined to change that. Hamer was a delegate of the Mississippi Freedom Democratic Party, which sought to displace the all-white Democratic delegation from Mississippi at the Democratic National Convention in Atlantic City in 1964. An uneducated sharecropper from the Delta, her speech was honest, unrehearsed, and delivered with emotion. It further demonstrated the need for political reform to give blacks a voice in the affairs of state and nation. Here are some of the more graphic excerpts.

June the 9th, 1963, I had attended a voter-registration workshop, was returning back to Mississippi. Ten of us was traveling by the Continental Trailway bus. When we got to [the town of] Winona, . . . I was carried to the county jail, and. . . . I was placed in a cell . . . where they had two Negro prisoners. The State Highway Patrolman ordered the first Negro to take the blackjack. The first Negro prisoner ordered me . . . to lay down on a bunk bed on my face, and I laid on my face. . . . I was beat by the first Negro until he was exhausted, and I was holding my hands behind me at that time on my left side because I suffered from polio when I was six years old. After the first Negro had beat until he was exhausted, the State Highway Patrolman ordered the second Negro to take the blackjack.

The second Negro began to beat and I began to . . . scream and one white man got up and began to beat me in my head and tell me to hush. . . .

All of this is on account we want to register, to become first-class citizens, and if the Freedom Democratic Party is not seated now, I question America, is this America, the land of the free [?] . . .

See Gary A. Donaldson, *The Second Reconstruction: A History of the Modern Civil Rights Movement* (Malabar, FL: Krieger, 2000), 105–107.

97.

THE ORGANIZATION OF AFRO-AMERICAN UNITY'S STATEMENT OF BASIC AIMS AND OBJECTIVES (1964)

In 1964, the year before his assassination, Malcolm X broke from the Nation of Islam and established the Organization of Afro-American Unity. John Henrik Clarke, a professor of History at Hunter College in Harlem and a close friend of Malcolm, wrote the OAAU's "Statement of Basic Aims and Objectives," which is herein excerpted.

We, the members of the Organization of Afro-American Unity gathered together in Harlem, New York. . . . Do hereby present this Charter.

I. ESTABLISHMENT

The Organization . . . shall include all people of African descent in the Western Hemisphere, as well as our brothers and sisters of the African continent.

II. SELF-DEFENSE

. . . We assert the Afro-American's right of self-defense.
The Constitution of the United States of America clearly affirms the right of every American citizen to bear arms. And as Americans, we will not give up a single right guaranteed under the Constitution. . . .

III. EDUCATION

. . . . The Organization . . . Must make the Afro-American community a more potent force for educational self-improvement.
. . . . We want Afro-American principals . . . We want Afro-American teachers . . . We want textbooks written by Afro-Americans. . . .

IV. POLITICS–ECONOMICS

. . . . The Organization . . . will organize the Afro-American community block by block to make the community aware of its power and potential; we will start immediately a voter-registration drive to make every unregistered voter in the Afro-American community an Independent voter; we propose to support and/or organize political clubs, to run Independent candidates for office, and to support any Afro-American already in office . . .

The Organization of Afro-American Unity will. . . . start a housing self-improvement program. We propose to support rent strikes . . .

V. SOCIAL

. . . . The Organization . . . believes that the Afro-American community must endeavor to do the major part of all charity work from within the community. . . .

Afro-Americans must. . . . take pride in the Afro-American community, for it is home and it is power.

VI. CULTURE

. . . . Our history and our culture were completely destroyed when we were forcibly brought to America in chains. And now it is important for us to know that our history did not begin with slavery's scars. . . .

Armed with the knowledge of our past, we can with confidence charter a course for our future. . . .

See John Henrik Clarke, ed., *Malcolm X: The Man and His Times* (New York: The Macmillan Company, 1969), 335–42.

98.

MALCOLM X'S IDEOLOGICAL TRANSFORMATION (1963–65)

The historical legacy of Malcolm X is controversial and complex. One of the fundamental ideologies of the Nation of Islam (NOI), which he had long preached, was black nationalism—the notion that African Americans must emigrate to Africa and set up a nation of their own. After he withdrew from the NOI, however, Malcolm modified his views on that issue somewhat, and consequently redefined the term "black nationalism." Here we see examples of his 1963 rhetoric as a spokesman for the NOI and his 1964 and 1965 modifications.

A desegregated theater or lunch counter won't solve our problems. Better jobs won't even solve our problems. An integrated cup of coffee isn't sufficient pay for 400 years of slave labor, and a better job in the white man's factory or position in his business is, at best, only a temporary solution. The only lasting or permanent solution is complete separation on some land that we can call our own.

The Honorable Elijah Muhammad teaches us that the race problem can easily be solved, just by sending these 22 million ex-slaves *back to our own homeland* where we can live in peace and harmony with our own kind. . . .—1963

I still believe that Mr. Muhammad's analysis of the problem is the most realistic, and that his solution is the best one. The means that I too believe the best solution is complete separation, with our people going back home, to our own African homeland.

But separation back to Africa is still a long-range program, and while it is yet to materialize, 22 million of our people are still here in America need better food, clothing, housing, education, and jobs *right now* . . . .

The political philosophy of black nationalism means: we must control the politics and politicians of our community. . . .
—1964

I used to define black nationalism as the idea that the black man should control the economy of his community, the politics of his community, and so forth. . . .

I had to do a lot of thinking and reappraising of my definition of black nationalism. . . .

[I]f you have noticed, I haven't been using the expression for several months. . . . I still would be hard pressed to give a specific definition of the over-all philosophy which I think is necessary for the liberation of the black people in this country.
—1965

See George Breitman, *The Last Year of Malcolm X: The Evolution of a Revolutionary* (New York: Pathfinder Press, 1967), 57, 59.

99.

THE "MOYNIHAN REPORT" (1965)

Daniel Patrick Moynihan, then assistant secretary of labor in the Lyndon Johnson administration, prepared this sociological study for the president at the height of the turbulent mid-1960s civil rights movement. In retrospect, it seems that Moynihan's report should not have been viewed as revolutionary, because it merely propounded what appears today to be common knowledge concerning the economic situation of African Americans contrasted with that of white Americans. At the time, however, it was seen as revolutionary because it proposed that the solution to the problem lay in the federal government taking responsibility for repairing the black family structure, which, Moynihan said, had been broken in the slave era and remained in disrepair ever since. Here are excerpts from the preface of the report.

In the decade that began with the school desegregation decision of the Supreme Court [*Brown v. Board of Education*, 1954], and ended with the passage of the Civil Rights Act of 1964, the demand of Negro Americans for full recognition of their civil rights was finally met.

The effort, no matter how savage and brutal, of some State and local governments to thwart the exercise of those rights is doomed. The nation will not put up with it—least of all the Negroes. . . .

The expectations of the Negro Americans will go beyond civil rights. . . . they will now expect that in the near future equal opportunities for them as a group will produce roughly equal results, as compared with other groups. This is not going to happen. Nor will it happen for generations to come unless a new and special effort is made. . . .

The racist virus in the American blood stream still afflicts us: Negroes will encounter serious personal prejudice for at least another generation. . . . three centuries of sometimes unimaginable mistreatment have taken their toll on the Negro people. The harsh fact is that as a group . . . in terms of ability to win out in the competitions of American life, they are not equal to most of those groups with which they will be competing. . . .

The most difficult fact for white Americans to understand is that in these terms the circumstances of the Negro American community in recent years has probably been getting *worse, not better*. . . . The gap between the Negro and most other groups in American society is widening.

The fundamental problem . . . is that of family structure. . . .

The thesis of this paper is that . . . measures that have worked in the past, or would work for most groups in the present, will not work here. A national effort is required . . . of the federal government in this area . . . : the establishment of a stable Negro family structure.

See Daniel Patrick Moynihan, *The Negro Family: The Case for National Action* (Washington, D.C.: Government Printing Office, 1965).

100.

THE VOTING RIGHTS ACT (1965)

Despite the lengthy attempt to enforce the Fifteenth Amendment in the Civil Rights Act of 1964, unresolved problems with black suffrage remained. Wanting to find the ultimate solution to these problems and dispense with the issue once and for all, President Johnson supported passage of a voting rights act that would leave no doubt about the constitutional right of African Americans to vote. This act represented the culmination of years of trial and error, and it succeeded in accomplishing Johnson's goal.

AN ACT To enforce the fifteenth amendment to the Constitution of the United States, and for other purposes.

Be it enacted by the Senate and House of Representatives of the United States of America in Congress assembled, That this Act shall be known as the "Voting Rights Act of 1965."

Sec. 2. No voting qualification or prerequisite to voting, or standard, practice, or procedure shall be imposed or applied by any State or political subdivision to deny or abridge the right of any citizen of the United States to vote on account of race or color.

Sec. 3. (a) Whenever the Attorney General institutes a proceeding under any statute to enforce the guarantees of the fifteenth amendment in any State or political subdivision the court shall authorize the appointment of Federal examiners by the United States Civil Service Commission in accordance with section 6 to serve for such period of time and for such political subdivisions as the court shall determine is appropriate to enforce the guarantees of the fifteenth amendment (1) as part of any interlocutory order if the court determines that the appointment of such examiners is necessary to enforce such guarantees or (2) as part of any final judgment if the court finds that violations of the fifteenth amendment justifying equitable relief have occurred in such State or subdivision: Provided, That the court need not authorize the appointment of examiners if any incidents of denial or abridgement of the right to vote on account of race or color (1) have been few in number and have been promptly and effectively corrected by State or local action, (2) the continuing effect of such incidents has been eliminated, and (3) there is no reasonable probability of their recurrence in the future.

(b) If in a proceeding instituted by the Attorney General under any statute to enforce the guarantees of the fifteenth amendment in any State or political subdivision the court finds that a test or device has been used for the purpose or with the effect of denying or abridging the right of any citizen of the United States to vote on account of race or color, it shall suspend the use of tests and devices in such State or political subdivisions as the court shall determine is appropriate and for such period as it deems necessary.

(c) If in any proceeding instituted by the Attorney General under any statute to enforce the guarantees of the fifteenth amendment in any State or political subdivision the court finds that violations of the fifteenth amendment justifying equitable relief have occurred within the territory of such State or political subdivision, the court, in addition to such relief as it may grant, shall retain jurisdiction for such period as it may deem appropriate and during such period no voting qualification or prerequisite to voting, or standard, practice, or procedure with respect to voting different from that in force or effect at the time the proceeding was commenced shall be enforced unless and until the court finds that such qualification, prerequisite, standard, practice, or procedure does not have the purpose and will not have the effect of denying or abridging the right to vote on account of race or color: Provided, That such qualification, prerequisite, standard, practice, or procedure may be enforced if the qualification, prerequisite, standard, practice, or procedure has been submitted by the chief legal officer or other appropriate official of such State or subdivision to the Attorney General and the Attorney General has not interposed an objection within sixty days after such submission, except that neither the court's finding nor the Attorney General's failure to object shall bar a subsequent action to enjoin enforcement of such qualification, prerequisite, standard, practice, or procedure.

Sec. 4. (a) To assure that the right of citizens of the United States to vote is not denied or abridged on account of race or color, no citizen shall be denied the right to vote in any Federal, State, or local election because of his failure to comply with any test or device in any State with respect to which the determinations have been made under subsection (b) or in any political subdivision with respect to which such determinations have been made as a separate unit, unless the United States District Court for the District of Columbia in an action for a declaratory judgment brought by such State or subdivision against the United States has determined that no such test or device has been used during the five years preceding the filing of the action for the purpose or with the effect of denying or abridging the right to vote on account of race or color: Provided, That no such declaratory judgment shall issue with respect to any plaintiff for a period of five years after the entry of a final judgment of any court of the United States, other than the denial of a declaratory judgment under this section, whether entered prior to or after the enactment of this Act, determining that denials or abridgments of the right to vote on account of race or color through the use of such tests or devices have occurred anywhere in the territory of such plaintiff. . . .

(b) The provisions of subsection (a) shall apply in any State or in any political subdivision of a state which (1) the Attorney General determines maintained on November 1, 1964, any test or device, and with respect to which (2) the Director of the Census determines that less than 50 percentum of the persons of voting age residing therein were registered on November 1, 1964, or that less than 50 percentum of such persons voted in the presidential election of November 1964.

A determination or certification of the Attorney General or of the Director of the Census under this section or under section 6 or section 13 shall not be reviewable in any court and shall be effective upon publication in the Federal Register. . . .

(d) For purposes of this section no State or political subdivision shall be determined to have engaged in the use of tests or devices for the purpose or with the effect of denying or abridging the right to vote on account of race or color if (1) incidents of such use have been few in number and have been promptly and effectively corrected by State or local action, (2) the continuing effect of such incidents has been eliminated, and (3) there is no reasonable probability of their recurrence in the future. . . .

Sec. 5. Whenever a State or political subdivision with respect to which the prohibitions set forth in section 4(a) are in effect shall enact or seek to administer any voting qualification or prerequisite to voting, or standard, practice, or procedure with respect to voting different from that in force or effect on November 1, 1964, such State or subdivision may institute an action in the United States District Court for the District of Columbia for a declaratory judgment that such qualification, prerequisite, standard, practice, or procedure does not have the purpose and will not have the effect of denying or abridging the right to vote on account of race or color, and unless and until the court enters such judgment no person shall be denied the right to vote for failure to comply with such qualification, prerequisite, standard, practice, or procedure: Provided, That such qualification, prerequisite, standard, practice, or procedure may be enforced without such proceeding if the qualification, prerequisite, standard, practice, or procedure has been submitted by the chief legal officer or other appropriate official of such State or subdivision to the Attorney General and the Attorney General has not interposed an objection within sixty days after such submission, except that neither the Attorney General's failure to object nor a declaratory judgment entered under this section shall bar a subsequent action to enjoin enforcement of such qualification, prerequisite, standard, practice, or procedure. Any action under this section shall be heard and determined by a court of three judges . . . and any appeal shall lie to the Supreme Court.

Sec. 6. Whenever (a) a court has authorized the appointment of examiners pursuant to the provisions of section 3(a), or (b) unless a declaratory judgment has been rendered under section 4(a), the Attorney General certifies with respect to any political subdivision named in, or included within the scope of, determinations made under section 4(b) that (1) he has received complaints in writing from twenty or more residents of such political subdivision alleging that they have been denied the right to vote under color of law on account of race or color, and that he believes such complaints to be meritorious, or (2) that, in his judgment (considering, among other factors, whether the ratio of nonwhite persons to white persons registered to vote within such subdivision appears to him to be reasonably attributable to violations of the fifteenth amendment or whether substantial evidence exists that bona fide efforts are being made within such subdivision to comply with the fifteenth amendment), the appointment of examiners is otherwise necessary to enforce the guarantees of the fifteenth amendment, the Civil Service Commission shall appoint as many examiners for such subdivision as it may deem appropriate to prepare and maintain lists of persons eligible to vote in Federal, State, and local elections. . . .

Sec. 7. (a) The examiners for each political subdivision shall, at such places as the Civil Service Commission shall by regulation designate, examine applicants concerning their qualifications for voting. An application to an examiner shall be in such form as the Commission may require and shall contain allegations that the applicant is not otherwise registered to vote.

(b) Any person whom the examiner finds, in accordance with instructions received under section 9(b), to have the qualifications prescribed by State law not inconsistent with the Constitution and laws of the United States shall promptly be placed on a list of eligible voters. A challenge to such listing may be made in accordance with section 9(a) and shall not be the basis for a prosecution under section 12 of this Act. The examiner shall certify and transmit such list, and any supplements as appropriate, at least once a month, to the offices of the appropriate election officials, with copies to the Attorney General and the attorney general of the State, and any such lists and supplements thereto transmitted during the month shall be available for public inspection on the last business day of the month and, in any event, not later than the forty-fifth day prior to any election. The appropriate State or local election official shall place such names on the official voting list. Any person whose name appears on the examiner's list shall be entitled and allowed to vote in the election district of his residence unless and until the appropriate election officials shall have been notified that such person has been removed from such list in accordance with subsection (d): Provided, That no person shall be entitled to vote in any election by virtue of this Act unless his name shall have been certified and transmitted on such a list to the offices of the appropriate election officials at least forty-five days prior to such election.

(c) The examiner shall issue to each person whose name appears on such a list a certificate evidencing his eligibility to vote. . . .

Sec. 8. Whenever an examiner is serving under this Act in any political subdivision, the Civil Service Commission may assign, at the request of the Attorney General, one or more persons, who may be officers of the United States, (1) to enter and attend at any place for holding an election in such subdivision for the purpose of observing whether persons who are entitled to vote are being permitted to vote, and (2) to enter and attend at any place for tabulating the votes cast at any election held in such subdivision for the purpose of observing whether votes cast by persons entitled to vote are being properly tabulated. Such persons so assigned shall report to an examiner appointed for such political subdivision, to the Attorney General, and if the appointment of examiners has been authorized pursuant to section 3(a), to the court.

Sec. 9. (a) Any challenge to a listing on an eligibility list prepared by an examiner shall be heard and determined by a hearing officer appointed by and responsible to the Civil Service Commission and under such rules as the Commission shall by regulation prescribe. Such challenge shall be entertained only if filed at such office within the State as the Civil Service Commission shall by regulation designate, and within ten days after the listing of the challenged person is made available for public inspection, and if supported by (1) the affidavits of at least two persons having personal knowledge of the facts constituting grounds for the challenge, and (2) a certification that a copy of the challenge and affidavits have been served by mail or in person upon the person challenged at his place of residence set out in the application. Such challenge shall be determined within fifteen days after it has been filed. . . .

(b) The times, places, procedures, and form for application and listing pursuant to this Act and removals from the eligibility lists shall be prescribed by regulations promulgated by the Civil Service Commission and the Commission shall, after consultation with the Attorney General, instruct examiners concerning applicable State law not inconsistent with the Constitution and laws of the United States with respect to (1) the qualifications required for listing, and (2) loss of eligibility to vote.

(c) Upon the request of the applicant or the challenger or on its own motion the Civil Service Commission shall have the power to require by subpoena the attendance and testimony of witnesses and the production of documentary evidence relating to any matter pending before it under the authority of this section. In case of contumacy or refusal to obey a subpoena, any district court of the United States or the United States court of any territory or possession, or the District Court of the United States for the District of Columbia, within the jurisdiction of which said person guilty of contumacy or refusal to obey is found or resides or is domiciled or transacts business, or has appointed an agent for receipt of service of process, upon application by the Attorney General of the United States shall have jurisdiction to issue to such person an order requiring such person to appear before the Commission or a hearing officer, there to produce pertinent, relevant, and nonprivileged documentary evidence if so ordered, or there to give testimony touching the matter under investigation, and any failure to obey such order of the court may be punished by said court as a contempt thereof.

Sec. 10. (a) The Congress finds that the requirement of the payment of a poll tax as a precondition to voting (i) precludes persons of limited means from voting or imposes unreasonable financial hardship upon such persons as a precondition to their exercise of the franchise, (ii) does not bear a reasonable relationship to any legitimate State interest in the conduct of elections, and (iii) in some areas has the purpose or effect of denying persons the right to vote because of race or color. Upon the basis of these findings, Congress declares that the constitutional right of citizens to vote is denied or abridged in some areas by the requirement of the payment of a poll tax as a precondition to voting.

(b) In the exercise of the powers of Congress under section 5 of the fourteenth amendment and section 2 of the fifteenth amendment, the Attorney General is authorized and directed to institute forthwith in the name of the United States such actions, including actions against States or political subdivisions, for declaratory judgment or injunctive relief against the enforcement of any requirement of the payment of a poll tax as a precondition to voting, or substitute therefor enacted after November 1, 1964. . . .

(d) During the pendency of such actions, and thereafter if the courts, notwithstanding this action by the Congress, should declare the requirement of the payment of a poll tax to be constitutional, no citizen of the United States who is a resident of a State or political subdivision with respect to which determinations have been made under subsection 4(b) and a declaratory judgment has not been entered under subsection 4(a), during the first year he becomes otherwise entitled to vote by reason of registration by State or local officials or listing by an examiner, shall be denied the right to vote for failure to pay a poll tax if he tenders payment of such tax for the current year to an examiner or to the appropriate State or local official at least forty-five days prior to election, whether or not such tender would be timely or adequate under State law. An examiner shall have authority to accept such payment from any person authorized by this Act to make an application for listing, and shall issue a receipt for such payment. The examiner shall transmit promptly any such poll tax payment to the office of the State or local official authorized to receive such payment under State law, together with the name and address of the applicant.

Sec. 11. (a) No person acting under color of law shall fail or refuse to permit any person to vote who is entitled to vote under any provision of this Act or is otherwise qualified to vote, or willfully fail or refuse to tabulate, count, and report such person's vote.

(b) No person, whether acting under color of law or otherwise, shall intimidate, threaten, or coerce, or attempt to intimidate, threaten, or coerce any person for voting or attempting to vote, or intimidate, threaten, or coerce, or attempt to intimidate, threaten, or coerce any person for urging or aiding any person to vote or attempt to vote, or intimidate, threaten, or coerce any person for exercising any powers or duties under section 3(a), 6, 8, 9, 10, or 12(e).

(c) Whoever knowingly or willfully gives false information as to his name, address, or period of residence in the voting district for the purpose of establishing his eligibility to register or vote, or conspires with another individual for the purpose of encouraging his false registration to vote or illegal voting, or pays or offers to pay or accepts payment either for registration to vote or for voting shall be fined . . . or imprisoned . . . or both. . . .

(d) Whoever, in any matter within the jurisdiction of an examiner or hearing officer knowingly and willfully falsifies or conceals a material fact, or makes any false, fictitious, or fraudulent statements or representations, or makes or uses any false writing or document knowing the same to contain any false, fictitious, or fraudulent statement or entry, shall be fined . . . or imprisoned . . . or both.

Sec. 12. (a) Whoever shall deprive or attempt to deprive any person of any right secured by section 2, 3, 4, 5, 7, or 10 or shall violate section 11(a) or (b), shall be fined . . . or imprisoned . . . or both.

(b) Whoever, within a year following an election in a political subdivision in which an examiner has been appointed (1) destroys, defaces, mutilates, or otherwise alters the marking of a paper ballot which has been cast in such election, or (2) alters any official record of voting in such election tabulated from a voting machine or otherwise, shall be fined . . . or imprisoned . . . or both.

(c) Whoever conspires to violate the provisions of subsection (a) or (b) of this section, or interferes with any right secured by section 2, 3 4, 5, 7, 10, or 11(a) or (b) shall be fined . . . or imprisoned . . . or both.

(d) Whenever any person has engaged or there are reasonable grounds to believe that any person is about to engage in any act or practice prohibited by section 2, 3, 4, 5, 7, 10, 11, or subsection (b) of this section, the Attorney General may institute for the United States, or in the name of the United States, an action for preventive relief, including an application for a temporary or permanent injunction, restraining order, or other order, and including an order directed to the State and State or local election officials to require them (1) to permit persons listed under this Act to vote and (2) to count such votes.

(e) Whenever in any political subdivision in which there are examiners appointed pursuant to this Act any persons allege to such an examiner within forty-eight hours after the closing of the polls that notwithstanding (1) their listing under this Act or registration by an appropriate election official and (2) their eligibility to vote, they have not been permitted to vote in such election, the examiner shall forthwith notify the Attorney General if such allegations in his opinion appear to be well founded. Upon receipt of such notification, the Attorney General may forthwith file with the district court an application for an order providing for the marking, casting, and counting of the ballots of such persons and requiring the inclusion of their votes in the total vote before the results of such election shall be deemed final and any force or effect given thereto. The district court shall hear and determine such matters immediately after the filing of such application. The remedy provided in this subsection shall not preclude any remedy available under State or Federal law.

(f) The district courts of the United States shall have jurisdiction of proceedings instituted pursuant to this section and shall exercise the same without regard to whether a person asserting rights under the provisions of this Act shall have exhausted any administrative or other remedies that may be provided by law

Sec. 13. Listing procedures shall be terminated in any political subdivision of any State (a) with respect to examiners appointed pursuant to clause (b) of section 6 whenever the Attorney General notifies the Civil Service Commission, or whenever the District Court for the District of Columbia determines in an action for declaratory judgment brought by any political subdivision with respect to which the Director of the Census has determined that more than 50 percentum of the nonwhite persons of voting age residing therein are registered to vote, (1) that all persons listed by an examiner for such subdivision have been placed on the appropriate voting registration roll, and (2) that there is no longer reasonable cause to believe that persons will be deprived of or denied the right to vote on account of race or color in such subdivision, and (b), with respect to examiners appointed pursuant to section 3(a), upon order of the authorizing court. A political subdivision may petition the Attorney General for the termination of listing procedures under clause (a) of this section, and may petition the Attorney General to request the Director of the Census to take such survey or census as may be appropriate for the making of the determination provided for in this section. The District Court for the District of Columbia shall have jurisdiction to require such survey or census to be made by the Director of the Census and it shall require him to do so if it deems the Attorney General's refusal to request such survey or census to be arbitrary or unreasonable. . . .

Sec. 16. The Attorney General and the Secretary of Defense, jointly, shall make a full and complete study to determine whether, under the laws or practices of any State or States, there are preconditions to voting, which might tend to result in discrimination against citizens serving in the Armed Forces of the United States seeking to vote. Such officials shall, jointly, make a report to the Congress not later than June 30, 1966, containing the results of such study, together with a list of any States in which such preconditions exist, and shall include in such report such recommendations for legislation as they deem advisable to prevent discrimination in voting against citizens serving in the Armed Forces of the United States.

Sec. 17. Nothing in this Act shall be construed to deny, impair, or otherwise adversely affect the right to vote of any person registered to vote under the law of any State or political subdivision. . . .

Approved August 6, 1965.

See 79 *Statues at Large*, 437.

101.

ELDRIDGE CLEAVER ON THE WATTS RIOT
(CIRCA 1965)

Here Eldridge Cleaver, a leader of the Black Panthers, explains how the Watts riot—which occurred just a week after passage of the Voting Rights Act—transformed a black community from a cultural backwater, in the popular perception, to a place of racial pride.

We used to use Watts as an epithet in much the same way as city boys used "country" as a term of derision. To deride one as a "lame," who did not know what was happening (a rustic bumpkin), the "in-crowd" of the time from L. A. would bring a cat down by saying that he had just left Watts, that he ought to go back to Watts until he had learned what was happening, or that he had just stolen enough money to move out of Watts and was already trying to play a cool part. But now, blacks are seen in Folsom saying, "I'm from Watts, Baby!"—whether true or no, but I think their meaning is clear. Confession: I too, have participated in this game, saying, I'm from Watts. In fact, I did live there for a time, and I'm *proud* of it . . .

See Eldridge Cleaver, *Soul on Ice* (New York: Dell Publishing, 1967), 27.

102.

JOHN HOPE FRANKLIN PUTS THE CIVIL RIGHTS MOVEMENT IN HISTORICAL PERSPECTIVE (1966)

Franklin, the dean of black historians, spent most of his long, distinguished career looking at the African American experience in history. Here, writing in the midst of the civil rights movement, he puts the movement up to the mid-1960s in historical perspective. He notes a transformation in the making in terms of white attitudes toward civil rights, racial inclusion, and tolerance for change.

While it is not possible to measure the influence of public opinion in the drive for equality, it can hardly be denied that over the past five or six years public opinion has shown a marked shift toward vigorous support of the civil rights movement. This can be seen in the manner in which the mass-circulation magazines as well as influential newspapers, even in the South, have stepped up their support of specific measures that have as their objective the elimination of at least the worst features of racism. The discussion of the problem of race over radio and television and the use of these media in reporting newsworthy and dramatic events in the world of race undoubtedly have had some impact. If such activities have not brought about the enactment of civil rights legislation, they have doubtless stimulated the public discussion that culminated in such legislation. . . .

The reading of American history over the past two centuries impresses one with the fact that ambivalence on the crucial question of equality has persisted almost from the beginning. If the term "equal rights for all" has not always meant what it appeared to mean, the inconsistencies and the paradoxes have become increasingly apparent. This not to say that the view that "equal rights for some" has disappeared or has even ceased to be a threat to the concept of real equality. It is to say, however, that the voices supporting inequality, while no less strident, have been significantly weakened by the very force of the numbers and elements now seeking to eliminate the two worlds of race.

See Talcott Parsons and Kenneth B. Clark, eds., *The Negro American* (Boston: Houghton Mifflin Company, 1966), 66–67.

103.

OPPOSING VIEWPOINTS ON INTEGRATION DURING THE CIVIL RIGHTS MOVEMENT (CIRCA 1966)

Two competing and contradictory voices springing from the civil rights movement were those of Dr. Kenneth B. Clark, a psychologist, and Stokely Carmichael, head of SNCC. Clark held the mainstream view that Dr. Martin Luther King, Jr., had always advocated; integration was the only real, viable option for African Americans. Carmichael walked in the vanguard of those who sought to instill racial pride and independence in black America through the slogan "Black Power."

There is no point in talk, regardless of how poetic it may be, about whether the Negro wants to integrate with America. He has no choice. He is involved, inextricably so, with America and he knows it. And the sensible Negro is the man who takes pride in this involvement and accepts it as a mandate to work for the change . . .

—Clark

It [integration] is not the solution to segregation because telling black people to integrate is telling them that they cannot get together and solve their own problems, that they need white people to solve the problems for them. It is telling them that they are inherently inferior. And it is telling them that white people are better. . . . Our goal has been fighting against white supremacy, not fighting for integration.

According to the advocates of integration, social justice will be accomplished by "integrating the Negro into the mainstream institutions of the society from which he has traditionally been excluded." . . . Thus the goal of the movement for integration was simply to loosen up the restrictions barring the entry of Negroes into the white community. . . . Black people must look beyond these goals, to the issue of collective power.

—Carmichael

Black power is a bitter retreat from the possibility of the attainment of the goals of any serious racial integration in America. . . . It is an attempt to make verbal virtue of involuntary racial segregation. . . . "Black power" is the contemporary form of the Booker T. Washington accommodation to white America's resistance to making democracy real for Negro Americans. While Booker T. made his adjustment to and acceptance of white racism under the guise of conservatism, many if not all of the "black power" advocates are seeking to sell the same shoddy moral product disguised in the gaudy package of racial militance.

—Clark

See J. A. Parker, *Angela Davis: The Making of a Revolutionary* (New Rochelle, New York: Arlington House, 1973), 36, 44, 46–47.

104.

THE PROPONENTS OF BLACK POWER REJECT THE GRADUAL APPROACH TO CIVIL RIGHTS (1967)

Stokely Carmichael, who later changed his name to Kwame Ture, began voicing the rhetoric of black power in 1966 as head of SNCC. He opposed the strategy of peaceful, nonviolent protest that most other civil rights leaders, including Martin Luther King, Jr., employed at the time, considering it little more than appeasement of white America. Here he and Charles Hamilton explain their opposition to the gradual, compromising approach to achieving racial equality.

Anything less than clarity, honesty and forcefulness perpetuates the centuries of sliding over, dressing up, and soothing down the true feelings, hopes and demands of an oppressed black people. Mild demands and hypocritical smiles mislead white America into thinking that all is fine and peaceful. They mislead white America into thinking that the path and pace chosen to deal with racial problems are acceptable to masses of black Americans. It is far better to speak forcefully and truthfully. Only when one's true self—white or black—is exposed, can this society proceed to deal with the problems from a position of clarity and not from one of misunderstanding.

Thus we have no intention of engaging in the rather meaningless language so common to discussions of race in America: "Granted, things were and are bad, but we are making progress"; "Granted, your demands are legitimate, but we cannot move hastily. Stable societies are best built slowly"; "Be careful that you do not anger or alienate your white allies; remember, after all, you are only ten percent of the population." We reject this language and these views, whether expressed by black or white; we leave them to others to mouth, because we do not feel that this rhetoric is either relevant or useful.

See Stokely Carmichael and Charles V. Hamilton, *Black Power: The Politics of Liberation in America* (New York: Random House, 1967), xvii–xviii.

105.

HUEY NEWTON AND BOBBY SEALE ON THE BLACK PANTHER PHILOSOPHY OF RACE RELATIONS (CIRCA 1967, 1968)

Bobby Seale and Huey Newton, the chairman and minister of defense, respectively, of the Black Panthers, address a misconception about the party that was common from its founding to its demise: that it was a hate group. Here they both state clearly on two different occasions that it was not.

We needed allies, and we believed that alliance with you whites—students and workers—was worth the risk. . . .

Everywhere I went in 1967 I was vehemently attacked by black students for this position; few could present opposing objective evidence to support their criticisms. The reaction was emotional: all white people were devils; they wanted nothing to do with them. I agreed that some white people could act like devils, but we could not blind ourselves to common humanity.

—Newton

When a man walks up and says that we are anti-white I scratch my head. . . . I say, "Wait a minute—let's back up a little bit. That's your game, that's the Ku Klux Klan's game." To hate me and murder me because of the color of my skin. I wouldn't murder a person or brutalize him because of the color of his skin. Yeah we hate something alright. We hate oppression that we live in. . . . If you got enough energy to sit down and hate a white person just because of the color of his skin, you're wasting a lot of energy. You'd better take some of that same energy and put it in some motion and start dealing with those oppressive conditions.

—Seale

See Judson L. Jeffries, *Huey P. Newton: The Radical Theorist* (Jackson: University Press of Mississippi, 2002), 18–19, 22.

106.

THE REPORT OF THE NATIONAL ADVISORY COMMISSION ON CIVIL DISORDERS (1968)

President Lyndon Johnson hastily created this "Kerner Commission," headed by Illinois Governor Otto Kerner, in 1967 to find the root causes of the wave of race riots that broke out all over the United States in that year and to try to find preventative solutions. The commission found that documenting what happened in the riots was much easier than determining what had caused them or formulating plans for the prevention of future riots. Here are excepts that show the relative impotence of the commission.

PREFACE

. . . Much of our report is directed to the condition of . . . Negroes and to the social and economic environment in which they live. . . .

In speaking of the Negro, we do not speak of "them." We speak of us—for the freedoms and opportunities of all Americans are diminished and imperiled when they are denied to some Americans. The tragic waste of human spirit and resources, the unrecoverable loss to the nation which this denial has already caused—and continues to produce—no longer can be ignored or afforded. . . .

This report is addressed to the institutions of government and to the conscience of the nation, but even more urgently to the minds and hearts of each citizen. The responsibility for decisive action, never more clearly demanded in the history of our country, rests on all of us. . . .

SUMMARY OF REPORT: CONCLUSION

One of the first witnesses to be invited to appear before this Commission was Dr. Kenneth B. Clark, a distinguished and perceptive scholar. Referring to the reports of earlier riot commissions, he said:

"I read that report . . . of the 1919 riot in Chicago, and it is as if I were reading the report of the investigating committee on the Harlem riot of '35, the report of the investigating committee on the Harlem riot of '43, the report of the McCone Commission on the Watts riot.

"I must again in candor say to you members of this Commission—it is a kind of Alice in Wonderland—with the same moving picture re-shown over and over again, the same analysis, the same recommendations, and the same inaction."

These words come to our minds as we conclude this report. We have provided an honest beginning. We have learned much. But we have uncovered no startling truths, no unique insights, no simple solutions. . . .

See Otto Kerner et al., *Report of the National Advisory Commission on Civil Disorders* (New York: Bantam Books, 1968), 29–34.

_____

107.

MARTIN LUTHER KING, JR.'S "I'VE BEEN TO THE MOUNTAIN TOP" SPEECH (1968)

On the evening before his assassination at the Lorraine Motel in Memphis in April 1968, King delivered what would be the last speech of his life, at the Memphis Masonic Temple. Prophetic in its implications, as if King knew the end of his life was nearing, the speech showed the civil rights movement's greatest leader at his best. Here are King's climactic closing words to the stirring oration.

We've got some difficult days ahead. But it doesn't matter with me now, because I've been to the mountain top. . . . I would like to live a long life; longevity has its place. But I'm not concerned about that now. I just want to do God's will. And He's allowed me to go up to the mountain. And I've looked over. And I've seen the promised land. I may not get there with you. But I want you to know tonight that we as a people will get to the promised land. And I'm happy tonight, I'm not worried about anything. I'm not fearing any man. Mine eyes have seen the glory of the coming of the Lord.

See Coretta Scott King, ed., *The Words of Martin Luther King, Jr.* (New York: Newmarket Press, 1983), 94.

108.

RALPH ABERNATHY ON THE DECLINE OF THE SCLC AND THE CIVIL RIGHTS MOVEMENT (CIRCA 1968)

Upon Martin Luther King, Jr.'s assassination in 1968, Abernathy assumed the mantle of leadership within the SCLC and thus, to some extent, within the civil rights movement in general. By that time, the movement had crested, however, and Abernathy was left leading both an organization and a movement in decline. Here he lists the reasons for that decline.

1. The first reason we declined in influence was our remarkable success—we had eliminated virtually all of the statutory barriers to our own advancement and equality. . . .

2. . . . Our shift of the battleground from South to North also cost us support. . . . When we went northward many non-southerners were outraged, because they had never thought of themselves as anything but exemplary in their race relations.

3. The doctrine of nonviolent protest had increasingly come under attack by newer and younger black leaders who neither understood what we were doing nor cared about the progress we had made. . . .

4. The focus of the later years was no longer on race alone but on the disparity between the rich and the poor; and there were many people who opposed racism as a matter of principle, but who didn't want to see the economic apple cart upset. . . .

5. Finally, after a decade of fighting for racial justice, many people, black and white, were weary of the struggle and were ready to give up, to lay down their swords and shields. . . .

See Ralph David Abernathy, *And the Walls Came Tumbling Down* (New York: Harper & Row, Publishers, 1989), 495–98.

109.

JULIUS LESTER ON THE IMPENDING RACE WAR (1969)

In this excerpt from the provocative book *Look Out, Whitey! Black Power's Gon' Get Your Mama!* (Grove Press, 1969), Lester, a member of SNCC and a Black Power advocate, speculates on the causes of the race war that he believes is likely to come.

To those who fearfully wonder if America has come to the point of a race war, the answer is not certain. However, all signs would seem to say yes. Perhaps the only way that it might be avoided would be through the ability of young white radicals to convince blacks, through their actions, that they are ready to do whatever is necessary to change America.

The race war, if it comes, will come partly from the necessity of revenge. You can't do what has been done to blacks and not expect retribution. The very act of retribution is liberating, and perhaps it is not accident that the symbolism of Christianity speaks of being washed in blood as an act of purification. Psychologically, blacks have always found an outlet for their revenge whenever planes have fallen, autos have collided, or just every day when white folks die. One old black woman in Atlanta, Georgia, calmly reads through her paper each day counting the number of white people killed the previous day in wrecks, storms, and by natural causes. When the three astronauts were killed in February, 1967, black people did not join the nation in mourning. They were white and were spending money that blacks needed. White folks trying to get to the moon, 'cause it's there. Poverty's here! Now get to that!

See Melvin Steinfeld, ed., *Cracks in the Melting Pot: Racism and Discrimination in American History* (Beverly Hills: Glencoe Press, 1970), 331–32.

110.

H. RAPP BROWN AND THE COMING BLACK
MESSIAH (1969)

Brown, the radical leader of SNCC, member of the Black Panthers, and later convert to Islam, believed that a race war was impending in the United States and that African Americans could expect a black "Christ" to emerge soon and lead his people to their destiny. This excerpt from his quasi autobiography shows why he became one of the most controversial figures of the civil rights movement.

My first contact with white america was marked by her violence, for when a white doctor pulled me from between my mother's legs and slapped my wet ass, I, as every other negro in america, reacted to this man-inflicted pain with a cry. A cry that america has never allowed to cease; a cry that gets louder and more intense with age; a cry that can only be heard and understood by others who live behind the color curtain. A cry? Or was it a scream? Whatever it was, we accepted it.

I had been born in "america, the land of the free." To insure my country's freedom, my father was somewhere fighting, for this was a year of the second war to end all wars—World War II. This was October 4, 1943, and victory was in the air. The world would now be safe for democracy.

But who would insure my freedom? Who would make democracy safe for Black people? America recognized long ago what negroes now examine in disbelief: every Black birth in america is political. With each new birth comes a potential challenge to the existing order. Each new generation brings forth untested militancy. America's ruling class now experiences what Herod must have at the birth of "Christ": "Go and search . . . and when ye have found him, bring me word again, that I may come and worship him also." America doesn't know which Black birth is going to be the birth that will overthrow the country.

See H. Rapp Brown, *Die Nigger Die!* (New York: The Dial Press, 1969), 1.

111.

A FORMER BLACK PANTHER REFLECTS ON
THE LEADERSHIP OF THE PARTY (CIRCA
1971)

Here Charles E. Jones interviews Jimmy Slater, a member of the Black Panther party for nine years, five of which he spent in Oakland, California, in close contact with party leaders. Jones asks Slater to explain the causes of the infighting among party leaders in 1971. After beginning his answer by blaming the FBI for infiltrating the party and disseminating misinformation from within, he goes on to note the shortcomings of Minister of Information Eldridge Cleaver, while praising Minister of Defense Huey Newton and party Chairman Bobby Seale.

CEJ: What was the nature of the factional conflict that hampered the Party in 1971?

JS: . . . . Eldridge Cleaver was one of the biggest contradictions in the Black Panther Party. When we were heading into the political arena, and he was out hollering and screaming these militaristic ideas, it was so counterrevolutionary until all it did was damage the Black Panther Party. The vast majority of the people in the community accepted what Eldridge Cleaver said, as though it represented the major body of the Black Panther Party, and it really didn't. It wasn't the idea of the vast majority of the Black Panther Party. Also, Eldridge pushed this militaristic line all the way to the hilt. I mean he got Bobby [Hutton] killed.

CEJ: What were your impressions of Dr. Huey P. Newton?

JS: Dr. Huey Newton I felt was a politically sound, great brother. He was a really positive leader. He had a lot of pressure put upon him, and it came from all sides and angles. I found that the brother happened to be one of the strongest individuals that I have known to go through all the negative things that were thrown at him. I felt Huey was one of the great leaders of the Black Panther Party, but this is not to overlook leaders like Bobby Seale and the other Central Committee members that had equal leadership qualities.

See Charles E. Jones, ed., *The Black Panther Party Reconsidered* (Baltimore: Black Classic Press, 1998), 151–52.

112.

JULIAN BOND ON BLACK CAPITALISM
(1972)

Bond, a Democrat, abhorred President Richard Nixon and most of his policies. Here he takes Nixon to task for his idea called Black Capitalism, which Bond clearly considered an unrealistic if not ridiculous attempt to win African American support for the Republican party.

The 1968 Presidential elections left us to be governed by a man who was not the choice of 90 per cent of American blacks, and who has yet to demonstrate that he has any concern for the poor or the black. We are ruled by a man who says he wants to rebuild our slums with black capitalism, which at best can only mean exchanging exploiters of one race for those of another.

. . . .

I think black people have got to be aware of and suspicious of attempts to turn us against our own interests. Take Mr. Nixon's black capitalism, for instance. As he explains it, black capitalism means that General Motors will be given tax credits to come into my community to set up a factory that will

839

hire and train black people. Now that is wonderful, but it is not black capitalism by any stretch of the imagination. That is white capitalism once again coming into the black community and taking the only thing we have to offer, which is our labor.

Instead, we ought to become interested in forms of community socialism. We ought to be interested in the kind of economic development in our communities that will not only give us jobs, but will give the community the profit as well.

See Julian Bond, *A Time to Speak, A Time to Act: The Movement in Politics* (New York: Simon and Schuster, 1972), 19, 22.

113.

THE EQUAL EMPLOYMENT OPPORTUNITY ACT (1972)

This act revised those sections of the Civil Rights Act of 1964 designed to help guard against racial discrimination in hiring and added a few new points. Because the document is so long and redundant with respect to the Civil Rights Act of 1964, only the new features are recorded here.

An Act
To further promote equal employment opportunities for American workers.
Be it enacted by the Senate and House of Representatives of the United States of America in Congress assembled, That this Act may be cited as the "Equal Employment Opportunity Act of 1972."

. . . .

Sec. 11.
Title VII of the Civil Rights Act of 1964 is amended by adding at the end thereof the following new section:
"NONDISCRIMINATION IN FEDERAL GOVERNMENT EMPLOYMENT
"Sec. 717.
(a) All personnel actions affecting employees or applicants for employment (except) with regard to aliens employed outside the limits of the United States) in military departments as defined in section 102 of title 5, United States Code, in executive agencies (other than the General Accounting Office) as defined in section 105 of title 5, United States Code (including employees and applicants for employment who are paid from nonappropriated funds), in the United States Postal Service and the Postal Rate Commission, in those units of the Government of the District of Columbia having positions in the competitive service, and in those units of the legislative and judicial branches of the Federal Government having positions in the competitive serv-

ice, and in the Library of Congress shall be made free from any discrimination based on race, color, religion, sex, or national origin.

"(b) Except as otherwise provided in this subsection, the Civil Service Commission shall have authority to enforce the provisions of subsection (a) through appropriate remedies, including reinstatement or hiring of employees with or without back pay, as will effectuate the policies of this section, and shall issue such rules, regulations, orders and instructions as it deems necessary and appropriate to carry out its responsibilities under this section. The Civil Service Commission shall

"(1) be responsible for the annual review and approval of a national and regional equal employment opportunity plan which each department and agency and each appropriate unit referred to in subsection (a) of this section shall submit in order to maintain an affirmative program of equal employment opportunity for all such employees and applicants for employment;

"(2) be responsible for the review and evaluation of the operation of all agency equal employment opportunity programs, periodically obtaining and publishing (on at least a semiannual basis) progress reports from each such department, agency, or unit; and

"(3) consult with and solicit the recommendations of interested individuals, groups, and organizations relating to equal employment opportunity. The head of each such department, agency, or unit shall comply with such rules, regulations, orders, and instructions which shall include a provision that an employee or applicant for employment shall be notified of any final action taken on any complaint of discrimination filed by him thereunder. The plan submitted by each department, agency, and unit shall include, but not be limited to

"(1) provision for the establishment of training and education programs designed to provide a maximum opportunity for employees to advance so as to perform at their highest potential; and

"(2) a description of the qualifications in terms of training and experience relating to equal employment opportunity for the principal and operating officials of each such department, agency, or unit responsible for carrying out the equal employment opportunity program and of the allocation of personnel and resources proposed by such department, agency, or unit to carry out its equal employment opportunity program. . . .

"(c) Within thirty days of receipt of notice of final action taken by a department, agency, or unit referred to in subsection 717(a), or by the Civil Service Commission upon an appeal from a decision or order of such department, agency, or unit on a complaint of discrimination based on race, color, religion, sex or national origin, brought pursuant to subsection (a) of this section, Executive 11478 or any succeeding Executive orders, or after one hundred and eighty days from the filing of the initial charge with the department, agency, or unit or with the Civil Service Commission on appeal from a decision or order of such department, agency, or unit until such time as final action may be taken by a department, agency, or unit, an employee or applicant for employment, if aggrieved by the final disposition of his complaint, or by the failure to take final action on his complaint, may file a civil action as provided in section 706, in which civil action the head of the department, agency, or unit, as appropriate, shall be the defendant.

"(d) The provisions of section 706 (f) through (k), as applicable, shall govern civil actions brought hereunder.

"(e) Nothing contained in this Act shall relieve any Government agency or official of its or his primary responsibility to assure nondiscrimination in employment as required by the Constitution and statutes or of its or his responsibilities under Executive Order 11478 relating to equal employment opportunity in the Federal Government."

Sec. 12.

Section 5018 (c) of title 5, United States Code, is amended by— . . .

(3) by adding immediately after paragraph (10) the last time it appears therein in the following new paragraph:

"(11) the Chairman of the Equal Employment Opportunity Commission, subject to the standards and procedures prescribed by this chapter, may place an additional ten positions in the Equal Employment Opportunity Commission . . . for the purposes of carrying out title VII of the Civil Rights Act of 1964."

Sec. 13.

Title VII of the Civil Rights Act of 1964 is further amended by adding at the end thereof the following new section:

"SPECIAL PROVISION WITH RESPECT TO DENIAL, TERMINATION, AND SUSPENSION OF GOVERNMENT CONTRACTS

"Sec. 718.

No Government contract, or portion thereof, with any employer, shall be denied, withheld, terminated, or suspended, by any agency or officer of the United States under any equal employment opportunity law or order, where such employer has an affirmative action plan which has previously been accepted by the Government for same facility within the past twelve months without first according such employer full hearing and adjudication under the provisions of title 5, United States Code, section 554, and the following pertinent sections: Provided, That if such employer has deviated substantially from such previously agreed to affirmative action plan, this section shall not apply: Provided further, That for the purposes of this section an affirmative action plan shall be deemed to have been accepted by the Government at the time the appropriate compliance agency has accepted such plan unless within forty-five days thereafter the Office of Federal Contract Compliance has disapproved such plan."

Sec. 14.

The amendments made by this Act to section 706 of the Civil Rights Act of 1964 shall be applicable with respect to charges pending with the

Commission on the date of enactment of this Act and all charges filed there-after.

Approved March 24, 1972.

See 79 *Statues at Large*, 437.

114.

ALICE WALKER ON THE "SOUTHERN REVOLUTION" OF THE 1960S (1973)

In these excerpts from an interview with John O'Brien, Walker, then living in Jackson, Mississippi, recounts parts of her experience in the civil rights movement while a student in Atlanta. The experience clearly helped shaped her worldview and no doubt contributed to her ability to pen the powerful, imaginative, provocative, but graphically realistic fiction for which she is renowned.

I believe in change: change personal, and change in society. I have experienced a revolution (unfinished, without question, but one whose new order is everywhere on view) in the South. . . .

A bit more about the "Southern Revolution." When I left Eatonton, Georgia [Walker's hometown], to go off to Spelman College in Atlanta (where I stayed, uneasily for two years), I deliberately sat in the front section of the Greyhound bus. A white woman complained to the driver. He—big and red and ugly—ordered me to move. I moved. But in those seconds of moving, everything changed. I was eager to bring an end to the South that permitted my humiliation. During my sophomore year I stood on the grass in front of Trevor-Arnett Library at Atlanta University and I listened to the young leaders of SNCC. John Lewis was there and so was Julian Bond. . . . Everyone was beautiful, because everyone . . . was conquering fear by holding the hands of the persons next to them. . . .

Less than ten years after all these things I walk about Georgia (and Mississippi)—eating, sleeping, loving, singing, burying the dead—the way men and women are supposed to do, in a place that is the only "home" they've ever known. There is only one "for coloreds' sign left in Eatonton, and it is on the black man's barber shop. He is merely outdated. Booster, if you read this *change* your sign!

See Henry Louis Gates, Jr., and K. A. Appiah, eds., *Alice Walker: Critical Perspectives, Past and Present* (New York: Amistad, 1993), 332–34.

115.

TONY MORRISON ON THE DUAL STRUGGLE
OF BEING BLACK AND FEMALE (1980)

In this excerpt from an interview with Anne Koenen, Morrison briefly shares her thoughts about the difficulty of being both a woman and an African American in a world dominated by the white race and by men, and how that dual struggle has influenced her writing.

It seems to me historically true that Black women have a special place in this culture which is not always perceived as an enviable one. One of the characteristics of black women's experience was that they did not have to choose between a career and a home. They did both. Also, in times of duress, and I have to be careful here because what I have to say may sound like "Racism is good for you"—it isn't—but in times of duress which is an interesting time for me as a writer because you can see more things—my characters are always in some huge crisis situation, I push them all the way out as far as they will go, as far as I can. . . . The dual responsibility that Black women had—when they were left, they didn't collapse. They didn't have crutches in the first place, so with nothing but themselves to rely on they just had to carry on. And that, I think, is absolutely extraordinary and marvelous.

See Danielle Taylor-Guthrie, ed., *Conversations with Toni Morrison* (Jackson: University Press of Mississippi, 1994), 72.

116.

JESSE JACKSON EXPLAINS HIS DECISION TO
RUN FOR PRESIDENT (1984)

This is an excerpt from Jackson's Address to the Democratic National Convention, held in San Francisco, 18 July 1984. Here Jackson identified himself essentially as a populist—a friend to the poor and dispossessed, and a candidate for the working class.

Tonight we come together bound by our faith in a mighty God, with genuine respect and love for our country, and inheriting the legacy of a great party, the Democratic Party, which is the best hope for redirecting our nation on a more humane, just and peaceful course.

This is not a perfect party. We are not a perfect people. Yet, we are called to a perfect mission: our mission to feed the hungry; to clothe the naked; to house the homeless; to teach the illiterate; to provide jobs for the jobless; and to choose the human race over the nuclear race. [Applause.] . . .

My constituency is the desperate, the damned, the disinherited, the disrespected, and the despised. They are restless and seek relief. They've voted in record numbers. They have invested faith, hope and trust that they have in us. The Democratic Party must send them a signal that we care. I pledge my best to not let them down. . . .

No generation can choose the age or circumstance in which it is born, but through leadership it can choose to make the age in which it is born, an age of enlightenment, an age of jobs and peace and justice. [Applause.]

Only leadership—that intangible combination of gifts, the discipline, information, circumstance, courage, timing, will and divine inspiration—can lead us out of the crisis in which we find ourselves. The leadership can mitigate the misery of our nation. Leadership can part the waters and lead our nation in the direction of the Promised Land. Leadership can lift the boats stuck at the bottom. . . .

I ask for your vote on the first ballot as a vote for a new direction for this Party and this Nation. [Applause.] A vote of conviction, a vote of conscience. [Applause.]

See www.pbs.org/wgbh/pages/frontline/jesse/speeches.

117.

JESSE JACKSON DESCRIBES HIS CHILDHOOD
(1988)

This is an excerpt from Jackson's Address to the Democratic National Convention, held in Atlanta, on 19 July 1988. Here Jackson describes a child born in obscurity and poverty who, now as a presidential candidate, truly cared for the poor working Americans of all races.

I have a story. I wasn't always on television. Writers were not always outside my door. When I was born late one afternoon, October 8th, in Greenville, South Carolina, no writers asked my mother her name. Nobody chose to write down our address. My mama was not supposed to make it, and I was not supposed to make it. You see, I was born of a teen-age mother, who was born of a teen-age mother.

I understand. I know abandonment, and people being mean to you, and saying you're nothing and nobody and can never be anything.

I understand. Jesse Jackson is my third name. I'm adopted. When I had no name, my grandmother gave me her name. My name was Jesse Burns until I was 12. So I wouldn't have a blank space, she gave me a name to hold me over. I understand when nobody knows your name. I understand when you have no name.

I understand. I wasn't born in the hospital. Mama didn't have insurance. I was born in the bed at [the] house. I really do understand. Born in a three-room house, bathroom in the backyard, slop jar by the bed, no hot and cold running water.

I understand. Wallpaper used for decoration? No. For a windbreaker. I understand. I'm a working person's person. That's why I understand you whether you're Black or White.

I understand work. I was not born with a silver spoon in my mouth. I had a shovel programmed for my hand.

My mother, a working woman. So many of the days she went to work early, with runs in her stockings. She knew better, but she wore runs in her stockings so that my brother and I could have matching socks and not be laughed at at school. I understand.

At 3 o'clock on Thanksgiving Day, we couldn't eat turkey because momma was preparing somebody else's turkey at 3 o'clock. We had to play football to entertain ourselves. And then around 6 o'clock she would get off the Alta Vista bus and we would bring up the leftovers and eat our turkey—leftovers, the carcass, the cranberries—around 8 o'clock at night. I really do understand.

Every one of these funny labels they put on you, those of you who are watching this broadcast tonight in the projects, on the corners, I understand. Call you outcast, low down, you can't make it, you're nothing, you're from nobody, subclass, underclass; when you see Jesse Jackson, when my name goes in nomination, your name goes in nomination. [Applause.]

I was born in the slum, but the slum was not born in me. [Applause.] And it wasn't born in you, and you can make it. [Applause.]

See www.pbs.org/wgbh/pages/frontline/jesse/speeches.

118.

MAYA ANGELOU ON THE "PLAGUE OF RACISM" (1993)

One of the most gifted poet-philosophers of recent times, Maya Angelou expresses her thoughts here about the ongoing problem of racism in present-day America.

The plague of racism is insidious, entering into our minds as smoothly and quietly and invisibly as floating airborne microbes enter into our bodies to find lifelong purchase in our bloodstreams. . . .

It is time for the preachers, the rabbis, the priests and pundits, and the professors to believe in the awesome wonder of diversity so that they can teach those who follow them. It is time for parents to teach young people early on that in diversity there is beauty and there is strength. We all should know that diversity makes for a rich tapestry, and we must understand that all the threads of the tapestry are equal in value no matter their color; equal in importance no matter their texture.

Our young must be taught that racial peculiarities do exist, but that beneath the skin, beyond the differing features and into the true heart of being, fundamentally, we are more alike, my friend, than we are unalike. . . .

See Maya Angelou, *Wouldn't Take Nothing for My Journey Now* (New York: Random House, 1993), 121, 124.

119.

AL SHARPTON ON THE FUTURE OF AMERICAN RACE RELATIONS (1996)

The controversial Sharpton emerged in the 1990s as a nationally recognized African American leader. In the tradition of Martin Luther King, Jr., Ralph Abernathy, and Jesse Jackson, he is an ordained minister who sees the civil rights issue as his primary area of ministry. Here he explains why the issue is so important to him.

From the time I graduated from high school . . . I would say I was acting, consciously, out of my understanding of the depth of the pervasiveness of racism in New York City and the nation. I acted out of emotion—primarily anger and rage at how a supposedly just society viewed and treated blacks and imposed a regime that greatly limited the life choices of most blacks. I saw how black people were shot down like dogs and demonized by the media and politicians. I, and the people I was working with, worked at and were successful in putting race on the front burner: we put the value of black life out as an issue in New York State, and we showed the nation the ugly face of northern racism. . . .

Americans are going to have to decide to accept that we are, literally, all in this together, in the same boat, and that the boat will sink or sail depending on our decisions. . . .

Whites and blacks in this country face an imperative to develop a language that will enable them to communicate openly and fairly about the problems facing all of us. . . .

This country is like a bickering family, and until we resolve some of those differences and find some common ground we will not be able to work together. . . . and begin the real work of providing a just and prosperous society for all our citizens, protecting the sick and the needy, and securing the as-of-now-uncertain future for our children and grandchildren and beyond. It is that serious, and I want to do my part in bring it to pass.

See The Reverend Al Sharpton, *Go and Tell Pharaoh* (New York: Doubleday, 1996), 3, 6–7.

120.

BILL CLINTON'S VISION FOR BRIDGING THE RACIAL DIVIDE (2001)

President Bill Clinton presided over what was arguably the most minority-friendly administration in American history. As he prepared to leave office in 2001, he reflected upon the progress his administration had made in bridging the racial divide over the preceding eight years, and he articulated his vision for completing the process. Here are the most salient points of his vision.

THE UNFINISHED WORK OF BUILDING ONE AMERICA

January 15, 2001

I hereby submit this message to the 107th Congress of the United States on the State of Race Relations in America. In it, I present my personal assessment of the current national mood concerning race relations and issue a set of concrete challenges that form what I call the unfinished business of building One America. This report is an outgrowth of my Administration's consistent emphasis on racial reconciliation, most clearly embodied in my Initiative on Race and our White House Office on One America. But it also stems from my own personal commitment to racial harmony that has its roots in the lessons and experiences of my childhood in the racially segregated south. I dedicate this report to countless civil rights champions of all colors who have struggled since the time of Frederick Douglass for an America free from the bondage of racial injustice.

Introduction

After eight years of service as President of the United States, I will relinquish that title on January 20, 2001, when George W. Bush takes the oath of office. But as a citizen, I will always try to serve my country and to advance the ideals that propelled me into public service more than two decades ago, none more important than racial reconciliation. It began for me with the crisis at Little Rock in 1957. I was only 11 years old at the time. Like most southerners then, I never attended school with a person of another race until I went to college. Though discrimination had always gnawed at me, it was the courage and sacrifice of those nine black children who endured constant attacks, both physical and emotional, to integrate Little Rock's Central High School, that made racial equality a driving commitment in my life. I came of age at the height of the civil rights struggles of the sixties: the 1963 March on Washington, the passage of the Civil Rights Act of 1964 and the Voting Rights Act of 1965. I vividly remember the assassinations of John F. Kennedy, Martin Luther King and Bobby Kennedy. Like any American who grew up in that era, my life was shaped by those triumphs and tragedies. And ever since,

I have been inspired to join with others to carry on the fight for racial justice, including justice for all Americans without regard to gender, ethnicity, sexual orientation, disability, or religion. Progress on this road is essential to our march toward the "more perfect union" of our founders' dreams.

For eight years, my Administration has worked to build social and economic bridges strong enough for all of us to walk across; to give all responsible citizens equal opportunity to cross those bridges; and to celebrate our great diversity while uniting around our common humanity, values, and concerns. In a nation where soon the only majority will be "American," I believe we need to talk about race in a new way—not just in terms of black and white, but of the essential worth and dignity of all people. Of course, racial tensions still exist in America. But, if we are ever going to overcome them, we must begin to focus more on the things that unite us than on those that divide us.

Let's start with the remarkable fact that we are recognized around the globe as the most successful multi-racial democracy in history, a model of peaceful co-existence in a world torn by ethnic, racial and religious conflict. With the current explosion of diversity in America, that image of ourselves is being tested as never before.

America is undergoing one of the greatest demographic transformations in history. We are a changing people. Just fifty years ago, whites made up 90 percent of our population and the Census Bureau used only three major categories to describe us: white, Negro, and "other." Those distinctions were often reduced to just white and non-white. Since then, there has been a rapid growth in our Hispanic, Asian American, and American Indian populations. According to the latest statistics from the Census Bureau, African Americans, with a population of 35 million, still constitute the largest racial or ethnic group in America. . . .

There is no majority race in Hawaii or Houston or New York City. In nine of our ten largest public school systems, over 75 percent of the students are minorities. In a little more than 50 years there will be no majority race in America.

This unprecedented infusion of diversity brings with it a complex and sometimes controversial set of issues. Who, for example, decides who is white and who is a person of color? What will the terms "majority" and "minority" mean when there is no majority race in America? And perhaps, most important, will the black-white schism that has so defined racial struggle in America morph into new minority versus minority divisions or can we build new coalitions for social change and equal opportunity across all racial lines?

As our nation grows more diverse and the world grows more interdependent, our diversity will either be the great problem or the great promise of the 21st century. Will we be two societies, "separate and unequal," as the Kerner Commission concluded 33 years ago? We have made progress that can be measured both in numbers and in the hearts and minds of Americans. We have the lowest minority unemployment rate ever recorded, record numbers of minority owned businesses, and minority educational progress among all racial and ethnic groups. Perhaps even more important, most of our children believe that racial harmony and respect for diversity is the only way for all us to live and prosper. We have not yet reached the dream of One America, but I believe in this century, we can and we will. But it will take honest discussion about where we are and where we want to go and vigorous, relevant efforts to deal with our remaining challenges.

This report is not intended to grapple with all aspects of the racial divide in America, but to point to a number of concrete steps we can take to equalize opportunity, maximize the great potential of our growing diversity, and accelerate our journey to building the One America of our dreams. I will offer recommendations in seven broad areas of unfinished business: Economic and Social Progress, Education, Civil Rights Enforcement, Criminal Justice Reform, Eliminating Health Disparities, Election Reform, and Civic Responsibility. I offer these recommendations in the hope that they will be helpful, not only to the 107th Congress and the new administration, but to all of us as we continue the work of healing the racial wounds of the past and pointing the way to a more just future of greater opportunity for all Americans.

We must keep working to connect the threads of our coat of many colors into the fabric of One America.

I. ECONOMIC AND SOCIAL PROGRESS

New Markets: Ensuring that the Benefits of Our Strong Economy Reach All

By any measure, America has prospered, both economically and socially over the last eight years. We are now experiencing the longest economic expansion in history. We have a balanced budget. We have turned decades of deficits into the biggest back-to-back surpluses in history. And we have achieved what many people once thought impossible: we are paying down our national debt. In fact, we are well on our way to making America debt-free by the year 2010—the first time this has happened since Andrew Jackson was President in 1835.

The rising tide of our strong economy is lifting all boats. Between 1980 and 1992 the bottom 60 percent of Americans saw little, if any, increase in income. Unemployment for African Americans and Hispanics reached record highs and the poverty rate for African Americans remained at or above 30 percent.

Today, for the first time in decades, wages are rising at all income levels. Not only did every major income group see double-digit income growth, but the lowest 20 percent saw the largest income growth since 1993. The unemployment rate for African Americans fell from 14.2 percent in 1992 to 7.6 percent today. . . .

Responsible Fatherhood

Economic empowerment alone is not enough to build strong communities. The most basic building block of strong communities is strong families. Every child deserves the love and support of both parents. Still, nearly one in three American children grows up without a father. These children are five times more likely to live in poverty than children with both parents at home. Clearly, demanding and supporting responsible fatherhood is critical to lifting all children out of poverty and is an important component of welfare reform. . . .

Recommendation: Pass a bipartisan fatherhood bill that provides grants to help low-income and non-custodial parents—mainly fathers—work, pay child support and reconnect with their children. . . .

II. EDUCATIONAL EXCELLENCE FOR ALL CHILDREN

When Vice President Gore and I came into office in 1993, we pledged to the American people that we would strengthen education at every level and challenge the status quo by investing more in and demanding more from our nation's schools. Because every child can learn and every child deserves the opportunity to realize his or her dreams, the promise of a world-class education must be available to all Americans regardless of their income, where they live, or the color of their skin. As we enter the 21st century, nothing could be more important than investing in the public schools that will prepare our children to be successful in an increasingly global economy. Too often in the past we accepted low expectations for some children, using labels and categories to excuse our failure to educate them.

During the last eight years we have clearly made progress in improving our schools and helping more children succeed. For example, African American high school graduation rates are virtually equal to those of whites for the first time. Test scores for African Americans students are up in virtually all categories . . . In addition, more minority students are being challenged by rigorous coursework, which is an important precursor to post-secondary education. Three times as many African American students took Advanced Placement (AP) exams in 1999 as took the tests in 1988 . . .

Access to post-secondary opportunities also continues to increase for minority students: the percentage of African American high school graduates who go on to college has increased from 50 percent in 1992 to 58.5 percent in 1997 . . .

These improvements show that our commitment to education over the past eight years is helping more of America's students succeed, but they also highlight the fact that much work remains to be done. . . .

Eight years ago, the debate on education was usually divided into partisan camps arguing over false choices. On one side were those who believed that money could solve all the problems in our schools, and who feared that setting high standards and holding schools and teachers and students accountable to them would only hold back poor children, especially poor minority children. On the other side, there were those who felt education was a state responsibility, and did not need a comprehensive national response—or the leadership of a federal Department of Education. They were willing to give up on our public schools and many of the children in them because they did not believe that we could ensure a world-class education for all students, and therefore, were unwilling to spend money trying. We believed both of those positions were wrong because every child can learn. There was plenty of evidence, even then, that high levels of learning were possible in even the most difficult social and economic circumstances. The challenge was to make the school transformation going on in some schools available and real in all schools. We sought to do this by both investing more in our schools and demanding more from them, with a simple proven strategy: higher standards, greater accountability, more investment, equal opportunity.

This strategy should continue to guide our efforts to improve education. Last year, for the first time, Congress failed to fulfill its obligation to reauthorize the Elementary and Secondary Education Act. In May of 1999 I sent Congress a proposal that would fundamentally change the way the federal government invests in our schools—to support more of what we know works, and to stop supporting what we know does not work. It would help put quality teachers in all classrooms; send report cards to all parents on the performance of each school; end social promotion, but offer help for students rather than blaming them when the system fails them; and require a plan to identify failing schools and improve them, or shut them down. I have also favored voluntary national tests in fourth grade reading and eighth grade math—developed in a nonpartisan and professional manner—as a way to measure student progress within and across state borders as the National Assessment of Educational Progress (NAPE) tests do today. Congress and the new Administration must act on this legislation, and I hope they will do it in a way that makes progress on accountability, while increasing key investments in what works.

The fundamental lesson of the last seven years, it seems to me, is that an education investment without accountability can be a real waste of money. But accountability without investment can be a real waste of effort. All schools need adequate resources to provide all of our children with a world-class education and yet too often, many schools in poor communities cannot meet this goal because they simply don't have the resources. Long-standing gaps in access to educational resources exist, including disparities based on race and ethnicity. That's why I am appointing a Presidential Commission on Resource Equity charged with gathering data on this problem and reporting to the President, Congress, and the nation on the best strategies to close this equity gap. . . .

We cannot close disparities in race if we do not close the remaining disparities in education. It is just that simple. This means expanding efforts to tie investment to accountability, so that every child, regardless of race, class, ethnicity, income or background, can get a first-class public school education. This is a founding principle of our country and it remains today perhaps the most important tool we have to give all our citizens the chance to make the most of their own lives.

Recommendation: Reauthorize the Elementary and Secondary Education Act so that federal education funds promote higher standards and accountability for results, put qualified teachers in all classrooms, and turn around all failing schools. Finish the job of hiring 100,000 teachers to reduce class size. Expand afterschool and summer school help to make sure all students reach high standards. Mentor disadvantaged youth to increase the chance they go to college. Provide tax credits to help build or modernize 5,000 schools. Act on the findings of the newly appointed Presidential Commission on Resource Equity, that is charged with finding ways to close the resource equity gap between schools in poor communities and those in more affluent ones.

III. CIVIL RIGHTS ENFORCEMENT

Despite all the progress we have made in tearing down walls of segregation and barriers of opportunity, an old enemy lurks in the shadows. It continues to poison our perceptions, undermine our progress and threaten our future. Racial equality has been our nation's constant struggle, predating the nation's founding by a century and a half. And race has been our constant struggle.

We were born with a Declaration of Independence which asserted that we are all created equal and a Constitution that enshrined slavery. We fought a bloody civil war to abolish slavery and preserve the union, but we remained a house divided and unequal by law for another century. We advanced across the continent in the name of freedom, yet in doing so we pushed Native Americans off their land, often crushing their culture, their livelihood and their lives. We eagerly recruited laborers from Asia to help build our fledgling economy but in a time of war, forcibly removed more than 100,000 Japanese Americans from their homes and into internment camps. Our Statue of Liberty welcomes poor, tired, huddled masses of immigrants to our shores, but each new wave has felt the sting of discrimination, and for many that discrimination has burdened their native-born children and grandchildren. We must face these harsh contradictions squarely as a critical first step to healing the wounds of our past and unleashing the power and promise of our future.

After I launched the national initiative on race in San Diego in 1997, people asked me why, in the absence of a great national crisis like Little Rock or the Rodney King riots, should the American people focus anew on the challenge of racial reconciliation. My answer is two-fold. First and foremost, our work is not yet done. And our present progress and confidence give us the best chance to finish it. We have moved out of the epicenter of racism that rocked our nation from the time of the conquest, slavery and Japanese internment until the great breakthroughs of the civil rights era, but we are still experiencing the aftershocks. Though people of color have more opportunities than ever today, we still see evidence of unequal treatment in the litany of disparities in jobs and wealth, in education and health, and in criminal justice, that so often still break down along the color line.

Second, building One America is not just a fancy slogan. It is a rallying cry in defense of our future. As we have seen so often in other parts of the world, ancient ethnic divisions in the age of the new global economy can rip nations apart. That has not, and will not, happen here in America. The main reason is our fundamental faith in freedom and equality, embodied in the words, if not always the actions, of our founders.

I believe it is also tied to our belief in a spiritual law common to every major world religion. We hear its echo in our call for One America. It is the law of oneness. E pluribus unum: Out of many, one. In Christianity it is expressed as loving thy neighbor as thyself. In Islam we are instructed to "Do unto all men as you wish to have done to you and reject for others what you would reject for yourself." The Talmud teaches us, "Should anyone turn aside the right of the stranger, it is as though he were to turn aside the right of the most high God." As a nation that takes pride in both the depth and diversity of religious expression, we must embrace racial reconciliation as a way to honor our highest spiritual values.

In 1998, my Advisory Board on race made this prescient observation: "Now, more than ever, racial discrimination is not only about skin color and other physical characteristics associated with race; it is also about other aspects of our identity, such as ethnicity, national origin, language, accent, religion, and cultural customs." While overt racial prejudice has diminished, the discrimination of today is often more camouflaged. In a sense, this makes it more dangerous: if you are denied a job, apartment, or prompt service in a store on the basis of bigotry that is never expressed, and even cloaked in politeness, then you have no signal telling you to object, to fight. In order to build One America, to finish the work that we have started, it is vitally important that all Americans understand that discrimination—intentional or not, obvious or camouflaged—still exists and that each of us has the opportunity and responsibility to help eradicate it. This is about more than enforcing laws. It is about living up to our values and keeping our promises.

With our unprecedented strength, it is all the more intolerable that there are still doors to opportunity that are padlocked by prejudice. That is why I have proposed substantial new investments to strengthen civil rights enforcement at the federal, state, and local levels. Although money by itself will not achieve our civil rights goals, a strong enforcement agenda depends on a sufficient level of resources. But we must act strategically to put the federal investments where they can be the most effective. That is why, for eight years, I have fought so hard for additional investments in civil rights enforcement. These funds are critical to helping the Justice Department expand investigations and prosecutions of criminal civil rights cases. HUD needs adequate resources to reduce housing discrimination and the Departments of Education, Agriculture and Labor will be able to improve and expand civil rights compliance and enforcement programs.

And as our comprehensive review of federal affirmative action programs revealed, affirmative action is still an effective and important tool for expanding educational and economic opportunity to all Americans.

The fact is, important gaps in civil rights law and their enforcement remain. We need to ensure equal opportunity for all Americans, regardless of race, ethnicity, religion, gender, disability or sexual orientation. To that end, I challenge the new Congress and Administration to pass the Employment Non-Discrimination Act (ENDA). I believe that the simple business of enforcing anti-discrimination laws should be a bipartisan commitment. We should be able to agree on at least this much: enforce the law and promote voluntary compliance with it.

Recommendation: Redouble our efforts to end all forms of discrimination against any group of Americans by expanding investments in civil rights enforcement and passing the Employment Non-Discrimination Act.

Eliminate Hate Crimes

There is nothing more important to the future of this country than our standing together against intolerance, prejudice, and violent bigotry. No American should be subjected to violence on account of his or her race, color, national origin, religion, sexual orientation, gender or disability. Americans of conscience were horrified by the vicious murder of James Byrd, Jr. in Jasper, Texas and the cowardly torture-murder of Matthew Shepard in Wyoming. But we must do more than shake our heads in shame; we must back up our outrage with tough sanctions against those who perpetuate these crimes. Hate crimes are criminal acts driven by bias against another person's race, religion, disability, sexual orientation, or ethnicity. In 1999, the FBI reported 7,876 incidents of such crimes. Of these, more than 60 percent were based on the victim's race or ethnicity. It is suspected that many more go unreported. I am proud that my Administration has stood strong against hate crimes through vigorous prosecution under the civil rights statutes, but there is much more to do.

Under Attorney General Janet Reno's leadership, the Department of Justice has been deeply committed to prosecuting and preventing hate crimes. At the first White House Conference on Hate Crimes in 1997, I announced the centerpiece of the Attorney General's Hate Crime Initiative: the formation of local working groups in each federal judicial district to improve the prosecution and prevention of hate crimes. The Justice Department has also developed three law enforcement training curricula on hate crimes: for patrol officers, investigators, and a mixed audience. Since December 1998, more than 500 law enforcement officers have been trained with this curricula.

We must also ensure that when hate crimes do occur, we have the law enforcement tools necessary to identify the perpetrators swiftly and bring them to justice. In this regard, we must pass the revised Hate Crimes Prevention Act, now called Local Law Enforcement Enhancement Act. Currently, the law requires we prove that the defendant committed an offense not only because of the victim's race, color, religion, or national origin, but also because of the victim's participation in one of six "federally protected activities."

The federally protected activity requirement has impeded our efforts to prosecute hate crimes. For example, the federal government can prosecute a violent, racially-motivated hate crime that occurs in a public school's parking lot, but we may lack jurisdiction if the crime occurs in a private yard across the street from the school. To point out another outrageous limitation, the federal government's ability to respond to a racially motivated attack that occurs in front of a convenience store may depend on whether or not the store has a video game inside.

Although the vast majority of prosecutions would continue to be brought at the state and local level, the federal statute needs to be fixed so that there are more tools to prosecute these heinous criminal acts. Our federal officers must have the authority to work in concert with state and local law enforcement agencies to end hate crimes.

In addition to removing jurisdictional barriers, the revised Hate Crimes Prevention Act will strengthen current law by giving Federal prosecutors the power to prosecute hate crimes committed because of the victim's sexual orientation, gender, or disability. The federal government did not have the legal jurisdiction to prosecute Matthew Shepard's murderers under current law. Because of the lack of jurisdiction, federal law enforcement was not able to provide significant resources to help local law enforcement in that case. The local sheriff's office had to furlough law enforcement officers because of the costs of the investigation and subsequent prosecution. With this new legislation, this would never have happened. Matthew, a 21-year-old college freshman, was beaten in the dead of night, tied to a fence, and left to die alone. At Matthew's funeral, his cousin predicted that "Matt will have made a difference in the lives of thousands." I want to make sure he does. Congress and the next Administration should enact a law that provides justice for all Americans.

Let me emphasize that with the enactment of the Hate Crimes Prevention Act, state and local law enforcement agencies will continue to take the lead in investigating and prosecuting all types of hate crimes. For instance, the Justice Department will continue to defer prosecution in the first instance to state and local law enforcement officials. The revised Hate Crimes Prevention Act will, however, strengthen our ability to work effectively as partners with state and local law enforcement, and to serve an important backstop function with regard to a wider range of hate-motivated violence than federal law currently permits. Many people say we don't need this legislation because hate crimes are covered by other state laws. But, as state prosecutors have pointed out repeatedly, a case can often be better made by federal authorities, and even more often, federal support for state agencies with limited resources is critical.

Opponents of the civil rights legislation in the 1960s often said, "You can't legislate morality." It is true that a statute cannot exorcise hate; that is a personal demon that calls for a moral cleansing. But law does have a function in proclaiming our values and differentiating right from wrong. In that sense, over time, law can squeeze hate out of our public lives and eventually out of all but the most diseased hearts. The starting point is to make violent acts of hate against our neighbors a federal crime. And we should do it.

Recommendation: Recognize that hate crimes do damage not only to the victims, but to the moral fiber of our nation. They are different from other crimes and they deserve to be treated as such. The new Congress and Administration should pass the revised Hate Crimes Prevention Act without further delay. . . .

IV. CRIMINAL JUSTICE REFORM

There is perhaps no area today in which perceptions of fairness differ so greatly based on race than in the administration of criminal justice. If you are white, you most likely believe the system is on your side; if you are a minority, you most likely feel the opposite. This is true at all levels of justice from what happens on the beat to what happens when the sentencing gavel is pounded.

The statistics are cause for concern: For example, in a recent survey, more than 7 out of 10 blacks said they believe that blacks are treated more harshly by the criminal justice system than whites, and more than 4 out of 10 whites agree. Furthermore, of those crime victims who do not report the incident to police, approximately twice as many blacks than whites say they don't report a crime because the police would not care or would be inefficient, ineffective, or biased. No system that is perceived as unfair can have the full trust of all our citizens, even if it is fair. This lack of trust becomes a cycle, separating the community even farther from the police. We cannot turn a blind eye to this breach of trust and confidence at all levels of the system. We must keep working until every citizen believes that justice is truly blind.

In the three decades before the start of the Clinton-Gore Administration, the violent crime rate had skyrocketed by 400 percent. Many thought that rising crime would never reverse. The soaring crime rate took a particularly devastating toll in communities of color. The year I took office, homicide victimization for young black men ages 18–24 years old was at its highest level on record and was over ten times higher than the rate for white men of the same age.

Our Administration took a new approach to fighting crime with innovative policies to help communities reduce crime and restore public safety: by funding 100,000 more community police for our streets; supporting community policing strategies so police could work closely with residents to develop solutions to local crime problems; imposing tough, targeted penalties for the most violent offenders; pushing common sense measures to keep guns out of the hands of criminals and children; and providing more after school programs to keep youth supervised and out of trouble.

As a result of these and other efforts, the incidence of crime has dropped to new lows. The homicide rate is at its lowest level in 33 years, gun crime has declined by 40 percent, and the overall crime rate has dropped for over 8 straight years—the longest continuous decline on record. Moreover, people of color have in many cases experienced the sharpest decreases in crime victimization. For instance, since 1993, the murder rate for African Americans has dropped 40 percent, compared to 28 percent for whites, and property crime victimization decreased 45 percent for Hispanic households as compared to 37 percent for non-Hispanics. These are remarkable achievements.

Despite recent and substantial decreases in crime across racial lines, persons of color remain significantly more likely than whites to be victims of crime, especially violent crime. Persons of color are also much more likely to live in fear of crime. No American should have to live that way. We must remember that in the poorest, highest crime neighborhoods in this country, the vast majority of people get up every day, go to work, obey the law, pay their taxes, and do the best to raise their kids. More than anywhere else, these communities—which are often communities of color—want, need, and deserve strong law enforcement to restore order, reduce crime, and help build stronger communities.

However, these same communities often have less trust in law enforcement—limiting its effectiveness where it is most needed. So, while we have attained historic reductions in crime, we must build on our successful strategy and develop additional ways to make every community even safer. And in doing so, we must strengthen trust and confidence in law enforcement and in the criminal justice system overall.

Community Policing and "Hot Spots"

First and foremost, we must reduce crime and restore order in communities of color where crime and fear of crime are greatest. Every American has the right to live in a safe community, and we should not be able to identify high-crime neighborhoods based on the race of the residents who live there. Community policing should serve as the cornerstone for our efforts. We must continue to add another 50,000 more community police to our nation's streets and spread the philosophy of community policing which brings local police and residents together in developing ways to best solve and prevent local crime problems and disorder. We should further expand this successful model to other areas of the criminal justice system including prosecution, with new community prosecutors working side-by-side with community police to address quality of life issues and help prevent crime before it starts.

I challenge the Congress and the next Administration to create a crime "hot spots" initiative—to target more resources to communities and neighborhoods that continue to have high crime rates or emerging crime problems. In crime "hot spots," federal, state and local law enforcement would work together to identify high-crime locations through technology such as computer mapping. There would also be an increase in policing of high-crime areas, especially during the hours when crime is most likely to occur.

Recommendation: Build on the success of community policing by creating partnerships with local prosecutors. Increase community policing in the disadvantaged areas that need them most, with more resources, including 1,000 community prosecutors and completion of our 50,000 Community Policing Initiative, and police officers targeted to crime "hot spots." . . .

Crime Prevention

And finally, we must prevent young people from becoming involved in crime and the criminal justice system in the first place. That means giving our youth alternatives to the streets, where they are often most at-risk for being involved in, or falling prey to gangs, drugs and crime. We must continue to increase the number of after school programs that help to provide adult supervision and activities for young people during the afternoon and early evening hours when juvenile crime peaks. And we must make sure that they have strong adult supervision, as well as role models and mentors.

As we work to further reduce crime across America, we also must strive to ensure fairness in the criminal justice system so that it has the complete confidence of all of our nation's citizens. To do this, we must address important issues underlying the present racial gap in trust and confidence in our criminal justice system, including racial profiling, sentencing policy, and the death penalty.

Recommendation: Help young people avoid crime by giving them something to say yes to, by dramatically expanding after-school programs and increasing support for mentoring, afterschool programs, adult supervision, and role models.

Racial Profiling

We know that in order for police to be truly effective in their work, they must have the trust and cooperation of the residents in their community. Yet, in many communities, especially minority communities, there remains a disturbing lack of trust in law enforcement among residents. Among the reasons for this distrust are reports of police misconduct such as racial profiling. The vast majority of law enforcement officers in this nation are dedicated public servants of great courage and high moral character who deserve the respect of citizens of all races. However, we cannot tolerate officers who mistreat law-abiding individuals and who bring their own racial bias to the job. Racial profiling is the opposite of good police work where actions are based on hard facts, not stereotypes. Simply stated, no person should be targeted by law enforcement because of the color of his or her skin. We must stop the morally indefensible and deeply corrosive practice of racial profiling. While some remedies are already available, we know we must do more. We know it is wrong. And it should be illegal, everywhere.

Recent polls show that while many individuals believe that law enforcement engages in racial profiling, there is very little data on traffic stops to determine where and when it is occurring. That is why I ordered federal law enforcement agencies to begin to collect data on the race, ethnicity and gender of individuals subject to certain stops and searches. Federal law enforcement should make such data collection permanent and expand it to include more sites so we can identify problem areas and take concrete steps to eliminate racial profiling anywhere it exists. In addition, I challenge state and local law enforcement to take similar action to collect data. The federal government can help by providing funding and technical assistance to help them in their efforts. We should also provide for more police integrity training and resources to promote local dialogue to strengthen trust between police and the residents they serve.

But I believe we should go a step further. Even with many of these remedies already in place, we know that racial profiling continues to occur. We must find a way to construct and pass a national law banning racial profiling so that every citizen is assured that no police department and no community will tolerate this terrible practice.

Recommendation: End the intolerable practice of racial profiling by continuing efforts to document extent of problem and passing a national law banning the practice of racial profiling.

Mandatory Minimum Sentencing

We must re-examine our national sentencing policies, focusing particularly on mandatory minimum sentences for non-violent offenders. With the prison and jail population at roughly two million, it is time to take a hard look at who we are sending to prison—and whether our sentencing policies make sense given current circumstances. Over the long term, we should not be satisfied when so many Americans, especially so many people of color, are behind bars for so long for nonviolent crimes, with so little hope of putting their lives back together when they get out. We must demand a system that actually works to reduce criminality and recidivism. . . .

One penalty I believe should be changed immediately is the 1986 federal law that creates a 100-to-1 ratio between crack and powder cocaine sentencing polices. This substantial disparity has led to a perception of racial injustice and inconsistency in the federal criminal justice system. Republican and Democratic Members of Congress alike have called for a repeal of this inequitable policy. Congress should revise the law to shrink the disparity to 10-to-1. . . .

The Death Penalty

Finally, I believe we bear a special obligation to do everything we can to ensure that the death penalty is administered fairly. Justice Department studies have found that minorities are over-represented as both victims and defendants in both the federal and state death penalty systems. While this does not necessarily show that these systems are fundamentally broken or that they discriminate, this information raises profoundly disturbing questions. . . .

Recommendation: Pass and sign legislation to provide greater access to post-conviction DNA testing and increased access to competent counsel for defendants in capital cases.

V. ELIMINATING RACIAL AND ETHNIC HEALTH DISPARITIES

Nowhere are the divisions of race and ethnicity more sharply drawn than in the health of our people. Despite notable progress in the overall health of the nation, there are continuing disparities in the burden of illness and death experienced by African Americans, Hispanics, American Indians and Alaska Natives, and Pacific Islanders, compared to the U.S. population as a whole. African Americans are 40 percent more likely to die from heart disease than whites. . . . We do not know all the reasons for these disturbing gaps. But we do know that overall these groups are less likely to be immunized against disease, less likely to be routinely tested for cancer, and less likely to get regular checkups. No matter what the reason, racial and ethnic disparities in health are unacceptable in a country that values equality and equal opportunity for all. Access to the best health care America has to offer is a new civil right for the 21st century.

That is why we have set a national goal to eliminate racial and ethnic health disparities in six key areas by the year 2010: infant mortality; diabetes; cancer; heart disease; HIV/AIDS; and immunizations. To reach this goal, my Administration launched a major preventive health outreach campaign focusing on diseases disproportionately affecting racial and ethnic minorities. We also initiated a public-private collaboration to address racial and ethnic health disparities; and secured approximately $40 million in 2000 and 2001 for programs to research the causes and devise solutions for these disparities.

In 1999, the Administration launched a new initiative to address HIV/AIDS in minority communities, which received $167 million in funds this year. Finally, in 2001, NIH will establish the Center for Research on Minority Health and Health Disparities, which will coordinate the over $1 billion NIH invests annually in minority health and health disparities research.

America has the best health care system in the world. But we can't take full pride in it until every American has an equal chance to benefit from its ever-expanding potential. That is why achieving our goal of eliminating racial and ethnic disparities in health by the year 2010 must be a priority of the new Congress and new Administration.

Recommendation: Eliminate key racial and ethnic disparities in health by 2010, by expanding investment in research into such disparities, in HIV/AIDS prevention, and in the treatment of diseases that disproportionately harm people of color.

VI. VOTING REFORM

If ever there was a doubt about the importance of exercising the most fundamental right of citizenship, it was clearly answered by the first presidential election of the 21st century. No American will ever again be able to seriously say, "My vote doesn't count." That election also revealed serious flaws in the mechanics of voting, and brought up disturbing allegations of voter intimidation that we thought were relics of the past. Too many people felt that the votes they cast were not counted and some felt that there were organized efforts to keep them from the polls. Both of these allegations must be fully investigated. But, whatever the outcome, we can and must take aggressive steps to improve voter turnout, and modernize and restore confidence in our voting system.

While voting is the sacred right and responsibility of every American, it carries even greater weight for those who have fought so long and hard for civil rights and equal justice in America. In many ways the struggle for civil rights and racial progress in America is analogous to the struggle for voting rights. And this struggle, too, has not been all black and white.

The Fifteenth Amendment declared "the right of citizens of the United States to vote shall not be denied or abridged by the United States or by any State on account of race, color or previous condition of servitude." But new barriers, like poll taxes and literacy tests, were erected to prevent blacks and poor whites from casting their ballots. It was not until that historic confrontation on Selma's Edmund Pettus Bridge and the monumental Selma to

Montgomery March that the Voting Rights Act of 1965, outlawing these racist impediments, was passed. . . .

Consider the fact that while our Declaration of Independence and Constitution proclaimed liberty and justice for all, originally this only applied to property-owning white males. Barbara Jordan once put it in stark terms, when she said of the Preamble to the Constitution, "'We the People'. It is a very eloquent beginning. But when the document was completed on the 17th of September in 1787, I was not included in that 'We the People.'" America's on-going efforts to right those wrongs is marked by the blood, sweat and tears of scores of voting rights warriors—from Frederick Douglass, Sojourner Truth and Elizabeth Cady Stanton to Martin Luther King, Willie Velasquez and Viola Liuzzo. Ms. Liuzzo was one of a number of white freedom riders who lost their lives at the hands of bigots while working with blacks in the south for equal voting rights in the 1960s.

The right to vote is not only a sacred testament to the struggles of the past. It is an indispensable weapon in our current arsenal of efforts to empower those who have traditionally been left out, particularly people of color. So much progress—from the passage of civil rights laws to the increase in the numbers of minorities holding elected office—is the direct result of citizens exercising their right to vote. And so many of the needed changes in public policy, including those I have outlined in this Message to Congress, require active support by voters. Otherwise little will change. But, today, too many of us take our right to vote for granted. In recent presidential elections in France, for example, nearly 85 percent of the eligible voters went to the polls on election day. In America, there aren't more than two states that ever have an 80 percent turnout, even during a presidential election when interest runs very high.

So, we must do more to ensure that more people vote and that every vote is counted. In an effort to restore confidence in our democracy, I recommend that the next President appoint a nonpartisan Presidential Commission on Electoral Reform. The Commission should be headed by distinguished citizens who can put country ahead of party, such as former Presidents Gerald Ford and Jimmy Carter. The Commission should gather the facts and determine the causes of voting disparities in every state, including disparities of race, class, ethnicity, and geography. The Commission should make recommendations to Congress about how to achieve a fair, inclusive, and uniform system of voting in national elections—including how to modernize voting technologies, establish uniform voting standards, prevent voter suppression and intimidation, and increase voter participation.

I believe such a Commission should also examine two other issues that haven't received as much attention, but could go a long way toward ensuring every American citizen the right to vote and the chance to exercise that right. First, we should declare election day a national holiday so that no one has to choose between their responsibilities at work and their responsibilities as a citizen. In other countries that do this, voter participation dwarfs ours, and the most fundamental act of democracy gets the attention it deserves. Second, we should give back the right to vote to those who have repaid their debt to society. Over the next decade, millions of Americans in the criminal justice system will serve out their sentences and re-enter society. These Americans are disproportionately poor and minority. We should be doing everything we can to make sure that they re-enter society as responsible citizens. That means making sure that those who leave the criminal justice system leave it drug-free, and get the training they need to hold down a job and do right by their communities and their families. But if we want them to live right and do right, we should give them the chance to earn back their rights—above all, the right to vote.

Recommendation: Appoint a non-partisan Presidential Commission on election reform to ensure a fair, inclusive and uniform system of voting standards, prevent voter suppression and intimidation and increase voter participation. Declare election day a national holiday. Give ex-offenders who have repaid their debt to society the chance to earn back the right to vote.

VII. CIVIC RESPONSIBILITY: BUILDING ONE AMERICA IS THE WORK OF EVERY AMERICAN

When violence and strife exploded in Los Angeles following the Rodney King verdict, countless residents and community leaders responded with inspiring efforts to build bridges that would not only heal wounds but create opportunity. When more than 190 black churches, white churches, synagogues, and mosques were burned or desecrated during 1995–1996, we witnessed an awe-inspiring outpouring of concern and assistance across all lines of race and faith and party. When Jasper, Texas, was shaken to its core by a hideous hate crime, residents and leaders worked tirelessly to hold together, and in doing so, taught us all that some evils can be conquered with understanding. What all these examples prove is that when communities are faced with a crisis, our better angels soar to the challenge. In those moments, America ceases to be a nation of people divided into categories of color. America at its best is people of all colors united for the common good.

As in so many other areas, racial reconciliation and building opportunity simply won't happen unless there is committed engagement by people in communities and institutions throughout the nation. But in the absence of a crisis, we may be tempted to leave this work to national leaders, such as politicians, clergy, business executives or the heads of nonprofit organizations. Such leaders can perhaps help set a tone, point out examples, offer support, and provide critical seed resources. But it takes all of us working together to prevent the kind of devastating crisis that pulls us together only after much pain and suffering. At the end of the day, we will make the most fundamental kind of progress when we work with our neighbors for change.

To help spur this work, I hope that in the coming years leaders of goodwill in individual communities will rededicate themselves to working together across racial and ethnic lines in community partnerships designed to help us build a more perfect union. In many areas, there may already be a vesting place, such as an active ecumenical council of faith leaders, or a human rights commission with broad-based public legitimacy. In other places, convening a group of leaders might require a special initiative by a mayor, a tribal leader, a newspaper publisher, an archbishop, a leading employer or the board of a civic organization.

Much of that work is already underway across America. And I am proud that my White House Office on One America is doing its part. In February, 1999, I launched the first-ever White House office specifically charged with keeping the nation focused on closing opportunity gaps and fostering racial reconciliation. Since its inception, the office has been instrumental in several efforts including the formation of "Lawyers for One America"—a group of attorneys who have committed to change the racial justice landscape through greater diversity within the legal profession and increased pro bono service.

The One America Office also convened corporate leaders at the White House, who pledged a renewed commitment to diversity in their workplaces and stronger efforts to close opportunity gaps. And the One America Office brought a broad cross-section of religious leaders to the White House to pledge that the faith community would focus more of its efforts on expanding diversity, ending racism and promoting racial reconciliation.

The White House Office on One America has helped focus and coordinate efforts throughout my Administration to build One America. It is my sincere hope that the next Administration will maintain this office and its noble purpose.

Our national service program, Americorps, has also played an important role, bringing together young people of all races and walks of life to work in all kinds of communities with all kinds of people. Since 1994, 150,000 young people have served as Americorps volunteers, meeting community challenges and moving us closer to One America. Last year, 49 of the nation's 50 governors—including President-elect Bush—urged Congress to reauthorize the National and Community Service and Trust Act. I hope Congress will answer their call, and keep Americorps members on the job.

Building One America requires a new kind of leadership. Instead of looking outward for signs of hope, we must first look in the mirror and know that change is our responsibility. Rooted in the heart, that wisdom has the power to connect us in ways that nourish our dreams for a future that is better than our past. Whether you are able to give guidance to a single child or lead a national movement for justice, it all begins with a personal commitment to racial reconciliation. As Dr. King once said, "No social movement rolls in on the wheels of inevitability. Every step toward the goal of justice requires sacrifice, suffering, and struggle; the tireless exertions and passionate concern of dedicated individuals."

Recommendation: Maintain the White House Office on One America, and reauthorize the National and Community Service Trust Act. Every American should become engaged in the work of expanding opportunity for all and building One America.

See www.ask.elibrary.com.

INDEX